property of
creature Named
Ephrem

Managerial Economics

THIRD EDITION

H. CRAIG PETERSEN
UTAH STATE UNIVERSITY

W. CRIS LEWIS
UTAH STATE UNIVERSITY

Managerial Economics

THIRD EDITION

MACMILLAN PUBLISHING COMPANY
NEW YORK
Maxwell Macmillan Canada
TORONTO
Maxwell Macmillan International
NEW YORK   OXFORD   SINGAPORE   SYDNEY

Editor: Jill Lectka
Production Supervisor: John Travis
Production Manager: Su Levine
Text Designer: Robert Freese
Cover Designer: Cathleen Norz
Cover illustration: Interactive Images, Inc.

This book was set in Palatino and Korinna type by Bi-Comp, Inc., and printed and bound by Donnelley-Harrisonburg. The cover was printed by Lehigh.

Macmillan Publishing Company
866 Third Avenue, New York, New York 10022

Macmillan Publishing Company is part
of the Maxwell Communication Group of Companies.

Maxwell Macmillan Canada, Inc.
1200 Eglinton Avenue East
Suite 200
Don Mills, Ontario M3C 3N1

LIBRARY OF CONGRESS CATALOGING IN PUBLICATION DATA

Petersen, Harold Craig.
    Managerial economics / H. Craig Petersen, W. Cris Lewis.—3rd ed.
        p. cm.
    Includes bibliographical references and index.
    ISBN 0-02-394762-4
    1. Managerial economics.   I. Lewis, W. Cris.   II. Title.
HD30.22.P45   1994
338.5'024658—dc20   92-46907
                                                                       CIP

PRINTING: 1 2 3 4 5 6 7 8   YEAR: 4 5 6 7 8 9 0 1

Preface

Managerial economics is an interesting and fundamental part of the business curriculum; however, it can be a very difficult course for some students. Mastering the subject requires a good understanding of how basic concepts of economics can be combined with tools of mathematics and statistics to analyze and make decisions involving scarce resources. But, in the process of studying managerial economics, students can get mired in the minutiae of data, graphs, equations, and definitions. One result is that they may fail to appreciate fully the value of economic principles as tools for decision making.

Part of the difficulty in teaching managerial economics can be explained by the limitations of existing textbooks. Some texts devote so much time to manipulating data, deriving equations, and explaining the subtleties of statistics that they leave students without a good grasp of basic economic principles. Others provide extensive discussions of these principles but are almost totally devoid of good examples which allow the student to see how these concepts can be applied.

Objectives

Managerial Economics, Third Edition, is written with two primary objectives in mind. First, it is intended that students will receive a complete and rigorous introduction to basic principles of microeconomics. Albert Einstein once commented that things should be made as simple as possible, but not more so. In this text we have tried to follow this counsel. Esoteric and peripheral points have been avoided in order to concentrate on fundamental economic principles. However, difficult concepts have been included when it was determined that they could provide important insights for decision making. Care has been taken to assure that the exposition of these concepts is as clear and uncomplicated as possible.

Our second objective in writing *Managerial Economics* is to demonstrate how applications of economic theory can improve decision making. This goal is realized by use of a concept/example format throughout the book. The approach involves first introducing basic concepts of managerial economics and then using these principles to analyze decisions faced by managers. In addition, numerous case studies and solved problems have been included in each chapter to illustrate important principles and to stimulate interest in related topics. The use of the concept/example format makes the text more readable and facilitates learning by allowing students to see how economic principles can be used in decision making.

Features

A course in Managerial Economics taught at one university may be quite different from that offered at another school. Although it is impossible to provide a text that will meet the preferences of all instructors, *Managerial Economics* is designed to be suitable for many uses. For an undergraduate course, coverage of the first thirteen chapters provides a good understanding of basic economic principles and their applications. For an MBA curriculum or a more comprehensive undergraduate course, additional topics can be selected from the remaining six chapters as time permits.

One of the most difficult choices we faced in writing *Managerial Economics* involved the level of mathematics to be used in the text. Some course instructors use calculus, while others prefer a graphical and algebraic presentation. We have opted for a compromise position. There are some topics that are more easily understood using calculus. Accordingly, basic calculus (usually nothing more than taking a derivative) is used to discuss selected concepts in some chapters. For those students who have not had calculus, the appendix to Chapter 2 provides the necessary background to follow these presentations. For courses with greater emphasis on calculus, there are calculus footnotes. In addition, most chapters have supplementary problems that are clearly designated as requiring calculus for their solution.

In addition to the concept/example format mentioned on the preceding page, *Managerial Economics* includes other special features to facilitate student learning. Each chapter has key concepts listed at the end of major sections. Together with the chapter outline and summary, these key concepts can aid in the review of material. Case studies interspersed throughout the chapters show how economic tools are relevant for decision makers. Solved problems included in the chapters are designed to provide guidance in working problems. Discussion questions and problems are included at the end of each chapter. Many chapters also include separate sets of problems requiring calculus and/or a microcomputer for their solution.

Changes in the Third Edition

We believe that students and instructors will benefit from the changes made in *Managerial Economics*. In addition to updating and revising many topics, there are several substantive changes in the third edition.

- *New Chapters:* Two completely new chapters have been added to the Third Edition of *Managerial Economics.* Chapter 11, Game Theory and Strategic Behavior, uses game theory to provide important insights into decision making by managers in oligopolistic industries. Chapter 16, Technological Change in a Global Economy, considers the effects of technology and presents techniques for technological forecasting.
- *New Topics:* In addition to the two new chapters, important topics have been included in existing chapters. These include multicollinearity and omitted variables problems associated with regression analysis, exponential smoothing, economies of scope, additional models of oligopoly behavior, product bundling, and locating the firm in a global economy.
- *Additional Problems:* In the Third Edition, the number of end of chapter problems has been significantly increased.
- *Additional Test questions:* The Instructor's Manual for the Third Edition includes about 50 percent more multiple choice questions and problems than the Second Edition.

Support Materials

The following support materials are available for use with *Managerial Economics, Third Edition:*

1. *STUDY GUIDE WITH COMPUTER SOFTWARE.* This guide includes a summary of key concepts and equations for each chapter. It also includes solved problems and exercises that are designed for computer solution.

   A unique feature of the study guide is the inclusion of the microcomputer program, TOOLS. This software contains routines for time value of money problems, multiple regression, statistics of a probability distribution, trend projection, input/output projections, linear programming, benefit-cost analysis, and other quantitative techniques that enable students to solve reasonably complex problems without tedious hand calculations. TOOLS is a menu-driven program that can easily be used by students without classroom instruction.
2. *INSTRUCTOR'S MANUAL.* The manual includes a summary of key concepts and equations for each chapter. It also includes answers for the discussion questions and solutions for problems found at the end of each chapter.
3. *TEST BANK.* Includes over 600 multiple-choice questions and 150 problems for instructor use in preparing examinations. A computerized version of the test bank is provided to adopters.

Acknowledgments

We are indebted to those who reviewed the manuscript for the first three editions of *Managerial Economics.* Their incisive comments have changed and, we believe, significantly improved the final product. Specifically, we express thanks to

Andrew Buck   Kenneth Lyon
Thomas Cate   Michael Magura
Donald Chaffee   J. Peter Matilla
Robert Crawford   John McKean
Clifford Dobitz   Louis Noyd
Thomas Edwards   John Peterson
Patricia Euzent   Jean Sandver
Robert Greer   Edward Sattler
Jonathan Hamilton   John Snyder
George Hoffer   Michael Vaughan

HCP
WCL

Brief Contents

Contents

II *Demand*   *67*

V   Pricing Decisions   393

Tables   *653–657*

Index   *659–664*

I

Getting Started

CHAPTER *1*

Introduction to Managerial Economics

Preview ─────────────────────────────────────

For most purposes, economics can be divided into two broad categories: microeconomics and macroeconomics. *Macroeconomics* is the study of the economic system as a whole. It includes techniques for analyzing changes in total output, total employment, the consumer price index, the unemployment rate, and exports and imports. Macroeconomics addresses questions about the effect of changes in investment, government spending, and tax policy on exports, output, employment, and prices. Only aggregate levels of these variables are considered. But concealed in the aggregate data are countless changes in the output levels of individual firms, the consumption decisions of individual consumers, and the prices of particular goods and services.

Although macroeconomic issues and policies command much of the attention in newspapers and on television, the microdimensions of the economy also are important and often are of more direct application to the day-to-day problems facing the manager. *Microeconomics* focuses on the behavior of the individual actors on the economic stage: firms and individuals and their interaction in markets.

Managerial economics should be thought of as applied microeconomics. That is, managerial economics is an application of that part of microeconomics focusing on those topics of greatest interest and importance to managers. These topics include demand, production, cost, pricing, market structure, and government regulation. A strong grasp of the principles that govern the economic behavior of firms and individuals is an important managerial talent.

In general, managerial economics can be used by the goal-oriented manager in two ways. First, given an existing economic environment, the principles of managerial economics provide a framework for evaluating whether resources are being allocated efficiently within a firm. For example, economics can help the manager determine if profit could be increased by reallocating labor from a marketing activity to the production line. Second, these principles help managers respond to various economic signals. For example, given an increase in the price of output or the development of a new lower-cost production technology, the appropriate managerial response would be to increase output. Alternatively, an increase in the price of one input, say labor, may be a signal to substitute other inputs, such as capital, for labor in the production process.

The tools developed in the following chapters will increase the effectiveness of decision making by expanding and sharpening the analytical framework used by managers to make decisions. Thus, a working knowledge of the principles of managerial economics can increase the value of both the firm and the manager.

This chapter sets the stage for the development of managerial economic skills. First, the interrelationships among consumers, firms, and resource owners in a market economy are outlined. Next, the nature and objective of the firm and the importance of profit as an incentive for firms to respond to consumer demands for output are discussed. Finally, the role of economics in decision making is considered.

The Circular Flow of Economic Activity

Individuals and firms are the fundamental participants in a market economy. Individuals own or control resources that have value to firms because they are necessary inputs in the production process. These resources are broadly classified as labor, capital, and natural resources. Of course, there are many types and grades of each resource. Labor specialties vary from street sweepers to brain surgeons; capital goods range from brooms to electronic computers. Most people have labor resources to sell, and many own capital and/or natural resources that are rented, loaned, or sold to firms to be used as inputs in the production process. The money received by an individual from the sale of these resources is called a factor payment. This income to individuals then is used to satisfy their consumption demands for goods and services.

The interaction between individuals and firms occurs in two distinct arenas. First, there is a product market where goods and services are bought and sold. Second, there is a market for factors of production where labor, capital, and natural resources are traded. These interactions are depicted in Figure 1-1, which describes the circular flow of income, output, resources, and factor payments in a market economy.

In the product market shown in the top part of the figure, individuals demand goods and services in order to satisfy their consumption desires.[1] They make these demands known by bidding in the product market for these goods and services. Firms, anxious to earn profits, respond to these demands by supplying goods and services to that market. The firm's production technology and input costs determine the supply conditions, while consumer preferences and income (i.e., the ability to pay) determine the demand conditions. The interaction of supply and demand determines the price and quantity sold. In the product market, purchasing power, usually in the form of money, flows from consumers to firms. At the same time, goods and services flow in the opposite direction—from firms to consumers.

The factor market is shown at the bottom of Figure 1-1. Here the flows are the reverse of those in the product. Individuals are the suppliers in the factor market. They supply labor services, capital, and natural resources to firms that demand them to produce goods and services. Firms indicate the strength of their desire for these inputs by bidding for them in the market. The flow of money is from firms to individuals, and factors of production flow from individuals to firms. The prices of these productive factors are set in this market.

Prices and profits serve as the signals for regulating the flows of money and

---

[1] It is necessary to distinguish between *want* and *demand*. Many individuals *want* goods and services but cannot afford to buy them. The term *demand* implies that the consumer has both the desire to have the good and the ability to buy it.

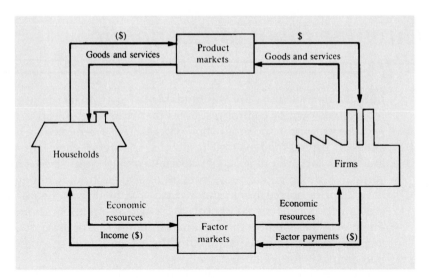

FIGURE 1-1 **Circular Flow of Income, Output, Resources, and Factor Payments.**

resources through the factor markets and the flows of money and goods through the product market. For example, relatively high prices and profits in the personal computer industry in the 1980s signaled producers to increase production and send more units of output to the product market. To produce more computers, more labor and capital were required. Firms raised the prices they would pay for these resources in the factor market to signal resource owners that higher returns were now available. The result was rapid growth in the personal computer industry as resources were bid away from other industries. In the early 1990s, this market became very competitive and prices fell substantially. While total unit sales increased, the profit on each computer was smaller, and some firms struggled to keep total profit at an acceptable level. Consumers benefitted greatly as better and more powerful computers became available at lower and lower prices.

In the market economy depicted by this circular flow, individuals and firms are highly interdependent; each participant needs the others. For example, an individual's labor will have no value in the market unless there is a firm that is willing to pay for it. Alternatively, firms cannot justify production unless some consumers want to buy their products. As a result, all participants have an incentive to provide what others want. All participate willingly because they have something to gain by doing so. Firms earn profits, the consumption demands of individuals are satisfied, and resource owners receive wage, rent, and interest payments. If an individual does not benefit by buying and selling in these markets, he or she is not required to do so. Thus one can be sure that no individual is made worse off by voluntary trade in these factor and product markets. Indeed, this is the essence of a market economy.

The Nature of the Firm

In order to earn profits, the firm organizes the factors of production to produce goods and services that will meet the demands of individual consumers and other firms. The concept of the firm plays a central role in the theory and practice of managerial economics. Thus a significant part of this text is focused on production, cost, and the organization of firms in the marketplace. These topics form the basis for what is known in economics as the theory of the firm. An understanding of the reason for the existence of firms, their specific role in the economy, and their objective provides a background for that theory.

The Rationale for the Firm[2]

In a free-market economy, the organization and interaction of producers (i.e., firms) and consumers is accomplished through the price system. There is no need for any central direction by government, nor is such central control or planning thought to be desirable. Within the firm, however, transactions and the organization of productive factors generally are accomplished by the central control of one or more managers. For example, workers subject themselves almost completely to management during the work period. Thus there is an apparent dichotomy in the organization of production in a market economy. The price system guides the decentralized interaction among consumers and firms, while central planning and control tend to guide the interaction within firms. This raises the question, Why is the production system not completely guided by price signals? That is, why do firms exist in a market economy?

Essentially, firms exist as organizations because the total cost of producing any rate of output is lower than if the firm did not exist. There are several reasons why these costs are lower. First, there is a cost of using the price system to organize production. The cost of obtaining information on prices and the cost of negotiating and concluding separate contracts for each step of the production process would be very burdensome. Firms often hire labor for long periods of time under agreements that specify only that a wage rate per hour or day will be paid for the workers doing what they are asked. That is, one general contract covers what usually will be a large number of transactions between the owners and workers. The two parties do not have to negotiate a new contract every time the worker is given a new assignment. The saving of the transactions costs associated with such negotiations is advantageous to both parties, and thus both labor and management voluntarily seek out such arrangements.

A secondary explanation for the existence of firms is that some government interference in the marketplace applies to transactions among firms rather than within firms. For example, sales taxes usually apply only to transactions between

---

[2] This section draws on the classic article by R. H. Coase, "The Nature of the Firm." *Economica*, November, pp. 386–405, 1937.

one firm and another. In some states, a construction company may have to pay sales tax on cabinets purchased from an independent cabinetmaker. By hiring that person, this tax is avoided and the cost of producing output is reduced. By internalizing some transactions within the firm that would otherwise be subject to those interferences, production costs are reduced. Because this is a secondary factor, firms would exist in the absence of such interference, but it probably contributes to there being more and larger firms.

Given that production costs are reduced by organizing production factors into firms, why won't this process continue until there is just one large firm, such as a giant General Motors or Exxon that produces all goods and services for the entire economy? There are at least two reasons. First, the cost of organizing transactions within the firm tends to rise as the firm gets larger. Logic dictates that the firm will internalize the lower-cost transactions first and then the higher-cost transactions. At some point, these internal transactions costs will equal the costs of transacting in the market. At that point, the firm will cease to grow. For example, all automobile producers in the world buy tires from companies that specialize in the production of rubber products. Surely, Ford and General Motors must have considered building plants to produce their own tires. It can be inferred that the cost of developing the new management skills required for such a different sort of production and the difficulty of managing an even larger and more complicated business must have been greater than the cost of continuing to buy tires from Goodyear, Michelin, and other producers.

Another example is legal services. Usually, attorneys are not an integral part of the production process but rather are needed periodically. It would be too costly for many firms to have full-time attorneys whose services would not be needed on a continual basis. So, rather than having a full-time lawyer employed by the firm, legal services are contracted on a when-needed basis. The cost of such an arrangement for most firms is lower. In contrast, large firms that have a continual need for legal services generally have an in-house legal staff.

A second factor constraining firm size is that an entrepreneur's organizational skill is limited. Resources within the company may not be efficiently allocated if the firm's size exceeds the manager's ability to control the operation. To overcome this problem, many large firms are organized into a group of divisions referred to as "profit centers." The management of each of these seeks to maximize that division's profit. By having a number of smaller organizations each being managed somewhat independently, the problem of limited ability to control the larger firm is at least partially overcome.

Both these reasons for a limit on the size of the firm fall under the heading of what economists have termed "diminishing returns to management." Stated another way, production costs per unit of output will tend to rise as firms grow larger because of limited managerial ability. It should be noted that many large firms recognize the problem of excessive size and decentralize by establishing a number of separate divisions or profit centers that act as individual firms.

KEY CONCEPTS

- The interaction of individuals and firms in a market economy can be described as a circular flow of money, goods and services, and resources through product and factor markets.
- Firms exist because the costs of production are lower and returns to the owners of labor and capital are higher than if the firm did not exist.
- Limits are imposed on the size of firms because the cost of organizing transactions rises as the firm becomes larger and because managerial ability is limited.

The Objective of the Firm

This book approaches microeconomics from the perspective of efficient management of a business or other organization. To be able to discuss efficient or optimal decision making requires that a goal or objective be established. That is, a management decision can only be evaluated against the goal that the firm is attempting to achieve. Traditionally, economists have assumed the objective of the firm is to maximize profit. That is, it is assumed that managers consistently make decisions in order to maximize profit. But profit in which period? This year? The next five years? Often, managers are observed making decisions that reduce current year profits in an effort to increase profits in future years. Expenditures for research and development, new capital equipment, and major marketing programs are but a few examples of activities that reduce profits initially but will significantly increase profits in later years.[3]

As both current and future profits are important, it is assumed that the goal is to maximize the present or discounted value of all future profits.[4] Formally stated, the goal or objective function for the firm is to

$$\text{maximize: } PV(\pi) = \frac{\pi_1}{1+r} + \frac{\pi_2}{(1+r)^2} + \cdots + \frac{\pi_n}{(1+r)^n} \tag{1-1}$$

where π_t is profit in time period t and r is an appropriate discount rate used to reduce future profits to their present value. Using the Greek letter Σ to indicate that each of the terms on the right-hand side of the equation have been added together, the objective function can be written as

$$\text{maximize: } PV(\pi) = \sum_{t=1}^{n} \frac{\pi_t}{(1+r)^t}$$

The present value of all future profits also can be interpreted as the value of the firm. That is, it is what a willing buyer would pay for the business. Thus, to

---

[3] Some managers who must report profit performance monthly or quarterly claim that the pressure for increased short-term profits may cause them to make decisions that increase these profits at the expense of long-term profit.

[4] Many students will have already studied the concept of present value. For those who have not, the concept is developed more fully in the appendix to this chapter.

maximize the discounted value of all future profits is equivalent to maximizing the value of the firm. The terms *profit maximization* and *value maximization* will be used interchangeably in the remainder of this book.

Maximizing versus Satisficing

Considerable controversy has developed about the "realism" of this assumed management goal. Advocates of alternative theories of the firm argue that the behavior of real-world managers is not always consistent with the profit-maximization goal. Other objectives are seen as being at least as important as profit maximization. Among the alternatives that have been identified are maximizing total revenue; maximizing employment tenure and departmental budget; maximizing executive salaries; achieving "satisfactory" profit levels; maximizing the manager's individual utility function; and maximizing market share subject to a satisfactory profit constraint. Indeed, an entire literature has developed on the subject of "satisficing" rather than "maximizing" management objectives.[5]

Some critics of the profit-maximization assumption argue that it is unrealistic because managers must function in an environment characterized by inadequate information and uncertainty about the outcome of any strategy that might be adopted. Therefore, as a practical matter, it is really impossible to maximize profit. Economist Fritz Machlup responded to this criticism by comparing managing a firm to driving a car.[6] When deciding whether to pass another car on a two-lane highway, a driver must consider a variety of conditions. A few of these include the speed of his car, the car that is to be passed, and that of any oncoming vehicles; the road conditions; the existence of any curves or intersections that may be upcoming; and lighting conditions. Obviously, to analyze this situation completely prior to passing the car ahead might require the assistance of a computer and several working days.

Clearly, however, the typical driver makes an intuitive evaluation of these conditions in a matter of a few seconds or less and makes a decision. Machlup contends that managers are seeking to maximize profit and simply react intuitively to a set of conditions characterized by incomplete information and uncertainty in the same manner as the automobile driver. Thus, while there may be additional information that would result in even greater profit, managers are striving to generate the greatest possible profit given the limited information available.

Although some managers may have other goals, most of the criticism leveled at the profit-maximization assumption may be irrelevant. Economics is less interested in how some managers really act than in understanding the economic environment in which managers must function and, more importantly, in developing a framework for predicting managerial responses to important changes in that environment.

---

[5] See H. A. Simon, "Theories of Decision Making in Economics," *American Economic Review*, 49(3):253–283, 1959; and R. M. Cyert and J. A. March, *A Behavioral Theory of the Firm* (Englewood Cliffs, N.J.: Prentice-Hall, 1963).

[6] F. Machlup, "Theories of the Firm: Marginalist, Behavioral, Managerial," *American Economic Review*, 57(1):1–33, 1967.

In this context, Machlup argues that it is fruitless to worry about how real-world business managers really behave and what their goals really are. The real question is: If we assume that firms attempt to maximize profit, will the principles of economics derived from that objective function explain the behavior of real-world firms? If the answer is yes, it really does not matter if the assumed goal is not entirely realistic. For example, suppose that there are two firms, A and B, that are identical except in one respect: The manager of A works 16 hours a day seven days a week, whereas the manager of B works only four days each week and leaves the office shortly after lunch each day to play golf. Because of manager A's commitment to work, it is probable that profits for firm A are greater than at firm B, but this difference in commitment to work and its effect on profit is not the issue. The fundamental question is: Will the two managers respond the same way to changes in economic conditions? If the price of their product increases, do both use the profit-maximizing strategy of increasing the rate of output? The manager of A may take action first because he is on the job most of the time, but the response should be the same for both firms.

Most economists agree that the principles of managerial microeconomics do indeed allow accurate predictions of managerial decisions, and that profit maximization provides a useful assumption in that context. Indeed, no general theory has yet proven to predict more accurately than the models based on profit maximization. Thus, in this book it will be assumed that the objective of the firm is to maximize profit or, equivalently, to maximize the value of the firm.

Constrained Decision Making

The essence of the science of economics is determining optimum behavior where that behavior is subject to constraints. As just discussed, profit maximization is constrained by the limited information available to the manager. In general, constraints on managerial decisions involve legal, moral, contractual, financial, and technological considerations. Legal constraints include the array of federal, state, and local laws that must be obeyed by all citizens, both individual and corporate. Areas where managers seem to be having some legal difficulty include environmental laws, especially those relating to pollution and the disposal of hazardous wastes, and employment law, including wrongful termination and sexual harassment matters. Moral constraints apply to actions that are not illegal but are sufficiently inconsistent with generally accepted standards of behavior to be considered improper. Contractual constraints bind the firm because of some prior agreement such as a long-term lease on a building or a contract with a labor union that represents the firm's employees.

Finally, there are financial and technological constraints. An example of a financial constraint occurs when a department of a firm is assigned a budget for the forthcoming production period and managers are given orders such as "maximize production subject to this budgeted amount." Technological constraints set physical limits on the amount of output per unit of time that can be generated by particular machines or workers. As will be shown in subsequent chapters, making optimizing decisions under financial or technological constraints is a fundamental part of managerial economics.

CASE STUDY _____

Adam Smith and the Invisible Hand

The eighteenth-century philosopher Adam Smith is regarded as the father of modern economics. He understood clearly how a decentralized market economy would function with little, if any, outside regulation required. In particular, he saw that by seeking to maximize their self-interest, the individual participants in this economy would achieve socially desirable results. In his book *An Inquiry into the Nature and Causes of the Wealth of Nations** (originally published in 1776), Smith writes

> It is not from the benevolence of the butcher, the brewer, or the baker that we expect our dinner, but from their regard to their own self-interest. We address ourselves, not to their humanity but to their self-love, never talk to them of our own necessities, but of their advantages.

The coordinating mechanism in the economy, the price system, was described by Smith as an "invisible hand" that guided private decisions in socially beneficial ways:

> Every individual endeavors to employ his capital so that its produce may be of greatest value. He generally neither intends to promote the public interest, nor knows how much he is promoting it. He intends only his own security, only his own gain. And he is in this led by an invisible hand to promote an end which was no part of his intention. By pursuing his own interest he frequently promotes that of society more effectually than when he really intends to promote it.

In addition to this rationale for a market system unfettered by outside (e.g., government)

* New York: Random House/Modern Library, 1985.

influence or control, Smith's example of the efficiencies associated with the mass production of pins provides insight into the role of the firm in market economy and the advantages of mass production.

> To take an example . . . the trade of the pin-maker; a workman not educated to this business . . . nor acquainted with the use of the machinery employed in it . . . could scarce, perhaps, with his utmost industry, make one pin in a day, and certainly could not make twenty. But in the way in which this business is now carried on not only the whole work is a peculiar trade, but it is divided into a number of branches, of which the greater part are likewise peculiar trades. One man draws out the wire, another straightens it, a third cuts it, a fourth points it, a fifth grinds it at the top for receiving the head; to make the head requires two or three distinct operations; . . . and the important business of making a pin is, in this manner, divided into about eighteen distinct operations. . . . I have seen a small manufactory of this kind where ten men only were employed making upwards of forty-eight thousand pins in a day. Each person, therefore, making a tenth part of forty-eight thousand pins, might be considered as making four thousand eight hundred pins in a day. But if they had all wrought separately and independently, and without any of them having been educated to this peculiar business, they certainly could not each of them have made twenty, perhaps not one pin in a day.

Even in 1776, Adam Smith could see the advantages of an economic system based on the self-interest of the individual participants and the development of firms to organize labor and capital for the purpose of low-cost mass production.

KEY CONCEPTS

- It is assumed that the objective of the firm is to maximize the present value of all future profits.
- Managerial decisions are subject to legal, moral, contractual, financial, and technological constraints.
- The principles of managerial economics allow accurate predictions of decision-making in business and other organizations.

The Concept of Economic Profit

Having determined that the goal of the firm is profit maximization, it is necessary to define the term *profit*. The conventional notion of profit is relatively straightforward: Profit is defined as revenues minus costs. But the definition of cost is quite different for the economist than for the accountant. Consider an individual who has an MBA degree and is considering investing $200,000 in a retail store that she would manage. The projected income statement for the year as prepared by an accountant is as shown:

Sales		$90,000
Less: Cost of goods sold		40,000
Gross profit		$50,000
Less: Advertising	$10,000	
Depreciation	10,000	
Utilities	3,000	
Property tax	2,000	
Miscellaneous expenses	5,000	30,000
Net accounting profit		$20,000

This accounting or business profit is what is reported in publications such as the *Wall Street Journal* and in the quarterly and annual financial reports of businesses. It is a meaningful concept as far as it goes—it just does not go far enough. Furthermore, the use of this concept may result in making the wrong decision.

The economist recognizes other costs, defined as implicit costs. These costs are not reflected in cash outlays by the firm, but are the costs associated with foregone opportunities. Such implicit costs are not included in the accounting statements but must be included in any rational decision-making framework. There are two major implicit costs in the preceding example. First, the owner has $200,000 invested in the business. Suppose the best alternative use for this money is a bank account paying a 5 percent interest rate. Therefore, this investment would return $10,000 annually. Thus, $10,000 should be considered as the *implicit* or *opportunity cost* of having the $200,000 invested in the retail store.

The second implicit cost includes the manager's time and talent. The annual wage return on an MBA degree from a reasonably good business school may be

$40,000 per year. This is the implicit cost of managing this business rather than working for someone else. Thus the income statement should be amended in the following way in order to determine economic profit:

Sales		$-90,000
Less: Cost of goods sold		40,000
Gross profit		$-50,000
Less: Explicit costs:		
Advertising	$10,000	
Depreciation	10,000	
Utilities	3,000	
Property tax	2,000	
Miscellaneous expenses	5,000	30,000
Accounting profit (i.e., profit before implict costs)		$-20,000
Less: Implicit costs:		
Return on $200,000 of invested capital	10,000	
Foregone wages	40,000	50,000
Net "economic profit"		$-30,000

From this broader perspective, the business is projected to lose $30,000 in the first year. The $20,000 accounting profit disappears when all "relevant" costs are included. Obviously, with the financial information reported in this way, an entirely different decision might be made on whether to start this business. Another way of looking at the problem is to assume that $200,000 had to be borrowed at 5 percent interest and an MBA graduate hired at $40,000 per year to run the store. In this case, the implicit costs become explicit and the accounting profit is the same as the economic profit (i.e., $-30,000) because all relevant costs have been considered.

Most decision makers are aware of this concept. The carpenter who works as an independent contractor rather than as an employee of another firm knows that his opportunity cost is the market wage rate for carpenters. The contractor's lament "I lost money on that job" may mean that his accounting profit was $100 per day when he could have made $150 per day working for someone else.

The important point of this discussion is that an entirely different signal may be given to management when the concept of economic profit is used. Sometimes the operation of economically unprofitable businesses is continued because of a failure to understand and properly include implicit costs. Rational decision making requires that all relevant costs, both explicit and implicit, be recognized. The concept of economic profit accounts for all costs and therefore is a more useful management tool than the more normally defined concept of accounting profit. In the following chapters, the economic definition of profit will be used, and the term *cost* is defined to include all relevant costs, both explicit and implicit.

EXAMPLE _____

Opportunity Costs

Sharon Smith is a full-time homemaker and also is an excellent seamstress. She has material for which she paid $5 per yard several years ago. The material has increased in value during that time and could be sold back to the local fabric shop for $15 per yard. Sharon is considering using that material to make dresses, which she would sell to her friends and neighbors. She estimates that each dress would require four yards of material and four hours of her time, which she values at $10 per hour. If the dresses could be sold for $90 a piece, could Sharon earn a positive economic profit by making and selling the dresses?

SOLUTION

The key to this decision is appropriately accounting for both Sharon's time (i.e., $10 per hour) and the true opportunity cost of the material, which is $15 per yard, the amount she could receive by selling it to the fabric shop. The profit calculation per dress would be as follows:

Revenue	$−90
Less: 4 hours of labor at $10/hr	40
4 yards of material at $15/yd	60
Economic profit	$−10

Clearly, making the dresses is not going to be profitable.

If Sharon had not included the value of her time and had used the historic price of $5 per yard as the cost of the material, she would have estimated a "profit" of $70 per dress; that is

Revenue	$90
Less: 4 yards of material at $5/yd	20
"Profit"	$70

This is not an accurate measure of profit because it fails to account for the true opportunity cost of Sharon's time and the opportunity cost of a yard of material. She could sell both in the market and make more than she could by producing the dresses.

_____

Profit in a Market System _____

Except for those who espouse the view that charity is the only virtue, contributors to output expect to be paid. Each workday, many people willingly spend about one-half of their waking hours in employment for which they are paid wages. Those who own land and structures will let others use those resources as long as rent is paid for their use. Owners of financial resources make their assets available in return for the payment of interest.

Of the total income generated in the U.S. economy each year, about 73 percent is in the form of wages. Rent accounts for 2 percent and interest comprises about 10 percent. Profit, although representing only 15 percent of national income, plays two primary roles in the functioning of the economic system. First, profit acts as a signal to producers to change the rate of output or to enter or leave an industry. Second, profit is a reward that encourages entrepreneurs to organize factors of production and take risk.

High profits in an industry usually are a signal that buyers want more output from that industry. Those profits provide the incentive for firms to increase output and for new firms to enter the market. Conversely, low profits are a signal that less output is being demanded by consumers and/or that production methods are not efficient. When demand for output decreases, firms reduce production of that product, and resources are made available for the production of other goods and services for which demand has increased. If low profits are an indication of inefficiency in production rather than inadequate demand, management is signaled to reorganize the production process or otherwise reduce costs.

It seems clear that profit is the objective of most managers and entrepreneurs. Although sometimes characterized by greed, avarice, misrepresentation, and outright lawbreaking, the desire for profit drives the market economy. But the quest for profit is no more selfish than the quest for higher wages. Profit is a residual income after other participants in production have been paid. The sellers of labor inputs want their payments before the final goods are sold to consumers. Generally, they do not want to share the risks. Thus it is not surprising that entrepreneurs will not commit time and resources to risky activities unless there is the prospect of earning a profit. One function of profit is to reward entrepreneurs for accepting the risk associated with their business decisions. Virtually all of these decisions carry the risk that money will be lost. Clearly, if there is a chance of a loss, there must be the chance for a gain in the form of profit; otherwise, such risks will not be taken.

Certain firms seem to be able to earn above-normal profits on a consistent basis. In some cases, they are continually innovative in developing new products, in reducing production costs on existing products, or in providing unusually good customer service. Although other firms may follow their lead and thus copy any new product or duplicate a production cost advantage, over time the truly innovative firm will have developed yet new products and production technology, thus maintaining its above-normal profit performance. In such cases, profit is playing a useful social function; it encourages firms to develop new products, to lower production costs, and to provide better service.

In other cases, firms may earn above-normal profit because they have monopoly power in a market. That is, for some reason, other firms are prevented from offering the same product or service for sale, thus allowing that firm to maintain high prices and profits. For example, Resorts International, Inc., was the first firm to be granted a gambling license in Atlantic City, New Jersey, when that activity was legalized in 1978. For three years, the firm made large profits. As soon as licenses were given to other firms, competition increased and Resorts' profit fell more than 50 percent. In another case, Bausch & Lomb, a large manufacturer of precision lenses, was given permission by the U.S. Food and Drug Administration (FDA) to produce and sell soft contact lenses. For several years the firm had a monopoly because no other firm was able to obtain FDA permission. During that period, prices of these lenses were very high as were profits for Bausch & Lomb. As soon as other firms were able to enter the market, both prices and profits declined.

In cases such as these, the above-normal profit is not socially useful. Indeed, a firm with monopoly power does not have as much incentive to hold down prices and production costs, to develop new products, or to provide good customer service as does a firm in a very competitive industry. However, in some industries, the lowest production cost can be achieved by having only one firm in the market. The generation and delivery of electric power is an example of such an industry. In most areas of the country, one firm is given a monopoly franchise but is subject to government regulation of price to ensure that "reasonable" prices are charged and that only a "fair" profit is earned. In this way, the advantage of low production cost is achieved without the above-normal profits usually associated with monopoly power.

Some critics of the capitalist system argue that profit is little more than a windfall gain that is randomly conferred on certain people. As such, they believe that it should be taxed away because it is "unearned." However, even if they were correct that profit is no more than a random windfall, the free enterprise system cannot work without profit. That is, no one will "play the game" (i.e., make investments in business) if there is no chance of winning a prize in the form of profit.

In a market characterized by many firms competing against one another, above-normal profits provide important signals but are not likely to be maintained over long periods of time. That is, firms already in the market respond to higher profits by increasing output, and new firms will have an incentive to enter the market as well. The result will be an increased supply of the product, lower prices, and, ultimately, lower profits. The result in competitive markets is that profits provide important signals but are somewhat transitory in nature.

CASE STUDY _____

William Henry Gates, III and the Microsoft Money Machine

Several years ago, when his fortune was a mere several hundred million dollars, a weekly magazine labeled Bill Gates as "America's richest 'nerd.'" In 1992, at age 36, he had passed Donald Trump, Ross Perot, and others to be listed as America's wealthiest person by *Forbes* magazine; the value of his holdings had grown to an estimated $6.3 billion. How did the free enterprise system help him to attain such phenomenal wealth?

After graduating from high school in Seattle in 1973, Gates went to Harvard. While there, he learned that the personal computer (PC) was in the development stage. He dropped out of school and threw himself completely into designing an operating system (the program that coordinates the hardware and software of the computer) for the PC. His system, MS-DOS (for Microsoft Disk Operating System), was so good that IBM agreed to use it in their line of personal computers. With IBM setting the industry standard, other computer manufacturers quickly adopted MS-DOS as well. Today it is estimated that more than 80 percent of all personal computers in the world use this system. Gates' firm, Microsoft, Inc., makes money on every computer sold with MS-DOS as the operating system. In 1992, the firm recorded $2.8 billion in revenue and $708 million in net profit. It ranks third in size in the industry, behind IBM and Hewlett-Packard. Gates's personal holdings of some 90 million shares of common stock represent about a 33 percent ownership share of the company.

Microsoft also produces programs for word processing, spreadsheets, and a variety of other applications. One of Gates's latest ventures has been to purchase the electronic reproduction rights to thousands of art and photographic works from museums and libraries around the world. These will be used as part of his plan for interactive home entertainment systems.

With extremely hard work, a creative mind, and a willingness to take risks, Gates has demonstrated how the market rewards the successful entrepreneur. He was able to produce what consumers wanted at a price they were willing to pay; the result was that both he and they are better off! This is the essence of the free-market economic system.

Economics and Decision Making

Where do the principles of microeconomics fit in the arena of managerial decision making? Nobel prize-winning economist Herbert Simon identifies the primary activities in decision making:[7]

1. Finding occasions for making decisions.
2. Identifying possible courses of action.
3. Evaluating the revenues and costs associated with each course of action.
4. Choosing that one course that best meets the goal or objective of the firm (i.e., that maximizes the value of the firm).

Thus the primary role of managerial economics is in evaluating the implications of alternative courses of action and choosing the best or optimal course of action from among those several alternatives.

Decision making in this context implies the need for optimizing behavior. The marketing vice-president strives to maximize sales revenue, the production manager attempts to minimize cost or maximize production, and the division president's goal is to maximize profit. As discussed in an earlier section, these management targets are constrained by other parameters relating to that decision. For example, production costs might be minimized by producing nothing, but this would be inconsistent with the firm's goal of profit maximization. A more

[7] H. A. Simon, "The Decision-Making Process" in *The Executive as Decision-Maker: The New Science of Management Decisions* (New York: Harper & Row, 1960).

typical goal for the production manager would be to minimize cost subject to producing a specified output rate, while the objective of the marketing vice-president would be to maximize sales subject to a given advertising budget.

The essence of efficient and rational management is constrained optimization. Virtually all choices and decisions are subject to limitations, and this is where the tools of managerial economics are most useful. The manager who can achieve the most despite those constraints will be rewarded with a high salary, stock options, and the other perquisites usually associated with success.

Optimization principles of managerial economics also are important in the not-for-profit sectors of the economy. For example, universities strive to maximize the value of teaching and research outputs subject to an annual budget constraint. Decisions about the level of tuition, the right mix of faculty and secretaries, and the balance between classrooms and laboratories will benefit from the correct application of the constrained optimization principles that are basic to economics.

KEY CONCEPTS

- Economic profit refers to revenues less all relevant costs, both explicit and implicit.
- Profit plays two roles in a market economy: (1) Changes in profit signal producers to change the rate of production, and (2) profit is a reward to entrepreneurs for taking risks, being especially innovative in developing new products, and reducing production costs.
- Firms can earn economic profits because they have monopoly power in a market. In general, such profits are not socially useful.
- The primary decision-making role of managerial economics is in determining the optimal course of action where there are constraints imposed on the decision.

Summary

Managerial economics can be viewed as an application of that part of microeconomics that focuses on such topics as risk, demand, production, cost, pricing, and market structure. Understanding these principles will help to develop a rational decision-making perspective and will sharpen the analytical framework that the executive must bring to bear on managerial decisions.

Individuals and firms interact in both the product and the factor markets. Prices of outputs and inputs are determined in these markets and guide the decisions of all market participants. The firm is an entity that organizes factors of production in order to produce goods and services to meet the demands of consumers and other firms. In a market system, the interplay of individuals and firms is not subject to central control. The prices of both products and factors of production guide this interaction. Within firms, however, activity is directed by managers. Central control within the firm is advantageous because transactions and information costs are reduced. The size of the firm is limited because transaction costs within the firm will rise as the firm grows and because management skill is limited.

It is assumed that the goal of the firm is to maximize the value of the firm or the present value of all future profits, defined as revenue less all costs, explicit and implicit. Opportunity costs such as the remuneration and interest that owners and managers have forgone on their labor and capital must be included as costs. Failure to account for these implicit costs may result in an inefficient allocation of resources. The objective of profit maximization is subject to legal, moral, contractual, financial, and technological constraints. Some economists argue that the firm's objective is a "satisfactory" level of profit rather than maximum profit.

Profit plays two primary roles in the free-market system. First, it acts as a signal to producers to increase or decrease the rate of output or to enter or leave an industry. Second, profit is a reward for entrepreneurial activity, including risk taking and innovation. In a competitive industry, economic profits tend to be transitory. The achievement of high profits by a firm usually results in other firms increasing their output of that product, thus reducing price and profit. Firms that have monopoly power may be able to earn above-normal profits over a longer period; such profit does not play a socially useful role in the economy.

A primary role of economics in management is in making optimizing decisions where constraints apply. In general, managerial economics will help managers to ensure that resources are allocated efficiently within the firm and that the firm makes appropriate reactions to changes in the economic environment.

Discussion Questions _____

1-1. Explain how firms and individuals participate and interact in the product market and in the factor market.

1-2. Describe the difference between the accounting and the economic concept of profit. How might accounting practices be changed to make financial statements and reports more useful for managerial decision making?

1-3. Explain how the principles of free-market economics that guide interrelations among firms and individuals might guide pricing and resource allocation decisions within the large, multiplant firm.

1-4. Why is it important to state a managerial objective? Could the assumption that managers' objective is profit maximization be useful even if their real objective is maximizing market share or their salaries?

1-5. What might be the objective or objectives of each of the following nonprofit institutions?
a. The college of business at a major state university.
b. A municipal police department.
c. The emergency room of a hospital.
d. A museum.

1-6. Explain the role of profit in a free-market economic system. How can such a small share of national income (about 15 percent) be such an important determinant of resource allocation?

1-7. Provide examples of managerial decisions that might reduce profits for the next few years but would increase the value of the firm. Explain.

1-8. Some argue that businesses need to be "socially responsible" (e.g., reduce pollution, employ more minority workers, cease buying from and selling to countries that are out of political favor, sell at lower prices to low-income people, etc.). Evaluate the effects on the firm of being socially responsible in a competitive environment. Can one firm in a market afford to be socially responsible if its competitors are not? Explain. Would you invest in a company that devoted a significant part of its resources to being socially responsible? Why?

1-9. Milton Friedman has argued that the realism of a model is not as important as its predictive ability. That is, a model of economic behavior that appears to be unrealistic but predicts well is superior to a model that seems more realistic but does not predict well. Do you agree? Why or why not?

1-10. In some large businesses, division managers must report profits monthly and, in some cases, more often. Some managers claim that the pressure to report favorable results continually on a month-to-month basis causes them to make decisions that will enhance short-term profit at the expense of profit in the long run. What actions might a manager take that would increase profit in the short run but that would reduce the present value of all future profits?

Problems

1-1. A recent engineering graduate turns down a job offer of $30,000 per year to start his own business. He will invest $50,000 of his own money, which has been in a bank account earning 7 percent in interest per year. He also plans to use a building he owns that has been rented to another business for $1,500 per month. Revenue during the first year was $107,000, while other expenses were

Advertising	$ 5,000
Rent	10,000
Taxes	5,000
Employees' salaries	40,000
Supplies	5,000

Prepare two income statements, one using the traditional accounting approach and one using the opportunity cost approach to determine profit.

1-2. Tempo Electronics, Inc., has an inventory of 5,000 unique electronic chips originally purchased at $2.50 each; their market value is now $5 each. The production department has proposed to use these by putting each one together with $6 worth of labor and other materials to produce a wristwatch that would be sold for $10. Should that proposal be implemented? Explain.

1-3. Smith, a college sophomore, generally spends his summers working on the university maintenance crew at a wage rate of $5.00 per hour for a 40-hour week. Overtime work is always available at an hourly rate of 1.5 times the regular wage rate. For the coming summer, he has been offered the pizza stand concession at the Student Union building, which would have to be open 10 hours per day, six days a week. He estimates that he can sell 100 pizzas a week at $6.00 each. The production cost of each pizza is $2.00 and the rent on the stand is $150 per week. Should Smith take the pizza concession? Explain.

Present Value Analysis

Many transactions involve making or receiving cash payments at various future dates. A home buyer trades a promise to make monthly payments for thirty years for a large amount of cash now to pay for a home. A person injured in an automobile accident accepts an insurance company's settlement of $1,000 per month for life as compensation for the damage associated with that injury. High-priced professional athletes offer their skills for multiyear, no-cut contracts. In all these cases, concepts relating to the time value of money are required to make sound decisions. The time value of money refers to the fact that a dollar to be received in the future is not worth a dollar today. Therefore, it is necessary to have techniques for measuring the value today (i.e., the present value) of dollars to be received or paid at different points in the future. This section outlines the approach to analyzing problems that involve payment and/or receipt of money at one or more points in time.

Understanding the following terms is essential to applying time value of money principles:

ANNUITY: a series of equal payments per period for a specified length of time. For example, the repayment of a loan by making forty-eight monthly payments of $200 each is a form of annuity.

AMOUNT: a specific number of dollars to be paid or received on a specified date.

PRESENT VALUE: the value today of an amount or an annuity, taking into consideration that interest can be earned.

Present Value of an Amount

The basic equation for the present value of an amount S is

$$PV = S \left[\frac{1}{(1 + i)^n} \right] \tag{1A-1}$$

The bracketed term

$$\left[\frac{1}{(1 + i)^n} \right]$$

is the present value of $1 in n periods if the interest rate is i percent. It is called the *present value interest factor* ($PVIF_{i,n}$).

As an example, what is the present value of $1,080 in one year if the interest rate is 8 percent per year? Substituting $S = 1,080$, $i = 0.08$ (i.e., the decimal equivalent of 8 percent), and $n = 1$ in equation (1A-1) yields

$$PV = \$1,080 \left[\frac{1}{(1.08)^1} \right] = \$1,000$$

Note that $1,000 would increase to $1,080 in one year at 8 percent interest. Thus, the present value concept explicitly takes account of the potential interest that could be earned.

Consider another problem. What is the present value of $100,000 to be received at the end of ten years if the interest rate is 10 percent? The problem can be expressed as

$$PV = 100,000 \left[\frac{1}{1.10} \right]^{10}$$

The present value interest factors ($PVIF_{i,n}$) for a range of interest rates and periods are given in Table I at the end of the book. Part of that table is reproduced as Table 1A-1.

Note that the present value factors decrease as the number of periods increases and as the interest rate increases. Because the interest rate is in the denominator of the present value equation, there is an inverse relationship between the present value and the interest rate. Further, the longer the period of time before an amount is paid, the lower the present value of any amount.

By reading down the "10%" column in Table 1A-1 to the row for $n = 10$ periods, the factor 0.3855 is found. This is the present value of $1 in ten years at 10 percent interest. Multiplying this factor by $100,000, we obtain

$$PV = 100,000(0.3855) = \$38,550$$

TABLE 1A-1 **Selected Present Value Interest Factors:**

$$PVIF_{i,n} = \left(\frac{1}{1 + i} \right)^n$$

	Interest Rate		
Periods	8%	10%	12%
1	0.9259	0.9091	0.8929
2	0.8573	0.8264	0.7972
3	0.7938	0.7513	0.7118
4	0.7350	0.6830	0.6355
6	0.6302	0.5645	0.5066
8	0.5403	0.4665	0.4039
10	0.4632	0.3855	0.3220

If 10 percent is the appropriate interest rate, $100,000 in ten years is equivalent to $38,550 today.

The process of reducing a future amount to its present value is often referred to as *discounting* because the present value is always less than the future amount. In this context, the interest rate used in present value problems is generally referred to as a *discount rate.*

Present Value of an Annuity

An *annuity* has been defined as a series of periodic equal payments. Although the term is often thought of in terms of a retirement pension, there are many other examples of annuities. The repayment schedule for a mortgage loan is an annuity. A father's agreement to send his son $200 each month while he is in college is another example. Usually, the number of periods is specified but not always. Sometimes retirement benefits are paid monthly as long as a person is alive. In other cases, the annuity is paid forever and is called a *perpetuity.*

It must be emphasized that the strict definition of an annuity implies equal payments. A contract to make 20 annual payments, which increase each year by, say, 10 percent, would not be an annuity. As some financial arrangements provide for payments with periodic increases, care must be taken not to apply an annuity formula if the flow of payments is not a true annuity.

The present value of an annuity can be thought of as the sum of the present values of each of several amounts. Consider an annuity of three $100 payments at the end of each of the next three years at 10 percent interest. The present value of each payment is

$$PV_1 = 100 \left(\frac{1}{1.10} \right)$$

$$PV_2 = 100 \left(\frac{1}{1.10} \right)^2$$

$$PV_3 = 100 \left(\frac{1}{1.10} \right)^3$$

and the sum of these would be

$$PV = 100 \left(\frac{1}{1.10} \right) + 100 \left(\frac{1}{1.10} \right)^2 + 100 \left(\frac{1}{1.10} \right)^3$$

or

$$PV = 100 \left[\left(\frac{1}{1.10} \right) + \left(\frac{1}{1.10} \right)^2 + \left(\frac{1}{1.10} \right)^3 \right]$$

Substituting the appropriate present value interest factors from Table 1A-1 and multiplying yields the present value of this annuity:

$$PV = 100(0.9091 + 0.8264 + 0.7513) = 100(2.4868) = 248.68$$

Although this approach works, it clearly would be cumbersome for annuities of more than a few periods. For example, consider using this method to find the present value of a monthly payment for forty years if the monthly interest rate is 1 percent. That would require evaluating the present value of each of 480 amounts!

In general, the formula for the present value of an annuity of A dollars per period for n periods and a discount rate of i is

$$PV = A\left(\frac{1}{1+i}\right)^1 + A\left(\frac{1}{1+i}\right)^2 + \cdots + A\left(\frac{1}{1+i}\right)^n$$

This can be written as

$$PV = A\left[\sum_{t=1}^{n}\left(\frac{1}{1+i}\right)^t\right] \tag{1A-2}$$

Equation (1A-2) is the general equation for the present value of an annuity. Recall that $\sum_{t=1}^{n}$ means the sum of n separate components, the first where $t = 1$, the second where $t = 2$, and so on, to $t = n$.

The term

$$\sum_{t=1}^{n}\left[\frac{1}{(1+i)^t}\right]$$

is called the *present value annuity factor* ($PVAF_{i,n}$). It is the present value of an annuity of $1 per period for n periods at a discount rate of i percent. Table II at the end of the book provides these factors for a variety of interest rates and periods. Part of that table is reproduced as Table 1A-2 here.

Consider the present value of an annuity of $3,522 per month for thirty months with an interest rate of 1 percent per month. Note that this problem differs from the first two examples because it considers monthly (not annual) payments and a monthly discount rate. This should not be confusing. The general problem refers to n periods and a discount rate of i percent *per period*. As long as the length of period (i.e., month, year, etc.) and the interest rate for that period correspond,

TABLE 1A-2 **Selected Present Value Annuity Factors:**

$$PVAF_{i,n} = \sum_{t=1}^{n}\frac{1}{(1+i)^t}$$

	Interest Rate		
Periods	*1%*	*2%*	*3%*
12	11.2551	10.5753	9.9540
24	21.2434	18.9139	16.9355
30	25.8077	22.3965	19.6004

the approach is straightforward. For example, if the periods are years, the interest rate must be a yearly rate.

The equation for the present value of this monthly annuity is

$$PV = 3{,}522 \left[\sum_{t=1}^{30} \left(\frac{1}{1.01} \right)^t \right]$$

The factor

$$\sum_{t=1}^{30} \frac{1}{(1.01)^t}$$

is the present value of an annuity of $1. From Table 1A-2, that value is 25.8077. Substituting that value and multiplying gives $PV = \$3{,}522(25.8077) = \$90{,}895$. This means that an amount of $90,895 invested at an interest rate of 1 percent per month would be just adequate to make thirty monthly payments of $3,522.

A similar problem might be stated in the following way. What is the present value of a series of 30 monthly payments of $150 if the interest rate is 24 percent per year? Note that the payments are monthly, but the interest rate is an annual rate. By dividing the annual interest rate by 12, the appropriate monthly rate is found (i.e., $24/12 = 2$). Thus the solution would be

$$PV = 150 \left[\sum_{t=1}^{30} \left(\frac{1}{1.02} \right)^t \right] = 150(22.3965) = \$3{,}359$$

With the advent of financial calculators, there is less need for actually using the present value equations and the tabular data on present value interest and annuity factors. However, it is essential that the principles underlying these financial calculations be understood.

KEY CONCEPT

- Given the interest rate per period (i), the number of periods (n), and the amount (S) or the annuity payment (A), there are two basic present value problems:

1. PRESENT VALUE OF AN AMOUNT: $PV = S \left[\dfrac{1}{(1 + i)^n} \right]$

PV is the present value of an amount S to be received (or paid) in n periods if the interest rate is i percent per period. The term $1/(1 + i)^n$ is the present value interest factor ($PVIF_{i,n}$).

2. PRESENT VALUE OF AN ANNUITY: $PV = A \left[\displaystyle\sum_{t=1}^{n} \frac{1}{(1 + i)^t} \right]$

Here PV is the present value of an annuity of A per period paid at the end of each of n periods if the interest rate is i percent per period. The term $\displaystyle\sum_{t=1}^{n} [1/(1 + i)^t]$ is the present value annuity factor $PVAF_{i,n}$.

Problems _____

1A-1. Robert Ryan, general manager of the Chicago Stars professional football team, is currently negotiating a new contract with Ronnie Smith, the team's star running back. Under league rules, Smith is now a free agent, which means that he is free to negotiate a contract with any other team in the league. Smith has presented Ryan with a final contract demand consisting of alternatives for a five-year contract. If Ryan does not agree to one of these, Smith will sign with another team. The alternative contract demands are

a. A $2,000,000 bonus payment immediately, a payment of $500,000 at the end of each of the next five years, and a deferred payment of $1,000,000 at the end of the fifth year of the contract.

b. A $500,000 bonus payment now, payments of $300,000 at the end of each of the next five years, and deferred payments of $200,000 each payable at the end of years 11 through 20.

Ryan has determined that Smith's value to the team over the next five years is about $3,000,000 (in terms of the present value of additional revenue from gate receipts and television discounted at 12 percent per year). Should Ryan accept one of Smith's contract demands, and if so, which one? Explain fully.

1A-2. A rich uncle gives you the choice of one of the following legacies:

a. $15,000 each year for the next twelve years.

b. $13,000 each year for the next eighteen years.

c. $11,000 each year for the next twelve years plus a lump-sum payment of $81,000 at the end of the eighteenth year.

Which would you take and why? Assume that the appropriate discount rate is 10 percent and all amounts would be received at the end of the year.

1A-3. Mighty-Lite, Inc., a manufacturer of plastic tables for institutional use, is considering a capital spending program involving annual expenditures of $100,000 for each of the next five years. The firm estimates that its annual profit of $100,000 would increase by 50 percent when the capital program was completed. Assuming the firm has a 20-year life and the appropriate interest rate is 12 percent, should the capital spending program be implemented?

1A-4. Andrew Construction borrows the entire cost of a new dump truck. The loan has an annual interest rate of 12 percent and calls for monthly payments of $1,000 over a five-year period. What is the cost of the truck?

1A-5. A couple borrows $10,000 to buy a car. The loan agreement specifies that monthly payments are to be made for four years. The annual interest rate is 12 percent. Determine the monthly payment.

1A-6. A firm develops a new product that will add $50,000 to profit each year for five years. If the discount rate is 10 percent per year, how much will this new product add to the value of the firm?

1A-7. It is estimated that the annual after-tax profits of the Microwave Corporation will be $500,000 per year for each of the next 30 years. Given a discount rate of 14 percent, what is the value of this firm?

CHAPTER 2

Basic Training

Preview _____

Just as the skilled craftsman needs tools to build a new home, the manager needs tools to assist in making decisions that will ultimately maximize the value of the firm. Increasingly, these tools are of the quantitative sort. Algebra, statistics, linear programming, and, to some extent, calculus are used in all the functional areas of business today. This is especially true for decision makers in production and finance, but even those in marketing and business law increasingly find these tools of value.

Many management decisions fall into the category of optimization problems. Optimization refers to finding the best way to allocate resources given an objective function. For example, a production manager may seek to maximize production for given inputs of capital and labor or to minimize the cost of producing a specified rate of output. In contrast, the president of the firm, who has a broader perspective, may want to organize the firm's labor and capital resources in order to maximize profit. Terms such as *minimize* and *maximize* imply an optimization problem. Sometimes managers seek optimal decisions by trial and error or other informal methods. In many situations, however, data on the firm and its market can be combined with quantitative analytical tools to scientifically determine the optimal management strategy.

The purpose of this chapter is to introduce basic quantitative tools that are commonly used in managerial decision making and to demonstrate their applications. In the first section, functional relationships are discussed, and a special set of functions—total, average, and marginal—is developed and applied to problems in managerial economics. Next, the nature and structure of an economic model is discussed. Typically, such models include several equations and conditions that constrain the nature of these functions. In the last section, basic principles of probability are developed, with emphasis on measures of central tendency and dispersion for probability distributions.

In addition, a review of the elements of calculus and their application to economics is included as an appendix. While all of the important concepts in managerial economics can be understood without using calculus, its use helps to understand important relationships and allows certain problems to be solved.

Functional Relationships: Total, Average, and Marginal _____

In mathematics, an equation of the form

$$y = f(x) \tag{2-1}$$

is read "*y* is a function of *x*." This means that the value of *y* depends on the value of *x* in a systematic way and that there is a unique value of *y* for each value of *x*. Usually the variable on the left-hand side of the equation, *y* in this case, is called the *dependent variable*. The variable on the right-hand side is called the *independent variable*.

Of course, y may depend on two or more independent variables, such as

$$y = g(x,z) \qquad \text{(2-2)}$$

or

$$y = h(x_1, x_2, \ldots, x_n) \qquad \text{(2-3)}$$

The letters f, g, and h have no specific meaning other than to indicate that a functional relationship exists between y and the independent variable or variables. Equation (2-1) is referred to as a univariate function because it has only one independent variable. Equations (2-2) and (2-3) are multivariate functions.

In many economic models, a special set of functional relationships called total, average, and marginal functions is used. Such functions are involved in the theory of demand, cost, production, and market structure. A basic command of these concepts is essential to understanding the principles of managerial economics.

The following production example will help in understanding these relationships. Suppose that there is a small building containing four machines and a stock of raw materials ready to be processed. Ten equally skilled and diligent workers are lined up outside ready to go to work in this factory. Unless the plant is completely automated, if there are no workers, output will be zero. As workers are added, output increases. The total amount of output associated with a particular input of labor working with those four machines is called the *total product of labor*. For example, the total product of one worker might be two units of output. As the labor input changes, so does total output. An example of a total product schedule is shown in the first two columns of Table 2-1.

As just indicated, one person working alone in this factory produces two units of output. Adding a second person and organizing the production system so that

TABLE 2-1 **Total, Average, and Marginal Product of Labor Schedules**

(1) Number of Workers (L)	(2) Total Product (Q)	(3) Average Product (AP)	(4) Marginal Product (MP)
0	0	—	
1	2	2.0	− 2
2	5	2.5	− 3
3	9	3.0	− 4
4	14	3.5	− 5
5	22	4.4	− 8
6	40	6.7	−18
7	57	8.1	−17
8	63	7.9	− 6
9	64	7.1	− 1
10	63	6.3	−1

the workers complement each other results in total product increasing to five units. The first worker is associated with a two-unit increase in output; having two workers instead of one will increase output by three units; three workers will increase output by four units; and so on. The change in output associated with a one-unit change in workers is called the *marginal product of labor*. Using the Greek capital letter delta (Δ) to indicate a change, the *marginal product function* (*MP*) can be defined as

$$MP = \frac{\Delta Q}{\Delta L} \qquad\qquad (2\text{-}4)$$

where Q represents output and L represents the input of labor.[1]

Note in Table 2-1 that for the first six workers, the marginal product increases as the rate of labor input increases. However, marginal product declines thereafter. That is, the sixth worker adds 18 units to output, but the seventh adds only 17 units and the eighth worker only 6. Finally, having ten workers actually causes output to decline; the marginal product associated with the tenth worker is negative. The point has been reached where there are too many workers in this plant. Perhaps they are getting in each other's way; in any event, the presence of ten workers has thwarted the achievement of efficient production.[2]

The *average product of labor function* (*AP*) measures the average output per unit of labor used. Average product is found by dividing total product by labor input. That is,

$$AP = \frac{TP}{L}$$

The total product function is plotted in Figure 2-1a, and the average and marginal product functions are shown in Figure 2-1b.[3] There are important relation-

---

[1] The marginal product function is the slope of the total product function. Slope can be defined as the change in the dependent variable divided by the change in the independent variable. Consider the function $y = 10 + 3x$. A one-unit change in x, say from $x = 5$ to $x = 6$, is associated with a three-unit change in y, from $y = 25$ to $y = 28$. Thus the change in y (i.e., Δy) is 3, and the change in x (i.e., Δx) is 1, so the slope is $\Delta y / \Delta x = 3/1 = 3$.

[2] That marginal product must ultimately decline as workers are added is clear in this example. The building has a finite amount of floor space. The change in output should be positive if one or two workers are added. But for some number of workers, output will be zero as workers fight for a place to stand rather than produce output. Therefore, beyond some rate of labor input, marginal product must decline.

[3] All three of the functions are drawn with graphs having the same units on both axes (i.e., output on the vertical axis and number of workers on the horizontal axis). Therefore, all three could have been included in the same graph. However, the range of total product (0 to 64) is so much greater than the range of average and marginal product that it is more descriptive to use two graphs. Note that the height of each interval on the vertical axis in Figure 2-2b is considerably greater than in Figure 2-2a. This allows the relationships among all three functions to be seen more clearly than if they were all drawn in the same graph. Note also that the horizontal axis in both graphs is exactly the same. This allows comparison of points on one graph that correspond to points on the other.

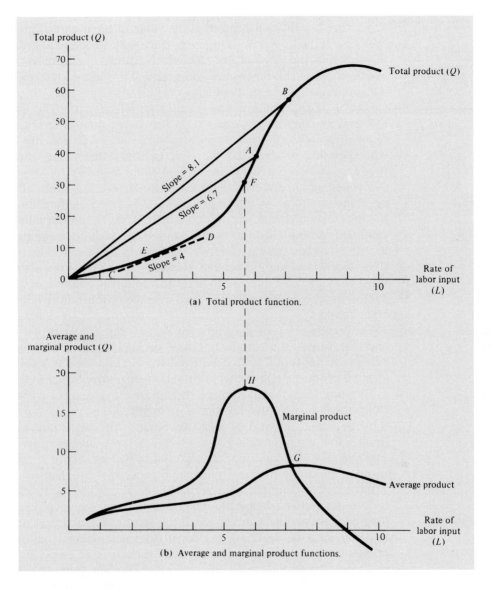

FIGURE 2-1 **The Product Functions.**

ships among the three functions that are true for all total, average, and marginal functions. First, the value of the average function at any point along that curve is equal to the slope of a ray drawn from the origin to the total function at the corresponding point. For example, from Table 2-1 it is known that the average product of six workers is 6.7. Thus, the slope of a line (OA) drawn from the origin to point A on the total product function has a slope of 6.7. Similarly, the average product of seven workers is 8.1; this is equal to the slope of a line drawn from the origin to point B on the total product function.

Another key relationship is that the value of the marginal function is equal to the slope of the line drawn tangent to the total function at a corresponding point. For example, the slope of line *CD*, which is drawn tangent to the total function at *E*, is about 4. This means that the marginal product corresponding to this point (i.e., between 2 and 3 units of labor) is 4.

Point *F* on the total function is called an *inflection point*. To the left of point *F*, the total function is increasing at an increasing rate; to the right of *F*, the total function is increasing but at a decreasing rate. Note that this inflection point, corresponding to about six workers, occurs at the point where the marginal product function is at a maximum (i.e., point *H* in Figure 2-1b).

If the marginal and average functions intersect, that point of intersection will be at the minimum or maximum point on the average function. In Figure 2-1b, the intersection occurs at point *G*, which is the maximum point of the average product function. The logic of this relationship is quite straightforward. Suppose that the average product for two workers is 2.5, and the marginal product of three workers is more than that average, say, 4. Thus the average product for three workers must increase to 3. If the additional output associated with hiring another worker is above the previous average product, the average product must be increasing.

Conversely, suppose that eight workers average 7.9 units of output per period, and that the marginal product of nine workers is only 1. This will cause average product to fall to 7.1. If an additional worker adds less to total output than the average product prior to that addition, average product must fall.

This logic leads to the following conclusion. For any set of average and marginal functions, if the marginal function is greater than the average function, the average must be rising. If marginal is below average, the average must be falling. This implies that the intersection of the two functions must occur where the average function is at a maximum or minimum. As will be shown in later chapters, this result is important in many managerial economics problems.

If the marginal function is positive, the total function must be rising. Note that it does not matter whether the marginal function is increasing or decreasing, as long as it is positive. Conversely, if the marginal function is negative, the total function must be declining. Again, it does not matter if marginal is rising or falling. If marginal is negative, the total function will be declining. For the data in Table 2-1 and Figure 2-1, the marginal product is positive for the first nine workers. It declines after the sixth worker but remains positive through the ninth. Note that total product increases until the tenth worker is added. The marginal product of the tenth worker is −1, and this negative marginal product is associated with a decline in total product.

Because the total function increases as long as the marginal function is positive and decreases when marginal is negative, it follows that total product is at a maximum when the marginal function is zero. In Figure 2-1 the maximum of the total product function occurs at nine workers. This point corresponds to the point where the marginal function intersects the horizontal axis, that is, where marginal changes from being positive to negative.

An understanding of total, average, and marginal relations is an important foundation for the effective study of managerial economics. Terms such as *average* cost, *marginal product*, and *total revenue* are integral parts of the manager's vocabulary, and the associated principles are some of the manager's most powerful tools.

CASE STUDY ————————————————————————————————————

Decision Making in the Public Sector: Marginal Analysis and Automobile Safety

Suppose a specific automobile model has so many engineering defects that the risk of having an accident is greatly increased. Although the car is no longer being manufactured, vehicles already on the road are expected to cause ten deaths during the next year. For simplicity, it is assumed that the engineering defects are so severe that none of the cars will be running after one year. The number of deaths can be reduced if the manufacturer recalls the cars and corrects some or all of the defects. Clearly, the more defects that are corrected, the greater will be the reduction in the number of deaths.

As shown in the table, the marginal cost of repairing and modifying these cars in order to

others require a substantial modification of the vehicle.

Suppose that the National Highway Traffic Safety Administration, a federal agency responsible for regulating automobile safety, uses marginal principles to make recall decisions and that the agency has determined that each life saved is worth $800,000 to society. That is, $800,000 is the marginal benefit associated with saving a life.

The benefits and costs of the recall/repair program shown in the table can be compared to make a decision. The marginal cost of saving the first life is $200,000 and the marginal benefit is $800,000. Thus it is clear that the manufacturer

Deaths	Marginal Cost of Death Prevention	Marginal Benefit of a Life Saved	Total Net Benefits
10	$1,000,000		
9	$1,200,000	$800,000	$1,600,000
8	$1,400,000	$800,000	$1,000,000
7	$1,600,000	$800,000	$1,200,000
6	$1,800,000	$800,000	$1,200,000
5	$1,000,000	$800,000	$1,000,000
4	$1,200,000	$800,000	$1,600,000
3	$1,400,000	$800,000	$1,000,000
2	$1,600,000	$800,000	$-800,000
1	$1,800,000	$800,000	$-1,800,000
0	$2,000,000	$800,000	$-3,000,000

reduce the number of deaths from ten to nine is $200,000, but marginal cost rises as the number of deaths decreases. For example, the marginal cost of going from one death to no deaths is $2,000,000. This cost rises because some of the defects are easily corrected, whereas

should be required to take some action. However, it is equally clear that it would be inefficient to attempt to eliminate all defects. For example, the marginal cost of going from one death to zero deaths is $2,000,000 but the marginal benefit is only $800,000.

The recall program should be designed to reduce those defects (and associated deaths) to the point where marginal benefits equal marginal costs. In this example, that equality occurs at six deaths. Note that total net benefits (a *net benefit* is defined as marginal benefit less marginal cost) are maximized ($1,200,000) at six deaths. Total benefits are $3,200,000 (i.e., four lives saved multiplied by $800,000 per life) and total costs are $2,000,000. To require additional repairs to reduce the number of deaths below six is not socially efficient because the costs exceed the benefits.

KEY CONCEPTS

- A functional relationship of the form

$$y = f(x_1, x_2, \ldots, x_n)$$

  means that there is a systematic relationship between the dependent variable y and the independent variables $x_1, x_2, \ldots, x_n$ and that there is a unique value of y for any set of values of the independent variables.
- For any total function (e.g., total product, total revenue, etc.) there is an associated marginal function and average function.
- The key relationships among the total, average, and marginal functions are
  1. The value of the average function at any point is the slope of a ray drawn from the origin to the total function.
  2. The value of the marginal function at any point is the slope of a line drawn tangent to the total function at that point.
  3. The marginal function will intersect the average function at either a minimum or a maximum point of the average function.
  4. If the marginal function is positive, the total function will be increasing. If the marginal function is negative, the total function will be decreasing.
  5. The total function reaches a maximum or minimum when the marginal function equals zero.

Economic Models

In the aerospace industry, small model airplanes are flown in wind tunnels to test the flight characteristics of full-sized planes having the same characteristics. In economics, graphs and / or equations are used to explain economic relationships and phenomena and to predict the effects of changes in such economic parameters as prices, wage rates, and the price of capital. Although such models are abstractions from reality and may seem unrealistic, they are useful in studying the way an economic system works. Just as it is not sound practice to build a radically new jet aircraft before a model is used to test its flight characteristics, an economic decision should not be made without having analyzed its implications by using an economic model.

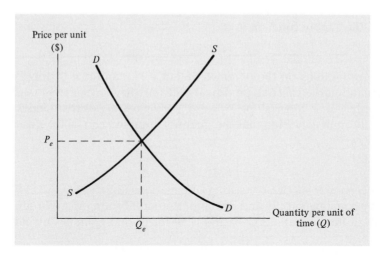

FIGURE 2-2 **Graphical Representation of Supply and Demand Analysis.**

An economic model usually consists of several related functions, some restrictions on one or more of the coefficients of these functions, and equilibrium conditions. Recall the concepts of supply and demand from introductory economics. As shown in Figure 2-2, the demand curve (*DD*) slopes downward from left to right and shows the quantity of output that consumers are willing and able to buy at each price. The negative slope implies that a larger quantity is demanded at lower prices than at higher prices. The supply curve (*SS*) shows the amount that firms will produce and offer for sale at each price. This curve has a positive slope because firms will supply a larger quantity at higher prices than at lower prices.[4]

Equilibrium in a market exists when the quantity demanded equals the quantity supplied. This is shown graphically as the intersection of the demand and supply functions in Figure 2-2. In this example, P_e and Q_e are the equilibrium price and quantity, respectively. In equilibrium there is no incentive for buyers or sellers to change price or the quantity. At point $\{P_e, Q_e\}$, buyers' demands are met exactly and suppliers are selling exactly the number of units they desire to sell at that price.

The above example is an economic model depicted graphically. A simple algebraic model can be used to describe exactly the same economic phenomenon and can do so more precisely. The quantity demanded (Q_d) and the quantity supplied (Q_s) are both functions of price. That is,

$$Q_d = f(P) \quad \text{and} \quad Q_s = g(P)$$

Suppose that the demand function is

$$Q_d = B + aP \quad \text{where } a < 0 \tag{2-5}$$

---

[4] The principles of demand and supply are discussed in greater detail in Chapters 3 and 9.

and the supply function is

$$Q_s = D + cP \quad \text{where } c > 0 \tag{2-6}$$

The restrictions on the parameters (i.e., $a < 0$ and $c > 0$) simply mean that the demand curve must slope downward (i.e., have a negative slope) and that the supply curve must slope upward (i.e., have a positive slope). By adding an equilibrium condition that the quantity supplied equals the quantity demanded, that is,

$$Q_d = Q_s \tag{2-7}$$

the economic model, consisting of equations (2-5), (2-6), and (2-7), is complete.

By equating supply and demand, the equilibrium price (P_e) can be determined. Substituting equations (2-5) and (2-6) for Q_d and Q_s in (2-7) yields

$$B + aP = D + cP$$

Solving for P, the equilibrium price is

$$P_e = \frac{D - B}{a - c} \tag{2-8}$$

The equilibrium quantity is found by substituting the equilibrium price into either the supply or demand function and solving for quantity. Using the demand function, the equilibrium quantity is

$$Q_e = B + a\frac{D - B}{a - c}$$

If the values of the parameters a, B, c, and D are known, the actual values of P_e and Q_e can easily be calculated. In Chapter 4, statistical methods used to estimate the numerical values of these parameters are reviewed.

Models of this type are used extensively in the study of economics. Indeed, one of the strengths of the discipline is that important and powerful results can be derived from models that are quite simple. To be sure, some economic models in advanced books are very complex. However, a thorough grasp of many of the key principles of economics can be obtained by applying rather basic concepts and models to business and social problems. Clearly, an important reason for studying managerial economics is to develop a set of economic models that can be used to analyze the many resource allocation problems faced by managers.

EXAMPLE ————————————————————————————————————

Determining Equilibrium Price and Quantity

Suppose parameters of the demand and supply equations have been estimated and that the equations are

$$Q_d = 14 - 2P$$

and

$$Q_s = 2 + 4P$$

Determine the equilibrium price and quantity.

SOLUTION   Note that the slopes of these functions meet the constraints specified in the chapter. That is, the demand function slopes downward and the supply curve slopes upward. Substituting the demand and supply functions in the equilibrium condition $Q_d = Q_s$ and solving for P_e yields

$$P_e = \frac{D - B}{a - c} = \frac{2 - 14}{-2 - 4} = 2$$

Substituting $P_e = 2$ into the demand function yields the equilibrium quantity

$$Q_e = 14 - 2(2) = 10$$

Thus the price–quantity combination $\{P_e = 2, Q_e = 10\}$ results in equilibrium in this market. This combination corresponds to $\{P_e, Q_e\}$ in Figure 2-2.

KEY CONCEPTS

- An economic model typically consists of several functional relationships, conditions or constraints on one or all of these functions, and one or more equilibrium conditions.
- Generally, economic models are used to demonstrate an economic principle, to explain an economic phenomenon, or to predict the economic implications of some change affecting one or more of the functional relationships.

Probability and Probability Distributions

Managers are often faced with making decisions that have the potential for a variety of outcomes. An outcome is a possible result of some action. For example, flipping a coin will result in one of two outcomes—heads or tails. A management decision to introduce a new product could result in a range of outcomes varying from wide consumer acceptance to no interest whatsoever. The quality of any decision will be enhanced by identifying the possible outcomes of the decision and then estimating the relative chances of each occurring. This listing of outcomes and the chance of each occurring is a *probability distribution* that can be evaluated using quantitative techniques. Often the chance of an outcome occurring will depend on the state of nature that prevails. The term *state of nature* refers to conditions in the business environment that will influence the outcome of a decision but that are not subject to control by the decision maker. For example, the condition of the general economy is a state of nature that will affect the outcomes of most business decisions.

Probability and probability distributions are an important part of the manager's tool kit. In this section, methods are developed to set up the probability distribution and then evaluate measures of central tendency and dispersion for that distribution. In Chapter 14, these principles are extended to analyze the concept of risk in decision making.

Probability

The *probability* of an event is the relative frequency of its occurrence in a large number of repeated trials. For example, in repeated tossing of a coin, a head will appear about one-half the time. That is, the relative frequency or probability of a head occurring is 0.50. In rolling a die, there are six possible outcomes, 1, 2, 3, 4, 5, 6. The relative frequency of any one of these outcomes is $1/6$, implying a probability of 0.167 for each outcome.

The probability of some events is known or can be computed with certainty. For example, the probabilities of most outcomes associated with rolling dice, drawing playing cards from a deck, and tossing coins are easily determined using standard principles of probability. Other probabilities are not easily determined mathematically but can be determined by repeating the process many times and observing how many times particular outcomes occur. For instance, there may be no mathematical way to estimate the probability of winning a particular game. But by playing the game many times and noting the number of times it is won, the probability of winning can be determined.

In other cases there is no accurate way to estimate probabilities except by using judgment. The weather forecaster's statement that "the probability of measurable precipitation tomorrow is 0.40" is based on an evaluation of how prevailing breezes, radar maps, and upper-air charts are associated with given weather conditions. Assessing the probability of a recession next year or a significant change in consumer preferences falls into the same category. Based on an analysis of current economic conditions, surveys of business capital-spending plans, and other information, a judgment can be made as to that probability. This judgment is necessarily subjective and may differ significantly among analysts, but predictions of this type are made daily by business managers, economists, and other decision makers.

Probability Distributions

For a decision or an experiment of some type with several possible outcomes, the probability of the *i*th outcome occurring is indicated by P_i, where

$$0 \le P_i \le 1 \quad i = 1, 2, \ldots, n \tag{2-9}$$

That is, the probability must take on a value in the range 0 to 1. Negative probabilities and those in excess of unity have no meaning. For example, if an event had a probability of 1.25, that would mean that it would occur more than 100 percent of the time!

Furthermore, the sum of the probabilities of all possible outcomes or events of an experiment must equal 1. That is,

$$\sum_{i=1}^{n} P_i = 1 \qquad (2\text{-}10)$$

This means that when the experiment is conducted (i.e., the dice rolled, the coin tossed, or the investment made), one of the outcomes must occur. It follows that the probability that an event will *not* occur is 1 minus the probability that it will occur. For example, if the probability of a 6 occurring when rolling a die is $\frac{1}{6}$, this implies that the probability of not rolling a six is $1 - \frac{1}{6} = \frac{5}{6}$. This corollary is useful because it is sometimes easier to find the probability of an event not occurring than the probability that the event will occur.

A listing of each outcome of an experiment and its probability defines a probability distribution. For example, the probabilities of tossing 0, 1, 2, or 3 heads in three tosses of a coin are shown in Table 2-2. In this example, X_i is the number of heads observed in each experiment of three tosses. Note that each probability is between 0 and 1 and that the sum of the probabilities is equal to 1.

Statistics of a Probability Distribution

For any probability distribution, there is a set of statistics or measures that describes or provides summary information about the distribution. The most important of these are measures of central tendency and dispersion. These have many applications in business, science, and engineering. In managerial economics they can be used to evaluate and compare the returns associated with alternative strategies and thus help to make sound managerial decisions.

EXPECTED VALUE. The first of these statistics is the expected value or mean of a probability distribution. Effectively, it is a weighted average of the outcomes using the probabilities of those outcomes as weights. The expected value is a measure of *central tendency* because in repeated trials of most experiments, the values of the outcomes tend to be concentrated around this statistic. For example, the expected value of the distribution for rolling two dice is 7. The range of

TABLE 2-2 **Probabilities Associated with Tossing a Coin Three Times**

Number of Heads (X_i)	Probability (P_i)
0	0.125
1	0.375
2	0.375
3	0.125

outcomes is 2 through 12, but the outcomes 6 through 8 occur much more often than the outcomes 2, 3, 11, or 12. This is because there are more combinations of the faces of the dice that yield 6, 7, or 8 than combinations that yield 2, 3, 11, or 12. There is only one combination $(1, 1)$ that yields 2, but there are six combinations $(1, 6)$, $(2, 5)$, $(3, 4)$, $(4, 3)$, $(5, 2)$, and $(6, 1)$ that yield 7.

The expected value (μ) of any probability distribution is computed by multiplying each outcome by its respective probability and then summing the products. Thus

$$\mu = P_1 X_1 + P_2 X_2 + \cdots + P_n X_n = \sum_{i=1}^{n} P_i X_i \qquad (2\text{-}11)$$

Recall the probability distribution for the number of heads observed in three tosses of a coin.

Heads	Probability
0	0.125
1	0.375
2	0.375
3	0.125

The expected value of this distribution is computed to be

$$\mu = 0.125(0) + 0.375(1) + 0.375(2) + 0.125(3) = 1.50$$

This means that if this experiment were repeated many times and the number of heads observed for each trial recorded, the average number of heads would be 1.50. Obviously, it is not possible to toss 1.5 heads on any trial. The expected value is not a particular outcome but is merely an average of the outcomes for a large number of repetitions of the experiment.

Understanding this principle and applying it when making managerial plans and decisions can be very profitable. The financial success of gambling casinos in Las Vegas and Atlantic City is evidence of the truth of this statement. The managers of these firms use the principles of probability to structure the gambling games played in their casinos. The payoffs to the players are always set so that the house wins more than an equal share of the amounts wagered. The return on a gambling game is often referred to as the expected payoff. It is computed by multiplying the probability of winning by the amount to be won and adding the product of the probability of losing and the amount to be lost. Consider a slot machine that costs $1 per play. The machine is programmed so that on average it returns $8 once in every ten plays for a net payoff of $7 (i.e., the $8 gross return less the $1 cost of playing the game). The probability distribution is as follows:

State of Nature	Outcome	Probability
Win	$7	0.10
Lose	−1	0.90

The expected payoff to the player is $\$-0.20$, that is,

$$\mu = 0.10(7) + 0.9(-1) = -0.20$$

A game is said to be fair if the expected return or payoff is zero. Clearly, the previous example is not a fair game; the player expects to lose $0.20 (equivalently, the casino expects to win $0.20) every time the slot machine is played. Gambling games in casinos are not fair in a statistical sense because the expected values are negative for the player.

STANDARD DEVIATION. The second statistic of interest measures the dispersion of possible outcomes around the expected value. This measure is called the standard deviation (σ) and is given by the equation

$$\sigma = \sqrt{\Sigma P_i(X_i - \mu)^2} \tag{2-12}$$

As just indicated, the standard deviation measures the variability of outcomes around the expected value of the distribution. If there is no variation in the outcomes, that is, if all $X_i = \mu$, then $\sigma = 0$. As the amount of variation about the expected value increases, the value of σ also increases.

The computation of σ for the probability distribution for tossing three coins is as follows:

$$\begin{aligned}\sigma &= \sqrt{0.125(0 - 1.5)^2 + 0.375(1 - 1.5)^2 + 0.375(2 - 1.5)^2 + 0.125(3 - 1.5)^2} \\ &= 0.87\end{aligned}$$

Because the standard deviation provides information about the dispersion of the individual values or outcomes around the expected value, this measure of variation can be of use in decision making. Suppose that a manager was considering two investment alternatives, A and B. The probability distributions for each are shown in Figure 2-3. Note that the expected value of profit (i.e., $100) is the same for both, but there is a much greater range of outcomes for B than A. This implies that σ_B is greater than σ_A (i.e., B is a riskier investment than A). Most decision makers will pick A, although there may be others who would select B because of differences in their preference for risk. The nature of these preferences is discussed in more detail in Chapter 14.

COEFFICIENT OF VARIATION. The third statistic is the coefficient of variation, which relates the variation of outcomes to the mean. It is defined as the ratio of the standard deviation to the expected value:

$$v = \frac{\sigma}{\mu} \tag{2-13}$$

This statistic provides a useful way to compare the variation to the expected value of a probability distribution. It measures variation per unit of expected value. The use of the coefficient of variation can be illustrated by considering two probability distributions, C and D, having the following statistics:

$$\mu_C = 100 \qquad \sigma_C = 50$$
$$\mu_D = 50 \qquad \sigma_D = 30$$

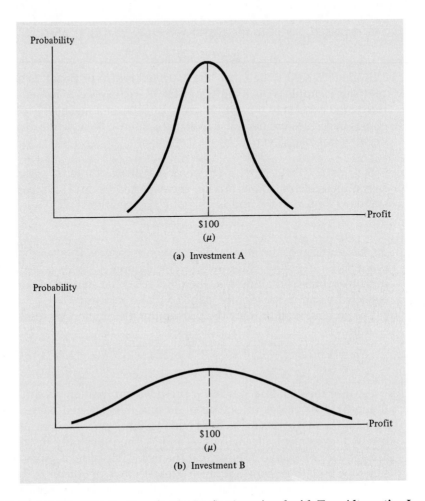

FIGURE 2-3 **Probability Distributions for the Profits Associated with Two Alternative Investments.**

Both the mean and standard deviation for distribution C are greater than for distribution D, but the coefficient of variation is less than C than for D. That is,

$$v_C = \frac{50}{100} = 0.5 < v_D = \frac{30}{50} = 0.6$$

This means that distribution C has less dispersion or risk relative to its mean than does distribution D. Thus not only does the absolute amount of risk (σ) have to be estimated and evaluated, but the level of that risk relative to the expected return on an investment should also be considered.

KEY CONCEPTS

- A probability distribution lists the possible outcomes of an experiment and the probability associated with each outcome.

- The probability of any outcome must be in the range $0 \leq P(X_i) \leq 1.0$, and the sum of the probabilities for all outcomes must equal 1.
- The expected value of a probability distribution ($\mu = \Sigma P_i X_i$) is a measure of the average outcome from repeated trials of an experiment.
- The standard deviation [$\sigma = \sqrt{\Sigma P_i (X_i - \mu)^2}$] measures the dispersion of outcomes around the expected value.
- The coefficient of variation ($v = \sigma/\mu$) is a measure of variation per unit of expected value.

Summary

A functional relationship such as $y = f(x_1, x_2, \ldots, x_n)$ means that the value of the dependent variable y depends on the values of the independent variables $x_1, x_2, \ldots, x_n$ in a systematic way and that there is a unique value of y for any set of values for those independent variables. Total, average, and marginal relationships are fundamental to understanding and using economics. The marginal function is the slope of the total function. The intersection of the marginal and average functions occurs at either the minimum or the maximum point of the average function.

An economic model generally consists of several related functions and certain conditions related to these functions. The model can be used to explain economic phenomena and to predict the effects of changes in one or more variables or functions. Often, simple models can be used to explain complex relationships and to derive powerful results. The effectiveness of managerial decision making can be enhanced significantly by using economic models.

An outcome is a possible result of some action. A state of nature is a condition that affects the outcome but cannot be controlled by the decision maker. The probability of an event happening is its relative frequency of occurrence. The probability of an outcome must be in the range $0 \leq P(x_i) \leq 1.0$ and the sum of all probabilities must equal one. The combination of all possible outcomes and their probabilities comprises a probability distribution. For any such distribution there is a set of statistics. The expected value or mean of a probability distribution measures central tendency. The standard deviation measures the dispersion of the outcomes, and the coefficient of variation provides information on the amount of dispersion relative to the central tendency of the distribution. The use of probability distributions and their associated statistics has wide applicability in managerial decision making.

Discussion Questions

2-1. Explain the concept of an economic model. Why do economists and managers use such models as part of the decision-making process?

2-2. Economists are not the only scientists to use models in their work. Describe how other disciplines use models or similar abstractions from reality in their work.

2-3. Explain the relationship among the total, average, and marginal functions. Intuitively explain why any intersection of the average and the marginal function will occur at a maximum or a minimum point on the average function.

2-4. The president of a major firm (who has had no training in managerial economics) complains during a board meeting that quantitative techniques are of little value because they are always subject to error and therefore should not be part of the decision-making process. If the chairman asked for your opinion, what would be your response?

2-5. Explain how principles of probability would be used to set the rules and payoffs for various gambling games in casinos.

2-6. Is the statement "y is a function of x" equivalent to saying that "y is caused by x"? In this context, critically evaluate the following statement: "The incidence of lung cancer is significantly higher for heavy smokers than for nonsmokers. Therefore, smoking causes cancer."

2-7. Explain how an insurance company could use its historical experience on deaths and accidents to set its insurance rates.

2-8. The General Mills Company has a number of brands of breakfast cereal on the market. Explain how you could use information on historic sales of these products to develop a probability distribution for the sales of a new brand of cereal.

Problems _____

2-1. Given the following supply and demand equations

$$Q_D = 100 - 5P$$
$$Q_S = 10 + 5P$$

a. Determine the equilibrium price and quantity.
b. If the government sets a minimum price of $10 per unit, how many units would be supplied and how many would be demanded?
c. If the government sets a maximum price of $5 per unit, how many units would be supplied and how many would be demanded?
d. If demand increases to

$$Q_D' = 200 - 5P$$

determine the new equilibrium price and quantity.

2-2. Given the following demand function

$$Q = 20 - 0.10P$$

where P = price and Q = rate of output, complete the table at the top of page 47. (Note that total revenue is equal to price times quantity.)

Quantity	Price	Total Revenue	Average Revenue	Marginal Revenue
1	_____	_____	_____	_____
2	_____	_____	_____	_____
3	_____	_____	_____	_____
4	_____	_____	_____	_____
5	_____	_____	_____	_____
6	_____	_____	_____	_____
7	_____	_____	_____	_____
8	_____	_____	_____	_____
9	_____	_____	_____	_____
10	_____	_____	_____	_____
11	_____	_____	_____	_____
12	_____	_____	_____	_____

2-3. Given the total cost function

$$TC = 150Q - 3Q^2 + 0.25Q^3$$

complete the following table by computing the total, average, and marginal costs associated with each quantity indicated.

Quantity	Total Cost	Average Cost	Marginal Cost
1	_____	_____	_____
2	_____	_____	_____
3	_____	_____	_____
4	_____	_____	_____
5	_____	_____	_____
6	_____	_____	_____
7	_____	_____	_____
8	_____	_____	_____
9	_____	_____	_____
10	_____	_____	_____
11	_____	_____	_____
12	_____	_____	_____

2-4. Using the data developed in Problems 2-2 and 2-3,
   a. Plot the total, average, and marginal functions for both revenue and cost. [*Note:* Use a two-part graph similar to Figure 2.1 that places the total function in the upper part and the average and marginal functions in the lower half. Also, it is conventional to plot the marginal values at the midpoint between the quantity values to which they relate. For example, the marginal revenue associated with going from two units of output to three units is $150. This value should be plotted midway between the two- and three-unit marks on the quantity (i.e., horizontal) axis.]

    b. What is true of the marginal revenue function at that level of output where total revenue is at a maximum?

    c. Determine total profit by subtracting total cost from total revenue at each rate of output. Plot this function in the upper part of your diagram.

    d. By comparing the marginal revenue and marginal cost curves and relating them to the profit curve, can you think of a rule the firm might use to determine that output rate that would maximize profit?

2-5. Determine the average function for each of the following total functions:
    a. Total revenue $= 100Q - Q^2$
    b. Total cost $= 1{,}000 + 10Q + 0.01Q^2$
    c. Total profit $= 50Q - 0.1Q^2 - 1{,}000$

2-6. Given the following total revenue (TR) and total cost (TC) equations, determine that output rate that would result in a breakeven (i.e., zero profit) situation for the firm.

$$TR = 51Q - Q^2$$
$$TC = 625 + Q$$

2-7. Do each of the following distributions meet the requirements for a probability distribution? Why or why not?

a.	X_i	$P(X_i)$	b.	Y_i	$P(Y_i)$	c.	Z_i	$P(Z_i)$
	-10	0.10		5	-0.20		-2	0.20
	-20	0.20		10	-0.40		-6	0.30
	-30	0.30		20	-0.40		-8	0.40
	-50	0.40		40	-0.40		-10	0.20

2-8. Given the following probability distribution

X_i	$P(X_i)$
2	0.10
4	0.20
6	0.30
8	0.30
10	0.10

Compute the expected value, standard deviation, and the coefficient of variation.

2-9. A firm is contemplating building a new factory that will have three possible levels of profit, depending on business conditions. The possible levels of profit and the probability of each occurring are

Profit	Probability
$-1{,}000$	0.20
$-5{,}000$	0.30
$-10{,}000$	0.50

Determine the expected value, standard deviation, and the coefficient of variation for this probability distribution.

Problems Requiring Calculus _____

2-10. Given the following function that relates total revenue (*TR*) to output (*Q*),

$$TR = 20Q - 2Q^2$$

determine
a. That rate of output that results in maximum total revenue.
b. The marginal revenue function.
c. The rate of output for which marginal revenue is zero.
d. Is there any connection between your answers to parts (a) and (c)? Explain.

2-11. Given the total cost function

$$TC = 100Q - Q^2 + 0.3Q^3$$

where Q = rate of output and TC = total cost, determine
a. The marginal and average cost functions.
b. The rate of output that results in minimum average cost.

2-12. Given the firm's demand function

$$Q = 55 - 0.5P$$

where P = price and Q = rate of output, and the total cost function

$$TC = 20 + Q + 0.2Q^2$$

where TC = total cost, determine
a. The total revenue function for the firm. (*HINT:* To find the total revenue function, solve the demand function for P and then multiply by Q.)
b. The marginal revenue and marginal cost functions and find that rate of output for which marginal revenue equals marginal cost.
c. An equation for profit by subtracting the total cost function from the total revenue function. Find the level of output that maximizes total profit. Compare your answer to that obtained in part (b). Is there any correspondence between these answers?

2-13. The profit function for a firm selling two products is

$$\pi = 50Q_1 - Q_1^2 + 100Q_2 - 4Q_2^2$$

where Q_1 and Q_2 represent output rates of products 1 and 2, respectively. Determine the profit maximizing output rates for the two products and the profit associated with these output rates.

Calculus and Managerial Economics

Many of the decisions facing managers fall into the category of optimization problems. For example, decisions relating to maximizing profit or minimizing cost clearly involve optimization. Often such problems can be solved graphically or by using algebra. In other cases, however, the solution requires the use of calculus. More importantly, in many cases calculus can be used to solve such problems more easily and with greater insight into the economic principles underlying the solution.

Consider a firm whose total revenues from sales are given by the function

$$TR = 20Q - Q^2$$

where Q represents the rate of output. Assume that the total cost of producing any rate of output is given by the equation

$$TC = 50 + 4Q$$

Given the firm's objective of maximizing profits (i.e., total revenue minus total cost), how much output should be produced? One approach would be to graph both the total revenue and total cost functions. The vertical distance between the two functions is profit. By identifying that point where this vertical distance is the largest, the profit-maximizing output is found. This is shown in Figure 2A-1, which shows profit is maximized by producing eight units of output ($Q = 8$).

An alternative approach is to develop a table showing revenue, cost, and profit at each rate of output. Such data are provided in Table 2A-1. The tabular method has the advantage of being somewhat more precise. That is, at an output rate of 8, total revenue is 96, total cost is 82, and profit is 14. From the graph in Figure 2A-1, these values can only be approximated.

The problem is that neither method is very efficient. What if the profit-maximizing output level is 8,000 or 8,000,000 instead of 8? The answer could be found using either approach, but finding that answer could have taken considerable

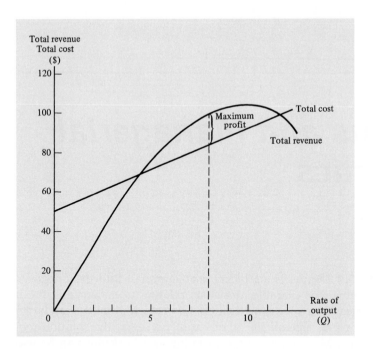

FIGURE 2A-1 **Total Revenue and Total Cost.**

time. What if there had been two outputs (Q_1 and Q_2) and three inputs (land, labor, and capital)? In this case, there would be no practical way to determine profit-maximizing output rates for Q_1 and Q_2 using these methods.

A more powerful technique is needed so that the solution process can be both precise and straightforward. Elementary calculus is easily adapted to optimization

TABLE 2A-1 **Total Revenue, Total Cost, and Total Profit**

Q	TR	TC	Profit (TR − TC)
0	0	50	−50
1	19	54	−35
2	36	58	−22
3	51	62	−11
4	64	66	−2
5	75	70	− 5
6	84	74	−10
7	91	78	−13
8	96	82	−14
9	99	86	−13
10	100	90	−10
11	99	94	− 5

problems in economics. Indeed, a few basic principles can be used in many different kinds of problems. The profit-maximization problem just outlined could have been solved quickly using the most elementary calculus. In the following pages, some basic principles of calculus are outlined and their application to economic problems is demonstrated.

The Derivative of a Function

From algebra recall that for the function $y = f(x)$, the slope of that function is the change in y (denoted by Δy) divided by a change in x (i.e., Δx). The slope sometimes is referred to as the *rise* (the change in the variable measured on the vertical axis) over the *run* (the change in the variable measured on the horizontal axis). The slope is *positive* if the curve slopes upward from left to right and *negative* if the function slopes downward from left to right. A horizontal line has a *zero slope*, and a vertical line is said to have an *infinite slope*. For a positive change in x (i.e., $\Delta x > 0$), a positive slope implies that Δy is positive, and a negative slope implies that Δy is negative.

The function $y = 10 + x^2$ is graphed in Figure 2A-2. To determine the average slope of this function over the range $x = 1$ to $x = 2$, first find the corresponding y values. If $x_1 = 1$, then $y_1 = 11$, and if $x_2 = 2$, then $y_2 = 14$. Then the slope is found by using the formula

$$\text{slope} = \frac{\Delta y}{\Delta x} = \frac{y_2 - y_1}{x_2 - x_1} = \frac{14 - 11}{2 - 1} = 3$$

In reality, this method determines the slope of a straight line through the points

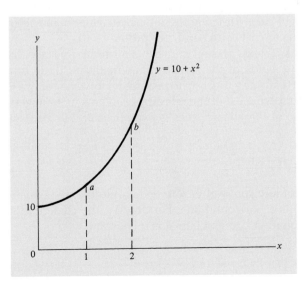

FIGURE 2A-2 **Graph of the Function** $y = 10 + x^2$.

a and *b* in Figure 2A-2. Thus, it is only a rough approximation of the slope of the function $y = 10 + x^2$, which actually changes at every point on that function. By making the interval smaller, a better estimate of the slope is determined. For example, consider the slope over the interval $x = 1$ to $x = 1.1$. If $x_1 = 1$, then $y_1 = 11$, and $x_2 = 1.1$ implies that $y_2 = 11.21$. Thus the slope is

$$\text{slope} = \frac{\Delta y}{\Delta x} = \frac{11.21 - 11}{1.1 - 1} = \frac{0.21}{0.10} = 2.1$$

By using calculus, the exact slope at any point on the function can be determined.

The first derivative of a function (denoted as dy/dx) is simply the slope of a function when the interval along the horizontal axis is infinitesimally small. Technically, the derivative is the limit of the ratio $\Delta y/\Delta x$ as Δx approaches zero, that is,

$$\frac{dy}{dx} = \lim_{\Delta x \to 0} \frac{\Delta y}{\Delta x}$$

Thus the calculus term dy/dx is analogous to $\Delta y/\Delta x$, but dy/dx is the precise slope at a point, whereas $\Delta y/\Delta x$ is the average slope over an interval of the function. The derivative can be thought of as the slope of a straight line drawn tangent to the function at that point. For example, the slope of the function $y = 10 + x^2$ at point *a* in Figure 2A-2 is the slope of the straight line drawn tangent to that function at *a*. The derivative of $y = f(x)$ is sometimes written as $f'(x)$.

What is the significance of this concept for managerial economics? Recall from the discussion of total and marginal relationships that the marginal function is simply the slope of the total function. Calculus offers an easy way to find the marginal function by taking the first derivative of the total function. Calculus also offers a set of rules for using these derivatives to make optimizing decisions such as minimizing cost or maximizing profit.

Standard calculus texts present numerous formulas for the derivative of various functions. In the hands of the skilled mathematician, these formulas allow the derivative of virtually any function to be found. However, only a few of these rules are necessary to solve most of the relevant problems in managerial economics. In this section each of these basic rules is explained and its use demonstrated.

The Derivative of a Constant

The derivative of any constant is zero. When plotted, the equation of a constant (such as $y = 5$) is a horizontal line. For any Δx, the change in y is always zero. Thus for any equation $y = a$, where *a* is a constant,

$$\frac{dy}{dx} = 0 \qquad\qquad\qquad (2A\text{-}1)$$

The Derivative of a Constant Times a Function

The derivative of a constant times a function is that constant times the derivative of the function. Thus the derivative of $y = af(x)$, where a is constant, is

$$\frac{dy}{dx} = af'(x) \tag{2A-2}$$

For example, if $y = 3x$, the derivative is

$$\frac{dy}{dx} = 3f'(x) = 3(1) = 3$$

The Derivative of a Power Function

For the general power function of the form $y = ax^b$, the derivative is

$$\frac{dy}{dx} = bax^{b-1} \tag{2A-3}$$

The function $y = x^2$ is a specific case of a power function where $a = 1$ and $b = 2$. Hence the derivative of this function is

$$\frac{dy}{dx} = 2x^{2-1} = 2x$$

The interpretation of this derivative is that the slope of the function $y = x^2$ at any point x is $2x$. For example, the slope at $x = 4$ would be found by substituting $x = 4$ into the derivative. That is,

$$\left(\frac{dy}{dx}\right)_{x=4} = 2(4) = 8$$

Thus when $x = 4$, the change in y is 8 times a small change in x.

The function $y = x^2$ is shown in Figure 2A-3. Note that the slope changes continually. The slope at $x = 4$ is 8. As x increases, the slope becomes steeper. For negative values of x, the slope is negative. For example, if $x = -3$, the slope is -6.

The Derivative of a Sum or Difference

The derivative of a function that is a sum or difference of several terms is the sum (or difference) of the derivatives of each of the terms. That is, if $y = f(x) + g(x)$, then

$$\frac{dy}{dx} = f'(x) + g'(x) \tag{2A-4}$$

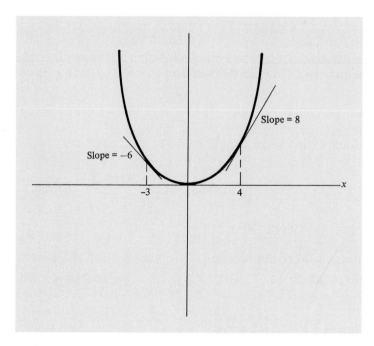

Slope = 8

Slope = −6

−3

4

FIGURE 2A-3 **Graph of Function $y = x^2$.**

For example, the derivative of the function

$$y = 10 + 5x + 6x^2$$

is equal to the sum of the derivatives of each of the three terms on the right-hand side. Note that the rules for the derivative of a constant, a constant times a function, and a power function must be used. Thus

$$\frac{dy}{dx} = 0 + (1)5x^0 + (2)6x^1 = 5 + 12x$$

Consider another function: $y = 2x^3 - 6x^{-2} - 4x + 10$

The derivative is $\dfrac{dy}{dx} = (3)2x^2 - (-2)6x^{-3} - 4 + 0$

$$= 6x^2 + 12x^{-3} - 4$$

The Derivative of the Product of Two Functions

Given a function of the form $y = f(x)g(x)$, the derivative dy/dx is given by

$$\frac{dy}{dx} = f'(x)g(x) + f(x)g'(x) \tag{2A-5}$$

That is, the derivative of the product of two functions is the derivative of the first function times the second function plus the first function times the derivative of the second.

For example, the derivative of the function

$$y = (x^2 - 4)(x^3 + 2x + 2)$$

is

$$\frac{dy}{dx} = (2x)(x^3 + 2x + 2) + (x^2 - 4)(3x^2 + 2) = 5x^4 - 6x^2 + 4x - 8$$

The Derivative of a Quotient of Two Functions

For a function of the form $y = f(x)/g(x)$, the derivative is

$$\frac{dy}{dx} = \frac{g(x)f'(x) - f(x)g'(x)}{[g(x)]^2} \tag{2A-6}$$

Given the function

$$y = \frac{x^2 - 3x}{x^2}$$

the derivative would be

$$\frac{dy}{dx} = \frac{x^2(2x - 3) - (x^2 - 3x)(2x)}{(x^2)^2} = \frac{3x^2}{x^4} = \frac{3}{x^2}$$

The Derivative of a Function of a Function

The function

$$y = (2x + 5)^3$$

is really two functions combined. That is, by writing

$$u = f(x)$$

where

$$u = 2x + 5$$

and

$$y = g(u)$$

where

$$y = u^3$$

it is seen that y is a function of a function. That is,

$$y = g(u) = g[f(x)]$$

This derivative is the derivative of y with respect to u and multiplied by the derivative of u with respect to x, or

$$\frac{dy}{dx} = \frac{dy}{du} \cdot \frac{du}{dx}$$

Now, using the rule for the derivative of a power function yields

$$\frac{dy}{du} = 3u^2 = 3(2x + 5)^2$$

and

$$\frac{du}{dx} = 2$$

so

$$\frac{dy}{dx} = [3(2x + 5)^2] \cdot 2 = 6(2x + 5)^2$$

Consider another example:

$$y = \frac{1}{\sqrt{x^5 + 2x + 6}}$$

which can be rewritten as

$$y = (x^5 + 2x + 6)^{-1/2}$$

In this case,

$$y = u^{-1/2}$$

and

$$u = x^5 + 2x + 6$$

so the solution is

$$\frac{dy}{du} = -\frac{1}{2}u^{-(1/2)-1} = -\frac{1}{2}u^{-3/2}$$

and

$$\frac{du}{dx} = 5x^4 + 2$$

Substituting $x^5 + 2x + 6$ for u and multiplying the two derivatives just given yields

$$\frac{dy}{dx} = \frac{dy}{du} \cdot \frac{du}{dx} = -\frac{1}{2}(x^5 + 2x + 6)^{-3/2}(5x^4 + 2)$$

These seven rules of differentiation are sufficient to determine the derivatives of all the functions used in this book. However, sometimes two or more of the rules must be used at the same time.

EXAMPLE _____

Finding the Marginal Function

Given a total revenue function

$$TR = 50Q - 0.5Q^2$$

and a total cost function

$$TC = 2,000 + 200Q - 0.2Q^2 + 0.001Q^3$$

find the marginal revenue and marginal cost functions.

SOLUTION   Recall that a marginal function is simply the slope of the corresponding total function. For example, marginal revenue is the slope of total revenue. Thus, by finding the derivative of the total revenue function, the marginal revenue function will be obtained:

$$MR = \frac{d(TR)}{dQ} = 50 - 2(0.5)Q^{2-1}$$

$$= 50 - Q$$

Similarly, the marginal cost function will be found by taking the first derivative of the total cost function:

$$MC = \frac{d(TC)}{dQ} = 0 + 200 - 2(0.2)Q^{2-1} + 3(0.001)Q^{3-1}$$

$$= 200 - 0.4Q + 0.003Q^2$$

KEY CONCEPTS _____

- The slope of a function $y = f(x)$ is the change in y (i.e., Δy) divided by the corresponding change in x (i.e., Δx).
- For a function $y = f(x)$, the derivative, written as dy/dx or $f'(x)$, is the slope of the function at a particular point on the function. Equivalently, the derivative is the slope of a straight line drawn tangent to the function at that point.

• By using one or more of the seven formulas outlined in this appendix, the derivative of most functions encountered in managerial economics can be found.

Higher-Order Derivatives

The derivative of a function sometimes is called the *first derivative* to indicate that there are higher-order derivatives. The *second derivative* of a function is simply the first derivative of the first derivative; it is written d^2y/dx^2 or f''. In the context of economics, the first derivative of a total function is the marginal function. The second derivative of the total function is the slope of the first derivative or the rate at which the marginal function is changing.

Higher-order derivatives are easy to find. One simply keeps taking the first derivative again. Given the function

$$y = 10x^3 + 3x^2 - 5x + 6$$

the first derivative is

$$\frac{dy}{dx} = 30x^2 + 6x - 5$$

and the higher-order derivatives are

$$\text{SECOND:} \quad \frac{d^2y}{dx^2} = 60x + 6$$

$$\text{THIRD:} \quad \frac{d^3y}{dx^3} = 60$$

$$\text{FOURTH:} \quad \frac{d^4y}{dx^4} = 0$$

The second derivative has an important application in finding the maximum and/or minimum of a function. This concept is explained in the following section.

Calculus and Optimization

Recall from the discussion of total and marginal relationships that if the marginal function is positive, the total function must be increasing; if the marginal function is negative, the total function must be decreasing. It was shown that if the marginal function is zero, then the total function must be at either a maximum or a minimum. In Figure 2A-4, a total function and its associated marginal function are shown. At point *a*, which corresponds to $x = x_1$, the total function is at a maximum and the marginal function is zero. At point *b*, corresponding to $x = x_2$, the total

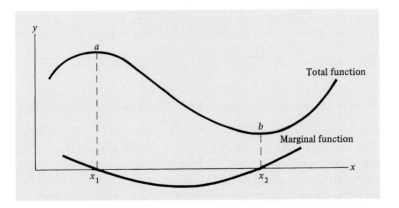

FIGURE 2A-4 **Relationship of Total and Marginal Functions at Minimum and Maximum Points.**

function is minimized and the marginal function is again zero. Thus the marginal curve is zero at both x_1 and x_2. However, note the difference in the slope of the marginal function at these points. At x_1, the marginal curve has a negative slope, whereas at x_2, the slope is positive.

Because the total function is at a maximum or a minimum (i.e., an extremum) when its slope is zero, one way to find the value of x that results in a maximum or a minimum is to set the first derivative of the total function equal to zero and solve for x. This is a better approach than the trial-and-error method used earlier. In that example, a total revenue function,

$$TR = 20Q - Q^2$$

and a total cost function,

$$TC = 50 + 4Q$$

were given. The problem was to find the rate of output, Q, that maximized profit. The total profit function (π) is found by subtracting total cost from total revenue:

$$\begin{aligned} \pi &= TR - TC \\ &= 20Q - Q^2 - 50 - 4Q \\ &= -Q^2 + 16Q - 50 \end{aligned}$$

The profit function will have a slope of zero where that function is at a maximum and also at its minimum point. To find the profit-maximizing output, take the first derivative of the profit function with respect to output, set that derivative equal to zero, and solve for output. That is, find the rate (or rates) of output where the slope of the profit function is zero.[5]

$$\frac{d\pi}{dQ} = -2Q + 16 = 0$$

$$2Q = 16$$

$$Q = 8$$

But will this output rate result in a profit maximum or a profit minimum? Remember, setting the first derivative equal to zero and solving results in an extremum, but it could be a maximum or a minimum. But Figure 2A-4 shows that if the total function is maximized, the marginal function has a negative slope. Conversely, a minimum point on a total function is associated with a positive slope of the marginal function.

Because the slope of the marginal function is the first derivative of that marginal function, a simple test to determine if a point is a maximum or minimum is suggested. Find the second derivative of the total function and evaluate it at the point where the slope of the total function is zero. If the second derivative is negative (i.e., the marginal function is decreasing), the total function is at a maximum. If the second derivative is positive at that point (i.e., the marginal function is increasing), the total function is at a minimum point.

In the profit-maximization problem just discussed, the second derivative of the profit function is -2, which is negative. Therefore, profit is maximized at $Q = 8$.

When finding the extremum of any function, setting the first derivative equal to zero is called the *first-order condition,* meaning that this condition is necessary for an extremum but not sufficient to determine if the function is at a maximum or a minimum. The test for a maximum or a minimum using the second derivative is called the *second-order condition.* The first- and second-order conditions together are said to be sufficient to test for either a maximum or a minimum point. These

---

[5] Sometimes the result of this optimization process is a quadratic equation, that is,

$$ax^2 + bx + c = 0$$

The solution (i.e., the value or values of x for which the equation is true) is given by the general equation

$$x_1, x_2 = \frac{-b \pm \sqrt{b^2 - 4ac}}{2a}$$

For example, given the quadratic equation
$$x^2 - 60x + 500 = 0$$
the solution is

$$x_1, x_2 = \frac{-(-60) \pm \sqrt{(-60)^2 - 4(1)(500)}}{2(1)}$$

or
$$x_1 = 50$$
$$x_2 = 10$$

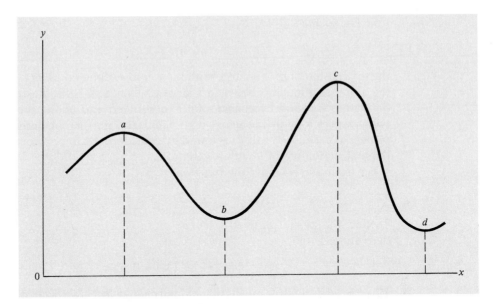

FIGURE 2A-5 **Graph of a Function Having Several Extrema.**

conditions are summarized as follows:

	Maximum	*Minimum*
First-order condition	$\dfrac{dy}{dx} = 0$	$\dfrac{dy}{dx} = 0$
Second-order condition	$\dfrac{d^2y}{dx^2} < 0$	$\dfrac{d^2y}{dx^2} > 0$

In some problems there will be two or possibly more points where the first derivative is zero. Therefore, all these points will have to be evaluated using the second-order condition to test for a minimum or a maximum. As shown in Figure 2A-5, a function could have several points, such as a, b, c, and d, where the slope is zero. Points a and c are relative maxima and b and d are relative minima. The term *relative* means that the point is an extremum only for part of the function. Point a is a maximum relative to other points on the function around it. It is not the maximum point for the entire function because the value of y at point c exceeds that at point a. To find the absolute maximum, the value of the equation must be determined for all relative maxima within the range that the function is defined and also at each of the end points.

The Partial Derivative

Many economic phenomena are described by multivariate functions (i.e., equations that have two or more independent variables). Given a general multivariate function such as

$$y = f(x, z)$$

the first partial derivative of y with respect to x, denoted as $\partial y / \partial x$ or f_x, indicates the slope relationship between y and x when z is held constant. This partial derivative is found by considering z to be fixed and taking the derivative of y with respect to x in the usual way. Similarly, the partial derivative of y with respect to z (i.e., $\partial y / \partial z$ or f_z) is found by considering x to be a constant and taking the first derivative of y with respect to z.

For example, consider the function

$$y = x^2 + 3xz + z^2$$

To find the partial derivative $\partial y / \partial x$ or f_x, consider z as a fixed and take the derivative. Thus

$$f_x = 2x^{2-1} + (3z) + 0 = 2x + 3z$$

This partial derivative means that a small change in x is associated with y changing at the rate $2x + 3z$ when z is held constant at a specified level. For example, if $z = 2$, the slope associated with y and x is $2x + 3(2)$ or $2x + 6$. If $z = 5$, the slope associated with y and x would be $2x + 3(5)$, or $2x + 15$.

Similarly, the partial derivative of y with respect to z would be

$$f_z = 0 + 3x + 2z^{2-1} = 3x + 2z$$

This means that a small change in z is associated with y changing at the rate $3x + 2z$ when x is held constant.

Optimization and Multivariate Functions

The approach to finding the maximum or minimum value of a multivariate function involves three steps. First, find the partial derivative of the function with respect to each independent variable. Second, set all the partial derivatives equal to zero. Finally, solve the system of equations determined in the second step for the values of each of the independent variables. That is, if

$$y = 4 - x^2 - 2z + xz + 2z^2$$

then the partial derivatives are

$$\frac{\partial y}{\partial x} = -2x + z$$

$$\frac{\partial y}{\partial z} = -2 + x + 4z$$

Setting these derivatives equal to zero

$$-2x + z = 0$$
$$-2 + x + 4z = 0$$

and solving these two equations simultaneously for x and z yields

$$x = \frac{2}{9}$$

$$z = \frac{4}{9}$$

These values of x and z minimize the value of the function. The approach to testing whether the optimizing solution results in a maximum or minimum for a multivariate function is complex and beyond the scope of this book. In this text, the context of the problem will indicate whether a maximum or minimum has been determined.

KEY CONCEPTS

- Higher-order derivatives are found by repeatedly taking the first derivative of each resultant derivative.
- The maximum or minimum point of a function [$y = f(x)$] can be found by setting the first derivative of the function equal to zero and solving for the value or values of x.
- When the first derivative of a function is zero, the function is at a maximum if the second derivative is negative or at a minimum if the second derivative is positive.
- For a function having two or more independent variables [e.g., $y = f(x, z)$], the partial derivative $\partial y / \partial x$ is the slope relationship between y and x, assuming z to be held constant.
- Optimizing a multivariate function requires setting each partial derivative equal to zero and then solving the resulting system of equations simultaneously for the values of each independent variable.

Problems

2A-1. Determine the first and second derivatives of each of the following functions.

a. $Y = 10$

b. $Y = 3X^2 + 4X + 25$

c. $Y = (X^2 - 4)(X^2 + 2X + 5)$

d. $Y = \dfrac{X^2 + 3X + 4}{X^2 - 4}$

e. $Q = 100 - 0.2P^2$

f. $R = 500Q(1 - 5Q)$

g. $Y = aX^2 + bX + c$

h. $C = 2{,}000 - 200X^2 + 3X^3$

i. $Y = (3X - 2)^2$

j. $Y = 3X^2(2X^3 - 2)^3$

2A-2. Determine all the first-order partial derivatives for each of the following functions.

a. $y = 3X^2 + 2XZ + Z^2$ b. $Q = 10K^{0.5}L^{0.6}$

c. $Q = 100P_1^{-1.2}P_2^{1.5}Y^{1.0}$ d. $C = 200 + 10X_1^2 + 2X_1X_2 + 3X_2^2$

2A-3. Given the multivariate function

$$Y = 50 + 18X + 10Z - 5XZ - 2X^2$$

determine the values of X and Z that maximize the function.

2A-4. The total revenue (TR) function for a firm is given by

$$TR = 1{,}000Q - 10Q^2$$

where Q is the rate of output per period. Determine the rate of output that results in maximum total revenue. (Be sure that you have maximized, not minimized, total revenue.)

2A-5. Smith and Wesson have written a new managerial economics book for which they receive royalty payments of 15 percent of total revenue from sales of the book. Because their royalty income is tied to revenue, not profit, they want the publisher to set the price so that total revenue is maximized. However, the publisher's objective is maximum profit. If the total revenue function is

$$TR = 100{,}000Q - 10Q^2$$

and the total cost function is

$$TC = 10{,}000 + 20Q + Q^2$$

determine

a. The output rate that will maximize total royalty revenue and also the amount of royalty income that Smith and Wesson would receive.

b. The output rate that would maximize profit to the publisher. Based on this rate of output, what is the amount of royalty income that Smith and Wesson would receive? Compare the royalty income of Smith and Wesson to that determined in part (a). (*HINT:* First determine a function for total profit by subtracting the cost function from the total revenue function.)

2A-6. A firm has determined that its annual profits depend on the number of salespersons it employs and the amount spent on advertising. Specifically, the relationship between profits, π (in millions), salespersons, S (in thousands), and advertising expenditures, A (in millions), is

$$\pi = -10 + 60S + 10A - 2S^2 - A^2$$

Determine the number of salespersons and the amount of advertising expenditures that would maximize the firm's profits.

II

Demand

Demand Theory and Analysis

Preview ───

Demand theory and analysis can be a source of many useful insights for business decision making. Indeed, it is difficult to overstate the importance of understanding demand. Ultimately, the success or failure of a business depends primarily on its ability to generate revenues by satisfying the demands of consumers. Firms that are unable to attract the dollar votes of consumers are soon forced from the market.

The fundamental objective of demand theory is to identify and analyze the basic determinants of consumer needs and wants. An understanding of the forces behind demand is a powerful tool for managers. Such knowledge provides the background needed to make pricing decisions, forecast sales, and formulate marketing strategies.

This chapter begins with a discussion of individual demand, market demand, and the demand faced by the firm. The focus then shifts to a basic concern of managers—the total revenue earned by the firm. Finally, the concept of elasticity is introduced as a tool for measuring the responsiveness of quantity demanded to changes in prices and income. Three elasticity measures are discussed: price elasticity, income elasticity, and cross elasticity.

Individual Demand ────────────────────────────

Consumer choice can be a difficult task in a modern economic system. In the United States and in other industrialized nations, tens of thousands of goods and services are offered for sale. But the purchases of most consumers are constrained by their income. Many would like to drive a Ferrari, dine at the best restaurants, and vacation in Europe. However, the relevant options often are a used Ford, a pizza, and a few days at the beach.

In determining what to purchase, individual consumers face a constrained optimization problem. That is, given their income (the constraint), they select that combination of goods and services that maximizes their personal satisfaction. Implicitly, these choices involve a comparison of the satisfaction associated with having a good or service and its opportunity cost, that is, what must be given up in order to obtain it. In a market economy, opportunity costs are reflected by prices. Thus prices act as signals to guide consumer decisions. A high price denotes a significant opportunity cost, while a lower price indicates that less must be given up.

One of the most basic concepts in demand theory is the *law of demand*. In its most simple form, this law states that there is an inverse relationship between price and quantity demanded—as price increases, quantity demanded will decrease. The law of demand can be explained in terms of substitution and income effects resulting from price changes. The substitution effect reflects changing opportunity costs. When the price of a good increases, its opportunity cost in terms of other goods also increases. Consequently, consumers may substitute other goods for the good that has become more expensive. The purchase of relatively more chicken and pork when beef prices increase is an example of a substitution effect.

Next consider the income effect. When the price of a good increases, the consumer's purchasing power is reduced. That is, at higher prices the individual cannot buy the same bundle of goods as before. For example, $30 will buy six pounds of chocolates at $5 per pound, but only five pounds at $6 per pound. The change in purchasing power is called an income effect because the price increase is equivalent to a reduction in the consumer's income.

CASE STUDY

The Law of Demand in Perkasie, Pennsylvania

Among the many environmental problems facing the United States is how to dispose of the vast amounts of garbage generated each day by households and businesses. In 1960, Americans discarded an average of 2.6 pounds of trash per person per day, but today the number is 3.6 pounds. As the volume of garbage grows, existing disposal sites are filling up, and it is becoming increasingly difficult to find new locations near urban areas for landfills.

One small community used the law of demand to ease its garbage collection problem. In 1987, residents of Perkasie, Pennsylvania, were paying an annual fixed fee of $120 per resident for garbage collection and discarding a daily average of 2.2 pounds of trash per person. Because the collection fee was fixed, the additional expense to residents of trash disposal was zero, and they had no financial incentive to conserve on the amount of trash they produced.

In 1988, Perkasie began charging by the bag for garbage collection. The city required that all trash be placed in special bags sold by the city. For example, a large bag had a capacity of about 40 pounds and sold for $1.50. Thus, the marginal cost to residents of generating additional trash increased from zero to about four cents per pound. Garbage that was not in an approved bag was not picked up. In addition, the city introduced a recycling program. Each household was given buckets to be filled with cans and bottles that were picked up every week. The city also arranged for newspapers to be collected once a month.

The result was predictable—people began to dump less trash. During the first year the program was in effect, trash collections per person declined to less than one pound per day. Perkasie citizens benefited because they paid 30 percent less than before, and the city reduced its garbage collection costs by 40 percent.

SOURCE: Adapted from *The Margin*, October 1989, p. 17.

Market Demand

Although choices by individuals are the basis of the theory of demand, it is total or market demand that is of primary interest to managers. The market demand for a good or service is the sum of all individual demands. For example, consider a market that consists of only two buyers. The demand curves for these two

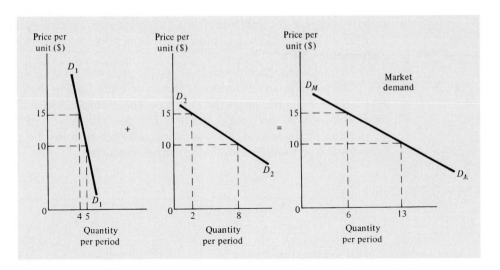

FIGURE 3-1 **The Market Demand Curve.**

consumers are depicted in Figure 3-1. These demand curves show the relationship between price and quantity demanded. Consumer 1's demand curve is shown in the first panel (D_1D_1) and that of consumer 2 in the second panel (D_2D_2). At a price of \$10, the individual quantities demanded are 5 and 8 units, respectively. Hence the total market demand (D_MD_M, as shown in the third panel) is 13 units. The market demand at any price is the sum of the individual quantities demanded at that price.

Graphically, the market demand curve is the horizontal summation of the individual demand curves. That is, for any given price, the market demand curve is the sum of the horizontal distances from the vertical axis to each individual demand curve.

Determinants of Market Demand

The effect of a change in price is depicted as a movement from one point to another *along* a particular demand curve. For example, in Figure 3-1, as price increases from \$10 to \$15, moving along the market demand curve D_MD_M depicts a decrease in quantity demanded from 13 to 6 units. A movement along the demand curve in response to a change in the price of a good or service is referred to as a *change in quantity demanded*.

The price of a good or service is not the only determinant of demand. However, in plotting a demand curve, it is assumed that other factors that affect demand are held constant. When these factors are allowed to vary, the demand curve will shift. Such shifts are referred to as *changes in demand*. A shift to the right is called an increase in demand, meaning that consumers demand more of the good or service at each price than they did before. A leftward shift indicates a decrease in demand. That is, less is demanded at each price than before.

In a market economy, firms must be responsive to consumer demands. Thus it is important that managers understand the determinants of demand. Some of the most important are consumer preferences, income levels, and prices of other goods.[1]

CONSUMER PREFERENCES   Obviously, an important determinant of demand is the preferences of consumers. These preferences can change rapidly in response to advertising, fads, and customs. There was a time when gloves were considered a must for the well-dressed woman. Today, gloves are usually worn only on special occasions. This change in preferences caused a decrease in the demand for gloves, meaning that fewer gloves are demanded at any given price. In contrast, pants for women have become more popular in recent years. In this case, the shift in preferences resulted in an increase in demand, with more women's pants now demanded at each price.

INCOME   Demand is also affected by the amount of income that consumers have available to spend. For most goods, an increase in consumer income would cause the demand curve for the product to shift to the right. For example, revenues from oil and gas leases recently left the state of Alaska with surplus revenues. The state responded by providing a cash grant to every resident of the state. Alaskans used much of this extra income to buy additional goods and services. That is, the increased income resulted in an increase in demand for many goods and services. More recently, lower oil prices have reduced incomes in Alaska. The result has been a decrease in demand for many goods and services.

PRICES OF OTHER GOODS   The demand for a good is often influenced by changes in the prices of other goods. The nature of the impact depends on whether the goods are substitutes or complements. *Substitutes* are goods that have essentially the same use. When the price of a good goes up, the demand for its substitutes is likely to increase. For example, 7-Up and Sprite are similar lemon-flavored soft drinks. An increase in the price of Sprite would cause people to purchase less of that beverage and consume more 7-Up. Thus the demand curve for 7-Up would shift to the right from DD to $D'D'$, as shown in Figure 3-2a. Note that more 7-Up is demanded at each price than before the shift.

Goods that are often used together are called *complements*. An increase in the price of one such good will cause the demand for its complement to decrease. Consider tennis rackets and balls. If the price of rackets increases, fewer people will play tennis. With fewer people involved in the sport, fewer tennis balls will be purchased. This outcome is illustrated by the leftward shift of the demand curve from DD to $D'D'$ in Figure 3-2b.

---

[1] Other factors, such as population, expectations, and government policies, can also affect demand. Although they may be important, for ease of exposition they are not considered here.

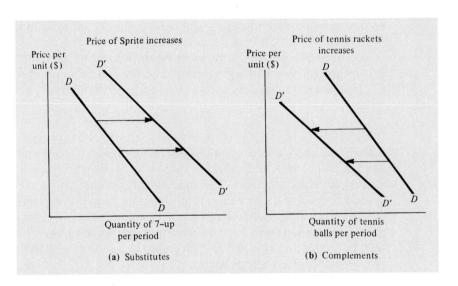

FIGURE 3-2 **Demand Curves for Substitutes and Complements.**

The Market Demand Equation

The market demand function can also be expressed mathematically. If the primary determinants of demand are the price of the product, income, consumer preferences, and the prices of other goods and services, the demand equation can be written as

$$Q_D = f(P, I, P_o, T) \tag{3-1}$$

where P is the price of the good or service, I is income, P_o represents the prices of other goods, and T is a measure of consumer tastes and preferences. Equation (3-1) suggests that there is a correspondence between the quantity demanded and the variables on the right-hand side. However, the equation implies only that there are general relationships. It says nothing about their nature and magnitude. For example, equation (3-1) provides no information about how quantity demanded would be affected by an increase in income. Quantifying this information requires that a functional form be chosen to represent the equation for market demand. The linear form is shown below.

$$Q_D = B + a_pP + a_II + a_oP_o + a_TT \tag{3-2}$$

The coefficients a_p, a_I, a_o, and a_T indicate the change in quantity demanded of one-unit changes in the associated variables. For example, a_p is the coefficient of price. Its interpretation is that, holding the other three variables constant, quantity demanded changes by a_p units for each one-unit change in price. In most cases, a_p will be negative. To illustrate, if $a_p = -2$ and price is measured in dollars, a $1 increase in price would be associated with a two-unit decrease in quantity demanded.

For many purposes it is useful to focus on the relationship between quantity demanded and the price of the good or service while holding the other variables constant. If I, P_o, and T are not allowed to vary, then demand is a function only of P. Hence the linear form of the demand equation can be written as

$$Q_D = B + a_p P \qquad (3\text{-}3)$$

where B represents the combined influence of all the other determinants of demand and $a_p \leq 0$. This simple demand equation is the basis for much of the analysis in the remainder of the chapter.

EXAMPLE _____

The Market Demand for Tests

Max, a graduating senior, has accumulated an impressive file of tests during his college career. But now he needs to sell his test collection to obtain money for his impending marriage. Three wealthy friends express interest in buying some of the tests. Max determines that their individual demand equations are as follows:

$$Q_1 = 30.00 - 1.00P$$
$$Q_2 = 22.50 - 0.75P$$
$$Q_3 = 37.50 - 1.25P$$

where the quantity subscripts denote each of the three friends and price is measured in dollars per test.

What is the market demand equation for Max's tests, and how many more tests can he sell for each one-dollar decrease in price? If he has a file of 60 tests, what price should he charge to sell his entire collection?

SOLUTION

Market demand, Q_m, is the sum of the individual demands. Thus

$$Q_m = Q_1 + Q_2 + Q_3 = (30.00 - 1.00P) + (22.50 - 0.75P) + (37.50 - 1.25P)$$

Simplifying yields

$$Q_m = 90.00 - 3.00P$$

Because P is measured in dollars, a one-dollar decrease in price will increase quantity demanded by three tests. To sell the entire 60-test collection, the price must be set such that $Q_m = 60$. That is,

$$60 = 90 - 3.00P$$

Solving this equation gives $P = \$10.00$. Substituting this price back into the individual demand equations gives $Q_1 = 20$, $Q_2 = 15$, and $Q_3 = 25$.

_____

Market Demand Versus Firm Demand

Thus far, the discussion has focused on market demand curves. But from the perspective of managers, it is the demand curve facing the individual firm that is most relevant in pricing and output decisions.

Where a firm is the only seller in a market, the relevant demand curve is the market demand curve. Consequently, the firm will bear the entire impact of changes in incomes, consumer preferences, and prices of other goods. Similarly, the pricing policies of the firm will have a significant impact on purchasers of the firm's product. But few businesses are the only sellers of a good or service. In the vast majority of cases, a firm supplies only part of the total market. Consequently, the demand curve faced by the individual firm is not the same as the market demand curve.

One major difference between firm and market demand is that additional factors affect demand at the firm level. Perhaps the most important factor is decisions made by competitors. For example, a price cut by one firm probably would decrease sales of rival firms unless those firms also reduced price. Similarly, an effective advertising campaign can increase a firm's sales at the expense of its competitors.

Another difference between firm and market demand is the quantitative impact of changes in tastes, income, and prices of other goods. Consider beef and pork as examples of substitute goods. Suppose the market demand equation indicates that a 1-cent per pound increase in the price of beef would increase the market demand for pork by 1 million pounds per year. Now consider the demand equation for a small meatpacker with a 1 percent market share of pork sales. Because the firm's share is a small fraction of the total market, the impact on the firm's sales resulting from the change in beef prices will be much less than the total market change. That is, if the demand equation for the small firm was estimated, the coefficient showing the effect of changes in the price of beef would be much smaller than the coefficient for the market demand equation. Similarly, the coefficients showing the effects of changes in tastes and incomes would also be less than for the market demand equation.

For the remainder of the chapter the discussion will focus on the demand curve faced by the individual firm. However, most of the concepts discussed are equally applicable to market demand curves.

KEY CONCEPTS _____

- A change in quantity demanded refers to a movement along a demand curve caused by a change in the price of the good or service.
- A change in demand is represented by a shift of the demand curve resulting from a change in consumer preferences, income, or prices of other goods.
- If two goods are substitutes, when the price of one good increases, demand for the other also increases.
- If two goods are complements, a higher price for one will cause a decrease in the demand for the other.

Total and Marginal Revenue _____

One indication of a firm's success is the total revenue generated by the sale of its products. Rankings of firm size are usually made on the basis of total revenue.

Similarly, growth is often expressed in terms of increases in total revenue. In that it reflects the ability of the firm to satisfy consumer demands, the use of total revenue as a measure of success has some merit.

The first two columns of Table 3-1 provide information about the demand faced by a firm. By multiplying price times quantity, the total revenue associated with each price–quantity pair is determined. These data are also shown in Table 3-1. Note that total revenue increases as price goes from $1 to $5 and then decreases for prices greater than $6. This suggests that sound pricing decisions require information about demand. In some cases higher prices may increase total revenue, whereas in other circumstances a price increase can have the opposite effect.

Table 3-1 also shows marginal revenue. Marginal revenue is defined as the change in total revenue associated with the sale of one more unit of the product. For example, as quantity goes from four to five, total revenue increases from $28 to $30. Hence the marginal or extra revenue associated with the fifth unit is $2. Note that marginal revenue declines as quantity increases. Beyond six units, marginal revenue is negative. The explanation stems from the inverse relationship between price and quantity. To sell extra units, the firm must reduce the price of all the units sold. Negative marginal revenue means that the dollars received from selling the extra unit are not sufficient to compensate for the dollars lost as a result of selling all other units at a lower price. Clearly, a firm should not increase output beyond the point where marginal revenue is zero.

The total and marginal revenue data of Table 3-1 can be plotted on a graph. If fractional units are allowed, the line has the appearance of a smooth curve, as shown in Figure 3-3. Note the relationship between the total and marginal revenue curves. As long as total revenue is increasing, marginal revenue is positive. At the maximum point on the total revenue curve, marginal revenue is zero. But beyond that point, marginal revenue is negative.

Figure 3-3 also shows the relationship between the marginal revenue curve and the demand curve. Note that the two curves intercept the price axis at the same point. Using calculus, it can easily be shown that for linear demand equations, the value of the slope of the marginal revenue curve is twice the value of the slope of the associated demand curve. Because the two curves have the same

TABLE 3-1 **Total and Marginal Revenue**

Price	Quantity	Total Revenue	Marginal Revenue
$10	1	$10	—
9	2	18	$8
8	3	24	6
7	4	28	4
6	5	30	2
5	6	30	0
4	7	28	−2
3	8	24	−4
2	9	18	−6
1	10	10	−8

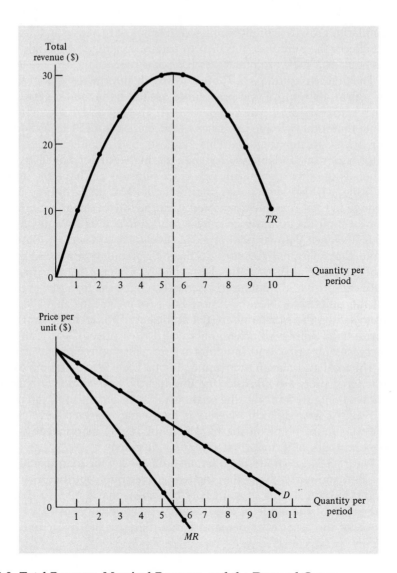

3-3 **Total Revenue, Marginal Revenue, and the Demand Curve.**

price intercept, this implies that the quantity intercept of the marginal revenue curve is exactly half that of the demand curve.

The marginal revenue equation can be derived from the demand equation. Suppose that the demand equation is given by $Q = B + a_p P$, where $a_p \leq 0$. Solving for price, the demand equation becomes

$$P = \frac{-B}{a_p} + \frac{Q}{a_p} \tag{3-4}$$

Multiplying by quantity gives

$$TR = PQ = -\frac{B}{a_p}Q + \frac{Q^2}{a_p} \tag{3-5}$$

Marginal revenue is the derivative of TR with respect to Q. Thus

$$MR = \frac{d(PQ)}{dQ} = -\frac{B}{a_p} + \frac{2Q}{a_p} \tag{3-6}$$

Note that the marginal revenue equation has the same intercept $(-B/a_p)$ as the demand equation and that the slope of marginal revenue, $2/a_p$, is twice the slope of the demand equation, $1/a_p$. Also note that $MR = 0$ at $Q = B/2$. This point corresponds to the maximum value of the total revenue function. For $Q < B/2$, marginal revenue is positive and total revenue is increasing. For $Q > B/2$, marginal revenue is negative and total revenue is decreasing.

KEY CONCEPTS

- Marginal revenue is the change in revenue associated with a one-unit change in output.
- Marginal revenue is zero at the quantity that generates maximum total revenue and negative beyond that point.
- For a linear demand curve, the absolute value of the slope of the marginal revenue curve is twice that of the demand curve.

Price Elasticity

In the preceding section it was demonstrated that higher prices do not always result in greater total revenue. A price change can either increase or decrease total revenue, depending on the nature of the demand function. The uncertainty involved in pricing decisions could be reduced if managers had a method of measuring the probable effect of price changes on total revenue. One such measure is *price elasticity of demand*, which is defined as the percentage change in quantity demanded divided by the percentage change in price. That is,

$$E_p = \frac{\%\,\Delta Q}{\%\,\Delta P} \tag{3-7}$$

where the symbol Δ is used to denote change. Thus, price elasticity indicates the percentage change in quantity demanded for a 1 percent change in price.

For example, suppose that a firm increases the price of its product by 2 percent and quantity demanded subsequently decreases by 3 percent. The price elasticity would be

$$E_p = \frac{-3\%}{2\%} = -1.5$$

Notice that E_p is negative. Except in rare and unimportant cases, price elasticity is always less than or equal to zero.[2] The explanation is the law of demand, which states that price and quantity demanded are inversely related. Thus, when the price change is positive, the change in quantity demanded is negative, and vice versa.

Point Versus Arc Elasticity

There are two approaches to computing price elasticities. The choice between the two depends on the available data and the intended use. Arc elasticities are appropriate for analyzing the effect of discrete (i.e., measurable) changes in price. For example, a price increase from $1 to $2 could be evaluated by computing the arc elasticity. In actual practice, most elasticity computations involve the arc method. The other choice is point elasticity. This approach can be used to evaluate the effect of very small price changes or to compute the price elasticity at a particular price. Point elasticities are important in theoretical economics.

ARC ELASTICITY   The percentage change in price is the change in price divided by price (i.e., $\Delta P/P$). Similarly, the percentage change in quantity demanded is the change in quantity divided by quantity (i.e., $\Delta Q/Q$). Thus price elasticity can be expressed as

$$E_p = \frac{\Delta Q/Q}{\Delta P/P} \tag{3-8}$$

By rearranging terms, equation (3-8) can be written as

$$E_p = \frac{\Delta Q}{\Delta P}\frac{P}{Q} \tag{3-9}$$

Note that P and Q specify a particular point on the demand curve, while $\Delta Q/\Delta P$ is the reciprocal of the slope of the demand curve. Thus the price elasticity will vary depending on where the measurement is taken on the demand curve and also with the slope of the demand curve.

The price and quantity information presented earlier in the chapter can be used to demonstrate the calculation of the arc price elasticity. Table 3-1 on page 77 indicates that at a price of $6, quantity demanded is 5 units. The table also shows that if the price increases to $10, quantity demanded will be 1 unit. Thus for a $4 increase in price, the change in quantity demanded is −4 units. That is,

$$\frac{\Delta Q}{\Delta P} = \frac{-4}{4} = -1$$

Determining the value of P/Q poses a problem. Which should be used, the price–quantity data before the price change or the price–quantity values after the price increase? The choice makes a significant difference in the computed price

[2] In some texts, price elasticities are multiplied by −1 to make them positive. This convention is not adopted here because it obscures the inverse relationship between price and quantity demanded.

elasticity. For example, if the initial data are used, then

$$E_p = \frac{\Delta Q}{\Delta P}\frac{P}{Q} = -1 \times \frac{6}{5} = -1.20$$

However, if the price–quantity data after the price change are selected, then

$$E_p = \frac{\Delta Q}{\Delta P}\frac{P}{Q} = -1 \times \frac{10}{1} = -10.00$$

In the first case, the price elasticity estimate indicates that a 1 percent increase in price results in a quantity decline of just over 1 percent. But the second estimate implies that the percentage impact on quantity demanded is 10 times that of the percentage price change.

The conventional approach used to calculate arc elasticities is to use average values for price and quantity. Thus arc price elasticity is defined as

$$E_p = \frac{Q_2 - Q_1}{(Q_2 + Q_1)/2} \bigg/ \frac{P_2 - P_1}{(P_2 + P_1)/2} \tag{3-10}$$

where P_1 and Q_1 are the initial price–quantity pair and P_2 and Q_2 are the price–quantity values after the price change. Simplifying and rearranging terms, equation (3-10) can be written as

$$E_p = \frac{Q_2 - Q_1}{P_2 - P_1}\frac{P_2 + P_1}{Q_2 + Q_1} \tag{3-11}$$

Now using the data from Table 3-1, the arc elasticity is computed to be

$$E_p = \frac{1-5}{10-6} \times \frac{10+6}{1+5} = -2.67$$

Thus as price increases from $6 to $10, the average change in quantity demanded per 1 percent change in price is −2.67 percent.

EXAMPLE

The Price Elasticity of Demand for Playing Cards

Suppose the market demand for playing cards is given by the equation

$$Q = 6{,}000{,}000 - 1{,}000{,}000P$$

where Q is the number of decks of cards demanded each year and P is the price in dollars. For a price increase from $2 to $3 per deck, what is the arc price elasticity?

SOLUTION

Using the market demand equation, the quantity demanded is 4,000,000 decks of cards at a price of $2. Similarly, it is determined that the quantity demanded is 3,000,000 decks at a price of $3 per deck. Note that in equation (3-11), $(Q_2 - Q_1)/(P_2 - P_1)$ is just $\Delta Q/\Delta P$. The market demand equation can be used to determine

$\Delta Q/\Delta P$. In that each \$1 increase in price causes a 1,000,000 decrease in quantity demanded, it is known that $\Delta Q/\Delta P = -1,000,000$. Thus the arc price elasticity is

$$E_p = -1,000,000 \times \frac{2+3}{4,000,000 + 3,000,000} = -0.71$$

This means that a one-percent increase in price will reduce quantity demanded by 0.71 percent.

POINT ELASTICITY   Now consider extremely small changes in price. For ΔP approaching zero, the term $\Delta Q/\Delta P$ can be written as dQ/dP, where dQ/dP is the derivative of Q with respect to P. Basically, dQ/dP expresses the rate at which Q is changing for very small changes in P. For a linear demand equation, dQ/dP is constant. For example, in the demand equation $Q = B + a_pP$, the derivative dQ/dP is a_p. Thus the rate of change for a small price change is the same as for large changes. Hence for linear demand equation, $dQ/dP = \Delta Q/\Delta P$.

For small price changes, P_1 and P_2 are approximately equal. Thus either price can be used in the calculation with no significant effect on the computed price elasticity. Hence the equation for point elasticity can be written as

$$E_p = \frac{dQ}{dP}\frac{P}{Q} \tag{3-12}$$

Equation (3-12) is used to calculate price elasticities at a particular point on the demand curve. For example, consider the price–quantity data used earlier in this section. It has already been determined that $dQ/dP = -1$. If price is \$6 and the quantity demanded is 5 units, the price elasticity is

$$E_p = \frac{dQ}{dP}\frac{P}{Q} = -1 \times \frac{6}{5} = -1.20$$

That is, for very small price changes above or below \$6, the percentage change in quantity demanded is -1.20 times the percentage change in price. Again, the minus sign denotes that there is an inverse relationship between price and quantity.

Point elasticities can also be computed from a demand equation. Suppose that the demand equation is as follows:

$$Q_D = 100 - 4P$$

Because the relationship is linear, dQ/dP is constant and equal to the rate of change in Q_D for each 1-unit change in P. Note that quantity demanded changes by -4 units for each unit increase in P. Thus $dQ/dP = -4$.

Suppose that $P = \$10$. Substituting this value into the demand equation yields $Q_D = 60$. Thus the point elasticity at $P = \$10$ is

$$E_p = -4 \times \frac{10}{60} = -0.67$$

The interpretation is that 1 percent increase in price causes a 0.67 percent reduction in quantity demanded.

Consider a second example using the same demand equation. Suppose that $P = \$20$, which implies that $Q = 20$. The equation is linear, so $dQ/dP = -4$, as before. Thus

$$E_p = -4 \times \frac{20}{20} = -4.0$$

That is, at $P = \$20$, a small change in price generates a percentage change in quantity demanded that is four times the percentage change in price.

Price Elasticity and Marginal Revenue

Table 3-2 reproduces the price, quantity, total revenue, and marginal revenue information from Table 3-1. It also shows the point price elasticity at each price. Note that the absolute value of the elasticities becomes smaller as prices decrease. At $P = \$10$, the elasticity is -10.00, while at $P = \$1$, it is -0.10.

Often, it is useful to classify demand relationships on the basis of price elasticities. The following classification scheme is frequently used:

IF:	THEN DEMAND IS SAID TO BE:
$E_p < -1$	Elastic
$E_p = -1$	Unitary elastic
$-1 < E_p \le 0$	Inelastic

Thus, based on the data in Table 3-2, at some price between $5 and $6, demand is unitary elastic because the price elasticity is equal to -1. For prices below this price, demand is inelastic. For higher prices, demand is elastic.

Figure 3-4 shows the demand and marginal revenue curves for the price–quantity data of Table 3-2. The figure has been labeled to show where demand is elastic, unitary elastic, and inelastic. The figure indicates that demand becomes less elastic at lower prices. This is a characteristic of linear demand curves. Because the curve is linear, dQ/dP is a constant. Thus price elasticity is determined by the value of P/Q. But as price decreases, P/Q also decreases. Consequently, the absolute value of E_p becomes smaller and demand becomes less elastic.

Figure 3-4 can be used to interpret the three elasticity categories. The figure

TABLE 3-2 **Price Elasticity, Total Revenue, and Marginal Revenue**

Price	Quantity	Price Elasticity	Total Revenue	Marginal Revenue
$10	1	−10.00	$10	—
9	2	−4.50	18	$8
8	3	−2.67	24	6
7	4	−1.75	28	4
6	5	−1.20	30	2
5	6	−0.83	30	0
4	7	−0.57	28	−2
3	8	−0.38	24	−4
2	9	−0.22	18	−6
1	10	−0.10	10	−8

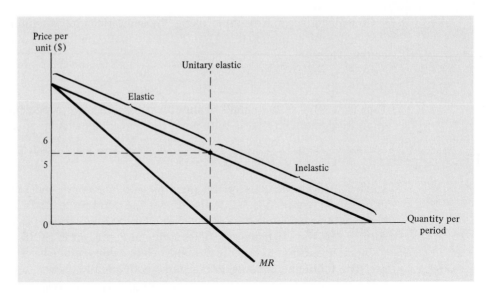

FIGURE 3-4 **Price Elasticity and Marginal Revenue.**

shows that the point of unitary elasticity corresponds to the point where the marginal revenue crosses the quantity axis. That is, marginal revenue is zero where demand is unitary elastic. The explanation is not difficult. Unitary elasticity means that a 1 percent increase in price causes quantity demanded to decrease by 1 percent. But total revenue is computed by multiplying price times quantity. Thus, if demand is unitary elastic, the increase in price is exactly offset by the decrease in quantity demanded. As a result, there is no change in total revenue—marginal revenue is zero.

Figure 3-4 also shows that marginal revenue is positive where demand is elastic and negative when demand is inelastic. Although the demand curve in Figure 3-4 is linear, these relationships are also true for nonlinear demand curves. The point where marginal revenue is zero always divides the elastic and inelastic regions of the demand curve.[3]

[3] However, it should be noted that there are some demand relationships for which marginal revenue is never zero. For example, consider a demand equation of the following form:

$$Q = P^a$$

Taking the derivative with respect to P yields

$$\frac{dQ}{dP} = aP^{a-1}$$

Thus the price elasticity is

$$E_p = (aP^{a-1})\frac{P}{Q} = \frac{aP^a}{Q}$$

But $P^a = Q$. Thus $E_p = a$. Because a is a constant, it follows that E_p is constant for all values of price and quantity. If $a < -1$, demand is elastic for all points on the curve. Thus marginal revenue is always positive. Conversely, if $a > -1$, demand is inelastic and marginal revenue negative. If $a = -1$, marginal revenue is zero and demand is unitary elastic for all price–quantity combinations.

The choice of the terms *inelastic* and *elastic* is appropriate when viewed in light of the relationship between price elasticity and marginal revenue. The word *inelastic* carries the connotation of something that is not flexible or responsive. Consider a vertical demand curve. For such a curve, quantity demanded is not affected by changes in price. That is, $dQ/dP = 0$ and thus $E_p = 0$. Such curves are sometimes referred to as completely inelastic.

In contrast, for a horizontal demand curve, quantity demanded is highly responsive to changes in prices. In fact, an arbitrarily small change in price causes an infinitely large change in quantity demanded. That is, $dQ/dP = -\infty$ and hence $E_p = -\infty$. Horizontal demand curves are said to be infinitely elastic. Although there are probably no goods or services for which market demand is infinitely elastic or completely inelastic, an understanding of these causes is useful in economic analysis. Also, individual producers may face demand curves that approach these extremes.

KEY CONCEPTS

- Price elasticity is defined as the percentage change in quantity demanded that results from a 1 percent change in price.
- Point elasticity is used where the price change is very small. Arc elasticity is appropriate for a larger change in price.
- Demand is elastic if $E_p < -1$, inelastic if $-1 < E_p \le 0$, and unitary elastic if $E_p = -1$.
- Demand is elastic where marginal revenue is positive, unitary elastic when marginal revenue is zero, and inelastic if marginal revenue is negative.

Determinants of Price Elasticity

Price elasticities have been estimated for many goods and services; Table 3-3 provides some examples. The short-run elasticities reflect periods of time that are not long enough for the consumer to adjust completely to changes in prices. The long-run values refer to situations where consumers have had more time to adjust.

Note the variation in elasticities in Table 3-3. The long-run demand for foreign travel by U.S. residents is elastic (i.e., $E_p = -4.10$). In contrast, the long-run demand for water is highly inelastic (i.e., $E_p = -0.14$). Electricity demand is inelastic in the short run, but elastic in the long run. In general, three factors determine the price elasticity of demand. They are (1) availability of substitutes, (2) proportion of income spent on the good or service, and (3) length of time.

AVAILABILITY OF SUBSTITUTES Products for which there are good substitutes tend to have higher price elasticities than products for which there are few adequate substitutes. Motion pictures are a good example. Movies are a form of recreation, but there are many alternative recreational activities. When ticket prices at the movie theater increase, these substitute activities replace movies. Thus the demand for motion pictures is relatively elastic, as shown in Table 3-3.

TABLE 3-3 **Estimates of Price Elasticity**

Good or Service	Estimated Price Elasticity	
Electricity	−0.13	Short run
Electricity	−1.89	Long run
Water	−0.14	Long run
Motion pictures	−3.69	Long run
Gasoline	−0.15	Short run
Gasoline	−0.78	Long run
Foreign travel	−4.10	Long run

SOURCES: H. S. Houthakker and L. D. Taylor, *Consumer Demand in the United States; Analysis and Projections* (Cambridge, Mass.: Harvard University Press, 1970), pp. 166–167; and J. L. Sweeney, "The Demand for Gasoline: A Vintage Capital Model," Department of Engineering Economics, Stanford University, 1975.

At the other extreme, consider the short-run demand for electricity. When the local utility increases prices, consumers have few options. The owner of an electrically heated home can turn down the thermostat, but the savings are limited by the desire to keep warm. The owner of an electric clothes dryer may try drying clothes on an outside line, but this option will not be very successful during the winter or for the residents of some apartment buildings. Similarly, there are not many short-run alternatives to using electricity for refrigeration and lighting. Hence the short-run demand for electricity is relatively inelastic.

PROPORTION OF INCOME SPENT   Demand tends to be inelastic for goods and services that account for only a small proportion of total expenditures. Consider the demand for salt. A one-pound container of salt will meet the needs of the typical household for months and costs only a few cents. If the price of salt were to double, this change would not have a significant impact on the family's purchasing power. As a result, price changes have little effect on the household demand for salt. In contrast, demand will tend to be more elastic for goods and services that require a substantial portion of total expenditures.

TIME PERIOD   Demand is usually more elastic in the long run than in the short run. The explanation is that, given more time, the consumer has more opportunities to adjust to changes in prices. Table 3-3 indicates that the long-run elasticity for electricity is more than ten times the short-run value. As indicated previously, in the short run, people living in an electrically heated home have few options to reduce electricity consumption. But over a longer period, they may switch to gas or improve the energy efficiency of the home. Similarly, higher electricity prices may ultimately cause consumers to use other energy sources for cooking and clothes drying.

CASE STUDY ────────────────────────────────

The Short-Run Versus Long-Run Demand for Gasoline

As shown in the following table, gasoline prices increased dramatically from 1973 to 1981. At first, consumers had little choice but to use about the same amount of gasoline and pay the higher prices. Some vacation trips were canceled and many commuters started going to work in buses or car pools, but the options were limited. From 1973 to 1975, average fuel consumption per vehicle declined from 736 to 685 gallons per year, a decrease of 7 percent. However, given more time to adjust, consumers were able to reduce the impact of higher gas prices. Smaller, fuel-efficient cars became popular and

the average miles per gallon of gasoline for passenger cars increased from 13.3 in 1973 to 15.7 in 1981. People also changed jobs or moved closer to their places of work. These and other changes in driving habits reduced the average miles driven per car from 9,800 to 8,700 over the same period. The net effect of these changes was that fuel consumption per vehicle in the United States declined from 736 to 555 gallons per year between 1973 and 1981, a reduction of nearly 25 percent. Clearly, the long-run demand for gasoline was more elastic than the short-run demand.

Gasoline Prices and Consumer Response

Year	Average Price of Gasoline	Average Miles per Gallon	Average Miles Driven per Vehicle per Year	Average Fuel Consumption (gallons)
1973	$0.40	13.3	9,800	736
1975	0.57	13.7	9,400	685
1977	0.62	14.1	9,600	680
1979	0.86	14.5	9,300	638
1981	1.31	15.7	8,700	555

SOURCE: U.S. Department of Commerce, Bureau of the Census, *Statistical Abstract of the United States* (Washington, D.C.: U.S. Government Printing Office, selected years).

Price Elasticity and Decision Making

Information about price elasticities can be extremely useful to managers as they contemplate pricing decisions. If demand is inelastic at the current price, a price decrease will result in a decrease in total revenue. Alternatively, reducing the price of a product with elastic demand would cause revenue to increase.[4] The

───────────────────────────────

[4] However, a price reduction is not always the correct strategy when demand is elastic. The decision must also take into account the impact on the firm's costs and profits. More will be said about pricing strategy in later chapters.

effect on total revenue would be the reverse for a price increase. However, if demand is unitary elastic, price changes will not change total revenues.

The relationship between elasticity and total revenue can be shown using simple calculus. Total revenue is price times quantity. Taking the derivative of total revenue with respect to quantity yields marginal revenue:

$$MR = \frac{d(TR)}{dQ} = \frac{d(PQ)}{dQ} = P + Q\frac{dP}{dQ} \qquad (3\text{-}13)$$

Equation (3-13) states that the additional revenue resulting from the sale of one more unit of a good or service is equal to the selling price of the last unit (P), adjusted for the reduced revenue from all other units sold at a lower price ($Q\,dP/dQ$). This equation can be written

$$MR = P\left(1 + \frac{Q}{P}\frac{dP}{dQ}\right) \qquad (3\text{-}14)$$

But note that $(Q/P)\,dP/dQ = 1/E_p$. Thus

$$MR = P\left(1 + \frac{1}{E_p}\right) \qquad (3\text{-}15)$$

Equation (3-15) indicates that marginal revenue is a function of the elasticity of demand. For example, if demand is unitary elastic, $E_p = -1$ then

$$MR = P\left(1 + \frac{1}{-1}\right) = 0$$

Because marginal revenue is zero, a price change would have no effect on total revenue. In contrast, if demand is elastic, $E_p < -1$ and $(1 + 1/E_p) > 0$. Hence, marginal revenue is positive, which means that, by increasing quantity demanded, a price reduction would increase total revenue. Equation (3-15) also implies that if demand is inelastic, marginal revenue is negative, indicating that a price reduction would decrease total revenue.

Some analysts question the usefulness of elasticity estimates. They argue that elasticities are redundant, in that the data necessary for their determination could be used to determine total revenues directly. Thus managers could assess the effects of a change in price without knowledge of price elasticity. Although this is true, elasticity estimates are valuable, in that they provide a quick way of evaluating pricing policies. For example, if demand is known to be elastic, it is also known that a price increase will reduce total revenues.

KEY CONCEPTS

- Demand tends to be less elastic if:
  There are few good substitutes available.
  Expenditures on the good or service account for a small proportion of total expenditures.
  Consumers have not yet had time to adjust fully to change in price.

- A price *increase* will have one of the following effects, depending on the price elasticity of demand:
  Total revenue will increase if demand is inelastic $(-1 < E_p \leq 0)$.
  Total revenue will decrease if demand is elastic $(E_p < -1)$.
  Total revenue will be unchanged if demand is unitary elastic $(E_p = -1)$.

EXAMPLE _____

How Much Tuition for College Students?

The board of trustees of a leading state university is faced with a critical financial problem. At present tuition rates, the university is losing $7.5 million per year. The president of the university, a well-known biologist, urges that tuition be raised $750 over the present $3,000 rate—a 25 percent increase. Based on the 10,000 students now attending the school, he projects that this increase would cover the $7.5 million shortfall in revenues.

Student leaders protest that they cannot afford a tuition hike, but the president responds that the only alternative is to cut back significantly on programs and faculty. The faculty supports the tuition increase as a means of preserving their jobs.

The students quickly realize that any appeal that involves compassion for their plight is likely to fall on deaf ears. Their only hope is to demonstrate that the tuition hike is not in the best interest of the university. What can they do?

SOLUTION

The university administration sees a tuition increase as a means of increasing total revenue. The board of trustees is likely to reject the administration's proposal only if the students can demonstrate that it would not achieve this purpose.

As part of a term paper, an economics major discovers a journal article that discusses the price elasticity of demand for a college education. The author of the article estimates that the elasticity for enrollment at state universities is −1.3 with respect to tuition changes. That is, a 1 percent increase in tuition would decrease enrollments by 1.3 percent. The data are current and the paper was written by a highly respected scholar.

Based on the elasticity estimate from the paper, the students calculate that the proposed tuition hike of 25 percent would decrease enrollment by 32.5 percent, or nearly 3,300 students. This would result in a decrease in total revenue from $30,000,000 at present (i.e., $3,000 × 10,000) to about $25,000,000 after the tuition increase (i.e., $3,750 × 6,700).

Faced with this startling information, the board of trustees asks the university president if cost savings from fewer students would compensate for the revenue drop. The president replies that most of the university's costs are independent of enrollment and hence there would not be a significant cost saving. By a unanimous vote, the board of trustees rejects the tuition increase and orders the president to find some other way to meet the revenue deficiency.

Income Elasticity

Income elasticities are used to measure the responsiveness of demand to changes in income. When other factors are held constant, the *income elasticity* of a good or service is the percentage change in demand associated with a 1 percent change in income. Specifically, the income elasticity of a good or service is defined as

$$E_I = \frac{\% \, \Delta Q}{\% \, \Delta I} = \frac{\Delta Q}{Q} \bigg/ \frac{\Delta I}{I} \tag{3-16}$$

where I denotes income. Rearranging terms, equation (3-16) can be written

$$E_I = \frac{\Delta Q}{\Delta I} \frac{I}{Q} \tag{3-17}$$

As with price elasticity, income elasticity can be expressed in either arc or point terms. Arc income elasticity is used when relatively large changes in income are being considered and is defined as

$$E_I = \frac{Q_2 - Q_1}{I_2 - I_1} \frac{I_2 + I_1}{Q_2 + Q_1} \tag{3-18}$$

where Q_1 and I_1 represent the initial levels of demand and income, and Q_2 and I_2 are the values after a change in income.

For example, suppose that the demand for automobiles as a function of income per capita is given by the equation

$$Q = 50,000 + 5(I)$$

What is the income elasticity as per capita income increases from \$10,000 to \$11,000? Substituting $I_1 = \$10,000$ into the equation, quantity demanded is 100,000 cars. Similarly, at $I_2 = \$11,000$, quantity demanded is 105,000 automobiles. Thus

$$E_I = \frac{105,000 - 100,000}{11,000 - 10,000} \times \frac{11,000 + 10,000}{105,000 + 100,000} = 0.512$$

The interpretation of this result is that over the income range \$10,000 to \$11,000, each 1 percent increase in income causes about a five-tenths of 1 percent increase in quantity demanded.

If the change in income is small or if income elasticity at a particular income level is to be determined, a point elasticity is appropriate. In this case, $\Delta Q/\Delta I$ is expressed as dQ/dI. Thus

$$E_I = \frac{dQ}{dI} \frac{I}{Q} \tag{3-19}$$

To illustrate, if $Q = 50,000 + 5I$ as before, each one-unit increase in income is associated with a five-unit increase in demand. Thus $dQ/dI = 5$. For $I = \$10,500$, demand is 102,500 units and the income elasticity is

$$E_I = 5 \times \frac{10,500}{102,500} = 0.512$$

Note that this value is identical to the arc elasticity between $10,000 and $11,000 of income. They are equal because demand is a linear function of income. Thus the rate of change in quantity does not vary as income increases. Hence the average rate of change between $10,000 and $11,000 is the same as the instantaneous rate of change at $10,500. However, for nonlinear demand equations, the arc and point elasticities at the midpoint of the arc are not necessarily equal.

Inferior Goods, Necessities, and Luxuries

Income elasticities can be either negative or positive. When they are negative, an increase in income is associated with a decrease in the quantity demanded of the good or service. Cheap hot dogs might be an example. Those living on tight budgets may be unable to afford any other kind of meat. But as their incomes increase, they give up hot dogs and switch to other types of meat, such as roast beef and steak. Thus the increase in income causes a decrease in demand for hot dogs. Goods with negative income elasticities are defined as inferior goods.

Normal goods and services have positive income elasticities. They can be further classified by the magnitude of E_I. If $0 < E_I \leq 1$, the percentage change in demand is positive but less than or equal to the percentage change in income. Such goods and services are referred to as necessities. That is, demand is relatively unaffected by changes in income. A good example is bread, a basic food item eaten by even the poorest families. As a family becomes more affluent, it will consume more bread, but the increase is usually not proportionate to the increase in income.

Finally, luxuries are goods and services for which $E_I > 1$. This means that the change in demand is proportionately greater than the change in income. For example, if $E_I = 4$, a 1 percent increase in income would cause a 4 percent increase in demand. Jewelry is an example of a luxury good. As individuals become wealthier, they have more disposable income. Thus purchases of necklaces, rings, and fine watches tend to represent a larger share of their incomes.

Income Elasticity and Decision Making

The income elasticity for a firm's product is an important determinant of the firm's success at different stages of the business cycle. During periods of expansion, incomes are rising and firms selling luxury items such as gourmet foods and exotic vacations will find that the demand for their products will increase at a rate faster than the rate of income growth. However, during a recession, demand may decrease rapidly. Conversely, sellers of necessities such as fuel and basic food items will not benefit as much during periods of economic prosperity, but will also find that their markets are somewhat recession-proof. That is, the change in demand will be less than that in the economy in general.

Knowledge of income elasticities can be useful in targeting marketing efforts. Consider a firm specializing in expensive men's colognes. Because such goods are luxuries, those in high-income groups would be expected to be the prime customers. Thus the firm should concentrate its marketing efforts on media that reach the more wealthy segments of the population. For example, advertising dollars should be spent on space in *Esquire* and the *New Yorker* rather than in the *National Enquirer* and *Wrestling Today*.

CASE STUDY

Engel's Law and the Plight of the Farmer

In the nineteenth century, a German statistician, Ernst Engel, etched his name in economic history by proposing what has become known as *Engel's law*. Engel studied the consumption patterns of a large number of households and concluded that the percentage of income spent on food decreases as incomes increase. That is, he determined that food is a necessity. His finding has repeatedly been confirmed by later researchers. Examples of estimated income elasticities are shown in the following table. Note that only beef has an estimated elasticity greater than unity.

One of the implications of Engel's law is that farmers may not prosper as much as those in other occupations during periods of economic prosperity. The reason is that if food expenditures do not keep pace with increases in gross domestic product, farm incomes may not increase as rapidly as incomes in general. However, this tendency has been partially offset by the rapid increase in farm productivity in recent years. In 1940, each U.S. farmer grew enough food to feed about 11 other people. Today, the typical farmworker produces enough to feed 80 people.

Estimates of the Income Elasticity for Selected Food Products

Food	Estimated Income Elasticity
Beef	1.05
Chicken	0.28
Pork	0.14
Tomatoes	0.24
Potatoes	0.15

SOURCES: D. B. Suits, "Agriculture." In W. Adams, ed., *Structure of American Industry*, 8th ed. (New York: Macmillan, 1990) and D. M. Shuffett, *The Demand and Price Structure for Selected Vegetables* (Washington, D.C.: U.S. Department of Agriculture, 1954, Technical Bulletin 1105).

KEY CONCEPTS

- Income elasticity is the percentage change in demand per 1 percent change in income.
- Negative income elasticities denote inferior goods. Normal goods are those with positive income elasticities. If $0 < E_I \leq 1$, the product is defined as a necessity. For luxuries, $E_I > 1$.

Cross Elasticity

Demand is also influenced by prices of other goods and services. The responsiveness of quantity demanded to changes in price of other goods is measured by *cross elasticity*, which is defined as the percentage change in quantity demanded of one good caused by a 1 percent change in the price of some other good. That is,

$$E_c = \frac{\% \, \Delta Q_x}{\% \, \Delta P_y} \qquad (3\text{-}20)$$

where x and y represent the goods or services being considered.

For large changes in the price of y, arc cross elasticity is used. The arc elasticity is computed as

$$E_C = \frac{Q_{x,2} - Q_{x,1}}{P_{y,2} - P_{y,1}} \frac{P_{y,2} + P_{y,1}}{Q_{x,2} + Q_{x,1}} \qquad (3\text{-}21)$$

where the subscript 1 refers to the initial prices and quantities and 2 to the final values. Suppose that demand for x in terms of the price of y is given by

$$Q_x = 100 + 0.5P_y$$

If P_y increases from \$50 to \$100, then, using the equation, it is determined that Q_x increases from 125 to 150 units. Thus the cross price elasticity is

$$E_C = \frac{150 - 125}{100 - 50} \times \frac{100 + 50}{150 + 125} = 0.27$$

The interpretation is that a 1 percent increase in the price of y causes a 0.27 percent increase in the quantity demanded of x.

Point cross elasticities are analogous to the point elasticities already discussed. For small changes in P_y,

$$E_C = \frac{dQ_x}{dP_y} \frac{P_y}{Q_x} \qquad (3\text{-}22)$$

Based on the demand equation $Q_x = 100 + 0.5P_y$, the derivative, $dQ_x/dP_y = 0.5$. At $P_y = \$20$, quantity demanded is 110 units. Hence the point cross elasticity is

$$E_C = 0.5 \times \frac{20}{110} = 0.09$$

Substitutes and Complements

Cross elasticities are used to classify the relationship between goods. If $E_C > 0$, an increase in the price of y causes an increase in the quantity demanded of x, and the two products are said to be *substitutes*. That is, one product can be used in place of (substituted for) the other. Suppose that the price of y increases. This means that the opportunity cost of y in terms of x has increased. The result is that consumers purchase less y and more of the relatively cheaper good x. Beef and pork are examples of substitutes. An increase in the price of beef usually increases the demand for pork, and vice versa.

When $E_C < 0$, the goods or services involved are classified as *complements* (goods that are used together). Increases in the price of y reduce the quantity demanded of that product. The diminished demand for y causes a reduced demand for x. Bread and butter, cars and tires, and computers and computer programs are examples of pairs of goods that are complements.

Cross elasticities are not always symmetrical. That is, the change in demand for good x caused by a change in the price of good y may not equal the change in demand for y generated by a change in the price of x. Consider the case of margarine and butter. One study determined that a 1 percent increase in the price of butter caused a 0.81 percent increase in demand for margarine. However, a 1 percent increase in the price of margarine increased demand for butter by only 0.67 percent.[5] Although the two elasticities are different, note that they are both positive, indicating that butter and margarine are substitutes.

Cross Elasticity and Decision Making

Many large corporations produce several related products. Gillette makes both razors and razor blades. Ford sells several competing makes of automobiles. Where a company's products are related, the pricing of one good can influence the demand for other products. Gillette probably will sell more razor blades if it lowers the price of its razors. In contrast, if the price of Fords is reduced, sales of Mercurys may decline. Information regarding cross elasticities can aid decision makers in assessing such impacts.

Cross elasticities are also useful in establishing boundaries between industries. Sometimes it is difficult to determine which products should be included in an industry. For example, should the manufacturing of cars and trucks be considered one industry or two? One way of answering such questions is to specify industries based on cross elasticities. This approach defines an industry as including firms whose products exhibit a high positive cross elasticity. Goods and services with negative or small cross elasticities are considered to belong to different industries. The definition of an industry might seem to be an unimportant matter, but the choice can have important implications. For example, the outcomes of antitrust cases alleging illegal monopolies are sometimes determined primarily by the industry definition used by the judges assigned to the case. This concept is discussed in greater detail in Chapter 19.

EXAMPLE _____

Using Elasticities in Decision Making

The R. J. Smith Corporation is a publisher of romance novels—nothing exotic or erotic—just stories of common people falling in and out of love. The corporation hires an economist to determine the demand for its product. After months of hard work and submission of an exorbitant bill, the analyst tells the company that demand for the firm's novels (Q_x) is given by the following equation:

$$Q_x = 12,000 - 5,000P_x + 5I + 500P_c$$

where P_x is the price charged for the R. J. Smith novels, I is income per capita, and P_c is the price of books from competing publishers.

[5] Wold, H. *Demand Analysis*. New York: Wiley, 1953.

Using this information, the company's managers want to

1. Determine what effect a price increase would have on total revenues.
2. Evaluate how sale of the novels would change during a period of rising incomes.
3. Assess the probable impact if competing publishers raise their prices.

Assume that the initial values of P_x, I, and P_c are $5, $10,000, and $6, respectively.

SOLUTION

1. The effect of a price increase can be assessed by computing the point price elasticity of demand. Substituting the initial values of I and P_c yields

$$Q_x = 12,000 + 5(10,000) + 500(6) - 5,000P_x$$

which is equivalent to

$$Q_x = 65,000 - 5,000P_x$$

Note that $dQ_x/dP_x = -5,000$. At $P_x = 5, quantity demanded is 40,000 books. Using these data, the point price elasticity is computed to be

$$E_p = -5,000 \times \frac{5}{40,000} = -0.625$$

Because demand is inelastic, raising the price of the novels would increase total revenue.

2. The income elasticity determines whether a product is a necessity or a luxury. It has already been determined that the initial quantity demanded at the given values of the price and income variables is 40,000. From the demand equation the derivative, $dQ_x/dI = 5$. Thus the income elasticity is

$$E_I = 5 \times \frac{10,000}{40,000} = 1.25$$

Because $E_I > 1$, the novels are a luxury good. Thus as incomes increase, sales should increase more than proportionately.

3. The demand equation implies that $dQ_x/dP_c = 500$. Thus it is known that E_C is positive, meaning that Smith's romance novels and books from competing publishers are viewed by consumers as substitutes. Computing E_C yields

$$E_C = 500 \times \frac{6.00}{40,000} = 0.075$$

Hence, a 1 percent increase in the price of other books results in a 0.075 percent increase in demand for R. J. Smith's romance novels.

KEY CONCEPTS

- Cross elasticity is the percentage change in quantity demanded of good x per 1 percent change in the price of good y.
- Cross elasticities are positive for substitutes and negative for complements.

Summary

Demand refers to the number of units of a good or service that consumers are willing and able to buy at each price during a specified interval of time. Market demand is the sum of all individual demands. A movement along the demand curve is caused by changes in price and is referred to as a change in quantity demanded. A change in demand is represented by a shift of the demand curve. Changes in demand can be caused by changes in tastes and preferences, income, and prices of other goods and services.

Marginal revenue is the change in total revenue per one-unit change in demand. Total revenue is increasing when marginal revenue is positive. Marginal revenue is zero at the point of maximum total revenue and total revenue is declining when marginal revenue is negative. For linear demand curves, the absolute value of the slope of the marginal revenue curve is twice that of the demand curve.

Elasticities measure the responsiveness of demand to various factors. Price elasticity is defined as the percentage change in quantity demanded per 1 percent change in price. Arc price elasticity is used to assess the impact of discrete changes in price. Point price elasticity is appropriate for very small price changes.

Demand is said to be elastic where $E_p < -1$ and inelastic for $-1 < E_p \leq 0$. Demand is unitary elastic if $E_p = -1$. Marginal revenue is positive where demand is elastic, zero for unitary elasticity, and negative for inelastic demand. Demand tends to be more elastic when (1) there are many substitutes for a good or service, (2) a substantial proportion of total income is spent on the product, and (3) the time period is longer.

Income elasticity is the percentage change in quantity demanded per 1 percent change in income. Inferior goods have negative income elasticities, while normal goods are those with positive income elasticities. For necessities, $0 < E_I \leq 1$. Luxuries are goods and services with income elasticities greater than 1.

Cross elasticity is defined as the percentage change in quantity demanded of one good per 1 percent change in the price of some other good. Cross elasticities are positive for substitutes and negative for complements. Goods with high positive cross elasticities are considered to be in the same market.

Discussion Questions

3-1. Suppose that the possession of marijuana was legalized in all states. What would happen to the demand for marijuana? Explain.

3-2. Why is the market demand curve usually less elastic than demand curves faced by the individual firms in that market?

3-3. The income elasticity for soft drinks is estimated to be 1.00. How could an executive of a bottling firm use this information to forecast sales?

3-4. The profit-maximizing price will never be set where demand is inelastic. True or false? Explain.

3-5. If demand is unitary elastic, what action could a manager take to increase total revenue? Explain.

3-6. Why would demand for natural gas be more inelastic in the short run than in the long run?

3-7. Which of the following pairs of goods are substitutes and which are complements? Explain.
  a. Insulation and heating oil.
  b. Hot dogs and mustard.
  c. Television sets and videocassette recorders.
  d. Rice and potatoes.

3-8. In a world with just two goods where all income is spent on the two goods, both goods cannot be inferior. True or false? Explain.

3-9. In 1984, tuition at Commonwealth College was $4,000 per year and enrollment was 5,000 students. By 1994, tuition had increased to $8,000, but enrollment had increased to 5,500 students. Does this change imply an upward-sloping demand curve? Explain.

Problems

3-1. It is known that quantity demanded decreases by two units for each $1 increase in price. At a price of $5, quantity demanded is ten units.
  a. What will be the quantity demanded if price is zero?
  b. Write an equation for quantity demanded as a function of price.
  c. Write an equation that expresses price as a function of quantity.
  d. Write an equation for total revenue.

3-2. A market consists of three people, A, B, and C, whose individual demand equations are as follows:

$$A: \quad P = 35 - 0.5Q_A$$
$$B: \quad P = 50 - 0.25Q_B$$
$$C: \quad P = 40 - 2.00Q_C$$

The industry supply equation is given by $Q_S = 40 + 3.5P$.
  a. Determine the equilibrium price and quantity.
  b. Determine the amount that will be purchased by each individual.

3-3. A market consists of two individuals. Their demand equations are $Q_1 = 16 - 4P$ and $Q_2 = 20 - 2P$, respectively.
  a. What is the market demand equation?
  b. At a price of $2, what is the point price elasticity for each person and for the market?

3-4. The demand equation faced by DuMont Electronics for its personal computers is given by $P = 10,000 - 4Q$.
  a. Write the marginal revenue equation.
  b. At what price and quantity will marginal revenue be zero?
  c. At what price and quantity will total revenue be maximized?

d. If price is increased from $6,000 to $7,000, what will be the effect on total revenue? What does this imply about price elasticity?

3-5. The demand for shirts produced by a Canadian manufacturer has been estimated to be $P = 30 - Q/200$.
a. Compute the point elasticity at $P = \$10$; at $P = \$15$.
b. How does the point elasticity vary with the price?

3-6. A manager believes that the demand for her product is given by the equation $P = 50 - Q/100$.
a. What is the arc elasticity of demand as price decreases from $12 to $10?
b. What is the arc elasticity of demand as price increases from $10 to $12?

3-7. For each of the following equations, determine whether demand is elastic, inelastic, or unitary elastic at the given price.
a. $Q = 100 - 4P$ and $P = \$20$.
b. $Q = 1500 - 20P$ and $P = \$5$.
c. $P = 50 - 0.1Q$ and $P = \$20$.

3-8. Sailright Inc. manufactures and sells sailboards. Management believes that the price elasticity of demand is -3.0. Currently, boards are priced at $500 and the quantity demanded is 10,000 per year.
a. If the price is increased to $600, how many sailboards will the company be able to sell each year?
b. How much will total revenue change as a result of the price increase?

3-9. Demand for a managerial economics text is given by $Q = 20,000 - 300P$. The book is initially priced at $30.
a. Compute the point price elasticity of demand at $P = \$30$.
b. If the objective is to increase total revenue, should the price be increased or decreased? Explain.
c. Compute the arc price elasticity for a price decrease from $30 to $20.
d. Compute the arc price elasticity for a price decrease from $20 to $15.

3-10. Write a demand equation for which the price elasticity of demand is zero for all prices.

3-11. A consultant estimates the price–quantity relationship for New World Pizza to be $P = 50 - 5Q$.
a. At what output rate is demand unitary elastic?
b. Over what range of output is demand elastic?
c. At the current price, eight units are demanded each period. If the objective is to increase total revenue, should the price be increased or decreased? Explain.

3-12. The price elasticity for rice is estimated to be -0.4 and the income elasticity is 0.8. At a price of $0.40 per pound and a per capita income of $20,000, the demand for rice is 50 million tons per year.
a. Is rice an inferior good, a necessity, or a luxury? Explain.
b. If per capita income increases to $20,500, what will be the quantity demanded of rice?

c. If the price of rice increases to $0.41 per pound and income per capita remains at $20,000, what will be the quantity demanded?

3-13. Acme Tobacco is currently selling 5,000 pounds of pipe tobacco per year. Due to competitive pressures, the average price of a pipe declines from $15 to $12. As a result, the demand for Acme pipe tobacco increases to 6,000 pounds per year.
a. What is the cross elasticity of demand for pipes and pipe tobacco?
b. Assuming that the cross elasticity does not change, at what price of pipes would the demand for pipe tobacco be 3,000 pounds per year? Use $15 as the initial price of a pipe.

3-14. The McNight company is a major producer of steel. Management estimates that the demand for the company's steel is given by the equation

$$Q_s = 5,000 - 1,000P_s + 0.1I + 100P_a$$

where Q_s is steel demand in thousands of tons per year, P_s is the price of steel in dollars per pound, I is income per capita, and P_a is the price of aluminum in dollars per pound. Initially, the price of steel is $1 per pound, income per capita is $20,000, and the price of aluminum is $0.80 per pound.
a. How much steel will be demanded at the initial prices and income?
b. What is the point income elasticity at the initial values?
c. What is the point cross elasticity between steel and aluminum? Are steel and aluminum substitutes or complements?
d. If the objective is to maintain the quantity of steel demanded as computed in part (a), what reduction in steel prices will be necessary to compensate for a $0.20 reduction in the price of aluminum?

3-15. The price of oil is $30 per barrel and the price elasticity is constant and equal to -0.5. An oil embargo reduces the quantity available by 20 percent. Use the arc elasticity formula to calculate the percentage increase in the price of oil.

Problems Requiring Calculus _____

3-16. The Inquiry Club at Jefferson University has compiled a book that exposes the private lives of many of the professors on campus. Economics majors in the club estimate that total revenue from sales of the book is given by the equation

$$TR = 120Q - 0.1Q^3$$

a. Over what output range is demand elastic?
b. Initially, the price is set at $71.60. To maximize total revenue, should the price be increased or decreased? Explain.

3-17. The demand equation for a product is given by

$$P = 30 - 0.1Q^2$$

a. Write an equation for the point elasticity as a function of quantity.
b. At what price is demand unitary elastic?

3-18. The demand equation for a product is given by

$$Q = \frac{20I}{P}$$

where I is income and P is price.

a. Write an equation for the point price elasticity. For what values of I and P is demand unitary elastic? Explain.

b. Write an equation for the point income elasticity. For what values of I and P is the good a necessity? Explain.

3-19. Given the demand equation, $Q = 12{,}000 - 10P^2$.

a. For this equation, write the expression for the point price elasticity of demand as a function of P.

b. Over what range of prices is the demand inelastic?

3-20. Consider the demand equation, $Q_x = 150 - P_xP_o$ where the subscripts x and o refer to two different goods.

a. For this equation, write the expression for the point price and cross elasticities of demand as a function of P_o and P_x.

b. What is the relationship between the price and cross elasticities?

CHAPTER 4

Regression Techniques and Demand Estimation

Preview —————————————————————————

In the previous chapter, demand analysis was introduced as a tool for managerial decision making. For example, it was shown that a knowledge of price and cross elasticities can assist managers in pricing and that income elasticities provide useful insights into how demand for a product will respond to different macroeconomic conditions.

In Chapter 3, it was assumed that these elasticities were known or that the data were already available to allow them to be easily computed. Unfortunately, this is not usually the case. For many business applications, the manager who desires information about elasticities must develop a data set and use statistical methods to estimate a demand equation from which the elasticities can then be calculated. This estimated equation can also be used to predict demand for the product, based on assumptions about prices, income, and other factors.

In this chapter, the basic techniques of demand estimation are introduced. The first major section considers regression analysis, which is a statistical method for fitting an equation to a data set. Regression analysis is used for demand estimation in this chapter and is also the technique used to estimate production and cost equations in later chapters. The second section describes the four basic steps involved in estimating a demand equation. Finally, three potential difficulties associated with regression analysis are discussed—omitted variables, the identification problem, and multicollinearity.

Regression Techniques ————————————————

Consider the simple demand equation $Q_d = B + aP$. The law of demand implies that the coefficient a should be negative, indicating that less of the product is demanded at higher prices. However, in making pricing decisions, it may not be sufficient to know that quantity demanded and price are inversely related. An estimate of the numerical value of a and also of the coefficient B may be required for decision making. Similarly, to fully understand the correspondence between inputs and outputs in production functions and between costs and output in cost functions, it is often necessary to quantify relationships between the variables. The most widely used technique in economics and many other sciences for estimating these relationships is the least-squares regression method. The basic elements of this technique are developed in this section.

Although the focus of this chapter is on estimation of demand, the example used in this section to introduce regression analysis is based on cost and output data. The reason for selecting a cost function is that it is somewhat easier to explain and to understand in a regression context than are price–quantity relationships. After the basics of least-squares analysis have been presented, the remainder of the chapter considers how the method is used to estimate demand functions.

Estimating Coefficients

Consider a firm with a fixed capital stock that has been rented under a long-term lease for $100 per production period. The other input in the firm's production process is labor, which can be increased or decreased quickly depending on the firm's needs. In this case, the cost of the capital input ($100) is fixed and the cost of labor is variable. The manager of the firm wants to know the relationship between output and cost, that is, the firm's total cost function. This would allow the manager to predict the cost of any specified rate of output for the next production period.

Specifically, the manager is interested in estimating the coefficients a and b of the function

$$Y = a + bX$$

where the dependent variable Y is total cost and the independent variable X is total output. If this function is plotted on a graph, the parameter a would be the vertical intercept (i.e., the point where the function intersects the vertical axis) and b would be the slope of the function. Recall that the slope of a total function is the marginal function. As $Y = a + bX$ is the total cost function, the slope, b, is marginal cost or the change in total cost per unit change in output.

Assume that data on cost and output have been collected for each of seven production periods and are reported in Table 4-1. Note that there is a cost of $100 associated with an output rate of zero. This represents the fixed cost of the capital input, which must be paid regardless of the rate of output. These data are shown as points in Figure 4-1. They suggest a definite upward trend, but they do not trace out a straight line. The problem is to determine the line that best represents the overall relationship between Y and X. One approach would simply be to "eyeball" a line through these data in a way that the data points were about equally spaced on both sides of the line. The coefficient a would be found by extending that line to the vertical axis and reading the Y-coordinate at that point. The slope, b, would be found by taking any two points on the line, $\{X_1, Y_1\}$ and

TABLE 4-1 **Hypothetical Data on Total Cost and Total Output**

Production Period	Total Cost (Y_i)	Total Output (X_i)
1	$100	0
2	150	5
3	160	8
4	240	10
5	230	15
6	370	23
7	410	25

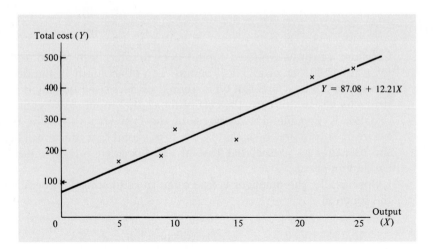

FIGURE 4-1 **Total Cost, Total Output, and the Estimated Regression Equation.**

$\{X_2, Y_2\}$, and using the slope formula

$$b = \frac{Y_2 - Y_1}{X_2 - X_1}$$

Although this approach could be used, the method is quite imprecise and can be employed only when there is just one independent variable. What if production cost depends on both the rate of output and the size of the plant? To plot the data for these three variables (total cost, output, and plant size) would require a three-dimensional diagram; it would be nearly impossible to eyeball the relationship in this case. The addition of another independent variable, say average skill levels of the employees, would place the data set in the fourth dimension, where any graphic approach is hopeless.

There is a better way. Statisticians have demonstrated that the best estimate of the coefficients of a linear function is to fit the line through the data points such that the sum of squared vertical distances from each point to the line is minimized. This technique is called *least-squares regression estimation*.

Based on the output and cost data in Table 4-1, the least-squares regression equation will be shown to be

$$\hat{Y} = 87.08 + 12.21X$$

This equation is plotted in Figure 4-1. Note that the data points fall about equally on both sides of the line.

Consider an output rate of 5. As shown in Table 4-1, the actual cost associated with this output level is 150. The value predicted by the regression equation, referred to as $\hat{Y}$, is 148.13. That is, $\hat{Y} = 87.08 + 12.21(5) = 148.13$. The deviation of the actual Y value from the predicted value (i.e., the vertical distance of the point from the line), $Y_i - \hat{Y}$, is referred to as the *residual* or the *prediction error*.

There are many values that might be selected as estimators of a and b, but only one of those sets defines a line that minimizes the sum of squared deviations [i.e., that minimizes $\Sigma(Y_i - \hat{Y}_i)^2$]. The equations for computing the least-squares estimators $\hat{a}$ and $\hat{b}$ are

$$\hat{b} = \frac{\Sigma(X_i - \overline{X})(Y_i - \overline{Y})}{\Sigma(X_i - \overline{X})^2} \tag{4-1}$$

and

$$\hat{a} = \overline{Y} - \hat{b}\overline{X} \tag{4-2}$$

where $\overline{Y}$ and $\overline{X}$ are the means of the Y and X variables.

Using the basic cost and output data from the example, the necessary calculations are shown in Table 4-2. Substituting the appropriate values into equations (4-1) and (4-2), the estimates of $\hat{b}$ and $\hat{a}$ are computed to be

$$\hat{b} = \frac{\Sigma(X_i - \overline{X})(Y_i - \overline{Y})}{\Sigma(X_i - \overline{X})^2} = \frac{6,245.71}{511.40} = 12.21$$

$$\hat{a} = \overline{Y} - \hat{b}\overline{X} = 237.14 - 12.21(12.29) = 87.08$$

Thus the estimated equation for the total cost function is

$$\hat{Y} = 87.08 + 12.21X$$

The estimate of the coefficient a is 87.08. This is the vertical intercept of the regression line. In the context of this example, $\hat{a} = 87.08$ is an estimate of fixed cost. Note that this estimate is subject to error because it is known that the actual fixed cost is \$100. The value of $\hat{b}$ is an estimate of the change in total cost for a one-unit change in output (i.e., marginal cost). The value of $\hat{b}$, \$12.21, means that, on average, a one-unit change in output results in a \$12.21 change in total cost. Thus $\hat{b}$ is an estimate of marginal cost.

TABLE 4-2 **Summary Calculations for Computing the Estimates $\hat{a}$ and $\hat{b}$**

Cost (Y_i)	Output (X_i)	$Y_i - \overline{Y}$	$X_i - \overline{X}$	$(X_i - \overline{X})^2$	$(X_i - \overline{X})(Y_i - \overline{Y})$
100	0	−137.14	−12.29	151.04	1,685.45
150	5	−87.14	−7.29	53.14	635.25
160	8	−77.14	−4.29	18.40	330.93
240	10	−002.86	−2.29	5.24	−6.55
230	15	−7.14	2.71	7.34	−19.35
370	23	132.86	10.71	114.70	1,422.93
410	25	172.86	12.71	161.54	2,197.05
$\overline{Y} = 237.14$ $\overline{X} = 12.29$				$\Sigma(X_i - \overline{X})^2$ $= 511.40$	$\Sigma(X_i - \overline{X})(Y_i - \overline{Y})$ $= 6,245.71$

KEY CONCEPTS

- The least-squares regression technique is used to estimate the coefficients of a function by fitting a line through the data such that the sum of squared deviations [i.e., $\Sigma(Y_i - \hat{Y}_i)^2$] is minimized.

- Estimates of the coefficients of the function $Y = a + bX$ are given by the equations

$$\hat{b} = \frac{\Sigma(X_i - \overline{X})(Y_i - \overline{Y})}{\Sigma(X_i - \overline{X})^2} \quad \text{and} \quad \hat{a} = \overline{Y} - \hat{b}\overline{X}$$

- The value of $\hat{a}$ estimates the vertical intercept or the estimated value of Y when $X = 0$. The value of $\hat{b}$ estimates the change in Y for a one-unit change in X.

EXAMPLE _____

Estimating the Demand for Lobster Dinners

The basic regression tools just discussed can also be used to estimate demand relationships. Consider a small restaurant chain specializing in fresh lobster dinners. The business has collected information on prices and the average number of meals served per day for a random sample of eight restaurants in the chain. These data are shown below. Use regression analysis to estimate the coefficients of the demand function $Q_d = a + bP$. Based on the estimated equation, calculate the point price elasticity of demand at the mean values of the variables.

City	Meals per Day (Q)	Price (P)
1	100	$15
2	90	18
3	85	19
4	110	14
5	120	13
6	90	19
7	105	16
8	100	14

SOLUTION

The mean values of the variables are $\overline{Q} = 100$ and $\overline{P} = \$16$. The other data needed to calculate the coefficients of the demand equation are shown below.

City	$Q_i - \overline{Q}$	$P_i - \overline{P}$	$(P_i - \overline{P})^2$	$(P_i - \overline{P})(Q_i - \overline{Q})$
1	0	−1	1	0
2	−10	2	4	−20
3	−15	3	9	−45
4	10	−2	4	−20
5	20	−3	9	−60
6	−10	3	9	−30
7	5	0	0	0
8	0	−2	4	0
			$\Sigma(P_i - \overline{P})^2 = 40$	$\Sigma(P_i - \overline{P})(Q_i - \overline{Q}) = -175$

As shown, the sum of the $(P_i - \overline{P})^2$ is 40 and the sum of the $(P_i - \overline{P})(Q_i - \overline{Q})$ is -175. Thus, using equations (4-1) and (4-2),

$$\hat{b} = -175/40 = -4.375 \quad \text{and} \quad \hat{a} = 100 - (-4.375)(16) = 170.$$

Hence, the estimated demand equation is $Q_d = 170 - 4.375P$. Recall from Chapter 3 that the formula for point price elasticity of demand is $E_p = (dQ/dP)(P/Q)$. Based on the estimated demand function, $dQ/dP = -4.375$. Thus, using the mean values for the price and quantity variables, $E_p = (-4.375)(16/100) = -0.7$.

Testing Regression Estimates

Once the parameters have been estimated, the strength of the relationship between the dependent variable and the independent variables can be measured in two ways. The first uses a measure called the coefficient of determination, denoted as R^2, to measure how well the overall equation explains changes in the dependent variable. The second measure uses the t-statistic to test the strength of the relationship between an independent variable and the dependent variable.

TESTING OVERALL EXPLANATORY POWER Define the squared deviation of any Y_i from the mean of Y [i.e., $(Y_i - \overline{Y})^2$] as the variation in Y. The total variation is found by summing these deviations for all values of the dependent variable. That is,

$$\text{total variation} = \Sigma(Y_i - \overline{Y})^2 \tag{4-3}$$

Total variation can be separated into two components: explained variation and unexplained variation. These concepts are explained below. For each X_i value, compute the predicted value of Y_i (denoted as $\hat{Y}_i$) by substituting X_i in the estimated regression equation:

$$\hat{Y}_i = \hat{a} + \hat{b}X_i$$

The squared difference between the predicted value $\hat{Y}_i$ and the mean value $\overline{Y}$ [i.e., $(\hat{Y}_i - \overline{Y})^2$] is defined as *explained variation*. The word *explained* means that the deviation of Y from its average value $\overline{Y}$ is the result of (i.e., is explained by) changes in X. For example, in the data on total output and cost used previously, one important reason the cost values are higher or lower than $\overline{Y}$ is because output rates (X_i) are higher or lower than the average output rate.

Total explained variation is found by summing these squared deviations, that is,

$$\text{total explained variation} = \Sigma(\hat{Y}_i - \overline{Y})^2 \tag{4-4}$$

Unexplained variation is the difference between Y_i and $\hat{Y}_i$. That is, part of the deviation of Y_i from the average value $(\overline{Y})$ is "explained" by the independent variable, X. The remaining deviation, $Y_i - \hat{Y}_i$, is said to be unexplained. Summing the squares of these differences yields

$$\text{total unexplained variation} = \Sigma(Y_i - \hat{Y}_i)^2 \tag{4-5}$$

The three sources of variation are shown in Figure 4-2.

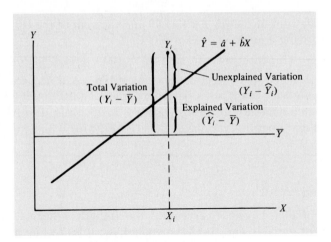

FIGURE 4-2 **Sources of Variation in a Regression Model.**

The *coefficient of determination* (R^2) measures the proportion of total variation in the dependent variable that is "explained" by the regression equation. That is,

$$R^2 = \frac{\text{total explained variation}}{\text{total variation}} = \frac{\Sigma(\hat{Y}_i - \overline{Y}_i)^2}{\Sigma(Y_i - \overline{Y})^2} \qquad (4\text{-}6)$$

The value of R^2 ranges from zero to 1. If the regression equation explains none of the variation in Y (i.e., there is no relationship between the independent variables and the dependent variable), R^2 will be zero. If the equation explains all the variation (i.e., total explained variation = total variation), the coefficient of determination will be 1. In general, the higher the value of R^2, the "better" the regression equation. The term *fit* is often used to describe the explanatory power of the estimated equation. When R^2 is high, the equation is said to fit the data well. A low R^2 would be indicative of a rather poor fit.

How high must the coefficient of determination be in order that a regression equation be said to fit well? There is no precise answer to this question. For some relationships, such as that between consumption and income over time, one might expect R^2 to be at least 0.95. In other cases, such as estimating the relationship between output and average cost for fifty different producers during one production period, an R^2 of 0.40 or 0.50 might be regarded as quite good.

Based on the estimated regression equation for total cost and output, that is,

$$\hat{Y}_i = 87.08 + 12.21 X_i$$

the coefficient of determination can be computed using the data on sources of variation shown in Table 4-3.

$$R^2 = \frac{\text{explained variation}}{\text{total variation}} = \frac{76{,}245.88}{79{,}942.86} = 0.954$$

TABLE 4-3 **Computing the Sources of Variation in a Regression Model**

Y_i	Total Variation $(Y_i - \overline{Y})^2$	$\hat{Y}_i$	Explained Variation $(\hat{Y}_i - \overline{Y})^2$	Unexplained Variation $(Y_i - \hat{Y}_i)^2$
100	18,807.38	87.08	22,518.00	166.93
150	7,593.38	148.13	7,922.78	1,003.50
160	5,950.58	184.76	2,743.66	613.06
240	10,008.18	209.18	781.76	949.87
230	10,050.98	270.23	1,094.95	1,618.45
370	17,651.78	367.91	17,100.79	1,004.37
410	29,880.58	392.33	24,083.94	312.23

$\overline{Y} = 237.14 \quad \Sigma(Y_i - \overline{Y})^2 = 79{,}942.86 \qquad\qquad \Sigma(\hat{Y}_i - \overline{Y})^2 = 76{,}245.88 \qquad \Sigma(Y_i - \hat{Y}_i)^2 = 3{,}668.41$
$\overline{X} = 12.29$

The value of R^2 is 0.954, which means that more than 95 percent of the variation in total cost is explained by changes in output levels. Thus the equation would appear to fit the data quite well.

EVALUATING THE EXPLANATORY POWER OF INDIVIDUAL INDEPENDENT VARIABLES The *t-test* is used to determine if there is a significant relationship between the dependent variable and each independent variable. This test requires that the standard deviation (or standard error) of the estimated regression coefficient be computed. The relationship between a dependent variable and an independent variable is not fixed because the estimate of b will vary for different data samples. The standard error of $\hat{b}$ from one of these regression equations provides an estimate of the amount of variability in $\hat{b}$. The equation for this standard error is

$$S_{\hat{b}} = \sqrt{\frac{\Sigma(Y_i - \hat{Y}_i)^2/(n-2)}{\Sigma(X_i - \overline{X})^2}}$$

where n is the number of observations. For the production-cost example used in this section, $n = 7$ and the standard error of $\hat{b}$ is

$$S_{\hat{b}} = \sqrt{\frac{3{,}668.41/5}{511.40}} = 1.19$$

The least-squares estimate of $\hat{b}$ is said to be an estimate of the parameter b. But it is known that $\hat{b}$ is subject to error and thus will differ from the true value of the parameter b. That is why $\hat{b}$ is called an estimate.

Because of the variability in $\hat{b}$, it sometimes is useful to determine a range or interval for the estimate of the true parameter b. Using principles of statistics, a 95 percent confidence interval estimate for b is given by the equation

$$\hat{b} \pm t_{n-k-1}S_{\hat{b}}$$

where t_{n-k-1} represents the value of a particular probability distribution known as *Student's t distribution*. The subscript $(n - k - 1)$ refers to the number of degrees of freedom, where n is the number of observations or data points and k is the number of independent variables in the equation. An abbreviated list of *t-values*

TABLE 4-4 **Selected Values of the Student's *t* Distribution for 95 Percent Confidence Interval**

Degree of Freedom	t-value
1	12.706
3	3.182
5	2.571
7	2.365
10	2.228
20	2.086
30	2.043
60	2.000
120	1.980
infinite	1.960

for use in estimating 95 percent confidence intervals is shown in Table 4-4.[1] In the example discussed here, $n = 7$ and $k = 1$, so there are five (i.e., $7 - 1 - 1$) degrees of freedom, and the value of t in the table is 2.571. Thus in repeated estimations of the output–cost relationship, it is expected that about 95 percent of the time the true value of parameter b will lie in the interval defined by the estimated value of b plus or minus 2.571 times the standard error of b. For the output-cost data, the 95 percent confidence interval estimate would be

$$12.21 \pm 2.571(1.19)$$

or from 9.15 to 15.27. This means that the probability that the true marginal relationship between cost and output (i.e., the value of b) within this range is 0.95.

If there is no relationship between the dependent and an independent variable, the parameter b would be zero. A standard statistical test for the strength of the relationship between Y and X is to check whether the 95 percent confidence interval includes the value zero. If it does not, the relationship between X and Y as measured by $\hat{b}$ is said to be statistically *significant*. If that interval does include zero, then $\hat{b}$ is said to be *nonsignificant*, meaning that there does not appear to be a strong relationship between the two variables. The confidence interval for $\hat{b}$ in the output-cost example did not include zero, and thus it is said that $\hat{b}$, an estimate of marginal cost, is statistically significant or that there is a strong relationship between cost and rate of output.

Another way to make the same test is to divide the estimated coefficient ($\hat{b}$) by its standard error. The probability distribution of this ratio is the same as Student's t distribution; thus this ratio is called a t-value. If the absolute value of this ratio is equal to or greater than the tabled value of t for $n - k - 1$ degrees of freedom, $\hat{b}$ is said to be statistically significant. Using the output-cost data, the t-value is

---

[1] A more complete list of *t*-values is found in Table III on page 659.

computed to be

$$t = \left|\frac{\hat{b}}{S_{\hat{b}}}\right| = \left|\frac{12.21}{1.19}\right| = 10.26$$

Because the ratio is greater than 2.571, the value of the t-statistic from Table 4-4, it is concluded that there is a statistically significant relationship between cost and output. In general, if the absolute value of the ratio $\hat{b}/S_{\hat{b}}$ is greater than the value from the table for $n - k - 1$ degrees of freedom, the coefficient $\hat{b}$ is said to be statistically significant.

KEY CONCEPTS

- The coefficient of determination, R^2, is a measure of the proportion of total variation in the dependent variable that is "explained" by the regression equation.
- A 95 percent confidence interval estimate of the parameter b is given by $\hat{b} \pm t_{n-k-1}S_{\hat{b}}$. If this interval does not include zero, $\hat{b}$ is said to be statistically significant, meaning that there is a strong relationship between the dependent and independent variables.
- The ratio of an estimated regression coefficient to its standard error (the t-statistic) can also be used to test the statistical significance of an independent variable.

Prediction Using Regression Equations

The regression equation can be used to predict or estimate the value of the dependent variable given the value of the independent variable.

The estimated total cost function,

$$\hat{Y} = 87.08 + 12.21X$$

can be used to make a point estimate of the cost of a particular rate of output, say 20, by substituting $X = 20$ and solving for $\hat{Y}$. Thus

$$\hat{Y} = 87.08 + 12.21(20) = 331.28$$

This means that the predicted cost of producing 20 units of output is \$331.28.

Recall that the actual output-cost data points do not lie on the regression line but are dispersed above and below that line. This means that a value predicted by the regression equation will be subject to error. That is, one would not expect the predicted values to be 100 percent accurate. The standard error of the estimate (S_e) is a measure of the probable error in the predicted values. The formula for this standard error is

$$S_e = \sqrt{\frac{\Sigma(Y_i - \overline{Y})^2 - \hat{b}\Sigma(X_i - \overline{X})(Y_i - \overline{Y})}{n - k - 1}} \tag{4-7}$$

The predicted value $\hat{Y}$ is called a *point estimate* of the value of the dependent variable to distinguish that estimate from a confidence interval estimate. The latter is a range of values that is expected to include the actual Y value 95 percent of the time. The standard error of the estimate is a fundamental part of the confidence interval estimate. For example, for a given predicted value of the dependent variable, $\hat{Y}$, the 95 percent confidence interval estimate is given by

$$\hat{Y} \pm t_{n-k-1}S_e$$

This means that 95 percent of the time the actual value of Y will fall within that range.

Suppose that management is considering a production run of 22 units of output and wants to know the estimated cost. Substituting 22 for X in the regression equation yields the point estimate:

$$\hat{Y} = 87.08 + 12.21(22) = 355.70$$

Using equation (4-7) and data from Tables 4-2 and 4-3, the standard error of the estimate is computed as

$$S_e = \sqrt{\frac{79,942.86 - (12.21)(6,245.71)}{5}} = 27.14$$

Thus, a 95 percent confidence interval estimate for the cost of producing 22 units of output is

$$\hat{Y} \pm 2.571(S_e) \quad \text{or} \quad 355.70 \pm 2.571(27.14)$$

Based on this statistical analysis, it is expected that in repeated production runs of 22 units, 95 percent of the time the cost will be in the range $285.92 to $425.48. Equivalently, only 5 percent of the time will the actual cost be higher than $425.48 or lower than $285.92.

CASE STUDY

The Value of a Poor Administrator

Many employees complain that their bosses do not deserve the large raises they receive each year, and college professors are no exception. If questioned, most faculty members could identify a department head, dean, provost, vice-president, or president they believe is receiving salary adjustments that do not correspond to that person's contribution to the institution.

Are undeserved raises the exception or the rule at colleges and universities? Is there a relationship between raises received by administrators and their job performance? Faculty members at the University of South Florida used regression analysis to evaluate this question.

Each year, administrators at the university are rated by the faculty using a five-point scale, where 1 equals very poor and 5 equals very good. About 20 percent of the faculty respond to the survey. To investigate the relationship between performance and pay, April 1990 ratings for 14 administrators were compared with the raises those same administrators received in August 1990. The equation used to estimate this relationship was $Y = B + aX$, where Y is the administrator's raise and X is the average rating of the individual.

Using ordinary least-squares regression, the estimated equation was $Y = 19,680 - 3,887X$. The sign of the coefficient of X implies that job performance and raises were inversely related at the University of South Florida in 1990. The coefficient of X is statistically significant and the R^2 is 0.30. The equation can be used to predict an administrator's raise based on the rating. For example, for a rating of 2, $Y = 19,680 - 3,887(2) = \$11,906$. The other predictions for raises are shown below.

Rating	Raise
Very poor (1.00)	$15,793
Poor (2.00)	11,906
Average (3.00)	8,019
Good (4.00)	4,132
Very good (5.00)	245

One interpretation of these findings is that the university's system for awarding raises is deeply flawed. How might the low response rate to the survey affect the validity of the conclusions?

Multiple Regression

Estimation of the parameters of an equation with more than one independent variable is called *multiple regression*. In principle, the concept of estimation with multiple regression is the same as with simple linear regression, but the necessary computations can be much more complicated. For an equation with three or more independent variables, the time required to calculate the values and the likelihood of an arithmetic error make computation by hand impractical. Consequently, virtually all regression analysis involving multivariate equations uses computers. There are dozens of programs available that can perform this task.

Because most economic relationships involve more than a simple relationship between a dependent and a single independent variable, multiple regression techniques are widely used in economics. For example, the demand for a product usually depends on more than just the price of the good. Other variables, such as income and prices of other goods can also have an influence. Thus, a simple regression equation involving only quantity and price would be incomplete and probably would result in an incorrect estimation of the relationship between quantity and price. This is because the effects of other variables omitted from the equation are not taken into account. Similarly, a regression equation that included only the rate of output as the determinant of costs could generate inaccurate results because other factors, such as input prices, also affect costs. The problem of omitted variables is discussed later in the chapter.

With multiple regression, it is important that the user understands how to interpret the estimated coefficients of the equation. Earlier in the chapter it was assumed that costs were a function of output. Now assume that costs are also determined by the price of labor. Thus, the multiple regression equation can be written as

$$Y = A + bX + cZ$$

where Y is total cost, X is output, Z is the price of labor, and A, b, and c are the coefficients to be estimated. The coefficients of X and Z indicate the effect on total cost of a one-unit change in each variable, holding the influence of the other variable constant. For example, b shows the change in total costs for a one-unit change in output, assuming that the price of labor stays the same.[2] The coefficient of Z estimates the effect of a unit change in labor price, assuming that the rate of output is unchanged.

KEY CONCEPTS _____

- A regression equation can be used to predict the value of the dependent variable for given values of the independent variable.
- The standard error of the estimate is a measure of the error in prediction.
- With multiple regression, each estimated coefficient measures the impact of one variable on the dependent variable, holding constant the influence of other variables.

Demand Estimation _____

Although the process can be very complex, regression analysis really involves just four steps: (1) development of a theoretical model, (2) data collection, (3) choice of a functional form, and (4) estimation and interpretation of results. In this section, these steps are described in the context of estimating a demand equation.

Development of a Theoretical Model

In using regression, the analyst must formulate a theoretical model of the economic relationships involved. This model should be based on sound economic theory and be expressed in mathematical terms. Fundamentally, the model-building process involves determining which variables should be included in the analysis and if there is a theoretical rationale for predicting the nature and magnitude of the relationships between variables. For example, if the objective is to estimate a demand equation, it would be reasonable to assume that quantity demanded is a function of the price of the good, income, prices of other goods, and tastes and preferences. Thus, the general form of demand equation could be written as

$$Q_d = f(P, I, P_o, T)$$

where P is the price of the good, I is income, P_o is the price of some other good, and T is a measure of tastes and preferences.

Economic theory can also be used to analyze the expected relationships between the dependent variable, Q_d, and the independent variables, P, I, P_o, and T. The law of demand states that price and quantity demanded are inversely related. For normal goods, income and quantity demanded would be positively related. With respect to the price of the other good, the relationship should be inverse if the two goods are complements and positive if they are substitutes. Without some

_____

[2] In mathematical terms, b is the partial derivative of Y with respect to X. Similarly, c is the partial derivative with respect to Z.

additional information on the variable used to measure tastes and preferences, the nature of that association cannot be predicted.

Prior knowledge, based on economic theory, about the relationships between variables can be used to assess the empirical results of regression analysis. If the signs of the estimated coefficients are inconsistent with the predictions of economic theory, then the process should be reexamined. For example, if the estimated coefficient of price is not negative, it is possible that the demand equation was incorrectly formulated or that there were errors in data collection and entry. Other possibilities are that relevant variables were omitted from the regression equation or that there is something unique about the good or service. At the very least, a coefficient with an unexpected sign is a signal that the analysis should be carefully reexamined.

Data Collection

To estimate demand, data for each of the variables that influence demand first must be obtained. These data may be collected from surveys, market experiments, or existing sources such as historical records of the firm or government publications. Either time-series or cross-section data may be used. Time-series data consists of period-by-period observations in a specific market for each of the variables that affect demand. Twenty months of data on quantity demanded, price, income, and prices of other goods from a single city would be an example of time series data that could be used to estimate a demand function.

In contrast, cross-section data are based on a number of markets at a single point in time. For example, cross-section data might consist of quantity demanded, income, price, and tastes and preferences for 100 different markets during a recent year. If the cross-section data exhibit variation from market to market, they can be used to estimate relationships between quantity demanded and the other variables.

KEY CONCEPTS

- The first step in regression analysis is to formulate a model based on economic theory.
- Economic theory can be used to evaluate the signs and magnitudes of estimated coefficients.
- Time series data consist of observations from a single market over a period of time. Cross-section data are based on information from a number of markets at a single point in time.

Choice of Functional Form

Equation (4-8) indicates a general relationship between quantity and the factors expected to influence demand. That is,

$$Q_d = f(P, I, P_o, T) \tag{4-8}$$

However, estimation using regression analysis requires the choice of a specific functional form for the equation. A linear equation is the simplest possible form. The linear equation corresponding to the general relationships of equation (4-8) is

$$Q_d = B + a_p P + a_I I + a_0 P_0 + a_T T \tag{4-9}$$

The linear form has several advantages. First, it can be estimated without modification—no transformations of the data are necessary. Second, the coefficients of the variables have a simple interpretation. If values of the other independent variables remain unchanged, each coefficient represents the change in quantity per unit change in the associated independent variable. Furthermore, the estimated changes are constant for each independent variable and unaffected by values of the other variables. These properties make computations much easier. For example, it is a simple matter to forecast the impact on quantity demanded of changes in per capita income. If per capita income increases by $1,000 and $a_I = 0.05$, the increase in quantity demanded will be $0.05 \times 1,000$, or 50 units per period.

It is also possible to calculate elasticities based on the estimated coefficients. The formula for point elasticity of demand is

$$E_p = \frac{dQ_d}{dP} \cdot \frac{P}{Q_d}$$

But $dQ_d/dP = a_p$. Thus, by selecting a value for P and using the estimated equation to compute Q_d, the elasticity for that price–quantity combination can be computed. Income and cross elasticities can be determined using the same general approach.

Various functional forms can be used for regression analysis. Other than the linear equation, probably the most common is the multiplicative functional form. For estimating demand, the multiplicative equation is

$$Q_d = BP^{a_p} I^{a_I} P_0^{a_o} T^{a_T} \tag{4-10}$$

In its present form, this equation cannot be estimated using ordinary least squares because it is not linear. However, there is a simple transformation of the equation that allows it to be estimated using least squares. First, take the logarithm of both sides of equation (4-10). The result is

$$\log(Q_d) = \log(BP^{a_p} I^{a_I} P_0^{a_o} T^{a_T})$$

But the logarithm of a product is just the sum of the logarithms. Thus,

$$\log(Q_d) = \log(B) + \log(P^{a_p}) + \log(I^{a_I}) + \log(P_0^{a_o}) + \log(T^{a_T})$$

The equation can be further simplified by noting that the logarithm of a number raised to a power is equal to that power times the logarithm of the number. Hence,

$$\log Q_d = \log B + a_p \log P + a_I \log I + a_o \log P_0 + a_T \log T \tag{4-11}$$

Because this equation is linear in terms of the logarithms of the original variables, the coefficients can be estimated using the ordinary least-squares method.

The coefficients a_p, a_I, a_o, and a_T in equations (4-10) and (4-11) have an important interpretation. Using calculus, it can easily be shown that they are the elasticities for the respective variables. Consider the price elasticity of demand. Taking the derivative of equation (4-10) with respect to price yields

$$\frac{dQ_d}{dP} = (a_p)BP^{a_p-1}I^{a_l}P_o^{a_o}T^{a_T}$$

Multiplying both sides of the equation by P/Q_d gives

$$E_p = \frac{dQ_d}{dP}\frac{P}{Q_d} = \frac{(a_p)BP^{a_p}I^{a_l}P_o^{a_o}T^{a_T}}{Q_d}$$

But

$$Q_d = BP^{a_p}I^{a_l}P_o^{a_o}T^{a_T}$$

Hence

$$E_p = a_p$$

Using an analogous approach, it can be shown that a_l is the income elasticity, a_o is the cross elasticity, and a_T is an elasticity measure for tastes and preferences. Thus, an advantage of the multiplicative form is that it yields estimates of elasticities. Note that in contrast to the elasticities from the linear equation, these elasticities are constant—they are unaffected by changes in the independent variables.

Another feature of the multiplicative form is that the change in quantity demanded per unit change in an independent variable is not constant as it is with the linear form. Rather, it is determined not only by the associated variable, but also by the values of the other independent variables. This makes computations using multiplicative equations somewhat more difficult but may be more realistic in depicting the relationship between the variables.

The choice of an appropriate functional form depends on the underlying theoretical model and the intended use of the results. If quantity demanded is thought to be a linear function of the independent variables, a linear form would be appropriate. In contrast, the multiplicative form may be a better choice if the objective is to estimate elasticities or to allow for nonlinear relationships between the variables.

CASE STUDY

The Pope and the Price of Fish

For over a thousand years the Catholic Church required that members abstain from eating meat on Fridays as an act of penance. Many Catholics responded by including fish as part of their Friday meals. The effect of this practice was to increase the demand for fish.

But in February 1966, Pope Paul VI authorized local bishops to end meatless Fridays. In December 1966, church leaders in the United States stipulated that members could eat meat on non-Lent Fridays (usually 46 Fridays during the year). With abstinence no longer required on these days, it was expected that Catholics would consume less fish and more meat. As a result, the price of fish, at least in the short run, should have decreased.

This hypothesis was examined by economist F. W. Bell. Noting that New England is 45 percent Catholic, he collected data on fish prices for seven different species consumed in that region before and after the change. He also collected data on other factors that affect fish prices, such as personal income and prices of meat and poultry. Using multiple-regression techniques to hold the effects of these other factors constant, Bell was able to assess the impact of the action by the church. His estimated equations are not reported here because they involved techniques beyond the scope of this book. However, the findings with respect to the Pope's decree are reported in the following table.

Species	Estimated Percent Decrease in Price Resulting from the Pope's Authorization to Eat Meat on Fridays
Sea scallops	−17
Yellowtail flounder	−14
Large haddock	−21
Small haddock (scrod)	−2
Cod	−10
Ocean perch	−10
Whiting	−20

Note that the percentage decrease in prices ranged from 2 percent for small haddock to 21 percent for large haddock. The average price decline for the seven species was 12.5 percent. Clearly, many Catholics enjoyed being able to have a steak on Fridays.

SOURCE: F. W. Bell, "The Pope and the Price of Fish." *American Economic Review*, December, pp. 1346–1350, 1968.

Estimation and Interpretation of Results

It has already been noted that many software packages are available for regression analyses. Most require little more than that the analyst specify the form of the equation to be estimated and input the data. The computer then performs the necessary calculations and provides results in a format that is usually relatively easy to interpret. Consider the estimation of the demand equation for a hypothetical good. The equation to be estimated is

$$Q_d = B + a_p P + a_I I + a_o P_o$$

and the price and income variables are measured in dollars.

Table 4-5 shows the output from the demand estimation problem. The estimated coefficient of the constant term suggests the quantity demanded if values of the other variables are zero. However, this coefficient has little economic meaning in most demand estimation problems. The other coefficients estimate the change in quantity demanded per dollar change in the associated independent variable. For example, the price coefficient is −4.9892. This estimate implies that if the other independent variables are held constant, a $1 change in the price of the good will result in a change in quantity demanded of almost five units.

In evaluating regression results, the estimated relationships between the variables should be considered in terms of economic theory. Note that the coefficient of price is negative. This implies an inverse relationship between price and quantity demanded, which is consistent with economic theory. Note also the coefficients

TABLE 4-5 **Sample Output for a Regression Problem**

		Variable		
	Constant	Price (P)	Income (I)	Price of Other Good (P_o)
Estimated coefficient	50.7836	−4.9892	0.0034	−1.2801
Standard error	10.2189	(−1.3458	0.0045	(−0.5890
t-statistic	(4.97)	(−3.71)	(0.76)	(−2.17)

Number of observations = 182 $R^2 = 0.6837$

of income and price of the other good. The signs of these coefficients could not be predicted using economic theory, but theory does provide information regarding their interpretation. The coefficient of income is positive, indicating that the item is a normal good. The "price of other good" coefficient is negative. Hence the two goods must be complements.

The standard errors reported in Table 4-5 indicate the precision of the estimates. Dividing the estimated coefficients by their standard errors gives the t-statistics. These can be used for hypothesis testing. A common hypothesis is that a coefficient is not significantly different from zero. As discussed earlier in the chapter, this hypothesis can be tested by comparing the computed t-statistics to the values shown for the t-distribution in Table 4-4 or in Table III on page 659.

For samples with more than about 120 observations (such as in Table 4-5), 95 percent of the t-distribution lies between +1.960 and −1.960. Thus t-statistics greater than +1.960 or less than −1.960 imply that the hypothesis that an estimated coefficient is equal to zero can be rejected with only a 5 percent probability of error. That is, the probability of erroneously concluding that a coefficient is not equal to zero is 5 percent or less.

In Table 4-5, the t-statistics for the constant term, price, and the price of the other good all have absolute values greater than 1.960. Thus the traditional interpretation is that these coefficients are significant (i.e., the probability of erroneously rejecting the hypothesis that they are equal to zero is less than or equal to 5 percent). In contrast, the t-statistic for the income variable is 0.76, meaning that there is more than a 5 percent probability of erroneously rejecting the hypothesis that the coefficient is equal to zero. Consequently, the income coefficient is referred to as nonsignificant.

Finally, the value of the coefficient of determination or R^2 indicates the overall explanatory power of the model. This number represents the proportion of total variation in the dependent variable explained by changes in the independent variables. The R^2 value from Table 4-5 is 0.6837. Thus about two-thirds of the total variation in quantity demanded is explained by price, income, and the price of the other good.

KEY CONCEPTS

- The functional form of an equation to be estimated should be selected based on the underlying economic theory and the intended use of the estimates.
- The estimated parameters of a linear equation indicate the impacts of a change in each independent variable.
- Without additional computation, the estimated parameters of multiplicative equations can be interpreted as elasticities.
- The estimated parameters of an equation are evaluated by examining their signs and magnitudes. The associated t-values are used to test hypotheses about statistical significance.

EXAMPLE

Interpreting an Estimated Demand Equation

A multiplicative demand function of the form

$$Q_d = BP_p^{a_p} I^{a_i} P_o^{a_o}$$

is estimated using cross-section data. The results are as follows:

	Constant	Variable		
		Price	Income	Price of Other Good
Estimated coefficient	0.02248	−0.2243	1.3458	0.1034
Standard error	0.01885	(−0.0563	0.5012	0.8145
t-statistic	(1.19)	(−3.98)	(2.69)	(0.13)
Number of observations = 224		$R^2 = 0.2515$		

1. How should the coefficients and the R^2 value be interpreted?
2. What will the quantity demanded be if the values of the independent variables are
   a. Price = $10.
   b. Income per capita = $9,000.
   c. Price of the other good = $15.
3. How much would quantity demanded change if price were decreased to $8 and the values of the other variables held constant?
4. Is demand elastic or inelastic? What effect would a price increase have on total revenue?
5. Are the two goods substitutes or complements?

SOLUTION

1. Because the functional form is multiplicative, the estimated coefficients represent elasticities. The price elasticity is −0.2243, indicating that demand is inelastic, and the income elasticity is 1.3458, suggesting that the good is a luxury. Both of these elasticity estimates are significantly different from zero. In contrast,

the coefficient of the "other good" price is positive but not significant. The implication is that there is a weak relationship between the two goods.

The R^2 reported for this problem is 0.2515. This is a rather low value, even for cross-section data. It means that only about one-fourth of the variation in demand can be explained by the model. Thus forecasts generated by the estimated equation are unlikely to be very accurate. A possible explanation for the low R^2 is that important explanatory variables have been omitted from the model.

2. In multiplicative form, the estimated equation is

$$Q_d = 0.02248P^{-0.2243}I^{1.3458}P_o^{0.1034}$$

A forecast of demand can be obtained by substituting in the given values for the independent variables. Making these substitutions, the quantity demanded is estimated to be 3,722 units.

3. The impact of reducing price can be estimated by recomputing quantity demanded for $P = \$8$, while holding the other variables constant. The resulting Q is 3,913. Hence the \$2 price decrease is estimated to increase quantity demanded by 191 units.

4. The coefficient of P is the estimated price elasticity. Because $a_p = -0.2243$, demand is inelastic and a price increase would increase total revenue.

5. The coefficient of P_o is positive, so the two goods are substitutes. However, the coefficient of P_o is not significant.

Problems with Regression Analysis ⎯⎯⎯⎯

Although regression analysis is a valuable technique for estimating demand functions and other economic relationships, serious problems can occur if the analyst is not careful in the formulation of the model and interpretation of results. Three potential pitfalls are discussed in this section—omitted variables, the identification problem, and multicollinearity.

Omitted Variables

It has already been observed that economic theory can be used to specify those variables that should be included in a regression equation. However, if there are variables that are omitted, the results of regression analysis can be misleading. The following example will help to explain the importance of including all the relevant variables.

It is hypothesized that the salary (S_i) of a major league baseball player depends on the number of times the player strikes out (K_i) during the season. It is assumed that the more times a player strikes out, the lower his salary would be. Hence the sign of the estimated regression coefficient is expected to be negative.

Based on data for 150 players, the following regression equation is estimated for annual salary (measured in thousands) and strikeouts in a season with the following result:

$$S = -242.21 + 7.72K \qquad R^2 = 0.44$$
$$(-5.32) + (2.51)$$

where the t-statistics are in parentheses. Note that the coefficient on strikeouts is positive and statistically significant because the t-statistic of 2.51 is greater than 1.96, the value of the t distribution in Table 4-4 that corresponds to 148 degrees of freedom. But this result suggests the nonsensical conclusion that players are paid more if they strike out more often! Because salary is measured in thousands of dollars, the coefficient 7.72 means that each additional strikeout is associated with an additional $7,720 in annual salary.

The problem is that a misspecified equation has resulted in a meaningless and misleading estimate of the relationship between strikeouts and salary. A better specification would have salary dependent on strikeouts and home runs (H). It is hypothesized that strikeouts are negatively related with salaries and that the coefficient of home runs should be positive. Using the same data on salaries and strikeouts, but adding data on home runs results in the following multiple-regression equation:

$$S = 231.4 - 0.64K + 8.57H \qquad R^2 = 0.92$$
$$(3.71) - (-0.33) + (6.44)$$

By including information on the number of home runs, the estimated relationship between strikeouts and salary changes dramatically. That relationship now is negative (as hypothesized), although the coefficient is not significantly different from zero. However, there is a very strong relationship between salary and home runs. The estimated coefficient (8.57) suggests that each home run is associated with an additional $8,750 in salary. Furthermore, this coefficient is statistically significant because the t-statistic is greater than 1.96.

Changing the specification of the equation resulted in an entirely different set of conclusions about how salary is related to performance. By including data on home runs, it is seen that the number of strikeouts is inversely related to salary. More importantly, the multiple-regression equation shows that salary is determined primarily by the number of home runs hit. Furthermore, in the first equation, R^2 was only 0.44, meaning that less than one-half the variation in the salary variable is explained. By including data on both strikeouts and home runs, R^2 increased to 0.92. The multiple-regression equation that includes both strikeouts and home runs fits the data much better.

The first equation failed to consider the number of home runs. By omitting this important information, the strange result was obtained that suggested strikeouts result in higher salaries. This erroneous conclusion resulted because many home run hitters tend to strike out quite often. Obviously, their high salaries are tied to home run production, not strikeouts. But by estimating the relationship between salary and strikeouts, it appeared that baseball players receive higher salaries for striking out more often.

The more complete analysis indicates that the number of strikeouts is relatively unimportant when the effect of home runs is considered. This suggests one of the advantages of the multiple-regression approach over simple regression. In multiple regression, the regression coefficient measures the net or partial effect of each independent variable while holding the effect of the other independent variables constant. In the example, the coefficient on home runs is 8.57, which means that while holding the effect of strikeouts constant, each additional home run is associated with an additional $8,570 in salary. The coefficient on strikeouts is -0.64. This means that after adjusting for the number of home runs, each additional strikeout is associated with $640 fewer dollars of salary.

When regression results are inconsistent with economic theory, the omission of important variables could be the cause. Consider a demand function estimated from 15 quarters of time series data from a particular market. The estimating equation is $Q_d = B + aP$. Assume that the estimated coefficient for price is positive and statistically significant. One explanation for this anomalous result could be that as price increased over time, so did income and the number of people in the market. Because price is positively correlated with income and with population, the coefficient of the price variable is reflecting increases in demand caused by the population and income changes. To separately identify these influences, additional variables should be included in the regression equation.

Identification

Related to the idea of omitted variables is the identification problem. Suppose that the following price and quantity information has been collected from a particular market. These data result from the interaction of supply and demand in the market. Specifically, they are the equilibrium prices and quantities observed for each year.

Year	Price	Quantity
1	10	100
2	8	120
3	6	140

In Figure 4-3a, the data have been plotted and a line fitted through the three points. Note that this line has a negative slope. If other factors that affect demand did not change over the three-year period and the supply curve shifted to the right from S_1 to S_2 to S_3, as shown in Figure 4-3a, then DD can be legitimately identified as a demand curve.

Alternatively, suppose that income, prices of other goods, or changes in tastes and preferences caused the demand curve to shift over time. In this case, the three points represent equilibrium prices and quantities determined by the intersection of different demand and supply curves, as shown in Figure 4-3b. Without more information, it is impossible to choose between the two possibilities; the separate demand curves cannot be identified.

The basic cause of this *identification problem* is that there is simultaneity between the supply and demand equations. That is, both the quantity demanded and the

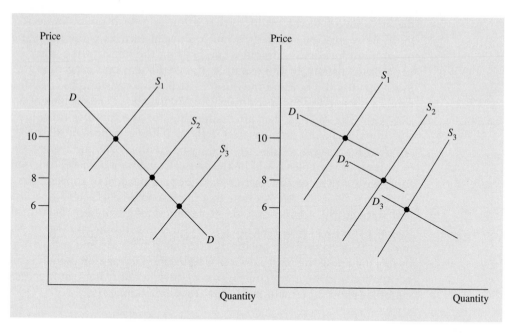

FIGURE 4-3a **Single Demand Curve.**   FIGURE 4-3b **Multiple Demand Curves.**

quantity supplied are affected by a change in the price of the good. Thus, the effects of price on quantity demanded and quantity supplied cannot be separately determined.

The key to identifying the true supply and demand relationships is to add one or more additional variables to each equation that are not included in the other equation. For example, assume that the problem involves the supply and demand for gasoline. The basic demand and supply model is

$$Q_d = B + d_1 P_g$$
$$Q_s = C + s_1 P_g$$
and $$Q_s = Q_d$$

where P_g is the price of gasoline and the equation $Q_s = Q_d$ is included because the observed data are equilibrium quantities and prices. The quantity demanded always equals the quantity supplied; thus there is no way to sort out the values of the parameters B, d_1, C, and s_1. Hence, neither function can be uniquely identified.

What is needed is another variable that affects only demand and one that affects only supply. Let income, I, be added to the demand equation and the price of crude oil, P_c, be added to the supply function. Now the three-equation model is

$$Q_d = B + d_1 P_g + d_2 I$$
$$Q_s = C + s_1 P_g + s_2 P_c$$
and $$Q_s = Q_d$$

Note that the dependent variables in this model are quantity and price of gasoline (even though price appears on the right-hand side of the equations). The two independent variables are income and the price of crude oil. Together, the three equations are referred to as the *structural form* of the model.

Because $Q_d = Q_s$, the demand and supply equations can be combined to form

$$B + d_1 P_g + d_2 I = C + s_1 P_g + s_2 P_c$$

Solving this equation for P_g gives

$$P_g = \frac{C - B}{d_1 - s_1} + \left\{\frac{s_2}{d_1 - s_1}\right\} P_c - \left\{\frac{d_2}{d_1 - s_1}\right\} I \qquad (4\text{-}12)$$

Substituting the expression for P_g back into the original demand equation and solving for quantity gives

$$Q = B + d_1 \left\{\frac{C - B}{d_1 - s_1}\right\} + \left\{\frac{d_1 s_2}{d_1 - s_1}\right\} P_c - \left\{\frac{d_2 s_1}{d_1 - s_1}\right\} I \qquad (4\text{-}13)$$

Equations (4-12) and (4-13) are called *reduced form* equations. Note that they are linear and that only the independent variables P_c and I appear on the right-hand side. Thus, these equations can be estimated using least squares because the simultaneity problem has been eliminated. The two equations look complicated but really are not. When estimated, they each have a constant term and a coefficient for each variable. If the following substitutions are made:

$$A = B + d_1 \left\{\frac{C - B}{d_1 - s_1}\right\}, \quad g_1 = \left\{\frac{d_1 s_2}{d_1 - s_1}\right\}, \quad \text{and} \quad g_2 = -\left\{\frac{d_2 s_1}{d_1 - s_1}\right\}$$

then equation (4-13) can be written as

$$Q = A + g_1 P_c + g_2 I$$

The estimated parameters A, g_1, and g_2 combine the effects of the coefficients from the structural equations. For example, g_1 shows the net effect of a change in the price of crude oil on the equilibrium quantity demanded of gasoline. Equation (4-12) is interpreted in a similar manner.

When one variable on the right side of a structural equation is simultaneously determined with the variable on the left side, one approach is to determine the reduced form equations of the model and use those equations for regression analysis. This method may be appropriate for estimating demand functions.

However, in actual practice, the simultaneity between quantity and price often is ignored and it is assumed that the price of the good is an independent variable. In this case, an equation of the general form

$$Q_d = f(P, I, P_o)$$

is used to estimate the demand function. Any shifts in demand are captured by including the income and other goods price variables. This approach is easier than working with a simultaneous equation model but may yield less accurate results.

Multicollinearity

The omitted variables and the identification problem discussed thus far have both involved the need to add additional variables to the regression equation. But there are situations where the problem is that there are too many variables. An important example is when two or more independent variables are highly correlated. This problem is referred to as *multicollinearity*.

Consider a student who has just completed a difficult course in American literature. So many books were assigned in the class that no one was able to finish all the reading. For an assignment in a statistics course, the student collected data on the grade performance and study habits of a random sample of 40 students who took the literature class. His hypothesis was that course grades should be positively related to the number of hours spent studying for the course and the amount of reading each person completed. Applying regression analysis to the data, the equation was estimated to be

$$G = 50.00 + 0.40H + 0.02P \qquad R^2 = 0.80$$
$$(2.80) + \ (0.80) + (1.35)$$

where G is the percentage grade, H is hours of study time, and P is total number of pages read. The t-statistics are in parentheses. Note that the coefficients of both H and P are positive, but neither is statistically significant. However, the R^2 is very high for cross-sectional data, suggesting the equation should be a good predictor of grades.

The problem with the analysis is that hours spent studying for the literature class and pages read are likely to be highly correlated. The more time students devote to the course, the more pages they will be able to read. In fact, the relationship probably will be nearly linear. That is, twice as many hours will probably result in about twice as many pages completed.

Multicollinearity causes problems in regression analysis. When two variables are highly correlated, it is difficult to identify the unique influence that each variable has on the dependent variable. For the example, more hours spent studying mean a better grade, but more study hours also allow more pages to be read and this also should result in a better grade.

When there is multicollinearity, the standard errors of the coefficients tend to be large and, hence, the t-statistics will be small. Consequently, the coefficients are less likely to be statistically significant. One solution to the problem of multicollinearity is to remove one of the highly correlated variables from the equation.

In the example, suppose that hours studied is dropped from the model. When the new equation is estimated, the results are

$$G = 60.00 + 0.03P \qquad R^2 = 0.75$$
$$(2.70) + (3.00)$$

Note that the revised equation still has a high R^2 and the coefficient of P is positive and statistically significant.

Multicollinearity is not always easy to detect. If two variables are almost perfectly correlated, most regression programs will indicate that they are unable to perform the analysis. But in other cases, there may be no error message and multicollinearity may go unnoticed. One approach is to check for pairs of independent variables that are highly correlated.

KEY CONCEPTS

- A misspecified regression equation can lead to erroneous conclusions about the relationship between variables.
- There may be an identification problem if price and quantity are simultaneously determined by supply and demand. The problem can be solved by including additional variables and using reduced form estimation.
- Multicollinearity results in large standard errors and small t-statistics for the estimated coefficients.

Summary

The least-squares regression technique can be used to quantify the relationship between a dependent variable and one or more independent variables. In simple regression, there is one independent variable, whereas with multiple regression, there are two or more independent variables. The estimated coefficients in a regression equation measure the change in the value of the dependent variable for each one-unit change in the independent variable, holding the other independent variables constant.

The coefficient of determination (R^2) is used to test the explanatory power of the entire regression equation. This statistic measures the proportion of the total variation in the dependent variable that is explained by variations in the independent variables. Hypotheses regarding the coefficients of individual independent variables are tested using the t-statistic, which is computed by dividing the estimated coefficient by its standard error. If the absolute value of this ratio is greater than the value taken from a table of the Student's distribution, the coefficient is said to be statistically significant. Regression equations can be used to make both point and interval estimates of the predicted value of the dependent variable for given values of the independent variables.

The first step in using regression analysis is to develop a theoretical model based on economic theory. This model can specify the data that should be collected and can also be used to interpret results. Regression analysis can be applied to either cross-section or time-series data. Linear estimating equations have the advantage of simplicity, but if a multiplicative equation is used to estimate the demand function, its coefficients are elasticities.

If relevant variables are excluded from a regression equation, the equation is said to be misspecified. The use of a misspecified equation may lead to incorrect conclusions about the relationships between the dependent and independent variables. Where price and quantity are simultaneously determined by supply and demand, it may be difficult to identify the demand function. This problem can be resolved by adding explanatory variables and using a reduced-form equation. When two or more independent variables are highly correlated, this multicollinearity may result in large standard errors and hence, small t-statistics for individual coefficients.

Discussion Questions

4-1. It is sometimes argued that quantitative techniques, such as multiple regression analysis, are of little value because they are always subject to error. Is this a valid argument?

4-2. A demand equation is estimated, but the coefficient of income is not significant. In using this equation to predict quantity demanded, should the income variable be omitted? Explain.

4-3. Why would coefficients of determination tend to be higher for time-series than for cross-section data?

4-4. What is the relationship between the sign of the estimated coefficient and the sign of the associated t-statistic? Explain.

4-5. In a demand function, what is the economic interpretation of a statistically significant coefficient for the price variable?

4-6. In transforming a multiplicative equation to a linear form, what would be the effect on the estimated coefficient of the price variable of using natural logarithms rather than logarithms to the base 10?

4-7. Data on average price and quantity over the last twelve months are used to plot a graph that is claimed to represent a demand function. Is this a valid interpretation? Explain.

4-8. Adding more independent variables to an estimating equation tends to increase the R^2. What problems could result from adding variables?

4-9. Is there any basis for choosing between a linear and a multiplicative equation for estimating a demand function? Explain.

Problems

4-1. Consider the following five data points:

X	−1	0	1	2	3
Y	−1	1	2	4	5

    a. Use regression analysis to calculate by hand the estimated coefficients of the equation $Y = B + aX$.

    b. Compute the standard error and the t-statistic for the coefficient of X.

4-2. Consider the following five data points:

X	−1.0	0.0	1.0	2.0	3.0
Y	−1.0	1.0	1.0	2.5	3.5

    a. Use regression analysis to calculate by hand the estimated coefficients of the equation $Y = B + aX$.

    b. Compute the coefficient of determination.

    c. What is the predicted value of Y for $X = 1.0$? For $X = 3.5$?

4-3. The following regression equation estimates the relationship between the number of cups of hot chocolate sold (H) and number of swimmers (N) at a beach:

$$H = 252.8 - 2.05N \qquad R^2 = 0.45$$
$$(2.06) - (-3.05)$$

(t-values are shown in parentheses.)

    a. Explain or interpret the regression coefficient of N, the t-value, and the coefficient of determination of this equation.

    b. How is it possible that more hot chocolate is sold when there are fewer people at the beach? Does this relationship suggest anything about the specification of the equation?

4-4. The vice-president of United Feeds, Inc., has provided the following quarterly price–quantity data for UF Superb, a horsefeed additive. He has asked that the demand equation for this product be estimated.

					Quarter					
	1	2	3	4	5	6	7	8	9	10
Price ($)	60	53	43	40	47	57	41	53	37	51
Quantity	83	93	100	108	97	80	105	86	110	90

    a. Use the ordinary least-squares regression method to estimate this function.

    b. The firm is considering a price increase to $66. Make a point and 95 percent confidence interval estimate of sales volume if this price increase is carried out.

4-5. Annual prices and beef consumption per capita in six cities are as follows:

City	Price per Pound	Consumption per Capita
1	$2.00	55
2	1.90	60
3	2.10	50
4	1.80	70
5	2.30	45
6	2.20	48

a. If a demand equation is to be estimated using these data, would the linear form (i.e., $Q = B + aP$) or the multiplicative form (i.e., $Q = BP^a$) be more appropriate? Explain.

b. Could the resulting equation be properly interpreted as a demand function? Explain.

4-6. The MacWend Drive-In has determined that demand for hamburgers is given by the following equation:

$$Q = 205.2 + 23.0A - 200.0P_M + 100.0P_C + 0.5Y$$
$$(1.85) + (2.64) - (-5.61) + (2.02) \quad + (4.25)$$

where Q is the number of hamburgers sold per month (in 1,000s), A is the advertising expenditures during the previous month (in $1,000s), P_M is the price of MacWend burgers (dollars), P_C is the price of hamburgers of the company's major competitor (dollars), and Y is income per capita in the surrounding community (in $1,000s). The t-statistic for each coefficient is shown in parentheses below each coefficient.

a. Are the signs of the individual coefficients consistent with predictions from economic theory? Explain.

b. If $A = \$5,000$, $P_M = \$1$, $P_C = \$1.20$, and $Y = \$20,000$, how many hamburgers will be demanded?

c. What is the advertising elasticity at $A = \$5,000$?

4-7. Motorland Recreational Vehicles estimates the monthly demand (Q) for its product is given by the equation

$$\log Q = 1.00 - 1.50 \log P + 3.00 \log Y \qquad R^2 = 0.21$$
$$(1.20) \; (-2.50) \quad + (0.02)$$

where P is price and Y is income per capita in thousands. The t-statistics are shown in parentheses and logarithms to the base ten were used to transform the equation.

a. Rewrite the expression as a multiplicative demand equation.

b. Based on the equation, is the product an inferior good, a necessity, or a luxury good? How much confidence do you have in your answer? Explain.

c. Is the equation likely to be useful in predicting demand for Motorland's product? Why or why not?

4-8. Data from 20 cities were used to estimate the demand for face lifts. The resulting regression equation was

$$Q_d = 50.000 - 0.001P + 0.002I \qquad R^2 = 0.55$$
$$(5.42) \qquad (-2.34) \quad (2.00)$$

where Q_d is face lifts per 1,000 population per year, P is the price in dollars, I is income in dollars, and the t-statistics are shown in parentheses.
 a. In determining statistical significance of the coefficients, what number should be used for degrees of freedom?
 b. Which of the coefficients are statistically significant at the 5 percent level?
 c. The mean values of P and I are $5,000 and $20,000, respectively. Compute the point price elasticity of demand.
 d. What is the predicted demand at the mean values of the independent variables?

Problems Requiring Calculus

4-9. The demand function for a product is estimated to be

$$Q_d = 10P^{-1.0}I^{2.0}P_o^{0.0}$$

and the mean values for P and I are $150 and $18,000, respectively.
 a. Predict the value for the dependent variables at the mean values of the independent variables.
 b. At the mean values, how much will a dollar change in price change the quantity demanded? What about a dollar change in income?

4-10. Economists on a skiing vacation in Aspen, Colorado, decide to study the demand for lift tickets in the area. Using multiple regression analysis, the demand equation is estimated to be

$$\log Q_t = 3.00 - 2.0 \log P_t + 0.5 \log S$$

where Q_t is quantity demanded per day, P_t is the price of a full day lift ticket, and S is accumulated snow depth in inches at the lodges. Using calculus, show that for small changes, a 1 percent increase in accumulated snow depth will increase daily lift ticket demand by 0.5 percent.

4-11. Starting with the general demand equation,

$$Q = bP_p^{a_p}I^{a_i}P_o^{a_o}$$

demonstrate that a_i is the income elasticity and a_o is the cross elasticity.

Microcomputer Problems

The following problems can be solved by using the microcomputer program tools, available with the study guide or by using other computer software.

4-12. Data on income (in thousands of dollars), education (years), experience (years), and age (years) for twenty people are shown here.

Person	Income	Age	Education	Job Experience
1	5.0	29	2	9
2	9.7	36	4	18
3	28.4	41	8	21
4	8.8	30	8	12
5	21.0	34	8	14
6	26.6	36	10	16
7	25.4	61	12	16
8	23.1	29	12	9
9	22.5	54	12	18
10	19.5	30	12	5
11	21.7	28	12	7
12	24.8	29	13	9
13	30.1	35	14	12
14	24.8	59	14	17
15	28.5	65	15	19
16	26.0	30	15	6
17	38.9	40	16	17
18	22.1	23	16	1
19	33.1	58	17	10
20	48.3	60	21	17

a. Use multiple regression analysis to estimate income as a linear function of age. Write the equation, t-statistics, and the coefficient of determination. Provide an explanation for the sign of the age coefficient.

b. Use regression analysis to estimate income as a linear function of education, job experience, and age. Write the equation, t-statistics, and the coefficient of determination. How do the results of part (b) explain the results from part (a)?

c. Use the results from part (b) to estimate income of a typical person who has 14 years of education, 10 years of job experience, and who is 45 years of age.

4-13. Data on grade point average and IQ were obtained for twelve high school students.

Grade Point Average	IQ	Grade Point Average	IQ
2.1	116	2.9	126
2.2	129	2.7	122
3.1	123	2.1	114
2.3	121	1.7	109
3.4	131	3.3	132
2.9	134	3.5	140

a. Use regression analysis to estimate the effect of IQ on grade point average. Write the equation, *t*-statistics, and the coefficient of determination. Is the result consistent with your prior expectations? Explain.

b. Forecast the grade point average for a student with an IQ of 120 and for a student with an IQ of 150. Which forecast do you have more confidence in? Why?

4-14. Data on electric power consumption (in billions of kilowatt-hours), GNP (in billions of dollars), and electricity prices (in cents per kilowatt-hour) for the period 1969–1983 are shown here.

Year	Consumption	GNP	Price
1969	407.9	$ 944.0	2.09¢
1970	447.8	992.7	2.10
1971	479.1	1,077.6	2.19
1972	511.4	1,185.9	2.29
1973	554.2	1,326.4	2.38
1974	555.0	1,434.2	2.83
1975	586.1	1,594.2	3.21
1976	613.1	1,718.0	3.45
1977	652.3	1,918.3	3.78
1978	679.2	2,163.9	4.03
1979	696.0	2,417.8	4.43
1980	734.4	2,631.7	5.12
1981	730.5	2,957.8	5.80
1982	732.7	3,069.3	6.44
1983	750.9	3,304.8	6.83

a. Using regression analysis, estimate consumption as a linear function of GNP, price, and the previous year's electricity consumption. (NOTE: assume 1968 consumption was $367.7 billion.) Write the equation, *t*-statistics, and the coefficient of determination. Are the signs of the estimated coefficients consistent with economic theory? Which of the coefficients are statistically significant at the 0.05 level?

b. In 1984, GNP was $3661.3 billion and the price of electricity was 7.16 cents per kilowatt-hour. Use the estimating equation from part (a) to predict electricity consumption for 1984.

4-15. Consumption of hamburgers (thousands of burgers per week) in twelve different cities is shown here. Prices of hamburgers, income per capita (in $1,000s), and prices of hot dogs for the cities, are also shown on the next page.

City	Hamburger Consumption	Hamburger Price	Income ($1,000s)	Hot Dog Price
1	50	$1.50	12.0	$1.80
2	80	1.35	14.2	1.55
3	95	1.25	15.0	1.45
4	105	1.20	16.0	1.35
5	70	1.40	13.8	1.60
6	85	1.30	14.3	1.50
7	55	1.50	13.3	1.70
8	60	1.45	13.3	1.70
9	75	1.35	13.7	1.60
10	90	1.25	14.5	1.50
11	100	1.20	15.2	1.35
12	65	1.45	13.6	1.65

a. Use regression analysis to estimate hamburger consumption as a multiplicative function of the price of hamburgers, income, and hot dog price. Write the equation, t-statistics, and the coefficient of determination. Which coefficients are significant at the 0.05 level?

b. Based on the estimates from part (a), what are the price, income, and cross elasticities? Is the cross elasticity consistent with economic theory? Explain.

CHAPTER **5**

Business and Economic Forecasting

Preview

Sources of Data
   Expert Opinion
   Surveys
   Market Experiments

Time-Series Analysis
   Trend Projection
   Exponential Smoothing

Barometric Forecasting
   Leading Indicators
   Composite and Diffusion Indices

Input/Output Analysis
   Transactions Matrix
   Direct Requirements Matrix
   Direct and Indirect Requirements Matrix
   Forecasting with an Input/Output Model

Summary

Discussion Questions

Problems

Preview

The vast majority of business decisions involve some degree of uncertainty—managers seldom know exactly what the outcomes of their choices will be. One approach to reducing the uncertainty associated with decision making is to devote resources to forecasting. Forecasting involves predicting future economic conditions and assessing their effect on the operations of the firm.

Frequently, the objective of forecasting is to predict demand. In some cases, managers are interested in the total demand for a product. For example, the decision by an office products firm to enter the home computer market may be determined by estimates of industry sales growth. In other circumstances, the projection may focus on the firm's probable market share. If a forecast suggests that sales growth by existing firms will make successful entry unlikely, the company may decide to look for other areas to expand.

Forecasts can also provide information on the proper product mix. For an automobile manufacturer such as General Motors, managers must determine the number of full-sized versus compact cars to be produced. In the short run, this decision is largely constrained by the firm's existing production facilities for producing each kind of car. However, over a longer period, managers can build or modify production facilities. But such choices must be made long before the vehicles begin coming off the assembly line. Accurate forecasts can reduce the uncertainty caused by this long lead time. For example, if the price of gasoline is expected to increase, the relative demand for compact cars is also likely to increase. Conversely, a projection of stable or falling gasoline prices might stimulate demand for larger cars.

Forecasting is an important management activity. Major decisions in large businesses almost always are based on forecasts of some type. In some cases, the forecast may be little more than an intuitive assessment of the future by those involved in the decision. In other circumstances, the forecast may have required thousands of work hours and tens of thousands of dollars. It may have been generated by the firm's own economists, provided by consultants specializing in forecasting, or be based on information provided by government agencies.

This chapter focuses on basic techniques of forecasting. The first section considers various methods for collecting the necessary data. Next is a discussion of time-series analysis. The third section considers barometric forecasting. The basic principles of input/output analysis are presented in the last section of the chapter.

Sources of Data

Forecasting requires the development of a good set of data on which to base the analysis. A forecast cannot be better than the data from which it is derived. Three important sources of data used in forecasting are expert opinion, surveys, and market experiments.

Expert Opinion

The collective judgment of knowledgable persons can be an important source of information. In fact, some forecasts are made almost entirely on the basis of personal insights of key decision makers. This process may involve managers conferring to develop projections based on their assessment of the economic conditions facing the firm. In other circumstances, the company's sales personnel may be asked to evaluate future prospects. In still other cases, consultants may be employed to develop forecasts based on their knowledge of the industry. Although predictions by experts are not always the product of "hard data," their usefulness should not be underestimated. Indeed, the insights of those closely connected with an industry can be of great value in forecasting.

Methods exist for enhancing the value of information elicited from experts. One of the most useful is the *Delphi technique*. Its use can be illustrated by a simple example. Suppose that a panel of six outside experts is asked to forecast a firm's sales for the next year. Working independently, two panel members forecast an 8 percent increase, three members predict a 5 percent increase, and one person predicts no increase in sales. Based on the responses of the other individuals, each expert is then asked to make a revised sales forecast. Some of those expecting rapid sales growth may, based on the judgments of their peers, present less optimistic forecasts in the second iteration. Conversely, some of those predicting slow growth may adjust their responses upward. However, there may also be some panel members who decide that no adjustment of their initial forecast is warranted.

Assume that a second set of predictions by the panel includes one estimate of a 2 percent sales increase, one of 5 percent, two of 6 percent, and two of 7 percent. The experts again are shown each other's responses and asked to consider their forecasts further. This process continues until a consensus is reached or until further iterations generate little or no change in sales estimates.

The value of the Delphi technique is that it aids individual panel members in assessing their forecasts. Implicitly, they are forced to consider why their judgment differs from that of other experts. Ideally, this evaluation process should generate more precise forecasts with each iteration.

One problem with the Delphi method can be its expense. The usefulness of expert opinion depends on the skill and insight of the experts employed to make predictions. Frequently, the most knowledgeable people in an industry are in a position to command large fees for their work as consultants. Or they may be employed by the firm, but have other important responsibilities, which means that there can be a significant opportunity cost in involving them in the planning process. Another potential problem is that those who consider themselves experts may be unwilling to be influenced by the predictions of others on the panel. As a result, there may be few changes in subsequent rounds of forecasts.

Surveys

Surveys of managerial plans can be an important source of data for forecasting. The rationale for conducting such surveys is that plans generally form the basis for future actions. For example, capital expenditure budgets for large corporations are usually planned well in advance. Thus a survey of investment plans by such corporations should provide a reasonably accurate forecast of future demand for capital goods.

Several private and government organizations conduct periodic surveys of plant and equipment expenditure plans. One of the most widely used is sponsored by McGraw-Hill, Inc. This survey is conducted twice yearly and includes corporations accounting for more than 50 percent of total investment in the U.S. economy. An even more comprehensive survey of capital expenditure plans is undertaken quarterly by the U.S. Department of Commerce. The results of this survey are reported in the Department's *Survey of Current Business*.

Useful data for forecasting can also be obtained from surveys of consumer plans. For example, the Survey Research Center at the University of Michigan polls consumers about their intentions to purchase specific products such as household appliances, housing, and automobiles. The results are used to project consumer demand and also to measure the level of consumer confidence in the economy. The U.S. Bureau of the Census also conducts surveys of consumer intentions.

If data from existing sources do not meet its specific needs, a firm may conduct its own survey. Perhaps the most common example involves companies that are considering a new product or making a substantial change in an existing product. But with new or modified products there are no data on which to base a forecast. One possibility is to survey households regarding their anticipated demand for the product. Typically, such surveys attempt to ascertain the demographic characteristics (e.g., age, education, and income) of those who are most likely to buy the product and how their decisions would be affected by different pricing policies.

Although surveys of consumer demand can provide useful data for forecasting, their value is highly dependent on the skills of their originators. Meaningful surveys require careful attention to each phase of the process. Questions must be precisely worded to avoid ambiguity. The survey sample must be properly selected so that responses will be representative of all customers. Finally, the methods of survey administration should produce a high response rate and avoid biasing the answers of those surveyed. Poorly phrased questions or a nonrandom sample may result in data that are of little value.

Even the most carefully designed surveys do not always predict consumer demand with great accuracy. In some cases, respondents do not have enough information to determine if they would purchase a product. In other situations, those surveyed may be pressed for time and be unwilling to devote much thought to their answers. Sometimes the response may reflect a desire (either conscious or unconscious) to put oneself in a favorable light or to gain approval from those conducting the survey. Because of these limitations, forecasts seldom rely entirely on results of consumer surveys. Rather, these data are considered supplemental sources of information for decision making.

CASE STUDY

The Use and Abuse of Survey Data

For years, firms have used consumer surveys to collect data on the demand for their products. A more recent trend has been the use of survey data to promote those products to potential customers. But where advocacy and persuasion are the goals, there may be a tendency to stretch the limits of good survey design and interpretation.

In some cases, the problem with a survey is that the questions have the effect of biasing the answers in a way that favors the products of the firm. A study sponsored by Levi Strauss asked college students to select which clothes they thought would be most popular during the coming year. The company announced that Levi's 501s were chosen as the most popular jeans. What the public was not told was that 501s were the only jeans on the list.

A Black Flag survey stated that, "A roach disk ... poisons a roach slowly. The dying roach returns to the nest and after it dies is eaten by other roaches. In turn, these roaches become poisoned and die." Survey respondents were then asked, "How effective do you think this type of product would be in killing roaches?" Provided with this "helpful" information, 79 percent said that the disk would be effective.

A sample that is not random can be used to generate survey results that are suspect. A Chrysler study showed that its cars were preferred to those of Toyota. However, none of the people in the sample owned a foreign car, suggesting that they may have been predisposed to buy U.S. automobiles. A survey sponsored by American Express and the French government concluded that it was untrue that the French are unfriendly. But the sample consisted of Americans who had visited France for pleasure more than once during the last two years—presumably people who have positive feelings about vacationing in France.

Sample bias was the cause of what is generally considered to be the most inaccurate political poll in U.S. history. In 1936, the *Literary Digest* predicted that Republican Alf Landon would be a big winner over Franklin D. Roosevelt in the presidential election of that year. But the sample consisted of those who had telephones, cars, or were subscribers to the magazine—all characteristics of high-income voters at that time. History records that Roosevelt was reelected to a second term by a landslide vote of the general population.

The selective use of data is not confined to Western society. In China a population census determined that the population of one province was 28 million. Five years later, the same province was found to have 105 million people. An astounding birth rate was not the cause. Rather, the first census was used for military conscription (hence, a small number was better) and the second was the basis for government aid to the victims of a famine in the regions (now a large estimated population was beneficial).

Market Experiments

A potential problem with survey data is that survey responses may not translate into actual consumer behavior. That is, consumers do not necessarily do what they say they are going to do. This weakness can be partially overcome by use of market experiments designed to generate data prior to the full-scale introduction of a product or implementation of a policy.

To set up a market experiment, the firm first selects a test market. This market may consist of several cities, a region of the country, or a sample of consumers taken from a mailing list. Once the market has been selected, the experiment may incorporate a number of features. It may involve evaluating consumer perceptions of a new product in the test market. In other cases, different prices for an existing product might be set in various cities in order to determine demand elasticity. A third possibility would be a test of consumer reaction to a new advertising campaign.

There are several factors that managers should consider in selecting a test market. First, the location should be of manageable size. If the area is too large, it may be expensive and difficult to conduct the experiment and to analyze the data. Second, the residents of the test market should resemble the overall population of the United States in age, education, and income. If not, the results may not be applicable to other areas. Finally, it should be possible to purchase advertising that is directed only to those who are being tested.

Market experiments have an advantage over surveys in that they reflect actual consumer behavior, but they still have limitations. One problem is the risk involved. In test markets where prices are increased, consumers may switch to products of competitors. Once the experiment has ended and the price reduced to its original level, it may be difficult to regain those customers. Another problem is that the firm cannot control all the factors that affect demand. The results of some market experiments can be influenced by bad weather, changing economic conditions, or the tactics of competitors. Finally, because most experiments are of relatively short duration, consumers may not be completely aware of pricing or advertising changes. Thus their responses may understate the probable impact of those changes.

KEY CONCEPTS

- The Delphi technique is an iterative technique that can be used to enhance the value of expert opinion.
- Surveys of consumer intentions require careful attention to wording, sample selection, and methods of administration.
- Market experiments provide actual data on consumer behavior. However, they are expensive, risky, and may be influenced by factors beyond the firm's control.

Time-Series Analysis

Regression analysis, as described in Chapter 4, can be used to quantify relationships between variables. However, data collection can be a problem if the regression model includes a large number of independent variables. When changes in a variable show discernable patterns over time, time-series analysis is an alternative method for forecasting future values.

The focus of time-series analysis is to identify the components of change in the data. Traditionally, these components are divided into four categories:

1. Trend.
2. Seasonality.
3. Cyclical patterns.
4. Random fluctuations.

A *trend* is a long-term increase or decrease in the variable. For example, the time series of human population in the United States exhibits an upward trend, while the trend for endangered species, such as the eagle, is downward. The *seasonal* component represents changes that occur at regular intervals. A large increase in sales of skis in the fall and early winter would be an example of seasonality.

Analysis of a time series may suggest that there are *cyclical patterns,* defined as sustained periods of high values followed by low values. Business cycles fit this category. Finally, the remaining variation in a variable that does not follow any discernable pattern is due to *random fluctuations*. Various methods can be used to determine trends, seasonality, and any cyclical patterns in time series data. However, by definition, changes in the variable due to random factors are not predictable. The larger the random component of a time series, the less accurate the forecasts based on those data.

Trend Projection

One of the most commonly used forecasting techniques is trend projection. As the name suggests, this approach is based on the assumption that there is an identifiable trend in a time series of data. Trend projection can also be used as the starting point for identifying seasonal and cyclical variations.

Table 5-1 is a time series of a firm's quarterly sales over a three-year time span. These data will be used to illustrate graphical and statistical trend projection and also to describe a method for making seasonal adjustments to a forecast.

GRAPHIC CURVE FITTING   Note that the data show generally increasing sales quarter by quarter. But a useful forecast usually requires greater precision than is implied by the statement "generally increasing sales." To be of value in forecasting, a numerical estimate of the increase in sales per quarter must be made. One way to make this estimate is to fit a line to the data graphically. Figure 5-1, a straight line is drawn through the data points in such a way as to reflect the trend of the data as accurately as possible.

The upward slope of the line reflects sales increases over time. By computing the slope of this trend line, it is possible to determine the average rate of increase per quarter. This value can be used to calculate sales in future periods. Alternatively, by extending the trend line beyond the last data point (i.e., the fourth quarter of 1993), the estimated sales can be read directly from the graph. Suppose that sales are to be forecast for the third quarter of 1994. Based on an extrapolation

TABLE 5-1 **Hypothetical Time-Series Sales Data**

Period Number	Quarter	Sales (millions)
1	1991:I	$300
2	1991:II	305
3	1991:III	315
4	1991:IV	340
5	1992:I	346
6	1992:II	352
7	1992:III	364
8	1992:IV	390
9	1993:I	397
10	1993:II	404
11	1993:III	418
12	1993:IV	445

of the data to that period, the graph indicates that sales are projected to be about $480 million.

STATISTICAL CURVE FITTING   One limitation of graphical curve fitting should be obvious—the accuracy of forecast depends on the analyst's ability to fit a curve to the data. A more sophisticated approach is to use statistical methods to fit the data to an equation of specified functional form. Basically, this involves using the ordinary least-squares concept developed in Chapter 4 to estimate the parameters of the equation.

CONSTANT RATE OF CHANGE   Suppose that an analyst determines that a forecast will be made assuming that there will be a constant rate of change in sales from one period to the next. That is, the firm's sales will change by the same amount between two periods. The time-series data of Table 5-1 are to be used to estimate that rate of change. Statistically, this involves estimating the parameters of the equation

$$S_t = S_0 + bt \tag{5-1}$$

where S denotes sales and t indicates the time period. The two parameters to be estimated are S_0 and b. The value of S_0 corresponds to the sales (vertical) axis intercept of the line in Figure 5-1. The parameter b is the constant rate of change and corresponds to the slope of the line in Figure 5-1.

Many hand calculators can estimate the parameters of equation (5-1). Specific procedures vary from model to model, but usually the only requirement is that the user input the data and push one or two designated keys. The machine then returns the estimated parameters. For the data of Table 5-1, the quarters would have to be inputted as sequential numbers starting with 1. That is, 1991: I would be entered as 1, 1991. II would be entered as 2, and so forth. Based on the data

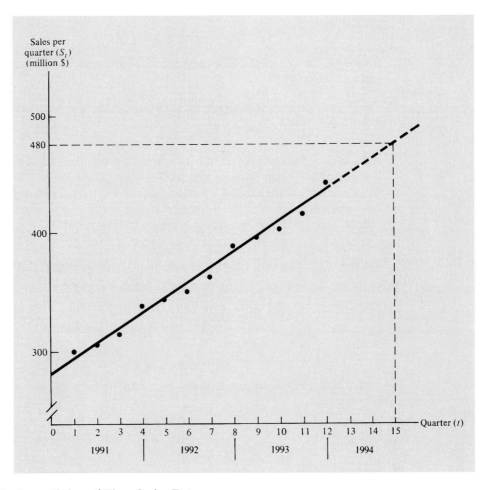

FIGURE 5-1 **Curve Fitting of Time Series Data.**

from the table, equation (5-1) is estimated as

$$S_t = 281.394 + 12.811t$$

The interpretation of the equation is that the estimated constant rate of increase in sales per quarter is \$12.811 million. A forecast of sales for any future quarter, S_t, can be obtained by substituting in the appropriate value for t. For example, the third quarter of 1994 is the 15th observation of the time series. Thus the estimated sales for that quarter would be $281.394 + 12.811(15)$, or \$473.56 million.

CONSTANT PERCENTAGE RATE OF CHANGE Now suppose that the individual responsible for the forecast wants to estimate a percentage rate of change in sales. That is, it is assumed that sales will increase by a constant percent each period. This relationship can be expressed mathematically as

$$S_t = S_{t-1}(1 + g)$$

Similarly,

$$S_{t-1} = S_{t-2}(1 + g)$$

where g is the constant percentage rate of change, or the growth rate. These two equations imply that

$$S_t = S_{t-2}(1 + g)^2$$

and, in general,

$$S_t = S_0(1 + g)^t \qquad (5\text{-}2)$$

As shown, the parameters of equation (5-2) cannot be estimated using ordinary least squares. The problem is that the equation is not linear. However, there is a simple transformation of the equation that allows it to be estimated using ordinary least squares.

First, take the logarithm of equation (5-2).[1] The result is

$$\ln S_t = \ln[S_0(1 + g)^t]$$

But the logarithm of a product is just the sum of the logarithms. Thus

$$\ln S_t = \ln S_0 + \ln[(1 + g)^t]$$

The right-hand side of the equation can be further simplified by noting that

$$\ln[(1 + g)^t] = t[\ln(1 + g)]$$

Hence

$$\ln S_t = \ln S_0 + t[\ln(1 + g)] \qquad (5\text{-}3)$$

Equation (5-3) is linear in form. This can be seen by making the following substitutions:

$$Y_t = \ln S_t$$
$$Y_0 = \ln S_0$$
$$b = \ln(1 + g)$$

Thus the new equation is

$$Y_t = Y_0 + bt \qquad (5\text{-}4)$$

which is linear.

The parameters of equation (5-4) can easily be estimated using a hand calculator. The key is to recognize that the sales data have been translated into logarithms. Thus, instead of S_t, it is $\ln S_t$ that must be entered as data. However, note that the t values have not been transformed. Hence for the first quarter of 1991, the data to be entered are $\ln 300 = 5.704$ and 1; for the second quarter, $\ln 305 = 5.720$ and 2; and so forth. The transformed data are provided in Table 5-2.

Using the ordinary least-squares method, the estimated parameters of equation (5-4), based on the data from Table 5-2 are

$$Y_t = 5.6623 + 0.0353t$$

But these parameters are generated from the logarithms of the data. Thus, for

---

[1] Either natural logarithms or logarithms to the base 10 can be used. In this section, natural logarithms (designated as ln) are used for all computations.

TABLE 5-2 **Natural Logarithms of Hypothetical Time-Series Sales Data**

Period Number (t)	Quarter	Natural Logarithm of Sales (in millions) (S_t)
1	1991:I	5.704
2	1991:II	5.720
3	1991:III	5.753
4	1991:IV	5.829
5	1992:I	5.847
6	1992:II	5.864
7	1992:III	5.897
8	1992:IV	5.966
9	1993:I	5.984
10	1993:II	6.001
11	1993:III	6.036
12	1993:IV	6.098

interpretation in terms of the original data, they must be converted based on the relationships $\ln S_0 = Y_0 = 5.6623$ and $\ln(1 + g) = b = 0.0353$. Taking the antilogs yields $S_0 = 287.810$ and $1 + g = 1.0359$. Substituting these values for S_0 and $1 + g$ back into equation (5-2) gives

$$S_t = 287.810(1.0359)^t$$

where 287.810 is sales (in millions of dollars) in period 0 and the estimated growth rate, g, is 0.0359 or 3.59 percent.

To forecast sales in a future quarter, the appropriate value of t is substituted into the equation. For example, predicted sales in the third quarter of 1994 (i.e., the fifteenth quarter) would be $287.810(1.0359)^{15}$, or \$488.51 million.

SEASONAL VARIATION IN TIME-SERIES DATA   Seasonal fluctuations in time-series data are not uncommon. In particular, a large increase in sales for the fourth quarter is a characteristic of certain industries. Indeed, some retailing firms make nearly half of their total sales during the Christmas holiday period. Other business activities have their own seasonal sales patterns. Electric utilities serving hot, humid areas have distinct peak sales periods during the summer months because of the extensive use of air conditioning, whereas those in colder regions may have peaks in winter. Similarly, housing sales drop off during the winter, but the demand for accountants' services increases in the first quarter as income tax deadlines approach.

A close examination of the data in Table 5-1 on page 142 indicates that the quarterly sales increases are not uniformly distributed over the year. The increases from the first quarter to the second, and from the fourth quarter to the first, tend to be small, while the fourth-quarter increase is consistently larger than that of other quarters. That is, the data exhibit seasonal fluctuations, as shown by the dashed line in Figure 5-2.

Pronounced seasonal variation can cause serious errors in forecasts based on time-series data. For example, Table 5-1 indicates that actual sales for the fourth quarter of 1993 were $445 million. But if the estimated equation is used to predict sales for that period (using the constant rate of change model), the predicted total is 281.394 + 12.811(12), or $435.13 million. The large difference between actual and predicted sales occurs because the equation does not take into account the fourth-quarter sales jump. Rather, the predicted value from the equation represents an averaging of individual quarters. Thus sales will be underestimated for the strong fourth quarter. Conversely, the predicting equation may overestimate sales for the other quarters.

The accuracy of the forecast can be improved by seasonally adjusting the data. Probably the most common method of adjustment is the *ratio-to-trend* approach.

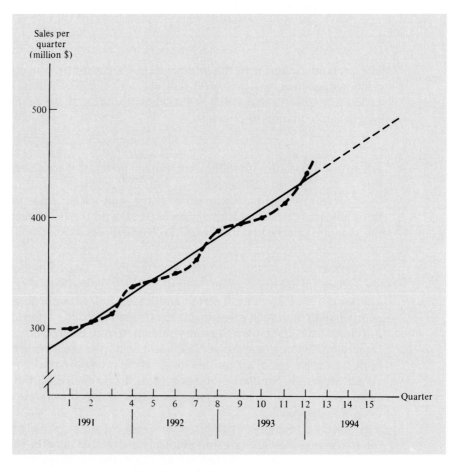

FIGURE 5-2 **Seasonal Variation in Time-Series Data.**

TABLE 5-3 **Seasonal Adjustment Using the Ratio-to-Trend Method**

Year	Forecasted Fourth-Quarter Sales	Actual Fourth-Quarter Sales	Actual/Predicted Fourth-Quarter Sales
1991	332.64	$340	Average = 1.022
1992	383.88	390	1.016
1993	435.13	445	1.023
			Average = 1.020

Its use can be illustrated using the data from Table 5-1. Based on the predicting equation,

$$S_t = 281.394 + 12.811t$$

actual and calculated fourth-quarter sales are shown in Table 5-3. The final column of the table is the ratio of actual to predicted sales for the fourth quarter. This ratio is a measure of the seasonal error in the forecast.

As shown, for the three-year period, average actual sales for the fourth quarter were 102 percent of the average forecasted sales for that quarter. The factor 1.02 can be used to adjust future fourth-quarter sales estimates. For example, if the objective is to predict sales for the fourth quarter of 1993, the predicting equation generates an estimate of $435.13 million. Multiplying this number by the 1.020 adjustment factor, the forecast is increased to $443.8 million, which is close to the actual sales of 445 million for that quarter. A similar technique could be used to make a downward adjustment for predicted sales in other quarters.

Seasonal adjustment can improve forecasts based on trend projection. However, trend projection still has some shortcomings. One is that it is limited primarily to short-term predictions. If the trend is extrapolated much beyond the last data point, the accuracy of the forecast diminishes rapidly. Another limitation is that factors such as changes in relative prices and fluctuations in the rate of economic growth are not considered. Rather, the trend projection approach assumes that historical relationships will not change.

KEY CONCEPTS

- Forecasts based on the assumption of a constant rate of change can be made by fitting time-series data to an equation of the general form

$$S_t = S_0 + bt$$

- Forecasts assuming a constant percentage rate of change involve estimating the parameters of the equation

$$S_t = S_0(1 + g)^t$$

- Forecast errors due to seasonal variation can be reduced using the ratio-to-trend adjustment method.

Forecasting Winning Performances in the Olympic Games

The Summer Olympics brings together the world's best athletes. In most events, there has been a general trend over the years for winning times, distances, weights, and scores to improve as training methods and equipment are perfected and more athletes become involved in the sport. The following table indicates the winning distance for the women's shotput and the winning time for the men's 400-meter race for the eleven olympics held between 1948 and 1988.

Winning Distance or Time

Year	Women's Shotput (meters)	Men's 400 Meters (seconds)
1948	13.75	46.2
1952	15.28	45.9
1956	16.59	46.7
1960	17.32	44.9
1964	18.14	45.1
1968	19.61	43.8
1972	21.03	44.7
1976	21.16	44.3
1980	22.40	44.6
1984	20.48	44.3
1988	22.24	43.9

Trend projection can be used to estimate the rate of improvement and forecast gold medal performances for future Olympic games. If the constant rate and percentage rate of change models are used to analyze the data, the results are as follows:

Women's Shotput
$Y_t = 13.932 + 0.830t$ — Forecast for 1992: 23.89 meters

$Y_t = 14.213(1.047)^t$ — Forecast for 1992: 24.59 meters

Men's 400 Meters
$Y_t = 46.353 - 0.235t$ — Forecast for 1992: 43.54 seconds

$Y_t = 46.358(0.995)^t$ — Forecast for 1992: 43.56 seconds

The analysis implies that the winning distance for the women's shotput has increased about eight-tenths of a meter, or nearly five percent per Olympics. The gold medal 400-meter time has decreased by about two-tenths of a second, or approximately one-half of one percent during each four-year interval.

The actual winning times for the 1992 Olympics in Barcelona, Spain, were 21.06 meters for the shotput and 43.5 seconds for the 400 meters. The trend projection equations for the 400 meters predict the 1992 winning time within five-hundredths of a second, but the forecasts for the women's shotput are much too high. The problem is that the rapid increases in distance in the earlier years (e.g., 1948 to 1972) have not been matched in more recent Olympics. In fact, the winning shotput distance for 1992 was about the same as it was in 1972. One possible explanation is that the gender and drug tests that are now required of athletes have reduced cheating in the field events. The failure of the shotput equations to accurately predict 1992 results indicates the need for the analyst to be aware of any conditions or events that could influence time-series data.

Exponential Smoothing

Trend projection is actually just regression analysis where the only independent variable is time. One characteristic of this method is that each observation has the same weight. That is, the effect of the initial data point on the estimated coefficients is just as great as the last data point. If there has been little or no change in the pattern over the entire time series, this is not a problem. However, in some cases, more recent observations will contain more accurate information about the future than those at the beginning of the series. For example, the sales history of the last three months may be more relevant in forecasting future sales than data for sales ten years in the past.

Exponential smoothing is a technique of time-series forecasting that gives greater weight to more recent observations. The first step is to choose a smoothing constant, α, where $0 < \alpha < 1.0$. If there are n observations in a time series, the forecast for the next period (i.e., $n + 1$) is calculated as a weighted average of the observed value of the series at period n and the forecasted value for that same period. That is,

$$F_{n+1} = \alpha X_n + (1 - \alpha)F_n \tag{5-5}$$

where F_{n+1} is the forecast value for the next period, X_n is the observed value for the last observation, and F_n is a forecast of the value for the last period in the time series. The forecasted values for F_n and all the earlier periods are calculated in the same manner. Specifically,

$$F_t = \alpha X_{t-1} + (1 - \alpha)F_{t-1} \tag{5-6}$$

starting with the second observation (i.e., $t = 2$) and going to the last (i.e., $t = n$). Note that equation (5-6) cannot be used to forecast F_1 because there is no X_0 or F_0. This problem is usually solved by assuming that the forecast for the first period is equal to the observed value for that period. That is, $F_1 = X_1$. Using equation (5-6), it can be seen that this implies that the second-period forecast is just the observed value for the first period, or $F_2 = X_1$.

The exponential smoothing constant chosen determines the weight that is given to different observations in the time series. As α approaches 1.0, more recent observations are given greater weight. For example, if $\alpha = 1.0$, then $(1 - \alpha) = 0$ and equations (5-5) and (5-6) indicate that the forecast is determined only by the actual observation for the last period. In contrast, lower values for α give greater weight to observations from previous periods.

Assume that a firm's sales over the last ten weeks are as shown in Table 5-4. By assumption, $F_2 = F_1 = X_1$. If $\alpha = 0.20$, then

$$F_3 = 0.20(430) + 0.80(400) = 406.0$$

and

$$F_4 = 0.20(420) + 0.80(406) = 408.8$$

The forecasted values for four different values of α are provided in Table 5-4. The table also shows forecasted sales for the next period after the end of the time-series data, or week 11. Using $\alpha = 0.20$, the forecasted sales value for the eleventh

TABLE 5-4 **Forecasts Based on Exponential Smoothing**

Week	Sales	$\alpha = 0.20$	$\alpha = 0.40$	$\alpha = 0.60$	$\alpha = 0.80$
t	x_t	F_t	F_t	F_t	F_t
1	400	400.00	400.00	400.00	400.00
2	430	400.00	400.00	400.00	400.00
3	420	406.00	412.00	418.00	424.00
4	440	408.80	415.20	419.20	420.80
5	460	415.04	425.12	431.68	436.18
6	440	424.03	439.07	448.67	455.23
7	470	427.23	439.44	443.47	443.05
8	430	435.78	451.67	459.39	464.61
9	440	434.62	443.00	441.76	436.92
10	420	435.70	441.80	440.70	439.38
11	—	432.56	433.08	428.28	423.88

week is computed to be

$$F_{11} = 0.20(420) + 0.80(435.7) = 432.56$$

Table 5-4 suggests why this method is referred to as smoothing technique. Consider the forecasts based on $\alpha = 0.20$. Note that the smoothed data show much less fluctuation than the original sales data. Note also that as α increases, the fluctuations in the F_t increase, because the forecasts give more weight to the last observed value in the time series.

CHOICE OF A SMOOTHING CONSTANT   Any value of α could be used as the smoothing constant. One criterion for selecting this value might be the analyst's intuitive judgment regarding the weight that should be given to more recent data points. But there is also an empirical basis for selecting the value of α. Remember that the coefficients of a regression equation are chosen to minimize the sum of squared deviations between observed and predicted values. This same method can be used to determine the smoothing constant.

The term $(X_t - F_t)^2$ is the square of the deviation between the actual time-series data and the forecast for the same period. Thus, by adding these values for each observation, the sum of the squared deviations can be computed as

$$\sum_{t=1}^{n} (X_t - F_t)^2$$

One approach to choosing α is to select the value that minimizes this sum. For the data and values of α shown in Table 5-4, these sums are

Smoothing Constant	Sum of Squared Deviations
0.20	6484.23
0.40	4683.87
0.60	4213.08
0.80	4394.52

These results suggest that, of the four values of the smoothing cconstant, α = 0.60 provides the best forecasts using these data. However, it should be noted that there may be values of α between 0.60 and 0.80 or between 0.40 and 0.60 that yield even better results.

EVALUATION OF EXPONENTIAL SMOOTHING   One advantage of exponential smoothing is that it allows more recent data to be given greater weight in analyzing time-series data. Another is that, as additional observations become available, it is easy to update the forecasts. There is no need to reestimate the equations, as would be required with trend projection.

The primary disadvantage of exponential smoothing is that it does not provide very accurate forecasts if there is a significant trend in the data. If the time trend is positive, forecasts based on exponential smoothing will be likely to be too low, while a negative time trend will result in estimates that are too high. Simple exponential smoothing works best when there is no discernable time trend in the data. There are, however, more sophisticated forms of exponential smoothing that allow both trends and seasonality to be accounted for in making forecasts.[2]

CASE STUDY

Forecasting Economic Growth and the Federal Deficit

Among the hundreds of time series collected and published by the federal government, two of the most important are the rate of real economic growth and the federal deficit. The numbers for these two series during the 1980s are shown here.

Year	Growth Rate in Real GDP (%)	Deficit (billions)
1980	−0.2	61.3
1981	−1.9	63.8
1982	−2.5	145.9
1983	−3.6	176.0
1984	−6.8	169.6
1985	−3.4	196.6
1986	−2.7	206.9
1987	−3.4	158.2
1988	−4.5	141.7
1989	−2.5	134.3

Based on these data, the growth rates and deficits for future years can be forecast using either trend projection or exponential smoothing. The estimated equations for the constant rate of change trend projection model are

$$Growth_t = 0.413 + 0.399t$$
$$Deficit_t = 93.913 + 8.385t$$

Using exponential smoothing, a smoothing constant is selected by examining the sum of squared deviations between the observed and forecasted values. For the 1980s data, it was found that the sum of squared deviations is minimized using α = 0.4 for the growth rate and α = 1.0 for the deficit. The choice of α = 1.0 for the deficit data implies that, with exponential smoothing, the best forecast of the next period is just the observed value for the previous period. In contrast, using growth data, the fore-

---

[2] See, for example, Makridakis, S., and Wheelwright, S. 1989. *Forecasting Methods for Management.* New York: Wiley, pp. 71–94.

cast for the last period is weighted more heavily than the actual value for the previous period.

The actual and forecasted values for 1990 are provided below. Note that none of the forecasts are close to the observed values for 1990. One explanation is that growth rates and deficits don't follow a regular pattern over time. Rather, they are determined by a variety of factors, such as fiscal and monetary policy and world economic conditions. As such, regression models that incorporate other variables should generate more accurate forecasts. However, even using very sophisticated econometric models, the track record for forecasting growth rates and deficits is not very impressive.

	Growth Rate	Deficit
Trend projection forecast	4.8	191.6
Exponential smoothing forecast	2.9	134.3
Actual value for 1990	0.9	161.3

KEY CONCEPTS

- Forecasts based on exponential smoothing are a weighted average of observed and predicted values for the previous period.
- Weights are determined by selecting a smoothing constant that minimizes the sum of squared deviations between the forecasted and observed values.

Barometric Forecasting

Trend projection and exponential smoothing use time-series data to predict the future based on past relationships. But if there is no clear pattern in a time series, the data are of little value for forecasting. An alternative approach is to find a second series of data that is correlated with the first. Hence, by observing changes in the second series, it may be possible to predict changes in the first. For example, suppose that a lumber company's sales exhibited large yearly fluctuations over the last decade—so large that any forecast based on a trend projection of sales is useless. But over the same period, it is also determined that the firm's sales were highly correlated with the number of housing starts. Thus if housing starts can be predicted, this information can be used to forecast lumber sales.

A time series that is correlated with another time series is sometimes called an *indicator* of the second series. Substantial time and effort have been expended searching for good indicators of economic trends. *Business Conditions Digest*, a monthly publication of the Department of Commerce, reports information on over 300 time series.[3] These data are closely followed by economists, managers, and financial analysts.

---

[3] U.S. Department of Commerce, *Business Conditions Digest* (Washington, D.C.: U.S. Government Printing Office, monthly).

Leading Indicators

If two series of data frequently increase or decrease at the same time, one series may be regarded as a coincident indicator of the other. For example, in Figure 5-3a series 1 is a coincident indicator of series 2 because the two series have their peaks and troughs in the same periods.

If changes in one series consistently occur prior to changes in another series, a leading indicator has been identified. In Figure 5-3b, series 1 can be considered a leading indicator of series 2 because the peaks and troughs of series 1 consistently occur before the corresponding peaks and troughs of series 2.

For purposes of forecasting, leading indicators are of primary interest. Much as a meteorologist uses changes in barometric pressure to predict the weather, leading indicators can be used to forecast changes in general economic conditions. Consequently, the use of such indicators is commonly referred to as *barometric forecasting*.

The value of a leading indicator depends on several factors. First, the indicator must be accurate. That is, its fluctuations must correlate closely with fluctuations in the series that it is intended to predict. Second, the indicator must provide adequate lead time. Even if two series are highly correlated, an indicator will be of little use if the lead time is too short. For example, because of the time needed to put idle steel furnaces into operation, a series that predicts changes in steel demand by, say, one week would not be a useful forecasting tool for managers in the steel industry. A third requirement is that the lead time be relatively constant.

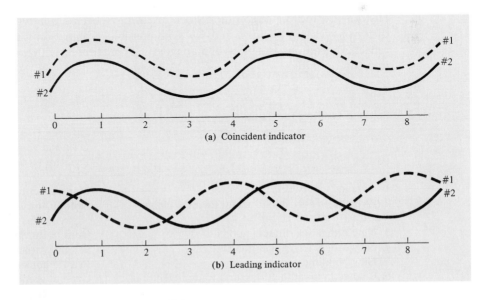

FIGURE 5-3 **Coincident and Leading Indicators.**

If a series leads another by six months on one occasion and by two years the next, the indicator will be of little use because it cannot provide useful forecasts.

Fourth, there should be a logical explanation as to why one series predicts another. If enough time series are studied, it is likely that a correlation can be found between pairs of series. However, unless there is a causal relationship between the two series, the historical pattern may not be very useful in forecasting future events because there is no reason to expect the pattern to be repeated. For example, it has been suggested that skirt lengths are a leading indicator of stock prices. Specifically, shorter skirts predict higher prices as measured by the Dow Jones Industrial Average. Some attempts have been made to explain this relationship, but they are not very convincing. Finally, an indicator's value is affected by the cost and time necessary for data collection. A time series that can be maintained only at a very high cost may not be worth the expense. Similarly, if there is a long delay before the data are available, the effective lead time of the indicator may be too short to be useful.

Table 5-5 lists selected leading indicators and an economic variable that each is used to predict. For some of the indicators, there is an obvious link between the two series. One example is new building permits and private housing starts. When a permit is issued, this indicates a strong commitment to build a new house. Thus changes in permits should be closely correlated to changes in housing starts. Clearly, housing permits represent a leading indicator because builders are legally required to have a permit before beginning construction. Similar arguments can be made to explain new orders as leading indicators of sales in the durable goods and capital equipment industries.

For some of the indicators, it is more difficult to explain the correlation between the two series. Consider stock prices as a predictor of general economic conditions. Historically, indices of common stock prices have been a relatively accurate predictor of cycles in business activity. One possible explanation is that stock prices reflect expectations and plans of managers and consumers, which are implemented in future months.

TABLE 5-5 **Selected Leading Indicators**

Leading Indicator	Economic Variable Predicted by the Indicator
1. Average workweek	Manufacturing output
2. Average weekly initial unemployment claims	State unemployment insurance payments
3. New orders for durable goods	Sales of durable goods
4. New orders for capital goods	Sales of capital goods
5. New building permits	Private housing starts
6. Change in manufacturing and trade inventories	General economic conditions
7. Industrial material prices	Consumer prices
8. Common stock prices	General economic conditions

Composite and Diffusion Indices

Although a time series showing the changes in stock prices may be somewhat useful in predicting general economic conditions, no single leading indicator yet identified comes close to having a perfect forecasting record. In addition, even when an indicator correctly predicts variations in economic activity, the lead time often shows considerable fluctuation. The basic problem is that any time series contains random fluctuations that do not conform to the general pattern of the data.

One way to improve barometric forecasting is by construction of an index. Such indices represent a single time series made up of a number of individual leading indicators. The purpose of combining the data is to smooth out the random fluctuations in each individual series. Ideally, the resulting index should provide more accurate forecasts. The most commonly used barometric forecasting indices are composite indices and diffusion indices.

COMPOSITE INDICES A composite index is a weighted average of individual indicators. The weights are based on the predictive ability of each series. That is, a series that does a better job of predicting would be given greater weight than a less accurate series. The index is interpreted in terms of percentage changes from period to period. For example, the most widely followed composite index is maintained by the U.S. Department of Commerce and is based on eleven leading indicators.

Each month the department reports the change in the index. Monthly swings have little significance, but sustained increases for several months are interpreted as a sign that general economic conditions are likely to improve. Conversely, successive declines in the index suggest that the economy is weakening.

DIFFUSION INDICES The same eleven leading indicators also are used by the Department of Commerce to construct a diffusion index. This index is a measure of the proportion of the individual time series that increase from one month to the next. For example, if eight of the indicators increased from June to July, the diffusion index for July would be 8/11, or 72.7 percent. When the index is over 50 percent for several months, the forecast is for improved economic conditions. As the index approaches 100 percent, the likelihood of improvement increases. Conversely, if less than 50 percent of the indicators exhibit an increase, a downturn is indicated.

The use of indices improves the accuracy of barometric forecasting. However, the prediction record of this technique is far from perfect. On several occasions the Department of Commerce indices have forecast recessions that failed to occur. Variability in lead time is another weakness. A third problem is that, while the barometric approach signals the likely direction of changes in economic conditions, it says little about the magnitude of such changes. As such, it provides only a qualitative forecast. Finally, although there has been much study on leading indicators of general economic conditions, the managers of individual firms may find it difficult to identify leading indicators that provide accurate forecasts for their specific needs.

KEY CONCEPTS

- The value of a leading indicator depends on the accuracy of prediction, length and stability of the lead time, and the cost and availability of data.
- Composite indices consist of a weighted average of several leading indicators.
- A diffusion index is calculated as the proportion of indicators that increase from one period to the next.

EXAMPLE

Calculating Composite and Diffusion Indices

Following are data for three leading indicators for a three-month period. The first month represents the base period, and the three series are to be given equal weight. Construct a composite and a diffusion index from the data.

Month	Leading Indicator I	Leading Indicator II	Leading Indicator III
1	400	30	100
2	425	29	110
3	460	33	135

SOLUTION
The diffusion index is generated by determining whether each series increased or decreased from month to month. For the second month, series I and III increased, but series II decreased. Hence the index is 66.7 for that month. During the third month, all of the series increased in comparison to month 2. Thus the index for that month is 100.

The composite index can be computed by first calculating the percentage changes (relative to the base month) for each series. Percentage changes during the second month were 6.25 percent for the first series, -3.33 percent for the second, and 10 percent for the third. Giving each series equal weight, the average percentage change was 4.31 percent. The value of the composite index for the first month is arbitrarily set to 100, so the index for the second month is 104.31. For the third month, the changes from the base period are $60/400 = 15$ percent, $3/30 = 10$ percent, and $35/100 = 35$ percent, respectively. Thus the average change is 20.0 percent. Hence the index for that month is 120.0.

Values for the two indices for each month are shown in the following table. Both indices suggest that economic conditions should improve in future months.

Month	Diffusion Index	Composite Index
1	—	100.00
2	66.70	104.31
3	100.00	120.00

Input/Output Analysis

Econometric models can be used to forecast changes in demand in one sector, but such models seldom have the detail necessary to assess the impacts of those changes on other sectors. But modern economic systems are highly interrelated. Changes in demand in one sector of the economy can have significant impacts on demand in other sectors. Some of these impacts are immediate and obvious. For example, steel, rubber, glass, and plastics are all important inputs in the production of motor vehicles. Thus an increase in the demand for automobiles would cause an increase in the demand for those four products.

The direct impact that automobile sales have on the demand for steel, rubber, glass, and plastics is augmented by secondary effects generated in still other sectors. Consider the resulting increase in demand for steel. As steel output increases to meet the requirements for producing automobiles, steel industry managers will find it necessary to purchase additional inputs. These may include iron ore, coal, and electricity. If the increase in demand is expected to be permanent, management may also decide to expand the capacity of their production facility by acquiring additional capital goods such as blast furnaces.

In turn, these secondary impacts will affect other parts of the economy. Over time, the increase in automobile demand may be the cause of change in hundreds of different industries. To the casual observer, many of these changes would seem unrelated to the production of automobiles.

Input/output analysis is a useful technique for sorting out and quantifying sector-by-sector impacts. This approach captures not only the direct effects but also related impacts in other parts of the economy. For example, an input/output matrix developed by the U.S. Department of Labor can estimate the impact of increased automobile sales on nearly 500 individual sectors in the U.S. economy.

Transactions Matrix

Input/output analysis is based on a table that indicates historic patterns of purchases and sales between industries. Data for this table are usually generated from surveying a sample of firms. A simple two-sector version of such a table is shown in Table 5-6. The two sectors identified in the table are manufacturing and agriculture. Within each sector are firms producing specific products. For example,

TABLE 5-6 **Two-Sector Input/Output Table**

	Sales to Manufacturing	+	Sales to Agriculture	+	Final Demand	=	Total Sales
Purchases from manufacturing	8	+	10	+	2	=	20
+	+		+				
Purchases from agriculture	6	+	12	+	12	=	30
+	+		+				
Valued added	6		8				
=	=		=				
Total sales	20		30				

the manufacturing sector might include firms making electronic components and also firms that produce television sets and computers. Similarly, the agriculture sector could include firms producing cotton and wool.

The rows of Table 5-6 show the disposition of each sector's output. Consider first the manufacturing sector that is depicted in the first row. If the numbers represent billions of dollars, the first element in the first row indicates that firms engaged in manufacturing sold $8 billion of their product to other manufacturing firms. An example of these "within-sector" transactions might be the sale of electronic components to a television manufacturer. The second element of the first row shows that $10 billion of manufactured goods were sold to firms in the agricultural sector. Together, these first two elements indicate total sales by manufacturing to other firms. Such sales are sometimes called *intermediate sales* because they represent output that is used as inputs for making products sold to consumers. The first two elements of the second row are interpreted in a similar manner. They show intermediate sales by the agriculture sector.

The third element of each row is designated as final demand and shows sales to ultimate consumers. Finally, the last element is total sales. This number is the sum of the intermediate sales and final demand and represents the total sales by the sector. Thus the $20 billion of total sales in manufacturing were made up of $18 billion in intermediate sales to other firms and $2 in sales to final consumers.

The columns of Table 5-6 indicates the use of revenues by each of the sectors. The elements in the first column show that firms in the manufacturing sector spent $8 billion to purchase intermediate goods from other manufacturing firms and $6 billion on goods from the agriculture sector. Subtracting that $14 billion amount from total sector sales of $20 billion leaves a residual of $6 billion. This amount is referred to as value added because it represents the difference between the value of inputs purchased and the product finally sold. Value added consists of payments to workers, owners of capital, and government.

The elements of the table indicating intermediate sales and purchases are of particular interest for input/output analysis. Together, they make up the transactions matrix of the model. Based on the numbers in Table 5-6, the transactions matrix is as shown in Table 5-7. In matrix notation, let this matrix be designated as X, where

$$X = \begin{bmatrix} 8 & 10 \\ 6 & 12 \end{bmatrix}$$

TABLE 5-7 **Transactions Matrix**

	Sales to Manufacturing	Sales to Agriculture
Purchases from manufacturing	8	10
Purchases from agriculture	6	12

Direct Requirements Matrix

If each element in a column of the transactions matrix is divided by the total sales of that sector's product, the result is the direct requirements matrix of an input/output model. The elements of each column of the direct requirements matrix can be interpreted as indicating the immediate or direct change in revenue for a sector generated by a $1 change in demand for the product of the sector represented by the column. The direct requirements matrix for the sample problem is shown in Table 5-8.

TABLE 5-8 **Direct Requirements Matrix**

	Manufacturing	Agriculture
Manufacturing sales per dollar	0.40	0.33
Agricultural sales per dollar	0.30	0.40

Consider the elements of the manufacturing column. They were computed by dividing the first column of the transactions matrix by total sales in manufacturing—$20 billion. The first element indicates that for each dollar of manufacturing sales, $0.40 of intermediate sales to other firms in the manufacturing sector are initially generated. The second element shows that $0.30 in sales by agricultural firms will be the direct result of each dollar of sales in the manufacturing sector. The elements of the second column have a similar interpretation with respect to each dollar of sales by the agricultural sector. Let the direct requirements matrix be designated as A. Thus

$$A = \begin{bmatrix} 0.40 & 0.33 \\ 0.30 & 0.40 \end{bmatrix}$$

Direct and Indirect Requirements Matrix

The direct requirements matrix shows the immediate or direct impact of changes in demand in a sector. But the elements of this matrix do not incorporate secondary and other impacts. For example, Table 5-8 indicates that the direct result of a $1 increase in agricultural sales would be a $0.33 increase in the demand for manufactured goods. However, such an increase would require that manufacturing firms purchase additional goods from other firms in the manufacturing and

TABLE 5-9 **Direct and Indirect Requirements Matrix**

	Manufacturing	Agriculture
Change in total demand in manufacturing	2.30	1.26
Change in total demand in agriculture	1.15	2.30

agricultural sectors. These purchases would stimulate still other purchases by firms in the two sectors. Thus the ultimate impact would be greater than predicted by the coefficient of the direct requirements matrix.

To take into account secondary impacts of changes in demand, input/output analysis requires computation of a direct and indirect requirements matrix. The derivation and calculation of this matrix are beyond the scope of this book, but conventionally it is designated by the notation $(I - A)^{-1}$, where A is the direct requirements matrix, I is the identity matrix, and the exponent denotes the inverse of a matrix.[4] For the example being considered, the direct and indirect requirements matrix is shown in Table 5-9.

The direct and indirect requirements matrix has a straightforward interpretation. The elements of each column indicate the change in total demand in each sector that would result form a $1 change in final demand for the sector designated by the column. For example, consider the first column. The first element shows that after all direct and secondary effects have been taken into account, a $1 change in final demand for manufactured goods will cause a $2.30 change in total demand in the manufacturing sector. The second element of the first column estimates that change in total demand in agriculture resulting from a $1 change in final demand for manufactured goods. In this case, the number is $1.15. Similarly, the elements of the second column show changes in total demand in each sector caused by a $1 change in final demand in the agricultural sector.

Forecasting with an Input/Output Model

The direct and indirect requirements matrix can be used to forecast sector-by-sector impacts of changes in final demand. For example, suppose that an increase in exports causes a $5 billion increase in final demand in the agricultural sector. After taking into account all the direct and secondary effects, what impact would this change have on total demand for manufactured and agricultural goods?

With respect to manufacturing, Table 5-9 shows that each $1 change in agricultural final demand causes a $1.26 change in the total demand for manufactured goods. Thus a $5 billion increase would increase total demand in manufacturing

[4] An identity matrix has 1s on its main diagonal and 0s for its other elements. It is analogous to the number 1 in arithmetic. The inverse of a matrix is a matrix that if multiplied by the original yields the identity matrix. The concept is analogous to the reciprocal in arithmetic.

by $5 billion × 1.26, or $6.30 billion. Similarly, the increase in total demand in the agriculture sector would be $5 billion × 2.30, or $11.50 billion.

Input/output analysis can also be used to forecast employment impacts. This is done by assuming a constant ratio of employment to total demand. To illustrate, assume that total demand in the manufacturing sector is $500 billion and the total number of workers in that sector is 5,000,000. Hence the employment ratio is 1 to $100,000. That is, one job exists for each $100,000 in total demand.

If this ratio is constant, one additional job in the manufacturing sector will be created for each $100,000 increase in total demand. Thus if a $5 billion increase in final demand for agricultural products causes a $6.3 billion increase in total demand in the manufacturing sector, the employment impact would be $6.3 billion divided by $100,000, or 63,000 new jobs. A similar computation could be made to estimate the employment increase in the agricultural sector.

EXAMPLE

Automobile Sales and the Demand for Glass

Assume that by 1997, automobile sales to consumers are forecast to be $10 billion greater than at present. A manufacturer of glass is contemplating a plant expansion and wants to know the probable effect of the increase in automobile demand on the total demand for glass. Union leaders in the industry want to know the employment impact.

The forecasts are to be based on a five-sector input/output model that includes sectors for glass and automobiles. The direct and indirect requirements matrix is as shown. The employment ratios are also shown. What will be the total demand and employment impacts in the glass industry of the projected increase in final demand for automobiles?

Direct and Indirect Requirements Matrix

	Steel	Automobiles	Computers	Glass	Electricity
Steel	1.034	0.334	0.008	0.010	0.010
Automobiles	0.008	1.010	0.009	0.002	0.007
Computers	0.003	0.004	1.110	0.001	0.100
Glass	0.009	0.090	0.048	1.004	0.005
Electricity	0.142	0.045	0.010	0.086	1.009

Employment Ratios

	Steel	Automobiles	Computers	Glass	Electricity
Jobs per million dollars of total sales	2.00	10.00	8.00	4.50	1.00

SOLUTION   The elements in the second column of the direct and indirect requirements matrix indicate the change in total demand resulting from a $1 change in final demand for automobiles. For the glass industry, the coefficient is 0.090. Thus a $10 billion increase in final demand for automobiles is estimated to increase total sales of glass by 0.090 × $10 billion, or $900 million. For the glass industry, the employment ratio is 4.5 jobs per $1 million in total sales. Thus the $900 million increase in total sales of glass is estimated to create 4,050 new jobs.

The construction of input/output models is a very expensive and time-consuming task. It would rarely be feasible for a firm to develop its own tables. Fortunately, several large models have been developed by various governmental agencies. Perhaps the most important is a 460-sector model of the U.S. economy maintained by the Department of Labor. The department also publishes employment ratios. This information is used by government analysts to evaluate impacts of public policy. It is also available for use by firms in forecasting. In addition, there are state and regional input/output models that can be used for forecasting on a more localized basis.

The major value of input/output analysis is that it takes into account interrelationships between sectors. However, the approach has limitations in addition to its high cost. A fundamental problem is that input/output forecasts are based on ratios that are assumed to be fixed. This assumption may not be very realistic in situations where rapid technological change is occurring.

KEY CONCEPTS

- Input/output analysis can be used to forecast the direct and indirect impacts of changes in one sector on other sectors of the economy.
- The transactions matrix shows the pattern of sales and purchases between sectors. The direct requirements matrix indicates the proportion of revenues used to purchase goods and services from each sector.
- The elements of the direct and indirect requirements matrix show the impact that a $1 change in final demand would have on total demand in each of the sectors of the model.
- Input/output analysis can be used to predict sector-by-sector sales and employment impacts.

Summary

Data for use in forecasting can be obtained from expert opinion, surveys, and market experiments. Forecasts of experts can be refined by procedures such as the Delphi technique, which uses an iterative process to aid individuals in assessing their judgments. Surveys of plans and attitudes by consumers and managers can be useful in forecasting. However, considerable care must be exercised to assure that the responses reflect subsequent consumer choices. Market experiments have an advantage over surveys because they provide information on actual consumer behavior. Their limitations include the risk of losing customers, high cost, problems of making consumers aware of changes, and inability to control all factors.

Variations in time-series data are the result of trends, seasonal fluctuations, cyclical patterns, and random factors. One method of analyzing a time series is trend projection. Basically, the technique involves estimating the coefficients that provide the best fit of data to a specified equation. The two most common equation forms estimate a constant rate of change and a constant percentage rate of change. Fitting the constant percentage rate of change equation requires that the data be inputted in logarithmic form. Forecasts based on trend projection of time-series data can be improved by adjusting for seasonal variations.

Another-time series technique for forecasting is exponential smoothing. Forecasts based on this approach are a weighted average of observed and predicted values for the last period. The weights are determined by choosing a smoothing constant that minimizes the sum of squared deviations between observed and forecasted values. Exponential smoothing works best when the time series does not have a strong time trend.

Barometric forecasting is based on time series that are correlated. If the changes in one series consistently occur prior to changes in another, a leading indicator has been identified. Useful leading indicators must be accurate, provide adequate and constant lead times, involve a logical explanation as to why one series predicts the other, and be available at reasonable cost. A composite index is a weighted average of several leading indicators. Diffusion indices measure the proportion of individual time series that increase from one period to the next.

Input/output analysis can be used to forecast the direct and indirect impacts of final demand changes in one sector on total demand in other sectors of the economy. The technique relies on data that show patterns of sales and purchases between sectors. These patterns are summarized in a transactions matrix. The direct requirements matrix is computed by dividing the columns of the transactions matrix by sector total sales. It shows the proportions of total revenues used to make purchases from the other sectors.

The direct and indirect requirements matrix is the basic tool used for forecasting with input/output analysis. Each number in a column shows the impact that a $1 change in final demand in one sector would have on total demand in each of the other sectors of the model. By assuming constant employment/total sales ratios, input/output analysis can also be used to estimate sector-by-sector employment impacts.

Discussion Questions _____

5-1. The manager of Harrison Toys assembles a panel of five experts to assist in formulating a sales forecast. The intent is to use the Delphi technique, but after examining the projections of the others, none of the experts are persuaded to make any changes in their initial forecasts. What conclusion might the manager draw from the inability of the experts to agree on a projection?

5-2. A business surveys its customers to generate information about the demand for a proposed new product. Under what circumstances might the customers understate their true demand for the product? When might they overstate their true demand? Explain.

5-3. To test consumer response, on January 1 a soft-drink manufacturer introduces a new brand in the Chicago market area. Over a three-month period, sales are slow and the company concludes that the product is unlikely to be profitable in nationwide marketing. Should the firm base its decision entirely on this experiment? Why or why not?

5-4. Using trend projection, how could a manager decide whether to use the constant-rate-of-change model rather than the constant-percentage rate of change?

5-5. Quarterly data from the beginning of 1983 to the end of 1993 are used to estimate the coefficients of the equation $S_t = S_0 + bt$, where S_t is sales in the tth quarter. No seasonal adjustments are made. How accurate are each of the following forecasts likely to be? Explain.

a. Annual sales of a tire manufacturer for the year 2000.

b. Fourth-quarter sales for 1994 for a retail gift store.

c. Fourth-quarter sales for 1994 for a newspaper publisher.

5-6. A particular composite and a diffusion index are constructed based on the same three times series of data. In a given month, could the composite index increase while the diffusion index decreased? Use a simple example to explain your answer.

5-7. Could the lead time necessary for an indicator to be useful in forecasting be longer in one industry than in another? Give an example.

5-8. The average work week is considered a leading indicator of general economic activity. Would longer workweeks predict an upturn or a downturn in economic activity? Explain.

5-9. A district manager proposes that her division develop its own state-level input/output model for use in forecasting. Is this a good idea? Why or why not?

5-10. A 20-sector input/output model gives value added as a percent of sales. Can this estimate be used to rank relative profitability of the sectors? Why or why not?

5-11. Would input/output analysis be useful in forecasting sales in a rapidly changing industry such as personal computers? Explain.

Problems

5-1. The management of Romano's Foods decides to test market a new frozen pizza. As the person in charge of the market experiment, what considerations should affect your decisions with respect to

a. The number and locations of cities in which the new pizza would be test marketed?

b. The duration of the experiment?

c. Pricing of the product?

5-2. Quarterly sales for Swarthmore Cycles are as follows:

Period	Sales	Period	Sales
1992:I	100	1993:I	130
1992:II	110	1993:II	135
1992:III	115	1993:III	145
1992:IV	125	1993:IV	150

a. Plot the sales data and graphically fit a straight line to the points.
b. In using the data for trend prediction, would the constant rate of change or the constant percentage change model be more appropriate? Explain.
c. Using a calculator or the computation methods described on pages 105–106 of Chapter 4, use the data to estimate the coefficients of the equation $S_t = S_0 + bt$, where S_t is sales in the tth quarter.
d. Use the data to estimate the coefficients of the equation $S_t = S_0(1 + g)^t$.

5-3. Based on quarterly data from 1990:I to 1993:IV, Highland Foods estimates that potato chip sales can be projected using the equation

$$S_t = 5{,}000{,}000 + 100{,}000t$$

where 1990:I is period 1. Actual fourth-quarter sales were as follows:

1990	5,450,000
1991	5,860,000
1992	6,270,000
1993	6,680,000

a. Project sales for the first three quarters of 1994.
b. Without using a seasonal adjustment, project sales for 1994:IV.
c. Project seasonally adjusted sales for 1994:IV.

5-4. The winning heights (meters) for the Olympic pole vault for 1948–1992 were analyzed using the two trend projection models. The estimated equations were

$$PV_t = 4.244 + 0.153t$$
$$PV_t = 4.289(1.033)^t$$

where PV_t is the forecasted winning height.
a. On average, how much has the winning height increased from one Olympics to the next? What has been the percentage increase?
b. Forecast the winning heights for 1976 and 1992.
c. The winning heights for 1976 and 1992 were 5.50 and 5.80 meters, respectively. Is there an explanation for the large differences between the forecasted and the actual values for 1992?

5-5. Over a six-year period, a firm's sales (millions) were $200, $220, $180, $200, $190, and $210.
a. Using a smoothing constant of 0.5, forecast sales for the next period.
b. Graph the original data. Based on the results from part (a), graph the fore-

casted sales. Do the smoothed results have less variability than the original data?

c. Forecast next period sales using smoothing constants of $\alpha = 1.0$ and $\alpha = 0.0$. What are the implicit assumptions associated with these smoothing constants?

5-6. The demand for newsprint over a ten-year period is shown in the following table. Also shown are three time series for the same time period.

Year	1	2	3	4	5	6	7	8	9	10
Quantity of newsprint	100	110	115	115	130	145	140	135	135	150
Series A	25	30	25	35	30	40	45	50	45	45
Series B	200	220	225	225	240	260	255	250	255	240
Series C	20	20	23	26	25	24	24	28	28	26

a. Which of the time series is a roughly coincident indicator of newsprint demand?

b. Which series is a leading indicator of newsprint demand? For the leading indicator, what is the lead time?

c. Based on the leading indicator, is newsprint demand likely to increase, decrease, or stay the same in period 11? Explain.

5-7. Each year, sector A purchases $5 million of goods from sector B and $10 million from sector C. Sector B makes annual purchases of $2 million from sector A and $8 million from sector C. Annual purchases of sector C are $3 million from sector A and $6 million from sector B. Within-sector purchases are $1 million for sector A, $4 million for sector B, and $5 million for sector C. Total sales in the sectors are $20 million, $20 million, and $30 million, respectively.

a. Write the transactions matrix for the three sectors.

b. How much is value added for sector A?

c. How much is final demand in sector A?

d. Write the direct requirements matrix for the model.

5-8. The Ohio Planning Commission has developed a four-sector regional input/output model with a direct and indirect requirements matrix as follows.

	Sector	1	2	3	4
Sector	1	1.20	0.45	0.90	0.60
	2	0.20	1.50	0.80	0.75
	3	0.89	0.63	1.10	0.10
	4	0.24	0.80	0.43	1.24

a. What is the interpretation of the element in the first row of the second column?

b. If final demand decreases by $5 million in sector 3, what will be the effect on total sales in sector 1?

c. The commission estimates that 1 ton of sulfur dioxide particles enters the atmosphere for each $10 million increase in total sales in sector 2. How much pollution will result from a $5 million increase in final demand in sector 1?

Microcomputer Problems

The following problems can be solved by using the microcomputer program TOOLS, available with the study guide or by using other computer software.

5-9. Electric power consumption data from 1969 to 1983 were provided in problem 4-14 on page 133. Those data are to be used for this problem.

a. Using trend projection, estimate the constant rate of change in electricity consumption between 1969 and 1983.

b. Based on the result from part (a), forecast electricity consumption for 1984. Actual U.S. consumption was 777.4 billion kilowatt-hours. What might account for the large prediction error?

5-10. Monthly sales for a firm over an eleven-month period are as shown.

Month	Sales	Month	Sales
January	$2,000	July	$1,550
February	1,350	August	1,300
March	1,950	September	2,200
April	1,975	October	2,775
May	3,100	November	2,350
June	1,750		

a. For smoothing constants of 0.2, 0.4, 0.6, and 0.8, compute predicted sales. What are the sums of squared deviations? What is the optimal smoothing constant?

b. Based on the result from part (a), forecast sales for December.

5-11. The gold-medal-winning heights (meters) for the men's high jump for 1948 to 1988 are shown here.

Year	Height	Year	Height
1948	1.98	1972	2.23
1952	2.04	1976	2.25
1956	2.12	1980	2.36
1960	2.16	1984	2.35
1964	2.18	1988	2.38
1968	2.24		

a. Use trend projection to estimate the constant rate of change and the constant percentage rate of change for the period 1948 to 1988.

b. Use the estimated trend projection equations to forecast the winning height for 1992.

c. Use exponential smoothing with a smoothing constant of $\alpha = 0.2$ and $\alpha = 0.8$ to forecast the winning height for 1992.

d. Which approach (trend projection or exponential smoothing) provides the most accurate forecast? Explain

5-12. Standard and Poor's provides a price index for stocks listed on the New York Stock Exchange. The index for 1972 to 1982 is shown here.

Year	Index	Year	Index
1972	109.2	1978	96.0
1973	107.4	1979	103.0
1974	82.9	1980	118.8
1975	86.2	1981	128.1
1976	102.0	1982	119.7
1977	98.2		

a. What was the estimated constant percentage rate of change per period?

b. Using the data, project the Standard and Poor's Index for 1983 and 1984.

c. The actual index for 1983 and 1984 was

Year	Index
1983	160.4
1984	160.5

Is trend projection a good tool for estimating future stock prices? Why or why not?

5-13. Quarterly profits data (in millions of dollars) for 1991:I to 1993:IV are shown here.

Period	Profit	Period	Profit
1991:I	−1.0	1992:III	+1.8
1991:II	−0.5	1992:IV	+2.4
1991:III	−0.0	1993:I	+2.7
1991:IV	+0.6	1993:II	+2.9
1992:I	+1.1	1993:III	+3.3
1992:II	+1.3	1993:IV	+3.6

a. Using trend projection, what is the estimated constant rate of change per period?

b. What happens when the trend projection program is used to estimate the constant percentage rate of change? Explain.

5-14. Each year sector A purchases $5 million of goods from sector B and $10 million from sector C. Sector B makes annual purchases of $2 million from sector A and $8 million from sector C. Annual purchases of sector C are $3 million from sector A and $6 million from sector B. Within-sector purchases are $1 million for sector A, $4 million for sector B, and $5 million for sector C. Total sales in each sector are $20 million, $20 million, and $30 million, respectively. Final demands are $14 million for sector A, $5 million for sector B, and $7 million for sector C.

   a. Using input/output analysis, what are the elements of the direct and indirect requirements matrix? What is the interpretation of the element in the second row and third column?

   b. Final demand in sector A increases by $2 million. What is the change in total demand for each sector?

   c. Starting from the original values, final demand decreased by $1 million each in sectors A and B and increases by $2 million in sector C. What is the change in total demand for each sector?

5-15. Consider the following four-sector transactions matrix:

	Sales to A	+	Sales to B	+	Sales to C	+	Sales to D	+	Final Demand	=	Total Sales
Purchases from A	8		10		5		7		10		40
Purchases from B	6		9		10		8		2		35
Purchases from C	10		5		2		3		15		35
Purchases from D	5		8		7		5		5		30
Value added	11		3		11		7				
Total sales	40		35		35		30				

   a. Write the direct and indirect requirements matrix. What is the interpretation of the element in the fourth column of the fourth row?

   b. If final demand in sector D increases by 5, what will be the changes in total demand for each sector?

   c. It is estimated that 50 jobs are created for each one-unit increase in total demand in sector A and 20 jobs for each one-unit increase in total demand in sector D. If final demand increased by 5 in sector D, how many additional jobs would be created in each of these two sectors?

III

Production and Costs

Production Theory

Preview

The firm is an entity that combines and processes resources in order to produce output that will directly or indirectly satisfy consumer demand. Firms range in size from the person who bakes apple pies at home for sale to neighbors to the largest multinational conglomerate. However, when reduced to the basics, all firms do the same thing—they employ resources to produce output that will be sold in the market. The goal of the firm is to maximize the profit earned from this activity.

The general production problem facing the firm is to determine how much output to produce and how much labor and capital to employ to produce that output most efficiently. Engineering information in the form of a production function and economic information on prices of outputs and inputs must be combined in order to answer those questions.

In this chapter a framework for understanding the economics of production is presented and a set of conditions for efficient production developed. In the first section, the concept of a production function is outlined. In following sections, techniques for determining cost-efficient production and input rates are determined. This is done for one variable input and then for two variable inputs. Next the concepts of returns to scale and economies of scope are discussed. Finally, techniques for statistical estimation of production functions are developed.

The Production Function

For simplicity, assume that all inputs or factors of production can be grouped into two broad categories, labor (L) and capital (K). The general equation for the production function is

$$Q = f(K, L) \tag{6-1}$$

This function defines the maximum rate of output (Q) per unit of time obtainable from a given rate of capital and labor input. Output may be in physical units such as automobiles or microcomputers, or it may be intangible, as in the case of medical care, transportation, or education.

The production function is really an engineering concept that is devoid of economic content. That is, it simply relates output and input rates. The production function does not yield information on the least-cost capital–labor combination for producing a given level of output, nor does it reveal that output rate that would yield maximum profit. The production function only shows the maximum output obtainable from any and all input combinations. Prices of the inputs and the price of output must be used with the production function to determine which of the many possible input combinations is best given the firm's objective.

The definition of the production function as defining maximum output rates is important. Obviously, firms can fail to organize or manage resources efficiently and produce less than the maximum output for given input rates. However, in a competitive environment, such firms are not likely to survive because competitors using efficient production techniques will be able to produce at lower cost, sell at lower prices, and ultimately drive inefficient producers out of the market. Thus only firms using the best production methods (i.e., maximizing production from any input combination) are considered in this chapter.

Economists use a variety of functional forms to describe production. The multiplicative form, generally referred to as a Cobb–Douglas production function,

$$Q = AK^{\alpha}L^{\beta} \qquad (6\text{-}2)$$

is widely-used in economics because it has properties representative of many production processes. It will be used as the basis for many of the examples found in this chapter.

Consider a Cobb–Douglas production function with parameters $A = 100$, $\alpha = 0.5$, and $\beta = 0.5$. That is,

$$Q = 100K^{0.5}L^{0.5} \qquad (6\text{-}3)$$

A production table shows the maximum rate of output associated with each of a number of input combinations. For example, given the production function (6-3), if two units of labor and four units of capital are used, maximum production is 283 units of output. If $K = 8$ and $L = 2$ the output rate will be 400. Table 6-1 shows production rates for various input-rate combinations applied to the production function (6-3).

Three important relationships are shown by the data in this production table. First, the table indicates that there are a variety of ways to produce a particular

TABLE 6-1 **Production Table for the Production Function $Q = 100K^{.5}L^{.5}$**

Rate of Capital Input (K)								
8	283	400	490	565	632	693	748	800
7	265	374	458	529	592	648	700	748
6	245	346	424	490	548	600	648	693
5	224	316	387	447	500	548	592	632
4	200	283	346	400	447	490	529	565
3	173	245	300	346	387	424	458	490
2	141	200	245	283	316	346	374	400
1	100	141	173	200	224	245	265	283
	1	2	3	4	5	6	7	8

Rate of Labor Input (L)

rate of output. For example, 245 units of output can be produced with any of the following input combinations:

Combination	K	L
a	6	1
b	3	2
c	2	3
d	1	6

This implies that there is *substitutability* between the factors of production. The firm can use a capital-intensive production process characterized by combination *a*, a labor-intensive process such as *d*, or a process that uses a resource combination somewhere between these extremes, such as *b* or *c*.[1] The concept of substitution is important because it means that managers can change the mix of capital and labor in response to changes in the relative prices of these inputs.

Second, in Table 6-1, if input rates are doubled, the output rate also doubles. For example, maximum production with one unit of capital and four units of labor is 200. Doubling the input rates to $K = 2$, $L = 8$ results in the rate of output doubling to $Q = 400$. The relationship between output change and proportionate changes in both inputs is referred to as *returns to scale*. In Table 6-1, production is characterized by constant returns to scale. This means that if both input rates increase by the same factor (e.g., both input rates double), the rate of output also will double. In other production functions, output may increase more or less than in proportion to changes in inputs. Returns to scale have implications for the size of individual firms and the number of firms in an industry. For example, in producing a product, if output increases more than in proportion to increases in inputs, that industry is likely to have only a few large firms. The U.S. automobile industry is an example. A more detailed discussion of the concept of returns to scale is included later in this chapter.

In contrast to the concept of returns to scale, when output changes because one input changes while the other remains constant, the changes in the output rates are referred to as *returns to a factor*. Note that in the table, if the rate of one input is held constant while the other is increased, output increases but the successive increments become smaller. For example, from Table 6-1 it is seen that if the rate of capital input is held constant at 2 and labor is increased from $L = 1$ to $L = 6$, the successive increases in output are 59, 45, 38, 33, and 30. As discussed below, this relationship holds for virtually all production processes and is the basis for an important economic principle known as the law of diminishing marginal returns.

In Table 6-1, changes in output are shown only for discrete changes in the inputs. That is, only integer values of capital and labor are used. If the input rates

[1] The term *capital intensive* refers to a production system where the ratio of capital to labor is relatively high. In a *labor-intensive* case, the capital-to-labor ratio would be relatively low.

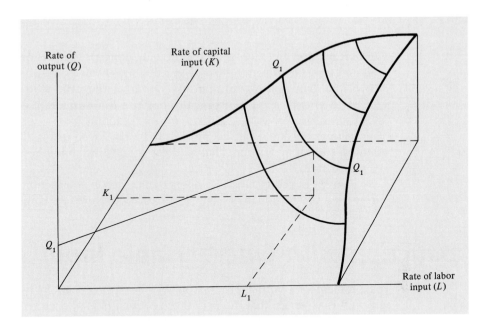

FIGURE 6-1 **The Production Surface.**

of capital and labor can be varied continuously (i.e., any value of K and L such as $K = 6.24$ or $L = 3.15$ is possible), a production function traces a smooth, continuous surface, such as that shown in Figure 6-1. In this three-dimensional diagram, capital and labor are shown on the K and L axes and output is measured on the vertical axis, which is perpendicular to the K, L plane. The rate of output generated by a given capital–labor combination is found by identifying the point representing an input combination (such as K_1 and L_1 in Figure 6-1) and drawing a perpendicular line up to the production surface. The height of this perpendicular line defines the rate of output Q_1 corresponding to the input combination K_1 and L_1. In general, any point on the production surface defines the maximum output possible from the input combination associated with that point.

Although the production table provides considerable information on production possibilities, it does not allow for the determination of the profit-maximizing rate of output or even the best way to produce some specified rate of output. For example, the production data in Table 6-1 show four different combinations of capital and labor that will generate 245 units of output. Which is the best combination? Similarly, of the infinite number of possible output levels, which one will result in maximum profit for the firm? The production function alone cannot answer these questions. As indicated previously, the production function, while a fundamental part of the decision-making process, is an engineering relationship and must be combined with data on the price of capital, labor, and output to determine the optimal allocation of resources in the production process.

KEY CONCEPTS _____

- The production function is an engineering concept that defines the maximum rate of output forthcoming from specified input rates of capital and labor.
- The Cobb–Douglas or multiplicative form of the production function, $Q = AK^\alpha L^\beta$, is widely used in economics because it accurately characterizes many production processes.
- Generally, a specified rate of output can be produced using different combinations of capital and labor. That is, there is substitutability between the factors of production.
- The concept of returns to scale refers to changes in production when all inputs are varied proportionately. Returns to a factor refers to changes in production associated with change in only one input.

Production with One Variable Input _____

The problem of optimal production will be approached in two ways. In this section it is assumed that the period of production is of such length that the rate of input of one factor of production is fixed. That is, the period is not long enough to change the input rate of that factor. The problem, then, is to determine the optimal rate of the variable input given the price of output, the price of the variable input, and the production technology as described by the production function. In the next section, both inputs will be allowed to vary, and the optimal rates of both variable inputs, capital, and labor will be determined.

The period of time during which one of the inputs is fixed in amount is defined as the short run. In contrast, all inputs are variable in the long run. The period of time for the short run will vary among firms. For some firms, such as a child's lemonade stand, the short run may be just long enough to run home for another cardboard box to augment the capital stock. For an electric utility company, the short run may be a number of years—the period of time necessary to plan and build a new generation unit.

Generally, at any point in time, the firm is operating in the short run. That is, the input rates of one or more factors are fixed. But most firms are continuously planning or considering changes in the entire scale of operation that would involve changes in all input rates. Thus it is said that the firm plans in the long run but operates in the short run. For example, an automobile manufacturer may have six plants with maximum production capacity of 1.5 million vehicles per year. To build a new plant may take several years. At any particular time, the firm operates the existing plants—a short-run decision, but based on current and projected demand conditions, the firm will plan to augment or reduce plant capacity in the future—a long-run decision.

The Product Functions

For a two-input production process, the total product of labor (TP_L) is defined as the maximum rate of output forthcoming from combining varying rates of labor input with a fixed capital input. Denoting the fixed capital input as $\overline{K}$, the total product of labor function is

$$TP_L = f(\overline{K}, L) \tag{6-4}$$

Similarly, the total product of capital function is written as

$$TP_K = f(K, \overline{L}) \tag{6-5}$$

Two other product relations are relevant. First, marginal product (MP) is defined as the change in output per one-unit change in the variable input. Thus, the marginal product of labor is

$$MP_L = \frac{\Delta Q}{\Delta L}$$

and the marginal product of capital is

$$MP_K = \frac{\Delta Q}{\Delta K}$$

For infinitesimally small changes in the variable input, the marginal product function is the first derivative of the production function with respect to the variable input. For the general Cobb–Douglas production function,

$$Q = AK^\alpha L^\beta$$

the marginal products are

$$MP_k = \frac{dQ}{dK} = \alpha A K^{\alpha-1} L^\beta$$

and

$$MP_L = \frac{dQ}{dL} = \beta A K^\alpha L^{\beta-1}$$

Second, average product (AP) is total product per unit of the variable input and is found by dividing the rate of output by the rate of the variable input. The average product of labor function is

$$AP_L = \frac{TP_L}{L} \tag{6-6}$$

and the equation for the average product of capital is

$$AP_K = \frac{TP_K}{K} \tag{6-7}$$

Consider a hypothetical production function. If capital is fixed at two units, the rates of output generated by combining various levels of labor with two units of capital (i.e., the total product of labor) are as shown in Table 6-2. The average and marginal product of labor are also shown in the table.

The total product function can be thought of as a cross section or vertical slice of a three-dimension production surface such as that shown in Figure 6-2a. Suppose the capital stock is fixed at K_1. The total product of labor function $f(K_1, L)$ is shown as the line starting at K_1 and extending through point a. Similarly, if the labor input is fixed at L_3, the total product of capital function is shown as the line beginning at L_3 and going through points a and b. Other total product

TABLE 6-2 **Total, Average, and Marginal Product of Labor for $K = 2$**

Rate of Labor Input (L)	TP_L	AP_L	MP_L
0	0	—	—
1	20	20	20
2	50	25	30
3	90	30	40
4	120	30	30
5	140	28	20
6	150	25	10
7	155	22	5
8	150	19	−5

functions are shown as the lines beginning at L_1, L_2, K_2, and K_3. If the cross section associated with $TP_K = f(K, L_3)$ was shown in a two-dimensional graph having output on the vertical axis and capital on the horizontal axis, it would appear as shown in Figure 6-2b.

Diminishing Marginal Returns

Consider a clothing manufacturer having a 5,000-square-foot building housing 100 sewing machines. Obviously, having only one or two workers in such a plant would be inefficient. As more labor is added, production should increase rapidly as more machines are placed in operation and better coordination achieved among workers and machines. However, as even more labor is added, the efficiency gains will slow and output will increase but at a slower rate (i.e., marginal product will decline). Finally, a point may be reached where adding more labor actually will cause a reduction in total output, that is, where marginal product becomes negative. Because only so many workers can be put in a finite space, enough labor could be added so that the production process would come to a standstill, reducing output to zero.

This example illustrates an important economic principle known as the *law of diminishing marginal returns*. This law states that when increasing amounts of the variable input are combined with a fixed level of another input, a point will be reached where the marginal product of the variable input will decline. This law does not result from a theoretical argument but is based on actual observation of many production processes. Virtually all studies of production systems have verified the existence of diminishing marginal returns.

Relationships Among the Product Functions

A set of typical total, average, and marginal product functions for labor is shown in Figure 6-3. Total product begins at the origin, increases at an increasing rate

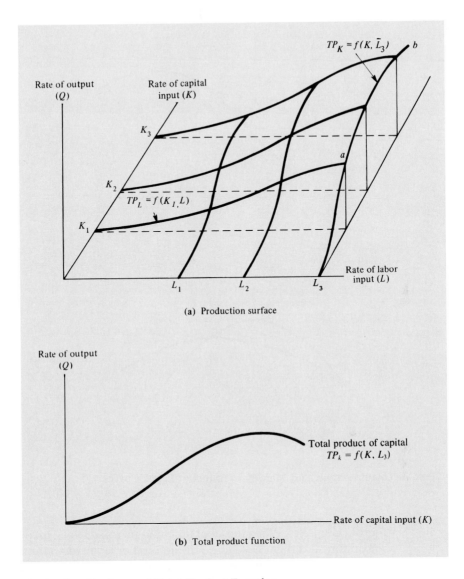

(a) Production surface

(b) Total product function

FIGURE 6-2 **Production Surface and Total Product Function.,**

over the range 0 to L_1, and then increases at a decreasing rate. Beyond L_3, total product actually declines. The explanation is as follows. Initially, the input proportions are inefficient—there is too much of the fixed factor, capital. As the labor input is increased from 0 to L_1, output rises more than in proportion to the increase in the labor input. That is, marginal product per unit of labor increases as a better balance of labor and capital inputs is achieved. As the labor input is increased beyond L_1, diminishing marginal returns set in and marginal product declines; the additional units of labor still result in an increase in output, but each increment

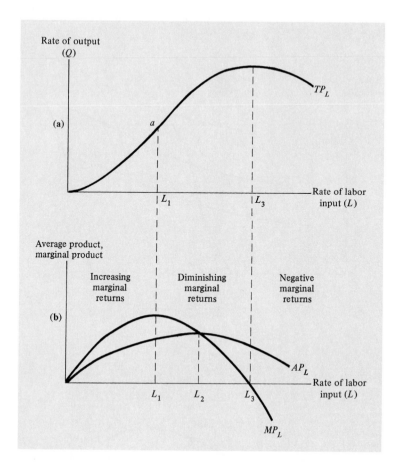

FIGURE 6-3 **Total, Average, and Marginal Product of Labor Curves.**

to output is smaller. When the labor input has increased to L_3, total product reaches a maximum, and then, beyond L_3, the amount of labor has become excessive and slows the production process with the result that total product actually declines.

Several relationships among the total, average, and marginal product functions are important:

1. Marginal product reaches a maximum at L_1, which corresponds to an inflection point (*a*) on the total product function. At the inflection point, the total product function changes from increasing at an increasing rate to increasing at a decreasing rate.

2. Marginal product intersects average product at the maximum point on the average product curve. This occurs at labor input rate L_2. Recall that whenever marginal product is above average product, the average is rising—it makes no difference whether marginal product is rising or falling. When marginal product is below average product, the average is falling. Therefore, the intersection must occur at the maximum point of average product.

3. Marginal product becomes negative at labor input rate L_3. This corresponds to the point where the total product curve reaches a maximum.

KEY CONCEPTS

- The short run is that period of time for which the rate of input use of at least one factor of production is fixed. In the long run, the input rates of all factors are variable. The firm operates in the short run but plans in the long run.
- In the short run, total product is the set of output rates obtained by combining varying rates of one input with a fixed rate of the other input.
- Marginal product is the change in output associated with a one-unit change in the variable input (i.e., $MP_L = \Delta Q/\Delta L$) or the first derivative of the production function with respect to the variable input (i.e., $MP_L = dQ/dL$).
- Average product is the rate of output produced per unit of the variable input employed (i.e., $AP_L = Q/L$).
- The law of diminishing marginal returns states that when increasing rates of a variable input are combined with a fixed rate of another input, a point will be reached where marginal product will decline.

Optimal Employment of a Factor of Production

The General Motors Corporation has a physical capital stock valued at about $36 billion. Consider this to be the fixed input for the firm. About 760,000 workers are employed to use this capital stock. What principles guide the decisions about the level of employment? In general, to maximize profit, the firm should hire labor as long as the additional revenue associated with hiring another unit of labor exceeds the cost of employing that unit. For example, suppose that the marginal product of an additional worker is four units of output and each unit of output is worth $10,000. Thus the additional revenue to the firm will be $40,000 if the worker is hired. If the additional cost of a worker (i.e., the wage rate) is $30,000, that worker will be hired because $10,000, the difference between additional revenue and additional cost, will be added to profit. However, if the wage rate is $45,000, the worker should not be hired because profit would be reduced by $5,000.

Formally stated, the basic principle is that additional units of the variable output should be hired until the marginal revenue product (*MRP*) of the last unit employed is equal to the cost of the input., The *MRP* is defined as marginal revenue times marginal product and represents the value of the extra unit of labor.[2] Thus labor is hired until MRP_L equals the wage rate (w):

$$MRP_L = w \qquad (6\text{-}8)$$

Similarly, if the labor input was fixed and the capital stock could be varied, capital would be employed until the marginal revenue product of capital equaled the

---

[2] In general, marginal revenue product is equal to $MR \cdot MP$. If price is constant, $P = MR$ and marginal revenue product is $P \cdot MP$.

price of capital (r), that is,

$$MRP_L = r \qquad (6\text{-}9)$$

Table 6-3 shows the total product, marginal product, total revenue, and marginal revenue product of labor for the production function $Q = 100\ K^5L^5$ and where the capital input rate has been fixed at four units and the price of output is $2. In the example, MRP_L can be determined either by multiplying each MP_L entry by $2 (the output price per unit) or by finding the change in total revenue for each one-unit increase in labor.

It is easily seen that the two methods are equivalent. Marginal revenue product is equal to marginal revenue multiplied by marginal product. That is,

$$MRP_L = MR \cdot MP_L$$

But

$$MR = \frac{\Delta TR}{\Delta Q}$$

and

$$MP_L = \frac{\Delta Q}{\Delta L}$$

Substituting, it is seen that

$$MRP_L = \frac{\Delta TR}{\Delta Q} \frac{\Delta Q}{\Delta L} = \frac{\Delta TR}{\Delta L}$$

Thus marginal revenue product can be written as the change in total revenue per one-unit change in the rate of labor input.

For infinitesimally small changes in the labor input, marginal revenue product is the first derivative of the total revenue function with respect to that input. That is,

$$MRP_L = \frac{d(TR)}{dL}$$

TABLE 6-3 **Total and Marginal Product, Total Revenue, and Marginal Revenue Product Functions for Labor for the Production Function** $Q = 100K^5L^5$, $K = 4$, and $P = \$2$

L	TP_L	MP_L	TR	MRP_L
0	0	—	$ 0	—
1	200	200	400	$400
2	283	83	566	166
3	346	63	692	126
4	400	54	800	108
5	447	47	894	94
6	490	43	980	86
7	529	39	1,058	78
8	565	36	1,130	72

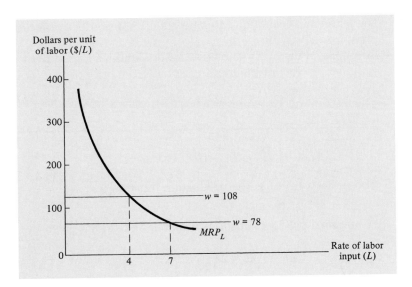

FIGURE 6-4 **The Optimal Quantity of Labor to Be Hired.**

The optimal rate of labor to be hired depends on the wage rate. If a unit of labor costs $108, then four units of labor are hired because the firm will hire labor only as long as MRP_L is greater than or equal to the wage rate. If the wage rate is lower, say $78 per unit of labor, seven units will be hired. Clearly, if the wage rate is lower, more labor will be purchased.

The marginal revenue product is the labor demand function for the firm. That is, it indicates the amount of labor that will be hired at any wage rate. In graphing the labor demand curve, the vertical axis is measured in dollars, and the horizontal axis is measured as the rate of labor input. The labor demand curve is downward sloping because of the law of diminishing marginal returns.

The MRP_L curve corresponding to Table 6-3 is shown in Figure 6-4. The horizontal line at $w = \$78$ in the figure can be thought of as the supply function for labor facing the firm. This horizontal supply curve means that the firm can hire all the labor it wants at $78 per unit. The optimum quantity of labor is determined by finding the intersection of the demand and supply functions, that is, the point where $MRP_L = w$. The figure shows that seven units of labor should be hired. If the wage rate increased to $108 (shown by the $w = 108$ line in Figure 6-4), the quantity of labor demanded by the firm would fall to four units. If the wage rate is higher than $108, less labor would be hired as the firm moved up the MRP_L curve.

KEY CONCEPTS

- Marginal revenue product (MRP) is found by multiplying the marginal product function by marginal revenue (i.e., $MRP = MR \cdot MP$).

- The marginal revenue product function for a productive factor is the demand curve for that factor.
- Additional units of a productive factor should be hired until the value of the marginal product of the input is equal to the price of that input.

EXAMPLE _____

The Optimal Labor Input Rate

Suppose that a firm has the production function

$$Q = 2K^{1/2}L^{1/2}$$

with marginal product functions for labor and capital given by

$$MP_L = \frac{dQ}{dL} = 2\left(\frac{1}{2}\right)K^{1/2}L^{1/2-1} = \frac{K^{1/2}}{L^{1/2}} \quad \text{or} \quad \sqrt{\frac{K}{L}}$$

and

$$MP_K = \frac{dQ}{dK} = 2\left(\frac{1}{2}\right)K^{1/2-1}L^{1/2} = \frac{L^{1/2}}{K^{1/2}} \quad \text{or} \quad \sqrt{\frac{L}{K}}$$

respectively. Assume that the capital stock if fixed at nine units (i.e., $K = 9$). If the price of output (P) is \$6 per unit, and the wage rate (w) is \$2 per unit, determine the optimal or profit-maximizing rate of labor to be hired. What labor rate is optimal if the wage rate increased to \$3 per unit?

SOLUTION   First, determine the MRP_L, assuming that K is fixed at 9 (note that $P = MR$):

$$MRP_L = P \cdot MP_L = P\sqrt{\frac{K}{L}} = 6\left(\sqrt{\frac{9}{L}}\right) = \frac{18}{\sqrt{L}}$$

Now, equate the MRP_L function and the wage rate and solve for L. That is, set

$$MRP_L = w$$

and substitute, yielding

$$\frac{18}{\sqrt{L}} = 2 \quad \text{or} \quad L = 81$$

Therefore, 81 units of labor should be employed.

If the wage rate increases to \$3 per unit of labor, the profit-maximizing condition $MRP_L = w$ would be

$$\frac{18}{\sqrt{L}} = 3$$

$$L = 36$$

This example shows that as the price of labor increases, the firm demands less labor. That is, the labor demand curve is downward sloping.

Production with Two Variable Inputs ⎯⎯⎯⎯

If both capital and labor inputs are variable, a different set of analytical techniques must be applied to determine optimal input rates. There are three ways the firm may approach the problem of efficient resource allocation in production. They are (1) maximize production for a given dollar outlay on labor and capital, (2) minimize the dollar outlay on labor and capital inputs necessary to produce a specified rate of output, or (3) produce that output rate that maximizes profit. For the profit maximization case, it will be shown that for each input, the marginal revenue product will equal the input price.

The first two problems are called *constrained optimization problems.* In problem (1), the constraint is a fixed dollar outlay for capital and labor. In problem (2), the constraint is a specified rate of output that must be produced. However, in problem (3), the firm seeks that output level that will maximize profit; there is no constraint on either the budget available for production or the output level to be produced.

In this section the approach to solving each of these problems is presented. A standard managerial economics technique using the concept of production isoquants and production isocosts is used to determine efficient input rate combinations for given production rates.

The Production Isoquant

In Figure 6-5, the three-dimensional production surface for the production function $Q = 100K^{0.5}L^{0.5}$ is shown. Think of an output rate, say $Q_1 = 490$, being specified and a "horizontal slice" cut through the production surface at that height. By cutting through the surface horizontally, the rate of output is held constant. This slice, denoted as Q_1Q_1, is a smooth curve that defines all combinations of capital and labor that yield a maximum production rate of 490. Two points on that isoquant, a and b, are used to show how the capital and labor input combinations are determined. Starting at point a, draw a perpendicular line from a to point a' on the capital–labor plane (i.e., the base of the diagram). Point a' denotes a capital input of 4 and labor input of 6. Repeating that process at b yields another capital–labor combination (3, 8) that also generates 490 units of output. If this process were repeated many times, it would trace out the smooth curve shown as the dashed curve $Q_1'Q_1'$ in the capital–labor plane. That curve is shown as the $Q = 490$ isoquant in the two-dimensional diagram in Figure 6-6.

Formally, an isoquant is the set of all combinations of capital and labor that yield a given output level. If fractional input units are allowed, there are an infinite number of points on any isoquant. Further, there is an isoquant through every point in the capital–labor space. Equivalently, there is an output rate corresponding to every combination of input rates. This implies that there are an infinite number of isoquants. For example, in addition to the isoquant for 490 units of output, isoquants for $Q = 200$ and $Q = 346$ are shown in Figure 6-6.

In general, isoquants are determined in the following way. First, a rate of output,

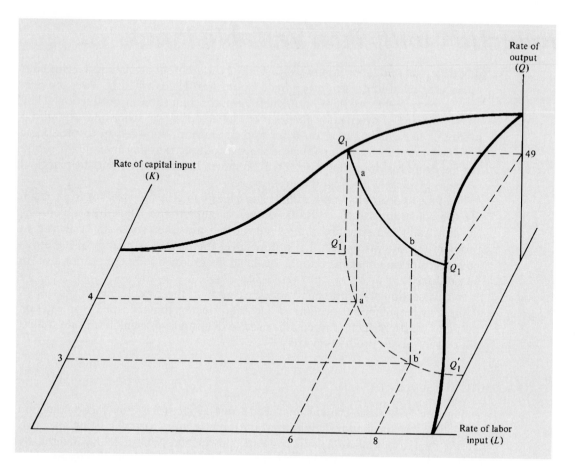

FIGURE 6-5 **Deriving an Isoquant from the Production Surface.**

say Q_o, is specified. Hence the production function can be written as

$$Q_o = f(K, L) \tag{6-10}$$

Those combinations of K and L that satisfy this equation define the isoquant for output rate Q_o.

The slope of the isoquant shows the rate at which one input can be substituted for the other such that the level of output remains constant. This slope is referred to as the *marginal rate of technical substitution* (*MRTS*). For example, consider points c, d, and e on the 200-unit isoquant in Figure 6-6. Moving from point c to d involves substituting one additional unit of labor for two units of capital. That is, the marginal rate of substitution of labor for capital averages $1:2$ over the range c to d. From point d to point e, it takes two units of labor to replace one unit of capital in order to maintain output at the 200 level. Thus the marginal rate of substitution of labor for capital is $2:1$ over the range d and e.

For most production functions, the isoquant is a smooth curve that is convex

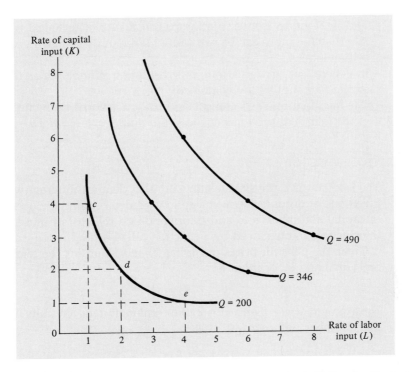

FIGURE 6-6 **Production Isoquants for Output Rates of 200, 346, and 490 for the Production Function Q = 100√KL.**

to the origin, as shown in Figure 6-6. The shape of this isoquant implies that inputs are imperfectly substitutable, and the rate of substitution declines as one input is substituted for another. For example, consider a factor having many machines but few workers. Adding an additional worker and reducing the number of machines may result in a much more efficient production system—that is, a relatively large increase in output would be obtained by adding that worker. But as more labor is added and machines removed, those efficiency gains fall. Thus is takes more and more workers to replace each machine.

It can be shown that the slope of an isoquant (i.e., the *MRTS*) is equal to the negative of the ratio of the marginal products, that is,

$$MRTS = -\frac{MP_L}{MP_K} \qquad (6\text{-}11)$$

This relationship will be useful later on in determining the optimal rates of capital and labor to be hired when both inputs are variable.

KEY CONCEPTS

- An isoquant shows all combinations of capital and labor input rates that will produce a specified rate of output.

- The slope of an isoquant is the marginal rate of technical substitution or the rate that one input can be substituted for another so that a given rate of output is maintained.
- In general, the marginal rate of substitution diminishes as more of one input and less of another are combined.
- The marginal rate of technical substitution is equal to the negative of the ratio of the marginal products of the two inputs. That is, $MRTS = -(MP_L/MP_K)$.

The Production Isocost

The isoquant is a physical relationship that denotes different ways to produce a given rate of output. The next step toward determining the optimal combination of capital and labor is to add information on the cost of those inputs. This cost information is introduced by a function called a production isocost.

Given the per-unit prices of capital (r) and labor (w), the total expenditure (C) on capital and labor input is

$$C = rK + wL \qquad (6\text{-}12)$$

For example, if $r = 3$ and $w = 2$, the combination of ten units of capital and five units of labor will cost \$40. That is,

$$40 = 3(10) + 2(5)$$

For any given cost, C_0, the isocost line defines all combinations of capital and labor inputs that can be purchased for C_0.

Rewrite equation (6-12) by solving for K as a function of L,

$$K = \frac{C_0}{r} - \frac{w}{r}L \qquad (6\text{-}13)$$

Equation (6-13) is an equation for a straight line where C_0/r is the vertical intercept and $-w/r$ is the slope. The ratio $-w/r$ is the rate that labor can be exchanged for capital in the market. For example, if $w = 2$ and $r = 3$, one unit of capital can be traded for 1.5 units of labor or one unit of labor can be traded for $\frac{2}{3}$ unit of capital.

Using the data from the preceding example ($w = 2$, $r = 3$, and $C = 40$), the isocost line becomes

$$40 = 3K + 2L$$

Solving for K yields

$$K = \frac{40}{3} - \frac{2}{3}L$$

or

$$K = 13.33 - \frac{2}{3}L$$

This information is shown as the \$40 isocost line in Figure 6-7. Note the intercept points on the capital and labor axes. If all of the \$40 budget is spent on capital,

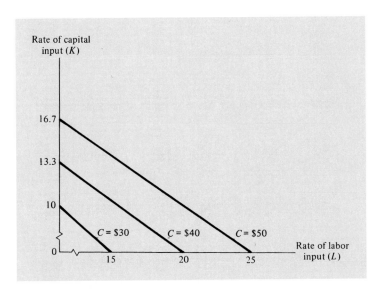

Rate of capital input (K)

16.7

13.3

10

C = $30   C = $40   C = $50

Rate of labor input (L)

0

15   20   25

FIGURE 6-7 **Isocost Lines for Budgets of $30, $40, and $50.**

13.3 units can be purchased. Conversely, if the budget is spent entirely on labor, 20 units can be obtained.

If the budget constraint is increased to, say, $50, the equation for the isocost equation becomes

$$50 = 3K + 2L$$

or

$$K = \frac{50}{3} - \frac{2}{3}L$$

Note that the intercept term on the capital axis has increased but the slope $(-\frac{2}{3})$ remains the same because the input prices are unchanged. That is, the new isocost has shifted outward but remains parallel to the $40 isocost. The capital and labor intercepts (K, L) are now (16.7, 0) and (0, 25). Similarly, a decrease in the budget from $40 to, say, $30 causes a parallel shift in the function toward the origin. These three isocost lines ($30, $40, and $50) are shown in Figure 6-7.

Now, consider how the isocost function shifts if an input price changes instead of the budget amount. Initially, assume that $C_0 = 40$, $w = 5$, and that r is variable. Thus the equation for the isocost is

$$K = \frac{40}{r} - \frac{5}{r}L$$

If r increases from, say, 2 to 3, the equation for the isocost changes from

$$K = \frac{40}{2} - \frac{5}{2}L$$

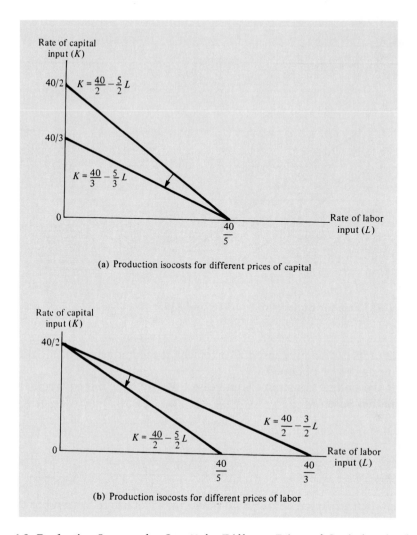

(a) Production isocosts for different prices of capital

(b) Production isocosts for different prices of labor

FIGURE 6-8 **Production Isocosts for C = 40 for Different Prices of Capital and Labor.**

to

$$K = \frac{40}{3} - \frac{5}{3}L$$

These isocosts are shown in Figure 6-8a. Note that both the vertical (capital) intercept and the slope of the isocost function have changed, but the horizontal or labor intercept is unchanged. That intercept is determined by the ratio C_0/w, which is not influenced by a change in the price of capital. Thus, as r changes, the isocost pivots about the point (40/5, 0), which is the horizontal intercept.

Conversely, if the price of capital is held constant at 2 and the price of labor changes from, say, 3 to 5, the $40 isocost function will pivot about the point (40/2) on the vertical axis, as shown in Figure 6-8b.

KEY CONCEPTS

- The isocost function is the set of all combinations of capital and labor that can be purchased for a specified total cost.
- Changes in the budget amount, C_0, cause the isocost line to shift in a parallel manner. Changes in either the price of labor or capital cause both the slope and one intercept of the isocost function to change.

Optimal Employment of Two Inputs

When both capital and labor are variable, determining the optimal input rates of capital and labor requires that the technical information from the production function (i.e., the isoquants) be combined with the market data on input prices (i.e., the isocost functions).

Consider the problem of minimizing the cost of a given rate of output. Specifically, suppose that the firm's objective is to produce ten units of output at minimum cost. To help analyze this problem, two production isoquants are shown in Figure 6-9. The infinite number of capital–labor combinations that yield an output of 10 are indicated by the 10-unit isoquant. Three of these combinations are indicated by points a, b, and c. Points a and c are on the $150 isocost and b is on the $100 isocost. Of these, clearly b is the best of the three in the sense of being the lowest cost. In fact, b is the absolute minimum cost combination of capital and labor. At point b, the 10-unit isoquant is tangent to the $100 isocost line. Note

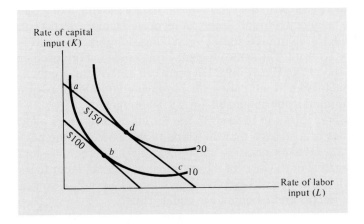

FIGURE 6-9 **Using Isocost and Isoquant Functions to Solve the Production Problem.**

that all other input combinations shown on the 10-unit isoquant would correspond to higher isocost curves, thus costing more than $100. That is, any other capital–labor combination on the 10-unit isoquant will be on a higher isocost line. Furthermore, there is no input combination that costs less than $100 that will produce 10 units of output.

At the tangency of the 10-unit isoquant and the $100 isocost, the slopes of the two functions are equal. Thus the marginal rate of technical substitution (i.e., the slope of the isoquant) equals the price of labor divided by the price of capital. That is,

$$MRTS = \frac{w}{r} \qquad (6\text{-}14)$$

Equation (6-14) is a necessary condition for efficient production. If this equality does not hold (such as at points a and c), there is some other combination of capital and labor inputs that will reduce the cost of producing 10 units of output. Equivalently, there is a way to move along the 10-unit isoquant to a lower isocost.

Consider a different production problem. Suppose that the objective is to maximize output given a budget constraint of $150. Now the choice of input combinations is limited to points on the $150 isocost function. In Figure 6-9 three points are shown on that isocost line, a, d, and c. These all satisfy the budget constraint, but they are on different isoquants. For example, output at points a and c is 10 units, but at point d output is 20 units. Clearly, d is the preferred point among these three because a higher rate of output is produced. In fact, d is the best of all points on the $150 isocost. No other combination of capital and labor that costs $150 will yield as much output. Again, at that optimal point, the isoquant is tangent to the isocost. Hence the same efficiency condition ($MRTS = w/r$) applies. That is, the marginal rate of technical substitution in production must equal the rate of exchange of labor for capital in the market.

Regardless of the production objective, efficient production requires that the isoquant be tangent to the isocost function. If the problem is to maximize output subject to a given cost, the solution is found by moving along the specified isocost until the tangency is found. If the problem is to minimize cost subject to an output constraint, the solution is found by moving along the specified isoquant until the tangency is found. The same efficiency rule holds in both problems. For example, consider point d in Figure 6-9. That point can be thought of either as the minimum-cost capital–labor combination for producing 20 units of output or as the point of maximum output obtainable on a $150 budget.

These principles can be used to test for efficient resource allocation in production. It has been shown that the slope of the isocost is the negative of the ratio of the wage rate and price of capital (i.e., $-w/r$) and that the slope of the isoquant is the negative of the ratio of the marginal product of labor to that of capital (i.e., $-MP_L/MP_K$). Further, it has been shown that at a point of tangency, the slopes of both the isocost and isoquant are equal. Thus

$$-\frac{MP_L}{MP_K} = -\frac{w}{r}$$

or

$$\frac{MP_L}{MP_K} = \frac{w}{r}$$

This condition must be met for efficient production.

Rewriting this efficiency condition as

$$\frac{MP_L}{w} = \frac{MP_K}{r} \tag{6-15}$$

suggests an important principle. For an input combination to be efficient, the marginal product per dollar of input cost must be the same for both inputs.[3] For example, consider the following inefficient situation. Assume that both w and r are equal to 2 but that the marginal product of labor is 10, compared to 8 for capital. Thus we have

$$\frac{10}{2} > \frac{8}{2}$$

This cannot be an efficient input combination. The firm is getting more output per dollar for funds spent on labor than on capital. But because the input prices are the same, labor can be traded for capital on a one-to-one basis. If one unit of capital is sold to obtain one unit of labor, the reduction of capital by one unit causes output to fall by 8, but increasing the labor input by one unit will increase output by 10. Thus the substitution of labor for capital would result in a net increase of two units of output at no additional cost.

The inefficient combination corresponds to a point such as a in Figure 6-9. At that point the ratio of capital to labor is too high. The profit-maximizing firm will substitute labor for capital by moving down the isocost line. Conversely, at a point such as c in Figure 6-9, the reverse is true—there is too much labor, and the inequality

$$\frac{MP_L}{w} < \frac{MP_K}{r}$$

will hold. That is, the firm generates more output per dollar spent on capital than from dollars spent on labor. Thus the firm should substitute capital for labor.

Suppose that the firm is producing at the inefficient point c in Figure 6-9. If the problem is to minimize the cost of producing a given rate of output, the firm would move from point c along the 10-unit isoquant to b, thereby reducing cost by $50 while maintaining the rate of production at 10 units. Alternatively, if the firm is maximizing output subject to a $150 cost constraint, it would move from c along the $150 isocost to point d, where that isocost is tangent to the 20-unit isoquant. Note that in the latter case, output would increase from 10 to 20 at no additional cost.

---

[3] This principle extends directly to production functions with more than two inputs. In general, efficient production requires that the ratio of marginal product to input price be equal for all inputs.

Profit Maximization

The efficiency condition just discussed is necessary but not sufficient for profit maximization. There are many points of tangency between isocosts and isoquants. For example, both points b and d in Figure 6-9 are efficient resource combinations. However, profits probably will be different at each point. Thus the problem is to determine that one point among the many efficient points that results in the largest profit. That the efficiency condition is necessary for maximum profit is obvious. If the firm is not operating at an efficient point, there will be some way to reduce the cost of that level of output and thereby increase profit. Thus only the efficient points defined by the tangencies of isocost and isoquant functions need to be considered.

To maximize profit, it is necessary to fall back on the rule for an efficient input rate when only one input is variable. That is, both inputs must be hired until the marginal revenue product equals the price of the input for both capital and labor. That is, the conditions for profit maximization are that

$$MRP_K = r \qquad\qquad (6\text{-}16)$$

and

$$MRP_L = w \qquad\qquad (6\text{-}17)$$

Marginal revenue product measures the additional dollars of revenue added by using one more unit of input. As long as MRP is greater than the cost of the input, profit can be increased by adding more of that input. That is, if an additional unit of an input adds more to revenue than that input cost, profits will increase, and those profits will increase until marginal revenue product equals the input price.

These conditions for a profit maximization imply that the condition for efficient production (i.e., $MP_L/P_L = MP_K/P_K$) will be met. This is shown by rewriting equations (6-16) and (6-17), that is,

$$MRP_K = r$$

and

$$MRP_L = w$$

as

$$P \cdot MP_L = w \qquad\qquad (6\text{-}18)$$

and

$$P \cdot MP_K = r \qquad\qquad (6\text{-}19)$$

Dividing equation (6-18) by (6-19) yields

$$\frac{MP_L}{MP_K} = \frac{w}{r}$$

and rewriting results in the efficiency condition

$$\frac{MP_L}{w} = \frac{MP_K}{r}$$

Therefore, if a firm is maximizing profit, it follows that it must be operating efficiently.

KEY CONCEPTS

- Efficient production requires that the isoquant function be tangent to the isocost function. At those points the marginal product per dollar of input cost is equal for both inputs. That is,

$$\frac{MP_L}{w} = \frac{MP_K}{r}$$

- If the condition for efficient production is not met, there is some way to substitute one input for the other that will result in an increase in production at no change in total cost.
- Profit maximization requires that inputs be hired until $MRP_K = r$ and $MRL_L = w$. The conditions also imply that $MP_L/w = MP_K/r$.

Changes in Input Prices

If the price of one input, say labor, increases, the firm will adjust the input mix by substituting capital for labor. If the price of labor declines, thus making labor relatively less expensive, labor will be substituted for capital. In general, if the relative prices of inputs change, managers will respond by substituting the input that has become relatively less expensive for the input that has become relatively more expensive.

The isoquant–isocost framework can be used to demonstrate this principle. Consider Figure 6-10 on page 198. Suppose the firm currently is operating at point a where 100 units of output are produced using the resource combination ($K = 10, L = 2$). This is an efficient resource mix because the 100-unit isoquant is tangent to the isocost line cc at point a. Assume that the firm's goal is to maximize production subject to a cost constraint (i.e., the firm is limited to resource combinations on a given isocost function).

Now, assume that the price of labor falls while the price of capital remains unchanged (i.e., labor has become relatively less expensive). The isocost pivots to the right from cc to the isocost cc'. The reduction in the price of labor means that the firm is able to increase the rate of production. Hence the firm moves from point a to point b, which is a new efficient resource combination. That is, the new isocost is tangent to the 120-unit isoquant at point b. Now nine units of capital and six units of labor are employed. Note that at point a, the efficient ratio of capital to labor was $5:1$. Now the efficient ratio of the two inputs is $3:2$. The reduction in the price of labor has caused the firm to substitute that relatively less expensive input for capital.

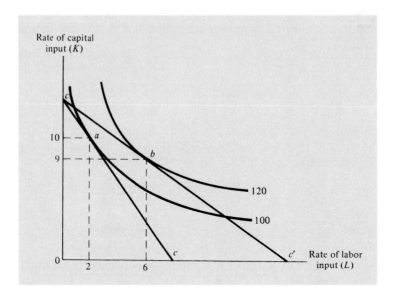

FIGURE 6-10 **Response of the Firm to a Decrease in the Price of Labor.**

CASE STUDY

Input Substitution in Response to Higher Energy Prices

The decade of the 1970s was one of rapidly rising prices for virtually all energy products. The price of gasoline, fuel oil, and natural gas increased much more rapidly than the prices of most other products and services. For example, during the period 1971–1980, the real price (i.e., the price adjusted for overall inflation) of crude oil, natural gas, and coal increased 240 percent, 347 percent, and 113 percent, respectively.

Because energy is an important input in many

Energy Consumption per Dollar of Value Added in Selected Industries

Year	Sector					
	All Manu-facturing	Paper	Organic Chemicals	Petroleum Refining	Steel	Aluminum
1971	52.5	316.2	277.9	631.4	314.7	418.5
1977	42.3	308.7	193.9	573.4	282.7	379.9
Percent change	−19.4	−2.4	−30.2	−9.2	−10.2	−9.2

SOURCE: U.S. Department of Commerce, Bureau of the Census, *Statistical Abstract of the United States* (Washington, D.C.: U.S. Government Printing Office, 1981).

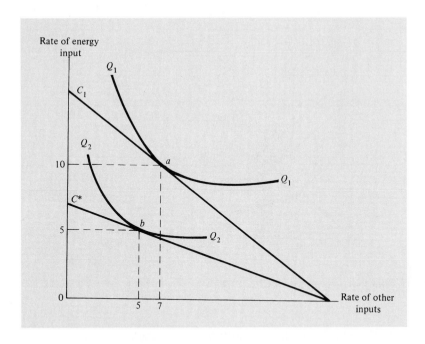

Effect of Increased Energy Cost on Optimal Input Rates.

production systems, principles of managerial economics predict that firms will substitute other inputs for the relatively more expensive energy products. In the figure, the input of energy is measured on the vertical axis, and a composite measure of other inputs is measured on the horizontal axis. Assume that before the increase in energy prices, a hypothetical firm is producing at point a, where the Q_1 isoquant is tangent to the C_1 isocost. The optimal input ratio is 10:7 or ten units of energy for every seven units of the "other input."

If the price of energy increased, the isocost would pivot downward from C_1 to C^*. The firm now will operate at point b, where the ratio of energy to other inputs is 5:5, or one unit of energy for every unit of the "other" input. Thus the result of the higher price of energy is that the firm has substituted other inputs for energy.

As shown in the preceding table, producers in the United States did reduce their dependence on energy by substituting other inputs for energy. As measured by energy consumption (thousand Btu) per dollar of value added, dependence on this input was reduced significantly. Even an energy-producing sector, petroleum refining, conserved on its use of energy by using relatively more of other inputs.

The Expansion Path

Consider the system of isoquants and isocosts shown in Figure 6-11. Suppose that a firm is producing 1,000 units of output using ten units of capital and ten units of labor (i.e., point a) and the input prices are $w = 2$ and $r = 2$. Thus the cost of this input combination is $40. At point a, the 1,000-unit isoquant is tangent

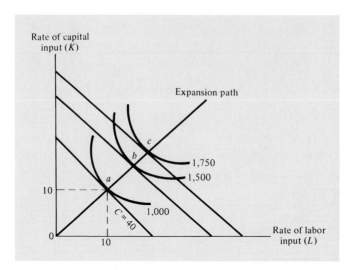

FIGURE 6-11 **The Expansion Path for the Firm.**

to the $40 isocost line. If output is to be increased, how much capital and labor will be hired? That is, how will the firm expand production? Clearly it will move to point b if 1,500 units are to be produced and then to point c if 1,750 units of output are to be produced. In general, the firm expands by moving from one tangency or efficient production point to another. These efficient points represent the expansion path. An expansion path is formally defined as the set of combinations of capital and labor that meet the efficiency condition $MP_L/w = MP_K/r$.

An equation for the expansion path can be determined by first substituting the marginal product functions and input prices into the efficiency condition, and then by solving for capital as a function of labor. For example, suppose that the production function is of the form $Q = 100K^{1/2}L^{1/2}$. The corresponding marginal product functions are

$$MP_L = \frac{dQ}{dL} = 50\frac{K^{1/2}}{L^{1/2}}$$

and

$$MP_K = \frac{dQ}{dK} = 50\frac{L^{1/2}}{K^{1/2}}$$

Substituting the marginal product equations in the efficiency condition $(MP_L/MP_K = w/r)$ yields

$$\frac{50\dfrac{K^{1/2}}{L^{1/2}}}{50\dfrac{L^{1/2}}{K^{1/2}}} = \frac{w}{r}$$

Solving for K gives:

$$K = \frac{w}{r}L \tag{6-20}$$

This expression is the equation for the expansion path for the production function $Q = 100K^{1/2}L^{1/2}$. If w and r are known, equation (6-20) defines the efficient combination of capital and labor for producing any rate of output. That is, it is an equation for an expansion path such as that shown in Figure 6-11. For example, if $w = 1$ and $r = 1$, the expansion path defined by equation (6-20) would be

$$K = L$$

If $w = 2$ and $r = 1$, the equation for the expansion path would be

$$K = 2L$$

If the expansion path is known, then knowing the isoquant–isocost system is not necessary to determine efficient production points. The firm will only produce at those points on the expansion path.

The expansion path indicates optimal input combinations, but it does not indicate the specific rate of output associated with that rate of input use. The output rate is determined by substituting the equation for the expansion path into the original production function. In the example, substituting the equation for the expansion path, $K = (w/r)L$, into the production function, $Q = 100K^{1/2}L^{1/2}$ yields

$$Q = 100 \left(\frac{w}{r}L \right)^{1/2} L^{1/2}$$

or

$$Q = 100L \left(\frac{w}{r} \right)^{1/2} \tag{6-21}$$

The two equations (6-20) and (6-21) have three unknowns: K, L, and Q. [Recall that the prices of labor (w) and capital (r) are assumed to be known.] If the value of K, L, or Q is given, the efficient rate of the other two variables can be calculated.

Consider the problem of determining the efficient input combination for producing 1,000 units of output if $w = 4$ and $r = 2$. The steps are as follows. First, substitute $Q = 1,000$, $w = \$4$, and $r = \$2$ into equation (6-21) and solve for L. Thus

$$1,000 = 100L \left(\frac{4}{2} \right)^{1/2}$$

$$L = 7.07$$

Then, substitute $L = 7.07$ into (6-20), the equation for the expansion path, to find K.

$$K = \left(\frac{4}{2} \right) 7.07$$

$$K = 14.14$$

Thus the input combination ($K = 14.14$, $L = 7.07$) is the most efficient way to produce 1,000 units of output.

How would the input mix change if the price of capital increased to $r = 4$ and the firm still wanted to produce 1,000 units of output? Again, substitute $Q = 1,000$ into equation (6-21) and solve for L:

$$1,000 = 100L \sqrt{\frac{4}{4}}$$

$$L = 10$$

Now substitute $L = 10$ into equation (6-20) and solve for K:

$$K = \left(\frac{4}{4}\right)L$$

$$K = 10$$

The new efficient combination is ($K = 10$, $L = 10$). The firm responded to the higher price of capital by substituting labor for capital. That is, the capital input was reduced from 14.14 to 10 and the labor input was increased from 7.07 to 10.

KEY CONCEPTS

- If the price of one or both inputs changes, the firm will respond by substituting the input that has become relatively less expensive for the other input.
- The firm expands production by moving from one efficient production point (where the isoquant and isocost functions are tangent) to another. These efficient points define the firm's expansion path.
- By using the production function and the production efficiency conditions together, the optimal level of capital and labor used to produce any rate of output can be determined. This expansion path determines the efficient input combinations for any output rate.

Economies of Scale and Scope

In general, the cost of producing and marketing products depends both on the scale (i.e., the amount of labor and capital employed) and the scope (i.e., the array of different goods and services produced) of the firm's operations. The relationship of per-unit costs to changes in these two factors are referred to as economies of scale and economies of scope.

Economies of Scale

A given rate of input of capital and labor defines the scale of production. Proportionate changes in both inputs result in a change in that scale. The term *returns to scale* refers to the magnitude of the change in the rate of output relative to the change in scale. For example, given the production function

$$Q = 100K^{.5}L^{.5}$$

if both capital and labor are 10, output will be 1,000. A doubling of both input rates to 20 will result in a doubling of output to 2,000. This proportionate response of output to change in inputs is defined as *constant returns to scale*.

In general, there is no reason to expect that output will always change in proportion to the change in inputs. Output might increase more than in proportion (*increasing returns to scale*) or less than in proportion (*decreasing returns to scale*). Returns to scale are formally classified as follows. Given the general production function

$$Q = f(K, L) \qquad (6\text{-}22)$$

if both inputs are changed by some factor λ, output will change by a factor h. That is,

$$hQ = f(\lambda K, \lambda L) \qquad (6\text{-}23)$$

If $h = \lambda$, the production function is said to be characterized by constant returns to scale because the change in output is proportional to the change in both inputs. If $h < \lambda$, there are decreasing returns to scale, and if $h > \lambda$, returns to scale are increasing.

There is a simple way to test for constant, decreasing, or increasing returns to scale. Solve the production function (i.e., determine the rate of output) for one set of input values, double both inputs, and again solve for output. If output doubled, the production function is characterized by constant returns to scale over that range of output. If output changed by less than twice the initial rate, decreasing returns to scale apply. Finally, if output more than doubled, the function exhibits increasing returns to scale.[4]

For production functions of the Cobb–Douglas type (i.e., $Q = AK^\alpha L^\beta$), the arithmetic sum of the exponents (i.e., $\alpha + \beta$) can be used to determine if returns to scale are decreasing, constant, or increasing. This is demonstrated by taking the basic Cobb–Douglas production function

$$Q = AK^\alpha L^\beta$$

and doubling both inputs, which will increase Q by a factor h, that is,

$$hQ = A(2K)^\alpha (2L)^\beta$$

Rewriting yields

$$hQ = 2^\alpha 2^\beta (AK^\alpha L^\beta)$$

or

$$hQ = 2^{\alpha+\beta}(AK^\alpha L^\beta)$$

But $Q = AK^\alpha L^\beta$. Hence the factor $h = 2^{\alpha+\beta}$ and will be less than 2, equal to 2, or greater than 2, depending on whether $(\alpha + \beta)$ is less than 1, equal to 1, or greater

---

[4] There are production functions that are characterized by increasing returns over part of the output range and decreasing returns over another part of the range. For these functions, this simple technique will test for the nature of returns to scale only for that part of the output range that is evaluated.

than 1, respectively. Thus the three possibilities are

Sum of Exponents ($\alpha + \beta$)	Returns to Scale
Less than one	Decreasing
Equal to one	Constant
Greater than one	Increasing

For example, the production function $Q = 10K^{0.5}L^{0.6}$ is characterized by increasing returns to scale because $\alpha + \beta$ (i.e., $0.5 + 0.6$) is greater than unity. In contrast, the function $Q = 20K^{0.4}L^{0.5}$ exhibits decreasing returns to scale because the sum of the exponents is 0.9.

The principle applies to Cobb–Douglas production functions with any number of inputs. Given a production function of the form $Q = AK_1^{\alpha}K_2^{\beta}L_1^{\delta}L_2^{\gamma}$, returns to scale would be decreasing, constant, or increasing if $\alpha + \beta + \delta + \nu$ is less than 1, equal to 1, or greater than 1, respectively.

There are several reasons why increasing returns to scale occur. First, technologies that are cost-effective at high levels of production generally have higher unit costs at lower levels of output. For example, the million-dollar machinery used for cutting and stamping auto bodies by General Motors would make little sense for a small custom car manufacturer. Geometric relations are another factor causing decreasing average costs. A gas company using 12-inch pipe has 3 cubic inches of pipe volume per square inch of pipe surface, while a firm with output sufficient to justify 24-inch pipe will have 6 cubic inches of volume per square inch of surface. The reduced cost per unit of pipe volume occurs because the materials requirement varies with the diameter of the pipe, while the volume varies with the square of the radius of the pipe. Thus the larger firm using bigger pipelines will have lower unit costs.

Two other causes of increasing returns are specialization of labor and inventory economies. As a firm becomes larger, the demand for employee expertise in specific areas grows. Instead of being generalists, workers can concentrate on learning all the aspects of particular segments of the production process. Usually, a worker who only has to perform one task can do it more rapidly and more accurately than one who must do many different jobs. Size also affects unit costs because larger firms may not have to increase inventories or replacement parts proportionately with size. For example, suppose that a small firm uses a machine that is critical to the firm's operations. Let the probability of a machine breakdown during a month be 10 percent. If a replacement is not readily obtainable from a nearby supplier, the firm may be forced to keep a backup on the premises. Suppose that a larger firm uses five of the same machines, each with a 10 percent probability of malfunctioning. The probability that two of those machines will break down in a month is 0.1×0.1, or 1 percent. The likelihood that the five machines will become inoperative is 0.1^5, which is essentially zero. Thus whereas the small firm may be required to have one backup machine for each operating machine, the larger firm may have a high degree of reliability with a much lower ratio of backup to operating machines and hence a lower per-unit cost.

Decreasing returns to scale may occur because the firm grows so large that management cannot effectively manage it. For example, the costs of gathering, organizing, and reviewing information on all aspects of a large firm may increase more rapidly than output. Further, managing large numbers of employees and coordinating the several divisions of a large firm may be difficult.

Economies of Scope

Firms often find that per-unit costs are lower when two or more products are produced. Sometimes the firm will have excess capacity that can be used to produce other products with little or no increase in its capital costs. One example is the firm that reconfigured its passenger planes each night by removing seats to haul packages and freight. Ski resorts have developed various warm-weather activities (e.g., Alpine slides, mountain bike paths, etc.) to allow them to use ski lifts on a year-round basis.

Other firms have taken advantage of their unique skills or comparative advantage in marketing to develop products that are complementary with the firm's existing products or that would simply be logical items for the firm's sales staff to sell on their regular calls on retail stores. For example, Proctor and Gamble, a large household products firm, sells all kinds of cleaning products, not just one or two. Sometimes these products are complements (e.g., laundry detergent, bleach, and fabric softeners), whereas other products are specialized substitutes.

If cost data are known, a quantitative measure of economies of scope can be determined. Consider a firm that can produce both stationary and notebook paper. The cost is $50,000 per 1,000 reams of stationary and $30,000 per 1,000 reams of notebook paper if the firm produces only one of these products. However, 1,000 reams of each type of paper can be produced for a total of $70,000 if both are produced together.

A measure of economies of scope (S) is

$$S = \frac{TC(Q_A) + TC(Q_B) - TC(Q_A, Q_B)}{TC(Q_A, Q_B)}$$

where $TC(Q_A)$ is the cost of producing product A alone, $TC(Q_B)$ is the total cost of producing Q_B units of product B alone, and $TC(Q_A, Q_B)$ is the total cost of producing both A and B. Given the data on the paper firm, the extent of economies of scope is

$$S = \frac{50,000 + 30,000 - 70,000}{70,000} = 0.14$$

or a 14 percent reduction in total costs associated with producing both products instead of just one. Clearly, a firm that can take advantage of economies of scope can have lower costs than other firms. In a competitive market, aggressive decision makers always will be looking for ways to capture such economies.

KEY CONCEPTS

- *Returns to scale* refers to the change in output relative to proportionate changes in inputs.
- Returns to scale are said to be:
  Increasing if output increases more than in proportion to the change in inputs.
  Decreasing if output increases less than in proportion to the change in inputs.
  Constant if the change in output is proportionate to the change in inputs.
- *Economies of scope* refers to per-unit cost reductions that occur when a firm produces two or more products instead of just one product.

Estimating the Production Function

The principles of production theory just developed are fundamental to an understanding of economics and provide an important conceptual framework for analyzing managerial problems. However, short-run output decisions and long-run planning often require more than just this conceptual framework. That is, quantitative estimates of the parameters of the production function are required for some decisions.

The general approach to estimating production functions is the same as that for most estimation problems. One of the first tasks is to select a functional form, that is, the specific relationship among the relevant economic variables. Although a variety of functional forms have been used to describe production relationships, only the Cobb–Douglas production function is discussed here. Recall that the general Cobb–Douglas function is of the form

$$Q = AK^\alpha L^\beta$$

where A, α, and β are the parameters that, when estimated, describe the quantitative relationship between the inputs (K and L) and output (Q).

The marginal products of capital and labor are functions of the parameters A, α, and β and the rates of the capital and labor inputs. That is,

$$MP_K = \frac{\partial Q}{\partial K} = \alpha AK^{\alpha-1}L^\beta$$

$$MP_L = \frac{\partial Q}{\partial L} = \beta AK^\alpha L^{\beta-1}$$

It was shown earlier that the sum of these parameters ($\alpha + \beta$) can be used to determine returns to scale. That is,

$(\alpha + \beta) > 1 \Rightarrow$ increasing returns to scale,
$(\alpha + \beta) = 1 \Rightarrow$ constant returns to scale, and
$(\alpha + \beta) < 1 \Rightarrow$ decreasing returns to scale.

Having numerical estimates for the parameters of the production function provides significant information about the production system under study. The marginal products for each input and returns to scale can all be determined from the estimated function.

The Cobb–Douglas function does not lend itself directly to estimation by the regression methods described in Chapter 4 because it is a nonlinear relationship. Technically, an equation must be a linear function of the parameters in order to use the ordinary least-squares regression method of estimation. However, a linear equation can be derived by taking the logarithm of each term. That is,

$$\log Q = \log A + a \log K + b \log L \tag{6-25}$$

That this is simply a linear relationship can be seen by setting

$$y = \log Q, \qquad A^* = \log A, \qquad X_1 = \log K, \qquad X_2 = \log L$$

and rewriting the function as

$$y = A^* + aX_1 + bX_2 \tag{6-26}$$

This function can be estimated directly by the least-squares regression technique and the estimated parameters used to determine all the important production relationships. Then the antilogarithm of both sides can be taken, which transforms the estimated function back to its conventional multiplicative form, as demonstrated in the following example.

EXAMPLE _____

Estimating a Production Function

Given the following data on output and inputs for ten production periods:

Production Period	Output (Q)	Capital (K)	Labor (L)
1	225	10	20
2	240	12	22
3	278	10	26
4	212	14	18
5	199	12	16
6	297	16	24
7	242	16	20
8	155	10	14
9	215	8	20
10	160	8	14

1. Estimate the parameters (A, α, and β) of a Cobb–Douglas production function using the least-squares regression method.
2. Use the estimated parameters to determine
   a. Returns to scale.
   b. Equations for the marginal product of labor and capital.
3. Calculate the marginal products of capital and labor for the input combination $\{K = 20, L = 30\}$.

SOLUTION   1. First, transform the production function by taking the natural logarithm of each term in the function, that is,

$$\ln Q = \ln A + \alpha \ln K + \beta \ln L$$

By transforming the output, capital, and labor data into logarithms, the least-squares regression method can be used to estimate the parameters. Using a standard multiple regression computer program, the following results were obtained:

$$\ln Q = 2.322 + 0.194 \ln K + 0.878 \ln L \qquad R^2 = 0.97$$
$$\ln Q = (12.66) + (3.74) \ln K + (14.09) \ln L \qquad R^2 = 0.97$$

The estimated parameters are $\alpha = 0.194$, $\beta = 0.878$, and the value of A is determined by taking the antilogarithm of 2.322, which is 10.2. The t-statistic for each estimated parameter is shown in parentheses below the estimate. Thus the estimated production function in its original functional form is

$$Q = 10.2 K^{0.194} L^{0.878}$$

2. Returns to scale are increasing because $\alpha + \beta = 1.072$ is greater than 1. The marginal product functions for capital and labor are

$$MP_K = \alpha A K^{\alpha-1} L^{\beta} = 0.194(10.2) K^{-0.806} L^{0.878}$$

and

$$MP_L = \beta A K^{\alpha} L^{\beta-1} = 0.878(10.2) K^{-0.194} L^{-0.122}$$

3. Substituting the estimated values for the parameters A, α, and β and the specified values of capital and labor ($K = 20$ and $L = 30$) yields the following marginal products:

$$MP_K = 0.194(10.2)(20)^{-0.806}(30)^{0.878} = 3.50$$
$$MP_L = 0.878(10.2)(20)^{0.194}(30)^{-0.122} = 10.58$$

These estimates mean that a one-unit change in capital with labor held constant at 30 would result in a 3.50-unit change in output, and a one-unit change in labor with capital held constant at 20 would be associated with a 10.58-unit change in output.

CASE STUDY

Empirical Estimates of Production Functions

There are many empirical studies of production functions in the United States and in other countries. One comprehensive study of a number of manufacturing industries was made by John R. Moroney. He estimated the production function

$$Q = A K^{\alpha} L_1^{\beta} L_2^{\gamma}$$

where K is the dollar value of capital, L_1 is production worker-hours, and L_2 is nonproduction worker-hours. The data were taken from the Census of Manufactures, a comprehensive cross-section survey of all manufacturing firms in the United States that is made every five years by the U.S. Department of Commerce.

A summary of the estimated values of the production elasticities (i.e., α, β, and γ) and R^2, the coefficient of determination, for each industry is shown in the following table.

Estimated Production Elasticities for 17 Industries

Industry	Estimate of α	β	γ	α + β + γ	R²
Food and beverages	0.555*	0.438*	0.076*	1.070*	0.987
Textiles	0.121	0.549*	0.335*	1.004	0.991
Apparel	0.128	0.437*	0.477*	1.041*	0.982
Lumber	0.392*	0.504*	0.145	1.041	0.951
Furniture	0.205	0.802*	0.103	1.109*	0.966
Paper and pulp	0.421*	0.367	0.197*	0.984	0.990
Printing	0.459*	0.045*	0.574*	1.079*	0.989
Chemicals	0.200*	0.553*	0.336*	1.090*	0.970
Petroleum	0.308*	0.546*	0.093	0.947	0.983
Rubber and plastics	0.481*	1.033*	−0.458	1.056	0.991
Leather	0.076	0.441*	0.523	1.040	0.990
Stone and clay	0.632*	0.032	0.366*	1.029	0.961
Primary metals	0.371*	0.077	0.509*	0.958	0.969
Fabricated metals	0.151*	0.512*	0.365*	1.027*	0.995
Nonelectrical machinery	0.404*	0.228	0.389*	1.020	0.980
Electrical machinery	0.368*	0.429*	0.229*	1.026	0.983
Transportation equipment	0.234*	0.749*	0.041	1.023	0.972

* Estimated parameter is statistically significant.

Note that the R^2 values are all very high. Even the lowest, 0.951 for the lumber industry, means that more than 95 percent of the variation in output is explained by variation in the three inputs. A test of significance was made for each estimated parameter, $\hat{\alpha}$, $\hat{\beta}$, and $\hat{\gamma}$, using the standard t-test. Those estimated production elasticities that are statistically significant at the 0.05 level are noted with an asterisk.

Of somewhat more interest, the sum of the estimated production elasticities $(\alpha + \beta + \gamma)$ provides a point estimate of returns to scale in each industry. Although the sum exceeds unity in fourteen of the seventeen industries, it is statistically significant only in the following industries: food and beverages, apparel, furniture, printing, chemicals, and fabricated metals. Thus only in those six industries can one be confident that there are increasing returns to scale. For example, in the furniture industry, a 1 percent increase in all inputs is estimated to result in a 1.109 percent increase in output.

SOURCE: J. R. Moroney, "Cobb–Douglas Production Functions and Returns to Scale in U.S. Manufacturing Industry," *Western Economic Journal 6* (December):39–51, 1967.

KEY CONCEPTS

- The Cobb–Douglas production function $Q = AK^{\alpha}L^{\beta}$ is frequently used to estimate production relationships.
- To estimate a Cobb–Douglas production function using the ordinary least-squares regression method, the function must be transformed into a linear

relationship by taking the logarithm of each term (i.e., $\log Q = \log A + \alpha \log K + \beta \log L$).

Summary

Firms buy capital and labor and transform them through the production process into output of goods and services to meet the demands of consumers and other firms. The production function is an engineering or technological concept that specifies the maximum rate of output obtainable with given rates of input of capital and labor. Decisions on optimal production rates and/or efficient input combinations require that data on input prices be combined with the information generated by the production function.

The short run is defined as the period during which the rate of input use of one factor of production is fixed. By varying the rate of input of the other factor, total, average, and marginal product functions are determined. The law of diminishing marginal returns states that as more of a variable input is combined with a fixed input, a point will be reached where marginal product declines. The marginal revenue product function (MRP), found by multiplying marginal product by marginal revenue, is the firm's demand curve for an input. The profit-maximizing firm will hire an input until MRP equals the price of the input.

An isoquant is derived from the production function and shows all combinations of labor and capital that will produce a given rate of output. The isocost line shows all combinations of capital and labor that can be purchased for a given cost. If one input price changes, the slope of the isocost line will change.

The firm faces one of three production problems: (1) maximize output subject to a cost constraint, (2) minimize cost subject to an output constraint, or (3) produce that output rate that will maximize profit. Regardless of the problem addressed, the optimal input combination is determined by the tangency of an isoquant and isocost curve. At that point the slope of the isoquant [the marginal rate of technical substitution (MRTS)] equals the ratio of the input prices. The firm's expansion path is defined as those points that satisfy the tangency condition.

For production to be efficient, the marginal product per dollar of input cost must be the same for all inputs. If that condition is not met, there is some way to substitute one input for the other and increase output at no additional cost. In addition, profit maximization requires that all inputs be hired until the marginal revenue product of each input equals the input's price.

The concept of returns to scale refers to the change in output associated with proportionate changes in all inputs. Such returns are increasing, decreasing, or constant, depending on whether output increases more than in proportion, less than in proportion, or in proportion to the input changes. Increasing returns to scale may be explained by production technology that is cost-efficient only at high output rates, specialization of labor, and by inventory economies. Decreasing returns to scale may occur when firms grow so large that they are difficult to manage. Economies of scope refer to a reduction in per-unit costs when a firm increases the number of products that it produces.

Decision making often requires a quantitative estimate of the parameters of the production function. Having quantitative estimates of the parameters of a production function allows determination of the marginal product of each input and economies of scale. For a Cobb–Douglas production function, returns to scale are constant, increasing, or decreasing, depending on whether the sum of the estimated exponents is equal to 1, greater than 1, or less than 1, respectively.

Discussion Questions

6-1. Explain the concept of a production function. Why is only having qualitative information about the production function inadequate for making decisions about efficient input combinations and the profit-maximizing rate of output?

6-2. Explain the law of diminishing marginal returns and provide an example of this phenomenon.

6-3. What is the difference between the short run and the long run? What are examples of a firm where the short run would be quite short (e.g., a few days or weeks) and where it would be quite long (e.g., several months or a year or more)? Explain.

6-4. What is meant by the statement that "firms operate in the short run and plan in the long run?" Relate this statement to the operation of the college or university that you are attending.

6-5. Legislation in the United States requires that most firms pay workers at least a specified minimum wage per hour. Use principles of marginal productivity to explain how such laws might affect the quantity of labor employed.

6-6. What would the isoquants look like if all inputs were nearly perfect substitutes in a production process? What if there was near-zero substitutability between inputs?

6-7. Explain why the isocost function will shift in a parallel fashion if the cost level changes, but the isocost will pivot about one of the intercepts if the price of either input changes.

6-8. Suppose wage rates at a firm are raised 10 percent. Use theoretical principles of production to show how the relative substitution of one input for another occurs as a result of the increased price of labor. Provide an example of how input substitution has been made in higher education.

6-9. When estimating production functions, what would be some of the problems of measuring output and inputs for each of the following?
a. A multiproduct firm.
b. A construction company.
c. An entire economy.

Problems

6-1. Use the production function

$$Q = 10K^{0.5}L^{0.6}$$

to complete the following production table.

Rate of Capital Input (K)

6	24.5			56.3		71.8
5						
4		30.3				
3					45.5	
2			27.3			
1	10.0					29.3
	1	2	3	4	5	6

Rate of Labor Input (L)

a. For this production system, are returns to scale decreasing, constant, or increasing? Explain.

b. Suppose the wage rate is $28, the price of capital also is $28 per unit, and the firm currently is producing 30.3 units of output per period using four units of capital and two units of labor. Is this an efficient resource combination? Explain. What would be a more efficient (not necessarily the best) combination? Why? (*HINT:* Compare the marginal products of capital and labor at the initial input combination.)

6-2. Use the data from problem 6-1 to answer the following questions.

a. If the rate of capital input is fixed at three and if output sells for $5 per unit, determine the total, average, and marginal product functions and the marginal revenue product function for labor in the following table.

L	TP_L	AP_L	MP_L	MRP_L
0				
1				
2				
3				
4				
5				
6				

b. Using the data from part (a), if the wage rate is $28 per unit, how much labor should be employed?

c. If the rate of labor input is fixed at 5 and the price of output is $5 per unit, determine the total, average, and marginal product functions for capital and the marginal revenue product of capital in the following table.

K	TP_K	AP_K	MP_K	MRP_K
0				
1				
2				
3				
4				
5				
6				

d. Using the data from part (c), if the price of capital is $40 per unit, how many units of capital should be employed?

6-3. International Publishing has kept the following data on labor input and production of textbooks for each of eight production periods.

Production Period:	1	2	3	4	5	6	7	8
Labor Input:	4	3	6	8	2	7	5	1
Output of Books (Total Product):	260	190	310	240	110	290	300	50

a. Use the data on labor input and total product to compute the average and marginal product for labor input rates from one to eight. (Assume that a zero labor input would result in zero output.)

b. Using two graphs similar to that of Figure 6.3, plot the total product function in the upper graph and average and marginal product functions in the lower graph. On the graph identify the rate of labor input: (1) where total output is at a maximum and the corresponding point where marginal product is zero; (2) where there is an inflection point on the total product function and the corresponding point where the marginal product function is at a maximum; and (3) where the slope of a line drawn through the origin to a point on the total product function would have maximum slope and the corresponding point where the average product curve is at a maximum.

c. Given that the objective of the firm is to maximize profit, can you determine from these data how much output should be produced? If not, what additional information would you need? Can you think of any circumstance where the firm would use more than six units of labor per period in this production process?

6-4. The marginal product of labor function for Central Milling Inc. is given by the equation

$$MP_L = 10 \left(\frac{K}{L}\right)^{0.5}$$

Currently, the firm is using 100 units of capital and 121 units of labor. Given the very specialized nature of the capital equipment, it takes six to nine months to increase the capital stock, but the rate of labor input can be varied daily. If the price of labor is $10 per unit and the price of output is $2 per unit, is the firm operating efficiently in the short run? If not, explain why, and determine the optimal rate of labor input.

6-5. For each of the following production functions, determine whether returns to scale are decreasing, constant, or increasing.
   a. $Q = 2K + 3L + KL$
   b. $Q = 20K^{0.6}L^{0.5}$
   c. $Q = 100 + 3K + 2L$
   d. $Q = 5K^{a}L^{b}$, where $a + b = 1$
   e. $Q = K/L$

6-6. The revenue department of a state government employs certified public accountants (CPAs) to audit corporate tax returns and bookkeepers to audit individual returns. CPAs are paid $31,200 per year, while the annual salary of a bookkeeper is $18,200. Given the current staff of CPAs and bookkeepers, a study made by the department's economist shows that adding one year of a CPA's time to auditing corporate returns results in an average additional tax collection of $52,000. In contrast, an additional bookkeeper adds tax collections of $41,600 per year.
   a. If the department's objective is to maximize tax revenue collected, is the present mix of CPAs and bookkeepers optimal? Explain.
   b. If the present mix of CPAs and bookkeepers is not optimal, explain what reallocation should be made. That is, should the department hire more CPAs and fewer bookkeepers or vice versa?

6-7. The production function for Superlite Sailboats, Inc., is

$$Q = 20K^{0.5}L^{0.5}$$

with marginal product functions

$$MP_K = 10\left(\frac{L}{K}\right)^{0.5} \quad \text{and} \quad MP_L = 10\left(\frac{K}{L}\right)^{0.5}$$

   a. If the price of capital is $5 per unit and the price of labor is $4 per unit, determine the expansion path for the firm.
   b. The firm currently is producing 200 units of output per period using input rates of $L = 4$ and $K = 25$. Is this an efficient input combination? Why or why not? If not, determine the efficient input combination for producing an output rate of 200.

6-8. For the production function $Q = 20K^{0.5}L^{0.5}$

determine four combinations of capital and labor that will produce 100 and 200 units of output. Plot these points on a graph and use them to sketch the 100- and 200-unit isoquants.

6-9. Suppose the price of labor is $10 and the price of capital is $2.5.

a. Use this information to determine the isocost equations corresponding to a total cost of $200 and $500.
b. Plot these two isocost lines on a graph.
c. If the price of labor falls from $10 per unit to $8 per unit, determine the new $500 isocost line and plot it on the same diagram used in part (b).

6-10. Consider two firms, A and B, with the following production functions:

Firm A: $Q_A = 100K^{0.8}L^{0.2}$ Firm B: $Q_B = 100K^{0.5}L^{0.5}$

a. If both firms use 25 units of capital and 25 units of labor, what is the output rate for each firm?
b. If the input prices are $r = \$1$ and $w = \$1$, is the input combination $K = 25$ and $L = 25$ efficient for firm A? For firm B?
c. If the input combination $K = 25$ and $L = 25$ is not efficient for either firm A or firm B, determine the efficient ratio of the two inputs for each firm. (*NOTE:* Do not calculate unique values for K and L but only the ratio of K to L that is efficient; that is, find the input ratio defined by the expansion path.)

6-11. The Economic Planning Department at International Chemicals, Inc. has used regression analysis to estimate the firm's production function as

$$\ln Q = 3 + 0.25 \ln K + 0.75 \ln L$$

where "ln" denotes the natural logarithm of the variable.

a. If the capital stock is fixed at 16, the price of labor is $200 per unit, and the price of the firm's only product, sulfuric acid, is $10 per unit, determine the rate of labor input that will maximize the firm's profit.
b. If both the capital and labor inputs are variable the price of labor is $200 per unit, and the price of capital is $100 per unit, determine the input rates for both labor and capital that will maximize profit.

Problems Requiring Calculus

6-12. Given the production function

$$Q = AK^{\alpha}L^{\beta}N^{\gamma}$$

where Q is the rate of output and K, L, and N represent inputs of capital, labor, and land, respectively, determine

a. The specific conditions under which returns to scale would be increasing, constant, and decreasing.
b. The equation for the marginal product function for each input.

6-13. A production process uses only one input, labor, and is described by the following production function:

$$Q = 25L^2 - \frac{L^3}{3}$$

(*NOTE:* This function is applicable only for labor input rates between 0 and 75.)

Over what output ranges are marginal returns increasing, decreasing (but still positive), and negative?

6-14. Squaretire, Inc., a small producer of automobile tires, has the following production function:

$$Q = 100K^{0.5}L^{0.5}$$

During the last production period, the firm operated efficiently and used input rates of 100 and 25 for capital and labor, respectively.

a. What is the marginal product of capital and the marginal product of labor based on the input rates specified?

b. If the price of capital was $20 per unit, what was the wage rate?

c. For the next production period, the price per unit of capital is expected to increase to $25 while the wage rate and the labor input will remain unchanged under the terms of the labor contract with the United Rubber Workers Local No. 25. If the firm maintains efficient production, what input rate of capital will be used?

6-15. Given the production function

$$Q = 30K^{0.7}L^{0.5}$$

and input prices $r = 20$ and $w = 30$,

a. Determine an equation for the expansion path.

b. What is the efficient input combination for an output rate of $Q = 200$? For $Q = 500$?

6-16. The production function for United Foodstuffs is

$$Q = 20K^{0.5}L^{0.5}$$

The initial prices of the inputs are $w = 20$ and $r = 30$. Under the labor contract with a national union, at least the current employment level of 300 workers must be maintained through the next production period. (However, more workers can be hired if necessary.)

a. In the previous production period, the firm produced 4,899 units of output. Assuming efficient production, what was the rate of capital input?

b. Because of the national recession, the desired level of output for the next production period is only 4,000 units. What is the optimal rate of capital input?

6-17. Output for the Cloverdale Farm in Southern Iowa is given by the production function

$$Q = 10L^{0.7}N^{0.3}$$

where Q is the rate of output, and L and N are the rates of labor and land, respectively. In the previous production period, the farm produced 2,633 units of output using 500 acres of land (the entire cropland available) and 200 units of labor. As the result of the farm's participation in a government soil-bank program, 100 acres must be left fallow (i.e., unused) in the next production period.

a. What will be the rate of output in the next period if the same labor input rate is used together with the reduced land input?

b. How much additional labor would be needed to maintain output at the rate achieved in the original period? Explain.

6-18. The following table shows the relationship between hours of study and final examination grades in each of three classes for a particular student who has a total of 15 hours to prepare for these tests. If the objective is to maximize the average grade in the three classes, how many hours should this student allocate to preparation for each of these classes? Explain your approach to this problem.

Managerial Economics		History		Chemistry	
Hours	Grade	Hours	Grade	Hours	Grade
0	40	0	50	0	30
1	50	1	60	1	50
2	59	2	69	2	60
3	67	3	77	3	66
4	74	4	84	4	71
5	79	5	90	5	74
6	83	6	95	6	76
7	86	7	96	7	77
8	88	8	97	8	77
9	89	9	97	9	77
10	89	10	97	10	77

6-19. Western Fabricating manufactures metal office furniture with the following production function:

$$Q = 20K^{0.1}L^{0.9}$$

The firm currently is efficiently using 20 units of capital and 50 units of labor.

a. What is the rate of output?

b. What are the relative prices of capital and labor (i.e., what is the ratio of the two input prices?) Can you determine the actual price of labor and capital? Explain.

c. If output sells for $200 per unit, can you determine the firm's profit? Why or why not?

Microcomputer Problems

The following problems can be solved by using the microcomputer program TOOLS, available with the study guide, or by using other computer software.

6-20. The capital and labor necessary to produce various quantities of bicycles are shown below.

Production Period	Quantity	Labor	Capital
1	1,100	65	40
2	660	35	15
3	1,200	75	45
4	1,000	60	30
5	900	55	30
6	840	45	25
7	1,050	60	35
8	500	30	10
9	1,130	65	45
10	700	40	15

a. Use regression analysis to estimate quantity as a multiplicative function of labor and capital. Determine the estimated equation, t-statistics, and the coefficient of determination. What are the marginal product equations? What does the equation imply about returns to scale?

b. Let the cost of capital be $15 and the wage rate be $20. Determine the equation for the expansion path. How much labor and capital should a firm use to produce 200 units of output efficiently?

6-21. Following are data on gross national product, labor input, and capital for the Taiwanese manufacturing sector for 1958–1972.

Year	GNP	Labor	Capital
1958	8911.4	281.5	120,753
1959	10,873.2	284.4	122,242
1960	11,132.5	289.0	125,263
1961	12,086.5	375.8	128,539
1962	12,767.5	375.2	131,427
1963	16,347.1	402.5	134,267
1964	19,542.7	478.0	139,038
1965	21,075.9	553.4	146,450
1966	23,052.0	616.7	153,714
1967	26,128.2	695.7	164,783
1968	29,563.7	790.3	176,864
1969	33,376.6	816.0	188,146
1970	38,354.3	848.4	205,841
1971	46,868.3	873.1	221,748
1972	54,308.0	999.2	239,715

a. Use regression analysis to estimate a Cobb–Douglas production function for Taiwan. Which coefficients are significant at the 0.05 level? What proportion of the variation in GNP is explained by variations in capital and labor?

b. Does the production process exhibit constant, increasing, or decreasing returns to scale? Explain.

CHAPTER 7

Cost Theory

Preview _____

The theory of cost, together with the principles of demand and production, constitute three of the basic areas of managerial economics. Few significant resource allocation decisions are made without a thorough analysis of costs. For the profit-maximizing firm, the decision to add a new product is made by comparing additional revenues to additional costs associated with that new product. Similarly, decisions on capital investment (e.g., new machinery or a warehouse) are made by comparing the rate of return on the investment with the opportunity cost of the funds used to make the capital acquisitions. Costs are also important in the nonprofit sector. For example, to obtain funding for a new dam, a government agency must demonstrate that the value of the benefits of the dam, such as flood control and water supply, exceeds the cost of the project.

This chapter focuses on those principles of cost theory integral to decisions about optimal price and output rates. In contrast to the traditional approach to costs where historic cost data are typically used, the economist focuses on the concept of opportunity cost. In the first section, this economic concept of cost is developed. Next, the link between production theory and the principles of cost is developed. It is shown that efficient resource combinations for producing specific rates of output can be translated into cost data. Cost functions are then developed for both the short-run and long-run cases. Then, two special cost-related topics are discussed—profit contribution analysis and the principle of operating leverage. Finally, the methods used to empirically estimate cost functions are developed and applied.

The Economic Concept of Cost _____

Because the term *cost* has different meanings, it is essential that the term be defined precisely. As suggested previously, the traditional definition tends to focus on the explicit and historical dimension of cost. In contrast, the economic approach to cost emphasizes opportunity cost rather than historical cost and includes both explicit and implicit costs.

Opportunity Costs

Fundamental to the managerial economist is the concept of opportunity cost. The best measure of cost of a consumer product or a factor of production is what must be given up to obtain that product or factor. For example, a consumer who pays ten dollars for dinner may have to give up going to a concert. The manager who hires an additional secretary may have to forgo hiring an additional clerk in the shipping department. Alternatively, the cost to society of adding another soldier to the army is not only the dollar outlay for salary, uniforms, and equipment but also the forgone output this individual would have produced as a civilian worker. In general, the opportunity cost of any decision is the value of the next best alternative that must be forgone.

The effective manager must view costs from this perspective. For example, budgeting is fundamental to most organizations. The very nature of that process implies that opportunity costs are incurred whenever budget resources are allocated to one department rather than another. A reallocation from the production department to the research and development group may result in new and better products in the future but at a cost of a lower production (and profit) rate for the current production period. Obviously, such a decision should be made only when management thinks that the potential for even greater profit in the future outweighs the reduced profit for the current period.

Explicit and Implicit Costs

Sometimes, the full opportunity cost of a business decision is not accounted for because of failure to include implicit costs. In general, *explicit costs* are those costs that involve an actual payment to other parties, while *implicit costs* represent the value of forgone opportunities but do not involve an actual cash payment. Implicit costs are just as important as explicit costs but are sometimes neglected because they are not as obvious. For example, a manager who runs his own business forgoes the salary that could have been earned working for someone else. This implicit cost generally is not reflected in accounting statements, but rational decision making requires that it be considered.

To see how reliance on historical rather than opportunity cost can lead to a poor decision, consider the following example. A bakery has an inventory of wheat that was purchased at $3 per bushel but that is now worth $5 per bushel. The firm is considering using this wheat to make a new whole wheat bread that will be sold to stores for $5 per unit (six loaves). Suppose that one bushel of wheat is required to make each unit of this new type of bread, while $1.50 of labor, energy, and other costs per unit of output are also incurred.

The traditional approach to cost would value the wheat input at $3 per bushel and estimate profit on the finished product to be $0.50 per unit, as shown in Table 7-1. In contrast, the economic approach to cost would value the wheat at the current market price of $5 per bushel. Analyzing the decision to product the new bread from this approach indicates a loss of $1.50 for each bushel. Note that the only difference in the two approaches is the value placed on the inventory of wheat.

Consider the same problem in another way. The money spent on the inventory of wheat is gone; now, how can the firm best use the inventory? That is, what will be the net revenue per bushel if the new bread is manufactured compared to selling the wheat inventory in the market without processing it? If the decision is made to manufacture the bread, the firm will have a net cash flow of $3.50 per bushel, that is, the $5 selling price less $1.50 of other costs. In contrast, if the wheat is simply sold rather than processed, the firm would receive a net cash flow of $5 per bushel. Clearly, selling the wheat rather than producing the bread

TABLE 7-1 **Traditional Versus Economic Approach to Determining Profit Per Unit of Output for a Bakery**

	Traditional Approach	Economic Approach
Price of finished product	$5.00	−$5.00
Less: Cost of wheat input	$3.00	−$5.00
Less: Other costs	$1.50	−$1.50
Net profit per unit	$0.50	−$1.50

is the better alternative because profits will be greater. The example demonstrates that the use of the correct cost concept is essential to sound decision making. It also suggests that costs incurred in the past are generally irrelevant when making decisions.

Normal Profit and Costs

In industries characterized by substantial competition, principles of economics predict that profits will be driven to zero in the long run. While this sounds inconsistent with the conventional idea that most firms report a profit each year, the apparent inconsistency disappears when the concepts of economic costs and economic profits are understood and used to measure revenues and costs.

Because all opportunity costs must be accounted for, the proper concept of cost includes a normal payment to all inputs, including managerial and entrepreneurial skills and capital supplied by the owners of the firm. A normal return to management or capital is the minimum payment necessary to keep those resources from moving to some other firm or industry. Thus cost includes a normal rate of profit. The term *economic profit* refers to profit in excess of these normal returns. That is, economic profit is defined as revenue less all economic costs.

A firm earning zero economic profit generally would show a positive profit on the income statement prepared by its accountants. This is because the normal returns to entrepreneurial skill and capital supplied by the owners are not included as costs on that statement. Unless otherwise indicated, the term *cost* will refer to all explicit and implicit costs, and the term *profit* will refer to revenues after all economic costs, including the normal returns just described, have been subtracted.

Marginal, Incremental, and Sunk Costs

Clearly, cost is an important consideration in decision making. But as the bakery example showed, it is essential that only those costs that matter be considered. Three types of cost need to be discussed: sunk costs, marginal costs, and incremental costs.

Sunk costs are expenditures that have been made in the past or that must be paid in the future as part of a contractual agreement. The costs paid for inventory and future rental payments on a warehouse that must be paid as part of a long-term lease are examples. In general, sunk costs are irrelevant in making decisions. For instance, suppose that the monthly rental payment on the warehouse is $1,000 but the firm finds it no longer needs the space. The firm offers to sublease the space but finds that the best offer is for $800 per month. Clearly, the firm should take that offer; the additional revenue, $800 per month, is greater than the additional cost, which is zero. The $1,000 per month payment is irrelevant because it must be made regardless of the decision to rent the warehouse space. In retrospect, the decision to enter the long-term lease was a mistake, but the costs associated with that decision are sunk and now irrelevant in the decision about what to do with the warehouse.

Marginal cost refers to the change in total cost associated with a one-unit change in output. This concept is integral to short-run decisions about profit-maximizing rates of output. For example, in an automobile manufacturing plant, the marginal cost of making one additional car per production period would be the labor, materials, and energy costs directly associated with that extra car. In contrast, the term *incremental cost* refers to the total additional cost of implementing a managerial decision. The costs associated with adding a new product line, acquiring a major competitor, or developing an in-house legal staff fall into the broader class of incremental costs. In a sense, marginal cost is that subcategory of incremental cost that refers to the additional cost associated with the decision to make marginal variations in the rate of output.

In the warehouse rental example, the only incremental costs the firm faces when subleasing the property may be the cost of preparing and negotiating the details of the new rental agreement. Clearly, the $1,000 per month sunk cost is not a component of incremental cost. It is essential that incremental cost measurement be done carefully so that all possible additional costs are included, but costs that are sunk are not included.

The Cost of Long-Lived Assets

Another area where accounting and economic definitions of cost diverge is for assets such as buildings, machinery, and other types of capital equipment that may last for a number of years. These are referred to as *long-lived assets*. The traditional approach to measuring the periodic cost of these assets is to combine historical cost and one of several depreciation methods to assign part of the historical cost to each year of the defined life of the asset so that the total expenses over that life will equal the historical cost. For example, using the straight-line depreciation method, an asset costing $1,000 and having a five-year life would be depreciated at the rate of $200 per year. Thus, the total historical cost will be exhausted entirely over this five-year period. The asset may have considerable value to the firm after this period, but this is not reflected in such an accounting statement. Often, tax guidelines and considerations dictate the decision on the depreciation method used. This approach to cost measurement is adequate if the objective is to have an arbitrary method for reporting on the flow of funds into and out of the business over some time interval or to meet income tax regulations. However, as a tool for managerial decision making, the approach is flawed.

In contrast, the economic approach determines the cost as the difference between the market value of the asset at the beginning and end of the period. If the market value of the machine just discussed was $1,000 at the beginning of the year and $600 at the end, the economic cost of using it for that period was $400, not $200, as indicated by the straight-line depreciation method. It is possible for some long-lived assets to actually increase in value over time, implying that their cost was negative for that period. This has been true for some buildings and other types of real estate.

KEY CONCEPTS

- Opportunity cost, the value of a resource in its next best use, is the best way to measure cost.
- Both explicit and implicit costs must be considered in decision making.
- Economic profit is revenue minus all costs, including normal returns to management and capital.
- In general, only incremental and marginal costs are relevant in decision making; sunk costs are of little or no importance.
- The economic cost of a long-lived asset during a period is the change in its market value from the beginning to the end of the period.

Production and Cost _____

A cost function relates cost to the rate of output. The basis for a cost function is the production function and the prices of inputs. Recall from Chapter 6 that the expansion path defines the efficient combination of capital and labor input rates for producing any rate of output. Thus the minimum cost of a specific level of output is found by multiplying the efficient rate of each input by their respective prices and summing the costs. The combination of that cost and the associated rate of output defines one point on the cost function.

In Chapter 6 it was shown that the production function, $Q = 100\ K^{.5}L^{.5}$, has an expansion path $K = (w/r)L$. Thus if the price of labor is 2 and the price of capital is 1, the expansion path would be $K = 2L$ and the firm would expand by adding inputs at the rate of two units of capital for each additional unit of labor. Table 7-2 shows a set of efficient labor–capital combinations, the rate of output associated with each combination, and the cost of those inputs. Columns (3) and (6) represent the long-run total cost schedule for this production function given that input prices are $w = 2$ and $r = 1$. This schedule shows the total cost of producing various rates of output. For example, the total cost of efficiently producing an output rate of 283 units per peirod is $8. That is, four units of capital at a price

TABLE 7-2 **Production and Cost Data**

(1)	(2)	(3)	(4)	(5)	(6)
				Cost	
K	L	Q	Capital	Labor	Total
2	1	141	$ 2	$ 2	$ 4
4	2	283	4	4	8
6	3	424	6	6	12
8	4	565	8	8	16
10	5	707	10	10	20

of $1 per unit and two units of labor at a price of $2 per unit would cost $8. The minimum cost of producing 424 units of output is $12. In this example it is a long-run function because both inputs are variable—there is no fixed factor of production.

In the short run, at least one factor of production is fixed, and the cost of that input is defined as *fixed cost*. Regardless of the rate of output, that cost does not change. That is, management has made a decision in the past that obligates the firm to pay certain costs that are independent of the rate of output. A long-term lease on a warehouse, an employment contract with an executive, and a collective bargaining agreement with a labor union are examples of commitments that may result in fixed costs. Fixed costs fall into the category of sunk costs.

As suggested in Chapter 6, the length of the operating period varies with the nature of the business. A child's lemonade stand may be able to vary all inputs in a matter of minutes. Conversely, adding additional capacity to a nuclear generating facility probably would take years. The length of this period depends on the degree of asset specialization, the economic life of the assets, the time necessary to order and install new capital equipment, and the amount of training that labor requires.

Asset specialization refers to the number of uses of an asset. For example, a nuclear generator can only be used to generate electricity in a nuclear power plant and is a very specialized asset. Thus it might be difficult to sell that generator because only another nuclear power plant could use it. Conversely, many trucks can be used to haul a variety of products and are rather unspecialized assets. If a firm decides that one of its trucks is no longer needed, it could easily be sold in the market and its cost eliminated.

Clearly, the longer the life of the asset, the longer the period defined as the short run. Buildings and some types of machinery may have an economic life of many years. Once in place, their costs may be fixed for a long period of time. Also, it may take months or even years to order and install certain types of capital equipment and/or to develop a particular set of skills in labor. In such cases the firm may find that part of the cost of its productive capacity is fixed for that period.

KEY CONCEPTS _____

- The long-run total cost of any rate of output is determined by the expansion path of the firm (which relates output rates and efficient input combinations) and the prices of the inputs.
- If one input is fixed, the firm is operating in the short run, and the costs associated with that input are called fixed costs. The costs associated with the nonfixed inputs are called variable costs.

Short-Run Cost Functions _____

Managerial decision making is facilitated by information that shows the cost of each rate of output. Both short-run and long-run cost functions are considered in this section.

Consider a production process that combines variable amounts of labor with a fixed capital stock, say, ten machines. In this process, the rate of production is changed by varying the rate of labor input. Assume that the firm can vary the labor input freely at a cost of $100 per unit of labor per period. Therefore, the expenditure for labor is the variable cost. If the ten machines are rented under a long-term lease at $100 per machine per production period, the fixed cost would be $1,000 per period. Table 7-3 summarizes the relevant production and cost data for this production process.

The total cost data from Table 7-3 are shown graphically in Figure 7-1a. Note that fixed cost is indicated by a horizontal line; that is, this cost is constant with respect to output. The total variable cost function (TVC) begins at the origin, increases at a decreasing rate up to an output rate between 3 and 4, and then increases at an increasing rate. Total cost (TC) has the same shape as total variable cost but is shifted upward by $1,000, the amount of fixed cost. These functions relate an output rate to the total cost of producing that output rate.

TABLE 7-3 **Short-Run Production and Cost Data**

Input Rate		Rate of Output	Total Fixed Cost	Total Variable Cost	Total Cost
Capital	Labor				
10	0	0	$1,000	$1, 0	$1,000
10	2.00	1	1,000	1,200	1,200
10	3.67	2	1,000	1,367	1,367
10	5.10	3	1,000	1,510	1,510
10	6.77	4	1,000	1,677	1,677
10	8.77	5	1,000	1,877	1,877
10	11.27	6	1,000	1,127	2,127
10	14.60	7	1,000	1,460	2,460
10	24.60	8	1,000	2,460	3,460

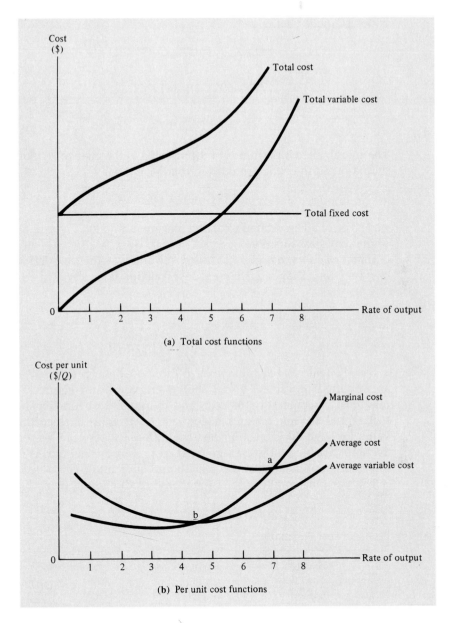

FIGURE 7-1 **Short-Run Cost Functions.**

Functions that indicate the cost per unit of output also can be determined. Often, these are more useful for decision making than are total cost functions. This is because managers must compare cost per unit of output to the market price of that output. Recall that market price is measured per unit of output. By dividing a total cost function by output, a corresponding per-unit cost function is determined. That is,

$$AVERAGE\ TOTAL\ COST: AC = \frac{TC}{Q} \tag{7-1}$$

$$AVERAGE\ VARIABLE\ COST: AVC = \frac{TVC}{Q} \tag{7-2}$$

$$AVERAGE\ FIXED\ COST: AFC = \frac{TFC}{Q} \tag{7-3}$$

The marginal cost per unit of output (MC) is the change in total cost associated with a one-unit change in output, that is,

$$MARGINAL\ COST: MC = \frac{\Delta TC}{\Delta Q} \tag{7-4}$$

As is true of all associated total and marginal functions, marginal cost is the slope of the total cost function.

Using calculus, marginal cost is determined as the first derivative of the total cost function. That is, if the total cost function is

$$TC = f(Q)$$

marginal cost would be

$$MC = \frac{d(TC)}{dQ} \tag{7-5}$$

Based on the total cost functions in Table 7-3, data for each per-unit cost function are reported in Table 7-4 and shown graphically in Figure 7-1b. The average total cost, average variable cost, and marginal cost functions are important in managerial decision making. In contrast, the average fixed cost function has little value for such decisions. Further, the difference between average total cost and average variable cost is average fixed cost. Thus the AC and AVC curves provide information on fixed cost per unit should such information be needed.

The per-unit cost functions for many production systems have the U shape

TABLE 7-4 **Per-Unit Cost Functions**

Output	Averaged Fixed Cost (AFC)	Average Variable Cost (AVC)	Averate Total Cost (AC)	Marginal Cost (MC)
0	—	—	—	
1	$1,000	$200	$1,200	$1,200
2	1,500	184	1,684	1,167
3	1,333	170	1,503	1,143
4	1,250	169	1,419	1,167
5	1,200	175	1,375	1,200
6	1,167	188	1,355	1,250
7	1,143	209	1,351	1,333
8	1,125	307	1,432	1,000

shown in Figure 7-1b. At low rates of production, there is too little of the variable input relative to the fixed input. As the variable input is increased, output rises rapidly, and the cost per unit falls. Initially, total cost increases but at a decreasing rate. This implies that marginal cost (the slope of total cost) is falling. Because of the law of diminishing marginal returns, additional units of the variable input result in smaller additions to output and ultimately marginal cost rises. When marginal cost exceeds average cost, the average cost function begins to rise.

As is true of all marginal and average functions, as long as marginal cost is below the average cost curve, the average function will decline. When marginal is above average, the average cost curve will rise. This implies that marginal cost intersects both the average total cost and average variable cost functions at the minimum point of the average curves (points a and b in Figure 7-1b).

EXAMPLE _____

Finding Minimum Average Variable Cost

Given the total cost function

$$TC = 1{,}000 + 10Q - 0.9Q^2 + 0.04Q^3$$

find the rate of output that results in minimum average variable cost.

SOLUTION   Marginal cost is the first derivative of the total cost function

$$\frac{d(TC)}{dQ} = MC = 10 - 1.8Q + 0.12Q^2$$

Now, find the total variable cost function (TVC) by subtracting the fixed cost component ($1,000) from the total cost function. That is,

$$TVC = 10Q - 0.9Q^2 + 0.04Q^3$$

Then find average variable cost (AVC) by dividing TVC by output (Q). That is,

$$AVC = \frac{TVC}{Q} = \frac{10Q - 0.9Q^2 + 0.04Q^3}{Q}$$

$$AVC = 10 - 0.9Q + 0.04Q^2$$

Because the minimum point of AVC occurs at its intersection with marginal cost, equate the AVC and MC functions and solve for Q. That is,

$$AVC = MC$$
$$10 - 0.9Q + 0.04Q^2 = 10 - 1.8Q + 0.12Q^2$$

Rearranging terms yields a quadratic equation

$$-0.08Q^2 + 0.9Q = 0$$

or

$$Q(-0.08Q + 0.9) = 0$$

which has the roots

$$Q_1 = 0 \quad \text{and} \quad Q_2 = 11.25$$

Disregarding the root associated with a zero output rate, it is seen that the minimum AVC is achieved at an output rate of 11.25 units.

Alternatively, the minimum point of AVC could be found by setting the first derivative of AVC equal to zero and solving for Q. That is,

$$\frac{d(AVC)}{dQ} = -0.9 + 0.08Q = 0$$

$$0.08Q = 0.9$$

$$Q = 11.25$$

KEY CONCEPTS

- Per-unit or average cost functions sometimes are more useful than total cost functions in making decisions. The average cost functions are found by dividing the relevant total cost functions by output, that is,

$$AVERAGE\ COST:\ AC = \frac{TC}{Q}$$

$$AVERAGE\ VARIABLE\ COST:\ AVC = \frac{TVC}{Q}$$

$$AVERAGE\ FIXED\ COST:\ AFC = \frac{TFC}{Q}$$

- Marginal cost per unit is the change in total cost associated with a one-unit change in output, that is,

$$MC = \frac{\Delta TC}{\Delta Q}$$

Long-Run Cost Functions

Firms operate in the short run but plan in the long run. At any point in time, the firm has one or more fixed factors of production. Therefore, production decisions must be made based on short-run cost curves. However, most firms can change the scale of their operation in the long run by varying all inputs, and in doing so, move to a preferred short-run cost function.

Recall from Chapter 6 that returns to scale are increasing, decreasing, or constant, depending on whether a proportional change in both inputs results in output increasing more than in proportion, less than in proportion, or in proportion to the increase in inputs. These three possibilities are shown in the left-hand panels of Figure 7-2.

There is a direct correspondence between returns to scale in production and the long-run cost function for the firm. If returns to scale are increasing, inputs are increasing less than in proportion to increases in output. Because input prices

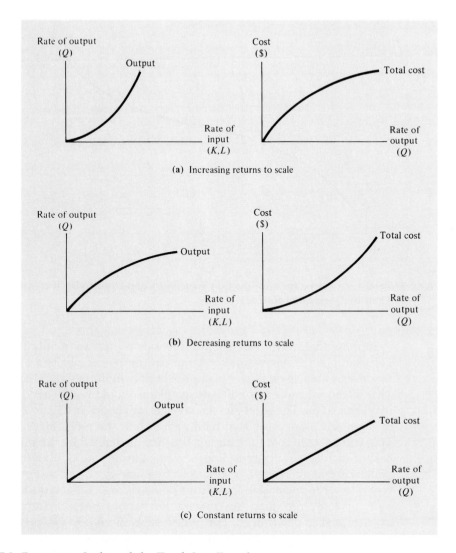

FIGURE 7-2 **Returns to Scale and the Total Cost Function.**

are constant, it follows that total cost also must be increasing less than in proportion to output. This relationship is shown in Figure 7-2a. If decreasing returns to scale apply, the total cost function increases at an increasing rate. Constant returns to scale implies that total cost will change in proportion to changes in output. The latter two relationships are shown in parts (b) and (c) of Figure 7-2.

The production process of many firms is characterized first by increasing returns and then by decreasing returns. In this case, the long-run total cost function first increases at a decreasing rate and then increases at an increasing rate, as shown in Figure 7-3. Such a total cost function would be associated with a U-shaped long-run average cost function.

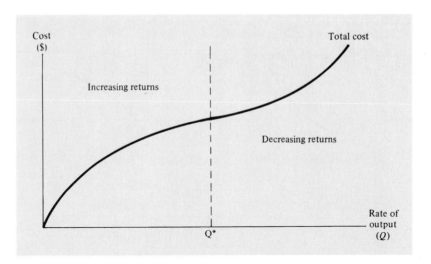

FIGURE 7-3 **Total Cost Curve for a Production Function Characterized by Increasing Returns, Then by Decreasing Returns.**

Suppose that a firm can expand the scale of operation only in discrete units. For example, the generators for large electric power plants are made in only a few sizes. Often, these power plants are built in multiples of 750 megawatts (MW). That is, output capacity of alternative plants would be 750 MW, 1500 MW, 2250 MW, and so on. The short-run average cost functions in Figure 7-4 (labeled SAC_1 through SAC_4) are associated with each of four discrete scales of operation. The long-run average cost function for this firm is defined by the minimum average cost of each level of output. For example, output rate Q_1 could be produced by plant size 1 at an average cost of C_1 or by plant size 2 at a cost of C_2. Clearly, the cost is lower for plant size 1, and thus point a is one point on the long-run average cost curve. By repeating this process for various rates of output, the long-run average cost is determined. For output rates of zero to Q_2, plant 1 is the most efficient and that part of SAC_1 is part of the long-run cost function. For output rates Q_2 to Q_3, plant 2 is the most efficient, and for output rates Q_3 to Q_4, plant 3 is the most efficient. The scallop-shaped curve shown in boldface in Figure 7-4 is the long-run average cost curve for this firm. This boldfaced curve is called an *envelope curve*. Firms plan to be on this envelope curve in the long run. Consider a firm currently operating plant size 2 and producing Q_1 units at a cost of C_2 per unit. If output is expected to remain at Q_1, the firm will plan to adjust to plant size 1, thus reducing per-unit cost to C_1.

Most firms will have many alternative plant sizes to choose from, and there is a short-run average cost curve corresponding to each. A few of the short-run average cost curves for these plants are shown in Figure 7-5. Only one point or a very small arc of each short-run cost curve will lie on the long-run average cost function. Thus long-run average cost can be shown as the smooth U-shaped curve

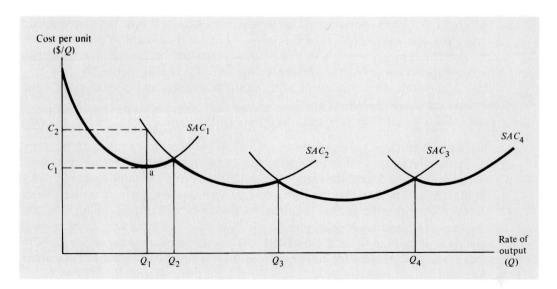

FIGURE 7-4 **Short-Run Average Cost Functions for Four Discrete Plant Sizes.**

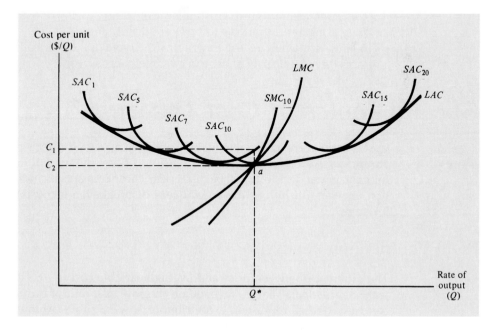

FIGURE 7-5 **Short-Run and Long-Run Cost Curves.**

labeled *LAC*. Corresponding to this long-run average cost function is a long-run marginal cost curve *LMC*, which intersects *LAC* at its minimum point *a*, which is also the minimum point of short-run average cost curve 10. The short-run marginal cost curve (SMC_{10}) corresponding to SAC_{10} is also shown. But $SMC_{10} = SAC_{10}$ at the minimum point of SAC_{10}. Thus at point *a* and only at point *a* the following unique result occurs:

$$SAC = SMC = LAC = LMC \qquad (7\text{-}6)$$

The long-run cost curve serves as a long-run planning mechanism for the firm. For example, suppose that the firm is operating on short-run average cost curve SAC_7 in Figure 7-5, and the firm is currently producing an output rate of Q^*. By using SAC_7, it is seen that the firm's cost per unit is C_2. Clearly, if projections of future demand indicate that the firm could expect to continue selling Q^* units per period at the market price, profit could be increased significantly by increasing the scale of plant to the size associated with short-run average curve SAC_{10}. With this plant, cost per unit for an output rate of Q^* would be C_2 and the firm's profit per unit would increase by $C_1 - C_2$. Thus total profit would increase by $(C_1 - C_2) \cdot Q^*$.

KEY CONCEPTS

- The firm's long-run average cost function will be
  Decreasing where returns to scale in production are increasing.
  Constant where returns to scale are constant.
  Increasing where returns to scale are decreasing.
- The long-run average cost function is the envelope curve consisting of points or arcs on a number of short-run average cost curves.

Special Topics in Cost Theory

Cost functions are essential to making effective managerial decisions about output and prices. At this point, several extensions of cost theory that have implications for managerial decisions will be discussed. These concepts include profit contribution analysis (including the special case of breakeven analysis), and operating leverage.

Profit Contribution Analysis

The difference between price and average variable cost ($P - AVC$) is defined as *profit contribution*. That is, revenue on the sale of a unit of output after variable costs are covered represents a contribution toward profit. At low rates of output, the firm may be losing money because fixed costs have not yet been covered by the profit contribution. Thus, at these low rates of output, profit contribution is used to cover fixed costs. After fixed costs are covered, the firm will be earning a profit.

A manager may want to know the output rate necessary to cover all fixed costs and to earn a "required" profit of π_R. Assume that both price and variable cost per unit of output (AVC) are constant. Profit (π) is equal to total revenue (PQ) less the sum of total variable costs ($Q \cdot AVC$) and fixed costs. Thus

$$\pi_R = PQ - [(Q \cdot AVC) + FC]$$

Solving this equation for Q yields a relation that can be used to determine the rate of output necessary to generate a specified rate of profit. That is,

$$Q = \frac{FC + \pi_R}{P - AVC} \qquad (7\text{-}7)$$

For example, suppose that FC = $10,000, P = $20, AVC = $15, and that the firm has set a required profit target of $20,000. To generate this profit, an output rate of 6,000 units is required; that is,

$$Q_R = \frac{\$10{,}000 + \$20{,}000}{20 - 15} = 6{,}000$$

A special case of this equation is where the required economic profit is zero, that is, π_R = 0. This output rate is called the breakeven point for the firm. (Recall that a zero economic profit means that normal returns are being earned by capital and other factors of production.) The breakeven rate of output, Q_e, is given by the equation

$$Q_e = \frac{FC}{P - AVC} \qquad (7\text{-}8)$$

Using the data just given, it is seen that the breakeven rate of output is 2,000; that is,

$$Q_e = \frac{\$10{,}000}{20 - 15} = 2{,}000$$

This example of breakeven analysis is shown graphically in Figure 7-6. Fixed cost is shown as the horizontal line at $10,000. Total cost is given by the equation

$$TC = FC + TVC$$

Because FC = 10,000 and variable cost per unit is 15, the total cost function is

$$TC = 10{,}000 + 15Q$$

Since price is constant, the total revenue function is

$$TR = 20Q$$

which is shown as a straight line through the origin having a slope of 20. The breakeven point occurs at an output rate of 2,000, which is at the intersection of the total revenue and total cost functions. At this point, both total revenue and total cost are $40,000.

This linear approach to profit contribution has been criticized because of the assumption that both price and average variable cost are constant. The price

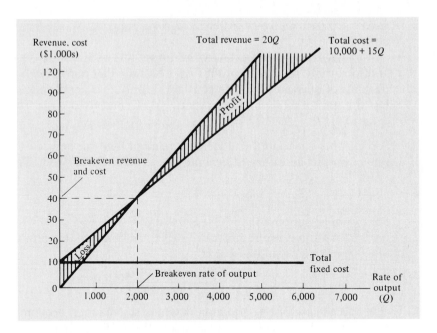

FIGURE 7-6 **Linear Breakeven Analysis.**

assumption is not unrealistic for many firms, as they are able to sell all they can produce at the going price. However, other firms, especially those where sales are large relative to the size of the market, may have to reduce price to sell more output. For some firms, the assumption of constant average variable cost may be unrealistic. However, if the price and average variable cost are roughly constant, at least over the limited range of output relevant to the problem, breakeven analysis is a useful tool for managerial decisions. However, care and judgment are required in its application.

EXAMPLE

Breaking Even on Microcomputer Software

MicroApplications Inc. is a small firm that specializes in the production and mail-order distribution of computer programs for microcomputers. The accounting department has gathered the following data on development and production costs for a typical program and the documentation (i.e., the manual) that must accompany the program.

Development costs (fixed):

Program development	$10,000
Manual preparation and typesetting	3,000
Advertising	$10,000
Total	$23,000

Variable costs per unit:

Blank disk	$ 2.00
Loading cost	0.50
Postage and handling	1.25
Printing of manual	$ 2.75
Total	$ 6.50

A typical program of this type, including the manual, sells for $40. Based on this information:

1. Determine the breakeven number of programs and the total revenue associated with this volume.
2. MicroApplications has a minimum profit target of $40,000 on each new program it develops. Determine the unit and dollar volume of sales required to meet this goal.
3. While this program is still in the development stage, market prices for software fall by 25 percent due to a significant increase in the number of programs being supplied to the market. Determine the new breakeven unit and dollar volumes.

SOLUTION

1. Based on fixed costs of $23,000, a price of $40 per unit, and variable costs per unit of $6.50, the unit volume required to break even is

$$Q_e = \frac{\text{fixed cost}}{P - AVC} = \frac{\$23,000}{\$40 - \$6.50} = 686.6$$

Total revenue at this output rate is determined by multiplying price times the breakeven quantity;

$$TR = PQ_e = 40(686.6) = \$27,464$$

2. The quantity necessary to meet the profit target of $40,000 is

$$Q_R = \frac{FC + \pi_R}{P - AVC} = \frac{23,000 + 40,000}{40 - 6.50} = 1,880.6$$

The associated total revenue is

$$TR = PQ_R = 40(1,880.6) = \$75,224$$

3. If the price declines by 25 percent to $30, the new breakeven quantity would be

$$Q_e = \frac{23,000}{30 - 6.50} = 978.7$$

The corresponding total revenue for this output rate is

$$TR = 30(978.7) = \$29,361$$

If the assumptions of constant price and average variable cost are relaxed, breakeven analysis can still be applied, although the key relationships (total revenue and total variable cost) will not be linear functions of output. Nonlinear total revenue and cost functions are shown in Figure 7-7. The cost function is conventional in the sense that at first costs increase but less than in proportion to output and then increase more than in proportion to output. There are two breakeven points, Q_1 and Q_2. Note that profit, the vertical distance between the total revenue and total cost functions, is maximized at output rate Q^*.

Of the two breakeven points, only the first, corresponding to output rate Q_1, is relevant. When a firm begins production, management usually expects to incur losses. But it is important to know at what output rate the firm will go from a loss to a profit situation. In Figure 7-7, the firm would want to get to the breakeven output rate Q_1 as soon as possible and then, of course, move to the profit-maximizing rate Q^*. However, the firm would not expand production beyond Q^* because this would result in a reduction of profit. No rational manager would ever increase the rate of production to the second breakeven rate Q_2, and therefore, that breakeven point is irrelevant.

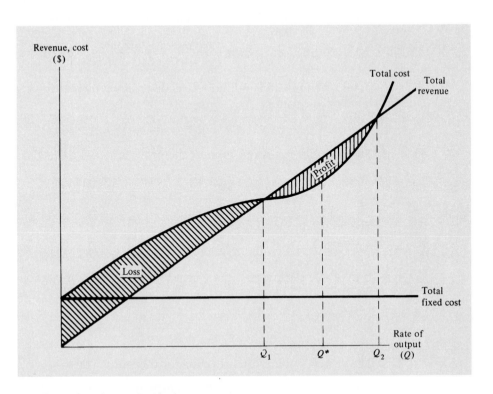

FIGURE 7-7 **Nonlinear Breakeven Analysis.**

KEY CONCEPTS

- The output rate that yields a specified rate of economic profit is found by dividing the required profit plus total fixed cost by profit contribution, that is,

$$Q_R = \frac{\pi_R + TFC}{P - AVC}$$

- Breakeven analysis is a special case of required profit analysis where the required profit is zero.

Operating Leverage

A firm is said to be *highly leveraged* if fixed costs are large relative to variable costs. For example, relatively large fixed costs may result from the firm having large amounts of borrowed money with large fixed-interest obligations. Also, firms may have large investments in fixed assets, such as plant and equipment, with heavy fixed expenses, including depreciation charges and/or lease payments that must be paid regardless of the rate of output.

A general characteristic of a highly leveraged firm is that it experiences more variation in profits for a given percentage change in output than does a less leveraged firm. This is because total cost for a highly leveraged firm will change less than in proportion to a change in output rate, and therefore profit will tend to change more than in proportion to output changes. Conversely, for a firm with little or no fixed cost, profit should change more nearly in proportion to output changes.

Leverage can be analyzed using the concept of *profit elasticity* (E_π), defined as the percentage change in profit associated with a 1 percent change in unit sales or rate of output. That is,

$$E_\pi = \frac{\% \text{ change in profit}}{\% \text{ change in unit sales}} \tag{7-9}$$

or

$$E_\pi = \frac{\frac{\Delta \pi}{\pi}}{\frac{\Delta Q}{Q}} = \frac{\Delta \pi}{\Delta Q} \cdot \frac{Q}{\pi} \tag{7-10}$$

For infinitesimally small changes in Q, the operating profit elasticity is

$$E_\pi = \frac{d\pi}{dQ} \cdot \frac{Q}{\pi}$$

If the price of output is constant regardless of the rate of output, operating profit elasticity depends on three variables: the rate of output, the level of total fixed costs, and variable cost per unit of output. This can be seen by substituting the equations for profit

$$\pi = PQ - (AVC)(Q) - TFC$$

and change in profit

$$\Delta\pi = P(\Delta Q) - (AVC)(\Delta Q)$$

into equation (7-10). That is,

$$E_\pi = \frac{[P(\Delta Q) - (AVC)(\Delta Q)]/[PQ - (AVC)(Q) - TFC]}{\Delta Q/Q}$$

Simplifying this equation yields a computational formula for the operating profit elasticity:

$$E_\pi = \frac{Q(P - AVC)}{Q(P - AVC) - TFC} \qquad (7\text{-}11)$$

Close inspection of this equation reveals that for two firms with equal prices, rates of output, and variable costs per unit, the firm having the greater total fixed cost will have the higher operating profit elasticity. This is because total fixed cost has a minus sign in the denominator in equation (7-11). The greater is total fixed cost, the smaller is the denominator and the higher is the value of E_π.

Table 7-5 shows profit and operating profit elasticity data for two firms, A and B, with differing total fixed costs and average variable costs. Note that leverage is greatest for smaller output rates and that it declines as output increases. At the same rate of output, the elasticity is always higher for firm B than for firm A. This is because B has higher total fixed costs and lower variable costs per unit than does A. Therefore, if both firms are producing the same output rate, for any change in output the percentage change in profit will be greater for B than for A. For example, at an output rate of 1,000, a 1 percent increase in output results in a 1.25 percent increase in profit for A, compared to a 2.0 percent increase for B. As the output rate increases, the difference in the elasticities between the two firms decreases.

TABLE 7-5 **Operating Profit Elasticity for Two Firms**

Firm A: Firm B:
  Price = $10.00   Price = $10.00
  AVC = $ 5.00   AVC = $ 2.00
  TFC = $ 1,000   TFC = $ 4,000

Rate of Output	Profit		Operating Profit Elasticity	
	Firm A	Firm B	Firm A	Firm B
1,000	4,000	4,000	1.25	2.00
1,500	6,500	8,000	1.15	1.50
2,000	9,000	12,000	1.11	1.33
2,500	11,500	14,000	1.09	1.25
3,000	14,000	16,000	1.07	1.20

Over time, profits for firm B will vary considerably more than for A. In a sense, the management of B has structured the firm so that it takes more risk. When the rate of output is high, profits will be greater at B than A. However, if economic conditions become unfavorable and output falls, profit will decline more rapidly for the highly leveraged firm B. If output continues to fall, firm B will incur losses before A will. In a prolonged period of low demand, the risk of bankruptcy is greater for B. Thus the operating profit elasticity can be used as an indicator of risk.

As will be shown in Chapter 14, usually there is a trade-off between risk and return. That is, greater returns are usually associated with greater risk, and vice versa. A management decision to become more leveraged (e.g., by incurring significant debt or a large capital investment program) effectively is a decision to accept greater risk for the chance to earn higher profit.

KEY CONCEPTS

- A firm is said to be highly leveraged if fixed costs are high relative to variable costs. In general, the use of leverage implies higher risk (i.e., more variability in profit over time).
- Leverage can be measured by operating profit elasticity, defined as the percentage change in profit associated with a 1 percent change in output.

Estimating Cost Functions

As discussed in the previous chapter, many managerial decisions require quantitative information about the firm's production function. This is also true for the firm's cost functions. Decision making generally requires that the manager go beyond knowing that the average cost function is U-shaped and that marginal cost is increasing to actually making estimates of the parameters of these cost functions. In this section, methods for estimating both short-run and long-run cost functions are developed.

Short-Run Cost Functions

Recall that in the short run some costs are fixed. Although these fixed costs should be identified and measured, they typically are not used to estimate the short-run cost function. The usual procedure is to estimate the total or average variable cost function and then, if necessary, add the fixed cost component to obtain the total or average cost function.

Suppose that accurate data on variable cost and output have been collected. The remaining tasks are to specify the appropriate functional form (i.e., the hypothesized relationship between cost and output), statistically estimate the parameters of that functional form using the standard multiple-regression technique, and then interpret the results.

If the relationship between cost and output is approximately linear, the functional form

$$TVC = b_0 + b_1Q \qquad (7\text{-}12)$$

may be used to estimate the cost function. If b_0 and b_1 are estimated, the average variable cost function would be given by

$$AVC = \frac{b_0}{Q} + b_1 \qquad (7\text{-}13)$$

and the marginal cost function by

$$MC = b_1 \qquad (7\text{-}14)$$

TVC, AVC, and MC curves that are consistent with this linear model are shown in Figure 7-8. These functions have the following properties: Total variable cost is a linear function; average variable cost declines initially and then becomes quite flat approaching the value of marginal cost as output increases;[1] and marginal cost is constant at b_1.

If the empirical data indicate a U-shaped average cost curve, the linear function just used will not capture that relationship between output and cost. Consequently, a quadratic total variable cost function of the form

$$TVC = c_0 + c_1Q + c_2Q^2 \qquad (7\text{-}15)$$

or a cubic cost function

$$TVC = d_0 + d_1Q + d_2Q^2 + d_3Q^3 \qquad (7\text{-}16)$$

is often used because functions of this type can capture the hypothesized nonlinear relationship. The parameters of both (7-15) and (7-16) can be estimated directly using the least-squares regression method.[2]

Although the shape of the quadratic and cubic functions will depend on the estimated parameters, conventional or typical estimated cost functions based on these functional forms are shown in Figures 7-9 and 7-10. The quadratic function (Figure 7-9) has the following properties: Total cost increases at an increasing rate; marginal cost is a linearly increasing function of output[3] (i.e., $MC = c_1 + 2c_2Q$); and average variable cost, found by dividing the total variable cost function by Q, is a nonlinear increasing function, i.e.,

$$AVC = \frac{c_0}{Q} + c_1 + c_2Q \qquad (7\text{-}17)$$

---

[1] Note that the ratio b_0/Q approaches zero as Q becomes large. Therefore, for high output rates, AVC will approach b_1, which is marginal cost.

[2] Equation (7-16) is nonlinear in the variables Q, Q^2, and Q^3, but it is linear in the parameters $d_0, d_1, d_2,$ and d_3. Therefore the ordinary last-squares regression method can be used without any transformation of the equation.

[3] Recall that marginal cost is the first derivative of the total variable cost function, equation. That is,

$$MC = \frac{d(TVC)}{dQ} = c_1 + 2C_2Q$$

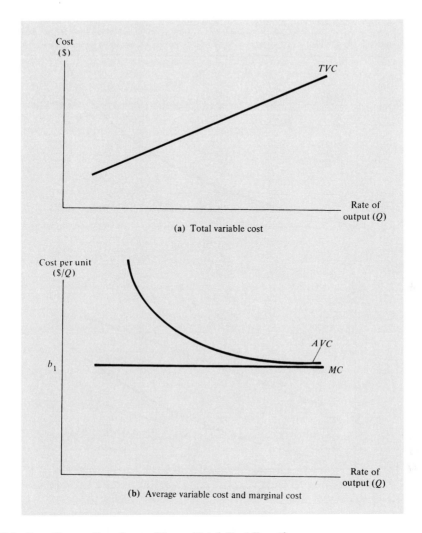

FIGURE 7-8 **Cost Curves Based on a Linear Total Cost Function.**

Typical total variable cost, average cost, and marginal cost curves based on a cubic function are shown in Figure 7-10. The characteristics of these functions are: Total variable cost first increases at a decreasing rate (up to output rate Q_1 in the figure), then increases at an increasing rate; and both marginal cost

$$MC = d_1 + 2d_2Q + 3d_3Q^2 \qquad (7\text{-}18)$$

and average variable cost

$$AVC = \frac{d_0}{Q} + d_1 + d_2Q + d_3Q^2 \qquad (7\text{-}19)$$

are U-shaped functions.

In Figure 7-10, the conventional relationships among the cost functions are

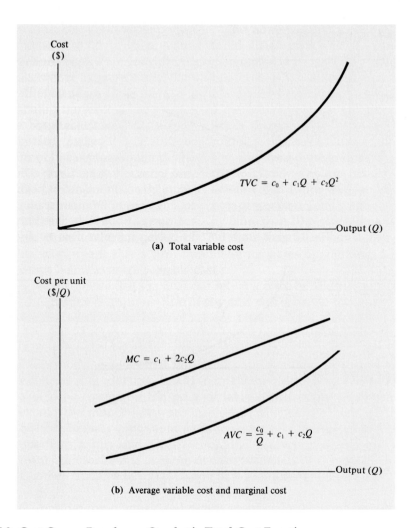

FIGURE 7-9 **Cost Curves Based on a Quadratic Total Cost Function.**

evident. For example, note the correspondence between the inflection point on
TVC (i.e., at output Q_1, where the rate of increase goes from decreasing to increasing) and the minimum point on marginal cost. Also, marginal cost intersects the
average variable cost function at the minimum point of the AVC curve.

Although there is empirical evidence to support a variety of cost relationships,
several studies of short-run cost functions have concluded that the marginal cost
curve is approximately horizontal, that is, that marginal cost is constant over a
fairly wide range of output rates. These empirical results would appear to be
inconsistent with conventional cost theory, which suggests that average cost
curves are U-shaped and that marginal cost functions are rising. This may be the
result of saucer-shaped marginal cost functions that do have negative slopes at
low rates of output and positive slopes at high output rates but are essentially
flat over fairly wide output ranges. As firms normally would be operating within

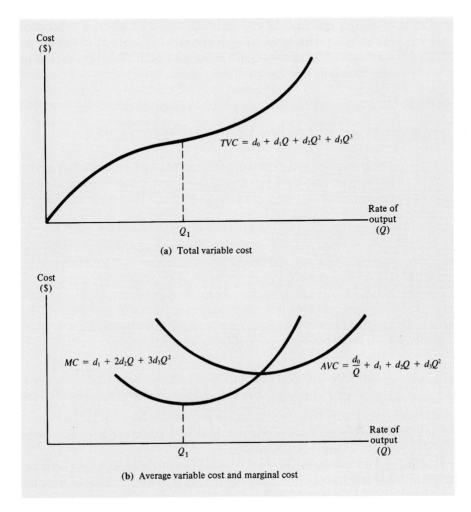

Cost
($)

$$TVC = d_0 + d_1Q + d_2Q^2 + d_3Q^3$$

Q_1

Rate of
output
(Q)

(a) Total variable cost

Cost
($)

$$MC = d_1 + 2d_2Q + 3d_3Q^2$$

$$AVC = \frac{d_0}{Q} + d_1 + d_2Q + d_3Q^2$$

Q_1

Rate of
output
(Q)

(b) Average variable cost and marginal cost

FIGURE 7-10 **Cost Curves Based on a Cubic Total Cost Function.**

that range (i.e., operating efficiently), all or most of the actual production rate
and cost data would show approximately constant marginal costs.

An alternative explanation for a flat marginal cost function is that the so-called
fixed inputs may not really be fixed. Recall from Chapter 6 that the marginal
product function declines because increasing amounts of the variable input are
being combined with fixed amounts of another input. Initially, returns to additional units of the variable factor may increase, but ultimately the law of diminishing marginal returns applies, and the marginal product function declines while
the marginal cost curve rises. But if the "fixed" input is not really fixed, the
fixed-variable input proportion may not change as output varies, and the law of
diminishing returns may not be observed. For example, a manufacturing firm
may have a fixed stock of machines, but the number in use may vary as the rate

of output changes. In that case, the ratio of labor to machines in use may be roughly constant even though the ratio of labor to the total stock of machines may vary considerably. If this is the case, both the estimated marginal and average cost functions may be quite flat.

EXAMPLE _____

Estimating and Using Cost Functions

The engineering department of Consolidated Chemicals has developed the following output-cost data for a proposed new plant to produce ammonium sulfate fertilizer:

Output	Total Cost
50	$1,870
100	1,920
150	1,990
200	1,240
250	1,440
300	1,940
350	2,330
400	3,100

a. Estimate the total cost function and then use that equation to determine the average and marginal cost functions. Assume a quadratic total cost function:
$$TC = c_0 + c_1 Q + c_2 Q^2$$

b. Determine the output rate that will minimize average cost and the per-unit cost at that rate of output.

c. The current market price of this fertilizer is $5.50 per unit and is expected to remain at that level for the foreseeable future. Should the plant be built?

SOLUTION   a. Using the ordinary least-squares regression method, the estimated function is
$$TC = 1,016 - 3.36Q + 0.021Q^2, \qquad R^2 = 0.99$$
$$(11.45)\ (-3.71)\ \ (10.71)$$

The t-statistics, shown in parentheses, indicate that the coefficients of each of the independent variables are significantly different from zero. The value for the coefficient of determination means that 99 percent of the variation in total cost is explained by changes in the rate of output.

The average cost function is
$$AC = \frac{TC}{Q} = \frac{1,016}{Q} - 3.36 + 0.021\,Q$$

and the marginal cost function is
$$MC = \frac{d(TC)}{dQ} = -3.36 + 0.042\,Q$$

b. The output rate that results in minimum per-unit cost is found by taking the first derivative of the average cost function, setting it equal to zero, and solving for Q.

$$\frac{d(AC)}{dQ} = -\frac{1,016}{Q^2} + 0.021 = 0$$

$$0.021 = \frac{1,016}{Q^2}$$

$$0.021\, Q^2 = 1,016$$

$$Q = 220$$

To find the cost at that rate of output, substitute 220 for Q in the average cost equation and solve.

$$AC = \frac{1,016}{220} - 3.36 + 0.021(220) = \$5.88$$

c. Because the lowest possible cost is \$5.88 per unit, which is \$0.38 above the market price, the plant should not be constructed.

Long-Run Cost Functions

Recall that the long-run average cost curve consists of points or small segments of each of a series of short-run average cost functions. A long-run cost function and associated short-run cost functions are shown in Figure 7-11. At any point

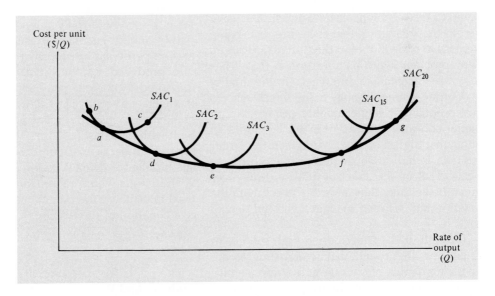

FIGURE 7-11 **Short-Run Average Cost Curves and the Associated Long-Run Average Cost Curve.**

in time, of course, a firm will be operating on one of these short-run functions. Estimating the long-run function requires: (1) obtaining data on each of a number of points on the long-run function (i.e., obtaining data on the relevant point on each of a number of short-run cost functions such as point *a*, *d*, *e*, *f*, and *g* on the short-run functions shown in Figure 7-11); (2) specifying the appropriate functional form; and (3) estimating the parameters of the function.

Either a time-series or a cross-section approach can be used, although most studies of long-run cost behavior have used cross-section data. One problem with time-series data on a single plant is that if the period is long enough for the scale to have changed, it is probably long enough for production technology and input prices to have changed as well. As suggested previously, a cross-section study must assume that firms are operating at that point on the short-run function that lies on the long-run function. For example, in Figure 7-11 accurate estimation of the long-run cost function would require that the firm represented by SAC_1 would be operating at point *a*. If the firm were operating at some other point, such as *b* or *c*, the estimate of the long-run average cost curve would be biased in an upward direction.

CASE STUDY

Returns to Scale in High School Education

Studies of per-student expenditures in the nation's schools have generally shown a tendency for these costs to increase as the number of students in the school increases. Such studies have led to the conclusion that there are decreasing returns to scale in the production of education. One problem with this approach is that it has not taken account of differences in the quality of output among schools. If the larger schools are producing a higher quality product (i.e., a better educated student), it is not legitimate to infer that higher cost per student in the larger schools is indicative of decreasing returns to scale. That is, the effect of quality differences must be held constant in order to estimate the relationship between average cost and school size.

Riew studied 102 accredited high schools in Wisconsin. He found that if adjustments are made for quality of education, there are significant economies of scale in producing high school education. Riew specified a general average cost function of the form:

average cost = *f*(number of students, quality)

Average cost per student (*AC*) was measured by expenditure per student and number of students by average daily attendance. Although output quality generally is measured by reference to particular attributes of the good or service produced, in Riew's study quality was measured by the characteristics of the schools that were surveyed. The following measures of quality were used: percentage of classrooms built within the last ten years; average teacher's salary; number of credit units offered; and average number of courses taught per teacher.

The least-squares regression technique was used to estimate the parameters of a quadratic cost equation of the form

$$AC = c_0 + c_1Q + c_2Q^2 + c_3V_1 \\ + c_4V_2 + c_5V_3 + c_6V_4$$

where *AC* is cost per student, *Q* is number of students, and V_1, V_2, V_3, and V_4 are the quality variables. After adjusting for quality differences among schools so that the effect of variables V_1

through V_4 are included in the constant term, the following net relationship between cost and number of students was estimated:

$$AC = 10.3 - 0.402Q + 0.00012Q^2 \qquad R^2 = 0.56$$
$$\qquad (6.38) \qquad (5.22)$$

The values of the t-statistics are shown in parentheses and indicate that both coefficients are significantly different from zero. The number of students that minimizes this function is found by setting the first derivative of the average cost function equal to zero and solving for Q. That is,

$$\frac{d(AC)}{dQ} = -0.402 + 0.00024Q = 0$$
$$Q = 1,675$$

Thus average cost is minimized for a school with 1,675 students.* When graphed, this estimated function is a U-shaped average cost curve having a minimum point at 1,675 students, as shown in the following figure.

* The second derivative of the average cost function is positive (i.e., 0.00024), this implys that AC is minimized for a school of this size.

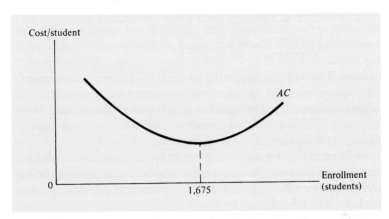

Cost/student

AC

Enrollment (students)

0   1,675

Relationship Between Cost per Student and Number of Students.

SOURCE: J. Riew. "Economies of Scale in High School Operations." Review of Economics and Statistics 48(3): 280–287.

KEY CONCEPTS

- Managerial decisions often require that quantitative estimates be made of the firm's cost functions.
- A quadratic cost function of the form $TVC = c_0 + c_1 Q + c_2 Q^2$ usually yields linear average and marginal cost curves.
- A cubic cost function of the form $TVC = d_0 + d_1 Q + d_2 Q^2 + d_3 Q^3$ yields U-shaped average and marginal cost curves.

Summary

The theory of cost is a fundamental concern of managerial economics. The best measure of resource cost is the value of that resource in its highest-valued alternative use (i.e., its opportunity cost). The concept of opportunity cost includes both explicit and implicit costs. Examples of the latter include the value of labor and capital contributed to the firm by the manager/owner.

The cost of long-lived assets during the production period is the difference in the value of that asset between the beginning and end of the period. Because the opportunity cost concept is used, economic cost includes a normal return or profit to the firm. A normal return is defined as the minimum payment necessary to keep resources from moving to other firms or industries. Marginal and incremental costs are fundamental to decision making. Sunk costs generally are irrelevant.

The cost function relates cost to specific rates of output. The basis for the cost function is the production function and the prices of inputs. In the short run, the rate of one input is fixed. The cost associated with that input is called fixed cost. The cost associated with the variable inputs is defined as variable cost. The total cost of any rate of output is equal to the total fixed cost plus the total variable cost of producing that output rate. Per-unit cost functions include average total cost, average variable cost, average fixed cost, and marginal cost. Often, the per-unit cost functions are more useful for decision making than are the total cost functions.

In the long run, all costs are variable. The long-run average cost curve is the envelope of a series of short-run average cost curves. If returns to scale are increasing, long-run average cost (LAC) will be decreasing. If returns to scale are decreasing, LAC will be increasing. The long-run cost functions are used for planning the optimal scale of plant size.

Profit contribution analysis is used to determine the output rate necessary to earn a specified profit rate. A special case of profit contribution theory is breakeven analysis, where the rate of output necessary to generate a zero rate of economic profit is determined.

A firm is said to be highly leveraged if fixed costs are large relative to variable costs. Leverage is measured by the profit elasticity or the percentage change in profit associated with a 1 percent change in output. In general, increased leverage implies more variability in profit over time and therefore greater risk.

Linear, quadratic, and cubic functional forms are used to estimate short-run cost functions. Both the quadratic and cubic functions can be used as functional forms if the cost data are consistent with the nonlinear cost curves suggested by economic theory. Long-run cost functions typically are estimated using cross-section data on costs in a number of plants. It must be assumed that the cost-output data observed on the short-run function of each plant also is a point on the firm's long-run cost function.

Discussion Questions

7-1. Three business school graduates decide to open a business, and all three devote their full time to its management. What cost would you assign to their time? Is this an explicit or implicit cost?

7-2. Why do increasing returns to scale imply a decreasing long-run average cost function and decreasing returns to scale imply an increasing long-run average cost function?

7-3. Why is the historic cost of inventory or capital equipment irrelevant for managerial decision making?

7-4. Virtually all firms report the value of capital equipment and real estate based on historical cost less accounting depreciation. Do you think the reported value of these assets would approximate their market value? Explain. Would reporting the true market value of these assets provide investors with better information? Why?

7-5. If a firm found it could only operate at a breakeven output rate, would it stay in business in the long run?

7-6. Is there a problem using accounting data based on historical cost and standard depreciation techniques to estimate economic cost functions? Explain.

7-7. Some empirical studies have suggested that the marginal cost function is approximately horizontal, but conventional cost theory suggests that the marginal cost curve is U-shaped. Provide an explanation for this apparent inconsistency.

7-8. United Pharmaceuticals, Inc. has spent $5 million developing and testing a new anti-baldness drug. The head of the marketing department now estimates that it will cost $3 million in advertising to launch this new product. Total revenue from all future sales is estimated at $6 million, and therefore, total costs will exceed revenue by $2 million. He recommends that this product be dropped from the firm's product offerings. What is your reaction to this recommendation? The head of the accounting department now indicates that $3.5 million of corporate overhead expenses also will be assigned to this product if it is marketed. Does this new information affect your decision? Explain.

Problems

7-1. Use the following data to compute total variable cost, total fixed cost, average total cost, average variable cost, average fixed cost, and marginal cost for each output rate shown. Also, use the information to determine equations for each of the total and per-unit cost functions.

Production Period	Rate of Output (Q)	Total Cost (TC)
1	10	1,800
2	0	1,000
3	4	1,320
4	2	1,160
5	7	1,560

7-2. Wyatt Motors has one fixed input, the long-term lease on its factory building, for which the rent is $5,000 per production period. Use the data shown here to determine average cost, average variable cost, and marginal cost for each output rate shown. Also, write equations for total cost, total variable cost, and marginal cost.

Q	Total Variable Cost
1	$1,000
2	2,000
3	3,000
4	4,000
5	5,000

7-3. Based on a consulting economist's report, the total and marginal cost functions for Advance Electronics, Inc., are

$$TC = 200 + 5Q - 0.04Q^2 + 0.001Q^3$$
$$MC = 5 - 0.08Q + 0.003Q^2$$

P. R. Swensen, president of the company, determines that knowing only these equations is inadequate for decision making. You have been directed to do the following:

a. Determine the level of fixed cost (if any) and equations for average total cost, average variable cost, and average fixed cost.
b. Determine the rate of output that results in minimum average variable cost.
c. If fixed costs increase to $500, what output rate will result in minimum average variable cost?

7-4. President Emert of Eastern State University had decided on a new budgeting system for all departments in the university. Historically, each department was provided with an annual budget that was essentially the same amount each year. Being a trained economist, the President has decided to allow student demand for courses to determine how the University's budget is to be allocated to departments. Each quarter, every department will receive $40 for each student credit hour (SCH) taught. For example, a three-credit course for fall quarter might enroll thirty-five students, thus generating 105 SCH. For offering that course, the department would receive $4,200 (i.e., $40 × 105 SCH).

The following table shows selected cost data for each of four university departments:

Department	Number of Faculty	Salary Cost (Fixed)	Variable Cost per SCH
Economics	10	$500,000	$3.00
English	15	510,000	2.00
Physics	8	380,000	7.00
Physical education	7	200,000	3.00

a. Determine the breakeven number of student credit hours for each department.

b. If the objective of each department is to maximize the size of its budget, what change in the type of course offerings and assignment of faculty to courses might result from such a budgeting system?

c. Suppose that student credit hours have been declining steadily for several years in physical education while they have been growing rapidly in economics. Given these trends, what advantages and disadvantages would the new budgeting system offer compared to the one used previously?

7-5. Ruby Vazquez has invested $80,000 in a hardware store. Business has been good, and the store shows an accounting profit of $10,000 for the last year. This profit is after taxes and after payment of a $20,000 salary to Ms. Vazquez. This salary is less than the $40,000 she could make at another job. Considering the risk involved in the hardware business, she believes that a 15 percent after-tax rate of return is appropriate for this type of investment.

a. Given this information, calculate the *economic* profit earned by Ms. Vasquez.

b. What accounting profit would the firm have to earn in order for the firm to break even in terms of economic profit?

7-6. Universal Dental Products, Inc. manufactures false teeth with a pliable base that allows one size to fit any mouth. A set of these dentures sells for $80. Fixed costs are $200,000 per production period and the profit contribution is 40 percent of price.

a. Determine the operating profit elasticity at output rates of 8,000, 10,000, and 12,000 units.

b. For the next production period, fixed costs will increase to $300,000 due to a major capital investment program, but the new and more efficient machinery will result in lower variable production costs so that variable cost per unit will be reduced by $8. If price is unchanged, recompute the operating profit elasticity at output rates of 8,000, 10,000, and 12,000 units.

c. What change in the risk–return trade-off has the company made by this capital investment program?

7-7. Space Dynamics, Inc. produces electronic components for an antimissile system. Each component sells for $900, average variable cost is constant at $700, and total fixed cost is $10,000.

a. Determine the breakeven rate of output.

b. Demonstrate that the profit elasticity declines as the output rate increases.

c. Show that for any rate of output, profit elasticity increases if fixed cost increases and this elasticity will decrease as variable cost per unit decreases.

7-8. Southern Airways, a small regional airline, has a daily late evening flight into Atlanta. The plane must be in Atlanta at 8:00 A.M. each morning for a flight to Richmond, Virginia. Unfortunately, the charge for a plane remaining overnight in Atlanta is $500. One alternative is to schedule a 9:00 P.M. flight to Gainesville, Florida (a one-hour trip), and a 6:00 A.M. flight back to Atlanta. There is no charge for the overnight stay at Gainesville. However, the flights to and from Gainesville will average only about ten passengers each at a one-way fare of $50. The operating cost of the plane is $600 per hour. The company's total fixed costs are allocated to each flight at the rate of $300 per hour. Should the plane stay in Atlanta overnight, or should flights to and from Gainesville be scheduled? Explain your decision.

7-9. A firm is considering the rental of a new copying machine. The rental terms of each of the three machines under consideration are given here:

| | Costs | | |
Machine	Monthly Fee		Per Copy
A	$1,000	+	$0.02
B	300	+	0.04
C	100	+	0.05

a. How many copies per month would the firm have to make for B to be a lower total cost machine than C?
b. For A to be lower cost than B?

7-10. During the last period, the sum of average profit and fixed costs for a firm totaled $100,000. Unit sales were 10,000. If variable cost per unit was $4, what was the selling price of a unit of output? How much would profit change if the firm produced and sold 11,000 units of output? (Assume average variable cost remains at $4 per unit.)

7-11. The economics department of Western Drilling, a producer of natural gas, has estimated the long-run total cost function for natural gas distribution to be

$$TC = 200Q - 0.004Q^3$$

where TC is total cost and Q is millions of cubic feet (MMCF) of natural gas per day.

a. Determine an equation for the long-run average cost of distributing natural gas and plot it on a graph over the range $10 \leq Q \leq 150$.
b. At present, Western produces but does not distribute natural gas. Interstate Pipeline is the only distributor of gas in the region, and it carries about 100 MMCF per day. Management at Western estimates the regional market will grow from 100 to 150 MMCF per day and thinks it might be able to capture about 50 percent of the increase in the size of the market. Interstate has the capacity to deliver 200 MMCF per day. Will Western be able to compete against Interstate in the distribution of gas? Explain. (Assume Interstate has the same total cost function as Western Drilling.)

Problems Requiring Calculus _____

7-12. Economists at Jensen Enterprises used time-series data to estimate the following total cost function for the firm:

$$TC = 200 - 2Q + 0.05Q^2$$

where TC is total cost and Q is the output rate.

   a. Determine an equation for the average cost function for Jensen Enterprises. Plot this function, and find the output rate that minimizes average cost.

   b. Is the production process at Jensen characterized by decreasing constant, or increasing returns to scale?

   c. If the market price of output is $4.32 per unit, is there a scale of plant that would allow the firm to earn an economic profit or, at a minimum, to break even?

7-13. Given the total cost function for Randle Enterprises:

$$TC = 100Q - 3Q^2 + 0.1Q^3$$

   a. Determine the average cost function and the rate of output that will minimize average cost.

   b. Determine the marginal cost function and rate of output that will minimize marginal cost.

7-14. Logan Manufacturing produces ball point pens. Fixed costs in each production period are $25,000, and the total variable cost (TVC) is given by the equation

$$TVC = 0.15Q + 0.1Q^2$$

where Q is the rate of output. What output rate would minimize average total cost?

7-15. Given the total cost function

$$TC = 1{,}000 + 200Q - 9Q^2 + 0.25Q^3$$

determine:

   a. The equation for each total and per-unit cost function (i.e., TVC, FC, AFC, AVC, AC, and MC).

   b. The lowest price for output that would allow the firm to break even.

   c. The lowest price for output that would allow the firm to cover average variable cost.

7-16. A firm sells its output for $20 per unit and has a total cost function

$$TC = 16 + 17Q - 9Q^2 + Q^3$$

Determine:

   a. The firm's total profit function.

   b. The firm's marginal cost function.

   c. The operating profit elasticity at output rates of 8 and 15 units.

Microcomputer Problems

The following problems can be solved using the microcomputer program TOOLS available with the study guide, or by using other computer software.

7-17. The quantity produced (in thousands) and the average cost (in dollars) of producing a toy at different plants are shown here.

Plant	Average Cost	Quantity	(Quantity)²
1	$0.75	100	10,000
2	0.40	200	40,000
3	0.50	140	19,600
4	0.60	260	67,600
5	0.45	160	25,600
6	0.55	120	14,400
7	0.70	280	78,400
8	0.45	180	32,400
9	0.40	220	48,400
10	0.45	240	57,600

a. Use regression analysis to estimate average cost as a linear function of quantity produced. Write the equation, t-statistics, and coefficient of determination. Does the equation exhibit increasing, decreasing, or constant returns to scale?

b. Use regression analysis to estimate average cost as a linear function of quantity and quantity squared (e.g., the quantity and quantity squared data for plant 1 would be 100 and 10,000, respectively). Determine the equation, t-statistics, and coefficient of determination. At what quantity is average cost a minimum? Over what range of output are increasing returns to scale indicated? What about decreasing returns to scale?

c. Using the results from part (b), what is the minimum output necessary to break even at a price of $0.55?

7-18. A plant has been operating for ten periods. The output rate and total cost for each period are shown here.

Period	O	TC
1	4	$ 1,300
2	12	1,700
3	21	4,400
4	16	2,900
5	30	10,500
6	11	1,900
7	6	1,250
8	27	9,500
9	19	3,550
10	8	1,400

a. Use the multiple regression technique to estimate the cubic total cost function:

$$TC = d_0 + d_1 Q + d_2 Q^2 + d_3 Q^3$$

(Hint: Create two additional variables, Q^2 and Q^3, and then regress TC on Q, Q^2, and Q^3.)

b. Use the estimated total cost function to derive equations for average cost and marginal cost.

c. Using the same data, compute average costs by dividing TC by Q for each of the ten periods. Using the computed average cost data, estimate the quadratic average cost function

$$AC = e_0 + e_1Q + e_2Q^2$$

How do your results compare with the estimated average cost equation from part (b)?

CHAPTER 8

Linear Programming

Preview

In Chapter 6, the concept of a constrained optimization problem was introduced. In general, such problems consist of an objective function and one or more constraints. For example, one problem addressed in that chapter is to minimize cost (the objective) subject to meeting a specified level of production (the constraint). The essence of economics is efficient resource allocation when resources are scarce. Specifying one or more constraints is simply a way of identifying this scarcity.

Linear programming (LP) is a technique for solving a special set of constrained optimization problems where the objective function is linear and there are one or more linear constraints. It is a powerful decision-making technique that has found application in a variety of managerial problems. Not only does linear programming have value in decision making, it also helps in understanding the concepts of constrained optimization and opportunity cost.

In the first section of this chapter, examples of problems that lend themselves to linear programming analysis are suggested. In the next two sections, different types of programming problems are considered. First, a profit-maximization problem is set up and solved and then a cost-minimization problem is considered. In each case, both a graphical and an algebraic approach to the solution are presented. Actually, most real-world programming problems are solved by computers, but it is important that the principles underlying the solutions be understood. The next section, on sensitivity analysis, shows how changes in one or more parameters of the linear programming problem affect the final solution. In the fifth section, a set of special considerations relevant to linear programming problems is presented. Finally, the concept of primal and dual linear programs is discussed.

Linear Programming Applications

Because all managers face constrained optimization problems, it should not be surprising that linear programming has many uses in business. The earliest applications were in production-related problems. For example, managers in multiproduct firms sought the combination of output rates for each of several products that would maximize profit subject to a limited number of machine-hours and worker-days. An alternative production problem might have been to find that combination of output rates that could be produced at minimum cost while meeting a specified set of orders and inventory requirements.

In the marketing area, linear programming is used to select the minimum-cost mix of radio, television, and magazine advertising that will meet constraints on the total number of people exposed to the advertising and the number in certain age, sex, and income classes. Financial managers use linear programming models to determine the least-cost method of financing the firm given such constraints as bank borrowing limitations and a maximum ratio of debt to equity. In addition, the technique is now being used to value leases, bonds, pension liabilities, and options on common stock.

Many transportation problems can also be solved by linear programming. Consider an automobile producer with several manufacturing plants and numerous dealers throughout the country. How should shipments of cars be made from plants to dealers to minimize total transportation costs? A special transportation variant of linear programming has been developed to solve problems of this type. Also, the airline industry has used linear programming to assign gates to flights in order to minimize the total walking distance of all passengers.

Linear programming has been widely used in agriculture. For example, dairy farmers and beef cattle producers have used the technique to determine the least-cost combination of feeds that would meet minimum nutrition requirements for their animals. Agribusiness managers also have used linear programming to determine the profit-maximizing allocation of land to different crops subject to such constraints as fixed land area, differing soil characteristics, and limited water availability.

These are but a few of the many constrained optimization problems that face managers. Historically, some managers used intuition and guesswork to make resource allocation decisions. In the era of scientific management, however, better techniques are available and should be used if the firm is to compete successfully. Linear programming is among the most important of these techniques.

The Linearity Assumption

All the important relationships in a linear programming problem must be linear. These often include the production, total cost, total revenue, and profit functions. The assumption that these functions are linear also means that it is assumed that there are constant returns to scale in production, that the price of output is constant for all output levels, and that input prices are constant regardless of the amount of input purchased. The combination of constant returns to scale and constant input prices implies that production cost per unit of output is constant. Further, the combination of constant per-unit cost and output price results in a constant rate of profit per unit of output.

Some critics of linear programming argue that the assumption of linearity is inconsistent with other aspects of economic theory that are based on U-shaped cost curves, production functions having other than constant returns to scale, and nonlinear profit functions. Although these critics have a point, cost and profit per unit may be constant over a limited range of output, and thus the assumptions underlying linear programming would be valid for that range. More important, the successful application of linear programming to many managerial problems suggests that the technique is a useful management tool. Even where the important relationships are not exactly linear, the programming approach still may be the best way to approximate optimal resource allocation.[1]

---

[1] There are nonlinear programming methods for problems involving nonlinear functions. For example, see D. Luenberger, *Linear and Nonlinear Programming*, Reading, MA: Addison-Wesley, 1989.

KEY CONCEPTS

- Linear programming is a widely used quantitative technique for solving constrained optimization problems where both the objective function and the constraints are linear.
- The linearity assumption means that there are constant output and input prices, constant returns to scale in production, and constant cost and profit per unit of output.

Constrained Profit Maximization

Many firms simultaneously produce several products in a plant. Management faces the problem of whether to produce more or less of one product (i.e., to allocate more or less resources to that product) relative to the others. That decision is based on a comparison of the profit earned on an additional unit of output relative to the opportunity cost of the resources devoted to producing that unit. Linear programming is well suited to solving problems of this type.

Structuring the Problem

Consider a firm that produces two products, A and B, that require processing on three different machines. During the production period, the number of hours available on each machine is limited. Assume that profit per unit of each output is constant for all relevant rates of output. The problem facing the firm is to determine the quantities of A and B (i.e., Q_A and Q_B) that will maximize profit but not require more than the limited number of machine hours available. Q_A and Q_B are referred to as *decision variables*.

The management's objective must be stated in the form of a function, hence, the term *objective function*. In this problem the objective function is

$$\pi = aQ_A + bQ_B \tag{8-1}$$

where π represents total profit and a and b are the profit per unit of A and B produced. Solving for Q_B yields

$$Q_B = \frac{\pi}{b} - \frac{a}{b}Q_A \tag{8-2}$$

Equation (8-2) describes a straight line where the vertical intercept is determined by the ratio of total profit to profit per unit of product B (i.e., π/b) and the slope is the negative of the ratio a/b, or the relative profitability of the two products. As both a and b are positive, the slope of the line will be negative.

Suppose that profit per unit of output is $3 for product A and $1 for product B. The profit or objective function is then

$$\pi = 3Q_A + 1Q_B$$

which can be rewritten as

$$Q_B = \pi - 3Q_A \tag{8-3}$$

If the rate of profit, π, is specified, equation (8-3) defines all combinations of Q_A and Q_B that yield that rate of profit. Thus equation (8-3) can be considered an isoprofit equation. For example, if $\pi = 90$, some of the combinations of Q_A and Q_B that yield that profit rate are

Q_A	Q_B
0	90
10	60
20	30
30	0

This \$90 isoprofit line is shown in Figure 8-1 together with the isoprofit lines for $\pi = 60$ and 120. The management problem is to attain the highest profit possible given the resource constraints facing the firm.

Recall that producing products A and B requires processing on three different machines. Let these machines be designated X, Y, and Z. Table 8-1 lists the hours

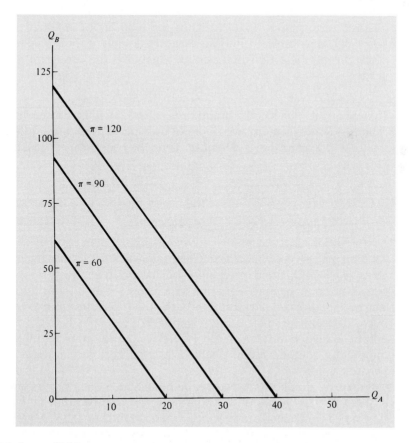

FIGURE 8-1 **Isoprofit Lines.**

TABLE 8-1 **Resource (Machine Time) Requirements Per Unit of Output and Total Machine Time Available**

| Machine | Hours of Machine Time Required Per Unit of Output for | | Total Hours of Machine Time Available |
	Product A	Product B	
X	1	3	90
Y	2	2	80
Z	2	0	60

of time per unit of output that are required on each machine and the hours of time available on each machine during the production period.

For example, on machine X each unit of product A requires one hour and each unit of B requires three hours. Thus, for any output rate, Q_A, the number of machine X hours required is $1Q_A$; for any output rate, Q_B, the number of hours required on machine X is $3Q_B$. Thus the total hours required on machine X is $1Q_A + 3Q_B$, and Table 8-1 indicates that this total is limited to no more than ninety hours during the production period. Therefore, the constraint for machine X is written

$$1Q_A + 3Q_B \leq 90 \qquad (8\text{-}4)$$

This inequality reflects the limited resource availability of machine time.

Both products require two hours of time per unit of output on machine Y and the total time available is 80 hours. Thus the constraint for machine Y is

$$2Q_A + 2Q_B \leq 80 \qquad (8\text{-}5)$$

Finally, product A requires two hours of time on machine Z per unit of output, but product B does not require the use of this machine, so the constraint is

$$2Q_A \leq 60 \qquad (8\text{-}6)$$

In addition, a set of nonnegativity requirements is added to assure that the solution makes economic sense. These requirements specify that all relevant variables (e.g., output and machine time) be positive. Negative values for either output or hours of time would be meaningless, but without these nonnegativity constraints, the mathematical approach could easily result in one or more values of the decision variables being negative. For example, because profit per unit of output is higher for A than for B, if the nonnegativity requirements were not imposed, a solution might result in a large positive value for Q_A and a large negative value for Q_B.

Requiring that both Q_A and Q_B be nonnegative (i.e., $Q_A \geq 0$ and $Q_B \geq 0$) also ensures that the hours of machine time will also be nonnegative. The hours of time on each machine are specified by constraints (8-4), (8-5), and (8-6). The only way that negative machine hours could occur would be for there to be negative values for the output rates Q_A and Q_B.

Now the linear programming problem is complete and can be stated as follows:

maximize: $\pi = 3Q_A + 1Q_B$ (objective function)

subject to: $\begin{aligned} 1Q_A + 3Q_B &\leq 90 & \text{machine } X \text{ constraint} \\ 2Q_A + 2Q_B &\leq 80 & \text{machine } Y \text{ constraint} \\ 2Q_B + 2Q_A &\leq 60 & \text{machine } Z \text{ constraint} \\ nn + Q_A, Q_B &\geq 0 & \text{nonnegativity constraints} \end{aligned}$

The Feasible Region

The next step is to determine the output rates Q_A and Q_B that can be produced without violating the constraints. The five constraints are shown graphically in Figure 8-2. Consider the first constraint, $Q_A + 3Q_B \leq 90$, which is shown as the machine X constraint in the figure. To draw this constraint, consider the relation as an equality and solve for Q_B, that is,

$$Q_B = 30 - \frac{1}{3}Q_A$$

This is the equation for a straight line that has a vertical intercept of 30 and a slope of $-\frac{1}{3}$. Now find two points on that line by setting $Q_A = 0$ and solving for $Q_B = 30$, yielding the point $(0, 30)$, and then by setting $Q_B = 0$ and solving for $Q_A = 90$, thus yielding a second point $(90, 0)$. These two points are sufficient to identify the line. Because it is a less-than-or-equal-to constraint, all values on or below this line meet the constraint. Similarly, all points on or below the line $2Q_A + 2Q_B \leq 80$ meet the machine Y constraint, and points to the left of $2Q_A \leq 60$ meet the constraint on hours available for machine Z. Finally, the nonnegativity requirements $Q_A, Q_B \geq 0$ restrict the allowable rates of the decision variables to the northeast quadrant, that is, where Q_A and Q_B are nonnegative.

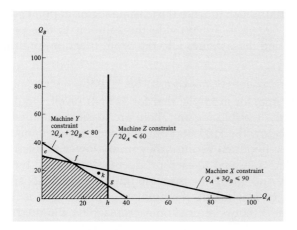

FIGURE 8-2 **The Feasible Region.**

In general, the feasible region consists of all values of the decision variables that satisfy all the constraints simultaneously. In this example, the feasible region of production is that set of combinations of the decision variables, Q_A and Q_B, that meets all five constraints. This set is shown as the shaded area in Figure 8-2. Any point on or within that boundary can be produced because all the constraints are satisfied. A point such as k is not in the feasible region because it does not satisfy the constraint for machine Y. The linear programming problem is to identify the one combination (Q_A, Q_B) within the feasible region that yields maximum profit.

KEY CONCEPTS

- All linear programming problems consist of an objective function, one or more resource constraints, and a nonnegativity constraint for each decision variable.
- The feasible region consists of all combinations of values for the decision variables that satisfy all of the constraints.
- The goal of linear programming is to find that point in the feasible region that optimizes (i.e., either maximizes or minimizes) the objective function.

Graphic Solution

Recall the problem of maximizing production subject to a budget constraint from Chapter 6. The budget constraint defined a feasible set of input combinations. The problem was to find the highest isoquant that touched that budget constraint. The linear programming problem discussed here is analogous to that production problem. Here the problem is to find the highest isoprofit line that still meets the constraints, that is, to find the highest isoprofit line that has at least one point in common with the feasible region.

In Figure 8-3, the feasible region is shown together with three isoprofit functions, which are depicted as dashed lines. The highest profit line that satisfies all of the constraints is $\pi = 100$, which touches the feasible region at point g. The coordinates of point g ($Q_A = 30$, $Q_B = 10$) provide the solution to this profit-maximizing problem. Substituting these values into the profit function confirms that profit is $100 at this point:

$$\pi = 3(30) + (10) = 100$$

Any higher profit line, for example, that for $150 of profit, would have no point in common with the feasible region. There are feasible combinations of Q_A and Q_B on profit lines below the $100 isoprofit line, such as point j on the $60 isoprofit line, but they are suboptimal because they imply lower profits.

The machine time allocated to each product is determined by multiplying the solution values Q_A and Q_B by the machine time requirements specified in Table 8-2. For example, for machine X, the number of hours used is $30 + 3(10)$, or 60 hours. The number of hours of time on each machine allocated to each product is shown in Table 8-2. Note that the available hours for machines Y and Z are all

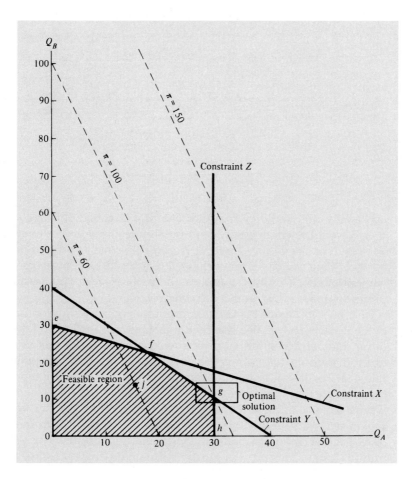

FIGURE 8-3 **Solving the Linear Programming Problem.**

used, but there are unused hours available for machine X. Producing 30 units of A requires 30 hours on machine X, and producing 10 units of B also requires 30 hours, for a total of 60 hours required. As there are 90 hours available, 30 hours remain unused. In the language of linear programming, it is said that the constraints for machines Y and Z are binding but there is slack in time for machine X. The constraint for X is said to be nonbinding. Note the optimal point (g) in Figure 8-3. That point lies on constraints Y and Z but is below the constraint for machine X. This also shows that all of the available hours on machines Y and Z are used but that there are unused hours on machine X.

The concept of binding and nonbinding constraints has implications for determining the opportunity cost of the limited resources. With regard to the specific problem, the available hours of time on machines Y and Z have an opportunity cost; if one or more of these hours were reallocated to some other

TABLE 8-2 **Hours of Machine Time Allocated to Each Product**

Machine	Hours of Time Allocated to		Hours Available	Slack Hours
	Product A	Product B		
X	30	30	90	30
Y	60	20	80	0
Z	60	0	60	0

use, total profit would be reduced. That is, reducing hours available on machine Y or Z would result in a reduction in the rate of one or both outputs Q_A and Q_B. The result of this reduced output would be a smaller profit. But there are thirty hours of time available on machine X that could be allocated to some other use without affecting profit. Thus those hours have zero opportunity cost as far as producing products A and B are concerned.

Also note in Figure 8-3 that the profit-maximizing solution occurs at a corner of the feasible region. Because both the objective function and the constraints are linear, the optimal solution always will occur at one of the corners.[2] By having to evaluate only the corner solutions, the number of computations is greatly reduced. For instance, in the example, points e, f, g, and h are the corners and therefore are the only points that need to be considered. In the computer programs written to solve linear programming problems, the approach is to pick one corner arbitrarily, evaluate the objective function at that point, and then systematically move to other corners that offer higher profits until no other corner yielding greater profit is found. This process greatly reduces the time necessary to determine the optimal solution.

In Figure 8-4, two different isoprofit lines, π_1, and π_2, are drawn. The optimal solution for the original profit equation,

$$\pi_1 = 3Q_A + Q_B$$

(labeled π_1 in the figure), has been shown to be at point g. For the other objective function, there is one dollar of profit for each unit of Q_A and two dollars of profit per unit of Q_B. Thus the profit equation is

$$\pi_2 = Q_A + 2Q_B$$

For profit function π_2, the optimal solution is at corner point f. The solution to any linear programming problem will always be at a corner point, and the slope of the objective function is critical in determining which corner point is optimal.

---

[2] It is possible that the highest isoprofit line will coincide with one of the sides of the feasible region, such as fg in Figure 8-4. In this case, points f, g, and all others in between are optimal in that they yield the same level of profit. Still a corner solution, f or g, will optimize the objective function. The possibility of multiple solutions is discussed in detail later in the chapter.

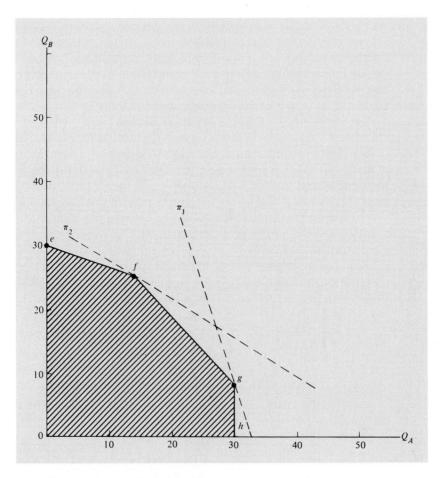

FIGURE 8-4 **The Feasible Region with Alternative Objective Functions.**

Algebraic Solution

The graphic approach just used demonstrates the conceptual solution to linear programming problems and actually could be used to solve some problems. However, if there are more than two decision variables, the graphic approach cannot be used. Fortunately, there is an algebraic technique that, at least conceptually, can be used to solve linear programs of almost any size.

The problem considered in the preceding section involved an objective function, three inequalities denoting the resource constraints, and the nonnegativity requirements. That is,

$$\text{maximize: } \pi = 3Q_A + 1Q_B$$

$$\text{subject to: } 1Q_A + 3Q_B \leq 90$$
$$2Q_A + 2Q_B \leq 80$$
$$2Q_B + 2Q_A \leq 60$$
$$+Q_A, Q_B \geq 0$$

As outlined earlier in this chapter, the general approach to solving the problem is to identify corners of the feasible region and then evaluate profits at each corner. Because the corners are defined by the intersection of the constraints, those corners can be found by identifying which constraints combine to form that corner and then solving those two constraint equations for the values of the decision variables Q_A and Q_B at that point of intersection.

Refer again to the feasible region shown in Figure 8-4. The only points that have to be evaluated are the corners e, f, g, and h. Technically, the origin, 0, is a corner of the feasible region, but it is obvious that profits cannot be maximized at that point. Also, point h can be dismissed as a possibility because point g yields the same output rate for A and a greater output rate for B; thus g is unequivocally better. Therefore, only points e, f, and g require consideration. Hence the linear programming problem can be solved by finding the values (Q_A, Q_B) at points e, f, and g, evaluating the profit rate at each, and selecting that combination that yields the greatest profit.

Point e is the intersection of constraint X with the vertical (Q_B) axis. Thus Q is determined by substituting $Q_A = 0$ (the equation for the vertical axis) into the first constraint,

$$0 + 3Q_B = 90$$

and solving for Q_B, yielding

$$Q_B = 30$$

Thus, at point e, the values of the decision variables are $Q_A = 0$ and $Q_B = 30$.

Point f is the intersection of constraints X and Y. By writing these constraints as equalities and solving them simultaneously, the value of Q_A and Q_B can be determined. The two equations are

$$Q_A + 3Q_B = 90$$
$$2Q_A + 2Q_B = 80$$

To solve for the values of Q_A and Q_B, first multiply the first equation by -2 and add the two equations:

$$\begin{array}{rcr} -2Q_A - 6Q_B = & -180 \\ \underline{2Q_A + 2Q_B = } & 80 \\ -4Q_B = & -100 \end{array}$$

Thus

$$Q_B = 25$$

Now, substitute $Q_B = 25$ into the first equation to find the value of Q_A. That is,

$$Q_A + 3(25) = 90$$

or

$$Q_A = 15$$

Thus, at point f, the values of the decision variables are $Q_A = 15$ and $Q_B = 25$.

Finally, point g is the intersection of constraints Y and Z. The values of Q_A and

TABLE 8-3 **Values of the Decision Variables and Profit at Each Corner Point**

| Corner Point | Decision Variables | | Profit |
	Q_A	Q_B	
0	0	0	0
e	0	30	30
f	15	25	70
g	30	10	100
h	30	0	90

Q_B are found by simultaneously solving the equations

$$2Q_A + 2Q_B = 80$$
$$2Q_B + 2Q_A = 60$$

which yields the solution $Q_A = 30$ and $Q_B = 10$.

Now, by substituting the values (Q_A, Q_B) at each corner into the profit function

$$\pi = 3Q_A + Q_B$$

the profit at each corner is determined. For example, at point f, $Q_A = 15$ and $Q_B = 25$. Therefore,

$$\pi = 3(15) + 1(25) = 70$$

The values of the decision variables and the associated profit rate at each corner are reported in Table 8-3. The values at the origin and point h have been included even though it is known that they cannot be profit-maximizing points.

Corner point g yields the highest profit ($\pi = 100$), and therefore the optimal solution for the firm is to produce 30 units of Q_A and 10 units of Q_B. This is the same solution obtained using the graphic approach.

As the linear programming problem becomes larger, the number of computations increases rapidly. For this reason, most solutions are found by using computers. It is not unusual for a problem to have ten, twenty, or more decision variables and literally dozens of constraints. It simply is not practical even to attempt to solve such problems without the aid of a computer. Numerous computer programs for solving linear programming problems are available and are easily used.

KEY CONCEPTS

- The graphic approach to solving a linear programming problem consists of graphing the feasible region (as defined by the system of constraints) and then shifting the objective function until an optimal solution is found at a corner of the feasible set.

- Solving a linear programming problem algebraically requires determining the values of the decision variables at each corner point of the feasible region and then evaluating the objective function for each set of the decision variables so determined.
- The solution to a linear programming problem will always occur at a corner point of the feasible region. This greatly simplifies the number of computations required to find the optimal solution.

Constrained Cost Minimization _____

Linear programming is an optimization technique for finding the set of values for the decision variables that maximizes or minimizes an objective function subject to one or more constraints. In the preceding section, a profit function was maximized subject to resource constraints in the form of a limited number of available machine hours. In this section the solution to a minimization problem is outlined. The approach is analogous to that used in the maximization problem.

Structuring the Problem

The example used here comes from agribusiness, where linear programming models have been widely used. Consider a producer of milk whose objective is to feed the milk cows adequately but to do so at minimum cost. Suppose that an adequate feed ration consists of a minimum of 40 units of protein, 60 units of calcium, and 60 units of carbohydrates.

The manager must determine how much of two feeds, A and B, to use. One ton of feed A contains one unit of protein, three units of calcium, and one unit of carbohydrates. One ton of feed B contains one unit of protein, one unit of calcium, and six units of carbohydrates. Let the price of feed A be $100 per ton and the price of feed B be $200 per ton. These basic data are summarized in Table 8-4.

The problem is to find the quantities of the two feeds, X_A and X_B (the decision variables), to be purchased so that the feed cost (C) will be minimized. Thus the problem is to minimize the objective function,

$$C = 100X_A + 200X_B$$

subject to the following minimum nutrition requirements or constraints:

$$1X_A + 1X_B \geq 40 \quad \text{(protein constraint)}$$
$$3X_A + 1X_B \geq 60 \quad \text{(calcium constraint)}$$
$$1X_A + 6X_B \geq 60 \quad \text{(carbohydrate constraint)}$$

and the usual requirement that all decision variables be nonnegative:

$$X_A \geq 0 \qquad X_B \geq 0$$

The constraints are plotted in a graph just as was done in the preceding problem. These constraints and the resultant feasible region are shown in Figure 8-5. Note that the feasible region extends upward and to the right of the constraints, in

TABLE 8-4 **Summary of Data for the Cost-Minimization Problem**

	Feed		
	A	B	
Price per ton	$100	$200	

	Units of Nutrients Per Ton of Feed		Minimum Units Required Per Period
	A	B	
Protein	1	1	40
Calcium	3	1	60
Carbohydrates	1	6	60

contrast to the preceding problem, where the feasible region extended to the left and below the resource constraints. This is due to the nature of the resource constraints. In the first problem, the resource constraints were all of the form "less than or equal to" (i.e., $\leq$), thus restricting feasible combinations of the decision variables to points on or below those constraints when shown graphically. In this problem the resource constraints are of the form "greater than or equal to," which restricts feasible combinations of the decision variables to points on or above those constraints.

To find the combination of feed inputs (X_A, X_B) that meets the nutrition requirements at minimum cost, think in terms of starting at the origin, making parallel

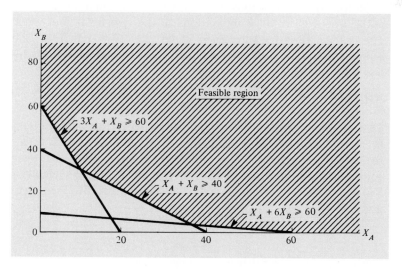

FIGURE 8-5 **Constraints and Feasible Region for the Cost Minimization Problem.**

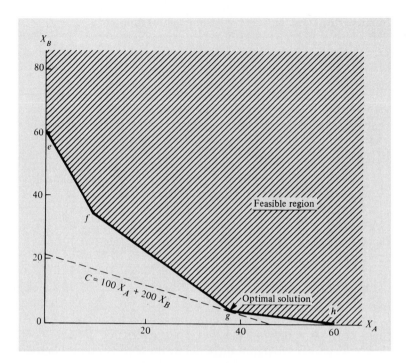

FIGURE 8-6 **Solving the Cost Minimization Problem.**

shifts in the cost equation $C = 100X_A + 200X_B$ in a "northeasterly" direction until that cost function touches a point in the feasible region. The solution is shown in Figure 8-6. The cost function first touches the feasible set at point g, corresponding to 36 tons of A and 4 tons of B. This is the optimal solution in the sense that it is the least-cost of all combinations of the two feeds that meet the constraints. The cost of these feed inputs is $4,400 [i.e., $C = 100(36) + 200(4)$]; there is no other combination of the two feeds (X_A, X_B) that satisfies the constraints and costs less than $4,400.

Algebraic Solution

The algebraic approach is essentially the same as that used for the profit-maximization problem. First, find the values of X_A and X_B at each corner of the feasible region (i.e., at points e, f, g, and h) by solving the two intersecting constraint equations simultaneously at each point. For example, consider point f in Figure 8-6, which is the intersection of the first two constraints. Writing these as equalities gives

$$X_A + X_B = 40$$
$$3X_A + X_B = 60$$

Subtracting the second from the first yields

$$-2X_A = -20$$

TABLE 8-5 **Values of the Decision Variables and Cost at Each Corner Point**

Corner Point	Decision Variables		Cost
	X_A	X_B	
e	0	60	$12,000
f	10	30	7,000
g	36	4	4,400
h	60	0	6,000

or

$$X_A = 10$$

Now, substituting $X_A = 10$ into the first constraint and solving for X_B yields

$$10 + X_B = 40$$

or

$$X_B = 30$$

Thus point f is ($Q_A = 10$, $Q_B = 30$). The next step is to evaluate the cost of that input combination by substituting X_A and X_B into the cost equation. Repeating this process at points e, g, and h yields the values of the decision variables and cost at each corner point. These are summarized in Table 8-5.

Clearly, the optimal solution is at point g. The manager should use 36 tons of feed A and 4 tons of feed B. There is no other input combination that can satisfy the constraints at a cost less than $4,400.

Whether the objective is minimizing or maximizing the objective function, the approach to solving the linear programming problem is essentially the same. First, use the constraints to determine the feasible region. Next, determine the values of the decision variables at each corner point of the feasible region. Then evaluate the objective function for each of those combinations, and select that combination that optimizes (i.e., minimizes or maximizes) that function.

CASE STUDY ———————————————————————————————————

Linear Programming and Hospital Staffing

The allocation of a staff of nurses of differing specialties to the various wards and other departments is a major problem in most hospitals. A large institution may have hundreds of nurses, ranging from practical nurses to surgical specialists. Some wards need nurses on duty 24 hours per day, whereas others may need only one shift. Further complicating the problem, some nurses can work in several areas, whereas others can only be assigned to one. In addition, provision must be made for periods of vacation and substitutes for nurses who are absent because of illness. Most hospitals use temporary staff and overtime work to fill in where members of the regular nursing staff are unavailable. Generally, this alternative is more costly than using regular staff at standard wage rates.

The job of scheduling nurses could be a nightmare in a large hospital. However, the very nature of the problem makes it amenable to solution by means of linear programming. The objective function is to minimize the cost of providing nurses subject to constraints on the number and type of nurses required in each area of the hospital during each shift and the number of nurses available at each relevant period of time.

The administrator at one Chicago hospital faced these problems as she scheduled the assignments for more than 300 nurses. Historically, this job was done by hand and required more than three days of work each month. The acquisition of a personal computer and some linear programming software allowed her to complete this task in an afternoon. Not only did she save considerable time in the process, but the hospital was able to reduce significantly the amount of overtime work and the hiring of temporary workers. Total wage costs were reduced by more than 10 percent, thus saving the hospital more than $1 million a year.

Sensitivity Analysis

Decision markers often are faced with questions of the what-if variety. For example, a production manager might be asked how the production process should be changed if the price of labor increased by 10 percent. That is, how should the mix of labor and capital be altered to adjust for the higher price of labor? Linear programming is an especially useful technique for answering questions of this kind. Given an original problem and its solution, it is a simple matter to change one or more of the parameters of that problem, solve it again, and then compare the original and new solutions. This is the essence of sensitivity analysis.

Consider the optimal feed ration problem in the previous section. Given the price of feed A of $100 per ton and the price of feed B of $200 per ton, it was determined that the combination of 36 tons of A and 4 tons of B is the least-cost combination (i.e., $4,400) of feeds that meets the nutrition constraints. Now, what if the price of feed A doubles to $200—what is the effect on least-cost input combination and its cost? Changing the price of feed A to $200 per ton and solving the problem again yields an optimal solution of 10 tons of A and 30 tons of B, with a total cost of $8,000. Doubling the price of feed A causes a substantial change in the optimal mix of feeds and a large increase in cost.

Sensitivity analysis also can be used to measure the effect of a change in one of the constraints. For example, in the original problem, what if new research indicated that the animals needed only 50 units of carbohydrates per day rather than 60? Changing the right-hand side of the third constraint from 60 to 50 and solving the problem yields a cost-minimizing solution of 38 tons of A and 2 tons of B, and that combination has a total cost of $4,200. Thus, that change in the constraint resulted in a cost reduction of $200.

Finally, if a new feed that had three units of protein, five units of calcium, and seven units of carbohydrates were introduced at a price of $210 per ton, what would be the new optimal mix of the three feeds? Using the original data but adding a new decision variable for this feed (X_C) and changing the constraints appropriately yields the following problem:

$$\text{Minimize: } C = 100X_A + 200X_B + 210X_C$$

$$\text{Subject to: } 1X_A + 1X_B + 3X_C \geq 40$$
$$3X_A + 1X_B + 5X_C \geq 60$$
$$1X_A + 6X_B + 7X_C \geq 60$$
$$X_A, X_B, X_C \geq 0$$

It can be shown that the new solution is zero units of both A and B and 13.33 tons of the new feed (i.e., $X_A = 0$, $X_B = 0$, and $X_C = 13.33$), with a total cost of $2,800. Thus, the new feed is used exclusively, and the total cost is reduced by $1,600 compared to the original solution.

As indicated by these examples, sensitivity analysis involves solving a linear programming problem, then changing one or more component parts of the problem, solving the problem again, and comparing the two solutions. The coefficients of the objective function, the coefficients of the constraints, and/or the resource amounts on the right-hand side of the constraints can be changed. Also, a decision variable or a constraint could be added to or deleted from the problem.

KEY CONCEPTS

- The algebraic solution to a linear programming problem requires that the coordinates of each corner point of the feasible solution be determined and then the objective function evaluated for each set of coordinates.
- Sensitivity analysis involves solving a linear programming problem, changing one or more components of the objective function or the constraints, solving the new problem, and then comparing the solutions.

EXAMPLE

The Transportation Problem

One area where linear programming has been especially useful is determining optimal shipping patterns. A typical problem is to determine the minimum cost for shipping output from manufacturing plants to dealers. In general, the problem is to determine how much to ship from each source or supply point to each destination or demand point such that the total shipping costs are minimized. The constraints are the maximum production rates at each source and the quantity demanded at each destination.

Consider the following hypothetical example. An automobile manufacturer with plants in Detroit and Los Angeles must supply its dealers in Atlanta, Chicago, and Denver. Assign an index i to each plant (e.g., 1 for Detroit and 2 for Los

Angeles) and an index j to each dealer (e.g., 1 for Atlanta, 2 for Chicago, and 3 for Denver). The data in the following table show the transportation cost per car from each plant to each dealer (i.e., C_{ij}), the maximum production per period at each plant, and the number of cars demanded at each dealership.

	Transportation Cost per Car			Number of Cars
Plant	Atlanta (1)	Chicago (2)	Denver (3)	Produced (Supply)
Detroit (1)	200 (C_{11})	100 (C_{12})	300 (C_{13})	3,000
Los Angeles (2)	400 (C_{21})	300 (C_{22})	200 (C_{23})	5,000
Number of cars demanded	3,000	4,000	1,000	

There are six decision variables, X_{ij} (where $i = 1, 2$, and $j = 1, 2, 3$), representing the number of cars shipped from each plant to each dealer. For example, X_{23} would refer to shipments from Los Angeles to Denver. The objective is to determine the number of cars to be shipped from each plant to each dealer that will minimize total shipping costs. That is, minimize

$$C = \sum_i \sum_j C_{ij} X_{ij}$$

The constraints are (1) the total number of cars shipped from each plant (e.g., $X_{11} + X_{12} + X_{13}$ would be total shipments from Detroit) must be equal to or less than the maximum output rate for that plant; and (2) shipments to each dealer (e.g., $X_{11} + X_{21}$ would be the number of cars shipped to Atlanta) must be at least as great as the quantity demanded.

Thus the linear program is to find those values of the decision variables X_{ij} that will minimize

$$C = 200X_{11} + 100X_{12} + 300X_{13} + 400X_{21} + 300X_{22} + 200X_{23}$$

subject to the production or supply constraints

$$X_{11} + X_{12} + X_{13} \leq 3,000$$
$$X_{21} + X_{22} + X_{23} \leq 5,000$$

the demand constraints

$$X_{11} + X_{21} \geq 3,000$$
$$X_{12} + X_{22} \geq 4,000$$
$$X_{13} + X_{23} \geq 1,000$$

and the nonnegativity constraints

$$X_{ij} \geq 0 \qquad i = 1, 2; \qquad j = 1, 2, 3$$

Clearly, this problem cannot be solved graphically and the algebraic approach would be cumbersome. However, the problem can be solved easily using a microcomputer to yield the following optimal values of the decision variables:

Least-Cost Shipment Pattern to

From	Atlanta	Chicago	Denver	Total Production
Detroit	$X_{11} = 3{,}000$	$X_{12} = 0$	$X_{13} = 0$	3,000
Los Angeles	$X_{21} = 0$	$X_{22} = 4{,}000$	$X_{23} = 1{,}000$	5,000
Total demand	3,000	4,000	1,000	

Note that the supply (production) and demand constraints are met. For example, total production is 3,000 in Detroit and 5,000 in Los Angeles, which are the maximum output rates in those plants. Further, the dealers in each city receive exactly the number of cars necessary to meet demand. The total transportation cost is $2,000,000. No other set of values for the decision variables would meet the constraints and result in lower transportation costs.

Special Problems in Linear Programming

There are several special situations that may be encountered in linear programming problems. Some do not pose a problem but generate rather curious results. In other cases, the result is that there is no optimal solution to the problem.

Multiple Solutions

If the objective function has the same slope as one of the constraints, the result will be an infinite number of optimal combinations of the decision variables. Consider the following problem:

$$\text{maximize: } \pi = 10X_1 + 5X_2$$

$$\text{subject to: } \begin{array}{ll} X_1 + 2X_2 \le 60 & \text{(constraint } A) \\ 2X_1 + X_2 \le 60 & \text{(constraint } B) \\ X_1 + 2X_2 \le 27 & \text{(constraint } C) \\ X_1 \ge 0, X_2 \ge 0 \end{array}$$

In this problem the objective function and constraint B both have a slope equal to -2. This can be seen by rewriting each of those relations as a function of X_2. That is,

$$\textit{PROFIT FUNCTION: } X_2 = \frac{\pi}{5} - 2X_1$$

$$\textit{CONSTRAINT B: } \quad X_2 \le 60 - 2X_1$$

The problem is shown graphically in Figure 8-7a.

The optimal level of the objective function is coincident with constraint B between points f and g. Thus all combinations of (X_1, X_2) in that interval yield

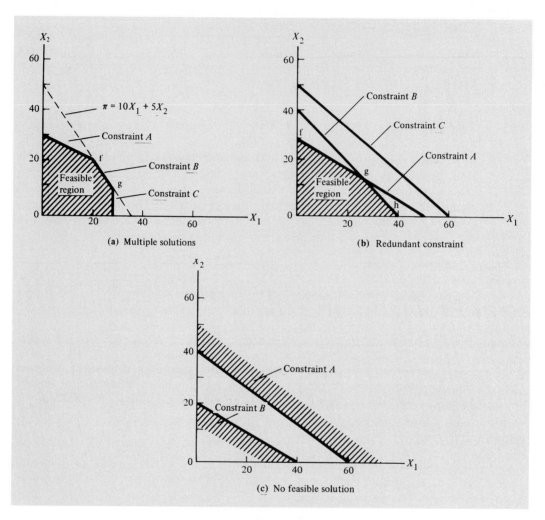

FIGURE 8-7 **Special Problems with Linear Programming.**

the same profit, and therefore all are equally profitable. This situation does not pose a problem, and the solution is exactly as outlined earlier. The corner solutions are evaluated and both f and g yield the same profit. Thus either can be used as the optimal solution.

Redundant Constraints

Sometimes, one or more constraints is unnecesary or redundant. Consider the following constraint set:

$$A:\ X_1 + 2X_2 \leq 50 \quad \text{(constraint } A\text{)}$$
$$B:\ X_1 +\ X_2 \leq 40 \quad \text{(constraint } B\text{)}$$
$$C: 5X_1 + 6X_2 \leq 300 \quad \text{(constraint } C\text{)}$$
$$X_1 \geq 0,\ X_2 \geq 0$$

The feasible region for these constraints is shown in Figure 8-7b. Note that this region is defined by constraints A, B, and the nonnegativity requirements. Constraint C is redundant because if either constraint A or B is satisfied, so is constraint C. This does not present a problem in solving the problem. It only means that the information contained in constraint C is irrelevant and therefore unnecessary. Because constraint C is nonbinding, the resource associated with that constraint has a zero opportunity cost. The solution would proceed as before by evaluating profit corner points f, g, and h.

No Feasible Solution

A serious problem arises when the set of constraints is such that there are no values of the decision variables that simultaneously satisfy all the constraints. The following constraints have been graphed in Figure 8-7c:

$$2X_1 + 3X_2 \geq 120 \quad \text{(constraint } A\text{)}$$
$$X_1 + 2X_2 \leq 40 \quad \text{(constraint } B\text{)}$$

Only points below $X_1 + 2X_2 = 40$ satisfy constraint B, and only points above $2X_1 + 3X_2 = 120$ satisfy constraint A. But there are no points that satisfy both these conditions simultaneously. Therefore, there is no feasible solution.

In a simple problem such as the example shown, the lack of a feasible solution is easily seen. However, in large linear programming problems with many constraints, there may be no way of knowing that there is no solution until the computer program is run. In such cases, obtaining a feasible solution means that one or more constraints must be modified. For example, additional hours of machine time may have to be acquired in order for any production to take place.

KEY CONCEPTS _____

- In some linear programming problems, multiple solutions and redundant constraints occur. Neither of these possibilities poses a problem for solving the linear program.
- Sometimes the constraints define a region for which there is no feasible solution. In this case, obtaining a solution (i.e., finding nonzero values of the decision variables that meet all the constraints) will require that one or more constraints be changed by augmenting the resource associated with those constraints.

The Dual Problem _____

It is known that when a resource constraint is binding, there is an opportunity cost associated with that resource. Consider a profit-maximization problem where the resource constraints are hours of time available on machines X, Y, and Z. Assume that the constraints or hours of time on machines Y and Z are binding. If one hour of time on either of those machines had to be given up, profit would fall. But if the constraint for hours of machine X is not binding, this means that there is a zero opportunity cost for this resource.

In terms of planning for expansion of facilities, it would be useful to have an estimate of the value or opportunity cost of time on machines Y and Z. For example, if the firm could hire one more hour of machine time, should it hire more of Y or Z? Suppose it was known that the opportunity costs of one hour of time on machines Y and Z are \$20 and \$10, respectively. This means that an additional hour on machine Y would add \$20 to profit in contrast to adding only \$10 to profit for an additional hour on machine Z. The dual linear program is a way to estimate the opportunity cost of the resource associated with each constraint.

For every linear programming problem (called the *primal problem*), there is an associated problem, referred to as the *dual problem*. If the objective of the primal problem is maximization of an objective function, the objective of the dual problem is minimization of an associated objective function and vice versa. For example, if the objective of the primal problem is to maximize production subject to a set of machine-hour constraints, the objective of the dual problem would be to minimize the cost of the resources (i.e., the machine hours) subject to a constraint on production. The dual and primal problems are said to be symmetric because a solution to one is a solution to both. For example, in the production problem used at the beginning of the chapter, the objective was to find the values Q_A and Q_B that maximized profit. Determining this combination (Q_A, Q_B) also determined the hours of time used on each machine. The dual problem would find that set of hours on each machine that minimized the cost of the resources devoted to the production of the outputs Q_A and Q_B. The solution to the dual problem would allocate the same number of machine-hours to each product as did the primal problem.

Structuring the Dual Problem

The interpretation of the dual will be made clearer by setting up, solving, and interpreting a dual problem. Recall the original profit-maximization problem on page 265. This will be referred to as the primal problem:

$$\text{maximize: } \pi = 3 Q_A + 1 Q_B$$
$$\text{subject to:}$$
$$1 Q_A + 3 Q_B \le 90$$
$$2 Q_A + 2 Q_B \le 80$$
$$2 Q_A + 0 Q_B \le 60$$

The dual problem is constructed by using the columns of the coefficients of the primal problem as shown by the dashed lines. Define three new variables C_x, C_y, and C_z that represent the opportunity cost of hours on machines X, Y, and Z, respectively. The objective function for the dual problem is to

$$\text{minimize: } C = 90C_x + 80C_y + 60C_z$$

That is, the objective is to minimize the opportunity cost of the firm's scarce resources (i.e., hours of machine time).

The first constraint in the dual problem is determined by the coefficients of Q_A from the first column of the primal problem. That is,

$$C_x + 2C_y + 2C_z \geq 3$$

meaning that the value of machine-hours used to produce one unit of product A must be at least as great as the profit on that unit of output. Thus one unit of output A requires one hour of time on machine X, two hours on Y, and two hours on Z, and those hours are valued at C_x, C_y, and C_z, respectively.

The second constraint is based on the coefficients in the second column in the primal problem. Hence

$$3C_x + 2C_y \geq 1$$

Note that output B does not require processing on machine z, so that there is no cost associated with that machine.

As with the primal problem, there are nonnegativity requirements for the dual, that is,

$$C_x, C_y, C_z \geq 0$$

These requirements constrain opportunity costs from being negative. A negative opportunity cost would make no sense because it would mean that profit could be increased by giving up the resource.

Solving the Dual Problem

The solution to the dual problem follows exactly the same steps as before. That is, identify the values of the decision variables at each corner, evaluate the objective function using each set of values of the C_i, and select that set that yields the minimum value for the objective function.

Because there are three variables, a graphic solution would require three-dimensional analysis and would be extremely difficult to draw and interpret. An algebraic approach is more straightforward, but with three constraints and three decision variables, even this approach can be cumbersome. The solution to this particular problem is simplified because it is known that constraint X in the original problem is not binding, and therefore the opportunity cost of machine X hours is known to be zero (i.e., $C_x = 0$). Thus the problem reduces to

$$\text{minimize: } C = 80C_y + 60C_z$$
$$\text{subject to: } 2C_y + 2C_z \geq 3$$
$$2C_y \geq 1$$
$$C_y, C_z \geq 0$$

Further, it is known that both constraints Y and Z are binding so that both C_y and C_z must be positive. As this can only occur at the intersection of the two constraints, consider the constraints as equalities and solve them simultaneously. That is,

$$2C_y + 2C_z = 3$$
$$2C_y + 2C_z = 1$$

Subtracting the second equation from the first yields

$$2C_z = 2$$

or

$$C_z = 1$$

and it follows that

$$C_y = 0.5$$

These values, $C_y = 0.5$ and $C_z = 1$, represent the opportunity cost per hour of time on machines Y and Z, respectively. That is, a one-hour reduction in time available on machine Y would reduce profit by $0.50 and on machine Z by $1.00.

Evaluating these costs using the objective function yields a cost of $100, that is,

$$C = 90(0) + 80(0.5) + 60(1)$$
$$= \$100$$

This minimum cost is the same as the rate of profit for the primal problem. That is, at the point of optimal resource allocation, profit equals the value or the opportunity cost of the resources being used to generate that profit.

Thus the linear programming analysis has established the opportunity cost of an hour of time on each machine as $C_x = 0$, $C_y = 0.50$, and $C_z = 1$. The value of each C_i is the increase in profit associated with one additional hour of time on the ith machine.

The opportunity cost of any resource is its value to the firm. The term *shadow price* is often used in the context of dual programming problems to describe this opportunity cost. That is, C_i in the problem is the shadow prices of the machine-hours. As the firm makes plans to add more machine capacity, it can compare the shadow price to the market or acquisition price of additional hours of machine time. If the shadow price exceeds the acquisition price, profit can be increased by acquiring more hours. Thus the dual problem provides direction to management when making decisions about expanding productive capacity.

CASE STUDY _____

Cost Minimization at Wellborn Cabinet, Inc.

Wellborn Cabinet, Inc. is an integrated producer of cabinets located in Ashland, Alabama. The cabinet industry is very competitive with numerous small producers located throughout the United States, and the entry of foreign producers is making conditions even more competitive. Unlike most of its competitors, Wellborn's operation includes a sawmill and drying kilns (for treating green wood) so that it can make its own lumber. Each year Wellborn purchases about $1.4 million in wood materials, including various types, sizes, and grades of logs (e.g., hardwood and common) and lumber (e.g., dry and green). The firm faced two questions: (1) Could raw materials costs be reduced while still maintaining the same rate of output of cabinets? and (2) Was the capacity of the sawmill and drying kilns adequate given that the firm's output would be increasing (i.e., did these two resources have a positive shadow price)?

The firm did not have the expertise to make the necessary analysis, so management sought help from faculty members in the School of Forestry at Auburn University. The professors determined that both questions could be answered using linear programming. That is, the optimal mix of logs and lumber could be determined by the primal problem and the shadow price of the sawmill and drying kilns computed by solving the dual problem.

The objective was to minimize the cost of procuring raw materials, and the objective function had 116 decision variables, including four types of lumber (i.e., grades 1 and 2 and types dry and green) and 112 different types of logs. The logs were classified by grade (i.e., hardwood and common), length (8, 10, 12, and 14 feet), and diameter (9 to 22 inches). There were 119 resource constraints in the model, as outlined here:

Resource	Number of Constraints
Sawmill capacity	1
Drying capacity	1
Wood requirements for cabinets	1
Supply of each type of log	112
Supply of each type of lumber	4

In addition, there were 116 nonnegativity requirements, one for each decision variable.

Solution of this linear programming problem indicated that total raw material cost would be minimized by meeting 88 percent of its wood requirements by buying only number 2 grade logs with a diameter of 9 to 15 inches and running these through the sawmill and drying kilns. The remaining 12 percent of its needs should be met by buying number 2 common green lumber. It was estimated that the company would save about $412,000 annually in the cost of raw materials; this would represent a 32 percent reduction from current levels. Also, a positive shadow price on the drying kiln constraint indicated that this facility was currently being used at capacity (i.e., there were no slack hours), and that it would have to be expanded if the output of cabinets were increased.

Some time after the study was completed, Paul Wellborn, the firm's president, wrote to the university: "We cannot follow the guidelines set forth by the model analysis 100 percent, but we are following it as closely as possible. We feel that we can look for a savings of up to $100,000 in this calendar year on solid wood raw materials purchases."

SOURCE: H. Carino and C. LeNoir, Jr. "Optimizing Wood Procurement in Cabinet Manufacturing," *Interfaces* (18:2), March–April 1988.

KEY CONCEPTS

- For every linear programming problem there exists an associated linear programming problem referred to as the dual problem.
- If the primal requires maximizing an objective function, the dual problem will involve minimizing an objective function.
- The solution to a dual problem results in estimates of the opportunity cost or shadow price of the resources that constrain the primal problem.

Summary

Linear programming is a technique for solving constrained optimization problems where the objective function and the resource constraints are linear. Although the early applications of this tool were in the production area, linear programming has been successfully used in marketing, finance, transportation, and most other functional areas of management. The assumption of linear relationships implies that there are constant returns to scale in production and that output and input prices are constant. These relationships imply that cost and profit per unit are constant for all levels of output.

Conceptually, linear programming problems can be solved graphically or algebraically. The graphic approach consists of identifying the feasible region and then shifting the objective function until an optimal solution is found at a corner of that feasible set. In the algebraic approach, the corners of the feasible set are identified and the values of the decision variables determined at those corners. Then the objective function is evaluated for each set of decision variables so identified and the maximum or minimum value selected. Sensitivity analysis involves solving a linear programming problem, then changing one or more parameters and comparing the original and new solutions.

If the objective function has the same slope as one of the constraints, multiple solutions to the linear program will occur. This poses no problem, as the standard solution techniques still will result in finding one of these several optimal solutions. In other cases, there is no feasible solution because the constraint system is such that there are no values of the decision variables that simultaneously satisfy all of the constraints. A resolution of this problem requires that one or more constraints be relaxed by augmenting the resources used in that constraint.

For every primal linear programming problem, there is an associated linear program referred to as the dual problem. If the primal problem requires maximizing an objective function, the dual linear program will be a minimization problem. The dual problem is structured using the columns of the primal problem. The solution to the dual problem results in estimates of the opportunity cost or shadow price of the resources that constrain the primal problem. The optimal solutions to the primal and dual problem yield the same value for the objective functions.

Discussion Questions

8-1. What assumptions about production, cost, and profit functions are implied in linear programming analysis?

8-2. In Chapter 6, isoquant and isocost functions are used to demonstrate how to maximize output subject to a budget constraint. Describe the differences between that approach and the linear programming approach to solving a problem where the objective is to maximize output subject to one or more machine-time constraints.

8-3. Explain the relationship between the primal and dual linear programming problems. If the primal problem is to maximize production subject to machine-time constraints, how would the dual problem be stated?

8-4. Why is it that the resource associated with a binding constraint has a positive opportunity cost but the resource associated with a nonbinding constraint has a zero opportunity cost?

8-5. Why do only the corner points of the feasible region need to be evaluated in solving a linear program?

8-6. List two managerial problems (other than those described in the chapter) where linear programming tools could be used.

8-7. If a firm's production function is characterized by increasing returns to scale, what problem does this pose for using linear programming methods to determine optimal solutions to production problems?

8-8. Consider a situation where the linear programming problem is to maximize the profits associated with producing two products subject to a limited number of hours of time available on each of a number of machines. If a change in technology results in a reduction of processing time required on each machine, explain in general terms how the feasible region of production will change and how the optimal production rates of the two products will change.

8-9. How could the principles of linear programming be used at your college or university to allocate resources more efficiently?

Problems

8-1. Graph the region that is defined by each set of inequalities listed here.

a. $3x + 2y \leq 150$
    $x + 2y \leq 80$
    $x \geq 0$
    $y \geq 0$

b. $2x + 2y \leq 100$
    $4x + 6y \leq 240$
    $2x + 5y \geq 100$
    $x \geq 0$
    $y \geq 0$

c. $10x + 5y \leq 50$
    $2y \leq 15$
    $3x \leq 9$
    $x \geq 0$
    $y \geq 0$

d. $x + y \leq 40$
    $2x + y \leq 60$
    $3x + 3y \geq 60$
    $x \geq 0$
    $y \geq 0$

8-2. Graph the feasible region defined by the following set of inequalities:

$$x + y \leq 40$$
$$2x + 4y \leq 100$$
$$3y \leq 60$$
$$x \geq 0$$
$$y \geq 0$$

Using a graphic approach, determine that point in the feasible region (i.e., the values of x and y) that maximizes each of the following objective functions:

a. $z = x + 3y$
b. $z = 6x + 4y$

8-3. Given the following linear program,

$$\text{maximize } \pi = 4Q_A + 3Q_B$$

subject to the following machine-time constraints:

$$Q_A + 2Q_B \leq 100$$
$$2Q_A + Q_B \leq 80$$

and the nonnegativity constraints

$$Q_A, Q_B \geq 0$$

a. Solve the program using both an algebraic and graphic approach. Check to be sure that the optimal values of the decision variables are the same for both solutions.
b. Set up the associated dual problem and solve algebraically. Check to be sure that the value of the optimized objective function is the same for both the primal and dual problems.
c. What is the opportunity cost of one hour of time on each of the machines?

8-4. The officer in charge of a military mess hall has been ordered to design a minimum-cost survival-type meal that could be used in the event of a serious emergency. The meal is to consist only of milk and ground beef but must provide the following nutrient units: calories—300, protein—250, and vitamins—100. The nutrient content per ounce of each food is as follows:

	Milk	Ground Beef	Minimum Units
Calories	20	15	300
Protein	10	25	250
Vitamins	10	4	100

Milk can be purchased at $0.02 per ounce, and the price of ground beef is $0.04 per ounce.

a. Use linear programming to determine the composition of the lowest-cost meal (i.e., ounces of milk and beef) and the cost of that meal.
b. Set up the associated dual problem and explain how the shadow price (i.e., the value) of calories, protein, and vitamins would be determined.

8-5. National Publishing produces textbooks in plants in Boston, Atlanta, St. Louis, Denver, and San Frnacisco, which are then shipped to distribution centers in Newark, Chicago, Dallas, and Los Angeles. National is publishing a new managerial economics text and must supply its distribution facilities. The relevant data on quantity demanded at each distribution center, production capacity at each plant, and cost of shipping a book from each plant to each distribution center are shown here:

	Distribution Center				
Manufacturing Plant	(1) Newark	(2) Chicago	(3) Dallas	(4) Los Angeles	Production Capacity
	Shipping Costs per Unit				
1. Boston	$0.20	$0.35	$0.40	$0.60	40,000
2. Atlanta	0.35	0.40	0.45	0.50	10,000
3. St. Louis	0.30	0.20	0.30	0.40	15,000
4. Denver	0.50	0.40	0.30	0.30	15,000
5. San Francisco	0.70	0.50	0.45	0.20	20,000
Demand	20,000	40,000	30,000	10,000	

The president of National wants to know how to supply each distribution center to minimize the total shipping costs of meeting the demands at each center. Set up the transportation linear program to solve this problem.

8-6. The economics department at Southern State University produces two products—teaching, measured in student credit hours taught (H), and research, measured in pages published in professional journals (P). In any academic term, the department has 8,250 faculty hours to devote to teaching and research activities. Teaching output is valued at $40 per credit hour and research output at $1,000 per page published in journals. It is estimated that it takes 2.2 faculty hours per quarter to produce one student credit hour and about 24 faculty hours per page published in a journal. In order to meet its mandate from the state legislature, the department must generate at least 1,800 student credit hours per quarter; to maintain credibility in the economics profession, the department must publish at least 120 pages of research output each quarter.
   a. Set up the linear programming problem and draw a graph of the feasible region.
   b. Solve the problem algebraically to determine how the department chairman should decide the output mix between credit hours and pages in order to maximize the value of departmental output.

8-7. The tax commission of a state government employs 150 CPAs, 250 bookkeepers, and 40 investigators to audit state income tax returns. All employees work 2,000 hours per year. The number of hours required of each type of labor to audit different types of tax returns and the average additional tax revenue collected as a result of the audit are as follows:

Type of Return	Required Time (Hours) for:			Additional Tax Revenue Collected Per Return Audited
	CPA	Bookkeeper	Investigator	
Individual	2	4	3	$ 350
Small business	4	7	10	900
Corporation	30	15	24	2,400

   a. Set up the linear programming problem to maximize the amount of additional tax revenue collected subject to constraints on time available by each type of worker.
   b. Solve this problem to determine the revenue-maximizing number of audits of each type of return.
   c. Set up, solve, and interpret the dual problem.
   d. If the agency were faced with a cut in its budget and had to reduce its work force, which type of worker (i.e., CPA, bookkeeper, or investigator) should be the first to be terminated? Explain.

e. What if the state legislature provided additional funds to the tax commission but specifically directed that they be used to hire five additional CPAs? How many additional audits could be performed? Is this decision by the legislature consistent with economic efficiency? Explain.

8-8. Unique Software, Inc. produces two different video games, Firedarter and Paramedic, for the children's market. Each Firedarter game produced requires 0.2 hours of inspection time, 0.1 hours of packaging time, and 2.0 hours of assembly time. Each unit of the Paramedic program requires 0.1 hours of inspection, 0.2 hours of packaging, and 2.4 hours of assembly. The profit per unit is $4 on Firedarter and $6 on Paramedic. There are 200 hours of inspection time available, 300 hours of packaging time, and 2,400 hours of assembly time.
   a. Solve this problem graphically.
   b. Solve this problem algebraically.
   c. What is the shadow price of assembly time? Explain.

8-9. Northwestern, Inc., a profit-maximizing firm, publishes textbooks using secretaries, editors, typesetters, and bindery workers. Given current staffing levels, a linear programming analysis has estimated shadow prices for each type of labor. The annual wage rates for these workers also are shown.

	Shadow Price	Annual Wage
Secretaries	$25,000	$20,000
Editors	48,000	35,000
Typesetters	20,000	25,000
Bindery	-0-	18,000

   a. Given its current budget, should Northwestern change its mix of workers? Explain.
   b. If Northwestern could add one worker, what type should it be? Why?

8-10. Set up the following linear programming problem graphically:
   Max: $Z = 5Q_x + 10Q_y$
   subject to:
   1. $Q_x + Q_y \leq 5$
   2. $2Q_x + 4Q_y \leq 20$
   3. $Q_x + 4Q_x \leq 4$
   4. $Q_y 2 + 4Q_y \leq 4$
   5. $+Q_x, Q_y \geq 0$
   a. Does constraint (2) affect the solution? Explain.
   b. Can a solution be found if the following constraint is added? Why or why not?
$$4Q_x + 8Q_y \geq 48$$

8-11. A firm has m plants, each with a maximum supply capacity per period, and n warehouses, each having a demand requirement. The shipping cost is c_{ij} per unit shipped from plant i to warehouse j.

a. How many terms will be in the objective function?
b. How many total constraints will there be?
c. Set up the general problem of minimizing total transportation costs subject to meeting the supply and demand constraints.

Microcomputer Problems

The following problems can be solved by using the microcomputer program TOOLS, available with the study guide, or by using other computer software.

8-12. The production of type A, B, and C transistors requires processing in each of five areas of a firm's manufacturing facility. The profit per unit on these products is $0.07, $0.06, and $0.08, respectively. The processing times required in each area (in minutes) and the total minutes available per production period are shown here.

Transistor	Time Required in Area (Minutes)				
	1	2	3	4	5
A	3	1	2	5	2
B	1	1	4	3	5
C	2	2	1	4	4
Total time available in area (minutes)	3,500	2,000	3,000	5,000	3,000

a. Determine the profit-maximizing production rates for the three products. What is the maximum profit?
b. Determine the shadow price (i.e., opportunity cost) of one minute of time in each of the production areas of the plant.

8-13. Skoshi Motors, Inc., has built two plants and three regional distribution centers in the United States and Canada. Use the following information to determine shipments from each plant to each warehouse and the production rate at each plant that will minimize transportation costs. What is the minimum cost?

Plant	Maximum Production Rate	Distribution Center	Number of Cars Required
Cincinnati	90,000	Seattle	70,000
Dallas	240,000	Los Angeles	120,000
		New York	140,000

To	Shipping Cost Per Car		
From	Seattle	Los Angeles	New York
Cincinnati	310	380	190
Dallas	260	190	290

8-14. Eastern Marketing must select a mix of advertising in order to reach a minimum of 1 million adult males, 2 million adult females, 0.5 million senior citizens, and 1.5 million children. The cost per unit and number of each type of person reached by the various advertising media are shown here. The cost per unit of advertising is: television, $200; radio, $15; magazines, $90; and newspapers, $30.

	Number of People Reached Per Unit			
	Television	Radio	Magazine	Newspaper
Adult males	100	5	50	30
Adult females	300	20	160	5
Senior citizens	40	10	5	25
Children	100	40	10	5

Determine the number of units of each kind of advertising that will meet the standards outlined at minimum cost. What is the minimum cost?

8-15. Hardcastle Builders, Inc., builds single-family houses and condominium apartments of various sizes. The profit per unit on each of these is as follows:

Condominium A $3,000
Condominium B $2,800
House C $3,900
House D $6,200

Because of a very tight labor market, Hardcastle has not been able to increase its number of skilled employees (i.e., carpenters, bricklayers, plumbers, and roofers). The following data indicate the units of time available for each of the workers and the number of units required for each type of housing unit built.

Labor Type	Units of Time Required per Unit for Each Housing Type				Units of Time Available
	Condo. A	Condo. B	House C	House D	
Carpenters	95	110	105	160	5,000
Bricklayers	40	50	45	70	4,000
Plumbers	20	50	60	90	2,500
Roofers	25	14	30	50	1,500

a. To maximize profit, how many units of each type of housing should be built? What is the maximum profit?

b. What is the shadow price per unit for each type of labor? Assuming that the wage rate is the same for all types of labor, and that the firm could add one unit of labor, what type should be hired?

c. What if the profit on house D falls to $2,000 per unit? How many units of each housing type should be built and what is the new maximum profit?

8-16. Mid-South Securities invests funds for a variety of institutional accounts. A new account, the Southern Teamsters Union, has $14,250,000 in cash to be invested. The union has specified that the following conditions must be met:

1. No more than 50 percent of the assets can be invested in common stock.

2. No more than 15 percent of the assets can be invested in any one common stock.

3. No more than 35 percent of the assets may be invested in Treasury bonds. The approved securities and the rate of return on each are shown here:

Common Stock		Fixed-Income Securities	
High-technology stocks		U.S. Treasury bonds 9%	
Ectotronics	12.5%	U.S. Treasury bills 7%	
Digital Products	11.4%	United Motor bonds 10.5%	
Floppy Disk Inc.	13.2%		
Other stocks			
Western Foods	10.8%		
Southern Steel	8.9%		
International Publ.	12.3%		

a. Determine the amount to be invested in a set of securities that will maximize the rate of return on the pension fund's assets while meeting the requirements just outlined.

b. What are the dollar and percentage returns on the total investment?

8-17. The Springfield school district consists of six neighborhoods and four schools. The capacity of each school, number of students in each neighborhood, and the costs of busing one student between each neighborhood and school are shown here. If the objective of the school district is to minimize transportation cost, how should the children be assigned to the schools?

			Neighborhood				
	1	2	3	4	5	6	School
School			Cost Per Student				Capacity
Adams	0.25	0.50	0.40	0.60	0.20	0.15	500
Hillcrest	0.30	0.40	0.50	0.20	0.40	0.30	1,000
Lincoln	0.40	0.30	0.20	0.60	0.35	0.40	800
Central	0.20	0.30	0.40	0.50	0.45	0.35	1,100
Total students in neighborhoods	300	700	500	400	800	700	

IV

Market Structure

Perfect Competition and Monopoly

Preview _____

One of the most important decisions made by managers is setting the price of the firm's product. If price is set too high, the firm will be unable to compete with other suppliers. But if the price is too low, the firm may not be able to earn a normal rate of profit.

Pricing decisions are affected by the economic environment in which the firm operates. An important dimension of this environment is the degree of competition faced by the firm. A firm in a very competitive market may have little or no control over price. In that case, managerial attention must be focused on the rate of output to be produced. Conversely, a firm that is the only seller of a product may have considerable freedom in setting price. In this chapter two market environments are considered: perfect competition and monopoly. These two cases can be thought of as extremes of market structure. For each case, economic theory is used to analyze pricing and output decisions of managers.

The first section of this chapter suggests criteria for categorizing market structures. The second and third sections discuss pricing and output decisions in perfectly competitive and monopoly market structures. The final section is a brief evaluation of the relevance of the perfect competition and monopoly models. Other market structures are considered in Chapter 10.

Market Structure _____

Managers must tailor their decisions to the specific market environment in which their firms operate. For example, a manager of a business that is the patent holder and only supplier of a new wonder drug will act differently than a manager of a firm trying to survive in the very competitive fast-food industry.

Because the decision-making environment depends on the structure of the market, it follows that no single theory of the firm can adequately describe all of the conditions in which firms operate. However, it does not follow that there must be a unique theory corresponding to every conceivable market structure. By categorizing markets in terms of their basic characteristics, it may be possible to identify a limited number of market structures that can be used to analyze decision making. Although there are many possible ways of categorizing market structures, four characteristics are frequently employed.

Number and Size Distribution of Sellers

The ability of an individual firm to affect the price and total amount of a product supplied to a market is related to the number of firms providing that product. If there are numerous sellers of nearly equal size, the influence of any one firm is likely to be small. In contrast, in a market consisting of only a few sellers, an individual firm can have considerable impact on price and total supply.

The size distribution of firms is also an important characteristic of market structure. When the market includes a dominant firm or a few large firms that provide a substantial proportion of total supply, those large businesses may be able to exert considerable influence over price and product attributes. For example, in the market for small business computers, IBM and Apple are dominant firms. The products of many smaller manufacturers are designed to be IBM- or Apple-compatible and their prices are influenced by the prices set by IBM and Apple. Conversely, in a market with firms of nearly equal size, individual sellers are likely to have less influence.

Number and Size Distribution of Buyers

Markets can also be characterized by the number and size distribution of buyers. Where there are many small purchasers of a product, all buyers are likely to pay about the same price. However, if there is only one purchaser, that buyer is in a position to demand lower prices from sellers. Similarly, if a market consists of many small buyers and one or a few firms making volume purchases, the larger firms may be able to buy at lower prices. For example, because of their sales volume, IBM and Apple may be able to obtain electronic components at prices below those of most competitors.

The market structures discussed in this chapter and in Chapter 10 assume that the market has a large number of small buyers. Situations where buyers can influence price are referred to as monopsonies or oligopsonies and are discussed in Chapter 13.

Product Differentiation

Product differentiation refers to the degree that the output of one firm differs from that of other firms in a market. Where products are undifferentiated, decisions to buy are made strictly on the basis of price. In these markets, sellers who attempt to charge a higher price are unable to sell their output. If there is no difference in price, the buyer has no preference as to sellers. Wheat is a good example of an undifferentiated product. Although there are several grades, all wheat of a given grade sells for the same price in a given market. Buyers are usually not told who produced the wheat, nor do they care. If properly graded, wheat from one supplier is as good as wheat from another.

At the other extreme, consider a product that is viewed by buyers as having unique characteristics. A new Rolls-Royce automobile is an example. Even the most naive car buyer would be unlikely to mistake a Rolls-Royce for a Ford. A Rolls-Royce has come to represent the ultimate in automobile luxury. As such, it commands a price that may be ten to fifteen times that of a new Ford.

Product differentiation is an important market characteristic because it indicates a firm's ability to affect price. If a firm's product is perceived as having unique features, it can command a premium price. However, products considered less desirable will be purchased only if the seller is willing to accept a lower price.

For example, consumers will pay extra for fresh San Francisco sourdough bread, but will buy day-old Wonder Bread only if the price is substantially reduced.

Conditions of Entry and Exit

Ease of entry and exit are crucial determinants of the nature of a market in the long run. When it is extremely difficult for new firms to enter, existing firms will have much greater freedom in making pricing and output decisions than if they must be concerned about new entrants who have been attracted by the lure of high profits. Consider a drug manufacturer that holds a patent that prohibits other firms from making the drug. If there are no close substitutes for the product, that firm will be essentially free from competition now and for the duration of the patent. Thus its managers can make pricing decisions without worrying about losing market share to new entrants. But if the drug can be easily copied, and if prices are substantially above costs, new firms may enter the market.

Ease of exit also affects managerial behavior. Suppose that certain firms in a market have been earning less than the normal rate of profit. If the resources used to produce the product can easily be transferred from one use to another, some of those resources will be shifted to other industries, where they can earn a higher rate of return. However, if the resources are highly specialized, they may have little value in another industry. For example, the track and terminals of an unprofitable railroad may have few alternative uses, and may only be sold for their salvage value. This makes exit more difficult and costly.

KEY CONCEPTS

- In markets where there are a large number of small buyers and sellers, individual firms have little control over price.
- By differentiating its product, a firm can gain some control over price.
- If it is easy for new firms to enter an industry, existing firms may have little freedom in their pricing decisions.

Perfect Competition

The term *perfect competition* is something of a misnomer. In a perfectly competitive world there really is no overt competition between economic units. As buyers and sellers make business decisions, they do not have to take into account the effect of their actions on other participants in the market. The reason is that the individual economic units in perfect competition are so small relative to the total market that their actions have no perceptible impact on other buyers and sellers. Hence decisions can be made without considering the reactions of others. In perfect competition, market participants do not compete against one another. Rather, they make decisions in an economic environment that they perceive as being fixed or given.

TABLE 9-1 **Market Structure Characteristics of Perfect Competition**

Number and size distribution of sellers	Many small sellers. No seller is able to exert a significant influence over price.
Number and size distribution of buyers	Many small buyers. No buyer is able to exert a significant influence over price.
Product differentiation	Product undifferentiated. Decisions to buy are made on the basis of price.
Conditions of entry and exit	Easy entry and exit. Resources are easily transferable among industries.

Characteristics

The concept of perfect competition can be defined in terms of the market structure characteristics of the preceding section. First, there must be a large number of sellers in the market with no single seller able to exert significant influence over price. This criterion is sometimes described in terms of sellers being *price takers* who can sell all that they can produce at the market-determined price. Graphically, this situation is depicted as sellers facing a horizontal demand curve. Similarly, the second requirement for perfect competition is that there are a large number of small buyers, each buyer being unable to influence price. That is, all buyers are price takers.

Third, perfect competition assumes easy entry and exit from an industry. If price is above cost, resulting in economic profits, resources can be mobilized to create new firms or to expand the production capacity of firms already in the industry. If profits are below average, resources can easily be transferred from the industry and used to produce other products at higher profit rates. Finally, under perfect competition, it is assumed that the product is totally undifferentiated. One firm's output cannot be distinguished from that of other producers. As a result, purchasing decisions are based entirely on price. If the firm sets its price above the market-determined level, it will be unable to attract buyers. Price cutting is unnecessary because producers can sell their total output at the market price.[1] Characteristics of perfectly competitive markets are summarized in Table 9-1.

The Equilibrium Price

In the preceding section, reference was made to the market-determined price. Although no single entity in a perfectly competitive market can affect price, the aggregate effect of the participants in the market is important in price determination. Indeed, the interaction of supply and demand determines the equilibrium price and the quantity to be exchanged.

Consider a hypothetical market for wheat. Each wheat producer has an individual supply schedule. Two such schedules are shown in Table 9-2. These schedules

[1] Sometimes the assumption of perfect knowledge regarding prices and technology is included as a fourth characteristic of perfect competition. For ease of exposition, it is not included here.

TABLE 9-2 **Market Supply Schedule**

	Quantity Supplied Per Period				
Price Per Bushel	Firm 1	+	Firm 2	=	Two-Firm Supply	× 10,000 =	Total Market Supply
$8	10,000		9,000		19,000		190 million
7	9,500		8,000		17,500		175 million
6	9,000		7,000		16,000		160 million
5	8,500		6,000		14,500		145 million
4	8,000		5,000		13,000		130 million
3	7,500		4,000		11,500		115 million

indicate the quantity of wheat that will be produced per period at different wheat prices. At each price the decision rule is the same: Additional wheat will be supplied only if the price is high enough to allow the supplier to earn at least a normal rate of profit on the incremental output. Table 9-2 shows that higher anticipated prices are necessary to induce the producers to supply more wheat.

For the moment, assume that the two supply schedules shown in Table 9-2 represent the only suppliers of wheat in the market. By adding the amount that each producer will provide at each price, the market supply schedule for wheat can be computed. This information appears in the fourth column of Table 9-2. For example, at a price of $6 per bushel, the first producer will supply 9,000 bushels of wheat per period and the second will supply 7,000 bushels per period. Thus the quantity supplied to the market at $6 is 16,000 bushels of wheat per period.

Now suppose that there are 10,000 wheat producers with supply schedules as shown in column 2, and another 10,000 with schedules like that of column 3. Thus the quantity of wheat supplied per period at each price will be 10,000 times the amounts shown in column 4 of Table 9-2, and the market supply schedule will be as shown in the last column of the table.

The supply data can be plotted to form the supply curve shown in Figure 9-1. The market demand curve is also shown. As discussed in Chapter 3, the market demand is the horizontal sum of the demands of individual buyers. The equilibrium price of wheat is P_e and is determined by the point of intersection of the supply and demand curves. If price is greater than P_e, there is excess supply. Producers will respond by cutting prices in order to sell the excess wheat. As the price falls, quantity demanded increases and quantity supplied decreases. Alternatively, excess demand exists when the price is below P_e. This causes consumers to bid up the price of wheat. As the price increases, buyers reduce their purchases and suppliers increase production. These forces continue to operate until supply and demand come into balance at the equilibrium price, P_e.

Consider the impact of any one seller on the market supply curve. Table 9-2 shows that at a price of $6, the amount supplied will be 160 million bushels of wheat per period. Suppose that a business like firm 1 in the table decides not to

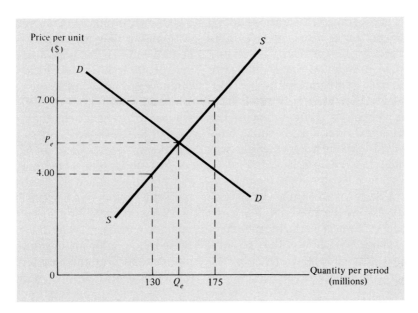

FIGURE 9-1 **Determination of the Market Price.**

produce. The effect would be to reduce supply, but only by 9,000 bushels or about six-thousandths of 1 percent of total supply. Thus the action of a single seller would have no measurable impact on the market. Although the supply function would shift to the left, the shift would be nearly impossible to detect and would have virtually no impact on the equilibrium price, P_e.

Now consider the effect of individual consumer demands. Suppose that there are 20,000 buyers, each with the same demand schedule. Should one buyer drop out of the market, the demand curve would shift to the left. But the shift would be so small as to have no observable impact. Once again, the market price would be essentially unaffected. Thus it is seen that in markets with large numbers of buyers and sellers, individual firms and consumers are unable to affect price. That is, they are price takers in the market.

CASE STUDY

Credit Cards and Perfect Competition

In 1992, over $500 billion purchases were charged on credit cards, and this total is increasing at a rate of over 10 percent per year. At first glance, the credit card market would seem to be a rather concentrated industry. Visa, MasterCharge, and American Express are the most familiar names, and over 60 percent of all charges are made using one of these three cards. But, on closer examination, the industry seems to exhibit most of the characteristics of perfect competition.

Consider first the number and size distribution of buyers and sellers. Although Visa, MasterCharge, and American Express are the choice of the majority of consumers, these cards do not originate from just three firms. In fact, there are over 5,000 enterprises (primarily banks and credit unions) in the United States that offer charge cards to over 80 million credit card holders. One person's Visa card may have been issued by his company's credit union in Los Angeles, while a next-door neighbor may have acquired hers from a Miami bank when she was living in Florida.

Credit cards are a relatively homogeneous product. Most Visa cards are similar in appearance, and they can all be used for the same purposes. When a charge is made, the merchant is unlikely to notice who it was that actually issued the card. Entry into and exit from the credit card market is easy, as evidenced by the 5,000 institutions that currently offer cards. Although a new firm might find it difficult to enter the market, a financially sound bank, even one of modest size, could obtain the right to offer a Visa or MasterCharge card from the parent companies with little difficulty. If the bank wanted to leave the field, there would be a ready market to sell its accounts to other credit card suppliers.

Thus, it would seem that the credit card industry meets most of the characteristics for a perfectly competitive market. However, in some ways the industry appears not to behave in a manner consistent with the model of perfect competition, which is developed in the following sections. This anomaly will be explained in a later case study in this chapter.

Profit-Maximizing Output in the Short Run

This section analyzes the profit-maximizing output of a profitable competitive firm in the short run. As discussed in Chapter 6, the short run is defined as a period of time in which at least one input is fixed. Often, the firm's capital stock is viewed as the fixed input. Accordingly, this analysis assumes that the number of production facilities in the industry and the size of each facility do not change because the period being considered is too short to allow businesses to enter or leave the industry or to alter the basic nature of their operations. The period of time that can properly be designated as the short run depends on the characteristics of the industry. For production of electric power, it may take as much as ten years to bring a new generating plant on line. In contrast, economic profits in service industries may attract new entrants in a matter of weeks.

DEMAND. The firm in perfect competition faces a horizontal demand curve at the market price for its product. This can be seen by evaluating the effect of the firm's decisions on market demand. Using wheat as an example, let the market demand equation be given by

$$Q_D = 170,000,000 - 10,000,000P \qquad (9\text{-}1)$$

The equation implies that quantity demanded per period is reduced by 10 million bushels per dollar increase in price. Suppose that the supply equation is given by

$$Q_s = 70,000,000 + 15,000,000P \qquad (9\text{-}2)$$

Equation (9-2) corresponds to the market supply data from Table 9-2 and indicates that a $1 price increase results in 15 million extra bushels of wheat being supplied per period.

Equating these supply and demand functions and solving for P and Q yield the equilibrium values. Specifically, price equals $4 and quantity is 130,000,000 bushels per period. Now assume that a supplier like firm 2, as shown in Table 9-2, leaves the market. The table implies that the supply equation for that single supplier is given by the equation $q_2 = 1,000 + 1,000P$. Subtracting q_2 from equation (9-2) gives a new equation for market supply:

$$Q'_s = 69,999,000 + 14,999,000P \qquad (9\text{-}3)$$

Solving equations (9-1) and (9-3) gives $P = \$4.0002$ and $Q = 129,998,000$. Note that the exit of one producer increased the equilibrium price by $0.0002 and reduced quantity by 2,000 bushels.

Thus, it is seen that the output decisions of individual producers have no significant impact on the market price. If the one supplier remains in the market, the equilibrium price will be $4. But if the small producer leaves the market, the price is still very close to $4. Graphically, this is portrayed by a horizontal demand curve at the $4 equilibrium price, as shown in Figure 9-2. The curve indicates that an individual firm can sell as much as it can produce at the given price. However, if the firm sets its price greater than $4, it will have no sales because consumers will purchase from other suppliers. Conversely, there is no reason to sell below $4 because the firm's total output can be sold at the market price of $4 per bushel.

COSTS. It is assumed that the firm has U-shaped average and marginal cost curves, as shown in Figure 9-2. The figure shows that as quantity increases from 0 to q_m units, average cost declines and then increases beyond that point. It is important to remember that the cost curves of Figure 9-2 include a normal rate of profit. Thus any time that the firm's price is greater than average cost, it is earning economic profit.

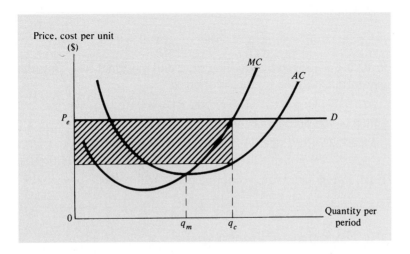

FIGURE 9-2 **Short-Run Profit-Maximizing Output in Perfect Competition.**

EQUILIBRIUM OUTPUT. Because price is determined in the market and the product is homogeneous, the only decision left to the manager of a firm in a perfectly competitive market is how much output to produce. The profit-maximizing output is determined where the extra revenue generated by selling the last unit (i.e., the market price) just equals the marginal cost of producing that unit. For a horizontal demand curve such as that of Figure 9-2, this condition is met by increasing the rate of production to q_c where price equals marginal cost. If the firm increases output beyond this point, the additional revenue, P_e, is less than the extra costs as shown by the marginal cost curve. In contrast, if production is reduced below q_c, the loss of revenues is greater than the reduction in costs and profits decrease. The output rate q_c represents the short-run equilibrium for the competitive firm in the sense that a profit-maximizing manager has no incentive to alter output as long as the demand and cost curves remain unchanged.

EXAMPLE

Pizza Profits

A new pizza place, Fredrico's, opens in New York City. The average price of a medium pizza in New York is $10 and, because of the large number of pizza sellers, this price will not be affected by the new entrant in the market. The owner of Fredrico's estimates that monthly total costs, including a normal profit, will be

$$TC = 1{,}000 + 2Q + 0.01Q^2$$

To maximize total profit, how many pizzas should be produced each month? In the short run, how much economic profit will the business earn each month?

SOLUTION   Taking the derivative of the total cost equation with respect to Q gives the marginal cost equation

$$MC = \frac{dTC}{dQ} = 2 + 0.02Q$$

Profit is maximized by equating price and marginal cost. Thus the profit-maximizing output is given by the solution to

$$10 = 2 + 0.02Q$$

which is 400 pizzas per month.

Economic profit is total revenue minus total cost, or

$$TR - TC = 10(400) - [1{,}000 + 2(400) + 0.01(400^2)] = \$600$$

Thus, in the short run, economic profit will be $600 per month.

Losses and the Shutdown Decision

Simply because profit maximization is the objective of managers is no guarantee that a firm will actually earn economic or even normal profits. Oversupply, poor management, or high costs may prevent a firm from operating profitably at any rate of output. That is, maximum profit may actually be negative.

The course of action adopted by managers of an unprofitable firm should be based on a consideration of the alternatives. One option would be to continue producing at the least unprofitable (i.e., smallest loss) rate of output. Another would be to shut down operations and produce nothing. The best choice is the alternative that minimizes the firm's losses.

In the short run, the consequences of shutting down versus continuing production are illustrated using the hypothetical data for a firm in perfect competition found in Table 9-3. Column (1) shows various rates of output that could be produced, and column (2) shows total fixed costs. By definition, these fixed costs are constant for all rates of output. In column (3) total variable costs are reported. The remaining data in the table have been computed from the information in the first three columns.

Recall that total costs are the sum of total variable costs and the total fixed cost. Marginal cost is the change in total cost (or total variable cost) resulting from a one-unit change in output. Average variable cost is total variable cost divided by quantity. Similarly, average total cost is total cost divided by quantity. Note that marginal, average variable, and average total costs first decrease and then increase. This is consistent with the discussion of costs in Chapter 7.

Now consider the optimal rate of output for a profit-maximizing firm facing a horizontal demand curve. The optimal quantity depends on the market-determined price. The decision rule is that the firm should produce an additional unit of output if the selling price is at least as great as the marginal cost of production.

For example, if the price is $5, the firm should produce seven units because the marginal cost of the seventh unit is $5. If price increases to $6, the optimal quantity would be eight units because the marginal cost of the eighth unit is $6. Similarly, at a price of $7, nine units should be produced.

What if the price declines to $3? Applying the same logic, it would seem that the firm should produce five units. But note that average variable cost at five

TABLE 9-3 **Short-Run Output and Cost Data**

(1) Quantity	(2) Total Fixed Cost	(3) Total Variable Cost	(4) Total Cost	(5) Marginal Cost	(6) Average Variable Cost	(7) Average Total Cost
0	$5	$ 0	$ 5	—	—	—
1	5	5	10	$5	$5.00	$10.00
2	5	9	14	4	4.50	7.00
3	5	12	17	3	4.00	5.67
4	5	14	19	2	3.50	4.75
5	5	17	22	3	3.40	4.40
6	5	21	26	4	3.50	4.33
7	5	26	31	5	3.72	4.42
8	5	32	37	6	4.00	4.63
9	5	39	44	7	4.33	4.88

units is $3.40 and total variable cost is $17. This $17 is an expense that could be avoided if the firm did not produce the five units of output. Because the firm sells output for $3 per unit, its total revenue is $15. Hence, by producing, the firm adds $15 to its total revenue but incurs additional (and avoidable) costs of $17. Adding the fixed cost of $5 to the avoidable loss of $2 results in a total loss of $7.

At a price of $3, producing at any other output rate would cause equal or greater losses. For example, cutting back to four units would also result in a total loss of $7, and expanding output to six units would increase the firm's loss to $8. However, the firm's managers do have one other option. They could shut down the firm's operations and produce nothing. In this case, there would be no revenue and no variable costs. The loss would be the $5 in fixed costs that must be paid whether or not the firm produces. Thus, by shutting down, the firm loses $5, compared to a minimum loss of $7 if any production takes place. In general, the decision rule is that a firm minimizes its losses by shutting down when price drops below average variable cost.

Now suppose that the firm can sell at a price of $4. Price equals marginal cost at a quantity of six units. Sale of six units will generate revenues of $24 and cause the firm to incur total costs of $26, for a net loss of $2. At any other rate of output, the losses are even greater. Is the optimal choice again to shut down, as it was at a price of $3?

If the firm shuts down, it must still pay the fixed costs of $5. However, by producing six units, the loss is only $2. Clearly, the firm minimizes its losses by continuing to produce. The key to the decision is an examination of price in relation to average variable cost. As long as price exceeds average variable costs, the firm is better off if it continues to produce. The reason is that revenue will be sufficient to cover variable costs and make a contribution to payment of the

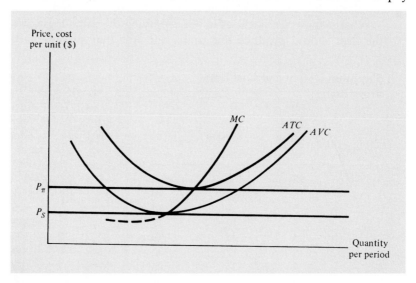

FIGURE 9-3 **Produce or Shutdown Decision.**

firm's fixed costs. In contrast, shutting down means that the firm's loss is the entire fixed cost.

This concept is illustrated in Figure 9-3. That portion of the marginal cost curve that lies above average variable cost represents the firm's supply curve. That is, it shows the profit-maximizing output at each price. When price drops below average variable cost (i.e., below P_s), the firm minimizes its losses by shutting down. If price is greater than average variable cost but less than average total cost, the firm earns less than a normal rate of profit but loses less than if its operations were shut down. Finally, for prices greater than or equal to average total cost (i.e., P_π or greater), the firm earns at least a normal rate of profit.

CASE STUDY

Texas Instruments' Exit from the Home Computer Market

The unfortunate experience of Texas Instruments (TI) in the home computer industry during the early 1980s illustrates the relationship between variable costs and the decision to produce or shut down. In mid-1980, TI was selling its basic home computer for $650. But cost-reducing technology and intense competition from firms such as Atari, Commodore, and Tandy drove market prices steadily downward. By mid-1982, TI had been forced to cut its price to $249, and by early 1983, the firm's basic computer could be purchased for just $149. Still, because TI's variable cost per unit was about $100, the firm was better off continuing to produce, even at this low price.

But improved technology and competitive pressures continued to push prices even lower. By the fall of 1983, market conditions required TI to reduce its price to $99. Because this level was less than the $100 variable cost, the firm stopped producing home computers. However, at the time of the shutdown decision, the company had almost 500,000 unsold computers on hand. Texas Instruments finally got out of the home computer business by dumping its remaining inventory onto the market at $49 per unit.

If the variable cost of producing a computer was $100, why would the firm be willing to sell its remaining machines for less than that amount? The explanation is that the $100 was a variable cost before the computers were produced, but a sunk cost afterward. Thus, the firm was better off selling the computers than keeping them as long as the $49 price was greater than the transportation and marketing expenses (the costs that were still variable) of selling each unit.

Texas Instruments was not alone in its exit from the home computer market. Atari, Mattel, and dozens of smaller companies also determined that their losses would be less if they shut down than if they continued to produce. In fact, the rate of exit from the home computer market in 1983 to 1985 was as rapid as the rate of entry in 1979 to 1982.

Two qualifications apply to the basic decision rule. First, the rule does not necessarily mean that managers should shut down operations every time price drops below average variable cost. In many cases, substantial costs are incurred when a production process is shut down and also when it is restarted. For example, in steel manufacturing several days may be required to bring a blast furnace up to operating temperature, and there are costs involved in laying off and recalling workers. Also, a firm that shuts down and then reopens may find that its customers are buying from other suppliers. These costs must be taken into account. They suggest that a decision to shut down will be made only if it is expected that price will remain below average variable cost for an extended period of time.

The second qualification involves the distinction between the short run and the long run. Note that the decision to shut down depends on whether the firm can make a contribution to its fixed cost by continuing to produce. But in the long run, there are no fixed costs. Buildings can be sold, equipment can be auctioned off, and purchase contracts will expire. Thus, in the long run, if price is expected to remain below average total cost, the firm will shut down and go out of business. Basically, the same decision rule applies to both the short and the long run—a firm should continue to produce as long as revenues exceed variable or avoidable costs.

EXAMPLE

Calculating the Shutdown Price

A bicycle manufacturer faces a horizontal demand curve. The firm's total costs are given by the equation

$$TVC = 150Q - 20Q^2 + Q^3$$

where Q is quantity.

Below what price should the firm shut down operations?

SOLUTION   Marginal cost is the derivative of total cost with respect to quantity. Thus

$$MC = \frac{dTVC}{dQ} = 150 - 40Q + 3Q^2$$

(handwritten: $\frac{d(AVC)}{dQ} = 0$)

The average variable cost equation is given by

(handwritten: $-20 + 2Q = 0$)

$$AVC = \frac{TVC}{Q} = \frac{150Q - 20Q^2 + 1Q^3}{Q} = 150 - 20Q + Q^2$$

(handwritten: $Q = 10$ #)

(handwritten margin note: stupid +)

The shutdown point is where price equals minimum average variable cost. But profit maximization requires that price also equal marginal cost. Thus by setting $MC = AVC$, the result is

$$150 - 40Q + 3Q^2 = 150 - 20Q + Q^2$$

Rearranging terms gives

$$-2Q^2 + 20Q = 0$$

which can be rewritten as

$$-2Q(Q - 10) = 0$$

Solving this equation gives $Q = 0$ or $Q = 10$. Substituting $Q = 10$ into the marginal cost equation gives

$$P = MC = 150 - 40(10) + 3(100) = 50$$

A similar substitution for $Q = 0$ yields $P = 150$. The relevant solution is the nonzero output. Thus if the price falls below \$50 per unit, the firm should shut down.

KEY CONCEPTS

- The firm in perfect competition maximizes profit by producing at the rate of output where price equals marginal cost.
- In the short run, managers of a firm should shut down the operation if price is below average variable cost.
- If price is greater than average variable cost but less than average total cost, the firm should continue to produce in the short run because a contribution can be made to fixed costs.

Profit-Maximizing Output in the Long Run

A key characteristic of the perfect competition model is ease of entry and exit. However, this assumption does not imply that such changes are instantaneous. It takes time for new firms to build facilities and for existing firms to increase output. Similarly, firms leaving an industry may experience delays in converting their resources to other uses. These problems of entry and exit are not considered in the short-run analysis.

In the long run, all inputs are variable. Firms can enter or exit an industry and can also change the size of their production facilities. As a result, although the output rate q_c in Figure 9-2 of page 305 represents the profit-maximizing decision in the short run, it may not be the optimal choice in the long run. Producing at q_c, the firm is earning economic profit. In the figure, per-unit economic profits are given by the vertical distance between the average cost curve and the demand curve at the output rate q_c. Total economic profit is shown by the shaded area. Because the average cost curve already includes a normal profit rate, the implication is that capital invested in the firm is earning substantially more than capital used in other sectors of the economy. Thus owners of capital have an incentive to withdraw their capital from those sectors yielding only a normal return and employ it in this industry where greater profits can be earned.

As additional capital flows into the industry, more output will be produced at each price. Thus the market supply curve, SS, shifts to the right to $S'S'$, as shown in Figure 9-4. This shift may result from more firms operating in the industry or the facilities of existing firms being expanded. It is useful to think of the supply shift as indicating that more of the product will be produced at any given price than before the inflow of capital. As the supply curve shifts to the right, the

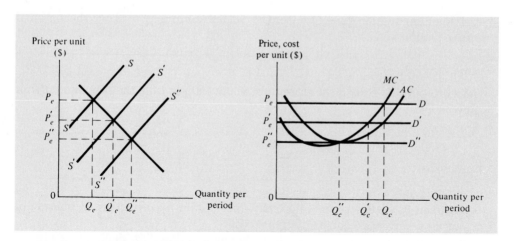

FIGURE 9-4 **Long-Run Profit-Maximizing Output.**

intersection of supply and demand causes a new equilibrium price, P'_e. This result is shown in Figure 9-4. At the lower price, the individual firm now faces a new horizontal demand curve, D'. But at the price, P'_e, the output rate Q_c no longer maximizes profit. At Q_c marginal cost is greater than incremental revenue. Now the firm maximizes profits by reducing the rate of output to Q'_c, where price again is equal to marginal cost.

Producing Q'_c units per period and selling at P'_e, the firm is less profitable than before, but it is still earning economic profit. This can be seen by observing that the firm's average revenue, P'_e, is greater than average cost at the output rate Q'_c. Thus there is an incentive for additional capital to flow into the industry. This additional capital expands capacity and causes further rightward shifts of the industry supply curve. The inflow of capital will continue until the supply curve is shifted to $S''S''$ and the equilibrium price is reduced to P''_e. Hence the demand curve faced by the individual firm is shown by curve P''_eD'' in Figure 9-4. In this situation, profit is maximized by producing Q''_c. Notice that at Q''_c, price is equal to marginal cost, but price is also equal to average cost. Thus the firm's average revenue just equals average cost. Hence the firm is earning a normal rate of profit, but there is no economic profit.

Because the return to capital in the industry is no higher than the return earned in other segments of the economy, there is no further incentive for capital to flow into the industry. However, because capital earns at least a normal return, there is no reason for owners to withdraw capital from the industry. Hence the output rate Q''_c, where price equals average cost, is the long-run equilibrium for the representative firm in this perfectly competitive industry.

Evaluation of Perfect Competition

Prices play a central role in economic theory. The price that a person is willing to pay for a good or service is a measure of the value attached to having one more unit of that product. If a person is willing to buy at a specified price, the implication is that nothing else could provide equal satisfaction for the same amount of money. Obviously, individuals differ in their valuation of products. Also, preferences are affected by how much of a good or service the person already has. Usually, additional units are considered less valuable than the initial units purchased.

Preferences for goods and services are depicted by a demand curve such as in Figure 9-5. The curve indicates the maximum amount that anyone will pay for each additional unit. For example, the curve shows that there is a consumer who would pay P_1 for the first unit, someone who would pay almost that price for the next unit, and so on.

The market equilibrium price, P_e, in Figure 9-5 is determined by the intersection of supply and demand. But only those consumers who value the product at least P_e (i.e., that part of the demand curve above P_e) will buy it at that price. Thus quantity demanded will be Q_e. But in perfect competition, everyone pays the same price. The implication is that all those who valued the product more than P_e receive more benefit than they paid for. This extra benefit is referred to as the consumer surplus. For each unit purchased, the consumer surplus in Figure 9-5 is the vertical distance between the demand curve and P_e. The total consumer surplus is the area of the shaded triangle, P_1CP_e.

Marginal costs are a measure of the opportunity cost of producing one more unit of the product. For example, to produce an additional automobile, fuel, labor, and capital must be diverted from other uses. The value of these inputs in those other uses is measured by their cost. The sum of these input costs is the marginal cost and represents the opportunity cost of producing an additional car, as shown by the supply curve in Figure 9-5.

The profit-maximizing firm in perfect competition will expand production until price equals marginal cost. Concurrently, buyers will purchase the firm's product

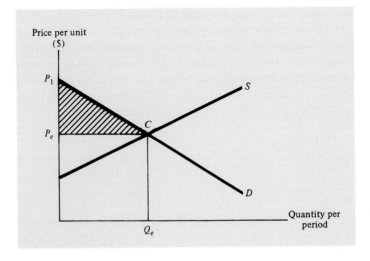

FIGURE 9-5 **Consumer Surplus.**

until price exceeds the relative value that they attach to the product. Because the price paid by the consumer is identical to the additional revenue received by sellers, the equilibrium output in perfect competition has the following characteristic: The value that the last buyer attaches to the last unit of output produced is just equal to the opportunity cost of producing that unit of output.

It is often suggested that perfect competition results in the right amount of the product being produced. The preceding argument is the justification for that statement. If the value of the last unit of output is less than the cost of its production, social welfare would be improved by shifting the resources used in producing that last unit to production of some other good or service. Conversely, if there are potential customers who attach a value to the product greater than its marginal cost and who are not being served because of insufficient production, resource allocation could be improved by increasing output.

Another way of thinking about this result is in terms of voluntary exchange. Firms and consumers will exchange goods and services only as long as both parties benefit from the trade. Thus increased voluntary exchange implies improved resource allocation. Voluntary exchange is maximized under perfect competition because output is increased until there are no consumers willing to pay the opportunity cost of producing an additional unit of the good.

A second consequence of perfect competition is that resources are efficiently allocated among alternative uses. Consider economic profits in long-run equilibrium. In the long run, individual firms earn no more than a normal rate of profit. If the rate of profit measures the productivity of resources in a given use, then whenever resources are earning a higher rate of return in one use than in another, resource allocation could be improved by shifting resources to the higher-return use. This is exactly what occurs in the long-run model of perfect competition. Resources flow into the competitive industry (entry) until economic profit is eliminated. Conversely, if the return in the competitive sector is less than the normal rate of return, resources leave the industry (exit) until the remaining resources are earning a normal rate of return.

A third characteristic of perfect competition in the long run is that production occurs at minimum cost. Recall that the profit-maximizing output is at the minimum point on the average cost curve. This result does not mean that competitive firms necessarily are more efficient than firms in other types of market structure. However, it does imply that, given the technology available to the firm, economic forces in perfect competition require producers to minimize the per-unit cost of production.

KEY CONCEPTS

- In the long run, economic profit is eliminated by the entry of new firms. The profit-maximizing rate of output occurs where price equals both marginal and average cost.

- Consumers who would have been willing to pay more than the market price receive a consumer surplus when they buy the product.
- In perfectly competitive markets, (1) the value of the last unit exchanged equals the opportunity cost of producing it, (2) capital moves to its highest valued use, and (3) production takes place at the minimum point on the average cost curve.

CASE STUDY

Credit Cards, Perfect Competition, and High Interest Rates

In an earlier case study in this chapter, it was argued that the credit card industry fulfills most of the criteria for a perfectly competitive market. But at least one aspect of the industry seems inconsistent with the competitive model just described.

Credit cards serve as a medium of exchange by allowing consumers to charge purchases rather than pay cash at the time of the transaction. If payment is made within thirty days, there is no finance charge. They also are a source of credit, whereby people can defer payment for a purchase for an extended period of time by paying interest. It is the high interest rates charged by credit card issuers that require explanation.

Economic theory suggests that competition should drive interest rates down as card offerers compete with one another for accounts. But the evidence of the 1980s and early 1990s suggests that credit card interest rates remained high while other rates were declining. In mid-1992, finance charges to credit card holders were typically 18 to 19 percent, while banks were paying just 4 to 5 percent on money deposited in savings and money market accounts. Why didn't competition among the suppliers of credit cards cause finance charges to adjust to a level consistent with the cost of money to banks?

The answer involves how consumers use their charge cards. Less than one-half of credit card holders actually pay finance charges in a given month and another one-fourth do not anticipate that they will have a balance that will require that they pay interest. Consequently, only the remaining one-fourth of card holders who expect to pay finance charges are likely to base their decision of which card to select on the interest rate that must be paid. The rest of the credit card users are more concerned about other features, such as where the card is accepted, the annual fee, and the credit limit.

Thus, in setting the interest rate for credit card accounts, banks will focus on the risk associated with those who frequently use their cards as a credit instrument. But who are these people likely to be? Often, those who incur substantial finance charges on their credit cards will be consumers with a relatively high risk of default—people who cannot get credit on favorable terms elsewhere, those who have difficulty managing money, or those with relatively low net worth. Hence, the explanation for high interest rates on credit card balances is that the rates are set to account for the risk associated with the one-fourth of card holders who are most likely to borrow. The majority of customers are largely unaffected by the high interest rates.

SOURCE: Ausubel, L. M., "The Failure of Competition in the Credit Card Market," *American Economic Review* (March 1991), pp. 80–81.

Monopoly

While conditions facing a monopolist are much different from those of firms in perfect competition, the two types of firms have at least one thing in common—they do not have to compete with other individual participants in the market. Sellers in perfect competition are so small that they can ignore each other and consider the market environment as given. At the other extreme, the monopolist is the only seller in the market and has no competitors.

Characteristics

Monopoly can be described in terms of the market structure characteristics discussed earlier in the chapter. First, there is only one seller in the market. This means that the demand curve faced by the monopolist is the downward-sloping demand curve for the market. Second, for a firm to continue as a monopoly in the long run, there must be factors that prevent the entry of other firms. Such barriers to entry are discussed in Chapter 10. Finally, the product of the monopolist must be highly differentiated from other goods. That is, there must be no good substitutes. The market structure characteristics of a monopoly are listed in Table 9-4.

Consider a small, isolated community that has only one supplier of concrete. Essentially, that firm has a monopoly position. When residents want concrete for foundations of new houses, they will have to buy from this monopolist. The high cost of transporting concrete makes it unlikely that concrete producers in other cities will be viable competitors. At the same time, there are few good substitutes for concrete foundations. Wood, stone, and cinder block are possibilities, but they are not as strong or as easy to use as concrete.

Profit-Maximizing Price and Output in the Short Run

Demand and cost curves for a monopolist are shown in Figure 9-6. As with the perfectly competitive firm, the cost curves depict first decreasing and then increasing average costs.

Because they face a horizontal demand curve, managers of firms in a perfectly competitive world have no control over price. They simply choose the profit-maximizing output. However, because the monopolist has a downward-sloping demand curve, as shown in Figure 9-6, managers must recognize that their output

TABLE 9-4 **Market Structure Characteristics of Monopoly**

Number and size distribution of sellers	Single seller
Number and size distribution of buyers	Unspecified
Product differentiation	No close substitutes
Conditions of entry and exit	Entry prohibited or difficult

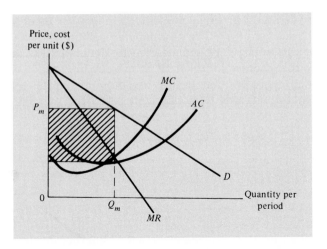

FIGURE 9-6 **Profit-Maximizing Price and Output for a Monopoly.**

decisions can influence price and vice versa. Because price must decrease in order to increase sales, an increase in output will require that the firm sell at a lower price. The effect of output changes on total revenues depends on the marginal revenue curve shown in Figure 9-6. If marginal revenue is positive, increasing output increases the total revenue. If marginal revenue is negative, total revenue is reduced by the increased output.

The criterion for maximizing profits is the same for the monopolist as for firms in perfect competition—output should be increased until the additional revenue equals the marginal cost. For the competitive firm, the price is unaffected by output, so the decision criterion is to produce until price equals marginal cost. For the monopolist, the equivalent criterion is to produce at Q_m in Figure 9-6 where marginal revenue equals the marginal cost. At this output, the monopolist charges what the market will allow, as indicated by the demand curve. In Figure 9-6, this price is P_m.

Profit-Maximizing Price and Output in the Long Run

Notice that producing Q_m units of output, the monopolist is earning economic profit, as indicated by the shaded area in Figure 9-6. If it were possible, other firms would enter the market to take advantage of the high rate of return. With other sellers in the market, the demand curve faced by the monopolist no longer would be the market demand curve. The firm's new demand curve would be relatively more elastic because the firm's output would represent a smaller share of total market sales and thus have a smaller effect on price. At the same time, part of the market and some of the economic profit earned by the monopolist would be captured by the new entrants. Ultimately, the market structure might evolve to an oligopoly (a small number of sellers) or even approach perfect competition. However, if the firm's monopoly position is the result of its control over scarce inputs such as mineral reserves, patents, unique managerial talent, or a choice location, entry by other firms may be impossible and the firm will maintain its monopoly position. In this case, economic profits may persist indefinitely. Thus Figure 9-6 may depict both the short-run and the long-run profit-maximizing price and output for a monopoly.

KEY CONCEPTS _____

- As the only seller, a monopolist faces the market demand curve. The profit-maximizing output is determined by the point where marginal revenue equals marginal cost.
- If entry by other firms is difficult, even in the long run, the monopolist can earn economic profits.

EXAMPLE _____

Computing Profit-Maximizing Price and Output for a Monopolist

Suppose that the total cost equation (TC) for a monopolist is given by

$$TC = 500 + 20Q^2$$

Let the demand equation be given by

$$P = 400 - 20Q.$$

Because total revenue is price times quantity, the total revenue equation is

$$TR = 400Q - 20Q^2$$

What are the profit-maximizing price and quantity?

SOLUTION   CALCULATION APPROACH.   The equations can be used to compute total cost and total revenue at various rates of output. In turn, these data are used to determine marginal cost and marginal revenue. The data for output rates from 1 to 11 are as follows:

Quantity	Total Cost	Total Revenue	Marginal Cost	Marginal Revenue	Profit
1	$1,520	$1,380	—	—	$−140
2	1,580	1,720	$ 60	$340	−140
3	1,680	1,020	100	300	−340
4	1,820	1,280	140	260	−460
5	1,000	1,500	180	220	−500
6	1,220	1,680	220	180	−460

Quantity	Total Cost	Total Revenue	Marginal Cost	Marginal Revenue	Profit
7	$1,480	$1,820	260	140	340
8	1,780	1,920	300	100	140
9	2,120	1,980	340	60	−140
10	2,500	2,000	380	20	−500
11	2,920	1,980	420	−20	−940

Note that marginal revenue exceeds marginal costs for the first five units, but that the marginal cost of the sixth unit (220) is greater than its marginal revenue. Hence profits will be maximized by producing five units of output. This result is verified by the profit data in the last column. Producing four units, total profit is $460, while total profit is $500 for five units. However, total profit is only $460 if the sixth unit is produced.

MATHEMATICAL APPROACH. The equation for marginal revenue is the derivative of the total revenue equation with respect to Q. Similarly, marginal cost is the derivative of total cost with respect to quantity. That is:

$$MR = \frac{dTR}{dQ} = 400 - 40Q$$

and

$$\frac{dTC}{dQ} = MC = 40Q$$

Profits are maximized by choosing the quantity where marginal revenue equals marginal cost. Thus

$$400 - 40Q = 40Q$$

Solving for Q gives five units as the profit-maximizing quantity. Substituting $Q = 5$ into the demand equation gives $P = \$300$.

Allocative Inefficiency and Income Redistribution

Assume that average costs and marginal costs are constant for all output levels, as shown in Figure 9-7. To maximize profit, the firm would equate marginal revenue to marginal cost, produce Q_m, and charge P_m. As an alternative, suppose that policymakers required the monopolist to use the competitive rule of equating price to marginal cost. In that case, the price would be P_c. Those consumers who value the product in excess of P_c would be purchasers resulting in total sales of Q_c. Because all consumers are charged the same price, most buyers would receive a consumer surplus as a result of their purchase. The dollar value of this surplus is the difference between their valuation of the product (as depicted by the demand curve) and the price, P_c. For example, in Figure 9-7, the person who values the product most highly receives a consumer surplus equal to the vertical distance

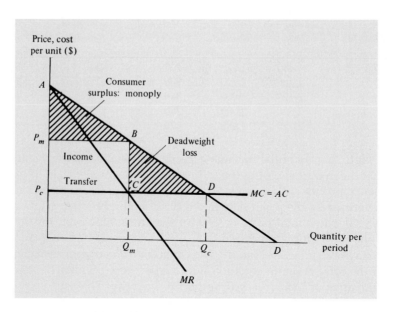

FIGURE 9-7 **Evaluation of Monopoly.**

AP_c. But the consumer who purchases the Q_cth unit receives no surplus because he or she attaches a value to the product just equal to the purchase price. Therefore, when output is determined based on the price equals marginal cost rule, the total consumer surplus is the area under the demand curve and above the price. In the figure this area is the triangle ADP_c.

Now consider output and price of the profit-maximizing monopolist. As indicated, the price will be P_m and the quantity will be Q_m. Although the price is higher than using the competitive pricing rule, there is still an area of consumer surplus created by those consumers who value the product above its price. The consumer surplus in the monopoly case is the area of the triangle ABP_m. This triangle is part of the consumer surplus under competition, ADP_c. The rectangle P_mBCP_c was also a part of the consumer surplus under competition, but now is economic profit earned by the monopolist. This economic profit represents a redistribution of income from consumers to producers. Whether or not this change is considered an improvement requires an assumption about the appropriate distribution of income and cannot be evaluated using efficiency criteria.

Finally, the last component of the consumer surplus under competition is the triangle BDC. This area is referred to as the allocative inefficiency or *deadweight loss* associated with monopoly. It represents the loss of consumer surplus stemming from monopoly pricing and is a net loss to society. No assumptions about the relative merits of consumers and producers or the distribution of income are required to assess this impact of monopoly. It is a loss suffered by consumers that is not captured by anyone.

The source of the allocative inefficiency can be identified using Figure 9-7. The monopolist produces until marginal revenue equals marginal cost. Expanding production beyond Q_m would result in reduced profit because the incremental revenues are less than the extra costs incurred. However, at the output rate, Q_m, the consumer is charged a price, P_m, that is greater than marginal cost. Thus only those consumers who attach a value to the product of at least P_m will purchase if price is set at that level.

Note that the last person to buy values the product at exactly P_m, but the cost of producing is given by the marginal cost curve and equals P_c. Hence the value to the last buyer is greater than the opportunity cost of production. Thus social welfare would be increased if more were produced. Specifically, expanding production by one unit would generate additional consumer surplus equal to the vertical distance between the demand curve and the marginal cost curve. Additional increases in output would create successively smaller consumer surplus gains until the output rate Q_c was reached. At that point there would be no additional consumer surplus. Thus the triangle BDC can be thought of as the loss of consumer surplus stemming from the output-restricting tendency of monopoly.

To summarize, relative to firms in perfect competition, monopolists produce too little output and set too high a price. Whereas competition results in the lowest price consistent with the survival of the firm, the monopolist charges the highest price consistent with profit maximization. From the perspective of society, resource allocation would be improved if more resources were used to produce the products provided by the monopolist. There is also an income distribution effect associated with monopoly, but an evaluation of this transfer depends on judgments regarding the relative needs of consumers and producers. Although economic analysis provides little assistance in judging this income transfer, its importance in public policymaking should not be underestimated. In political debate, a legislator's call to take action against the abuses of monopoly is not commonly based on esoteric notions of allocative inefficiency as discussed in a textbook. Rather, it is more likely to focus on the alleged unfairness of the income redistribution from consumers to owners of the monopoly.

KEY CONCEPTS

- Monopoly pricing results in allocative inefficiency because not enough output is produced.
- Monopoly pricing also causes a redistribution of income from consumers to the owners of the monopoly.

CASE STUDY

The Price of Caviar and the Fall of Communism

Many products produced in the now-defunct USSR were considered inferior by Western standards. However, one area where the Soviets excelled was in the production of caviar. In the Volga River, near the Caspian Sea, the water temperature and degree of salinity are a perfect spawning ground for the sturgeon whose eggs produce the world's most prized caviar.

During the nearly seven decades of communist rule, the Soviet state maintained a near monopoly over the harvest, processing, and marketing of this delicacy. The result was a textbook example of the restricted output, high prices, and income redistribution associated with monopoly control over a market.

Until 1991, the Soviet Bureau of Fisheries made virtually all decisions about sales of Russian caviar. In a typical year, about 2,000 tons of caviar were harvested. Of this amount, the Bureau allowed only 150 tons to be exported. By restricting the amount available to foreign consumers, the price was maintained at an extremely high level. For example, in Moscow, the black market price for top-grade black caviar in 1991 was about $5 per kilogram. But the same caviar could easily have been sold for $500 to $1,000 per kilogram in New York City. Clearly,

the monopoly arrangement caused a substantial redistribution of income from New York restaurant and delicatessen patrons to the Soviet state. During the period of communist rule, caviar was a much-needed source of hard currency for the government.

One effect of the breakup of the USSR in 1991 was to increase competition in the caviar market. The two largest Soviet fisheries now are under the control of two different republics, Russia and Kazakhstan. In addition, fishermen on the Caspian Sea have begun to bypass the government and establish their own export businesses. The results were as predicted by economic theory. Prices dropped by 20 percent in one year. Unless caviar suppliers succeed in forming a cartel to fix prices, further price declines will occur.

Technical Inefficiency and Rent Seeking

There are at least two other negative consequences of monopoly. The first has come to be known as *technical inefficiency*. In discussing both perfect competition and monopoly in this chapter, it was assumed that the goal of managers is to maximize profit. A necessary condition for profit maximization is that costs be minimized for the output rate selected. Consequently, all cost curves shown in the figures represent minimum cost production. For firms in a competitive market, this is a reasonable assumption because the manager may have no choice. In the long run, prices are driven down until perfectly competitive firms earn only a normal rate of profit. Hence, those businesses that are inefficient will not be able to survive in competition with more efficient rivals because they will earn inadequate profits to sustain their operations. In a competitive market, cost minimization is a necessity.

However, a monopolist may not be under the same constraint. Earning economic profits, the manager of a firm that is insulated from competition has some discretion with respect to cost minimization. If costs increase, the survival of the monopoly firm will not be in jeopardy because the business has a cushion of economic profits. But there is a trade-off. Any increase in costs resulting from waste will reduce economic profits earned by the firm.

Why would a manager sacrifice profits by permitting the firm to operate inefficiently? There are several possible reasons. One is that cost minimization requires effort. The search for least-cost resources and the most advanced technology can be difficult. A manager, particularly one who is salaried and not a stockholder of the firm, may choose to go home a little earlier or take a little longer lunch rather than devote full effort to managing. Another explanation is that firms are run by people and people are likely to make mistakes. Decisions are made under conditions of uncertainty by individuals of different capabilities who experience stress and illness. Sometimes these choices may not be wise when judged from the perspective of hindsight.

Labor contracts are another source of technical inefficiency. When workers are hired, the agreement usually is concerned with inputs—the number of hours to be worked. A new employee provides his or her time but usually does not commit to a specified level of effort. Just as managers prefer leisure to work, so do employees. A primary task of management is to monitor performance, but this is not a costless task. Consequently, in many organizations, there is considerable slack.

Although managers may permit technical inefficiency, it is not consistent with the objectives of stockholders. Every dollar wasted is a dollar in reduced profit. To the extent that a firm's stockholders can constrain the behavior of managers, the problem of technical inefficiency will be reduced. But in today's economic system, stockholder control is often limited. Most large firms have thousands of stockholders, and any single individual or group does not control a large proportion of the stock. This separation of ownership and control provides opportunities for technical inefficiency where monopoly power exists.

Yet another consequence of monopoly is the tendency for *rent-seeking* behavior. The ability of a monopolist to earn economic profit is a valuable possession. Any rational person should be willing to pay to obtain and maintain this privilege. If a firm earns $1 million in economic profits per year, the value of its monopoly position is worth up to that amount. That is, the owners of the firm would be willing to spend up to $1 million each year to assure a continued flow of profits. When resources are expended to seek or maintain monopoly profits, this behavior is referred to as rent seeking.

Rent-seeking behavior does not increase the amount of goods and services produced. Remember that economic profit represents a transfer of wealth from consumers to stockholders. But rent seeking is an attempt to capture these economic profits. Hence, the resources used do nothing more than alter the distribution of income. Sometimes rent seeking may be directed toward obtaining income from consumers. If other cases, the purpose may be to obtain economic profits currently being earned by another firm.

Rent seeking results in a deadweight loss because there is no new productive activity. The analogy may be a bit overstated, but rent seeking has been likened to the activities of a burglar. The thief expends time and effort to break into a person's house, and the potential victims install burglar alarms and locks to prevent theft. But all these efforts either facilitate or prevent changes in the existing distribution of income. The burglar's purpose is to acquire the possessions of the victim and the victim's intent is to avoid losing what she already has. Rent seeking is much the same. Nothing new is created. All of the effort is to change the division of the existing pie.

Rent-seeking behavior can take many forms. Often it involves government officials. Choices of policy makers can significantly affect the distribution of income. The location of a defense base in an area or the award of a contract to a firm can mean millions of dollars to the beneficiaries. Changes in tax laws can increase or decrease profits by huge amounts. The decisions of regulatory bodies on who will be allowed to enter an industry or procedures to be followed in conducting business can have an enormous impact on profitability.

But, unlike the Ten Commandments, public policy is not etched in stone. Decisions can be affected by activities of groups and individuals. Legislators are constantly besieged by lobbyists, who argue for favorable legislation. Tens of millions of dollars are spent each year on campaign contributions. A firm may engage in a costly public relations campaign to improve its image with policy makers.

Rent seeking can also have a darker side. Because the stakes are so high, bribes for favorable legislative or agency treatment may be offered. Firms may resort to espionage activities to get ahead of competitors. The legal system may be utilized to harass competitors or to forstall legislation or regulations that could have an adverse effect on the firm.

Waste from rent seeking can actually exceed the total amount of economic profit that could be earned. Although no single firm would spend more than it expects to gain, where there are several contending firms, there efforts may offset one another and exceed the potential prize. The outcome is analogous to shoppers during a sale in a china store. In their attempt to get the best buy, they may break more dishes than they purchase.

Technical inefficiency and rent-seeking behavior imply that the observed rate of profit for monopolists may not be high. As shown in Figure 9-8, economic

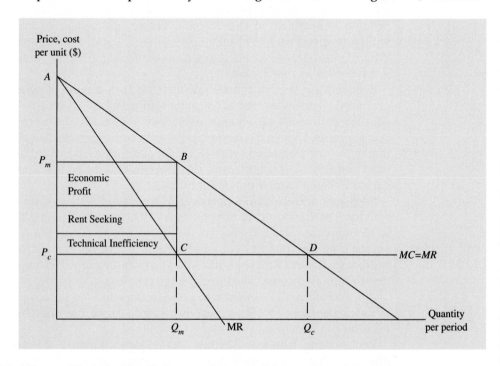

FIGURE 9-8 **Effects of Technical Inefficiency and Rent Seeking on Economic Profits.**

profits may be absorbed by these two sources of deadweight loss. The rectangle $P_m BCP_c$ represents economic profit that could be earned by a monopolist. But where costs are allowed to increase and resources are used to obtain or maintain a monopoly position, the amount of economic profit could be much smaller, as shown in the figure. In fact, it is possible that inefficiency and rent seeking could consume all the economic profit and the monopolist would earn only a normal return.

KEY CONCEPTS

- If a firm has market power and there is separation of ownership from control, technical inefficiency may result because of the failure of managers to minimize costs.
- Rent seeking involves the use of resources to acquire or maintain monopoly profits. Rent seeking involves a deadweight loss to society because no additional goods or services are produced.

Relevance of Perfect Competition and Monopoly

Over 70 years ago, economist Frank Knight wrote: "In view of the fact that practically every business is a partial monopoly, it is remarkable that the theoretical treatment of economics has related so exclusively to complete monopoly and perfect competition."[2] Since that time, important contributions have been made to the analysis of alternative market structures. However, classroom time typically is still heavily weighted toward discussing the extremes of competition and monopoly. What is the rationale for such emphasis?

The assumptions of the model of perfect competition are very restrictive. Few markets would meet the requirements of many small sellers, easy entry and exit, and an undifferentiated product. Certain parts of the agricultural sector are the most likely candidates. For example, in the Midwest grain exchanges, there are many buyers and sellers of wheat. Wheat of a given grade is relatively homogeneous. Compared to activities such as electricity production, resources can enter and leave agriculture without great difficulty. However, to claim that resources are perfectly mobile strains credibility. All in all, it is not easy to think of many circumstances where the requirements for perfect competition are closely approximated.

It is also difficult to think of examples of pure monopoly. In most communities the local electric and telephone utilities usually fit the definition of being single sellers of their product. However, there may be substitutes for their products that reduce the monopoly power of these firms. For example, an electric utility does face competition from substitute energy sources. Consumers usually have the

[2] Knight, F. *Risk, Uncertainty and Profit*. Chicago: University of Chicago Press, 1985, p. 193.

option of heating their homes and water, cooking, and drying clothes with gas instead of electricity. Large industries may generate their own electricity if the rates of the local utility become too high. There are fewer substitutes for telephone service. Still, technological advances and pricing policies can make it advantageous for large firms to construct facilities that bypass the local telephone network. And, in the future, cable systems may compete with telephone companies in some areas.

If there are few, if any, examples of pure monopoly and perfect competition, why expend the time and effort required to discuss these extreme conditions? In many applications, it is useful to think of perfect competition and pure monopoly as extremes, with other market structures positioned in between. Although there may be few industries at either extreme, there are many that have most of the characteristics of perfect competition or monopoly. Hence the value of the extreme models is that they serve as benchmarks. Industries that approximate perfect competition are likely to function much like those in the perfectly competitive model. In contrast, those that have many of the characteristics of monopolies will generate monopoly-like results. Indeed, the monopoly model may be applicable in many situations where producers sell a differentiated product and believe that they have some control over price. In addition to providing information on the likely behavior and result of specific market structures, the extreme models of competition and monopoly provide guidance in making public policy. As a general rule, economists favor policies that move industries toward the competitive end of the spectrum.

KEY CONCEPTS _____

- Perfect competition serves as a benchmark and a guide for public policy.
- The monopoly model may be applicable in situations where a producer has some power over price.

Summary _____

Market structures can be characterized on the basis of four characteristics: (1) number and size distribution of sellers, (2) number and size distribution of buyers, (3) product differentiation, and (4) ease of entry and exit. The model of perfect competition assumes a large number of small buyers and sellers, undifferentiated products, and ease of entry and exit. Firms in a perfectly competitive market face a demand curve that is horizontal at the equilibrium price. This price is determined by the interaction of the market supply and demand curves. Because they have no control over price, the objective of managers is to determine the rate of output that maximizes profit.

The profit-maximizing output for the perfectly competitive firm occurs where price equals marginal cost. In the short run, firms in perfect competition may earn economic profit. But if price drops below average variable cost, the firm should shut down. However, in the long run, entry of new firms and/or plant expansion drive price down and eliminate the economic profit. Perfect competition results in efficient allocation of resources because production occurs at minimum average cost, voluntary exchange is maximized, and capital is employed in its highest value use.

The monopolist is a single seller of a differentiated product. Entry into the market is difficult or prohibited. As the single seller, the monopolist has power over price. The decision rule for maximizing profits is to produce until marginal revenue equals marginal cost and then charge the price that the demand curve will allow. Because entry is restricted, the monopolist may earn economic profits in both the short and the long run.

Consumer surplus is the difference between what consumers are willing to pay for a product and the price that must be paid to purchase it. The principle of consumer surplus can be used to demonstrate that monopoly pricing causes allocative inefficiency because too little of the product is produced. Monopoly pricing also results in a redistribution of income from consumers to the stockholders of the firm.

If a firm has market power and there is a separation of ownership and control, technical inefficiency can also occur because the firm's managers will not be required to minimize costs. When monopolists use resources to acquire or maintain economic profits, this is referred to as rent-seeking behavior. Because no additional goods or services are produced, rent seeking imposes a deadweight loss on society. The combination of technical inefficiency and rent seeking may cause the economic profit earned by a monopolist not to appear excessive.

Few market structures meet the restrictive assumptions for perfect competition or monopoly. Still, these economic models are useful because the performance of many industries approximates the outcomes of perfect competition or monopoly. Also, the perfectly competitive model is often used as a benchmark for evaluating the performance of actual markets and as a guide for public policy.

Discussion Questions

9-1. Why is concrete sold in local markets, while cement powder is sold in a national market?

9-2. Does product differentiation always refer to real differences between products? Use an example to explain your answer.

9-3. Does ownership of very specialized capital equipment affect ease of exit from an industry? Why or why not?

9-4. How would risk affect the normal rate of profit in an industry?

9-5. Suppose that firms in a perfectly competitive industry are earning less than a normal rate of profit. In the long run, what price adjustments will occur in this industry? What will cause these adjustments?

9-6. Basically, perfectly competitive firms and monopolists use the same rule to determine the profit-maximizing output. True or false? Explain.

9-7. Firms in a perfectly competitive market do not have to compete with the other individual firms in the market. True or false? Explain.

9-8. In the long run, firms in a perfectly competitive market produce at the minimum point on their average cost curves. However, the long-run profit-maximizing output for a monopolist will not be at the point of minimum average cost. Does this mean that competitive firms can produce at a lower average cost than the monopolist? Explain.

9-9. How is the deadweight loss from monopoly affected by the slope of the demand curve?

9-10. Do non-profit institutions, such as universities, ever engage in rent-seeking behavior? Give an example.

Problems

9-1. Suppose the market supply and demand equations for plywood are given by

$$Q_s = 20,000 + 30P$$

and

$$Q_D = 40,000 - 20P$$

a. Graph the supply and demand equations and show the equilibrium price and quantity.

b. Determine the equilibrium price and quantity algebraically.

c. Suppose an increase in housing starts results in a new demand equation,

$$Q'_D = 50,000 - 20P$$

What is the new equilibrium price and quantity?

9-2. The market supply and demand equations for plywood are the original equations used in problem 9-1. The plywood industry is perfectly competitive, and the marginal cost equation for one firm, High Country Plywood, is given by

$$MC = 200 + 4Q$$

a. What is the short-run profit-maximizing output rate for High Country Plywood?

b. Average cost is given by

$$AC = \frac{1,000}{Q} + 200 + 2Q$$

In the short run, how much economic profit will the firm earn?

9-3. Tyson Brothers Manufacturing is currently earning economic profit. However, the market for the firm's product is perfectly competitive, so the economic profit is not expected to persist in the long run. Tyson's total and marginal cost functions are given by

$$TC = 500Q - 20Q^2 + Q^3$$

and

$$MC = 500 - 40Q + 3Q^2$$

a. At what output rate will average costs be a minimum?

b. If the cost curves for all other firms in the market are the same as Tyson's, determine the long-run equilibrium price.

9-4. The equilibrium price in a perfectly competitive market is $10. The marginal cost function is given by

$$MC = 4 + 0.2Q$$

The firm is presently producing 40 units of output per period. To maximize profit, should the output rate be increased or decreased? Explain.

9-5. The market supply and demand curves for a product are given by

$$Q_s = 3{,}000 + 200P$$

and

$$Q_D = 13{,}500 - 500P$$

The industry supplying the product is perfectly competitive. An individual firm has fixed costs of $150 per period. Its marginal and average variable cost functions are

$$MC = 15 - 4Q + \frac{3Q^2}{10}$$

and

$$AVC = 15 - 2Q + \frac{Q^2}{10}$$

a. What is the profit-maximizing rate of output for the firm?
b. What is the maximum total profit for the firm?

9-6. United Electric is the sole supplier of electricity to the community of Lakeview. Managers of the firm estimate that the demand for electricity is given by

$$P = 200 - 4Q$$

The firm's marginal cost equation is given by

$$MC = 4Q$$

a. What is the profit-maximizing price and quantity?
b. Can economic profit be determined from the information given? Why or why not?

9-7. A consultant estimates that the demand for the output of Marston Chemical is represented by the equation

$$Q = 2{,}000 - 50P$$

a. If the managers of Marston decide to maximize total revenue instead of profit, at what output rate should the firm operate? What is the revenue-maximizing price?
b. Will the revenue-maximizing output be greater than or less than the profit-maximizing output rate? Explain.

9-8. The demand equation faced by a monopolist for a product is given by

$$Q = 50 - 5P$$

A price of $5 is charged for the product.

a. Using this information, draw a graph that shows the consumer surplus.

b. Compute the amount of consumer surplus generated by sale of the product.

9-9. Lyon Concrete is a monopoly supplier of concrete in northern Arkansas. Demand for the firm's concrete is given by

$$P = 110 - 4Q$$

Marginal cost is constant and equal to 10.

a. What are the profit-maximizing price and output?

b. What is the deadweight loss resulting from Lyon's monopoly?

c. Compared to pricing at marginal cost, how much income is redistributed from consumers to the owners of the monopoly?

9-10. Show that the profit-maximizing quantity for a monopolist will always lie in the elastic region of the demand curve.

9-11. The demand equation for a monopolist is given by $P = 50 - 2Q$ and the marginal cost is $10.

a. Compute the deadweight loss associated with monopoly pricing.

b. If $P = 50 - 4Q$, what is the deadweight loss?

c. Based on your answers to (a) and (b), how is the deadweight loss related to the slope of the demand curve?

9-12. The market price faced by a firm in a perfectly competitive market is $50 and marginal cost is given by $10 + 2Q$.

a. What is the profit-maximizing rate of output?

b. How does a $1 increase in the price affect the optimal output?

c. How does a $1 increase in the marginal cost at each output rate affect the optimal output?

Problems Requiring Calculus

9-13. The manager of Biswas Glass Company estimates that total revenue from the sale of her firm's product is given by the equation:

$$TR = 300Q - \frac{Q^2}{2}$$

The total cost equation is estimated to be

$$TC = 5,000 + 60Q + Q^2$$

a. What is the profit-maximizing price and output rate? What is the amount of economic profit?

b. At what output rate is average cost a minimum? At this output rate, what is the amount of economic profit?

9-14. For a perfectly competitive firm, the market price is $16. The total cost equation is

$$TC = \frac{Q^3}{3} - 5Q^2 + 40Q$$

Use calculus to determining the profit-*maximizing* and the profit-*minimizing* rates of output. Explain.

9-15. Michelle's Mints is a small chain of candy stores. Cross-section data from the stores were used to estimate the demand equation. Holding income and prices of other goods constant, the demand equation is estimated to be

$$P = 12Q^{-1/3}$$

where P is price per found and Q is pounds sold per day per store. The marginal cost of supplying the candy is constant and equal to $2 per pound.
a. What is the point price elasticity of demand?
b. What are the profit-maximizing price and quantity?

9-16. The manager of a small candy shop operating in a perfectly competitive market determines that his average cost for chocolates is given by $10 - .2Q + .005Q^2$, where Q is in pounds per month. The market price of chocolates is expected to remain at $8 per pound. How many pounds per month should he produce? Explain.

9-17. The plant manager of a firm producing a specialized brand of caviar believes that her total revenues are given by $TR = 1000Q - Q^2$ and that total costs are $TC = -200Q - Q^2 + Q^3$. What are the profit-maximizing price and quantity for the firm?

CHAPTER 10

Monopolistic Competition, Oligopoly, and Barriers to Entry

Preview

Chapter 9 developed models of price and output determination for two important types of market structures: monopoly and perfect competition. But most markets have neither the single seller required to meet the definition of a monopolist nor the large number of small sellers and undifferentiated product necessary to qualify as perfectly competitive. Where the number of sellers is large and the product differentiated, the model of monopolistic competition is a useful tool for analyzing price and output decisions. When there are only a few sellers, oligopoly theory can provide important insights for decision making.

The first section of this chapter develops the model of monopolistic competition. The second considers oligopoly theory in its various forms. In the third section, the relationship between market structure and barriers to entry is examined.

Monopolistic Competition

The models of perfect competition and monopoly are useful, but there is a need to bridge the gap between these extreme forms of market structure. An important contribution is the model of monopolistic competition developed by Edward Chamberlin.[1] Chamberlin observed that even in markets with a large number of sellers, the products of individual firms are rarely homogeneous. For example, consider men's shoes. In a large city there may be hundreds of shoe stores. But men's shoes may be highly differentiated in the minds of consumers. This product differentiation may reflect materials and workmanship of the shoes sold in a particular store, or it may be the result of effective advertising. The manner in which the store displays the shoes can be another source of product differentiation. An establishment with thick carpet and soft music may have an advantage over a firm that stocks its merchandise on shelves like a warehouse. Location is another source of product differentiation. Sellers in a nearby mall will be more likely to obtain a consumer's business than stores on the other side of town.

Characteristics

The theory of monopolistic competition has elements of both monopoly and perfect competition. Like perfect competition, it is assumed that there are a large number of small sellers. Thus the actions of any single seller do not have a significant effect on other sellers in the market. Also, like perfect competition, it is assumed that there are many buyers and that resources can easily be transferred into and out of the industry. However, the model of monopolistic competition resembles the monopoly models in that products of individual firms are consid-

---

[1] Chamberlin, E. *The Theory of Monopolistic Competition*. Cambridge, Mass.: Harvard University Press, 1962.

TABLE 10-1 **Market Structure Characteristics of Monopolistic Competition**

Number and size distribution of sellers	Many small sellers. Actions of individual sellers go unheeded by other firms.
Number and size distribution of buyers	Many small buyers.
Product differentiation	Slightly differentiated. Product of one firm is a fairly close substitute for that of other sellers.
Conditions of entry and exit	Easy entry and exit.

ered to be slightly differentiated. That is, the product of one firm is assumed to be a close, but not a perfect substitute for that of other firms. The result is that each firm faces a demand curve with a slight downward slope, implying that the individual firm has some control over price. Although increasing its price will cause the firm to lose sales, some consumers will be willing to buy at the higher price because the product is slightly differentiated from that of competitors. The characteristics of monopolistic competition are summarized in Table 10-1.

Profit-Maximizing Price and Output in the Short Run

Managers of firms in monopolistic competition determine the rate of output, product attributes, and advertising expenditure that maximizes profits. To simplify the discussion, it is assumed that advertising and product attributes have already been determined. Therefore, determining the profit-maximizing rate of output and price are the remaining decisions for managers. Chamberlin's monopolistic competition model also assumes that all firms have similar demand and cost curves. Thus it is possible to consider a "representative" or "typical" firm. The demand, marginal revenue, and cost curves for such a firm are shown in Figure 10-1.

The results of monopolistic competition in the short run are similar to those of monopoly. The profit-maximizing output rate occurs at Q_c, where marginal revenue equals marginal cost. The corresponding price (as determined by the demand curve, D) is P_c. Like a monopolist, a firm in monopolistic competition may earn short-run economic profit. Recall that economic profit per unit is price minus average cost. Thus total economic profit is shown by the shaded area in Figure 10-1.

Profit-Maximizing Price and Output in the Long Run

In the long run, monopolistic competition generates results similar to those of perfect competition. Because entry into the industry is easy, economic profit induces other firms to enter the market. For example, the success of a video rental

skip

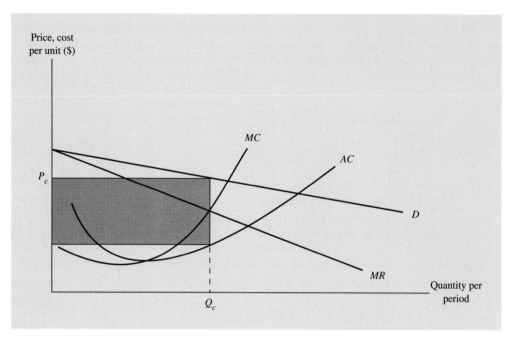

FIGURE 10-1 **Short-Run Profit Maximization in Monopolistic Competition.**

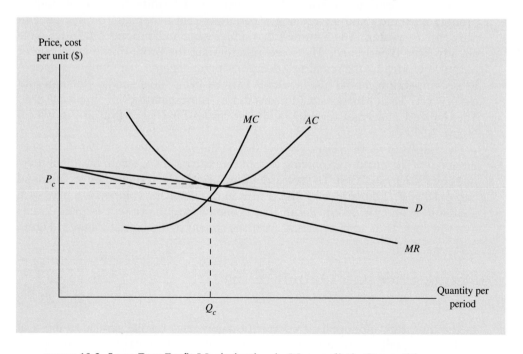

FIGURE 10-2 **Long-Run Profit Maximization in Monopolistic Competition.**

outlet in a community may entice other firms to provide this service. Because an inventory of movies is the major prerequisite for entry, new suppliers may include bookstores, gas stations, grocery stores, or other businesses. As this entry occurs, the market shares of existing firms decrease. Thus the demand curve faced by these firms shifts down and to the left, until it becomes as shown in Figure 10-2.

As in the short run, the representative firm maximizes profit by equating marginal revenue and marginal cost. In Figure 10-2, profit maximization requires setting price at P_c and producing Q_c units of output per period. Note that the demand and average cost curves are tangent at this price–quantity combination. This implies that price and average cost are equal and so there is no economic profit. Thus there is no incentive for new firms to enter the market. Similarly, because the representative firm is earning a normal return, firms will not exit the market. Hence P_c and Q_c represent the long-run equilibrium for firms in monopolistic competition.

EXAMPLE

In the Long Run They're All Dead

DOGGONE, a pet mortuary in Chicago, offers complete funerals for dogs. The pet funeral business in Chicago is monopolistically competitive. The manager of DOGGONE has determined that the firm's demand equation is given by $P = 309.75 - Q$ and the long-run total cost equation is $TC = 400Q - 20Q^2 + Q^3$, where Q is the number of funerals per month.

What is the long-run equilibrium price and quantity and how much economic profit will the firm earn?

SOLUTION

In monopolistic competition in the long run, price will be driven down to average cost. The average cost equation is computed by dividing total cost by quantity. Thus, the optimal quantity is the solution to $P = AC$, or

$$P = 309.75 - Q = 400 - 20Q + Q^2 = AC$$

Rearranging terms yields the quadratic equation

$$Q^2 - 19Q + 90.25 = 0$$

which has the single solution, $Q = 9.5$. Substituting this quantity into the demand equation gives $P = 309.75 - 9.50 = \$300.25$. Because price equals average cost, economic profit is zero.

Figure 10-2 on page 336 shows that, in monopolistic competition, marginal revenue must equal marginal cost at the optimal output. For the demand and total cost equations of this problem, $MR = 309.75 - 2Q$ and $MC = 400 - 40Q + 3Q^2$. Substituting $Q = 9.5$ into these two equations gives $MR = MC = 290.75$. Hence, this condition also is fulfilled.

Evaluation of Monopolistic Competition

It is sometimes suggested that firms in monopolistic competition are inefficient. Figure 10-2 shows that the profit-maximizing output does not occur at the minimum point on the firm's average cost curve. Thus it can be argued that the firm is operating at an inefficient output rate. In contrast, in Chapter 9 it was demonstrated that the long-run equilibrium rate of output in perfect competition occurs at the point of minimum average cost.

The difference in the two outcomes is the result of the downward-sloping demand curve in monopolistic competition. Remember, the long-run equilibrium is the point of tangency of the demand and average cost curves. But because the demand curve is not horizontal, the tangency point cannot be at minimum average cost. However, this result does not necessarily imply inefficiency. The downward slope of the demand curve is the result of product differentiation in the market. Presumably, these differences are of value to consumers as they select goods that meet their particular needs. For example, although name-brand canned goods are likely to cost more than generic brands, many buyers are willing to pay the extra price as an assurance of quality. In general, the validity of the claim that monopolistic competition is inefficient depends on a comparison of the benefits derived from product differentiation and the increased costs caused by differentiated products.

KEY CONCEPTS _____

- Firms in monopolistic competition have some control over price because their products are differentiated.
- As with perfect competition, there may be economic profits in the short run, but there are no long-run economic profits in monopolistic competition.

CASE STUDY _____

Competition in the Video Rental Industry

A good argument can be made that today's market for the rental of video cassettes is monopolistically competitive. Even in medium-size cities, there usually are many places where a movie can be rented. Some of these outlets focus exclusively on video rentals, but many music stores, gas stations, and grocery stores also have movies available for rent. In fact, the typical video outlet in a metropolitan area in the United States now has six competitors within a three-mile radius. Although there are some large firms in the industry, market concentration is relatively low—chains with as many as 50 outlets have only a 15 percent share of the total market.

Product differentiation is also a characteristic of the video rental industry. While it is true that a particular movie from one store is identical to the same movie from another outlet, sellers can differentiate themselves in other ways. A music store may offer tapes and CDs in addition to movies, while a grocery store provides the opportunity to pick up a movie along with needed food items. An outlet that only rents video cassettes may have the advantage of maintaining a huge selection of movies.

The video industry also meets the entry and exit requirements for monopolistic competition. The basic requirement to become a participant is to have display space, an inventory of tapes, and a computer system for record keeping. New movies are easily available from distributors, and there is a rather active market for the inventories of firms who wish to exit the market.

The history of the video rental industry is consistent with the predictions of the model of monopolistic competition. During the early 1980s, there were far fewer outlets than today. Because of the lack of competition, tapes rented for as much as $8 per day, and the business could be extremely profitable. Some early entrants had profits as high as 80 percent of sales. But entry occurred rapidly, and prices dropped precipitously. Today the prices of new releases are as low as $1.49, and older movies can be rented for less than a dollar a day. The decline in prices has also affected profits. Video rental outlets in the 1990s are fortunate if profits are 10 percent of sales, and many firms have been forced to leave the market because of their losses. Because competition has eliminated economic profits, the rate of entry into the industry is much less than in previous years. In the future, rental outlets will face additional competition from cable television, which has begun to implement the technology to give viewers the opportunity to select a movie of their choice from the convenience of their own homes.

skip

Oligopoly — *start Reading.*

The term *oligopoly* comes from the Greek words *oligos* and *polis* and means, literally, few sellers. Oligopoly is a common form of market structure in modern economic systems. The cereal, automobile, and steel industries in the United States would all qualify. However, oligopolies exist at the local as well as the national level. For example, although there are thousands of gas stations scattered throughout the nation, the typical consumer considers only a few nearby stations. Other sellers who are farther away may offer lower prices or better service, but proximity is probably the dominant consideration. Hence the market for gasoline faced by the individual consumer could be described as an oligopoly.

Characteristics

An oligopoly involves an unspecified number of buyers but only a small number of sellers. There is no precise limit on the number of sellers that a market can have and still be characterized as an oligopoly. The key issue is not numbers, but rather the reaction of sellers to one another. In the three forms of market structure described thus far, there was no need for sellers to be concerned about the actions of individual competitors. The monopolist has no rivals, while firms in perfect and monopolistic competitive markets are too small to have a significant impact on other firms. In contrast, the actions of each firm in an oligopoly do affect the other sellers in the market. Price cutting by one firm will reduce the market share of other firms. Similarly, clever advertising or a new product line may increase sales at the expense of other sellers.

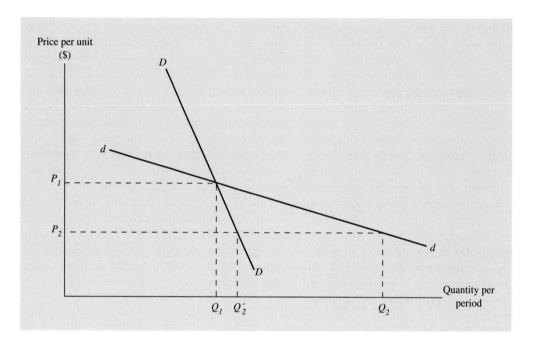

FIGURE 10-3 **Demand Curves for an Oligopolist.**

Figure 10-3 shows how the actions of rivals can affect the demand curve faced by oligopolists. If one firm reduces its price and the other firms in the market do not respond, the price cutter may substantially increase its sales. This result is depicted by the relatively elastic demand curve, *dd*. For example, a price decrease from P_1 to P_2 will result in a movement along *dd* and increase sales from Q_1 to Q_2 as customers take advantage of the lower price and abandon other suppliers. However, if the price cut is matched by other firms, the increase in sales will be less. Since other firms are selling at the same price, any additional sales must result from increased demand for the product. Thus the effect of the price reduction is a movement down the relatively less elastic demand curve, *DD*. Now the price reduction from P_1 to P_2 only increases sales to Q_2'.

Clearly, the responses of competitors can have a significant impact on the outcome of managerial decisions in an oligopoly market. Consequently, decision making in an oligopoly is much more difficult than in other market situations.

The other two characteristics that categorize market structure are product differentiation and condition of entry and exit. The product sold in an oligopoly can be homogeneous or differentiated. If the product is homogeneous, the market is said to be a pure oligopoly. The steel and copper markets in the United States would fit into this category. If the product is not homogeneous, the market is a differentiated oligopoly. The automobile and television industries are examples of differentiated oligopolies.

With respect to condition of entry, for an oligopolistic market structure to persist in the long run, there must be some factor that prevents new firms from entering

TABLE 10-2 **Market Structure Characteristics of Oligopoly**

Number and size distribution of sellers	Small number of sellers. Each firm must consider the effect of its actions on other firms.
Number and size distribution of buyers	Unspecified.
Product differentiation	Product may be either homogeneous or differentiated.
Conditions of entry and exit	Entry difficult.

the industry. For example, a drug manufacturer might hold a patent that legally prevents other firms from producing the drug covered by the patent. Market structure characteristics of oligopoly are summarized in Table 10-2.

The most distinctive feature of an oligopolistic industry is that sellers must recognize their interdependence. That is, the action of one seller may affect another and thus cause that seller to respond in ways that will affect the first seller. But oligopolists are likely to deal with this interdependence in different ways, depending on the specific nature of the industry. In some cases, most actions of competitors will be ignored. In other situations, a price war may occur in response to a seemingly innocuous price change. Many factors, such as industry maturity, nature of the product, and methods of doing business, can affect the way firms respond to actions of rivals. The difficulty of formulating models of oligopoly stems from the many ways that firms interact. Consequently, there is no general model of oligopoly. There are, however, models that analyze oligopoly decisions on the basis of specific assumptions about the interaction between firms. Several models that reflect specific aspects of oligopolistic interdependence are discussed in this section.

Price Rigidity: The Kinked Demand Model

Early students of oligopoly noted that prices in some markets sometimes remained unchanged for long periods of time. For example, the price of steel rail was set at $28 per ton in 1901 and did not change for 15 years. Between 1922 and 1933, the price remained at $43. Similarly, sulfur prices hovered within a few cents of $18 per ton between 1926 and 1938. This apparent price rigidity led Paul Sweezy to suggest that oligopolists behave as if facing a kinked demand curve.[2] Such a curve is shown in Figure 10-4.

The kink in the demand curve stems from an asymmetry in the response of other firms to one firm's price change. Suppose that the price initially is at P_k, the point of the kink in the demand curve. Sweezy argued that if one firm raised its price, other sellers might not follow the increase. The result would be that the firm would lose a significant amount of sales. This is shown in Figure 10-4 as a relatively elastic demand curve above the existing price, P_k.

[2] Sweezy, P. "Demand Conditions Under Oligopoly." *Journal of Political Economy*, August 1939, pp. 568–573.

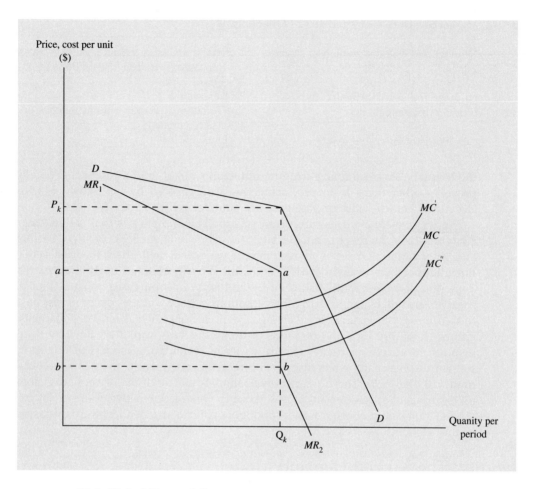

FIGURE 10-4 **Kinked Demand Curve.**

In contrast, if the firm reduces its price below P_k, it is likely that the other firms will follow suit in an attempt to maintain their market shares. As a result, the price cut by the original firm will not add much to its sales. Figure 10-4 depicts this outcome as a relatively inelastic demand curve below P_k.

Associated with the demand curve is a marginal revenue curve. For a linear demand curve, the absolute value of the slope of the corresponding marginal revenue is twice as great. Note that the kinked demand curve of Figure 10-4 consists of two linear curves joined at P_k. Marginal revenue for prices above the kink is given by MR_1. For those below the kink, it is MR_2. At the point of the kink, the marginal revenue curve is a vertical line that connects the two segments.[3]

---

[3] Because the demand curve of Figure 10-4 has a kink at Q_k, the marginal revenue curve is said to be discontinuous at Q_k. The vertical line, ab, represents this discontinuity.

The model assumes that the firm has a U-shaped marginal cost curve, MC, as shown in Figure 10-4. As with previous models, the profit-maximizing output is determined by equating marginal cost and marginal revenue. This output rate is Q_k, and the price (as given by the demand curve at Q_k) is P_k. Note that the profit-maximizing solution occurs at the kink because it is in the region where marginal revenue and marginal cost intersect.

Now suppose that increases in input prices cause the marginal cost curve to shift upward to MC'. Profit maximization requires that marginal revenues again be set equal to marginal costs. But for the marginal cost curve MC', the optimal output is still Q_k, and the optimal price is still P_k. Although the marginal cost has increased, there is no change in the profit-maximizing price and quantity. The explanation is the vertical section of the marginal revenue curve found at the kink in the demand curve. Even though the marginal cost curve shifted upward, it still intersects marginal revenue in the region where that curve is vertical. Hence there is no change in the optimal output rate and price in response to the input price increase.

Similarly, assume that more efficient production techniques or lower input prices allowed the marginal revenue curve to shift downward, as shown by MC'' in Figure 10-4. As long as the new marginal cost curve intersects the vertical portion of the marginal revenue curve, there will be no change in the profit-maximizing price and quantity. The firm will continue to produce Q_k units and the price will remain at P_k. For price and quantity to change, the marginal cost curve must shift enough to cause it to intersect the marginal revenue either above point a or below point b.

The important implication of the kinked demand curve model is that firms in oligopolistic market structures could experience substantial shifts in marginal costs and still not vary their prices. This theoretical result is consistent with Sweezy's observation that some oligopolistic markets exhibit very stable prices.

CASE STUDY

Something's Rigid in Denmark

An interesting and well-documented example of price rigidity involved a leather tannery in Denmark. While interviewing the managers of Danish firms about their pricing policies, an economist discovered a firm that charged a higher price for dyed shoe leather than it did for black leather. The price differential had existed since 1890, when dyed leather was more expensive to make. However, by the time of the interview, the dyed shoe leather had become less costly to produce. Queried as to why the pricing policy had not been changed, the firm's manager responded:

> Perhaps we ought to raise the price of black leather somewhat and lower the price of dyed leather to a corresponding degree, but we dare not do so. The fact is that we shall then run the risk of being unable to sell black leather shoes, whereas our competitors will also reduce their prices for dyed shoes.*

* B. Fog, *Industrial Pricing Policies* (Amsterdam: North-Holland, 1960), p. 130.

The manager's explanation is consistent with the kinked demand curve model. An increase in the price of black leather shoes, unmatched by competitors, was perceived as resulting in a substantial loss of sales. In contrast, a price cut on dyed shoes was expected to result in a price cut by competitors and, hence, little increase in sales. Thus the price differential between black and dyed shoes was maintained even though relative costs had changed.

The kinked demand curve model can be criticized on at least two grounds. First, although it explains the reluctance of oligopolists to change prices, it provides no insight in understanding how the price was originally determined. Thus the model is incomplete at best. Second, empirical research has not verified the predictions of the model. George Stigler studied pricing in seven oligopolies.[4] He found that firms in these industries were just as likely to match a price increase by a competitor as they were to follow a rival's cut in price.

When first proposed, Sweezy's kinked demand curve model was hailed as a general theory of oligopoly. Today, it is viewed in a more limited perspective as one of several descriptions of oligopoly behavior. In markets where the important firms are of nearly equal size, the product is homogeneous, and sellers are not yet certain how rivals will react, the kinked demand curve model can be a useful tool for understanding pricing particles. Where these conditions are not met, this approach is less useful.

KEY CONCEPTS

- The kinked demand curve model of oligopoly is based on the assumption that rivals will match price reductions, but not price increases.
- The kinked demand curve model predicts that price changes will be infrequent in oligopolistic markets.

End

Interdependence: The Cournot Model

skip

The distinctive feature of the different oligopoly models is the way they attempt to capture the interdependence of firms in the market. Perhaps the best known is the Cournot model, which was developed by a French mathematician in the early 1800s. Although the basic model is rather simplistic, it provides useful insights into industries with a small number of sellers.

COURNOT DUOPOLY Consider a product for which demand is given by the equation $P = 950 - Q_T$, where Q_T is the total amount produced by all of the suppliers in the market. Assume that the marginal and average costs are constant

[4] Stigler, G. J. "The Kinky Oligopoly Demand Curve and Rigid Prices." *Journal of Political Economy,* October 1947, pp. 432–449.

and equal to \$50. The assumption of constant costs is not critical to the analysis, but it simplifies the calculations and makes the insights of the model more obvious.

As a starting point, think about the results of having a monopolist in this market. A single firm would select its output by equating marginal revenue and marginal cost. For the demand equation given, the corresponding marginal revenue equation is $MR = 950 - 2Q_T$. Thus, the profit-maximizing quantity is the solution to

$$950 - 2Q_T = 50$$

or $Q_T = 450$. Substituting this rate of output back into the demand equation gives $P = \$500$.

Next consider a perfectly competitive market. In this situation, prices are driven to costs. Hence, the optimal quantity is determined by $P = MC$, which is the solution to

$$950 - Q_T = 50$$

or $Q_T = 900$. The corresponding price is $P = \$50$. As predicted by economic theory, price is higher and the rate of output lower for a monopoly supplier than in a perfectly competitive market.

Now consider a market that has two sellers—a duopoly. In analyzing this case, an assumption must be made regarding how the two firms respond to one another. The Cournot model assumes that each firm chooses a rate of output to maximize its profits, in the belief that the other firm will continue to produce the same rate of output as it did in the previous period. Although each firm will, in all probability, change its output from period to period, the two firms are assumed to remain oblivious to this adjustment.

For the duopoly case, Q_T in the demand equation $P = 950 - Q_T$ is the sum of the output produced by the first firm, q_1, and the second firm, q_2. Because firm 1 believes that firm 2 will not change its rate of output, firm 1 will behave like a monopolist in determining its profit-maximizing quantity. That is, because q_2 is assumed constant, the marginal revenue equation for firm 1 is

$$MR_1 = \frac{dTR}{dq_1} = \frac{d[(950 - q_1 - q_2) \cdot q_1]}{dq_1} = 950 - q_2 - 2q_1.$$

Similarly, firm 2 uses $MR_2 = 950 - q_1 - 2q_2$. In both cases, the profit-maximizing rate of output is determined by setting marginal revenue equal to marginal cost. That is,

$$\text{Firm 1} \qquad 950 - q_2 - 2q_1 = 50$$
$$\text{Firm 2} \qquad 950 - q_1 - 2q_2 = 50$$

Solving each equation for the output of the firm gives

Firm 1	$q_1 = 450 - 0.5q_2$	(10-1)
Firm 2	$q_2 = 450 - 0.5q_1$	(10-2)

Equations (10-1) and (10-2) show the rate of output for each firm based on the output the managers expect the other firm to produce. For example, if firm 2 is expected to produce 200 units, the profit-maximizing rate of output for firm 1 will be 350 units. Similarly, if firm 1 is expected to produce 200 units, then firm

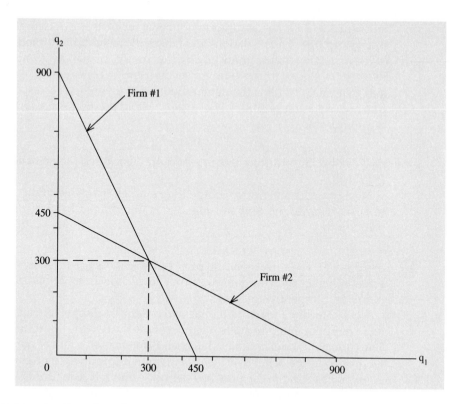

FIGURE 10-5 **Reaction Functions for Cournot Duopolists.**

2 will produce 350 units. Equations (10-1) and (10-2) are referred to as reaction functions because they describe how each firm reacts to the output choice of the other. These reaction functions are portrayed graphically in Figure 10-5.

At some point in time, suppose that firm 1 assumes that firm 2 will produce 200 units of output. Based on its reaction function, firm 1 will produce 350 units. If firm 1 produces 350 units, firm 2's reaction function specifies that it should then produce 275 units. But at an output rate of 275 units from firm 2, firm 1's quantity of 350 units is no longer optimal, so it will alter its output based on its reaction function. When firm 1 changes, then firm 2 needs to make an adjustment. As long as the output of one firm is different than that used by the other in selecting its optimal quantity, there will be adjustment.

The market will reach an equilibrium when each firm's output expectation about the other turns out to be correct. Mathematically, this is determined by simultaneously solving equations (10-1) and (10-2). This can be done by substituting $450 - 0.5q_2$ for q_1 in equation (10-2), which gives

$$q_2 = 450 - 0.5(450 - 0.5q_2)$$

or $q_2 = 300$. Substituting this value into equation (10-1) yields $q_1 = 300$. Thus, when each firm produces 300 units, the market has reached an equilibrium. This result can also be shown graphically. Note that in Figure 10-5, the two reaction

TABLE 10-3 **Outputs, Prices, and Profits for Cournot Oligopolists**

Number of Firms	Total Output	Price	Profit
1	450	$500	$202,500
2	600	350	180,000
4	720	230	129,600
8	800	150	80,000
16	847	103	44,891
32	873	77	23,571
64	886	64	12,404
128	893	57	6,251
1,000	899	51	899

curves intersect at 300 units of output for each firm. This point of intersection is the graphical equivalent of solving equations (10-1) and (10-2) simultaneously.

THE COURNOT MODEL WITH n FIRMS   Although the duopoly market structure is the easiest, the Cournot approach can be used to analyze industries with more than two firms. The mathematics will not be developed here, but for an industry with n firms, the total equilibrium output for a Cournot oligopoly is given by

$$Q_n = Q_c \left(\frac{n}{n + 1} \right) \qquad (10\text{-}3)$$

where $n \geq 1$ and Q_c is the output resulting from a perfectly competitive market. In the previous section, it was determined that $Q_c = 900$. For the case of a monopoly, $n = 1$. Thus, equation (10-3) implies that a monopolist's output would be 450 units and the combined output of two duopolists ($n = 2$) would be 600 units. These are the same values that were calculated in the previous section. In general, note that as n becomes large, the value of $n/n + 1$ approaches unity. This means that as the number of firms in the market increases, the combined output of those firms approaches that of a perfectly competitive market. But as output increases because of more firms participating in the market, the demand equation, $P = 950 - Q_T$, implies that price must decrease. Thus, the Cournot model suggests that increased competition, as measured by the number of firms in the market, drives prices down toward costs.

Table 10-3 shows outputs, prices, and economic profits for different numbers of firms in a Cournot oligopoly. Profits were computed by multiplying output times (price − marginal cost). Note that economic profits decline as the number of firms increases and that maximum profit is obtained when there is a single seller in the market.

KEY CONCEPTS

- In the Cournot model, each firm makes its output decision assuming that other firms will produce the same amount as before.
- As the number of firms increases, the Cournot result approaches the equilibrium result for perfect competition.

End skip

start Read.

Cartels and Collusion

In oligopolistic industries, vigorous price competition among firms tends to drive prices down and to reduce profits. Consequently, in such industries there is a strong incentive for managers to avoid price competition. One alternative is to collude and set prices at or near the monopoly level.

Although there may be difficulties in formulating an agreement or in dividing the profit, successful collusion can result in substantial benefits for all of the firms involved. Thus, there is a natural tendency for collusion to occur in such industries. This tendency may take the form of explicit price-fixing agreements, price leadership, or other practices that reduce competition between the firms in the market. The exact nature of the collusion in an industry is determined by the specific characteristics of the market and by constraints imposed by government policy. Still, a useful model of oligopoly behavior can be formulated based on the assumption that many managerial decisions are directed toward avoiding active competition and maintaining pricing discipline in the industry.

COLLUSION AND CHEATERS Although successful collusion can improve the profitability of all the firms in an industry, any one firm can benefit still more by cheating on the agreement. For example, if the managers in an industry collude and raise prices, an individual firm will be able to increase its share of the market and its total profit by offering a price slightly below that charged by other firms.

The benefits of cheating on a collusive agreement are illustrated by Figure 10-6. Consider a firm participating in an oligopolistic market. Assume that the firms in the market all agree to charge a price P_1. If average and marginal costs are constant and equal, as illustrated by the figure, economic profit earned by each member of the cartel is shown by the rectangle P_1abc.

If every firm in the industry reduces its price, the demand curve faced by the individual firm will be aD, as shown in Figure 10-6. This curve is relatively inelastic because any increase in sales for the firm associated with lower prices must result from increased demand for the industry's product.

Now assume that one firm cheats on the collusive agreement and unilaterally reduces its price to P_2. If the price cut is undetected and unmatched, the demand curve faced by this firm will be ad and quantity demanded will increase from Q_1 to Q_2. This increase results from sales of the product to new customers and from sales to customers who previously purchased from other firms.

By selling at a lower price, P_2, the firm will lose profits on the Q_1 units that it was selling at the higher price. But this loss will be more than recouped by profits on the additional sales, $Q_2 - Q_1$. The loss is shown in Figure 10-6 as the shaded rectangle P_1aeP_2. But the gain is the much larger shaded rectangle, $efgb$. Hence, by cheating, the firm is able to earn additional economic profits. A similar opportunity is available to all the other firms in the industry.

As long as the other firms adhere to the price-fixing agreement, the cheater will continue to earn additional profit. Eventually, however, other firms will become aware of the actions of the cheater and will reduce their prices. When this occurs, the price-fixing agreement starts to fall apart. Unless there is a mecha-

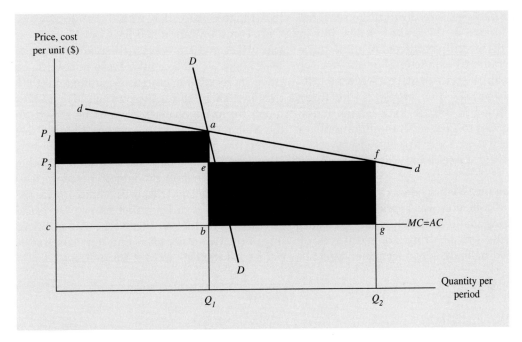

FIGURE 10-6 **Benefits of Cheating on a Collusive Agreement.**

nism for restoring price discipline in the industry, the firms may revert to active price competition.

KEY CONCEPTS

- By colluding to avoid price competition, firms in oligopolistic markets can increase the total profit to be shared.
- Individual firms can gain even more by setting a slightly lower price and increasing their market share at the expense of other members of the cartel.

CASE STUDY

Raising the Price of Unleavened Bread: The Matzo Conspiracy

For 3,000 years, matzo has been used by Jewish people to commemorate Moses' leading the children of Israel out of bondage in Egypt. This flat, unleavened bread is eaten at Passover to symbolize a departure so hasty that the Israelites couldn't wait for their bread to rise.

For many years, the ancient tradition of eating matzo bread at Passover has provided a small number of producers with a profitable business. Because the product has religious significance, demand for matzo tends to be rather insensitive to price and to changes in economic conditions.

For seven decades, three firms dominated the market for matzo in the United States. But in May 1991, the executive officers of these three firms were indicted by a federal grand jury for colluding to fix the price of matzo. A few months later, Manischewitz, the largest of the three firms, was fined $1,000,000 by a federal judge and also agreed to give several million dollars more in cash and food to charities to settle several private price-fixing cases that were pending.

The suit against Manischewitz alleges that the origin of the collusion was a price war in Chicago involving gefilte fish. When the price cutting on gefilte spread to matzo, executives of the three leading matzo producers met together to arrange a truce that would stabilize prices. Once communication had been established, the executives went a step further and began to meet together on a regular basis to collude on price increases for matzo. Beginning in 1981, they met each fall for five years to decide how much the price of matzo would be raised for the following Passover season. During that period, the price of matzo increased by nearly 38 percent, while the price index for all other food items increased by only 25 percent.

Although the antitrust action ended price fixing of matzo, it did not result in lower prices to consumers. In 1991, Manischewitz acquired one of the two other firms and now controls 90 percent of the U.S. market for matzo.

Price Leadership

U.S. antitrust laws make explicit collusion difficult and potentially costly. As a result, oligopolists sometimes use other methods to avoid active competition. One of the most prevalent is price leadership. Basically, price leadership occurs when one firm initiates changes in price and the other firms in the industry follow the lead of the first firm. Frequently, the practice of price leadership in an industry first occurred during a period when large price fluctuations and cutthroat pricing were the rule. As a result of price leadership, price changes came to be made infrequently and in ways designed to maintain price discipline in the industry. Two forms of price leadership are considered here: dominant firm and barometric price leadership.

DOMINANT FIRM PRICE LEADERSHIP   Consider an industry consisting of a single large firm and several smaller firms. The large firm may have achieved its position by being the first seller in the industry, because it has lower costs resulting from scale economies, or by virtue of superior management skill. Whatever the reason, assume that the firm is now able to dictate prices in the industry. Smaller firms that fail to conform may find themselves in a price war that they cannot survive. However, because the price dictated by the dominant firm is likely to be higher than would result from active competition, the small firms probably will earn more profit by allowing the dominant firm to take the lead in price setting. From the perspective of the industry leader, a closely followed pattern of price leadership eliminates the cost of enforcing industry price discipline. Also, if a large firm is too aggressive in competing in a market, it may be prosecuted for illegal monopolization under antitrust statutes.

Figure 10-7 describes pricing and output decisions with dominant firm price leadership. Let $D_T D_T$ represent total demand. If the small firms in an industry

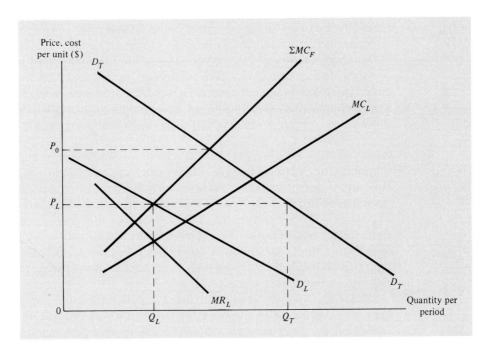

FIGURE 10-7 **Price and Output with Dominant Firm Price Leadership.**

look to the dominant firm to establish price, they can be viewed as price takers. As such, their behavior is similar to firms in perfect competition. If they can sell all they produce at the market price, they maximize profits by producing until price equals marginal cost. The implication of this assumption is that the marginal cost curve for each small firm shows the output that it will produce at various prices established by the dominant firm. Thus the total output supplied by all the small firms is the sum of their marginal cost curves. This curve is shown in Figure 10-7 as $\Sigma\, MC_F$.

If the dominant firm is content to set a price and let its small rivals supply as much as they want, the large firm can be thought of as supplying the residual demand. For example, if the price is set at P_0, the small firms will meet total market demand and the dominant firm will have no sales because there is no residual demand. It is obvious, therefore, that price will be set below P_0. The demand curve faced by the industry leader can easily be determined for any price level. It is the horizontal distance between the total demand curve, $D_T D_T$, and the $\Sigma\, MC_F$ curve. The leader's demand curve is shown on Figure 10-7 as $D_L D_L$. The associated marginal revenue curve is MR_L.

The curve MC_L is the dominant firm's marginal cost curve. It is shown as being below the $\Sigma\, MC_F$ curve to indicate a cost advantage of the price leader. Because the small firms follow the lead of the dominant seller, the dominant firm acts as a monopolist. Taking $D_L D_L$ as the firm's demand curve, it maximizes profits by choosing that rate of output where marginal revenue equals marginal cost. Thus output for the price leader will be Q_L. The profit-maximizing price, P_L, is determined by the price leader's demand curve. At this price, output of the small firms is determined from the $D_T D_T$ and $D_L D_L$ curves to be $Q_T - Q_L$ units.

Dominant firm price leadership is less common today than in years past. At one time, firms such as U.S. Steel, Firestone, Alcoa, and IBM were the acknowledged price setters in their markets. Over time, however, market growth, technological change, new U.S. producers, and foreign competition have reduced their dominance. Although still leaders, their relative importance has diminished.

BAROMETRIC PRICE LEADERSHIP Price leadership can occur even if there is no dominant firm in a market. Where price changes occur only in response to clear and widely understood changes in market conditions, a pattern of barometric price leadership may evolve. For example, suppose that a union wage settlement has increased labor costs in the industry or that fuel costs have risen. Either of these events will increase costs. One firm in the industry may take the lead in announcing that, due to higher costs, it is necessary to increase prices. Because the price hike reflects industry-wide cost changes, other firms are likely to follow suit and increase their prices.

Similarly, if stagnating sales are being experienced by all firms, one seller may announce a price cut to stimulate the demand for its product. If it is well understood that the price reduction is a response to changing market conditions and not an attempt to increase market share at the expense of competitors, the action is unlikely to precipitate a price war. Rather, other firms will match the first firm's price change in an orderly and nonthreatening manner.

With barometric price leadership, it is not necessary that the same firm always function as the price leader. The critical requirement for being a leader is the ability to interpret market conditions and propose price changes that other firms are willing to follow. Thus it may be somewhat misleading to define this pattern of behavior as price leadership. Rather, it represents an accepted and legal method of signaling a need for price changes.

KEY CONCEPTS

- Dominant firm price leadership involves a single firm setting its profit-maximizing price and the other firms in the industry charging the same price.
- Barometric price leadership is a method of signaling that changes in costs or demand require a price change.

CASE STUDY

Reestablishing Price Discipline in the Steel Industry

Until the early 1960s, U.S. Steel was the leader in setting prices in the steel industry. However, in 1962, a price increase announced by U.S. Steel provoked so much criticism from customers and elected officials, especially President John F. Kennedy, that the firm became less willing to act as the price leader. As a result, the industry evolved from dominant firm to barometric price leadership. This new form involved one firm testing the waters by announcing a price change and then U.S. Steel either confirming or rejecting the change by its reaction.

In 1968, U.S. Steel found that its market share was declining. The company responded by secretly cutting prices to large customers. This action was soon detected by Bethlehem Steel, which cut is posted price of steel from $113.50 to $88.50 per ton. Within three weeks, all of the other major producers, U.S. Steel included, matched Bethlehem's new price.

The lower industry price was not profitable for the industry members. Consequently, U.S. Steel signaled its desire to end the price war by posting a higher price. Bethlehem waited nine days and responded with a slightly lower price than that of U.S. Steel. U.S. Steel quickly dropped its price to Bethlehem's level. Having been given notice that U.S. Steel was once again willing to play by industry rules, Bethlehem announced a price increase to $125 per ton. All of the other major producers quickly followed suit and industry discipline was restored. Note that the price of $125 per ton was higher than the original price of $113.50.

Market Structure and Barriers to Entry

Many factors can contribute to the existence of a particular market structure. However, in the long run, conditions of entry may be the most important determinant. Difficulties encountered in entering an industry are often referred to as *barriers to entry.*

There is some disagreement among economists as to what constitutes a barrier to entry. Bain argues that entry barriers should be defined in terms of any advantage that existing firms hold over potential competitors.[5] In contrast, Stigler contends that for any given rate of output, only those costs that must be borne by new entrants but that are not borne by firms already in the industry should be considered in assessing entry barriers.[6]

Two examples illustrate the difference in philosophy. Suppose that one firm had control over all the iron ore deposits in the United States. As a result, new entrants into the steel industry could get ore only by transporting it from Canada or another foreign supplier. Transportation costs would cause potential competitors to have higher costs of producing steel than those of the existing firm. This disadvantage could prevent the new firms from successfully entering the market. Both the Bain and the Stigler criteria for a barrier to entry are satisfied in this example. Alternatively, assume that iron ore deposits are equally available to the existing and the potential new firms, but that the existing firm is large enough to take advantage of highly efficient production technologies. If new entrants build plants of small scale, their costs may be so high that they cannot sell steel

---

[5] Bain, J. S. *Barriers to New Competition.* (Cambridge, Mass.: Harvard University Press, 1956), pp. 3–5.

[6] Stigler, G. J. *The Organization of Industry.* (Homewood, Ill.: Richard D. Irwin, 1968), pp. 67–70.

at a price competitive with the established firm. That is, successful entry requires construction of plants that are large enough to take advantage of economies of scale. Bain would consider this condition a barrier to entry because of the difficulties in coordinating and raising capital for large-scale entry. However, Stigler's definition would not recognize scale economies as an entry barrier because the old and the new firms both face the same cost conditions. That is, for any given rate of output produced, the cost per unit would be the same for the new entrant as for an existing firm.

From a strictly conceptual point of view, the Stigler position that entry barriers should be confined to problems faced by new, but not existing, firms has appeal. But the Bain definition is the more useful of the two approaches. By including all factors that impede entry into an industry, it provides a better framework for understanding the determinants of market structure.

Sources of Barriers to Entry

Although there are many possible factors that restrict entry, this discussion focuses on four of the most important. The first is product differentiation. A firm that has convinced consumers that its product is significantly better than the product of new entrants has an advantage. The new firm may be forced to sell its product at a lower price that may not generate an adequate profit. There is no requirement that the product really be superior, only that consumers perceive it as more desirable. For example, some aspirin manufacturers have extolled the virtues of their product for decades. The result is that the typical consumer has a subjective feeling that Bayer and other well-advertised aspirins are superior to other brands—despite their being chemically identical. The ability of firms such as Bayer to differentiate their product allows them to capture a larger share of the market, charge higher prices, and earn economic profit. Even if new firms were to spend as much on advertising each year as Bayer, it would be unlikely that they could ever catch up. Bayer's long tenure in the market has generated strong consumer loyalties that are difficult for new firms to overcome. Thus a barrier to entry exists.

A second restriction on entry is control of inputs by existing suppliers. If potential entrants cannot easily obtain the capital, raw materials, and labor needed to produce their product, entry may be difficult. Examples include scarcity of natural resources, locational advantages, and managerial talent.

Legal restrictions such as patent protection are a third source of entry barriers. In some industries, patents held by existing firms make it virtually impossible for other businesses to produce a comparable product. Exclusive franchises granted by government are another form of legal restriction. For example, an electric company may have a legal right to be the sole supplier of electricity in its service area.

Scale economies are a fourth source of barriers to entry. As shown in Figure 10-8, if the production process exhibits economies of scale, a large, existing firm, producing at an output rate of Q_E, will have lower average costs than a new firm attempting to enter the industry on a small scale, such as Q_N. As a result, the new

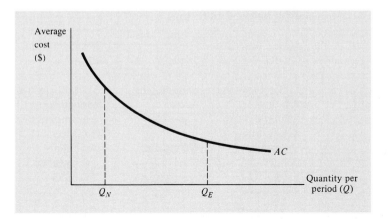

FIGURE 10-8 **The Long-Run Average Cost Curve for a Production Process Characterized by Economies of Scale.**

entrant may not be able to operate profitably at a price that allows existing firms to earn substantial economic profit. At the same time, any effort to enter the industry on a larger scale may be frustrated by difficulties of obtaining capital and putting together the necessary organization. Thus the ability of existing firms to expand gradually as compared to the need for new entrants to start out with considerable production capacity can be a substantial advantage for existing firms. A good example is the automobile industry. Because of the economies of scale associated with the manufacture and sale of automobiles, no new domestic producer has successfully entered the industry in over fifty years.

Spectrum of Market Structures

As discussed in Chapter 9, there are few markets that can properly be categorized as being either perfectly competitive or true monopolies. The majority of markets lies in the intermediate range characterized by monopolistic competition and oligopoly. Table 10-4 shows a spectrum of market structures and representative industries in each category. Although agriculture is listed under perfect competition, it does not meet all the requirements for that designation. Rather, it is an industry that comes very close to being perfectly competitive. Similarly, electric and gas companies may have legal monopolies in their service areas, but they still face some competition from substitute services. Thus, even they are not true monopolies.

Note that two types of oligopolies are shown in Table 10-4. The first type (listed in the third column) consists of a small number of firms of nearly equal size. The second type (shown in the fourth column) has a dominant firm. These dominant firms are shown in parentheses with each industry and supply a large share of total industry output. For example, several firms manufacture film in the United

TABLE 10-4 **Market Structures of Selected Industries**

Perfect Competition	Monopolistic Competition	Oligopoly	Dominant Firm Oligopoly	Monopoly
Agriculture	Movie theaters	Automobiles	Aircraft (Boeing)	Electric and
Futures	Printing	Cereal	Canned soup	gas
trading	Retailing	Cigarettes	(Campbell)	utilities
	Restaurants	Beer	Film (Kodak)	
	Dresses	Oil refining	Detergents	
	Poultry	Steel	(Procter &	
	Yarns	Newspapers	Gamble)	
	Sheet metal	Chewing gum		

States. But Kodak is clearly the dominant firm in that industry. The market shares of other U.S. film manufacturers are small.

KEY CONCEPTS

- In the long run, barriers to entry may be the most important determinant of market structure.
- Sources of entry barriers include control of scarce inputs, product differentiation, legal factors, and scale economies.
- Most markets resemble monopolistic competition and oligopoly more than perfect competition and monopoly.

CASE STUDY

Barriers to Entry: New York Taxi Drivers and Australian Fishermen

To limit the number and regulate the operations of taxicab drivers, in 1937 the city of New York required all cab drivers to purchase a license. These licenses were called medallions and were sold for $10 each. At that time, 11,787 medallions were issued and no additional licenses have been granted in the intervening years. Thus, those who own the medallions are part of a taxi service monopoly in New York. A legal barrier to entry exists, which prevents others from entering this market.

Although the supply of licensed taxicabs has not changed, the demand for taxi service has increased dramatically since 1937. As a result, the medallions have become extremely valuable because ownership of a medallion confers upon the owner an opportunity to earn economic profits. Essentially, a taxicab license is worth the present value of the future profit stream that it can generate. By the late 1980s, New York City taxi medallions were selling for over $100,000.

The legal barrier to entry in New York City has resulted in an excess demand for taxi service that has caused problems. Nonlicensed cabs cruise the streets of New York and illegally pick up passengers. Sometimes their presence results in violent confrontations with medallion drivers. Another difficulty is that licensed drivers, with ample opportunities in downtown New York, are often unwilling to pick up or deliver customers to bad neighborhoods or outlying areas. One solution has been to authorize a limited number of nonmedallion cars. These vehicles can respond to a telephone request for taxi service but are not allowed to pick up people who want to hail a cab from the street.

New York taxis are not the only example of monopoly resulting from a barrier to entry created by governmental restrictions. In Australia, offshore fishing is regulated by the Department of Fisheries. In order to fish Australia's coastal waters, fishermen must obtain a license from the department. But only a limited number of licenses are issued and, once obtained, the license grants a permanent right to fish in a specified area. The purpose of licensing is to prevent the region from being depleted by overfishing.

Because their number is restricted, these licenses can be extremely valuable. For example, one fishing area off the southern coast of Australia is a prolific source of giant prawns. But only thirty-nine boats are authorized to operate there. Consequently, licenses have sold for more than $900,000. This high price can be justified by the $400,000 to $500,000 in prawns that can be harvested during each year's 120-day fishing season.

Summary

Chamberlin's model of monopolistic competition assumes ease of entry and exit and a large number of small sellers. It differs from perfect competition by viewing sellers as providing products that are slightly differentiated. Thus firms have some control over price. In the short run, profits are maximized by equating marginal revenue and marginal cost and there are economic profits. In the long run, entry of new firms causes prices to fall and eliminates economic profits. The theory of monopolistic competition has a limited scope of application, but the model makes a useful contribution to economic analysis by calling attention to the importance of product differentiation.

Oligopolistic market structures have many buyers but only a small number of sellers. The product may be either differentiated or undifferentiated. Typically, entry into the industry is somewhat difficult. An important difference between oligopoly and other market structures is that oligopolists recognize their interdependence. Thus, in making decisions, managers must consider the effect on other firms and the probable response of those firms.

There is no single theory that describes all aspects of oligopoly behavior. However, specific models capture certain elements. The kinked demand curve model assumes that competitors will follow price reductions but not price increases. The implication is that price changes will be infrequent in oligopolistic markets.

In the Cournot model of oligopoly, each firm makes its profit-maximizing output decision on the assumption that other firms will not change their rate of output. Using the Cournot assumption, it can be shown that output increases and the price decreases as the number of firms in the market increases.

Oligopolists have an incentive to collude and avoid aggressive competition. By collusion, the firms can increase their total profit. But individual firms can gain even more if they cheat on a collusive agreement. The success of a cartel depends on its ability to detect and punish cheaters.

Price leadership is a substitute for illegal collusion. Where there is a dominant firm, that supplier will charge its profit-maximizing price and smaller firms will charge the same price. Barometric price leadership involves firms signaling each other that changes in demand or costs require a price change.

Barriers to entry are probably the most important long-run determinant of market structure. Entry barriers can result from control of scarce inputs, product differentiation, legal factors, and economies of scale.

End Read.

Discussion Questions

10-1. Is product differentiation important in the breakfast cereal industry? Explain.

10-2. Which of the following markets could be considered monopolistically competitive? Explain.
   a. Network television.   b. Low-priced pens.
   c. Restaurants.   d. Automobiles.

10-3. In monopolistically competitive markets, why is the firm's demand curve assumed to be relatively more elastic in the long run than in the short run?

10-4. Monopolistic competition assumes slightly differentiated products, but the average and marginal cost curves used in the analysis are those of a typical or representative firm. Are these assumptions consistent? Explain.

10-5. Suppose that there are 5,000 firms selling candy by mail to people in the Pacific Northwest. Could this market be characterized as monopolistically competitive? If 5,000 firms are selling concrete in the same region, could that market be considered monopolistically competitive? Explain.

10-6. Why might oligopolists be more likely to match a price cut than a price increase by a competitor?

10-7. Contracts for electric generating equipment are often awarded on the basis of sealed bids. As an employee of the U.S. Department of Justice, what would you look for as an indication of price fixing in the electric machinery industry?

10-8. Why would smaller firms be content to let a large firm practice dominant firm price leadership in an industry?

10-9. Accumulated experience may allow firms that have been producing for many years to have lower costs than new entrants in a market. Would this learning by doing be a barrier to entry as defined by Bain? What about using Stigler's definition of entry barriers?

10-10. Are service industries more likely to be near the monopoly or the competitive end of the spectrum of market structures? Why?

Problems

10-1. In Gotham City the movie market is monopolistically competitive. In the long run, the demand for movies at the Silver Screen theater is given by the equation

$$P = 5.00 - 0.002Q$$

where Q is the number of paid admissions per month. The average cost function is given by

$$AC = 6.00 - 0.004Q + 0.000001Q^2$$

a. To maximize profit, what price should the managers of Silver Screen charge? What will be the number of paid admissions per month?

b. How much economic profit will the firm earn?

10-2. EnviroEast can produce recycled paper at a constant marginal cost of $0.50 per pound. Currently, the firm is selling 500,000 pounds each year at $0.60 per pound. Managers of EnviroEast are considering increasing the price to $0.90 per pound. Demand elasticity is constant and equals -0.6 if the price increase is matched by competitors and -4.0 if it is not matched. Management believes there is a 70 percent chance that other firms will follow EnviroEast's lead and increase their prices.

a. If managers are risk neutral, should the proposed price change be implemented? Explain.

b. Write an equation for the expected change in profit as a function of the probability that the price increase will be matched by the other firms. What probability would make a risk-neutral manager indifferent to the change?

10-3. The price of steel is currently at $400 per ton. Pennsylvania Steel faces a kinked demand curve with a demand equation

$$P = 600 - 0.5Q$$

for prices above the present price of $400 and

$$P = 700 - 0.75Q$$

for prices below $400. The firm's marginal cost curve is given by an equation with the general form

$$MC = a + bQ$$

a. If $a = 50$ and $b = 0.25$, graph the demand, marginal revenue, and marginal cost curves. Using the graph, determine the profit-maximizing quantity for Pennsylvania Steel.

b. Starting from $a = 50$, how much can the constant term of the marginal cost equation increase before the profit-maximizing quantity decreases? How much can the coefficient decrease before the profit-maximizing quantity increases?

10-4. At present, the price of copper tubing is $1 per foot. Lyon Inc. is considering entering the industry by building a facility that will produce 40 million feet of tubing per year. It is estimated that the average cost curve for manufacturing copper tubing is given by the equation

$$AC = 1.21 - 0.010Q + 0.0001Q^2$$

where AC is average cost per foot (including a normal profit) and Q is millions of feet per year.

a. If the price of copper tubing remains unchanged, should Lyon Inc. build the planned production facility? Why or why not?
b. At a price of $1 per foot, what is the rate of output per year necessary to earn at least a normal profit?
c. Suppose the probability is 0.7 that the price will stay at $1 per pound and 0.3 that Lyon's entry will cause the price to drop to $0.90 per pound. If managers are risk neutral, should they build the production facility? Why or why not?

10-5. The demand for spring water is given by $P = 1000 - Q_T$, where Q_T is the total amount of the product sold. The marginal cost is zero. The firms in the market behave like Cournot oligopolists.
a. If there are two firms, determine the reaction functions for each firm. What will be the equilibrium price and equilibrium total output?
b. What would be the price and output for a monopolist?
c. What would be the price and output if there were six firms in the market?

10-6. The market demand for television sets is given by

$$P = 1,000 - 10Q$$

The industry consists of one large firm, which acts as a price leader, and two smaller firms, which act as followers. The summed marginal cost equation for the smaller firms is

$$\Sigma MC_F = 2.5Q_F$$

The large firm's marginal cost equation is

$$MC_L = 1Q_L$$

If the objective is to maximize profit,
a. What price will the dominant firm charge?
b. What price will the two smaller firms charge?
c. What will be the market share of the large firm?

10-7. Wyngate, a small manufacturing firm, is considering building a plant capable of producing 25 million wood pencils per year. Economies of scale are the only important barrier to entry in the industry. It is estimated that the average cost function is given by

$$AC = 100,000 - 1,000Q + 10.0Q^2$$

where Q is measured in millions of pencils per year. The current wholesale price of pencils is $75,000 per million, and this price will not be affected by the entry of Wyngate into the industry. What is the minimum output rate necessary to allow a firm to earn at least a normal profit? Will Wyngate be able to successfully enter the industry?

Problems Requiring Calculus

10-8. Southern Inc. operates in a monopolistically competitive market. The demand equation faced by Southern is given by $P = 350 - Q$ and the firm's long-run total cost equation is given by $TC = 355Q - 2Q^2 + 0.05Q^3$.

a. What are the equilibrium price and rate of output for the firm?
b. Compute the economic profit earned by the firm.
c. Determine whether the equilibrium rate of output calculated in part (a) meets the marginal revenue equals marginal cost test.

10-9. The demand for spring water is $P = 1,000 - Q_T$ and marginal cost is zero. There are two firms in the market, and each firm believes that the other will respond to a one-unit decrease in output by increasing its output by one-half unit. For example, if firm 1 reduces output by one unit, firm 2 will respond by increasing its output by one-half unit.
a. Compute the marginal revenue equations for each firm.
b. Compute the reaction functions for each firm.
c. What will be the equilibrium price and the total output for the industry? How do the price and output compare to those computed for the Cournot duopoly in problem 10-5?

10-10. For Jensen Associates, profit as a function of advertising is given by the following equation:

$$\text{Total Profit} = 500 + 50A - A^2$$

where A is units of advertising and each advertising unit costs $4.
(a) Mathematically determine the optimal rate of advertising.
(b) Now suppose that quantity discounts are available for purchases of advertising and that the marginal cost of an additional unit of advertising is given by

$$MC_A = 60 - 3A$$

Determine the profit maximizing rate of advertising. Explain.

CHAPTER *11*

Start Read.

Game Theory and Strategic Behavior

Preview

Introduction to Game Theory
> The Payoff Matrix
> Nash Equilibrium
> Dominant Strategies
> Dominated Strategies
> Maximin Strategies
> Mixed Strategies

Game Theory and Oligopoly
> Noncooperative Games: The Prisoner's Dilemma
> Cooperative Games: Enforcing a Cartel
> Repeated Games: Dealing with Cheaters
> Sequential Games: The Advantage of Being First

Strategic Behavior
> Present versus Future Profits: Limit Pricing
> The Value of a Bad Reputation: Price Retaliation
> Establishing Commitment: Capacity Expansion
> Preemptive Action: Market Saturation

Summary
Discussion Questions
Problems

Preview _____

The distinguishing characteristic of oligopolistic markets is that managers must consider the effects of their decisions on other firms and also must anticipate how managers of those other firms will respond. Basically, life in an oligopoly can be interpreted as a high-stakes game where the objective is to earn economic profits by outguessing your rivals. In fact, important insights into oligopolistic markets have been achieved by using a method of analysis called game theory.

The first section of this chapter introduces basic concepts of game theory. The second illustrates how game theory can be used to understand and predict the behavior of managers in oligopolies. The final section of the chapter considers strategies that are used to prevent entry in a market.

Introduction to Game Theory _____

Game theory was developed in the 1950s by mathematician John von Neumann and economist Oskar Morgenstern. The technique was designed to evaluate situations where individuals and organizations can have conflicting objectives. It can be used to analyze a broad range of activities, including dating and mating strategies, parlor games, legal and political negotiations, and economic behavior. For example, in wage negotiations between unions and firms, a primary objective of the management team is to keep the total wage bill as small as possible, while union negotiators want to maximize wage payments. In peace talks between two nations at war, each country wants to arrange a settlement that is to its advantage. And during courtship, both men and women may adopt complicated and sometimes devious strategies based on their individual objectives. In all of these situations, game theory could be used to analyze the bargaining process between the two parties.

Over time, game theory has evolved to become a very broad and complex subject. Consequently, only the most basic elements can be presented here. However, even these fundamental concepts can provide valuable insights into business behavior. In this section, the nomenclature and structure of game theory are introduced. Although the political and courtship applications of the techniques probably are more interesting, the discussion is limited to the use of game theory in an economic setting.

The Payoff Matrix

At the heart of game theory are the concepts of strategies and payoffs. A *strategy* is a course of action taken by one of the participants in a game, and the *payoff* is the result or outcome of the strategy. Consider the simple example of two children engaged in a penny-flipping game. One child tosses the coin and the other calls it. If a head or tail is correctly predicted, then the caller gets the penny. If not, the other person wins the coin. In this situation, the strategy is the caller's choice of a head or a tail, and the payoff or outcome is that either the caller wins a penny or the coin tosser wins the coin.

In this simple game, the coin tosser is a passive participant, and the outcome depends on the caller's choice and the result of a random flip of the coin. In more complicated games, the outcome may depend not only on the choice made by one person, but also on the strategies selected by one or more other participants.

Consider a market with two competing firms whose objective is to increase their profits by price changes. Assume that each firm has two possible strategies—it can either maintain its price at the present level or it can increase its price. In this game, there are four possible combinations of strategies—both of the firms increase their prices, neither firm increases its price, firm 1 increases its price but firm 2 does not, and firm 2 increases price but the other firm does not.

The results for each of the four combinations of strategies are shown in Table 11-1. The first number in each cell is the profit for firm 1, and the second value is the corresponding profit for firm 2. Table 11-1 is referred to as a *payoff matrix* because it shows the outcomes or payoffs that result from each combination of strategies adopted by the two participants in the game.

Nash Equilibrium

In discussing models of perfect competition and monopoly in Chapter 9, the focus was on determining equilibrium conditions. These conditions were the rates of output that allowed the firms to maximize profits. Because the equilibriums represented the best the firms could do, there was no reason to change. For both of these market structures, the profit-maximizing equilibrium was the rate of output where marginal revenue equaled marginal cost. Actions of the other firms in the market were irrelevant because they had an insignificant impact on the firm (perfect competition) or because there were no other firms (monopoly).

But the payoffs shown in Table 11-1 depend not only on the pricing alternative chosen by each firm, but also on the strategy selected by the other firm. If firm 1 decides not to raise prices, it will have $10 million in profits if firm 2 also does not change its price and $100 million if firm 2 implements a price increase. If firm

TABLE 11-1 **Payoff Matrix (millions)**

		Firm 2	
		No Price Change	Price Increase
Firm 1	No Price Change	10, 10	100, −30
	Price Increase	−20, 30	140, 35

1 raises prices, profits will be $-20 million if the other firm makes no change and $140 million if firm 2 does increase its price.

The objective of each firm is to do the best if can based on what the other firm does. Faced with the payoff matrix of Table 11-1, is there an equilibrium result? Suppose that firm 1 does not change its price. In this situation, the optimal strategy for firm 2 is also no price change because it will earn $10 million in profit, compared to a loss of $30 million if it increases prices. Note that if firm 2 does not change prices, the best strategy for firm 1 is to hold the line on prices.

Thus, for the payoff matrix of Table 11-1, no price changes is an equilibrium because neither firm can benefit by increasing its price if the other firm does not. This result is referred to as a Nash equilibrium (for mathematician John Nash). A *Nash equilibrium* is defined as a set of strategies such that none of the participants in the game can improve their payoff, given the strategies of the other participants. For the game described in Table 11-1, firm 1's choice not to raise prices is optimal if firm 2 doesn't raise prices and vice versa. In Chapter 10, the equilibrium for a Cournot duopoly was determined. That result also was a Nash equilibrium because each firm was producing the optimal rate of output based on the output for the other firm. Consequently, neither firm had any incentive to change.

A limitation of the concept of Nash equilibrium is that there can be more than one equilibrium. For example, in Table 11-1, if firm 1 were to increase its price, then firm 2 would earn more profit by increasing its price than by leaving its price unchanged. Similarly, if firm 2 were to initiate a price increase, firm 1 will earn $40 million more by matching the increase. Thus, both firms increasing their price is also a Nash equilibrium. The actual outcome of the game depends on which action occurs first. Because no price change is the initial condition, the expected outcome of this game would be that prices would not change. For some games, there may be no Nash equilibrium. In these cases, participants may continuously switch from one strategy to another.

KEY CONCEPTS

- A strategy is a course of action that can be used by a player in a game.
- The payoff matrix indicates the outcomes of all the possible combinations of strategies in a game.
- A Nash equilibrium is a set of strategies such that none of the players in a game can improve their payoff, given the strategies of the other participants.

Dominant Strategies

For the payoffs in Table 11-1, the optimal strategy for each firm depends on the strategy selected by the other firm. But in some situations, one firm's best strategy may not depend on the choice made by other participants in the game. In this case, that firm has a *dominant strategy*. Consider the payoff matrix shown in Table 11-2.

If firm 1 does not change prices, firm 2's best strategy is to also make no price adjustment. But, based on the profit numbers from Table 11-2, if firm 1 increases

TABLE 11-2 **Dominant Strategy (millions)**

		Firm 2	
		No Price Change	Price Increase
Firm 1	No Price Change	10, 10	100, −30
	Price Increase	−20, 30	140, 25

its price, firm 2 is still better off with no price change because profit will be $30 million, compared to $25 million if it increases price. Hence, firm 2's dominant strategy is to hold prices at the existing level, regardless of what firm 1 does. When one player has a dominant strategy, the game will always have a Nash equilibrium because that player will use that strategy and the other will respond with its best alternative. For the payoffs in Table 11-2, firm 1's best response to no price change by firm 2 is also not to change its price.

In the analysis of games, the first step is to determine if any participant has a dominant strategy. If such a strategy exists, then the outcome of the game should be easily determined because the player will use the dominant strategy, and other participants will adopt their best response. If there is no dominant strategy, the next step is to search for other Nash equilibriums. If there are none, it may still be possible to analyze the game using other techniques.

CASE STUDY

Indiana Jones and the Holy Grail

Among the most popular movies of recent years are the Indiana Jones sagas. In *Indiana Jones and the Last Crusade*, it is revealed that the hero is a great adventurer but not an astute student of game theory. Near the end of the movie, Jones, his father, and the Nazis are at the site of the Holy Grail. Because the pair refuse to help, the Nazis shoot the father, knowing that he can be saved only by taking a drink from the sacred cup.

Indiana Jones makes his way to the Grail but finds that it is located among hundreds of other chalices. Drinking from the right cup brings eternal life, but a sip from any other causes instant death. The Nazi leader impatiently drinks from the wrong cup and dies, while Indiana Jones makes a well-reasoned (but risky) choice of a chalice, which does turn out to be the Holy Grail. His father also drinks from the cup and is healed of his mortal wound.

Jones should be applauded for his courage but given a failing mark in economics for not recognizing he had a dominant choice. The best strategy was to give the drink to his father without tasting it first. If the cup was the Holy Grail, his father would be saved. Hence, he would have been as well off as by trying it himself and then giving the life-giving fluid to his father.

However, if Jones drank first and it was not the Holy Grail, both would die—Indiana from the liquid and his father from the wound. But if the wrong cup were given to his father first, he would die, but Indiana Jones would be spared.

Giving the cup to his father first is no worse than tasting it first if the Holy Grail is selected and better if it is not. Thus, this was the dominant strategy and should have been selected.

SOURCE: This example is taken from A. Dixit and B. Nalebuff. *Thinking Strategically*. (New York: Norton, 1991), pp. 59–60.

Dominated Strategies

Many games do not have a dominant strategy for any player. In fact, dominance is the exception rather than the rule. However, it may be possible to simplify a game by eliminating dominated strategies. A *dominated strategy* is an alternative that yields a lower payoff than some other strategy, no matter what the other players in the game do.

Consider a single play in a football game in which the goal of the offense is to gain as many yards as possible and the goal of the defense is to minimize the yards gained. Assume there is time for just two more plays, and the team with the ball wants to use the first play to get as close to the goal line as possible to try a field goal. The offense has two strategies—to run or to pass. The options for the defense are to defend against the run, to protect against the pass by dropping back their linebackers, or to defend against a pass by using a quarterback blitz. The outcomes of these offensive and defensive strategies are shown in Table 11-3. Each number in the cells shows yards gained by the offense.

Neither team has a dominant strategy. For the offense, this can be seen by noting that the run gains more ground against the blitz but less against the other two defenses. For the defense, there is no strategy that will always give up less yardage than the others. However, the defense does have one strategy that is dominated. Table 11-3 shows that the blitz yields more ground against both the run and the pass than either of the other two defenses. The implication is that the defense should either counter the run or drop back its linebackers but should not blitz.

TABLE 11-3 **Dominated Strategy**

		Defensive Strategy		
		Defense Against Run	Linebackers Back	Blitz
Offensive Strategy	Run	2	6	14
	Pass	8	7	10

End. Read.

Whenever there is a dominated strategy, the game can be simplified because the dominated strategy should always be avoided. Thus, by reducing the number of viable options, it may be easier to identify an equilibrium or to use other techniques to analyze the outcome.

Maximin Strategies

Thus far, the analysis of market structures has assumed that managerial decisions focus on maximizing profits. But in highly competitive situations, such as an oligopoly, von Neumann and Morgenstern suggested that decision makers might adopt a risk-averse strategy of assuring that the worst possible outcome is as beneficial as possible, regardless of what other decision makers do. This decision rule is referred to as a *maximin strategy* because it specifies that each player in the game will select the option that maximizes the minimum possible profit (or other desirable outcome).

Consider the following example. The two firms in a duopoly are each thinking about introducing a new product. The profit outcomes for the four possible combinations of strategies are shown by the payoff matrix in Table 11-4. If the firms are trying to maximize profit, the matrix has two Nash equilibriums—the two cases where one firm introduces a new product but the other does not. For example, if firm 1 markets the new product, firm 2 will earn $2 million if it follows suit, but profit will be $3 million if it does not. If firm 2 does not introduce a new product, the first firm will earn $2 million more if it markets the new product than if it does not. Hence, the bottom left-hand cell of the matrix is a Nash equilibrium. Using similar logic, the top right-hand cell is also an equilibrium.

But the maximin decision criterion is not a pure profit-maximizing strategy. Rather, it is designed to avoid highly unfavorable outcomes. In applying this principle, each firm first determines the minimum profit that could result from each strategy it could choose. As shown in the table, for firm 1, this is $3 million

TABLE 11-4 **Maximin Strategy (millions)**

		Firm 2		Firm 1
		No New Product	New Product	Minimum
Firm 1	No New Product	4, 4	3, 6	3
	New Product	6, 3	2, 2	2
	Firm 2 Minimum	3	2	

if the firm does not introduce the new product and $2 million if it does. The numbers are the same for firm 2.

The second step is to select the maximum of the minimums. The result is that neither firm should introduce a new product because they will be guaranteed a profit of at least $3 million by adopting this strategy. Note that the maximin outcome is not one of the two Nash equilibriums. The reason is that loss avoidance rather than profit maximization was the criterion used for decision making.

CASE STUDY _____

Texaco and Pennzoil

In January 1984, the Pennzoil Corporation offered to buy 40 percent of Getty Oil's stock for $128.50 per share. Getty's board of directors agreed, but then Texaco stepped in and offered $128 per share for 100 percent of the Getty stock. The Getty directors reversed their approval of Pennzoil's bid and sold the company to Texaco.

Pennzoil promptly sued Texaco for breach of contract. The case was tried in Texas, and in 1985, a jury awarded Pennzoil $10 billion in damages—the largest award in U.S. history. Texaco immediately appealed the verdict, and by the fall of 1987, the case was on its final appeal before the U.S. Supreme Court. Before a decision was announced by the Court, Pennzoil made an offer, which was accepted by Texaco, and the suit was settled in December 1987 for $3 billion.

With some oversimplification, Pennzoil's offer to settle a $10 billion lawsuit for $3 billion can be viewed as a maximin problem. That is, the company wanted to maximize the minimum possible payment from Texaco. Assume there were just two possible outcomes from the Supreme Court—either the $10 billion jury award would be affirmed or it would be overturned and nothing would be awarded. Also assume that Pennzoil's managers had just two options—to wait for the Court's decision or to make an offer they believed Texaco would accept.

If Pennzoil waited for the Supreme Court decision, the outcome would be $10 billion if the jury verdict was affirmed and zero if it was not. By settling out of court, the minimum payment would be $3 billion. Thus, Pennzoil's maximin decision strategy was to make the settlement offer.

The use of the maximin strategy was a logical choice by Pennzoil. If the Supreme Court reversed the jury award and the firm received nothing, Pennzoil's managers would have been criticized for not reaching a settlement. Indeed, they could have been sued for failing to act in the best interest of the firm's stockholders. By offering to settle, they were guaranteed at least $3 billion and avoided the potential criticism and/or litigation.

Mixed Strategies

In all of the games discussed, it has been assumed that each participant selects one course of action. This approach is called a *pure strategy*. But in many games, a pure strategy would be a very poor choice. For example, think about the duel between a baseball pitcher and hitter. If the pitcher throws all curves or all fastballs, a major league batter would have a good chance of getting a hit. To be effective, the pitcher must keep the hitter off balance by throwing a mixture of curves and fastballs. This approach is referred to as a *mixed strategy*.

Table 11-5 depicts the payoffs for the pitcher and hitter. Low percentages favor the pitcher, and high values are the objective of the batter. Note that a batter is more successful when he can anticipate the pitch, and the pitcher is more likely to succeed if he can fool the hitter.

If the pitcher throws all fastballs, the batter will look only for this pitch and will hit .400. Any pitcher who throws only curve balls will also be facing a .400 hitter. Clearly, either of these two pure strategies would be a disaster for the pitcher. The best strategy is to throw a mixture of fastballs and curves. Similarly, the hitter cannot succeed by always anticipating one pitch. Any batter who always goes to the plate looking for a curve will find his average hovering around .200 because pitchers will throw him fastballs, and one who anticipates only fastballs will do no better because he will receive a steady diet of curves.

For the payoff matrix shown in Table 11-5, there are no pure strategies that result in a Nash equilibrium. However, there are equilibrium mixed strategies. If the hitter randomly alternates between anticipating a fastball and a curve on a 50–50 basis and the pitcher randomly throws a mixture of 50 percent fastballs and 50 percent curves, the hitter's batting average will be .300. This is because each of the four payoffs in the matrix will occur 25 percent of the time. Thus, the expected frequency of base hits will be .25(40%) + .25(20%) + .25(20%) + .25(40%) = 30%.

Suppose the batter adopts a strategy other than anticipating that fastballs and curves are equally likely. If the pitcher continues to throw a random assortment of 50 percent of each pitch, the hitter will guess wrong more often than right, and his average will drop below .300. Thus, given the pitcher's strategy, the best approach for the batter is to anticipate a random 50–50 assortment.

In contrast, if the batter continues to assume that fastballs and curves are equally likely and the pitcher throws a different mix, the hitter's average will still be .300. For example, suppose the pitcher throws 60 percent fastballs and 40 percent curves. The probability of each payoff in Table 11-5 will now be

Expect fastball and fastball thrown: $.50 \times .60 = .30$
Expect fastball and curveball thrown: $.50 \times .40 = .20$
Expect curveball and fastball thrown: $.50 \times .60 = .30$
Expect curveball and curveball thrown: $.50 \times .40 = .20$

TABLE 11-5 **Mixed Strategies (percent base hits)**

		Pitcher	
		Throws Fastball	Throws Curve
Hitter	Anticipates Fastball	40%	20%
	Anticipates Curve	20%	40%

Multiplying these probabilities by the payoffs for each of the cells in the table, the expected frequency of hits will be .30(40%) + .20(20%) + .30(30%) + .20(40%) = 30%. Surprisingly, this result does not depend on the mixture of fastballs and curves used by the pitcher. As long as the batter continues to anticipate that curves and fastballs are equally likely, the hitter's average will be .300 regardless of what strategy the pitcher selects. Thus, the game has many Nash equilibriums. When mixed strategies are allowed, every game with a finite number of players and a finite number of strategies has at least one equilibrium.

Mixed strategies can be important in many settings. Sometimes they are used to reduce costs. Consider the Internal Revenue Service and its tax audit procedure. It would be extremely expensive to audit every income tax return, so the IRS chooses individuals at random (after using some preselection criteria) for audits. Although the vast majority of returns are not audited, the possibility of an audit encourages tax compliance among the general population.

KEY CONCEPTS

- If a player has a best option, regardless of what other players do, this is referred to as a dominant strategy.
- A dominated strategy is an alternative that always has a lower payoff than some other strategy.
- The maximin criterion involves maximizing the minimum desirable outcome of a game.
- A pure strategy involves always making the same choice, while mixed strategy requires randomly mixing different alternatives.

Game Theory and Oligopoly

Game theory can be used to analyze specific situations faced by managers in oligopolistic markets. This section considers four specific applications. The first is noncooperative games, which is used to illustrate how firms in an oligopoly can find themselves in a situation that is nonoptimal for all participants. The discussion of cooperative games shows how businesses can work together to avoid such situations, and the evaluation of repeated games presents methods for dealing with cheaters. Finally, sequential games are discussed to illustrate advantages that can come from being first to act in a business setting.

Noncooperative Games: The Prisoner's Dilemma

A game is considered *noncooperative* if it is not possible to negotiate with other participants and enter into some form of binding agreement. When U.S. firms in oligopolistic markets use pricing strategies to compete for profits, they usually are engaged in noncooperative games because they are legally prohibited by antitrust laws from coordinating their prices.

In some cases, noncooperatives games can result in outcomes that are undesirable for the participants and also for society. One example is the *Prisoner's Dilemma*. This model takes its name from the story of two people who were jailed for a crime they allegedly committed. The two suspects are separated and interrogated by the police. Each is told that if she does not confess and the other person does, she will be convicted and put in jail for 15 years. But if she does confess and implicates her friend, then the jail sentence will only be five years. However, because the evidence is circumstantial, if neither confesses, it will be impossible to get a conviction and neither person will go to jail. The payoff matrix for this game is shown in Table 11-6.

Because the two prisoners are interrogated separately, they have no idea whether the other person will confess or not. Hence, this is an example of a noncooperative game. If the suspects are risk averse, they may adopt a minimax decision criterion. This is similar to the maximin strategy discussed earlier, except that now the outcomes are undesirable. Consequently, the minimax approach involves minimizing the maximum jail sentence they could receive.

For suspect 1, the strategy of not confessing involves a maximum jail term of 15 years, while a confession would result in no more than five years in jail. Thus, the maximum sentence is minimized by confessing. The same is true for suspect 2, which implies that the minimax solution is for both people to confess. But note that if neither person confesses, neither will go to jail. Although not confessing is the best joint strategy, because they are involved in a noncooperative game and cannot influence what the other person does, they end up with a decidedly nonoptimal outcome.

The Prisoner's Dilemma model can be used to explain a number of interesting phenomena in business. One example is the resource waste from advertising in oligopolistic markets. For simplicity, assume that there are just two firms and that managers can choose a high level of advertising or a low level. Also assume that the managers are risk averse and that their objective is to maximize the minimum profit earned by their firms. That is, they use the maximin rule (maximin because the outcome is profit, which is a desirable outcome). Should managers select the low or the high level of advertising?

TABLE 11-6 **Prisoner's Dilemma (Years in Jail)**

		Suspect 2		Person 1 Maximum
		Don't Confess	Confess	
Suspect 1	Don't Confess	0, 0	15, 5	15
	Confess	5, 15	5, 5	5
	Person 2 Maximum	15	5	

TABLE 11-7 **Advertising and Resource Waste (millions)**

		Firm 2	
		Low-Level Advertising	High-Level Advertising
Firm 1	Low-Level Advertising	$30, $30	$10, $40
	High-Level Advertising	$40, $10	$20, $20

The payoff matrix for the four possible combinations of advertising strategy are shown in Table 11-7. If firm 1 advertises at a low level, its profit will be $30 million if the second firm also advertises at a low level and $10 million otherwise. Thus, minimum profit from low-level advertising is $10 million. Table 11-7 shows that a high level of advertising will guarantee firm 1 at least $20 million in profit. Hence, the maximin strategy for firm 1 is to advertise extensively. Similar logic suggests that firm 2 will also choose the high advertising option.

Both firms will opt for high-level advertising, and the result is a profit of $20 million for each company. However, note that a joint decision not to advertise would have been more profitable for each firm because profit would have been #30 million. But neither firm dares to select this choice because of the possibility that the other might select the high-advertising strategy and leave it with only $10 million in profit. The result is that both firms earn less profit and waste resources on mutually offsetting advertising. Although much simplified, this analysis provides insight into the dilemma faced by oligopolists.

The Prisoner's Dilemma is applicable to many game situations. One of the most important is the arms race between the Soviet Union and the United States. Each country spent trillions of dollars on missiles and acquired the capability to destroy the other nation many times over. These expenditures came at the expense of other programs, such as education, medical research, and housing. But neither country was willing to reduce its spending for fear that the other would gain a military advantage.

Cooperative Games: Enforcing a Cartel

In *cooperative games* it is possible to negotiate and enforce agreements that bind the participants in the game to a particular strategy. For example, the two suspects mentioned earlier were in a noncooperative game because they had no way of knowing what the other person was going to do. If they had been allowed to jointly decide on their strategies and had some means of assuring that the other did not renege, neither would have confessed and they could have avoided spending any time in jail. In the advertising version of the Prisoner's Dilemma, if the firms could have signed a binding contract pledging that they would use the low advertising strategy, they each would have earned $10 million more in profit. With the arms race, years were spent trying to negotiate an arms limitation treaty. But, because there was no satisfactory way to verify compliance by the other side, the buildups continued.

The experience of the cigarette industry during the 1960s is an interesting example of how a noncooperative game was turned, by government policy, into a cooperative game. Historically, the major cigarette manufacturers had spent large sums on TV advertising to promote their products. Much of this advertising was mutually offsetting, so the firms probably were in the Prisoner's Dilemma just described. They would have been better off if they had reduced their advertising expenditures, but no one firm could afford to do so unless there was some assurance that their lead would be followed by the other firms.

In 1968, the federal government banned the advertising of cigarettes on television. Initially, the companies fought the ban, but it soon became apparent that any lost sales were more than made up by the savings in advertising. In fact, there is some evidence that sales actually increased because stations were no longer required by the Federal Communications Commission to air anti-smoking ads that warned of the dangers of cigarettes. With its 1968 ban, the government did for cigarette manufacturers what they were unable to do for themselves— enforce a reduction in advertising.

KEY CONCEPTS

- In noncooperative games, it is not possible to negotiate and enforce agreements.
- The Prisoner's Dilemma model illustrates that the result of a game can be undesirable for all of the participants.
- In a cooperative game, agreements can be enforced. Such games may be a way to avoid the Prisoner's Dilemma.

Repeated Games: Dealing with Cheaters

Even if enforced agreement is not possible, firms may be able to escape the Prisoner's Dilemma if the action is a *repeated game*; that is, if it is played many times. Consider the advertising example shown in Table 11-7. If the game is played once, neither firm will adopt a low advertising level because the other could select high advertising, capture most of the profit, and the game would be over. Even if each firm agrees to hold down advertising, unless there is some way to enforce this agreement, the high-advertising equilibrium is likely to occur.

But if the advertising decision is made repeatedly, the outcome may change. A firm that reneges on an agreement and heavily advertises the first time the game is played will find that the other firm will respond by increasing its advertising in the second period. Thus, the cheater's advantage will be temporary, and profits for both firms will be low for the second period. In addition, the fact that cheating occurred once should cause the other firm to be more cautious in the future. With repeated games, reputations are important in determining the outcome.

end

What is the optimal strategy for firms playing noncooperative repeated games? A general answer depends on the nature of the game, but an experiment by Robert Axelrod provides interesting insights.[1] He proposed a tournament of two-person repeated Prisoner's Dilemma games with high and low prices as the two alternatives. He invited game theorists from all over the world to submit computer programs that embodied strategies for playing. Programs were paired against each other and the game was repeated a large number of times.

The result was surprising. The winning strategy was an approach described as "tit-for-tat." Basically, it was that each firm should mimic its rival's behavior from the previous period. If one firm cheats and cuts prices, the other firm responds by cutting prices in the next period. If one firm cooperates by raising prices, the other firm also raises prices. The experiment was later repeated with a larger number of contestants, but tit-for-tat again proved to be the optimal strategy.

In the real world, the advantage of tit-for-tat is that it embodies four principles that are important in any good strategy. First, it is simple, reducing the chance that it will be misunderstood. Second, tit-for-tat never initiates cheating, which could cause a breakdown in cooperation. Third, it never rewards cheating by allowing such behavior to go unpunished. Finally, tit-for-tat is forgiving because it allows cooperation to be quickly restored.

Unfortunately, tit-for-tat can break down if the players know for sure how many times the game will be repeated. The explanation is quite simple. Although cooperation can increase profits, a firm can gain even more if it cheats the last time the game is played because there is no opportunity for retaliation. But the same is true for the other player, so both firms should cheat on the last play. If cheating will occur on the last round, there is no reason to cooperate on the next to the last round, and so on. The result may be that each play of the game degenerates into a Prisoner's Dilemma.

Sequential Games: The Advantage of Being First

In the games described so far, it has been implicitly assumed that both players reveal their strategies simultaneously. In a *sequential game*, one of the players acts first and then the other responds. Entry into a new market is an example of a sequential game. The new firm decides whether or not to enter, and the existing firm then decides whether to ignore the new firm or try to prevent entry.

For sequential games, there may be an advantage to the player who acts first. Think about two firms contemplating the introduction of nearly identical new products. The first firm to get the product to the market is more likely to be successful because it can develop brand loyalties and may be able to associate the product with the firm in the minds of consumers. Also, if consumers invest time in learning to use the product of the first firm, users will be less willing to retool and use a similar product from some other supplier. Word processing and spreadsheet software are good examples. Users who are proficient in one program are unlikely to switch to other programs unless they offer significant advantages.

[1] Axelrod, R. *The Evolution of Cooperation*. (New York: Basic Books 1984).

TABLE 11-8 **Sequential Games (millions)**

		Firm 2	
		No New Product	Introduce New Product
Firm 1	No New Product	$2, $2	$-5, $10
	Introduce New Product	$10, $-5	$-7, $-7

The advantage of moving first is shown by Table 11-8. Each firm is faced with the decision of whether or not to introduce a new product. Assume that the firms use the maximin criterion. If the firms must announce their decisions independently and simultaneously, the maximin criterion specifies that neither should introduce a new product and that each firm will earn $2 million.

Now assume that firm 1 has research and development advantages that give it the option of introducing its product first. With firm 1 already in the market, firm 2's optimal strategy is to stay out because it will lose only $5 million, compared to $7 million if it enters. Consequently, firm 1 will earn $10 million as the only supplier. Clearly, firm 1 has benefitted by being the first mover in the market.

KEY CONCEPTS

- The optimal strategy in a repeated game may be different than the optimal strategy for a game that is only played once.
- A tit-for-tat strategy of mimicking the last choice of the other player may be effective in repeated games.
- In sequential games, where one player selects a strategy and the other responds, there is often advantage to being first.

Strategic Behavior

In the previous chapter, barriers to entry were identified as probably the most important determinant of market structures. But the four traditional barriers to entry described in that chapter (e.g., economies of scale, product differentiation, control over scarce inputs, and legal factors) are primarily the result of basic conditions that exist in each market. As such, the number of firms in an industry would be determined by how those conditions affect entry in each industry. Over time, markets where entry was not difficult would have many sellers, and those with significant barriers to entry would be dominated by a small number of firms.

But this passive view of barriers to entry is too simplistic. Businesses are run by managers, and these individuals will react aggressively if they believe that entry could significantly affect the profitability of their firms. These reactions may take the form of strategic behavior designed to deter entry. Although it is not possible to describe all of the options available to managers, this section considers some of the strategic responses that may be used to thwart entry.

Present versus Future Profits: Limit Pricing

Based on the discussion in Chapter 1, it is assumed that long-run profit maximization is the goal of managers. This objective is achieved by maximizing the present value of profits over some planning horizon. To this point, however, the analysis of managerial pricing decisions has focused on maximizing profit in a single period. But the price that maximizes profits in one period may not be consistent with long-run profit maximization. In this section, long-run pricing strategies are considered.

Bain suggested that setting prices to limit entry describes the pricing practice of many firms.[2] His model assumes that monopolists or firms in an oligopoly pursue a pricing strategy designed to prevent new firms from entering the industry. The approach is illustrated by Figure 11-1. Consider a monopolist facing the market demand curve, DD, and assume that increasing returns to scale provide a cost advantage for large firms. This cost advantage is depicted in Figure 11-1 by an average cost curve that is downward sloping to the output rate Q_x.

To maximize profit in a single period, the monopolist should increase production until marginal revenue equals marginal cost. This implies an output rate of Q_m and a price of P_m. At that price and output rate, the monopolist will earn economic profit for the period. But unless there are substantial barriers to entry, the lure of profit will cause new firms to enter the industry. A potential barrier to entry is the cost advantage of the large firms. That is, because of scale economies, the monopolist producing at Q_m will have lower costs than a new firm that will produce at output rates less than Q_m. However, by setting the profit-maximizing price, the monopolist makes it possible for new firms to enter on a relatively small scale and still earn at least a normal profit. For example, suppose a potential entrant believes that the monopolist will not reduce its price if a new firm enters the market. Thus if the price is P_m, a new entrant could earn a normal profit by producing at an output rate as low as Q_e. This can be seen by observing that at the output rate Q_e, the price, P_m, equals average cost.

Although a single new entrant may have little effect on the rate of profit earned by the monopolist, if the managers of the monopoly continue to use a pricing strategy that maximizes short-run profit, it is likely that additional firms will enter the market. Over time, the increased competition will force the firm to reduce its price and will also reduce the market share and economic profit of the firm.

Alternatively, the firm could utilize a pricing strategy designed to prevent entry.

[2] Bain, J. S. "A Note on Pricing in Monopoly and Oligopoly." *American Economic Review*, March 1949, pp. 448–464.

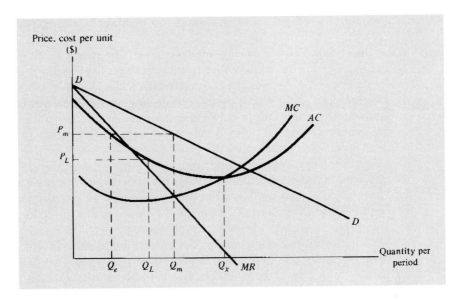

FIGURE 11-1 **Entry Limiting Pricing.**

This approach would require that in each period, managers set a price below the level that maximizes short-run profit. For example, as shown in Figure 11-1, the price might be set at P_L. At this price, new firms entering the industry and producing at output rate less than Q_L could not earn a normal profit. Thus the pricing strategy establishes a barrier to small-scale entry. Although new firms still may enter the market, the size requirement makes entry more difficult and

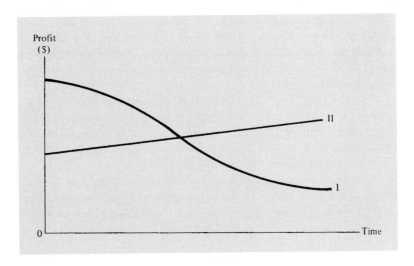

FIGURE 11-2 **Profit Streams Associated with Alternative Pricing Strategies.**

therefore less likely than if the short-run profit-maximizing price, P_m, had been set.

Using *entry-limiting pricing*, managers alter the firm's profit stream, as shown in Figure 11-2. Economic profit resulting from setting the profit-maximizing price in each period is depicted by the profit stream labeled I. Note that economic profit is substantial in the initial period but declines as new firms enter the market. In contrast, entry-limiting pricing generates a relatively constant profit stream over the planning horizon. In fact, if the market is growing, profit may actually increase over time. This is shown by the profit stream labeled II.

In contrast to entry-limiting pricing is Stigler's *open oligopoly model*.[3] Stigler observed that the objective of managers is to maximize the present value of profit. In some cases, this may be achieved by setting a price designed to deter entry. But in other circumstances, profits will be maximized in the long run by setting a high price that provides substantial economic profit in initial periods and then allowing profit to decline as new firms enter the market. In its extreme form, the open oligopoly model might involve setting the profit-maximizing price in each period. In this case, the profit stream would be as shown by I in Figure 11-2.

The optimal long-run pricing strategy is the one that maximizes the present value of profit. Examining the two profit streams in Figure 11-2, it is not obvious which should be chosen. Profit stream I has a high initial profit, but earnings decline rapidly over time. In contrast, profit stream II has less initial profit but shows a slight increase over time.

Basically, the optimal strategy depends on the discount rate used by managers to determine the present value of profit. A high discount rate gives less weight to profits in the future. Thus a high discount rate would cause the present value of profit stream I to be relatively greater. Conversely, a low discount rate would be more favorable to the entry-limiting approach associated with profit stream II.

The importance of the discount rate in selecting a pricing strategy can be illustrated by a simple example. Suppose that the two profit streams involve only three periods and the annual profit is as shown in Table 11-9. The first profit stream shows rapidly decreasing profit and is consistent with the open oligopoly model. Profit stream II has constant profit, as might result from entry-limiting pricing.

Assume that the discount rate is 20 percent and profit is received at the end of the period. In this case, the present value of profit stream I is $106 million, which is greater than the present value of II, which is $105 million. But if the discount rate is 10 percent, the result is reversed. Now the present value of II is $124 million, whereas that of I is only $121 million.

Clearly, the appropriate long-run strategy depends on how managers perceive future profits. Managers with a short planning horizon and those who view short-term profits as paramount would be more likely to behave in a manner consistent with the open oligopoly model. Conversely, those who have a longer time horizon

---

[3] Stigler, G. J. *The Theory of Price* (New York: Macmillan, 1987), Chapter 13.

and use a lower discount rate would be more likely to pursue entry-limiting pricing.

TABLE 11-9 **Alternative Profit Streams**

Period	Profit Stream I (millions of dollars)	Profit Stream II (millions of dollars)
1	80	50
2	40	50
3	20	50

CASE STUDY _____

Saudi Arabia and World Oil Prices

The Organization of Petroleum Exporting Countries (OPEC) is a cartel consisting of 13 of the world's most important oil-producing nations. Oil ministers from each member of the alliance meet on a regular basis, and their primary objective is to influence world oil prices by establishing maximum production quotas for the cartel and for each country. When oil prices are low, reductions in OPEC production can significantly increase world oil prices. Conversely, if OPEC members increase their supply, prices tend to decline.

But the history of OPEC suggests that agreements on production levels have often been difficult to formulate. Although there are exceptions, countries such as Iraq and Iran have usually advocated lower production quotas, which would result in high world oil prices. In contrast, Saudi Arabia has traditionally supported more moderate prices. It is sometimes alleged that the Saudi position is politically motivated by that nation's ties to the United States, which is a large importer of oil. Although political considerations may be a factor, the limit-pricing model can also be used to explain Saudi policy.

Saudi Arabia is the world's largest petroleum producer. Its known reserves of 162 billion barrels represent one-fourth of all known oil

resources, and the present rate of production can be maintained for over fifty years. In normal times (the Persian Gulf War was an exception), Saudi oil revenues are sufficient to sustain a high standard of living for Saudi citizens. In contrast, some other Middle East oil producers, notably Iran and Iraq, have an immediate need for increased revenues to rebuild their economies, which have been ravaged by war and embargoes.

By supporting the advocates of high prices, Saudi Arabia could increase its short-term oil revenues. But Saudi policy makers must also consider the long-term effects of high prices. Economic theory predicts that higher prices will increase quantity supplied because they will allow high-cost oil to be recovered that was not profitable at lower prices.

The problem with higher prices is that oil is just one part of the global energy market. As petroleum prices increase, consumers will shift to other forms of energy, such as nuclear, natural gas, and coal. Higher oil prices may also allow other forms of energy, such as solar, geothermal, and nuclear fusion, to be economically viable. In addition, consumers will respond to higher prices by finding ways to conserve on energy use. Thus, the long-term effect of higher petroleum prices may be reduced demand for oil because of substitution. If large capital expenditures have been made to develop other energy sources, markets for oil may be permanently lost even if prices decline.

Saudi Arabia's oil reserves are intended to provide the bulk of that nation's export revenues for many years. Thus, Saudi decision makers must adopt pricing policies that will preserve the future demand for petroleum. A limit-pricing approach, which makes it less profitable to substitute other energy forms for oil, is consistent with this objective. In contrast, for countries such as Iran and Iraq, which have critical needs for increased short-term oil revenues, the open oligopoly approach is a rational pricing strategy.

The Value of a Bad Reputation: Price Retaliation

The purpose of limit pricing is to reduce the likelihood of entry by keeping prices at a low level over a long period of time. Another strategic response to the threat of entry is to retaliate by reducing prices when entry actually does occur or if it appears imminent. When the perceived danger has diminished, prices can be increased to whatever level management views appropriate for market conditions.

An interesting example of price retaliation involved General Foods and Proctor and Gamble. In the early 1970s, General Foods, with its Maxwell House brand, had a 43 percent market share of the noninstant (ground) coffee market in the eastern United States. During the same period, Proctor and Gamble's Folger's brand was the leading seller in the West but was not distributed in most areas of the East.

In 1971, Proctor and Gamble began to advertise and distribute Folger's in selected eastern cities. This effort was initiated in General Food's Youngstown, Ohio, sales district, which included the cities of Cleveland and Pittsburgh. The response of General Foods to the new entrant was to increase its advertising and cut prices for Maxwell House coffee in this region. At times, the price was actually less than the price of producing the coffee. Profit figures indicate the impact of the price cuts. Profits as a percent of sales dropped from a preentry level of plus 30 percent in 1971 to a negative 30 percent in 1974. When Proctor and Gamble reduced its promotional activities for Folger's coffee in the area, the price of Maxwell House coffee was increased and General Foods' profit rates quickly returned to their previous level.

General Foods also responded to entry in its eastern markets by aggressively reducing prices in midwestern cities where Maxwell House and Folger's were both being marketed. When Proctor and Gamble moved into the Youngstown region, General Foods cut prices and increased its advertising in Kansas City. When Proctor and Gamble became less aggressive in Youngstown, prices and promotional efforts for Maxwell House were allowed to return to prior levels in the Midwest.

Reducing prices every time entry occurs or appears likely to occur would be a costly proposition for the existing firms in a market. But a few applications of this strong medicine can have a significant preventative effect. If a firm establishes a consistent pattern of reacting to entry by drastically reducing prices, then potential rivals may become convinced that they will face the same response and decide not to compete. Thus, by firmly establishing a reputation for dealing harshly with all new entrants, the firm may create an effective barrier to entry.

EXAMPLE _____

Evaluating Price Retaliation

Wild Tides is a water park in Southern Georgia. The firm has fixed costs of $500,000 per year, a variable cost per customer of $5, receives an average of $15 in revenue per admission, and has 100,000 customers each year.

At present, the firm is the only water park in the area, but Wild Tides management has learned that another facility is being planned for a nearby community. After the competing park opens, management expects that to get 100,000 patrons to Wild Tides each year, prices would have to be reduced and that the average revenue would drop to $12.50.

Management believes that if it immediately reduces prices and keeps them at a lower level for two years, it can prevent the other water park from ever opening. The necessary price cut would reduce average revenue to $8 but would increase attendance to 120,000 customers per year. After two years, prices would be raised to their previous level and revenues would again average $15 for 100,000 patrons.

Assume that Wild Tides uses a discount rate of 10 percent and a planning horizon of ten years, and that profits are received at the end of each year. Also assume that if prices are reduced for two years, there will be no entry for the remaining eight years of the planning period. Should the firm cut prices?

SOLUTION   The optimal strategy can be determined by computing the present value of profits for each alternative. If prices are not reduced and entry occurs, revenues will be $1,250,000 per year and variable costs will be $500,000 per year. Subtracting out the $500,000 fixed cost, profit per year will be $250,000. Using a 10 percent discount rate and a ten-year planning horizon, the present value of profits would be $1,536,142.

With price cutting to prevent entry, revenues will be $960,000 (i.e., $8 × 120,000) and variable costs will be $600,000 (i.e., $5 × 120,000). Subtracting the $500,000 fixed cost, profit in each of the first two years will be $−140,000. For the next eight years of the planning period, revenue per customer will be $15 for each of the 100,000 attendees and profits will be $500,000 per year. When these amounts are discounted, the present value of profits is $1,961,540. Because price retaliation gives a greater present value of profits, it is the optimal strategy.

KEY CONCEPTS _____

• Limit pricing involves setting lower prices, which make small-scale entry difficult.

- A firm that always retaliates with price reductions when faced with a new entrant may use its reputation to deter entry.
- In evaluating limit pricing and price retaliation, the present value of profits resulting from alternative strategies should be considered.

Establishing Commitment: Capacity Expansion

The threat of price retaliation against new entrants may not be credible if existing firms are unable to produce enough output to meet extra demand resulting from lower prices. In particular, in a rapidly growing market, a new entrant may be able to survive by serving new customers that the existing firms cannot supply with their present production capacity. A strategic response by established firms to prevent this from occurring would be to invest in additional capacity. Once this investment has been made, it becomes a sunk cost and places existing firms in a position to expand their production at relatively low cost. The existence of excess capacity provides a strong signal that the established firms can (and probably will) reduce prices as a strategic response to entry in their market.

Investment in excess capacity reduces the profits earned by an existing firm. Hence, this investment will be undertaken only if management believes that the certain and immediate loss of profit from making the investment is less than the expected future profit loss resulting from entry. Table 11-10 illustrates this trade-off. Suppose a monopolist must choose between building a small plant and a large plant and that a second firm must decide whether to enter the market. Profit outcomes for each firm for each of four possible scenarios are shown in the table.

If the monopolist builds the small plant, the competitor will enter because its profit will be $4 million, as opposed to zero if entry does not occur. But the larger plant will give the existing firm the ability to reduce its prices and still meet total market demand. Consequently, the new firm will not be able to cover its costs and will experience a loss of $4 million. Thus, if the large plant is built, the better strategy for the new firm is to stay out of the market.

For the monopolist the better strategy is to construct the small plant, restrict output, and continue as the only supplier. But this option is not viable because it will induce entry, and the monopolist's profit will be only $4 million. But if management is confident that the large plant will deter entry, its construction is the best strategy for the monopolist because profit will be $8 million.

TABLE 11-10 **Capacity Expansion as a Deterrent to Entry**

	New Entrant Profit	*Monopolist Profit*
Small plant		
Entry	−$4 million	$4 million
No entry	−$0	$12 million
Large plant		
Entry	$−4 million	$−4 million
No entry	−$0	−$8 million

Preemptive Action: Market Saturation

Just as the total amount of productive capacity can affect the rate of entry, the geographic location of that capacity can also cause barriers to entry. When costs of transporting a good are high relative to its value, consumers who are not close to a production facility may be required to pay substantially higher prices to have the good delivered to their location. Thus, firms that locate closer to those consumers will have a cost advantage and should be able to attract those customers.

This situation is depicted in Figure 11-3a. A monopolist has a production facility at point E, as shown. Although the monopolist may be able to reduce prices and prevent entry near point E, high transportation costs may allow new entrants located at point N_1 to underprice the monopolist and capture the demand of customers who are located near N_1. Having successfully entered on the geographic fringe of the market, the new supplier may, over time, be able to expand its position and challenge the existing firm in other areas, such as N_2.

One entry-deterring strategy for the existing firm would be to disperse its production facilities, as shown in Figure 11-3b. By the existing firm spreading its plants throughout the market area, the opportunity for the new entrant to take advantage of high transportation costs is greatly reduced. Although the monopolist may lose some of the benefits of economies of scale from this dispersion, the ability to prevent or reduce the likelihood of entry may cause management to decide that geographic market saturation is a viable long-run strategy.

The analysis of geographic saturation can also be applied to product characteristics. Now consider the circles of Figure 11-3 as representing possible characteristics of a product such as automobiles. Cars may be small, medium-sized, or large, convertible or hardtop, loaded with accessories or spartan, high performance or fuel-efficient. Let point E in Figure 11-3a represent a monopolist producing a single type of car. For example, in the early days of the U.S. automobile industry, Henry Ford only produced the Model T and allowed his customers to select any color they wanted as long as they wanted black. Initially, Ford experienced great success in the market, but eventually the company's market share declined as its

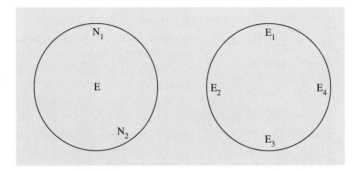

FIGURE 11-3 **Market Saturation.**

competitors introduced models with new features that were not available on the Model T. This entry is shown in Figure 11-3a, by the points N_1 and N_2 on the fringes of the diagram.

Ford's dominance of the market might have been extended if it had opted for the strategy illustrated by Figure 11-3b of filling the market characteristic space with a variety of models. If Ford had provided more options at the outset, new firms would have had more difficulty carving out their positions in the market. However, another manufacturer first recognized the potential of producing many different varieties of automobiles and responded to saturate the product space. Cadillacs were targeted for the luxury market, Chevrolets for the low-price buyer, and Buicks, Oldsmobiles, and Pontiacs for the middle price range. Each make was available in several models, and options could be selected to meet the specific wants of individual customers. As a result, Ford lost market share and General Motors for many years was the dominant automobile manufacturer in the United States.

CASE STUDY

Brand Proliferation in the Cereal Industry

A perusal of grocery store shelves indicates the large number of brands that are available from each of the three major cereal manufacturers—General Mills, General Foods, and Kellogg's. For example, just a partial list of the cereals produced by Kellogg's includes

Corn Pops	Mueslix
Frosted Flakes	Raisin Bran
Mini Buns	Rice Krispies
Just Right	Product 19
Corn Flakes	Kenmei Rice Bran
Fruit Loops	Double Dip Crunch
Crispix	Low Fat Granola
Special K	Smacks
Frosted Bran	Bran Flakes
All Bran	Raisin Squares
Nut and Honey Os	Cracklin' Oat Bran
Apple Jacks	Frosted Mini-Wheats

The cereal industry is of particular interest because an antitrust case was filed by the Federal Trade Commission alleging that the major manufacturers had attempted to prevent entry into the market by engaging in the "proliferation of brands." In this case, the issue involved not only filling the product market space with cereals brands of every conceivable type, but also saturating shelf space.

In modern supermarkets, there is competition for scarce shelf space. Only a certain amount of area in a store is allocated for cereals. Thus, if more of that space is used for the brands of the major manufacturers, then less will be available for cereals from smaller companies. Because they had filled the shelf space with their products, General Foods, Kellogg's, and General Mills were accused of saturating the market and creating a barrier to entry. Because they had so many different brands, the FTC also argued that product market saturation constituted a barrier to entry.

The case attracted considerable attention from politicians, who felt that pursuing this issue was a waste of money. Ultimately, the FTC dropped the case. Still, the episode illustrates the concept of market saturation.

KEY CONCEPTS ───────────────────────────────

- Investment in additional capacity may act as a barrier to entry because it allows a firm to increase production at low variable cost.
- Firms may be able to deter entry by saturating the geographic market with production facilities or the product market with brands or models.

Summary ───────────────────────────────

Game theory is a technique used to analyze situations where individuals or organizations have conflicting objectives. Payoff matrices indicate the outcomes of all the possible combinations of strategies in a game. A pure strategy involves always selecting one course of action, while a mixed strategy involves one participant randomly using different strategies. A Nash equilibrium is defined as a situation where none of the players can improve their payoff, given the strategies of the other players. A game may have more than one Nash equilibrium. If mixed strategies are allowed, every game has at least one equilibrium.

If a player has a strategy that is best, regardless of what other players do, this is called a dominant strategy, and it should always be used. Dominated strategies always yield a lower payoff than some other strategy. The analysis of games can be simplified by eliminating dominated strategies. Risk-averse decision makers may use the maximin criterion, which involves maximizing the minimum profit or other desirable outcome. If the outcome is undesirable, the minimax strategy would be the corresponding choice. This criterion specifies that the strategy to be chosen should minimize the maximum undesirable outcome.

A game is noncooperative if it is not possible to negotiate with other players and enter into a binding agreement on the strategies to be employed. Noncooperative games may result in undesirable equilibriums. One example, the Prisoner's Dilemma, can be used to explain many phenomena, such as overadvertising by oligopolists. The Prisoner's Dilemma outcome may be avoided in cooperative games where agreements can be enforced.

A study by Axelrod determined that the most effective strategy in repeated games may be tit-for-tat, which involves always selecting the choice used by the other player in the previous round. In sequential games, where one player acts first and then the other responds, there may be an advantage to being first.

Firms often engage in strategic behavior to deter new entry. One approach is to keep prices at a low level, which makes small-scale entry more difficult. Price retaliation when entry occurs or if it appears likely is another strategy. A firm that gains a reputation for aggressive price cutting may be able to effectively discourage entry. In evaluating both of these strategies compared to a policy of setting the monopoly price and letting entry occur, the present value of profits for each option should be compared.

The threat to cut prices must be credible to be effective. A firm that invests in capacity expansion signals potential entrants that it is able to meet the demand that would result from lower prices. Once the capacity is in place, variable costs of increasing production are low. Firms may also be able to deter entry by situating their production facilities to saturate the geographic space. Market saturation may also involve filling the product space with many different brands or models.

Discussion Questions

11-1. Consider the Cournot model discussed in Chapter 10. Is the solution to that problem a Nash equilibrium? Why or why not?

11-2. If one participant in a two-person game has a dominant strategy, will that person always receive a greater payoff from the game than the player who does not have a dominant strategy? Explain.

11-3. Reread the Indiana Jones case study. How might ethical or personal values have affected the choice made by Jones?

11-4. Under what conditions might a maximin strategy be a rational criterion for a manager to use in decision making?

11-5. Suppose a baseball pitcher adopted a strategy of throwing a fastball, then a curve, then a fastball, and so on. Is this mixed strategy? Would it be effective? Why or why not?

11-6. How could the Prisoner's Dilemma model be used to explain a price war between duopolists?

11-7. Would a manager who was two years from retirement be more likely to favor a limit pricing or an open oligopoly model? Explain.

11-8. How could the retaliation model be used to explain the tactics used by Israel and other nations in dealing with terrorists?

11-9. In general, how could a firm evaluate whether an investment in excess capacity to deter entry would be profitable?

11-10. How would brand loyalty for a product affect the success of a product market saturation strategy?

Problems

11-1. Two firms can either reduce their prices or keep them at the present level. If firm A cuts prices, it will earn $10 million in profit if firm B also cuts prices and $20 million if firm B does not change prices. If firm A makes no price change, it will earn $0 if firm B reduces prices and $5 million if firm B makes no price change. The outcomes for firm B are the same as for firm A.
a. Develop the payoff matrix for this game.
b. Does the game have a Nash equilibrium?
c. Does either firm have a dominant strategy? Explain

11-2. Two firms produce a homogeneous product for which variable costs are zero. The market demand for the product is given by $P = 100 - 4Q_T$, where Q_T is total output of both firms. Determine the Nash equilibrium output and price.

11-3. Consider the mixed strategy game involving the pitcher and batter described on pages 370–372. If the hitter considers a curve and a fastball to be equally likely, prove that any mixed strategy is optimal for the pitcher. Hint: Set up the problem in terms of the probability, P_p, that the pitcher will throw a fastball.

11-4. Two manufacturers of the same product must independently decide whether to build a new production facility. The profit payoff matrix is shown here.
a. If they both use the maximin decision criterion, what will be the outcome?
b. Does either firm have a dominant strategy? Explain.

Firm 2

	Don't Build	Build
Don't Build	5, 5	0, 10
Build	10, 0	4, 4

Firm 1

11-5. A single decision maker has four strategies, each with four undesirable outcomes (i.e., bigger numbers are worse), as shown here.
a. If he is highly risk averse, which strategy will he choose? Explain.
b. If he is risk neutral and knows that each outcome is equally likely, which strategy will he choose? Explain.

Outcomes

	1	2	3	4
A	10	20	30	30
B	50	10	100	8
C	60	40	40	40
D	200	0	40	50

Strategies

11-6. The manager of a firm has four strategies with four possible desirable outcomes for each, as shown here.
a. If there are any dominated strategies, rewrite the matrix to show the relevant choices faced by the decision maker.

b. Which strategy would a maximin decision maker select? Explain.

Outcomes

	1	2	3	4
A	10	20	70	30
B	50	10	30	8
C	60	40	40	40
D	5	15	60	25

Strategies

11-7. Phyzz Inc. is considering introduction of a new soft drink. Sparkle Corporation may introduce a similar drink. If Phyzz does not market the drink, its profit will be $100 million if Sparkle does not enter the market and $80 million if Sparkle does introduce a drink. If Phyzz enters, profits will be $120 million if Sparkle does not and $90 million if Sparkle introduces a drink.
   a. Set up the pay all matrix. If the choices are made independently and simultaneously, what should Phyzz's highly risk-averse managers do?
   b. If Sparkle moves first to introduce the drink, what will be Phyzz's optimal strategy? Explain.

11-8. Green Vista golf course charges $20 per round and has 200,000 golfers play the course each year. Fixed costs for the enterprise are $1 million, and the variable cost is $5 per round. If a competing course opens in another part of the city, the price would have to be reduced to $16 to keep the number of rounds at 200,000. Management believes that entry could be permanently prevented if the price were reduced to $12 for three years. At this price, rounds played would increase to 220,000. Management uses a six-year planning horizon for decision making. Assume all amounts are received or incurred at the end of the year.
   a. If the discount rate is 5 percent, what is the optimal strategy for the firm?
   b. How would a higher discount rate affect the optimal pricing strategy? What about a longer planning horizon?

11-9. The manager of the McRod Corporation is considering pricing strategies for its fishing equipment. One option is to make entry difficult by charging relatively low prices. A profit stream for the next five years using this option is shown on the next page. The second option is to set higher prices and allow entry to occur. The five-year profit stream associated with this pricing strategy is also shown. Assume that profits are received at the end of the year and that the objective of the firm is profit maximization over the planning horizon.

	Profit	
Year	*Limit Entry*	*Allow Entry*
1	100	130
2	100	110
3	100	90
4	100	70
5	100	50

Which pricing strategies should be selected if the manager uses
a. A discount rate of 5 percent and a five-year planning horizon?
b. A discount rate of 10 percent and a five-year planning horizon?
c. A discount rate of 5 percent and a three-year planning horison?
d. A discount rate of 10 percent and a three-year planning horizon

V

Pricing Decisions

CHAPTER 12

Pricing of Goods and Services

Preview —————————————————————————————————

Of the decisions made by a manager, none is more critical to the success of a firm than setting the price of output. The immediate and obvious effect of pricing choices is reflected in short-run profits. But prices set today also can have an important impact on future profits. Indeed, pricing decisions frequently are a major factor in determining a firm's long-term success or failure.

The material presented in the previous chapters makes the pricing decision appear deceptively simple. If the firm has some control over price, the rule is to produce until marginal revenue equals marginal cost and charge the price indicated by the demand curve for that quantity. But, as always, economic theory involves simplifications of reality. A large corporation might produce several hundred products that are sold in many different markets. Sometimes, the price set for one of these products can affect the demand for other products sold by the firm. For example, the price the Gillette Corporation sets for razors may affect the quantity of blades demanded that fit these razors, and vice versa. Similarly, production decisions relating to one product may affect the manufacturing or marketing costs of other products.

This chapter provides a broader perspective for pricing decisions. The first section discusses firms with multiple products and considers both demand and production interdependencies. The second and third sections examine price discrimination and product bundling. Section Four considers the advantages of peak load pricing. Finally, the fifth section introduces cost-plus pricing and demonstrates that this practice is consistent with profit maximization.

Pricing of Multiple Products ——————————————————

Procter & Gamble started in 1837 as a partnership selling soap to residents of Cincinnati, Ohio. Today, the firm has annual sales of over $27 billion and sells hundreds of products throughout the world. Procter & Gamble's most popular brands are shown in Table 12-1.

Some of these products are unrelated. For example, the demand for Pringle's Potato Chips is unlikely to be affected by the price of Tide. Similarly, production costs of Pringle's are independent of the amount of Tide produced. However, demand and production of other Procter & Gamble brands are interrelated. Clearly, Luvs and Pampers would be considered substitutes by consumers of disposable diapers. As such, the price of Luvs affects the demand for Pampers and vice versa. Also, the two competing brands share the same production facilities. Thus if pricing decisions are based partially on costs, prices will be dependent on how costs are allocated between the two products.

When firms produce several products, managers must consider the interrelationships between those products. Pricing techniques for multiproduct firms are considered in this section.

TABLE 12-1 **Popular Brands Produced by Procter & Gamble**

Laundry and Cleaning Products	Personal Care Products	Food Products
Cascade	Bounty	Crisco
Cheer	Camay	Crush
Comet	Charmin	Duncan Hines
Dash	Crest	Folger's
Downy	Head & Shoulders	Hires
Ivory Liquid	Ivory Soap	Jif
Mr. Clean	Luvs	Pringle's
Spic and Span	Pampers	
Tide	Pepto-Bismol	
	Scope	
	Sure	

Products with Interdependent Demands

Products with interdependent demands are either substitutes or complements. For substitutes, such as Luvs and Pampers, a price increase for one good tends to increase the demand for the other. However, the magnitude of the increase also depends on the number of substitutes available from other suppliers. For goods that are complements, a price increase tends to reduce the demand for the other good. Options that can be added to new cars are a good example of complements. Sales of antilock brakes, power windows, and stereo systems by an automobile manufacturer are dependent on the number of vehicles sold by the company. If the price of the basic automobile is increased, vehicle sales will decline and the demand for options will also decrease.

Correct pricing decisions require that demand interdependencies be taken into account. Instead of setting each price in isolation, the impact of each price on the demand for other products produced by the firm must be considered. The basic objective of the manager should be to determine prices that maximize total profit for the firm rather than profit earned by individual products.

When demands are interrelated, insight into managerial decisions can be gained by considering the marginal revenue equations for the products. Consider a firm that produces only two goods, X and Y. Assume that sales of X have an impact on the demand for Y and vice versa. In terms of marginal revenue, this assumption can be stated mathematically as

$$MR_X = \frac{dTR_X}{dQ_X} + \frac{dTR_Y}{dQ_X} \tag{12-1}$$

and

$$MR_Y = \frac{dTR_Y}{dQ_Y} + \frac{dTR_X}{dQ_Y} \tag{12-2}$$

Equation (12-1) indicates that marginal revenue associated with changes in the quantity of X can be separated into two components. The first, dTR_X/dQ_X, represents the change in revenues for good X resulting from a one-unit increase in sales of good X. The second, dTR_Y/dQ_X, reflects the demand interdependency. It indicates the change in revenue from the sale of good Y caused by a one-unit increase in sales of good X. Equation (12-2) has a similar interpretation in terms of a one-unit increase in sales of good Y.

The signs of the interdependency terms, dTR_Y/dQ_X and dTR_X/dQ_Y, depend on the nature of the relationship between X and Y. If the two goods are complements, both terms will be positive, and increased sales of one good stimulate sales for the other. Conversely, if the two goods are substitutes, the two terms will be negative because additional sales of one good reduce sales of the other.

Clearly, the firm must consider demand interdependencies in order to make optimal pricing and output decisions. Assume that goods X and Y are complements. In determining the profit-maximizing rate of output for good X, if the effect of sales of X on the demand for Y is not considered, output of X would be increased only until dTR_X/dQ_X equals the marginal cost of producing X. But, as can be seen from equation (12-1), dTR_X/dQ_X understates the actual incremental revenue generated by selling an additional unit of X. Specifically, revenue also is affected by dTR_Y/dQ_X, which is positive if the two goods are complements. Thus, when demand interdependence is taken into account, profit maximization requires a greater rate of output for good X. In fact, output of X should be increased until

$$\frac{dTR_X}{dQ_X} + \frac{dTR_Y}{dQ_X} = MC_X$$

where MC_X is the additional cost incurred by the firm in producing an additional unit of good X. Similarly, for goods that are substitutes, it can easily be shown that ignoring the demand interdependency will cause too many units of output to be produced.

CASE STUDY

Turkey Prices at Thanksgiving

For most American families, roast turkey is an important part of their Thanksgiving festivities. Although pumpkin pie, potatoes and gravy, and cranberry sauce are a traditional part of the meal, it is the size and taste of the turkey that determine the quality of the dining experience.

For many years, most families ate turkey only at Thanksgiving and Christmas. Today, turkey is recognized as a highly nutritious and relatively inexpensive meat and is eaten throughout the year. Turkey consumption has risen from 5.5 pounds per capita during the 1950s to about 20 pounds per person in the 1990s. However, demand for turkey still increases dramatically in November and December as families prepare for the holidays.

Economic theory predicts that when the demand for a product increases, the price should also increase. This is exactly what happens at the wholesale level. In early November, turkey producers raise their prices in anticipation of increased purchases by grocery stores and restaurants. For example, in 1991, the average wholesale price of turkey was 61 cents per pound. But during the fourth quarter of that year, the wholesale price averaged 63 cents.

Higher wholesale prices for turkey should result in a higher price at the retail level, but this is not the case. Typically, the price that shoppers pay for turkey is actually less around Thanksgiving and Christmas than during the rest of the year. The reason is that turkey is often used as a loss leader to entice customers into the store. Retailers assume that any losses they experience on turkey can be more than recouped as shoppers buy all of the other items that they need for the holiday season. Basically, the store owners recognize the interdependence between the demand for turkey and the other products they sell. Because of this complementary relationship, turkey prices are kept low.

Joint Products

Products can be related in production as well as demand. One type of production interdependency exists when goods are jointly produced in fixed proportions. The process of producing beef and hides in a slaughterhouse is a good example of fixed proportions in production. Each carcass provides a certain amount of meat and one hide. There is little that the slaughterhouse can do to alter the proportions of the two products.

When goods are produced in fixed proportions, they should be thought of as a "product package." Because there is no way to produce one part of this package without also producing the other part, there is no conceptual basis for allocating total production costs between the two goods. These costs have meaning only in terms of the product package. This idea is shown by Figure 12-1a. Note that the figure identifies two demand curves, one for hides and one for beef. Although the two goods are produced together, their demands are independent. However, there is a single marginal cost curve for both products. This reflects the fixed proportions of production, that is, the marginal cost is the cost of supplying one more unit of the product package.

Where goods are jointly produced, pricing decisions should take this interdependency into account. Figure 12-1a indicates how profit-maximizing prices and quantities are determined. MR_B and MR_H are the marginal revenue curves for beef and hides. But when an additional animal is processed at a slaughterhouse, both the beef and the hide become available for sale. Hence the marginal revenue associated with sale of a unit of the product package is the sum of the marginal revenues. This sum is represented by the line MR_T in Figure 12-1a. MR_T is determined by adding MR_H and MR_B for each rate of output. Graphically, it is the vertical sum of the marginal revenue curves of the two products.

The profit-maximizing rate of output, Q_0, is determined by the intersection of MR_T and MC. The profit-maximizing prices, P_H and P_B, are specified by the demand curves for each good at output rate Q_0.

In Figure 12-1a, note that both MR_H and MR_B are positive at Q_0. In contrast, Figure 12-1b was drawn so that MR_H is negative at the profit-maximizing quantity.

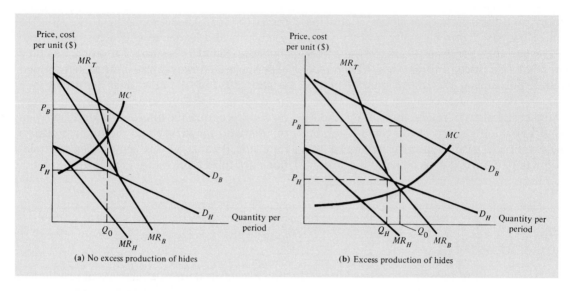

FIGURE 12-1 **Pricing of Joint Products.**

The implication is that sale of an extra hide reduces the revenues received from that product. Clearly, in this situation, Q_0 cannot be the optimal rate of output for hides. A firm should never produce at an output rate where marginal revenue is negative. But a problem arises because the products are jointly produced. Thus cutting back on production of hides would mean reduced supplies of beef for which marginal revenue is positive.

In cases such as that shown in Figure 12-1b, the profit-maximizing choice for beef is to sell Q_H at a price of P_H. Although Q_0 hides will be produced, sales should not be made beyond the point where marginal revenue is negative. Thus only Q_H should be sold and the price set at P_H. Unless costs of disposal or storage are high, the excess hides should be withheld from the market.

EXAMPLE

Calculating the Profit-Maximizing Prices for Joint Products

A rancher sells hides and beef. The two goods are assumed to be jointly produced in fixed proportions. The marginal cost equation for the beef-hide product package is given by

$$MC = 30 + 5Q$$

The demand and marginal revenue equations for the two products are

BEEF	HIDES
$P = 60 - 1Q$	$P = 80 - 2Q$
$MR = 60 - 2Q$	$MR = 80 - 4Q$

What prices should be charged for beef and hides? How many units of the product package should be produced?

SOLUTION

Summing the two marginal revenue equations gives

$$MR_T = 140 - 6Q$$

The optimal quantity is determined by equating MR_T and MC and solving for Q. Thus

$$140 - 6Q = 30 + 5Q$$

and, hence, $Q = 10$.

Substituting $Q = 10$ into the demand curves yields a price of $50 for beef and $60 for hides. However, before concluding that these prices maximize profits, the marginal revenue at this output rate should be computed for each product to assure that neither is negative. Substituting $Q = 10$ into the two marginal revenue equations gives $40 for each good. Because both marginal revenues are positive, the prices just given maximize profits. If marginal revenue for either product is negative, the quantity sold of that product should be reduced to the point where marginal revenue equals zero.

KEY CONCEPTS

- If a firm produces two goods that are substitutes, the optimal rate of output for each good is less than the rate that would maximize profit if there were no demand interdependence.
- If a firm produces complementary goods, the optimal rates of output are greater than if there were no interdependence.
- For products produced jointly in fixed proportions, output should be increased until the sum of the marginal revenues equals the marginal cost of the product package.

Fully Distributed versus Incremental Cost Pricing

Some costs are clearly related to the provision of a particular product or service. For example, meters on homes are there for the sole purpose of measuring the amount of electricity used in the house. No one could seriously challenge an accounting system that assigned the costs of those meters to residential electricity customers. However, other costs may not be clearly attributable to a particular product or service. High-voltage transmission lines fit into this category. Electricity for residential users is transmitted to urban areas over such lines. These facilities are also used to serve industrial and commercial customers. But if any two of the three classes of customers stopped using electricity, the same high-voltage transmission lines would still be required to continue serving the remaining customers.

For an electric utility, expenses associated with high-voltage transmission are referred to as *common costs*. Because the facilities are necessary to provide service to each class of customers, any allocation of these common costs is essentially arbitrary. In fact, the concept of allocating common costs really is a contradiction in terms. It involves allocating costs that already have been determined to be conceptually unassignable to any specific product or service.

Despite the problems, many businesses make extensive use of a practice called *fully distributed cost* pricing. This approach allocates a portion of the firm's common costs to each product or service. That is, all common costs are distributed among the products and services of the firm. Then the price of each is set so that it covers the designated portion of common costs plus costs that are directly related to the provision of the product or service.

As mentioned previously, any assignment of common costs must be arbitrary. But the real problem with this method of pricing is that the choice of allocation scheme may have an important effect on the price set and hence the quantity demanded of the goods and services provided by the firm. A scheme that allocates a small portion of common costs to a product will result in a lower price and greater quantity demanded for that product than will a method that apportions a larger fraction of such costs to the product.

Consider the following example. A firm provides two services, temporary secretarial help and data processing. The firm has $10 million of common costs that must be paid even if neither service is provided. Provision of the first service is very labor intensive, and 80 percent of all labor costs involve the secretarial workers. In contrast, data processing is capital intensive, and 80 percent of all capital costs involve this service.

The firm's management decides to base prices on fully distributed costs. Two allocation schemes are proposed. The first is to apportion common costs on the basis of labor costs resulting from each service. The second approach allocates common costs in proportion to the amount of capital investment that can be attributed directly to supplying each service.

Note how the alternative methods would affect the price set for each service. An allocation based on labor costs would result in 80 percent, or $8 million of common costs being assigned to temporary secretarial help. Thus the price set for this service would have to be relatively high to cover the common costs. But the data processing service with its relatively smaller labor expense would be priced lower because only 20 percent, or $2 million of common cost would be allocated to that service. Conversely, an apportionment based on investment would have the opposite effect. Because data processing is capital intensive, a large fraction of common costs would be assigned to that service and hence the price set for data processing would be higher and that of temporary secretarial assistance lower than with the first allocation scheme.

Although a firm must recover its common costs, it is not necessary that the price of each product be high enough to cover an arbitrarily apportioned share of common costs. Proper pricing does require, however, that prices at least cover the incremental cost of producing each good. Incremental costs are additional costs that would not be incurred if the product were not produced. As long as the price of a product exceeds its incremental costs, the firm can increase total profit by supplying that product. Hence decisions should be based on an evaluation of incremental costs.

The contrast between fully distributed and incremental costs in pricing can be illustrated by considering railroad passenger service. Suppose a railroad has a route that carries passengers between San Francisco and San Diego. The managers are considering an intermediate stop in Los Angeles. The rails, locomotives, and passenger cars already exist, so the primary additional expense would be the energy cost of transporting extra passengers and the establishment of terminal facilities in Los Angeles.

Assume that competition from bus travel between San Francisco and Los Angeles limits the fare that can be charged by the railroad for the trip. Specifically, the managers of the railroad believe that the fare cannot be greater than $30. Should the new service be offered?

One member of the management team argues that the decision should be based on fully distributed costs and that the San Francisco–Los Angeles service should not be offered unless fares will cover direct costs plus a share of the common costs. For a railroad, the primary common costs would include the rails between the two cities and the engines and cars. Based on the common cost allocation method used by the railroad, it is determined that the fare would have to be at least $40. Thus with fully distributed costs as a standard for pricing, the service would not be offered because the fare would be higher than for bus transportation.

Using incremental costs to evaluate and price the service is advocated by another member of the management team. This person's analysis suggests that with the rail lines in place and trains already operating between San Francisco and San Diego, the additional expense of transporting a passenger from San Francisco to Los Angeles would be only $15. The implication is that the service should be offered and priced between $15 and $30 per trip.

Clearly, the decision regarding the service should be based on incremental analysis. Both the railroad and its patrons could benefit from adding the stop in Los Angeles. If the ticket price is set higher than $15, the total profits of the firm would increase. Travelers between San Francisco and Los Angeles would benefit because an alternative form of transportation becomes available. Even the customers going from San Francisco to San Diego could benefit. Although the San Francisco–Los Angeles fare would not be high enough to cover its full share of common costs, any price in excess of $15 could provide a contribution to common costs. Thus the price of traveling from San Francisco to San Diego could be reduced.

Where common costs are involved, all of a firm's products and services cannot be priced at their incremental cost. In aggregate, prices must be set high enough to allow the firm to recover its common costs. However, the example demonstrates that it is not necessary that each product cover an arbitrarily determined share of those costs. As long as the price of a new product exceeds its incremental cost, total profit can be increased by providing the product.

The choice between incremental and fully distributed costs is far from academic. Frequently, poor choices are made by managers who insist that every price must cover fully distributed costs. But clearly, the proper approach by managers attempting to maximize profit is to make decisions based on incremental costs.

CASE STUDY

What Constitutes Unfair Competition?

The Louisville and Nashville Railroad filed a petition with the Interstate Commerce Commission requesting permission to lower its freight rates for a particular route from $11.86 to $5.11 per ton. The firm's objective was to be able to meet competition from a company hauling freight by truck and barge. The railroad had substantial costs that could not be clearly allocated to specific routes. Fully distributed costs for the route in question were $7.59 per ton, but incremental costs were only $4.69. Because the truck–barge operation had few fixed costs, its fully distributed and incremental costs were nearly equal—about $5.19 per ton.

The railroad argued that a rate of $5.11

should be allowed because the $4.69 in incremental costs would be covered. The competing truck–barge company contended that the proposed rail rates were unfair because they were less than the $7.59 per ton that represented the firm's fully distributed costs. In this case, the Interstate Commerce Commission based its decision on fully distributed costs and rejected the railroad's proposal for a rate reduction.* For many years, such decisions by the ICC made it difficult for railroads to compete with other modes of transportation. But since the early 1980s, railroad shipping rates have been deregulated, giving the firms more latitude in price setting.

* Ingot Molds, Pa., to Steelton, Ky., 326 ICC 77 (1965).

Ramsey Pricing

No product should be supplied by a firm unless its incremental revenues are expected to exceed its incremental cost. But if there are common costs, managers must also decide which products will be priced above incremental cost and how much above. For unregulated, profit-maximizing firms, the rules presented in this and other chapters can be used to make such decisions. But for regulated firms limited to a maximum rate of profit and for nonprofit enterprises expected to just cover their costs, some other approach may be necessary. One such method is Ramsey pricing.[1]

[1] The name is in recognition of pioneering work by economist Frank Ramsey. See F. Ramsey. ''A Contribution to the Theory of Taxation.'' *The Economic Journal* 37 (March 1927): 27–61.

Assume that an enterprise produces two products, X and Y, that the demand for good X is more elastic than demand for good Y, and that marginal costs are constant. If X and Y are priced at marginal cost (P_x and P_y, respectively), then, as shown in Figure 12-2, quantity demanded will be Q_x for X and Q_y for Y. However, because none of the enterprise's common costs are included in marginal costs, total revenue will be less than total cost.

For the enterprise to cover its total costs, at least one of the two goods must be priced above marginal cost. But it was shown in Chapter 9 that any deviation from marginal cost pricing results in allocative inefficiency. If efficiency is the objective, there is a need for a "second-best" pricing scheme that allows the enterprise to at least break even while minimizing the adverse effect on resource allocation.

If an enterprise is providing several goods, Ramsey pricing suggests guidelines for the price that should be charged for each good. Because all prices cannot equal marginal costs, the question is how far to set the price of each good above or below marginal cost for that good. In its most simple form, Ramsey pricing requies that price deviations from marginal costs by inversely related to the elasticity of demand. That is, for goods with very elastic demand, the price should be set close to marginal cost. Conversely, for goods with relatively inelastic demand, the price should deviate more from marginal cost. In terms of Figure 12-2, the price of X should be closer to its marginal cost than the price of good Y. For example, a price of P'_x results in quantity demanded of Q'_x, and P'_y corresponds to Q'_y. The shaded area in each panel is the amount that each good contributes to the recovery of the enterprise's common costs. Note that good Y makes a much greater contribution than good X.

The rationale for the Ramsey rule is easy to understand. If demand is elastic,

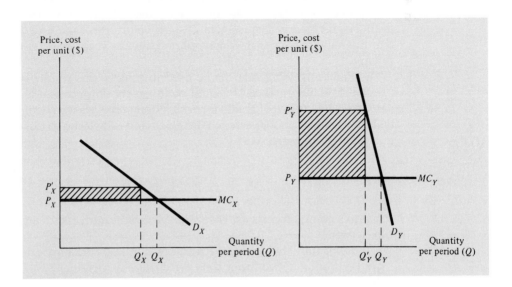

FIGURE 12-2 **Ramsey Pricing**

increasing the price causes a substantial reduction in quantity demanded. But if demand is highly inelastic, large changes in price will result in little change in the quantity demanded. In the extreme, if the demand were totally inelastic (a vertical demand curve), there would be no change in quantity demanded as price increased. Hence if deviations from marginal cost pricing are greatest for those goods with inelastic demand, the resource misallocation will be minimized.

Ramsey pricing is sometimes criticized because the largest deviations from marginal cost pricing are imposed on those with the fewest alternatives (i.e., least elastic demand). Although this is true, the more relevant point is that there really is no alternative to using some variant of Ramsey pricing. There is a limit to the contribution to common costs that can be obtained from the sale of goods with elastic demand. If large price increases are imposed on such goods, consumption will decline substantially as buyers shift to alternative goods. The net result is that the firm will obtain little contribution to fixed costs from goods with elastic demand.

Many nonprofit enterprises receive subsidies from tax revenues or charitable contributions. Where such subsidies are provided, revenues from sales do not have to cover the firm's total costs. However, the concept of Ramsey pricing may still be relevant for such enterprises. Even with a subsidy, prices set equal to marginal costs may not allow the enterprise to cover its total costs. However, by using the Ramsey principle, managers could set prices that would recover the necessary amount while minimizing the adverse effect on resource allocation.

In some situations, if prices are equated to marginal costs, the revenues of an enterprise (sales plus subsidies) might exceed its total costs. This could occur if the subsidy were very large or if decreasing returns to scale caused marginal costs to be greater than average total costs. In this case, the organization would be earning economic profit. But such an outcome is not generally consistent with the notion of a nonprofit enterprise. Thus there would be a need to reduce prices until total revenue just equals total cost. As before, this should be done in a manner that minimizes changes in consumption patterns in comparison to marginal cost pricing.

The Ramsey pricing rule can be used to achieve this result. The deviations of prices below marginal costs should be inversely proportional to the elasticity of demand. Thus prices of goods for which demand is elastic should be priced near their marginal cost. Conversely, where demand is inelastic, prices should be lower in relation to marginal cost.

KEY CONCEPTS

- A firm's common costs are those that cannot be assigned to any single product or service.
- The use of fully distributed costs can lead to poor pricing decisions. A product can be profitably produced if its price exceeds incremental costs of supplying the product.
- Ramsey pricing is a second-best alternative that can be used when marginal cost pricing is not feasible.

- A simple version of Ramsey pricing specifies that price deviations from marginal cost should be inversely related to the elasticity of demand.

EXAMPLE _____

Using Ramsey Pricing

Consider an enterprise that supplies two goods, X and Y. For ease of exposition, assume that the marginal cost of providing each is constant and equal to $10. However, also assume that the firm has common costs of $99 per period and that these costs must be recovered. Further suppose that demand elasticities are -0.1 for Y and -1.0 for X, and that if prices are equated to marginal costs, ten units of each product will be sold each period. However, note that if prices equal marginal costs, the firm will incur a loss of $99 per period. What prices for X and Y would allow the firm to recover its fixed and marginal costs while minimizing the adverse effect on resource allocation?

SOLUTION

The pricing problem is how to increase prices to recover the $99 in common costs while minimizing the changes in consumption patterns in comparison to those with marginal cost pricing. The Ramsey principle suggests that since demand is more inelastic, product Y should be priced higher in relation to marginal cost than should product X. One simple formulation of Ramsey pricing uses the inverse elasticity rule. This specifies that departures from marginal cost should be inversely proportional to elasticity of demand. In this example, since elasticity for Y is one-tenth that of X, the deviation of the price of Y from its marginal cost should be ten times the deviation of the price of X from its marginal cost.

Using the inverse elasticity rule, the solution is to price product Y at $20 and X at $11. Note that a 100 percent increase in the price of Y will decrease quantity demanded by only 10 percent (because the demand elasticity equals -0.1), to nine units. The 10 percent increase in the price of X will decrease quantity demanded by 10 percent (because elasticity equals -1.0), also to nine units. Now each unit of Y sold makes a $10 contribution to common costs for a total of $90. Each unit of X sold makes a $1 contribution for a total of $9. Together, this pricing approach allows the enterprise to recover its common costs of $99. This objective is achieved with minimal impact on the pattern of consumer demand. For both goods, the reduction in quantity demanded is only one unit as compared to marginal cost pricing.

_____

Intermediate Products (Transfer Pricing)

Vertical integration is common in modern economic systems. A firm is said to be vertically integrated when it operates at more than one stage of the production process. For example, some steel producers mine coal and iron, transport the ore on boats owned by the firm, use the coal as an energy source to transform the iron into steel ingots, shape the steel ingots into finished products, and distribute those finished products to consumers. The fabricated steel products received by the consumers are final goods. In contrast, the coal, iron ore, steel ingots, and undelivered steel products are referred to as *intermediate goods.* That is, they are goods or materials that will be needed as inputs at a later stage of the firm's operations.

By taking advantage of scale economies, avoiding possible supply disruptions, and by bringing complementary aspects of the production process together, a vertically integrated company may be more efficient than several small firms each operating at a single stage of the production process. However, greater size resulting from vertical integration can cause control problems. Top management may find it difficult to become familiar with each stage of the operation or a cumbersome bureaucracy may develop that makes it difficult to implement decisions.

One method of dealing with such problems is to organize vertically integrated firms into semiautonomous divisions. Each of these divisions has its own function and its own management. Each management team is rewarded based on the performance of the division. In some cases, the evaluation is based on the profit earned by the unit. But in an integrated firm, determining the amount of profit that should be credited to a division producing an intermediate product is a difficult task. The problem is that if the unit's function is to provide an input for the next stage of the production process, revenue will depend on the price that is charged for the intermediate good. A high price will increase profits of the unit at the earlier stage of production, whereas a low price will make the later production stage appear more profitable.

A more serious problem is that an incorrect price set for an intermediate good can affect the total profit earned by the firm. Specifically, if the decision makers in each division attempt to maximize profits for their units, the total profit of the firm might be reduced. Thus it is important that prices of intermediate products be set so as to maximize overall profits rather than division profit. This objective may require that top-level management be involved in pricing intermediate goods.

The following discussion provides guidelines for the pricing of intermediate products, sometimes referred to as transfer pricing. For simplicity, it is assumed that there are only two stages of production. In the first, rolls of paper are manufactured as an intermediate product. In the second, paper is cut into writing tablets and sold to final consumers. Two alternative situations are considered. The first occurs when an external market exists for the good. That is, the division making rolls of paper can sell its output to buyers outside the firm and the unit requiring the paper has alternative sources of supply. The second case is when there is no external market and paper can be bought and sold only between the two divisions of the firm. In this case, there is no market-determined price for the rolls of paper.

EXTERNAL MARKET   Assume that the writing tablet division of the integrated firm has the option of obtaining paper from the paper manufacturing division or from independent suppliers. Similarly, the paper manufacturing unit can sell to the writing tablet division or to other buyers. Also assume that the external market is perfectly competitive. This implies that the two units can buy or sell as much as they want at the market-determined price.

With a perfectly competitive external market, there really is no price decision to be made. The paper manufacturing unit, like a competitive firm, faces a horizontal demand curve at the market-determined price. If the managers of that unit attempt to maximize profits, they will increase production until price equals marginal cost. If the paper manufacturing division tries to charge a price in excess of the market price, the writing tablet unit should buy paper from independent suppliers. But if the final product division is unwilling to pay the market price, the paper rolls can be sold on the open market.

Where an external market exists, it is not necessary that the output of the paper manufacturing division equal the input demand for the tablet unit. If there is an excess supply of paper rolls, it can be sold to other firms. Similarly, if the firm's internal supply of paper is insufficient, the tablet division can buy from other producers.

NO EXTERNAL MARKET If no external market exists or if the divisions are not allowed to trade with other firms, a conflict may arise regarding the proper price to be charged for paper. The paper manufacturing unit may benefit from a higher price, while the division that makes tablets may benefit from a lower price. However, the goal of top management is to determine the price for paper that results in maximum profit for the combined firm.

The optimal price of both the intermediate and the final good can be determined using Figure 12-3. The demand and marginal revenue curves for writing tablets are D_w and MR_w, respectively. The marginal cost of producing the paper necessary to make a writing tablet is MC_p, while the marginal cost involved in transforming the paper into a tablet is MC_t. Hence from the perspective of the firm, the marginal cost of each additional tablet is the sum of MC_p and MC_t, which is designated as MC_w. Thus, for the combined firm, the profit-maximizing choice is to produce

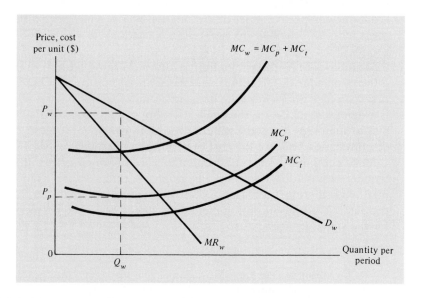

FIGURE 12-3 **Pricing Intermediate Goods with No External Market.**

where $MR_w = MC_w$, or at an output rate of Q_w per period. The corresponding price would be P_w.

Because Q_w is the profit-maximizing output of writing tablets for the combined firm, the price set for the intermediate product (paper) must cause the managers of the writing tablet division to produce Q_w tablets and the managers of the paper division to supply an amount of paper consistent with producing Q_w tablets.

The solution is for top management to require the paper unit to set its price equal to the marginal cost of producing paper. This directive will cause the tablet division to view $MC_w = MC_p + MC_t$ as its marginal cost curve and select Q_w as the profit-maximizing quantity and P_w as the price. At the same time, by setting a price of P_p for paper, the paper division will supply the exact amount of product necessary to produce Q_w tablets.   *End Red·*

KEY CONCEPTS

- If there is a perfectly competitive external market for an intermediate good, market forces will cause the price of the good to approach marginal cost, and no managerial pricing decision will be necessary.
- In the absence of an external market, profit maximization requires that the price of each intermediate good be set equal to its marginal cost.

Start Red·

Price Discrimination

Frequently, the same book is sold at a much lower price in South America and Europe than in the United States. This practice is an example of price discrimination and is designed to increase the total profit of the book publisher. From an economic perspective, price discrimination occurs when price differences between consumers or markets do not reflect variations in the cost of supplying the product.[2]

Sometimes price discrimination involves charging a uniform price when costs differ. Consider the firm that advertises an all-you-can-eat buffet for $9.95. The first customer is a jockey who does little more than pick at the salads. The second is a defensive tackle for the Dallas Cowboys, who requires 10,000 calories a day just to maintain his body weight. The uniform price of $9.95 constitutes price discrimination because the cost of serving the two customers differs markedly.

More commonly, price discrimination occurs when prices differ even though costs are essentially the same. Physicians' services are an example. For a given treatment, there is no reason to believe that costs depend on the income of the recipient. Yet high-income patients are sometimes charged more than the poor for the same services.

---

[2] The legal interpretation of price discrimination differs somewhat from the economist's definition. The legal status of price discrimination is discussed in Chapter 19.

Necessary Conditions for Price Discrimination

⑦ Three conditions must be met before a firm can successfully practice price discrimination. First, the firm must have at least some control over price. Obviously, a price taker in a perfectly competitive market is not in a position to engage in price discrimination. ② Second, it must be possible to group different markets in terms of the price elasticity of demand in each. It will be shown later in the section that firms can increase total profit by charging relatively higher prices in markets where demand is less elastic.

③ Finally, the firm's markets must be separable, meaning that products cannot *Can't be resold.* be purchased in one market and then resold in another. Suppose that a firm has identified two markets and charges a high price in the first and a lower price in the second. If the two markets are not separable, price discrimination cannot be successful. Either consumers will go to the low-priced market and make their purchases, or enterprising individuals will buy in the low-priced market and resell at a price below that established by the firm in the high-priced market. In either case, the price differential between the markets will disappear as prices decline in the first market and increase in the second.

CASE STUDY _____

Price Discrimination and the Airlines

Finding the lowest airfare can be a bewildering experience. On any day, there are tens of thousands of different fares available. With a full 150-seat aircraft flying between two U.S. cities, it would not be uncommon for the passengers to have paid 30 different fares for their seats. In some cases, these differences at least partially reflect amenities associated with higher price tickets. For example, first-class passengers have more leg room and better meals. But in other cases, different prices are charged for the same travel experience. During the summer of 1992, a regular coach round-trip ticket from Chicago to San Francisco cost $800, but promotional pricing by the airlines allowed some passengers to make the same journey for only $200. Once on board the plane, service was identical—same cramped seats, same bland meals, and same inconvenient restrooms.

For many years, the airlines have used what they call yield management to increase their profits. This practice involves both price discrimination and marketing. The price discrimination component is based on variations in price elasticities for different types of customers. Typically, business flyers have less elastic demands because they must meet with suppliers and customers at specific times and in specific locations. Often, these trips are made on relatively short notice. Airlines take advantage of this situation by setting higher prices for tickets that do not require advance purchase. In contrast, vacation travelers often choose between many destinations (including some that do not involve air travel) and plan their trips far in advance. Because these discretionary travel demands are more price sensitive, airlines advertise some seats at lower prices if passengers are willing to buy their tickets seven to thirty days in advance.

The marketing aspect of yield management strategies involves determining how many low-priced seats to offer. Although airlines are required to set aside at least some seats at the promotional price, they have considerable latitude in determining exactly how many they will allocate to each flight. Flights that usually are full will not have many low-cost seats, while on those that have a history of excess capacity, airlines will offer many such seats in the attempt to draw additional customers. Determining the most profitable mix of seat prices is a complex and ongoing process for the airlines. Computers are used to continuously reevaluate and alter the optimum composition of prices based on the latest information. It is possible for a potential customer to call a travel agent on a Tuesday and be told that there are no promotional fares available on a flight and for another person to call the agent on Wednesday and obtain the low-cost fare on the same flight.

Although airline pricing practices have the appearance of price discrimination, there are other factors that should be considered. Many low-cost fares involve restrictions. The ticket may have to be purchased in advance, a Saturday night stay at the location may be required, and the ticket could be nonrefundable. A purchaser of a regular coach fare ticket does not face these constraints. Thus, it could be argued that the tickets represent different services and that the higher price for the regular fare reflects the additional convenience associated with that ticket.

Types of Price Discrimination

There are many forms of price discrimination, but the standard method of classification identifies three types or degrees of discrimination. Their common characteristic is that they allow the firm to capture part of the consumer surplus that would have resulted from uniform pricing.

FIRST-DEGREE DISCRIMINATION   Figure 12-4a shows the demand curve faced by a monopolist. The curve indicates the maximum price that can be obtained for successive units of output. For example, the first unit, Q_1, could command a maximum price of P_1, the second could be sold for a maximum of P_2, and so on. To simplify the discussion, it is assumed that marginal cost is constant and equal to average cost.

First-degree price discrimination involves charging the maximum price possible for each unit of output. Thus the consumer who attaches the greatest value to the product is identified and charged a price of P_1. Similarly, the consumers willing to pay P_2 for the second unit and P_3 for the third are identified and required to pay P_2 and P_3, respectively. With first-degree price discrimination, the profit-maximizing output rate is where the marginal cost and demand curves intersect. In Figure 12-4a, this occurs at Q_D. At this point, the maximum price that can be obtained for the product is just equal to the marginal cost of production. Any attempt to sell more than Q_D units would reduce profits because price would have to be less than marginal cost. Conversely, any rate of output less than Q_D would not maximize profits because the additional units could be sold (as shown by the demand curve) at prices greater than the marginal cost.

First-degree discrimination is the most extreme form of price discrimination and the most profitable pricing scheme for the firm. Because buyers are charged

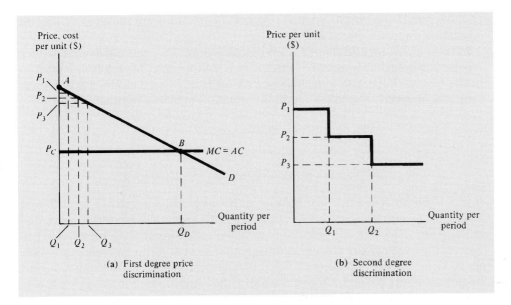

FIGURE 12-4 **First- and Second-Degree Price Discrimination.**

the maximum price for each unit of output, no consumer surplus remains. As defined in Chapter 9, consumer surplus is the difference between the price a consumer is willing to pay and the actual price charged for the good or service. The maximum consumer surplus results when there is no price discrimination and price is set equal to marginal cost. In Figure 12-4a, this maximum consumer surplus is shown as the area of the triangle AP_cB. In contrast with first-degree price discrimination, there is no consumer surplus because AP_cB is captured by the firm as economic profit.

First-degree discrimination is not common because it requires that the seller have complete knowledge of the market demand curve and also of the willingness of individual consumers to pay for the product. In addition, the seller must be able to segment the market so that resale between consumers cannot take place. These requirements are seldom met in actual market situations. However, one possible case involves the sale of Treasury bonds by the federal government. In selling these bonds, the government requires each prospective buyer to submit a sealed bid. Those conducting the auction determine a minimum bid. All the bids that exceed the minimum are accepted and the bidders are obligated to buy at the price they indicated in their bid. Thus, through this process, the government attempts to extract the maximum price that each buyer is willing to pay.

SECOND-DEGREE DISCRIMINATION Second-degree price discrimination is an imperfect form of first-degree discrimination. Instead of setting different prices for each unit, it involves pricing based on the quantities of output purchased by individual consumers. This is illustrated by Figure 12-4b. For each buyer, the first

Q_1 units purchased are priced at P_1, the next $Q_2 - Q_1$ units are priced at P_2, and all additional units are priced at P_3.

In most cases, second-degree price discrimination involves goods and service whose consumption is metered. Electricity is an example. Many electric utilities in the United States use a declining-block tariff in pricing electricity. A typical tariff might specify the following monthly rates for blocks of usage:

First 100 kilowatt-hours	$0.12 per kwh
Next 300 kilowatt-hours	$0.10 per kwh
All additional kilowatt-hours	$0.08 per kwh

It should be observed that just because different prices are charged for different blocks of consumption, this does not necessarily imply second-degree price discrimination. The high rate for the first 100 kilowatt-hours may be intended to recover the fixed costs of serving a customer, such as billing and metering. As such, the $0.12 for the first 100 kilowatt-hours may not involve price discrimination. But if kilowatt-hours beyond 300 cost the utility the same amount to provide as those in the second block, then price discrimination is being practiced.

In addition to electricity, second-degree price discrimination often is used in setting rates for water, gas, and time-share computer usage. It is also practiced by fast-food establishments. For example, a seller may offer soft drinks for $1.00, with refills available at $0.50. This pricing policy reflects the fact that the second drink is less valuable to the customer and will be purchased only at a lower price.

THIRD-DEGREE DISCRIMINATION   The most common type of price discrimination is third-degree discrimination. It involves separating consumers or markets in terms of their price elasticity of demand. This segmentation can be based on several factors. Often, third-degree price discrimination occurs in markets that are geographically separated. The practice of selling books at a lower price outside the United States is an example. Evidently, buyers in other countries have greater elasticities of demand than do U.S. buyers. At the same time, costs of collecting and shipping books make it unprofitable for other firms to buy in foreign countries and resell in the United States.

Discrimination can also be based on the nature of use. Telephone customers are classified as either residential or business customers. The monthly charge for a phone located in a business usually is somewhat higher than for a telephone used in a home. The explanation is that business demand is less elastic than residential demand. An individual without a telephone may be able to use a pay phone or go to a neighbor's house to make a call, but for many businesses a telephone is an absolute necessity.

Finally, markets can be segmented based on personal characteristics of consumers. Age is a common basis for price discrimination. Most movie theaters charge a lower price for children than they do for adults. But there is no difference in the cost of providing service to the two groups—one seat is required for each

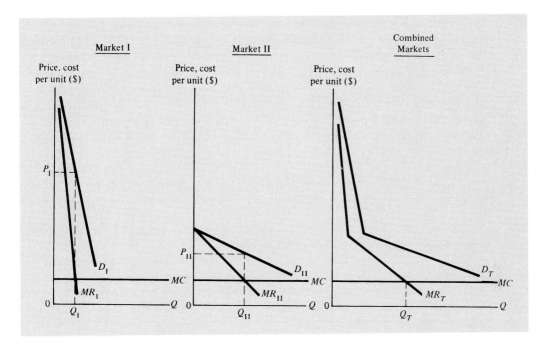

FIGURE 12-5 **Third-Degree Price Discrimination.**

patron regardless of age. The reduced price for children is based on differing demand elasticities. The assumption is that, with less money to spend, a child's demand for movies is more price sensitive than an adult's.

Figure 12-5 is used to show how profit-maximizing prices and quantities are determined with third-degree price discrimination. Consider a firm selling in two markets, I and II. To simplify the discussion, it is assumed that marginal costs are equal and constant in both markets. Demand is assumed to be less elastic in market I than in market II. The marginal revenue curves for the individual markets are MR_I and MR_{II}, respectively.

The combined demand curve for the two markets is also shown in Figure 12-5. It represents the sum of the demands in each of the markets at each price. The combined marginal revenue curve is also shown and was computed as the sum of marginal revenues in each market. For the firm, the optimal total output is at Q_T, the point where $MR_T = MC$. Once the profit-maximizing total output has been determined, the next step is to determine the output rates and prices in each market.

Because marginal costs are constant, the decision rule for allocating output is that the marginal revenue should be equal in the two markets. That is, the extra revenue obtained from selling an additional unit in the first market should be the same as that received from selling one more unit in the second market. If the two are not equal, the firm could increase its revenue and profit by allocating additional output to the market with greater marginal revenue. In Figure 12-5, equating marginal revenue to marginal cost means that Q_I units of output should be sold at a price of P_I in market I and Q_{II} units at a price of P_{II} in market II.

Note that a higher price is charged in market I, where demand is relatively less elastic. This relationship is true in general and is easily explained. Where demand is less elastic, consumers are less sensitive to price, meaning that relatively high prices can be charged. Conversely, in markets where demand is more elastic, the quantity demanded is more sensitive to price. Hence the profit-maximizing price is lower.

KEY CONCEPTS

- Price discrimination occurs when variation in prices for a product in different markets does not reflect variation in costs.
- The three criteria for successful price discrimination are market power, separable markets, and variation in demand elasticity among markets.
- First-degree price discrimination consists of charging the maximum price for each unit. In second-degree discrimination, prices are based on the quantity purchased by consumers.
- Third-degree discrimination usually requires setting a higher price in markets with less elastic demand. Markets may be segmented on the basis of geography, use of the product, or personal characteristics of consumers of the product.

EXAMPLE

Third-Degree Price Discrimination and Profits

A firm sells in two markets and has constant marginal costs of production equal to $2 per unit. The demand and marginal revenue equations for the two markets are as follows:

MARKET I	MARKET II
$P_I = 14 - 2Q_I$	$P_{II} = 10 - Q_{II}$
$MR_I = 14 - 4Q_I$	$MR_{II} = 10 - 2Q_{II}$

Using third-degree price discrimination, what are the profit-maximizing prices and quantities in each market? Show that greater profits result from price discrimination than would be obtained if a uniform price were used.

SOLUTION   With price discrimination, the condition for profit maximization is

$$MR_I = MR_{II} = MC$$

Because marginal cost is equal to $2, the optimal quantities are the solutions to the equations:

$$MR_I = 14 - 4Q_I = 2 \quad \text{which implies that } Q_I = 3$$

and
$$MR_{II} = 10 - 2Q_{II} = 2 \quad \text{which implies that } Q_{II} = 4$$

Optimal prices are obtained by substituting the profit-maximizing quantities into the demand equations. Thus $P_I = 8$ and $P_{II} = 6$.

Profits in each market are equal to total revenue $(P \cdot Q)$ minus total costs $(MC \cdot Q)$. Hence

$$\text{profit}_I = \$24 - \$6 = \$18 \quad \text{and} \quad \text{profit}_{II} = \$24 - \$8 = \$16$$

Hence combined profit for the two markets is $34.

To compute profits in the absence of price discrimination, the combined demand and marginal revenue equations must be computed. The first step is to express the demand equations in terms of quantities. Thus

$$Q_I = 7 - \frac{P}{2} \quad \text{and} \quad Q_{II} = 10 - P$$

Note that the subscript has been dropped from price because the same price is to be charged in each market. Adding the two demand curves gives

$$Q_T = 17 - \frac{3}{2}P$$

The corresponding marginal revenue equation is calculated by solving for P and using the principle that the marginal revenue function for a linear demand curve has the same intercept and twice the slope. Thus

$$P = 11\frac{1}{3} - \frac{2}{3}Q_T \qquad \text{Assume MC=AC ?}$$

and

$$MR_T = 11\frac{1}{3} - \frac{4}{3}Q_T$$

Equating marginal revenue to marginal cost gives

$$11\frac{1}{3} - \frac{4}{3}Q_T = 2$$

which implies that $Q = 7$. Substituting $Q = 7$ into the combined demand equation yields $P = 6\frac{2}{3}$. Hence profit without price discrimination is

$$P \cdot Q - MC \cdot Q = \$46\frac{2}{3} - \$14 = \$32\frac{2}{3}$$

But price discrimination resulted in total profit of $34. Thus it has been shown that profit can be increased by the use of price discrimination.

Find Real.

Product Bundling

In the movie *Five Easy Pieces*, actor Jack Nicholson enters a diner and asks for toast and coffee. The waitress curtly informs him that toast is not available, even though the restaurant has both bread and a toaster. To obtain his toast, Nicholson is forced to order a chicken salad sandwich without the chicken, mayonnaise, and lettuce. Although a little unusual, this is a form of product bundling. *Bundling* is the practice of selling two or more products together for a single price. When the products are only available as a package, the pricing strategy is referred to as *pure bundling*. If at least some products can also be purchased separately, then the firm is using *mixed bundling*.

Bundling is a common practice. College and professional sports teams offer season ticket packages that include seats for popular games that are likely to be sold out, together with seats for other games that have less fan appeal. Cultural arts series are often marketed in the same way. Many restaurants offer complete meals that include appetizers and desert. Car manufacturers provide vehicles with features such as air conditioning, antilock brakes, cassette decks, and airbags as standard equipment at "no extra" price. Computer companies often include certain software, such as an operating system and a word processor, with the machines that they sell.

Why is bundling such a common strategy? One reason is that firms can reduce their production and marketing costs by packaging goods and services in this way. For example, General Motors can customize its facilities to manufacture automobiles with a limited number of option packages. Successful college football teams such as Notre Dame can reduce their ticket sale costs because they have many season ticket holders. The waiters and waitresses at restaurants that offer only complete meals are spared much of the time required for customers to make decisions about each individual component of the meal.

But product bundling can be profitable even where there are no cost savings. Like price discrimination, bundling allows firms to increase their profits by extracting additional consumer surplus. However, in some situations, bundling may be preferable to price discrimination because it requires less information about tastes and preferences of consumers.

A simple example will be used to illustrate how bundling can increase profits. Because of their extremely high production costs, television series rarely make money for their producers when they are first seen on TV. The real payoff comes if the program lasts two or three years so that there are enough episodes produced to allow them to be sold to individual stations, which rely on reruns to meet their programming needs.

Consider a firm that has acquired the rights to fifty episodes each of two popular programs—*Murphy Brown* and *Star Trek*. Suppose stations in two different cities are contemplating the distributor's offerings and that the maximum prices they will pay, often referred to as the *reservation price,* for a fifty-episode series are as shown here:

	Murphy Brown	Star Trek
Memphis, Tenn.	$250,000	$150,000
Seattle, Wash.	$150,000	$250,000

The hypothetical numbers were set up so that the preferences of the two stations would be negatively correlated. Note that, presumably because of local tastes and preferences, the station in Memphis has a higher reservation price for *Murphy Brown* than for *Star Trek*. In contrast, the Seattle station attaches more value to *Star Trek*.

Because preferences of the two stations are negatively correlated, the distributor can increase its profit by bundling. If the firm prices the two series separately, the maximum amount it could charge (and still sell to both stations) would be $150,000 for each program, and total revenue would be $600,000. Now suppose the firm bundles the series and sets a price of $400,000 for the two. Each station will buy the package because the price does not exceed the sum of the reservation prices of the stations for the two series. But total revenue to the distributor will be $800,000. By bundling, the firm earns an additional $200,000.

If demands for the series had not been negatively correlated, bundling would not have been advantageous. For example, assume that the reservation prices for the two stations were as follows:

	Murphy Brown	*Star Trek*
Memphis, Tenn.	$150,000	$200,000
Seattle, Wash.	$200,000	$250,000

In this case, the firm could charge $150,000 for *Murphy Brown* and $200,000 for *Star Trek* and earn a total of $700,000. But the highest package price that could be charged is $350,000 per station, and this would generate the same amount of revenue. For bundling to be profitable, there must be at least some consumers whose preferences are negatively correlated with others. If there are consumers who have a high reservation price for one good but place a low value on the second, there must be other consumers whose reservation price for the second good is higher than for the first.

KEY CONCEPTS _____

- Pure bundling involves selling two or more products together for the same price.
- If reservation prices are negatively correlated, bundling can increase profits by capturing part of the consumer surplus.

Peak-Load Pricing _____

A firm selling in many markets at the same time can increase its profit by using price discrimination. Similarly, a firm that uses the same facility to supply several markets at different points in time can increase total profits by use of peak-load pricing. Basically, peak-load pricing involves charging a higher price for consumers who require service during periods of peak demand and a lower price for those who consume during low- or off-peak periods.

Pricing of long-distance telephone calls is a good example. Most long-distance calls are for business purposes and are placed on weekday afternoons. As a result, the switching facilities and lines provided by telephone companies are designed to meet demand during this peak period. In contrast, fewer calls are made late at night and on weekends. But these off-peak calls use the same facilities necessary for peak-period calls. To induce consumers to shift their calling patterns to periods of low demand, phone companies offer substantial discounts for late-night and weekend long-distance calls. If successful, costly additions to capacity can be postponed and existing facilities used more efficiently. As a result, both the company and its customers can benefit. The firm will have reduced costs and hence increased profit. Off-peak customers will pay lower rates. Even peak-period customers may benefit in the long run because the firm's facilities will be more efficiently utilized.

The fundamental principle of peak-load pricing is that those who impose the greatest demand on a firm for production capacity should be those who pay for most of that capacity. The traditional theory of peak-load pricing is discussed below.

Peak-load pricing may be appropriate if three conditions are met in producing a good or service. First, the product cannot be storable. For example, in the case of long-distance telephone calls, the service involves direct communication between two or more people. Calls cannot be stored for use at a later time. A busy executive in Portland would not consider a recorded message from an associate in New York to be an acceptable substitute for a telephone call received during business hours. Second, the same facilities must be used to provide the service during different periods of time. Again using long-distance telephone service as an example, this condition is met because calls placed at different times use the same lines and switching equipment. The third condition is that there must be variation in demand characteristics at different periods of time. Long-distance calls also meet this requirement. Demand is greater during business hours than at other times. In addition, demand for business calls at any given time is usually less elastic than is the demand for personal calls.

To illustrate the concept of peak-load pricing, assume that demand for telephone calls during a day can be divided into two periods of equal length.[3] Period 1 is a time of low demand and extends from 7 P.M. to 7 A.M. Period 2 is from 7 A.M. to 7 P.M. and is the time of peak demand. Let demand for telephone calls in period 2 be greater at all prices than demand in period 1. That is, at any given price the quantity demanded is greater in period 2 than in period 1.

Also assume that only labor and capacity costs are incurred in providing telephone service. Let b represent labor cost per unit of service, where b is assumed not to vary by the period or by the demand for service. Similarly, let B represent

---

[3] This discussion is based on an article by P. O. Steiner, "Peak and Efficient Pricing." *Quarterly Journal of Economics*, 71 (November 1957), pp. 585–610.

the rental cost of a unit of capacity, with B assumed constant with respect to the amount of capacity purchased. That is, the first unit of capacity costs $\$B$, and all additional units cost the firm $\$B$.

Let the price paid for telephone service be the sum of the labor cost and the capacity cost (which includes a reasonable return on capital). Because the labor cost per unit of service is assumed to be constant, it can be subtracted from the price in each period without altering the results of the analysis. Figure 12-6 depicts the two demand curves, D_1 and D_2, after the labor cost has been subtracted. As a result, the vertical scale starts with b (the labor cost) instead of zero. Because labor costs have been netted out, Figure 12-8 can be considered a graph of the demand for telephone capacity. Hence each point on the two demand curves indicates the amount of capacity that the firm's customers demand at a given price of capacity.

The D_T curve in Figure 12-6 is the result of vertically summing the two individual demand curves (i.e., adding the vertical distances above the horizontal axis at each point along the horizontal axis). Remember that the demands are noncompeting and hence the same capacity is used to provide service in each of the two periods. The individual demand curves can be interpreted as indicating the willingness of consumers to pay for capacity during each period. For example, consumers in period 1 will pay P_1 per unit for $\overline{X}$ units of capacity and consumers in period 2 will pay P_2 for $\overline{X}$ units. Because the capacity is usable to serve consumers in each period, the total value or demand for $\overline{X}$ units of capacity is $P_T = P_1 + P_2$.

Efficient resource allocation suggests that capacity should be added until the value of the last unit is just equal to the cost of obtaining it. The cost of each unit of capacity is B. The total value of capacity is read from the D_T curve and indicates

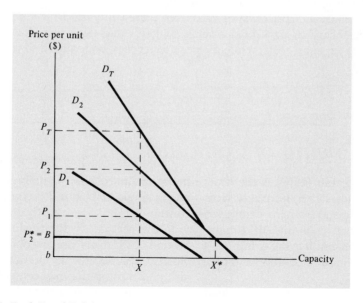

FIGURE 12-6 **Peak-Load Pricing.**

that at a cost of B, X^* units of capacity should be employed. The peak-load pricing problem is to determine who should pay for the X^* units of capacity. Notice that even if the cost of capacity were zero, less than X^* units of capacity would be required to meet the demand in period 1. Thus the selection of X^* units provides no benefits to consumers in period 1. The implication is that they should not be required to pay for capacity. Users in that period would properly be charged only the labor cost, b, per unit of telephone service consumed.

In contrast, because period 2 users attach a positive value to X^* units of capacity, they should be assessed the cost. Specifically, the value of capacity in period 2 is $P_2^* = B$. By assigning this cost to period 2 users, the marginal cost of capacity can be recovered. Thus the total price of telephone calls to period 2 users should be $P_2^* + b$ and to period 1 users, b.

Notice the basic principles involved in this scheme of peak-load pricing. Because the off-peak users place no value on the marginal units of capacity, they pay only the labor cost; the capacity charge is paid by the users who require the capacity. In general, peak-load pricing charges all or most capacity costs to peak-period users and charges off-peak users a price based on the noncapacity costs of serving them.

KEY CONCEPTS

- Peak-load pricing can be used to reduce costs and increase profits if
- 1. The same facilities are used to provide a product or service at different periods of time.
- 2. The product or service is not storable.
- 3. Demand characteristics vary from period to period.
- The theory of peak-load pricing suggests that peak-period users should pay most capacity costs, while off-peak users may be required to pay only variable costs.

CASE STUDY

Peak-Load Pricing of Computer Time

The central processing unit (CPU) is the heart and brain of a computer. Input/output devices transmit information to and from the computer, and storage devices such as on-line disks maintain files of information, but it is the computer's CPU that manages the entire operation and processes the data.

The three criteria for successful peak-load pricing are met by CPU time at large computational facilities. First, usually a computer has only a single CPU, but this equipment is in use constantly. Thus the same facility is used to provide the service at different periods of time. Second, CPU time not used is lost forever—clearly, the service is not storable. Finally, although a computational center may be able to provide the same service at 3 A.M. as at 3 P.M., late-night service is often not as desirable to the customer. As a result, demand for CPU time is usually much greater during the day than it is at night. The figure depicts demand for CPU time at a hypothetical computer facility during a 24-hour period. The solid line illustrates the usage pattern when the price per second of CPU time does not change with the time of day. Note that demand is very low during the early morning hours, begins to increase around 7 A.M., peaks in the afternoon, and declines in the evening. The result is that the facility is very busy at some times and virtually idle during other periods.

To encourage the use of the computer during off-peak hours, many computational facilities have implemented peak-load pricing. Although the specifics differ among centers, these pricing policies specify relatively high prices during period of peak demand and much lower prices during off-peak early-morning hours. For example, at one university computer facility, CPU time is priced as follows:

Day	Time Period	Cost per Second
Monday–Friday	8 A.M.–1 P.M.	$0.03
Monday–Friday	1 P.M.–5 P.M.	0.06
Monday–Friday	5 P.M.–1 A.M.	0.01
Monday–Friday	1 A.M.–8 A.M.	0.002
Saturday–Sunday	8 A.M.–5 P.M.	0.01
Saturday–Sunday	5 P.M.–8 A.M.	0.002

The weekend rates also apply to holidays. Note that CPU time at peak hours (weekdays from 1 to 5 P.M.) is thirty times more costly than during off-peak hours (weekday evenings from 1 to 8 A.M. and weekends and holidays from 5 P.M. to 8 A.M.). As a result, computer usage has declined during peak periods and is much greater during the off-peak hours. This change, resulting from peak-load pricing, is depicted by the dashed line in the figure. By reducing demand at peak periods, the facility may be able to postpone purchases of additional computing capacity.

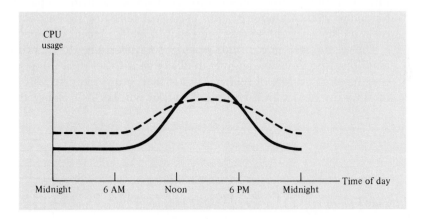

CPU Demand During a 24-Hour Period.

Cost-Plus Pricing

The traditional assumption of economic theory is that firms attempt to maximize profits and that this objective is accomplished by increasing production until marginal revenue equals marginal cost and then charging a price determined by the demand curve. But, in actual practice, many firms use cost-plus pricing. Basically, this approach involves setting prices that cover the cost of purchasing or producing a product plus enough profit to allow the firm to earn its target rate of return.

The remainder of this section considers why cost-plus pricing is so popular and how it is implemented. The section also examines the apparent conflict between the cost-plus and marginal revenue equals marginal cost pricing rules.

Mechanics of Cost-Plus Pricing

Two steps are involved in cost-plus pricing. First, the cost of acquiring or producing the good or service must be determined. The total cost has a variable and a fixed component. In either case, costs are computed on an average basis, That is,

$$AC = AVC + AFC \tag{12-3}$$

where

$$AVC = \frac{TVC}{Q} \quad \text{and} \quad AFC = \frac{TFC}{Q}$$

and AC is average total costs, AVC is average variable cost, TVC is total variable cost, AFC is average fixed cost, TFC is total fixed cost, and Q is the number of units produced. But there is a problem in making the computations. With cost-plus pricing, quantity is used to calculate the price, but quantity is determined by price. This problem is avoided by using an assumed quantity. Typically, this rate of output is based on some percentage of the firm's capacity. For example, for many years General Motors used cost-plus pricing and computed average costs on the assumption that sales would be 80 percent of capacity.

The second step in cost-plus pricing is to determine the markup over costs. As mentioned previously, the overall objective is to set prices that allow the firm to earn its targeted rate of return. Thus if that return requires X of total profit, the markup over costs on each unit of output will be X/Q. Hence the price will be

$$P = AVC + AFC + \frac{X}{Q} \tag{12-4}$$

EXAMPLE _____

Cost-Plus Pricing of Automobiles

An automobile manufacturer estimates that total variable costs will be $500 million and total fixed costs will be $1 billion in the next year. In setting prices, it is assumed that sales will be 80 percent of the firm's 125,000-vehicle-per-year capacity, or 100,000 units. The target rate of return is 10 percent, which is to be earned on an investment of $2 billion. If prices are set on a cost-plus basis, what price should be charged for each automobile?

SOLUTION   A target return of 10 percent on $2 billion requires that the firm earn a total profit of $200 million. Computations are based on assumed sales of 100,000 vehicles.

Thus average fixed cost, average variable cost, and profit per unit are

$$AFC = \frac{\$1 \text{ billion}}{100,000} = \$10,000$$

$$AVC = \frac{\$500 \text{ million}}{100,000} = \$5,000$$

$$\frac{X}{Q} = \frac{\$200 \text{ million}}{100,000} = \$2,000$$

Hence if profit of $2,000 per vehicle is added to the $15,000 in average fixed and variable costs, the price will be $17,000 per car.

Evaluation of Cost-Plus Pricing

Cost-plus pricing has some important advantages that help explain its appeal. First, it may contribute to price stability. This is a desirable result because price changes can be expensive and may provoke undesirable reactions by competitors. Second, the formula used in cost-plus pricing is simple and easy to use. As will be discussed later, the necessary information is less than for marginal revenue equals marginal cost pricing. Finally, cost-plus pricing provides a clear justification for price changes. A firm desiring to increase its price can point to cost increases as the reason.

However, cost-plus pricing has been criticized on a number of points. One alleged problem is that it is based on costs and does not take demand conditions into account. This shortcoming is compounded by the fact that the cost data used may be the wrong costs. Instead of using incremental or opportunity costs, cost-plus prices often rely on historical or accounting data. In addition, most applications of the procedure are based on fully distributing common costs to the various goods produced by the firm. Problems with prices based on fully distributed costs were discussed earlier in the chapter.

Cost-Plus Pricing and Economic Theory

At first glance, cost-plus pricing would appear to be inconsistent with economic theory that assumes profit maximization. Moreover, the wide use of cost-plus pricing seems to make analysis based on the marginal revenue equals marginal cost decision rule largely irrelevant. However, the conflict may be more apparent than real. There is reason to believe that use of cost-plus pricing is simply a tool used by businesses in pursuing the goal of long-run profit maximization. As such, cost-plus prices can be shown to be related to, although not identical to, prices based on marginal revenues and marginal costs.

A comparison of the two approaches to pricing starts with a consideration of costs. Although it is true that cost-plus pricing is based on average rather than marginal costs, frequently long-run marginal and average costs are not greatly different. This is especially true in many retailing activities. Thus use of average costs as a basis for price determination may be considered a reasonable approximation of marginal cost decision making.

The second step in the comparison involves the target rate of return and the resulting markup. How does a manager determine whether the target should be 10 percent or 20 percent? Basically, the decision involves management's perception of demand elasticity and competitive conditions. An example would be grocery stores. The intense competition among these firms holds down profits. As a result, the typical markup for most food items is only about 12 percent over cost.

If the markup over cost is based on demand conditions, cost-plus pricing may not be inconsistent with profit maximization. This can be shown mathematically. Marginal revenue is the derivative of total revenue with respect to quantity. Thus

$$MR = \frac{d(TR)}{dQ} = \frac{d(PQ)}{dQ} = P + \frac{dP}{dQ}Q$$

But $P + \dfrac{dP}{dQ}$ can be rewritten as $P\left(1 + \dfrac{dP}{dQ}\dfrac{Q}{P}\right)$. Note that $(dP/dQ)(Q/P)$ is $1/E_p$, where E_p is price elasticity of demand. Thus

$$MR = P\left(1 + \frac{1}{E_p}\right) \tag{12-5}$$

Profit maximization requires that $MR = MC$. As a simplifying assumption, let $MC = AC$. Thus the profit-maximizing price is the solution to

$$P\left(1 + \frac{1}{E_p}\right) = AC$$

which can be written as

$$P\left(\frac{E_p + 1}{E_p}\right) = AC$$

Solving for P yields

$$P = AC\left(\frac{E_p}{E_p + 1}\right) \tag{12-6}$$

Equation (12-6) can be interpreted as a cost-plus or markup pricing scheme. That is, the price is based on a markup over average costs. The markup, $E_p/(1 + E_p)$, is a function of the price elasticity of demand. As demand becomes more elastic, the markup becomes smaller.[4] For example, if $E_p = -1.5$, the markup is 3.0. But for $E_p = -4.0$, the markup is only 1.33 times average cost.

Thus cost-plus pricing may simply be the mechanism by which managers pursue profit maximization. Most managers have limited information on demand and costs. Obtaining the additional information necessary to generate accurate esti-

---

[4] If $E_p = -1.0$, the markup is undefined, and if $-1 < E_p < 0$, the markup becomes negative. However, these cases are irrelevant because the profit-maximizing firm will never operate on the inelastic portion of its demand curve. The reason is clear. As long as marginal revenue is positive, demand is elastic. But the profit-maximizing firm produces where marginal revenue equals marginal cost. Because marginal cost is positive, marginal revenue is also positive and demand is elastic at the profit-maximizing rate of output.

mates of marginal costs and revenues may be prohibitively expensive. Hence cost-plus pricing may be the most rational approach in maximizing profits.

KEY CONCEPTS

- Cost-plus pricing is widely used by managers and involves a markup over the average cost of acquiring or producing a product.
- Cost-plus pricing may stabilize prices and provide a justification for price changes.
- The markup used in cost-plus pricing is determined by demand elasticities and competition. Markups are lower where demand is more elastic and competition is intense.
- Cost-plus pricing may simply represent the decision rule used by managers in pursuit of profit maximization.

CASE STUDY

Cost-Plus Pricing at Wendy's

Many managers use some variation of the cost-plus method for setting prices. But the markup over costs must be based on their perception of what the market will bear. Fast-food establishments are a good example. The following excerpt describes the approach to price setting used by Peter Salg, who owns several Wendy's restaurants in Colorado.

> To determine the prices of menu items, Mr. Salg looks at his costs, particularly his food costs. His "target food cost" lies between 30 and 31 percent of the retail price of a meal. That target has changed over the years; in 1986, it was 28 to 29 percent.
>
> Mr. Salg charges prices that will yield food costs as a percent of price within his target. For some items such as beverages, food costs are only 20 percent of the price of the item. For others—like hamburgers—food costs make up nearly half of the sale price. Mr. Salg tries to keep his overall food cost for a typical meal in the 30 to 31 percent range.
>
> If he notices food costs going over 31 percent

of total sales, he considers raising his prices. Before he'll do so, however, he "takes a walk down to McDonald's to see what they're doing."

> If he finds that the spread on the price between his price and McDonald's price for a hamburger has reached ten cents, he'll experiment by raising his price by a nickel. If the extra nickel fails to produce enough revenue to bring him within his food cost target, he'll try raising the prices of some of his other items.
>
> "I don't raise my prices unless I have to," Mr. Salg says. "Every time I raise my price I lose customers." With only a small price change, such as an extra nickel for a hamburger, he expects only a small loss of customers. "But an increase in the price of a burger by fifteen cents causes a tremendous reduction in traffic."
>
> Demand isn't as responsive to price for his salad bar, Mr. Salg observes. "The price of lettuce fluctuates drastically—so much that I've sometimes had to increase the price of a salad by 30 cents. But such increases have hardly dented the number of salads I've sold."

SOURCE: S. Tregarthen and T. Tregarthen. "Hard Times for Fast Food." *The Margin*, 4(Nov./Dec. 1988): 13–15.

Summary

Modern corporations may produce hundreds of different products. When the demand for products is interrelated, the firm should take this interdependence into account. When a firm produces complementary goods, the output rate of each good should be greater than if no demand interrelationship existed. For substitutes, output rates should be less than if the goods were independent.

Some goods are jointly produced in fixed proportions. Profit maximization requires that the two goods be considered as a product package. Thus the rate of output should be increased until marginal cost equals the sum of marginal revenues obtained from selling an additional unit of the product package.

Not all costs are clearly attributable to a particular good or service. Attempts to allocate such common costs are arbitrary. Decisions based on fully distributed costs can result in inefficient resource allocation; incremental costs are a better guide. A good or service can be profitably produced if its price exceeds the incremental cost of supplying it.

If an enterprise has common costs, marginal cost pricing may not be feasible. Ramsey pricing is a second-best alternative that allows the firm to recover its costs while minimizing adverse effects on allocative efficiency. A simple version of Ramsey pricing specifies that deviations from marginal costs should be inversely proportional to the demand elasticities of the goods or services.

Vertical integration causes intermediate goods to be transferred from one division of a firm to another. However, profit maximization for the combined firm requires that those intermediate products be correctly priced. When a perfectly competitive external market exists, market forces will cause price to equal marginal cost. Hence the intermediate product will be appropriately priced. If there is no external market, management should set the price of the intermediate good at marginal cost.

Price discrimination occurs when variation in price for a product sold in different markets does not correspond to differences in costs. The three conditions for successful price discrimination are market power, variation in the elasticity of demand, and separable markets. First-degree price discrimination involves charging each consumer the maximum amount that he or she is willing to pay. Second-degree discrimination occurs when prices vary depending on the amount purchased. Third-degree discrimination separates markets in terms of elasticity of demand. The segmentation may be based on location, use, or personal characteristics. Usually, higher prices are charged when demand is less elastic.

Product bundling is a pricing scheme that allows firms to capture part of the consumer surplus. Pure bundling involves the selling of two or more products only as a package. If the reservation prices of consumers are negatively correlated, firms can use bundling to increase their profits.

Peak-load pricing can reduce costs and increase profits. The practice is appropriate when three conditions are met. First, the same facilities must be used to provide a product or service at different times. Second, the product or service must not be storable. Third, demand characteristics of consumers must vary from period to period. With peak-load pricing, peak-period consumers will pay most of the capacity costs, while off-peak users will be charged a price based on variable costs.

Cost-plus pricing is widely used by firms. This practice involves setting price as average cost plus a markup designed to provide a target rate of return. Advantages of cost-plus pricing include stable prices, a simple formula for pricing, and a clear justification for price changes. Problems include the use of historical and fully distributed costs rather than marginal costs and an apparent failure to take demand conditions into account in price setting.

On closer investigation, it can be shown that markups are related to demand elasticity and competition. Less elastic demand and lack of competition are associated with high markups over cost, while the reverse is true for markets characterized by more elastic demand and intense competition. Faced with a lack of information about demand and costs, it may be that cost-plus pricing is simply the method by which managers pursue profit maximization.

Discussion Questions

12-1. Macmillan Manufacturing produces razor blades and razors. Propose a pricing strategy that would allow the firm to maximize its profit on the two goods. Explain.

12-2. Why should goods produced in fixed proportions be regarded as a product package in developing production and pricing strategies?

12-3. Should a sheep-ranching operation consider lamb and wool as a product package? Why or why not?

12-4. What is meant by the statement that "the assignment of common costs must, by definition, be arbitrary"?

12-5. Generating equipment is used to provide electric power to both residential and industrial customers. Assume that total consumption by residential users is twice that of industrial consumers. In setting prices, would it be appropriate to assign two-thirds of the cost of the generating equipment to the residential users? Why or why not?

12-6. The managers of a firm are considering offering a new service. The proposed price of the new service would be greater than its incremental cost but would not cover fully distributed costs. As a user of services already provided by the firm, should you favor or oppose the new service? Explain.

12-7. How does the presence or absence of external markets affect the role played by top management in pricing intermediate products produced by a vertically integrated firm?

12-8. If an intermediate product is available from a perfectly competitive industry, why would a vertically integrated firm produce the product internally? That is, what is the advantage of vertical integration is this case?

12-9. A city has only one furniture store. Is it likely that the store could successfully practice price discrimination? Why or why not?

12-10. How is bundling similar to price discrimination? Which requires more information about consumer preferences?

12-11. Are the three conditions necessary for peak-load pricing met in the case of movies shown in theaters? Explain.

12-12. How can peak-load pricing improve resource allocation?

12-13. How can cost-plus pricing be reconciled to the "marginal revenue equals marginal cost" rule of economic theory?

Problems

12-1. A small firm traps rabbits for their fur and feet. Each rabbit yields one pelt and two feet (only the hind feet are used to make good-luck charms). The demand for pelts is given by

$$P_P = 2.00 - 0.001Q_P$$

and the demand for rabbit's feet is given by

$$P_F = 1.60 - 0.001Q_F$$

The marginal cost of trapping and processing each rabbit is $0.60.

a. What are the profit-maximizing prices and quantities of pelts and rabbit's feet?

b. If the demand for rabbit's feet is $P_F = 1.00 - 0.001Q_F$, what are the profit-maximizing prices and rates of output?

12-2. Mike's Shear Shop provides 4,000 haircuts each month at an average price of $5.00 per haircut. The common costs of operating the store at $12,000 per month. The business is considering hiring a photographer who would take pictures of customers after they had their hair cut. The price of the photographs would be $2.50 and it is estimated that 2,000 customers would purchase the service each month. The total extra cost of the photographic service is 1,000 + 1Q per month, where Q is the number of photographs sold.

a. If the decision is to be based on incremental revenue and incremental cost, should the service be offered? Explain.

b. If the decision is to be made on the basis of fully distributed costs and if the $12,000 in monthly common costs are to be apportioned based on the revenues from haircuts and photos sold each month, should the new service be offered? Why or why not?

12-3. Write-Right, a vertically integrated firm, produces both paper and writing tablets. The demand for tablets is given by

$$P_T = 1.00 - 0.001Q$$

where Q is the quantity of tablets. The marginal cost of producing the paper necessary for each tablet is

$$MC_P = 0.20 + 0.001Q$$

It costs the firm $0.10 to make the paper into a writing tablet. If there is no external market for the paper, what transfer price should top management set for the paper?

12-4. A firm has found a way of using first-degree price discrimination. Demand for its product is given by

$$P = 20 - 2Q$$

Marginal cost is constant and equal to $6.

a. With first-degree discrimination, what will be the profit-maximizing rate of output? How much economic profit will the firm earn?

b. What will be the profit-maximizing rate of output if the firm does not discriminate and sets one price for all customers? How much economic profit will the firm earn in this case?

12-5. Smith Distributing sells videocassettes in two separable markets. The marginal cost of each cassette is $2. For the first market, demand is given by

$$Q_1 = 20 - 5P_1$$

The demand equation for the second market is

$$Q_2 = 20 - 2P_2$$

a. If the firm uses third-degree price discrimination, what will be the profit-maximizing price and quantity in each market? How much economic profit will the firm earn?

b. If the firm charges the same price in both markets, what will be the profit-maximizing price and total quantity? How much economic profit will the firm earn?

12-6. Global motors sells its automobiles in both the United States and Japan. Due to trade restrictions, a vehicle sold in one country cannot be resold in the other. The demand functions for the two countries are

$$\begin{array}{ll} \text{U.S.} & P = 30,000 - 0.40Q \\ \text{Japan} & P = 20,000 - 0.20Q \end{array}$$

The firm's total cost function is $TC = 10,000,000 + 12,000Q$. What price should Global charge in each country in order to maximize profit? What will be the total profit?

12-7. A firm produces two products, A and B. Demands are independent and marginal costs are zero. The products are sold to three consumers, and each must be charged the same price.

a. For the following reservation prices, can profits be increased by bundling? Explain. What is the maximum profit?

	Good A	Good B
Consumer 1	$50	$40
Consumer 2	$60	$35
Consumer 3	$70	$50

b. For the reservation prices shown here, what is the profit-maximizing price strategy? Explain. What is the maximum profit?

	Good A	Good B
Consumer 1	$50	$60
Consumer 2	$60	$60
Consumer 3	$70	$50

12-8. The manager of a sporting goods store uses cost-plus pricing to determine the profit-maximizing price of bicycles. The cost of a bicycle to the store is $80. The manager estimates that the price elasticity of demand is -3.0. What is the profit-maximizing price?

12-9. Grasscutter Inc. makes a product used to trim lawns. The firm has fixed costs of $100,000 per year. Management expects to sell 2,000 units per year, and at that rate of output, total variable costs will be $50,000. The firm uses cost-plus pricing to earn a target rate of return on an investment of $200,000. If the price is set at $100, what is the target rate of return?

Problems Requiring Calculus

12-10. The House of Music sells low-cost turntables and speakers. The total revenue equation for sales of the two products is given by

$$TR = 200Q_T - 6Q_T^2 + 100Q_S - 4Q_S^2 + Q_TQ_S$$

where Q_T and Q_S are quantities of turntables and speakers, respectively. The marginal cost of turntables is $20 and the marginal cost of speakers is $10.
a. Are the two goods substitutes or complements?
b. What is the profit-maximizing rate of output for each good?
c. What would be the profit-maximizing rate of output if there were no demand interdependence between the two goods?

12-11. Culture Extravaganza produces ballets in Boston and New York. Monthly total revenues are given by

$$TR_B = 1,000Q_B^{0.5}$$

and

$$TR_N = 2,000Q_N^{0.5}$$

where Q_B is the monthly number of Boston patrons and Q_N is the monthly number of New York ballet attendees. Salaries of the performers are based on attendance, and the firm estimates that the marginal cost is $10 per attendee in each city.
a. If Culture Extravaganza attempts to practice third-degree price discrimination, what will be the profit-maximizing prices and rates of output in each city?
b. Will the firm earn more profit using price discrimination than if a uniform price is set? Explain.

12-12. A firm produces two types of calculators, x and y. The revenue and cost equations are shown below with Q_x and Q_y measured in thousands of calculators per year.

$$\text{Total revenue} = 2\,Q_x + 3\,Q_y$$
$$\text{Total cost} = Q_x^2 - 2\,Q_xQ_y - 2\,Q_y^2 + 6\,Q_x + 14\,Q_y + 5$$

a. To maximize profit, how many of each type of calculator should the firm produce?
b. What is the maximum profit the firm can earn?

CHAPTER 13

Pricing and Employment of Inputs

Preview ───

Individuals earn income by selling resources to firms. The firm uses these resources to produce the goods and services demanded by consumers. Of critical importance to both the individual and the firm is the price of a unit of the resource. The analysis presumes that the distribution of resources among individuals is given. That is, the ownership of land, capital resources, and human resources (i.e., the education, training, and experience embodied in labor) has already been determined. Given this initial distribution, the level and distribution of income are determined by the price of each resource unit: These include the wage rate per hour of labor, the rent per acre of land, and the profit per unit of capital. Clearly, input prices are also important to the firm because they are a critical factor in determining the amount and mix of resources employed. This chapter focuses on the determination of those input prices and how firms decide how much of an input to employ.

The price of a productive input is determined by supply and demand, just as is the price of output. However, the firm's demand for an input is a derived demand. Firms demand capital, labor, and land not because they have value as such, but because those resources can be used to produce goods and services that have value to consumers. Thus, the demand for inputs is dependent on the demand for the goods and services those inputs are used to produce; hence the use of the term *derived demand*.

The first part of this chapter focuses on the determination of input prices and the amount of an input to be employed. Two different market structures are considered. In the second section, the correspondence between output and input decisions is outlined. The next two sections include an introduction to the concept of economic rent and a discussion of the reasons for significant income differentials among workers. The role of labor unions in input markets is analyzed in the fifth section. Both the economics of collective bargaining and the objectives of labor unions are considered. Minimum wage laws are analyzed in the final section.

Input Pricing and Employment ─────────────────────

The analytical framework for studying the demand for productive inputs is based on the theory of production developed in Chapter 6. Recall that efficient production requires that the ratio of marginal product to input price be equal for all inputs. For example, if capital and labor are the only inputs, the efficiency condition is

$$\frac{MP_K}{r} = \frac{MP_L}{w} \tag{13-1}$$

where MP_K and MP_L are the marginal products of capital and labor and r and w are the prices of those inputs.

If one input, say capital, is held constant, it can be shown that the ratio of input price to marginal product is equal to marginal cost. Thus for labor

$$\frac{w}{MP_L} = MC \tag{13-2}$$

Recall that the profit-maximizing firm must increase output, and therefore the employment of inputs, to the point where marginal cost equals marginal revenue. Thus, in equilibrium, the ratio of input price to marginal product (i.e., marginal cost) must equal marginal revenue. That is,

$$\frac{w}{MP_L} = MR \tag{13-3}$$

Multiplying both sides of equation (14-3) by MP_L yields

$$w = MR \cdot MP_L \tag{13-4}$$

or

$$w = MRP_L \tag{13-5}$$

which indicates that the profit-maximizing firms should hire an input until the price of the input equals the marginal revenue product (*MRP*) of that input.

The *MRP* function is the firm's input demand function. Consider the *MRP* function shown in Figure 13-1. It can be used to determine the rate of labor input

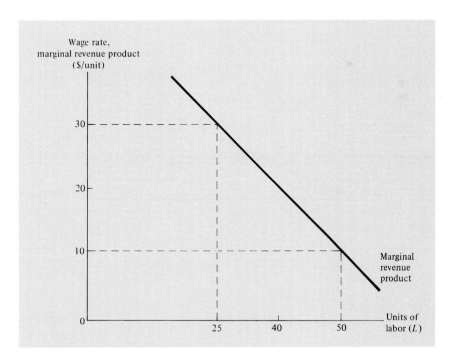

FIGURE 13-1 **Marginal Revenue Product Function for Labor.**

that will be hired at any wage rate. For example, if the wage is $10 per unit, 50 units of labor are employed; at $30 per unit, only 25 units will be employed.

The input demand function (i.e., the marginal revenue product or *MRP* function) is determined by multiplying marginal product by marginal revenue. Because of the law of diminishing marginal returns, the marginal product function will be decreasing, at least in the range that is relevant for the firm. Further, the firm's marginal revenue function will either be horizontal, as in the case of the perfectly competitive firm, or downward sloping. Thus, because the input demand function is found by multiplying the marginal revenue function by the marginal product function, the input demand function must be downward sloping.

The firm sells goods and/or services in the product market and buys inputs in the factor market. The structure of both of these markets will influence the price of the input and the amount employed. The circumstance of the firm on the output side of the market (i.e., whether the firm is a perfect competitor, oligopolist, or monopolist) will affect the firm's input demand function, whereas the market structure on the supply side will influence the input supply curve facing the firm. In this section, input pricing and employment decisions are considered for the following types of firms: (1) a firm that is a monopolist in the product market and a perfect competitor in the input market and (2) a firm that is a monopolist in the product market and a monopsonist in the input market.

The key difference in analyzing the effect of differing conditions in the product

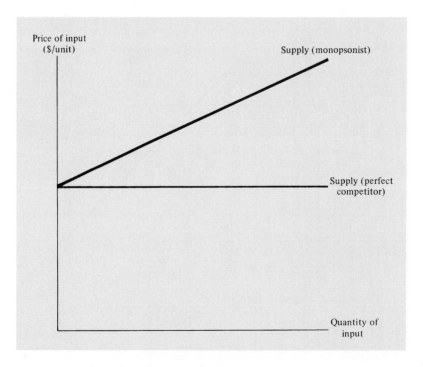

FIGURE 13-2 **Input Supply Functions Facing a Perfect Competitor and a Monopsonist.**

market is that price and marginal revenue are constant for the perfect competitor. In contrast, the demand curve facing the monopolist is downward sloping, which implies that the marginal revenue function also has a negative slope.

A perfect competitor in an input market is one of many buyers of the input. No one buyer has any influence on the price of the input. This implies that the input supply function is horizontal (i.e., perfectly elastic), meaning that any firm can buy as much of that input as desired without influencing the price. Thus the input price facing a perfect competitor in an input market is constant. In contrast, the input supply function facing the monopsonist or single buyer of an input is upward sloping. Additional inputs are obtainable only at higher prices. For example, a large firm in a small town may employ a substantial share of the local labor force. Thus, as a near-monopsonist, any significant increase in the firm's employment of labor would require an increase in the wage rate. Examples of these supply curves for a perfect competitor and a monopsonist are shown on the previous page in Figure 13-2.

KEY CONCEPTS

- The demand for a productive input is derived from the demand for the goods and services that input is used to produce.
- The demand function for an input is derived from the condition for efficient production. In general, an input should be employed until the input price equals the marginal revenue product of the input.
- Firms that are perfectly competitive in input markets face a horizontal input supply function. Monopsonists face an upward-sloping input supply function.

Market Structure I: Monopolist (Product Market)—Perfect Competitor (Input Market)

If the firm is a monopolist, or at least has some degree of market power, it faces a downward-sloping demand function for its output. Thus the marginal revenue curve lies below the demand function. In this case, the firm's demand for labor, as shown by the marginal revenue product function, will decline more rapidly than if price equaled marginal revenue. Because the firm in this example is a perfect competitor in the input market, the supply function is horizontal.

Table 13-1 shows hypothetical values for a firm's total product, marginal product, and marginal revenue. The resulting marginal revenue product or input demand function is shown in the right-hand column of the table. This demand is computed by multiplying each entry for marginal product by the corresponding marginal revenue per unit entry.[1] As MRP_L is the net addition to the firm's total

---

[1] Recall that marginal revenue is defined as the change in total revenue divided by a one-unit change in output. When the rate of labor input increases from 0 to 1, output increases from 0 to 10, and total revenue increases from 0 to 50. Therefore, marginal revenue per unit over that interval averages $50/10 or $5.00.

TABLE 13-1 **Total Product, Marginal Product, and Marginal Revenue Product of Labor for a Monopolist**

(1) Rate of Labor Input	(2) Total Product	(3) Marginal Product	(4) Output Price	(5) Total Revenue	(6) Marginal Revenue	(7) Marginal Revenue Product
0	0	—	—	—	—	—
1	10	10	$5.00	$ 50.00	$5.00	$50.00
2	19	9	4.50	85.50	3.94	35.50
3	26	7	4.00	104.00	2.64	18.50
4	30	4	3.75	112.50	2.13	8.50
5	32	2	3.60	115.20	1.35	2.70
6	33	1	3.50	115.50	0.30	0.30

revenue associated with an additional unit of labor, MRP_L also could be determined as the change in total revenue [in column (5)] associated with a one-unit change in labor.

The input demand function and the supply function are shown in Figure 13-3. If the market price of input is $8.50, the firm will employ four units of labor

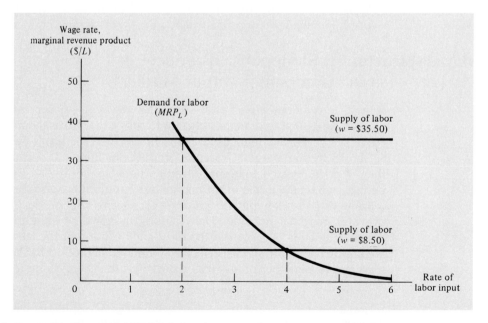

FIGURE 13-3 **Determination of the Optimal Employment of Labor: Competitive Input Market.**

because at that input rate, the marginal revenue product is just equal to the wage rate. If the price of labor increased to $35.50, the firm would employ only two units.

Market Structure II: Monopolist (Product Market)—Monopsonist (Input Market)

Now consider a hypothetical firm that not only is a monopolist in the product market but also is the only buyer of labor in the area. An electric utility company with a large generating facility near a small town could be an example of such a firm. The company may have a franchise as the only seller of electricity in the region and could be the only important employer of labor. Therefore, the firm is both a monopolist and a monopsonist. If this firm's output rate is to increase, it must hire more labor. But because the firm faces an upward-sloping supply curve, hiring more of an input will require that the price of that input be increased.

A labor supply schedule facing the firm is shown in the first two columns of Table 13-2. Also shown is the firm's marginal expenditure on labor function, which is defined as the change in total expenditure on labor associated with a one-unit change in the rate of labor input. Note that to hire more labor, the firm must offer a higher wage rate, and this higher rate must be paid to all inputs hired. Thus the marginal expenditure on input function lies above the supply curve, reflecting both the higher price necessary to attract new workers and the higher price that must be paid to those already working.

The relevant functions for determining the optimal labor input rate are the marginal revenue product function (from Table 13-1 on page 438) and the marginal expenditure on labor function (from Table 13-2). These data are summarized in Table 13-3. To maximize profit, the firm will employ labor until the marginal revenue product equals the marginal expenditure on labor. In Table 13-3 the marginal revenue product equals marginal expenditure when the rate of labor

TABLE 13-2 **Labor Supply, Total Expenditure, and Marginal Expenditure on Labor for a Monopsonist**

Rate of Labor Input	Labor Price Per Unit	Total Expenditure on Labor	Marginal Expenditure on Labor
0	—	$ 0	—
1	$ 5.50	5.50	$ 5.50
2	8.00	16.00	10.50
3	11.50	34.50	18.50
4	15.00	60.00	25.50
5	18.50	92.50	32.50
6	22.00	132.00	39.50

TABLE 13-3 **Marginal Revenue Product and Marginal Expenditure on Labor**

Rate of Labor Input	Marginal Revenue Product	Labor Price Per Unit	Marginal Expenditure on Labor
0	—	—	—
1	$50.00	$ 5.50	$ 5.50
2	35.50	8.00	10.50
3	18.50	11.50	18.50
4	8.50	15.00	25.50
5	2.70	18.50	32.50
6	0.30	22.00	39.50

input is three, which is the profit-maximizing input rate. This result is also shown in Figure 13-4, where the MRP_L function intersects the marginal expenditure function at point c, which corresponds to $L = 3$. Note that the wage rate paid labor, $11.50, which is determined by the labor supply function, is less than the marginal revenue product of labor. A monopsonist is able to hire workers at a wage less than the value of their contribution to output. This led to claims that firms with monopsony power exploit labor.

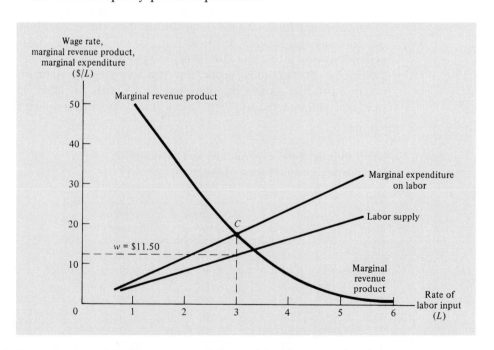

FIGURE 13-4 **Determination of the Wage Rate and Optimal Employment of Labor: Monopsonist.**

CASE STUDY _____

Economic Profits, Monopsony, and the Professional Sports Industry

Admission prices to most professional sports events are relatively expensive. One reason is that most major league teams have monopoly power in the market they serve. For example, in baseball, only in the metropolitan areas of Chicago, New York, San Francisco, and Los Angeles are there two teams; in all other cities there is only one provider of major league baseball entertainment. While there may be substitutes, such as high school, college, and semiprofessional teams, judging by attendance and ticket prices, these products are considered inferior to the major league brand of baseball.

Not only are most major league sports franchises monopoly sellers of baseball entertainment, they have traditionally been monopsony buyers of the services of the players. By using a system of drafting new players, each team was given the exclusive right to negotiate with the players it selected. The draft reduced the competition for the player's services and held wages down. To maintain this monopsony right, the league also used a reserve clause. Every player was required to sign a standard contract that contained a provision reserving the team's right to that player's services during the next season. The combination of the draft and the reserve clause effectively tied a player to one team forever. He could be traded to another team but was not free to shop around among other teams for a better salary.

In baseball, this system existed for about 70 years, but has now been substantially weakened, largely as the result of one owner failing to pay a bonus to a player. In 1974, Jim "Catfish" Hunter, an outstanding pitcher for the Oakland Athletics, claimed that he had not been paid one-half of the $100,000 specified by his contract.

He took the matter to arbitration, as required under baseball rules, and argued that he should be paid the remaining $50,000 and that he should be declared a free agent, thus allowing him to negotiate with any and all of the other teams. He won on both issues and subsequently signed a long-term contract with the New York Yankees for $750,000 per year—more than seven times his 1974 salary. The increase indicates that Oakland was paying him substantially less than his marginal revenue product!

This development was not lost on other players. In 1975, Andy Messersmith of the Los Angeles Dodgers and Dave McNally of the Baltimore Orioles both played without signing a contract. Then they went to arbitration, arguing that the reserve clause in their contract for the prior year was now nonbinding, as it only applied to the 1975 season. The arbitrator agreed, and both were declared free agents who could negotiate with any team.

After Messersmith and McNally signed contracts similar to that obtained by Hunter, other players realized the effect of the reserve clause in holding down salaries and demanded that a new contract system be developed. Negotiations between the players' association and management broke down over this issue, and a 17-day strike occurred during spring training in 1977. Both sides finally agreed to an arrangement wherein a player was tied to a team for six years (later reduced to five years), after which he automatically became a free agent. The result was a tremendous escalation in players' salaries; by 1992, the average exceeded $1,000,000 per year. Baseball owners were still charging monopoly prices, but they were now sharing the economic profits with the players.

KEY CONCEPTS _____

- A firm that is a perfect competitor in an input market faces a horizontal input supply function. Profit maximization for such firms requires that an input be increased until its marginal revenue product equals the price of the input.
- A firm that has market power in input markets faces an upward-sloping input supply function. The determination of the profit-maximizing price–quantity combination for the input is made by equating the firm's marginal revenue product and marginal expenditure on input functions.

The Correspondence Between Output and Input Decisions _____

The managerial decision about how much to produce is made simultaneously with the decision about how much input to employ. Suppose that the capital stock is fixed ($\overline{K}$) and the firm is jointly deciding the rate of output (Q) and the amount of labor to employ (L). Given the production function

$$Q = f(\overline{K}, L) \tag{13-6}$$

if either Q or L is specified, the other variable is determined. Thus in a technical sense, the firm has only one decision to make.

This can be shown in another way. Suppose that the firm is a perfect competitor in both the output and input markets. Profit maximization requires that the firm increase output until the price of output (P) equals marginal cost (MC), and efficient input resource utilization requires that labor be hired until the marginal revenue product (MRP) equals the unit price of labor (w). It can be shown that these two efficiency conditions,

$$P = MC \tag{13-7}$$

and

$$MRP_L = w \tag{13-8}$$

are equivalent; that is, if one is met, so is the other.

Recall that for the perfect competitor, the marginal revenue product is equal to marginal product multiplied by output price (P). Thus equation (13-8) can be rewritten as

$$MP_L \cdot P = w$$

Now divide both sides of this equation by the marginal product of labor (MP_L), yielding

$$P = \frac{w}{MP_L} \tag{13-9}$$

But the ratio of the wage rate to marginal product is simply marginal cost, so the condition specified by equation (13-9) is identical to that in equation (13-7). Thus the rule $P = MC$ implies that $MRP_L = w_L$, and vice versa. Although it is not demonstrated here, the profit maximization rules for a monopolist, $MR = MC$ and $MRP_L = w$, are also equivalent.

KEY CONCEPTS

- The decision to produce a given rate of output implies a decision to hire a certain rate of capital and labor and vice versa.
- The condition for a profit-maximizing output rate (i.e., $MR = MC$) is equivalent to the condition for a profit-maximizing input rate (i.e., MRP = input price).

Economic Rent

Rent is defined as a payment to any factor of production that has a relatively fixed supply. The term is often used to describe a return to land and reflects the notion that there is a fixed amount of land available.[2] As shown in Figure 13-5, when the supply of an input is fixed, the supply function is a vertical line. As a result, the price of that input or its rent is entirely determined by demand. If the demand curve is D_1, the price will be P_1. If the demand curve increases to D_2, the price will increase to P_2. Note that regardless of the change in price, the amount of the input supplied is unchanged.

Economic rent is a payment to a factor of production in excess of the minimum amount necessary to induce that factor into employment. Suppose that Q_1 in

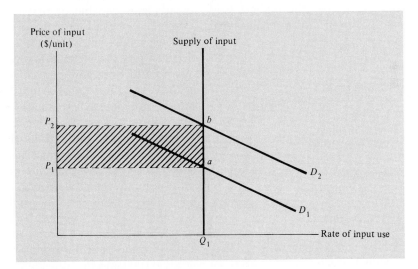

FIGURE 13-5 **Determination of the Input Price (Rent) When Supply Is Perfectly Inelastic.**

[2] Although in a strict sense the total amount of land in the world is fixed, from an economic perspective land is not fixed in supply. The relevant dimensions of the land input are the amount and quality of land in use. Both of these dimensions of the land input are variable. There is much land that is not used for any economic purpose. Periodically, some of this land is developed for agricultural or other uses, and thus the supply of land actually is increased in an economic sense.

Figure 13-5 represents the number of undeveloped acres in a particular tract of land. Assume that the cost of developing and marketing this land is equal to P_1. If the demand function is below D_1, the land will not be used because the market price would be less than the cost of supplying it. Only if the price is at least P_1 will the land be offered for use. Thus P_1 is said to be the *reservation price* for this input. At this price, the land is employed but there is no economic rent. If demand increased to D_2, the price would increase to P_2 and the rent would be the shaded rectangle defined by P_1P_2ba.

Only when the market price of an input is above the reservation price is there an economic rent paid. Because this return is over and above the amount necessary to employ the input, economic rent is sometimes said to be unearned. If part or all of this rent were taxed away, it would not change the resulting resource allocation.

CASE STUDY

Economic Rent in Professional Baseball

The previous case study discussed how the loss of monopsony power by the owners of major league baseball teams allowed player salaries to increase.

The All-Salary Team (i.e., the highest paid players at each position) for a recent year included the following:

Position	Player (Team)	Annual Salary
First base	Will Clark (San Francisco)	$4,750,000
Second base	Ryne Sandberg (Chicago Cubs)	6,475,000
Shortstop	Barry Larkin (Cincinnati Reds)	5,700,000
Third base	Kelly Gruber (Toronto Blue Jays)	4,633,000
Left field	Bobby Bonilla (New York Mets)	6,200,000
Center field	Kirby Puckett (Minnesota Twins)	5,200,000
Right field	Joe Carter (Toronto Blue Jays)	5,500,000
Catcher	Benito Santiago (Florida Marlins)	3,400,000
Pitcher	Dwight Gooden (New York Mets)	5,916,000

Certainly, a large part of these salaries represent economic rent. The following conceptual model explains how that rent would be determined. Suppose that there are a fixed number of atheletes capable of playing major league baseball and that each will do something other than play baseball unless the salary is at least $30,000 per year. Hypothetical demand and supply functions for these athletes are shown in the case figure. Note the unusual shape of the supply function. For these athletes, the supply function is horizontal at a price of $30,000 and then is vertical. This reflects the requirement that the typical athlete must have this much in salary per year to attract him to play baseball; otherwise, he would take another job. The $30,000 represents the opportunity cost of playing baseball and is the player's reservation price. Any return above that level is an economic rent. The intersection of demand and supply occurs at $1,000,000 and the athletes are each paid this wage rate. Of this amount, $970,000 is economic rent and $30,000 represents the payment necessary to attract these workers away from other jobs.

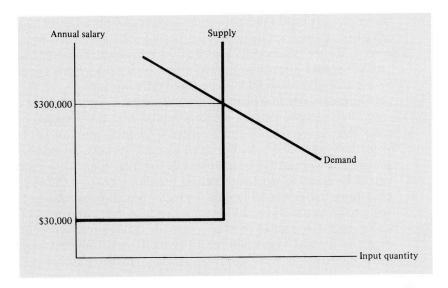

Economic Rent and Professional Baseball.

Wage and Income Differentials _____

There are large variations among the wage rates paid to different kinds of labor. Many unskilled workers are paid the federal minimum wage rate and others apparently have so little to offer employers that they are unable to find employment even at this low wage rate. In contrast, it is not unusual for senior lawyers to be paid $200 or more per hour, skilled surgeons may be paid several thousand dollars for an operation that may take less than an hour, and the salaries of some professional athletes are thousands of dollars per game. Why are there such large differentials in wage rates? Are they the result of market imperfections, such as a lack of information about prices and availability of competing services, or are there economic reasons that explain this phenomenon? Actually, there are important forces on both the demand and supply sides of the input market that explain most of the differences. These economic forces are considered in this section.

Demand-Side Considerations

All persons are not created equal. Differences in aptitude, intellectual ability, strength, and other individual attributes mean that some workers are more productive than others. The more productive workers add more to output and to the revenue of the firm. That is, their marginal revenue product is higher than for other workers. Therefore, they are able to command higher wage rates.

Some workers, such as salespersons and assembly line workers, are paid in direct proportion to their output. Thus their compensation is tied directly to their marginal revenue product, and the more productive workers will automatically receive higher wages than will their less productive counterparts. Even where pay is not tied directly to output in a formal sense, firms generally pay higher wages and salaries to their more productive workers.

Of course, some firms have plant-wide or even industry-wide wage rate schedules that prescribe that all workers in a certain job category be paid the same rate. Thus one might find differences in productivity among workers who are paid the same wage rate. But even in these cases, it is expected that the more productive workers will earn more in the long run. These workers will be the first to be asked to work overtime at premium rates, and the better workers will tend to be promoted to higher-paying supervisory positions. Furthermore, the less productive workers will be terminated if their contribution to output is significantly below that of their counterparts. Therefore, even in firms where there might be a fixed wage rate for all workers in a category, productive workers generally will earn significantly more than will their less productive associates.

Supply-Side Considerations

Adjustments in the supply of workers will also result in differential wage rates among jobs. Consider two jobs, A and B, where the skill and training requirements are much different. For example, job A may be a clerk in a retail clothing store that requires a high school education, whereas job B requires a college degree in electrical engineering. Clearly, it will be more costly for a person to prepare for job B. The cost of attending college for four or more years, including the opportunity cost of the lost income during that period, is substantial. That investment in education will not be made unless there is an expectation of higher earnings than can be earned in job A.

The wage adjustment for this required training is made on the supply side of the market. Considerably fewer high school graduates would attend college if they did not expect to increase their earning power. That is, fewer workers will make the necessary investment unless there is the prospect of higher earnings than can be earned in comparable jobs that do not require this training. Thus the supply function will be such that in any given wage, far fewer workers will offer their labor for sale for job B than for job A.

Other factors that result in supply-side adjustments in wage rates include risk of death or injury, working conditions, job content, and hours of work. Jobs that involve health risks, poor working conditions, unusual working hours, and/or tedious or strenuous work generally must pay a higher wage rate than jobs with more desirable characteristics. For example, holding constant other factors, a job that required heavy lifting in a very dirty place on the graveyard shift (midnight to 8 A.M.) would probably have to pay a premium wage rate to attract applicants. As in the preceding example, the wage adjustment for these job characteristics is made on the supply side of the market. At any given wage rate, more labor will be supplied to a firm offering a job with desirable characteristics than to a firm offering a less desirable job. Managers are aware of these factors and offer higher wages for less desirable jobs.

KEY CONCEPTS

- Economic rent is defined as the return to a factor of production in excess of the payment necessary to keep the factor in its current employment.
- Wage differentials among workers reflect demand-side considerations, such as greater productivity, and supply-side forces, including training requirements, health risks, and working conditions.

CASE STUDY

The Premium for Accepting Risk

The typical answer to the question "What value do you place on your life?" would be that it is of infinite value. Few people would offer to give up their life in return for a monetary gain except under the most extraordinary circumstances. Indeed, one of the arguments for a military draft is that military service is so risky that it is not possible to attract adequate volunteers by offering higher pay and benefits. However, the success of the all-volunteer military in the United States has disproved that notion.

Reflection on individual behavior, particularly with respect to job selection, suggests that people will take all kinds of risks to obtain economic and other kinds of rewards. Some recreational thrills, such as skydiving, hang-gliding, and skiing, can only be obtained by assuming a significant risk of injury. Many drivers exceed the speed limit to conserve on time. In fact, even driving at the speed limit is risky. To eliminate all deaths from vehicle accidents might require speed limits below 10 mph and vehicles built like Army tanks. For most people, the opportunity cost of eliminating traffic deaths is simply too high, and they are willing to take their chances at or above current speed limits. Furthermore, people regularly accept work in occupations that involve significant risk of injury. For example, those who repair the steam systems of nuclear power plants often are paid as much as $100 for a few minutes of work. The reason is because of the exposure to radiation that increases the risk of cancer and other diseases.

Many civilian occupations are more risky than being in military service during a war. During the Vietnam War, an average of about 7,000 U.S. servicemen were killed each year. At that time, there were some 3 million men and women in the military forces. Thus the death rate was about 2.33 per 1,000 employed in that field. Thaler and Rosen studied death rates and income differentials for a number of high-risk jobs. Several of these jobs, including guards and lumberjacks, had annual death rates higher than that for a military force at war! Jobs such as firefighter and police officer, where risk is often publicized, are actually less risky than a number of other jobs. Annual death rates per 1,000 employees for some of these occupations are shown here.

Occupation	Annual Death Rate Per Thousand Workers	Occupation	Annual Death Rate Per Thousand Workers
Firemen	0.44	Mine workers	1.76
Police officers	0.78	Lumberjacks	2.56
Electricians	0.93	Guards	2.67
Crane operators	1.47		

SOURCE: R. Thaler and S. Rosen, "The Value of Saving a Life: Evidence from the Labor Market," in N. E. Terlecky, ed., *Household Production and Consumption* (New York: Columbia University Press—National Bureau of Economic Research, 1975), pp. 265–298.

Thaler and Rosen also analyzed the incremental annual wage associated with these jobs. This increment measures the trade-off people are willing to make between risk and income. On average, it was found that about $700 in additional annual wages are needed to offset the additional risk associated with the incidence of one more death per 1,000 workers per year. The death rate for lumberjacks (2.56) suggests that the average worker would have to be paid about $1,800 dollars per year in additional annual wages (i.e., 2.56 × $700) to accept the additional risk compared to a job where the risk of death is near zero.

Labor Unions

About 16 percent of the nonagricultural labor force in the United States are members of labor unions. Where workers are organized, the nature of management–worker negotiations is different than for firms without labor unions. The union may act as a monopolist, that is, as a single seller of labor to the firm.

In this section two topics related to labor unions are considered. First, the economics of collective bargaining between firms and labor unions are discussed. The second considers alternative objectives that might influence labor union behavior.

Labor Unions and Collective Bargaining

Labor unions represent workers in negotiations with management concerning wage rates, fringe benefits, and working conditions. Where the workers of a firm are members of a union, wages are not set unilaterally by management in response to market conditions. Rather, they are determined by negotiations between management and union representatives. Of course, general labor market conditions, including wage rates for comparable workers (both union and nonunion) in other firms and industries influence these negotiations.

In some industries, collective bargaining is done on an industry-wide basis. Representatives from the major companies comprise an industry bargaining team and the labor union has a bargaining team that represents the workers. The result is similar to a bilateral monopoly situation where a single seller faces a single buyer in a market. The industry negotiating team acts as a monopsonist or the sole buyer of labor in the industry, and the union acts as a monopolist or the sole seller of labor in the industry.

The relevant labor demand and supply functions for such a situation are shown in Figure 13-6. Consider the union as a seller of labor. Industry demand for this labor is shown by the demand curve DD, the marginal revenue product of labor, and MR is the marginal revenue curve associated with the labor demand curve. The supply function for labor is shown by line SS, and the marginal expenditure for labor is shown by ME.

If it could act without restraint, the industry bargaining team would maximize profit by equating the labor demand curve and the marginal expenditure curve

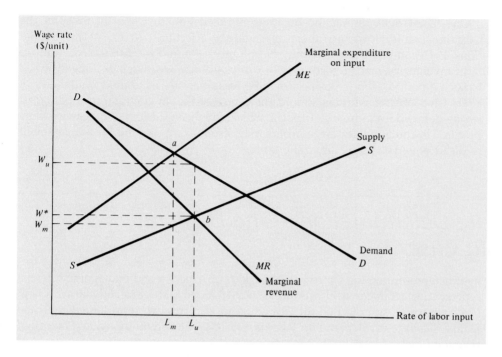

FIGURE 13-6 **Wage Rate and Employment Determination for a Bilateral Monopoly.**

at point a and would hire L_m units of labor. At this input rate, the marginal revenue product is equal to the marginal expenditure on labor. The price or wage rate is determined by the point on the supply curve corresponding to the quantity L_m, that is, W_m. Note that this wage is less than the marginal revenue product, meaning that workers are not paid their marginal contribution to output.

In contrast, assume that a labor union acting as a monopoly seller of labor wants to maximize the total surplus paid to industry workers. In Figure 13-6, the area below the wage rate but above the supply curve can be thought of as a surplus paid to workers over and above the amount necessary to have them offer their labor for sale. In a sense, it is a form of economic rent. For example, workers would offer L_u units of labor for sale at a wage of W^*. That is, W^* corresponds to that point on the labor supply curve where L_u units of labor are offered for sale. If they are paid a wage above W^*, they are earning a surplus. The total surplus accruing to all workers is maximized by equating the marginal revenue function and the supply curve at point b to determine the quantity hired of L_u and a wage rate of W_u. The wage rate W_u is that point on the industry labor demand curve corresponding to quantity L_u. Not surprisingly, the union approach results in a higher wage rate and more workers employed than occurs if the management objective is followed.

The exact result of the bargaining process is indeterminate. If management has much more bargaining power than the union, the wage rate may end up being close to W_m. Conversely, if the relative power lies with the labor union, the negotiations may result in a wage rate closer to W_u.

One factor determining the outcome is the negotiating skill of those at the bargaining table. However, other forces will also affect the outcome of the negotiations. For example, if the economy is in a recession and the firms have built up large inventories, management may be in a position to weather a prolonged strike. In such a period, labor's position may be weak because of limited availability of alternative jobs for workers should there be a strike. In contrast, in a period of strong demand for industry output, a strike may mean the loss of otherwise large profits. This potential for large profits may also make it difficult for management to plead poverty at the bargaining table.

EXAMPLE

Wage Rate Determination—The Bilateral Monopoly Case

Teams representing the United Steelworkers of America and management teams representing all major steel producers in the United States are negotiating a new labor contract. Assume that all workers and all firms are represented by these teams. The industry demand for labor is $w = 200 - 2L$ and the associated marginal revenue function is

$$MR = 200 - 4L$$

The supply curve for labor and marginal expenditure or labor function are

$$w = 8 + 4L \qquad \text{and} \qquad ME = 8 + 8L$$

where w is the daily wage rate and L is the number of workers employed in thousands. Determine the wage rate and level of employment that will result from these negotiations.

SOLUTION

Because virtually all firms and workers are represented by the two teams, this is a bilateral monopoly problem. As such, the solution will depend on the relative bargaining power of the two groups and their negotiating skills, and a unique solution does not exist. However, two extreme solutions can be determined.

First, assume that management is able to dominate the negotiations and dictate the terms of the contract. The amount of labor hired is determined by equating the labor demand and marginal expenditure functions

$$200 - 2L = 8 + 8L$$

and solving for L:

$$L = 19.2$$

The wage rate is found by substituting $L = 19.2$ into the labor supply function

$$w = 8 + 4(L) = 8 + 4(19.2)$$

or

$$w = 84.80$$

If the union is able to dictate terms of the negotiations, the quantity of labor hired would be found by equating the marginal revenue and labor supply functions and solving for L, that is,

$$200 - 4L = 8 + 4L$$

or

$$L = 24$$

The wage rate would be determined by substituting $L = 24$ into the labor demand function:

$$w = 200 - 2L = 200 - 2(24)$$

or

$$w = 152$$

The union solution, of course, has both a higher wage rate and a greater employment than the management solution. In general, neither side would be able to dictate the terms of the agreement, and therefore the actual solution would lie somewhere between these two extremes.

Union Objectives

In the bilateral monopoly example, it was assumed that the goal of the union is to maximize the net surplus to its members. This surplus is maximized where the marginal revenue curve intersects the supply curve. Note that this approach is analogous to the monopolist maximizing profit by equating marginal revenue and marginal cost. In a sense, the labor union is a monopolist in this labor market and the supply function serves as the marginal cost curve.

Obviously, the union may have other objectives. For example, it may want to have all union members fully employed or it may want to maximize the aggregate income of the membership. To analyze the implications of these alternative goals, consider the demand for labor function and the associated marginal revenue function shown in Figure 13-7. Suppose that there are L_2 workers in the union. To keep all these workers employed requires that the firm bargain for a wage rate of W_2, the wage rate associated with L_2 on the demand curve.

Conversely, if the objective is maximizing aggregate wages, the union would want to move to L_1, the point where the MR curve intersects the horizontal axis. The wage rate associated with this point is W_1, again determined by the demand curve. In this case, however, there is an unemployment problem, as $L_2 - L_1$ members of the union will not be employed. Which members are to be unemployed? Will it be those with the least seniority or those with the fewest skills? This is a difficult problem for union leaders to resolve, but it is clear that some union leaders have bargained for and obtained wage agreements that have led to unemployment for a significant number of the union members. For example, shortly after organizing as the United Mine Workers, coal miners bargained for and won much higher wage rates, but at the cost of a significantly higher unemployment rate for mine workers.

There are still other objectives the union leaders may have, such as maintaining their positions of leadership and power in the union. Usually, objectives of union

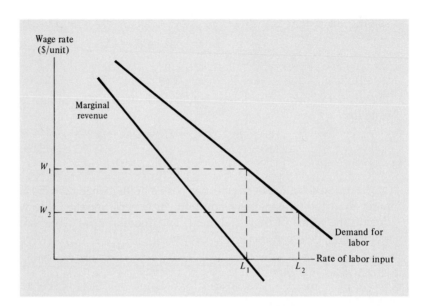

FIGURE 13-7 **Employment with Different Assumptions About Labor Union Objectives.**

leaders are stated in vague terms such as "higher wages," "better working conditions," or "more job security," and it is very difficult to identify the true objectives of the union. The final result of collective bargaining may reveal more about the true objectives than would any statement by union leaders.

KEY CONCEPTS

- Collective bargaining can be thought of as a bilateral monopoly situation where the firm acts as a monopsonist or the sole buyer of labor and the union acts as a monopolist or the sole seller of labor.
- The outcome of collective bargaining will depend not only on the relevant demand and supply functions but also on the relative bargaining skill and strength of management and union leaders.
- Alternative labor union objectives include full employment of all members of the union, maximization of the net surplus to workers, and maximization of aggregate wages paid to members.

Minimum Wage Laws

Managers in the United States and in many other countries work in an environment where government has set a minimum hourly wage rate for most workers. Such laws generally require that workers be paid not less than a specified rate per hour. Although many economists argue that such laws reduce total employment, especially for young workers with limited job skills, these laws have persisted for decades. The appropriate managerial response to a minimum wage law is the focus of this section.

Consider a firm that operates in product and input markets that are both perfectly competitive. The firm's labor demand (MRP_L) function and the supply curve for labor are shown in Figure 13-8. Initially, assume that the wage rate (w_0) has been set in the market and the firm's only decision is the amount of labor to hire. This amount is determined by the intersection of the demand function with the horizontal supply curve and results in a labor input rate of L_0 units per period.

If a government-mandated minimum wage rate is imposed at any wage rate less than w_0, it has no effect on the amount of labor employed or the market wage rate. However, if a minimum wage rate higher than w_0, say w_m, is legislated, that rate effectively becomes the supply function of labor facing the firm. The firm uses the same profit-maximizing rule (i.e., employ labor until $MRP_L = w_m$) but now employs only L_m units. Employment by the firm has been reduced by $L_0 - L_m$ units per period. While those workers who have kept their jobs are better off because their wage rate has increased, other workers are worse off because they are no longer employed.

Labor unions have generally supported increases in the minimum wage. This is somewhat curious because the vast majority of union workers earn substantially more than the minimum wage. One explanation is that skilled workers are a substitute for unskilled workers. Therefore, the cross-price elasticity between the quantity of skilled union labor employed and the wage rate for unskilled labor is positive. If the price of unskilled work increases because of a higher minimum wage, the demand for skilled workers should increase, resulting in higher wages for them. Thus one possible result of a higher minimum wage is more unemployed low-wage workers and more employed skilled workers who will be paid a higher wage than before.

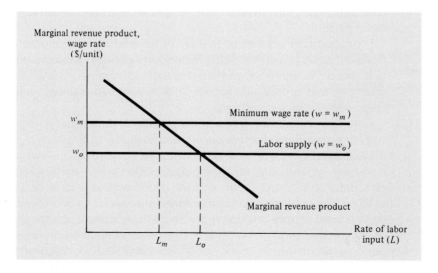

FIGURE 13-8 **Managerial Response to a Minimum Wage Law.**

KEY CONCEPTS ───────────────────────────────────────

- Minimum wage laws generally require that firms pay workers at least a specified wage rate per hour.
- For firms that are perfect competitors in the labor market, a minimum wage rate that is set above the market wage rate will reduce the amount of labor the firm will employ.

Summary ───────────────────────────────────────

Input prices are determined by the interaction of supply and demand. The demand for inputs is derived from the demand for the output that those inputs are used to produce. The marginal revenue product function, computed by multiplying marginal revenue and marginal product, is the firm's input demand function.

Determining input prices is important because these prices are used in deciding on the optimal mix of labor, capital, and natural resources to be employed by the firm. The approach to input price determination depends on the structure of both the input and output markets. A perfect competitor in an input market faces a constant input price. Thus the only decision made by the firm is the quantity of the input to be employed. A monopsonist has market power in the input market and thus faces an upward-sloping input supply function. The input price and quantity employed by the monopsonist are determined by the intersection of the input demand function with the firm's marginal expenditure on input function.

There is a unique correspondence between output and input decisions. A decision to produce a given rate of output implies a decision to hire certain rates of capital and labor input and vice versa. The condition for a profit-maximizing output rate (i.e., marginal cost equals marginal revenue) is equivalent to the condition for a profit-maximizing input rate (i.e., marginal revenue product equals input price).

Economic rent is a return to a factor of production in excess of the minimum payment necessary to keep that factor in its present employment. Wage differentials among workers reflect both demand-side forces, such as differences in productivity, and supply-side factors, such as required training requirements, health risks, and working conditions.

Collective bargaining refers to the process of determining wage rates and other working conditions through negotiation between labor union representatives and management from one or several firms. In some cases, collective bargaining can be thought of as a bilateral monopoly situation where the firm acts as a monopsonist, the sole buyer of labor, and the union acts as a monopolist, the sole seller of labor. The outcome of collective bargaining will depend not only on the relevant demand and supply functions but also on the relative bargaining skill and strength of management and union leaders. Objectives of labor unions include full employment of all members of the union, maximization of aggregate wages paid to members, and maximization of the net surplus to workers.

Minimum wage laws require that firms pay labor at least a specified wage per hour. If this wage is above that prevailing in a perfectly competitive labor market, the firm will reduce the amount of labor hired and unemployment will result.

Discussion Questions

13-1. What determines the mix of labor and capital used by the firm to produce output? Explain.

13-2. Explain why the term *derived demand* is used to describe the demand for factors of production.

13-3. Provide an intuitive explanation for the profit-maximizing rule that the firm should hire an input until the marginal revenue product of the input is equal to the additional cost of the input.

13-4. Why is the input supply function horizontal for a perfect competitor in the input market and upward sloping for a monopsonist?

13-5. Why is it that there is no unique input price and quantity of input hired in the bilateral monopoly case? What factors will play a role in determining that price and quantity?

13-6. Given that a firm should always be producing efficiently, explain why it is impossible for management to separate the decisions about the rate of output to be produced and the rates of capital and labor to be employed?

13-7. The annual salary of many players in the National Basketball Association is more than $1,000,000. Is it "right" for these athletes to make many times more than the average American worker? If that average salary were reduced by one-half, how many players do you think would leave the NBA for other occupations? Explain.

13-8. For many years the United States and other countries used a draft system to maintain required personnel levels in their military forces. During most of the period when the draft existed, earnings in military service, including such fringe benefits as housing and meals, were substantially less than in comparable civilian occupations. Supporters of the draft system argued that military service was sufficiently dangerous that regardless of the wage rate, there would not be adequate volunteers. Do you agree or disagree with this position? Explain.

13-9. The leader of a major labor union claims that the union's objective is full employment for all members. Despite an unemployment rate of 15 percent for workers in this union, labor negotiators are demanding a 15 percent increase in wage rates for each of the next three years. Workers in other industries have been receiving wage increases of 8 or 9 percent per year. Are the actions of the union negotiators consistent with the alleged objective of the union? Explain.

Problems

13-1. Suppose that the demand and supply functions for unskilled labor in an economy are

$$DEMAND: L_d = 10 - 0.5w$$
$$SUPPLY: L_s = 6 + 0.9w$$

where L is millions of workers and w is the hourly wage rate.

a. Determine the equilibrium wage rate and number of workers employed.
b. If the U.S. Congress sets a minimum wage of $4.25 per hour, what will be the wage rate and the quantity of labor employed? Compared to your answer for part (a), how many workers will lose their jobs?
c. If the minimum wage rate is set at $5.00, what will be the wage rate, the number of workers employed, and the number unemployed? Compare these answers to those in part (a).

13-2. Suppose the demand for centers on NBA basketball teams is given by the equation

$$L_d = 400{,}000 - 2w$$

while the supply of centers is given by the function

$$L_s = \begin{cases} 32 \text{ if } w \geq \$40{,}000 \\ 0 \text{ if } w < \$40{,}000 \end{cases}$$

where L is number of players and w is the annual salary.
a. Graph the demand and supply functions.
b. Determine the equilibrium wage rate for a center in the NBA.
c. Suppose a sudden drop in attendance and number of television viewers shifted the demand function to

$$L_d^* = 300{,}000 - 3w$$

How would the annual salary change? Would the number of workers playing professional basketball be any different than before the demand curve shifted?
d. Based on the supply function, what is your best estimate of the opportunity cost of playing center in the NBA?

13-3. Consider a firm in a perfectly competitive output market where the price of the product is $10 per unit. Given the following information on the total product of labor function, determine the firm's demand schedule for labor (i.e., MRP_L) by completing the table.

Quantity of Labor	Total Product	Marginal Product	Marginal Revenue Product
0	0	—	—
1	21		
2	30		
3	38		
4	42		
5	43		
6	40		

Suppose this firm is a monopsonist that faces the following labor supply schedule. Use these data to determine the firm's total and marginal expenditure on labor schedules.

Wage Rate	Quantity of Labor Supplied	Total Expenditure on Labor	Marginal Expenditure on Labor
20	0	_____	—
22	1	_____	_____
25	2	_____	_____
30	3	_____	_____
35	4	_____	_____
40	5	_____	_____
50	6	_____	_____

Use these data to determine how much labor the firm should employ. What will the wage rate be? Explain.

13-4. Demonstrate that, for a monopolist, the profit-maximizing condition that marginal revenue equals marginal cost (i.e., $MR = MC$) implies that the marginal revenue product of capital must equal the price of capital (i.e., $MRP_K = r$).

13-5. A team representing management of all firms in the automatic widget industry is currently negotiating a new three-year contract with the leaders of the United Widget Workers of America (UWW) labor union. The industry demand function for labor (i.e., the marginal revenue product of labor) is

$$MRP_L = 20 - 2L$$

the marginal revenue function associated with the demand curve is

$$MR = 20 - 4L$$

and the labor supply and marginal expenditure on input functions facing the industry are

$$W = 5 + 2L$$
$$ME = 5 + 4L$$

where L is the number of workers in thousands and W is the hourly wage rate.
a. If the management team can dominate the negotiations and dictate the terms of the agreement, what wage rate and level of employment will be determined?
b. If the labor union team can dominate the negotiations and dictate the terms of the agreement, what wage rate and level of employment will be determined?

13-6. The supply of apartments in a city is fixed at 2,000 units; no new units can be built because of shortage of water. The demand for these units is given by $Q_d = 5,000 - 5P$ where P is the monthly price of a unit and Q is number of units. The reservation price for each unit is $300 per month.
a. Determine the equilibrium monthly price of an apartment.
b. What is the economic rent per unit and the total economic rent?
c. A government rent-control ordinance is passed, limiting the monthly price to $400 per month. Determine the number of units demanded at this price.

How might apartment owners respond to a situation when the quantity demanded exceeds the quantity supplied, but when rent cannot be increased?

13-7. Assume that all jobs are identical except for the risk of being killed at work. If a job with zero risk of death pays $20,000 per year, determine the annual wage in each of the jobs listed here. (Use the information provided on page 448 regarding the additional amount necessary to compensate for the risk of being killed.)

Occupation	Annual Death Rate Per Thousand Workers
Police officer	0.78
Crane operator	1.47
Mine worker	1.76
Guard	2.67

Problem Requiring Calculus

13-8. The market demand and supply functions for Rhubarb Field Dolls are

$$Q_D = 2,000 - 250P$$

and

$$Q_S = 600 + 100P$$

where Q_D is quantity demanded, Q_S is quantity supplied, and P is the price.

Adamco Inc. manufactures these dolls using the following production function:

$$Q = K^{0.5}L^{0.5}$$

where Q is the rate of output, K is capital, and L is labor. Adamco is the largest employer in a small town and faces the following labor supply function:

$$w = 0.5L_S$$

where w is the wage rate.

If the capital input is fixed at 225, determine the profit-maximizing labor input, rate of output, and wage rate.

VI

Long-Term Planning Decisions

CHAPTER 14

Risk and Decision Making

Preview _____

Before introducing new products, managers undertake consumer surveys, assess product lines of their competitors, and closely check estimated production costs. These actions are taken to increase the information base on which the decision will be made. Still, there are few sure things in the world of management. Many spectacular failures have occurred despite management having taken all possible steps to ensure success. It is simply not possible to predict consumer behavior or changes in production technology with complete accuracy. Every decision carries with it the prospect that something will go wrong and that instead of earning large profits as expected, losses are incurred. Despite all of the modern techniques, learning to make decisions where there are risk and uncertainty is the essence of modern management.

In marketing goods and services, firms often try to reduce the risk faced by potential buyers. For example, the Ford Motor Company offers a three-year or 36,000-mile warranty on most important parts of its cars and trucks. The Mauna Kea Beach Hotel in Hawaii offers its guests one free night of lodging if it rains for 30 minutes on any day that the guest is at the hotel. These actions reduce the risk to the customer, but they increase it for the firm.

Managerial decisions are made in different risk environments. In the case of decision making under certainty, all relevant dimensions of the decision are known. For example, in Chapter 8 a linear programming problem was formulated in terms of deciding how much of each of two products should be produced given a specified profit rate for each and specified processing time required for each product on each of these machines. All of the relevant information was assumed to be known with certainty. The result was a unique solution that maximized the firm's profit. That is, there was only one relevant outcome of this decision.

In decision making under uncertainty, there are several, perhaps many, outcomes of a decision, but the probability of each of those outcomes occurring is unknown. For example, a firm may be considering the production of an altogether new product. Because consumers have had no experience with the product, there is no way to estimate the potential demand for it. The marketing department may undertake various market surveys in an attempt to estimate how many people might buy the product, but it is doubtful that much confidence can be placed in such efforts. There may be no way to provide anything but some rough guesses about demand.

Finally, decision making under risk applies when all significant outcomes of a decision are known as the probability of each outcome occurring. For example, consider the drilling of a well in an already proven oil field. Suppose that 100 wells have been completed, of which ten are producing 2,000 to 3,000 barrels per day (BPD), 40 are producing 5,000 to 10,000 BPD, and the remaining 50 are producing 10,000 to 15,000 BPD. This kind of historical experience allows the decision maker some basis for assessing the probability of success of the new well.

The focus of this chapter is on decision making under risk. The objective will be to develop guidelines for making rational decisions given the decision maker's attitude about (i.e., preference for) risk. First, the concept of risk is formally defined, and then the principles of probability developed in Chapter 2 are used to quantitatively measure risk. Next, the role of risk in making decisions is analyzed; basic to this is an understanding of the concept of the manager's preference for risk. Then methods for adjusting decisions for risk are developed and applied. Finally, the use of decision trees is explained.

The Concept of Risk

The analysis of risk is based largely on the concepts of probability and probability distributions that were developed in Chapter 2. First, terms such as *strategy*, *state of nature*, and *outcome* need to be defined. A strategy refers to one of several alternative plans or courses of action that could be implemented in order to achieve a managerial goal. For example, a manager might be considering three strategies designed to increase profits: (1) build a new, more efficient plant that will allow production at lower cost; (2) develop a new marketing program designed to increase sales volume; or (3) redesign the product in order to allow lower-cost production and increased sales due to greater consumer acceptance. A state of nature refers to some condition that may exist in the future that will have a significant effect on the success of any strategy. In making the decision about building a new plant, an important state of nature is the economic climate expected to prevail for the next few years. In this context, the possible states of nature might be (1) recession, (2) normal business conditions, or (3) economic boom. An outcome specifies the gain or loss (usually measured in dollars) associated with a particular combination of strategy and state of nature. For instance, the outcomes associated with the decision to build a new plant might be the present value of all future net profits. Finally, a payoff matrix shows the outcome associated with each combination of strategy and state of nature. An example of a payoff matrix is shown in Table 14-1. For example, if a new plant is built and a recession occurs, the loss is estimated to be $40 million. Conversely, the combination of a new marketing program and normal business conditions would yield an estimated

TABLE 14-1 **Payoff Matrix: Profits (Millions) for Each Strategy–State of Nature Combination**

Strategy	*State of Nature (Economic Conditions)*		
	Recession	*Normal*	*Boom*
New plant	$−40	$25	$40
New marketing program	−20	35	70
New product design	−15	30	60

profit of $35 million. If the probabilities of each state of nature are known, then the combination of those probabilities and the payoffs for each strategy constitute a probability distribution.

Risk refers to the amount of variability among the outcomes associated with a particular strategy. Where there is only one probable outcome of a decision, there is said to be little risk; where there are many possible outcomes with substantially different dollar returns, there is said to be substantial risk. For example, a manager with $1 million to invest may be faced with two alternatives. She could buy a one-year Treasury bill yielding 6 percent interest. At the end of a year, the $1 million investment will return $1,060,000. The only risk associated with this investment is that the federal government might be unable to pay its debts. This is so unlikely that there is essentially no risk associated with this investment (i.e., there is only one outcome). Indeed, Treasury bills are often referred to as a riskless investment.

The second alternative is the drilling of an oil well in an unproven field. If oil is found, the well will immediately be worth $50 million, the present value of all net profits from selling this oil. If oil is not found, the well will be worth nothing. This is a risky investment because there is great variability in the range of possible outcomes. In general, the greater the variation in outcomes, the greater is the risk. Thus the definition of risk is based on the variation of the outcomes of a particular decision.

KEY CONCEPTS

- Risk exists when there is a range of possible outcomes associated with a decision and the probabilities of those outcomes occurring are known. If those probabilities are not known, the decision maker is said to face uncertainty.
- A strategy is a plan or course of action designed to achieve a management goal.
- A state of nature refers to a condition that may exist in the future that will have a significant effect on the success of a strategy.
- An outcome is the gain or loss associated with a particular combination of strategy and state of nature.
- A payoff matrix lists the outcomes associated with each strategy–state of nature combination.

Risk and Decision Making

Having defined risk and reviewed some of the related terminology, the task now is to develop quantitative measures of return and risk and to show how they are applied in decision making. Because individuals have different preferences concerning risk taking, it is also important that such preferences be identified and their effect on decisions evaluated. Obviously, individuals respond to the same risky choices in different ways. For example, a few people are willing to risk death or serious injury in their recreational pursuits (e.g., hang gliding), while others prefer a game of Monopoly. One reason for these preferences is their attitude about risk. Rational decision making requires that the expected return be determined, the risk be measured, and that there be information about the manager's preference for risk.

Risk–Return Evaluation Statistics

Recall from Chapter 2 that three statistics were developed to describe a probability distribution. Given a set of outcomes, X_i, and the probability of each occurring, P_i, these statistics are

Expected value or mean:

$$\mu = \sum_{i=1}^{n} P_i(X_i) \tag{14-1}$$

Standard deviation:

$$\sigma = \sqrt{\sum_{i=1}^{n} P_i(X_i - \mu)^2} \tag{14-2}$$

Coefficient of variation:

$$\nu = \frac{\sigma}{\mu} \tag{14-3}$$

These statistics have a direct application in measuring the expected return and risk associated with any business decision for which a set of outcomes and their probabilities have been determined. The expected value, the standard deviation, and the coefficient of variation will be referred to as risk–return evaluation statistics.

Suppose that two investments, I and II, are being considered. Both investments require an initial cash outlay of $100 and have a life of five years. The dollar returns on each depend on the rate of inflation over the five-year period. Of course, the inflation rate is not known with certainty, but suppose that the collective judgment of economists is that the probability of no inflation is 0.20, the probability of moderate inflation is 0.50, and the probability of rapid inflation is 0.30. The outcomes are defined as the present value of net profits for the next five years. These outcomes for each state of nature (i.e., rate of inflation) for each investment are shown in Table 14-2.

Analysis of these investments can be made by calculating and comparing the three evaluation statistics for each alternative. The expected value (μ) is an estimate of the expected dollar return for the investment. Because risk has been defined in terms of the variability in outcomes, the standard deviation (σ) is a measure of risk associated with the investment. The larger σ is, the greater the risk. Risk per dollar of expected return is measured by the coefficient of variation (ν).

TABLE 14-2 **Probability Distributions for Two Investment Alternatives**

State of Nature	Probability (P_i)	Outcome (X_i)
Investment I		
No inflation	0.20	100
Moderate inflation	0.50	200
Rapid inflation	0.30	400
Investment II		
No inflation	0.20	150
Moderate inflation	0.50	200
Rapid inflation	0.30	250

The evaluation statistics for each investment alternative are computed as follows:

INVESTMENT I

$$\mu_1 = \sum_{i=1}^{n} P_i X_i = 0.2(100) + 0.5(200) + 0.3(400) = 240$$

$$\sigma_1 = \sqrt{\sum_{i=1}^{n} P_i(X_i - \mu)^2} = \sqrt{0.2(100 - 240)^2 + 0.5(200 - 240)^2 + 0.3(400 - 240)^2}$$

$$= 111.36$$

$$\nu_1 = \frac{\sigma_1}{\mu_1} = \frac{111.36}{240} = 0.46$$

INVESTMENT II

$$\mu_{II} = 0.2(150) + 0.5(200) + 0.3(250) = 205$$

$$\sigma_{II} = \sqrt{0.2(150 - 205)^2 + 0.5(200 - 205)^2 + 0.3(250 - 205)^2} = 35.00$$

$$\nu_{II} = \frac{35.00}{205} = 0.17$$

The expected return for investment I of $240 is higher than for II ($205), but I is a riskier investment because $\sigma_I = 111.36$ is greater than $\sigma_{II} = 35$. Also, risk per dollar of expected returns for I ($\nu_{II} = 0.46$) is higher than for II ($\nu_{II} = 0.17$). Which is the better investment? The choice is not clear. It depends on the investor's attitude about taking risks. A young entrepreneur may well prefer I, whereas an older worker investing a few dollars in a retirement account where risk ought to be minimized might prefer II. The entrepreneur is in a better position to absorb a loss if it occurs and is probably accustomed to investing in risky ventures.

KEY CONCEPT _____

- Given a probability distribution for the outcomes of a business decision, the statistics of that distribution can be used to evaluate return and risk:

—The expected value or mean is a measure of expected return.
—The standard deviation is a measure of risk.
—The coefficient of variation is a measure of risk per dollar of return.

Risk Preference

Generally, higher returns are associated with higher risk. Indeed, the essence of economics is making choices where there is a trade-off. Virtually all investment choices require giving up expected returns for higher risk or taking more risk in the expectation of a greater expected return. Thus, any decision will reflect the manager's attitude or preference for risk, and these preferences differ substantially among individuals. For example, some investors are so averse to taking risk that they keep all their assets in bank deposits insured by the federal government. Others are willing to risk all they own and can borrow to finance extremely risky ventures such as drilling oil wells or buying contracts in the fast-moving commodities market. There must be a reward for taking risk, and this comes in the form of higher returns. The following example will help to explain the concepts of risk and risk preference.

Consider the following gamble: "I will toss a coin ten times. If a head appears each time, you must pay me $1,000. If tails appear one or more times, I will pay you a dollar." Most people would reject this offer even though it is a fair game. That is, if the game were played many times, the amount lost would equal the amount won. However, the nature of the game is such that on any one trial the player could lose a large amount and stands to win only a small amount. The probability distribution for the return or payoff for each outcome of the game is shown in Table 14-3. The probability of a head appearing on ten consecutive tosses of a coin is given by $(\frac{1}{2})^{10}$ or 0.001. The probability that there is at least one tail in ten tosses is 1 minus the probability that there would be ten heads or $(1.0 - 0.001) = 0.999$. These probabilities multiplied by their associated payoffs yield an expected value of zero; therefore, it is fair game.

To understand why most people would reject this gamble, one must understand the concept of preference for risk. It is assumed that individuals can associate satisfaction with money. More money usually means more satisfaction, although for many people each additional dollar brings less satisfaction than the previous dollar did. Economists use the term *utility* as a measure of satisfaction. Although an individual's satisfaction is virtually impossible to measure, it will be assumed that this can be done for a hypothetical individual. This assumption will make it

TABLE 14-3 **Probability Distribution and Expected Value for Coin-Tossing Example**

Outcome	Probability	Payoff	Probability × Payoff
Ten heads	0.001	$-1,000	$-1.00
At least one tail	0.999	+ 1	+1.00
		Expected payoff =	0

easier to develop several important concepts. One relationship between utility and money is shown in Figure 14-1a. The curve shows that relationship just suggested; that is, utility increases as money increases but at a continually decreasing rate. Thus, the function is concave to the horizontal axis. A person having a concave utility function is said to be *risk averse*.

Suppose that this person has $10,000 and is offered the opportunity to bet $5,000 on the toss of a coin. If a head is tossed, she wins $5,000; if a tail is tossed, she loses $5,000. She now faces the choice of having $10,000 with certainty if she chooses not to bet (this option is called the *certain prospect*) or of having $15,000 with probability 0.5 or $5,000 with probability 0.5. The latter option is called the *uncertain prospect*. The expected monetary value of the uncertain prospect is

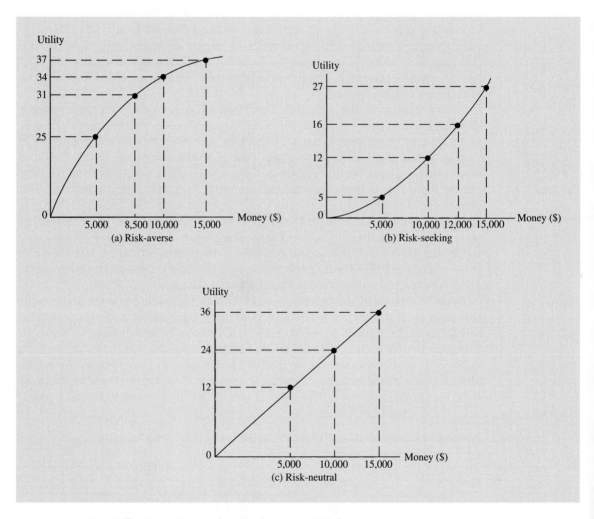

FIGURE 14-1 **Utility Functions and Attitude Toward Risk.**

$10,000, that is,

$$\mu = 0.5(\$5{,}000) + 0.5(\$15{,}000) = \$10{,}000$$

which is the same as the dollar value of the certain prospect.

Now, consider the analysis in terms of the utility associated with each dollar payoff. For a risk-averse person, the dollar payoffs are translated into utility by using a function like that shown in Figure 14-1a. The certain prospect (i.e., having $10,000) is associated with a utility of about 34. The expected value in utility of the uncertain prospect is determined as follows. A $5,000 payoff corresponds to a utility value of 25, and a $15,000 outcome is associated with a utility of 37. Thus, by substituting these utility values for the payoffs, the expected value in terms of utility is computed as

$$\mu = 0.5(25) + 0.5(37) = 31$$

This is less than the utility (34) associated with certain prospect. Thus, this utility-maximizing person prefers the certain prospect and chooses not to accept the wager.

Note that an amount of $8,500 with certainty also would yield a utility level of 31. This amount is said to be the *certainty equivalent* of the gamble. The individual would pay up to $1,500 (i.e., the difference between the expected value of the gamble and the certainty equivalent) in order to avoid the gamble. This suggests a formal definition of risk aversion. If the certainty equivalent of the gamble is less than the expected dollar value of the gamble the person is said to be risk averse.

Next, consider a risk-seeking person whose utility function has a continually increasing slope, as shown in Figure 14-1b. Here each additional dollar increases utility more than did the previous dollar. The utility level associated with the certain prospect of $10,000 is 12. The expected utility for the uncertain prospect is 16; that is,

$$\mu = 0.5(5) + 0.5(27) = 16$$

where the utility levels associated with $5,000 and $10,000 are 5 and 27, respectively. This expected value of utility for the uncertain prospect is greater than the utility (12) associated with the certain prospect. Thus this person would prefer the uncertain prospect even though the expected dollar returns are the same. The certainty equivalent of the gamble is $12,000, determined by the amount of money associated with a utility level of 16 on the utility function. In this case, the individual would pay up to $2,000 to take the gamble.

In general, if the certainty equivalent of the gamble is greater than the expected dollar value of the gamble, the individual is said to be *risk seeking*.

Finally, in the risk-neutral case depicted in Figure 14-1c, the expected value of the utility associated with an uncertain prospect is equal to that of a certain prospect where both have equal expected dollar values. The expected utility associated with the uncertain prospect is 24; that is, 0.5(12) + 0.5(36) = 24. The utility associated with the certain prospect of $10,000 also is 24. Thus, the certainty equivalent of the gamble ($10,000) equals the expected value of the gamble; this person is said to be *risk neutral*.

The concept of the preference for risk can be formalized in the following way. At any time, an individual has a given level of wealth, W, which is known with certainty. The utility of that wealth is also known with certainty if the utility function is specified. Assume the initial level of wealth is $100, and that the utility function for this person is given by the natural logarithm of wealth, i.e.,

$$U = \ln W$$

This is simply a mathematical function used to describe this individual's transformation of wealth into utility or satisfaction. Note that the utility of the initial wealth of $100 is 4.61 (i.e., $\ln(100) = 4.61$). Now assume the individual is faced with a gamble that has the following probability distribution:

Outcome (X_i)	Probability (P_i)
−80	0.5
+80	0.5

This is a fair game because the expected outcome is zero.

After the game is played, the individual's wealth is either $20 or $180, depending on which outcome occurs. That is, either $80 is won or $80 is lost from the initial wealth of $100. The expected wealth if the game is played is $100, i.e.,

$$E(W) = 0.5(20) + 0.5(180) = 100$$

which has a utility of 4.61, i.e., the *utility of expected wealth* is

$$U[E(W)] = \ln[E(W)] = \ln(100) = 4.61$$

The *expected utility of wealth* is determined as

$$
\begin{aligned}
E[U(W)] &= 0.5[U(20)] + 0.5[U(180)] \\
&= 0.5[\ln(20)] + 0.5[\ln(180)] \\
&= 4.10
\end{aligned}
$$

Given these probabilities and the outcomes, the expected wealth is $100. The utility of expected wealth is simply the utility generated if this person had $100. In contrast, after the game is played the person actually will have either $20 or $180 in wealth. Each of these amounts of wealth has a level of utility (i.e., $\ln(20) = 3.00$ and $\ln(180) = 5.19$). By multiplying each of these utility levels by the appropriate probability, the expected utility of wealth is determined.

Now, the preference for risk can be formally defined. An individual is said to be risk averse if, when faced with a gamble, the utility of expected wealth is greater than the expected utility of wealth, i.e., if

$$U[E(W)] > E[U(W)] \implies Risk\ Aversion$$

Clearly, the individual in the preceding example is risk averse by this definition.

An individual is said to be risk seeking if the utility of expected wealth is less than the expected utility of wealth, i.e.,

$$U[E(W)] < E[U(W)] \implies Risk\ Seeking$$

Finally, if the utility of expected wealth is equal to the expected utility of wealth, the individual is said to be risk neutral, that is,

$$U[E(W)] = E[U(W)] \implies Risk\ Neutrality$$

These principles can be demonstrated with reference to the utility function $U = \ln W$ shown in Figure 14-2. Note that the utility is shown at the initial wealth level ($100) and at $20 and $180, the levels of wealth after the game is played. The notion that $U[E(W)] > E[U(W)]$ is another way of saying that this person would prefer wealth of $100 with certainty to a gamble that had an expected wealth of $100. The risk associated with the gamble has reduced utility.

Notice that the expected utility of wealth of 4.10 could also be achieved by having a certain wealth level of $60.04, the certainty equivalent of the gamble. This risk-averse individual would be willing to pay up to $39.96 (i.e., the difference between expected wealth given the gamble and the certainty equivalent of the gamble) to avoid taking the gamble. This difference is called the risk premium. The fact that risk-averse persons are willing to pay up to the level of the risk

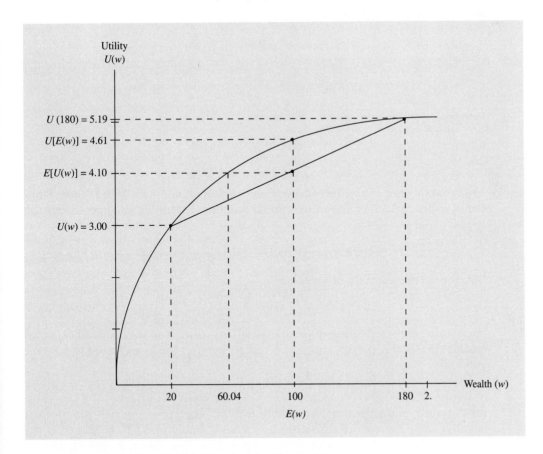

FIGURE 14-2 **Utility–Wealth Function for $U = \ln W$.**

premium to avoid gambles (such as the risk of loss from automobile accidents, home fires, etc.) creates a market for insurance. As we will see, because some people are risk seekers in some circumstances (i.e., they have negative risk premiums), a market for gambling also exists. That is, firms will respond to risk-averse persons' willingness to pay positive premiums to avoid risk by providing insurance on automobiles, homes, and lives.

Other firms respond to the willingness of risk-seeking individuals to pay negative premiums for taking risk by providing various gambling games. The gambles involved can be either explicit or implicit. An explicit gamble is one where the individual seeks out a risk decision such as a bet on a horse race or the purchase of common stock. An implicit gamble occurs when the risk is incidental to the primary activity. For example, a homeowner faces the risk that her house might burn down. This gamble is not sought out but rather is implicit in the decision to purchase the home. While the risks arise in different ways, they are dealt with in exactly the same manner by the rational decision maker.

Consider another example, involving a person who has initial wealth of $200 and a utility function given by

$$U = W + \frac{W^3}{10,000}$$

Assume that this person faces a gamble where he will win $100 with probability 0.5 or lose $100 with probability 0.5. The probability distribution is shown here:

Probability	Outcome (X_i)	Wealth (W_i)	$U(W_i)$
0.5	+100	300	3,000
0.5	−100	100	200

Note that this is a fair game because the expected value (in dollars) is zero. Thus, the expected wealth is $200, the original amount. The utility of expected wealth is 1,000, that is,

$$U[E(W)] = U(200) = 200 + \frac{(200)^3}{10,000} = 1,000$$

But, the expected utility of wealth is

$$E[U(W)] = 0.5[U(300)] + 0.5[U(100)]$$
$$= 0.5(3,000) + 0.5(200) = 1,600$$

Because the expected utility of wealth (1,600) is greater than the utility of expected wealth (1,000), this person is clearly a risk seeker and can be expected to take the gamble.

This example is depicted graphically in Figure 14-3. Note that expected utility of wealth of 1,600 also could be achieved by a certain wealth level of $239. Thus, the certainty equivalent of the gamble is $239. Therefore, the risk premium is negative (i.e., the expected wealth, given the gamble of $200, is less than the certainly equivalent wealth of $239). This means that this risk-seeking person would pay up to $39 to take the gamble.

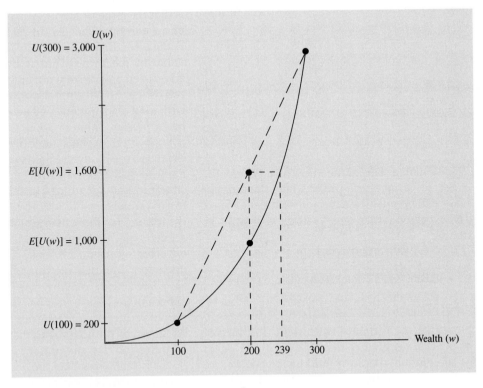

FIGURE 14-3 **Utility–Wealth Function for** $U = W + \dfrac{W^3}{10,000}$.

There are many people who are risk seekers, especially when small amounts of money are involved; they are willing to pay a premium for a gambling opportunity. The success of casinos in Las Vegas and Atlantic City is clear evidence that a market for gambling exists.

CASE STUDY ————————————————————————————————————

The State Lottery

In recent years, a number of states have developed lotteries in order to generate more revenue for government programs, especially education. In a typical state lottery, of each dollar wagered, about $0.05 is used for administrative expense, $0.45 is used for state government programs,

and $0.50 goes into the pool for prizes for the winners.

Consider a lottery program that generates $1 million a week by selling 1 million tickets at $1 each. A typical distribution of the prize pool of $0.5 million is shown here.

Prize Value (X_i)	Number of Prizes	Probability of Winning (P_i)	Total Prize Value
$150,000	1	0.000001	$150,000
75,000	2	0.000002	150,000
25,000	4	0.000004	100,000
5,000	10	0.000010	50,000
2,000	25	0.000025	$ 50,000
			$500,000

This is not a fair game (i.e., one where the expected value of the prize equals the amount wagered) because the expected value is not zero. The expected return on a $1 ticket is only $0.50, that is,

$$\mu = \sum_i P_i X_i = 0.000001(150,000) +$$

$$0.000002(75,000) + 0.000004(25,000)$$
$$+ 0.000010(5,000) + 0.000025(2,000)$$
$$+ 0.999958(0) = \$0.50$$

Note that the certainty equivalent (the $1 cost of a ticket) is greater than the expected value of the gamble. Because millions of people are willing to play these games regularly implies that their behavior should be characterized as risk seeking, at least when the wagers are for a small amount of money.

Another interesting dimension of these games is that the large prizes often are paid in the form of an annuity. That is, the $150,000 first prize in the preceding example may reflect the present value of the award, but it might actually be advertised as a prize worth more than $300,000 consisting of 20 annual payments of $15,000 each. At a discount rate of 8 percent, this annuity has a present value of about $150,000.

Supporters of the state lottery concept argue that it is a relatively painless way for the government to generate more revenue for important state programs. Unlike a tax that one is forced to pay, purchasers of lottery tickets voluntarily contribute to the government. Further, it is argued that if people understand that the expected return on a $1 ticket is only $0.50, one must conclude that the fun and the excitement associated with playing are greater than the expected loss.

Some critics of state lotteries claim that people do not really understand the probabilities of winning and that the present value of the large prizes is really less than the amount advertised. Further, there is good evidence that the largest share of the revenue from these programs comes from low-income people; for example, it is estimated that about 75 percent is paid by those earning less than $15,000 per year.

KEY CONCEPTS

- In general, investments that offer higher expected returns also involve greater risk.
- Behavior is said to be
  - Risk averse if the certainty equivalent of a gamble is less than the expected value of the gamble.
  - Risk neutral if the certainty equivalent of a gamble is equal to the expected value of the gamble.
  - Risk seeking if the certainty equivalent of a gamble is greater than the expected value of the gamble.
- Alternatively, behavior is
  - Risk averse if the utility of expected wealth is greater than the expected utility of wealth.

—Risk neutral if the utility of expected wealth is equal to the expected utility of wealth.

—Risk seeking if the utility of expected wealth is less than the expected utility of wealth.

Risk Aversion and Insurance

Firms and individuals buy insurance to protect against the financial loss associated with a variety of risks, including fire, theft, floods, earthquakes, and death. The market for insurance exists because people are risk averse. Consider a manager who knows that his fireworks manufacturing firm will earn a net profit of $100,000 each year but also faces a probability of 0.5 that the plant will burn down. Assume that if the plant burns down, it will cost $80,000 to replace. Now there are two possible outcomes: (1) the plant burns down, so net returns are $100,000 − $80,000 = $20,000; or (2) the plant does not burn down, so the net return is $100,000. Each outcome has a 0.5 probability of occurrence. The expected monetary value is $60,000, as shown in Table 14-4. Essentially, the manager is facing a gamble.

Suppose that manager's utility function is similar to that shown in Figure 14-4. Point A corresponds to the outcome associated with the plant burning down (i.e., a dollar payoff of $20,000 and utility = 100) and point B corresponds to the "no fire" outcome, when the dollar payoff is $100,000 and the utility is 200. Thus the expected utility for this uncertain prospect is 150. That is,

$$\mu = 0.5(100) + 0.5(200) = 150$$

Now the certainty equivalent is $40,000 (i.e., $40,000 with certainty generates a utility level of 150, as shown by point C in Figure 14-4). So the decision maker would be indifferent between a certain prospect of an income of $40,000 and the gamble just described, having an expected dollar value of $60,000.

This suggests that the profit-maximizing (but risk-averse) manager would pay up to $60,000 for a fire insurance policy on the factory because having this policy would guarantee a certain outcome of $40,000 whether or not the plant burned down. That is, the manager would know with certainty that the firm would net $40,000 (i.e., $100,000 in profit less the $60,000 insurance premium). If there is a fire, the insurance company will rebuild the factory at no cost to the firm.

Now consider the situation from the insurance company's perspective. The expected payout by the insurance company is determined by multiplying the probability of a fire by the dollar loss, that is, $0.5 \times \$80,000 = \$40,000$. This claim

TABLE 14-4 **Probability Distribution and Expected Value of Net Profit**

Event	Outcome	Probability	Outcome × Probability
Fire	$ 20,000	0.5	$10,000
No fire	100,000	0.5	$50,000
			$\mu = \$60,000$

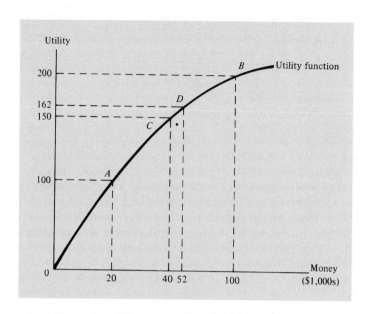

FIGURE 14-4 **Utility–Money Function for a Risk-Averse Manager.**

plus, say, 20 percent for operating expenses and profit suggests that a fire insurance policy for the plant could be offered for about $48,000. The result is that the manager of the fireworks company could actually have a certain outcome of $52,000 ($100,000 profit less the $48,000 insurance premium). This outcome, shown as point *D* in Figure 14-4, has a utility level of 162 and is preferred to the utility level 150 that corresponds to the uncertain prospect. Thus, in this example, the manager can choose between the certain prospect of having a utility level of 162 or an uncertain prospect with an expected utility of 150. Clearly, the rational manager would opt for the certain prospect involving insurance.

Although utility is impossible to measure, the best evidence that most people are risk averse is the existence of a large number of insurance companies and the variety of risks that they insure against. For example, private firms have issued policies that insure pianists' hands and dancers' legs. Ski resorts can buy insurance to protect against a lack of snow, and insurance companies paid more than $150 million in claims when rocket malfunctions sent two communications satellites into the oblivion of outer space.

CASE STUDY _____

Preference for Risk Among Physicians

Jury awards and out-of-court settlements of $1 million or more are not uncommon in malprac- tice suits against medical doctors. Because one mistake could mean financial ruin, virtually all doctors carry insurance against the risk of malpractice claims. Some in the so-called high-risk specialties, such as obstetrics and orthopedic surgery, face premiums in excess of $50,000 per year.

It is estimated that medical doctors pay about $4 billion each year for insurance protection against malpractice claims. Of this amount, only about 35 percent, or $1.4 billion, is paid out to injured people. The remaining 65 percent ($2.6 billion) goes for insurance company operating expenses and profits. A large part of the expenses are legal fees to hire lawyers to defend doctors who are sued and payments to the many expert witnesses (including economists) who testify in malpractice suits. Thus the average physician pays an insurance premium of about $3 for every dollar of loss expected. This suggests risk-averse behavior on the part of physicians.

Consider a hypothetical physician whose annual income is $100,000 after all expenses except malpractice insurance. Assume that the award for any successful malpractice suit would be $100,000 and that the probability of that occurring is 0.10. Thus the expected loss in any one year is $10,000 (i.e., 0.10 × $100,000). Suppose that the cost of an insurance policy against this risk is $30,000.

If the doctor buys an insurance policy, risk has been eliminated and net income would be $70,000, that is, $100,000 less the $30,000 insurance premium. If insurance is not purchased, income will be (1) $100,000 with probability 0.9; or (2) zero, in the case where an injured patient wins a lawsuit with probability 0.10. Thus the expected value of the risky alternative is $90,000, that is,

$$\mu = 0.9(\$100,000) + 0.1(0) = \$90,000$$

If the decision were based solely on the expected value of dollar returns, the physician would not buy the insurance. But assume that the doctor is risk averse, as indicated by the utility function

$$U = 40I - 0.2I^2$$

where I is income in thousands. Again, this is simply a mathematical relationship that allows income to be translated into utility for this person. The utility associated with the certain income of $70,000 is 1,820, that is,

$$U = 40(70) - 0.2(70)^2 = 1,820$$

which is higher than the expected utility (μ) associated with not having insurance. The latter is determined in the following way. First, the probability distribution is outlined and the two income possibilities ($100,000 and zero) are converted into utility.

Event	Probability	Income	Utility
No suit	0.9	$100,000	2,000
Suit	0.1	0	2,000

Then the expected value (in terms of utility) is computed:

$$\mu = 0.9(2,000) + 0.1(0) = 1,800$$

Thus this doctor is willing to spend $30,000 each year for insurance against possible claims having an expected value of only $10,000. Clearly, this is risk-averse behavior.

That virtually all doctors have malpractice insurance suggests that they are risk averse. However, there may be another explanation. Hospitals can be held responsible for a doctor's malpractice. As a result, almost all hospitals require that doctors have malpractice insurance before they are allowed to use the hospital. This reduces the risk of loss for the owners of the hospital. Because having hospital privileges is essential for most medical practices, one would find that even risk-seeking physicians would have insurance. Thus the high proportion of doctors who have malpractice insurance could be the result of risk-averse hospital administrators forcing their risk preferences on physicians.

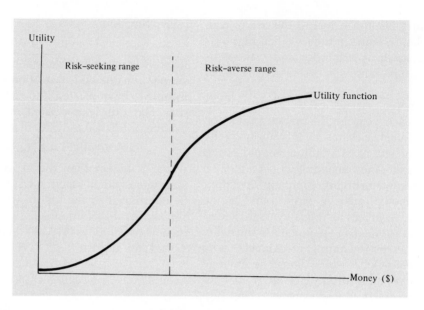

FIGURE 14-5 **Friedman–Savage Utility Function.**

Gambling and Insuring: A Contradiction?

Individual behavior is generally defined as either risk averse, risk neutral, or risk seeking. Thus one might expect to find risk-averse individuals spending their time reviewing their insurance coverage and to find risk-seeking persons in casinos in Las Vegas or Atlantic City. But if a survey were made, it probably would show that many people both buy insurance and engage in gambling games of one sort or another. For example, it is probably true that most people who engage in gambling in Las Vegas drove there in insured cars and live in insured homes. This appears to be a contradiction, as it suggests that people are risk seeking and risk averse at the same time. Actually, there is no contradiction, but a complete explanation is beyond the scope of this book. Suffice it to say that this behavior depends on the type of gambling games available and the nature and cost of insurance that can be purchased.

One rather simple explanation for this phenomenon is offered by Friedman and Savage,[1] who argue that the utility function may look as shown in Figure 14-5. It describes the person who is risk seeking when small amounts of money are involved and risk averse when larger amounts may be at risk. A person having such a utility function would engage in gambling games for relatively small amounts of money but would insure against large losses, such as those associated

[1] M. Friedman and L. Savage. "The Utility Analysis of Choices Involving Risk." *Journal of Political Economy*, 56 (1948), 279–304.

with a house fire or automobile accident. A utility function of this type is a sufficient condition for a rational person to gamble and have insurance at the same time.

EXAMPLE ———

Risk Preference and Decision Making

Consider the problem facing a manager who must choose between two investments, A and B, each having an initial cost of $10. The probability distributions for the payoffs for each investment are shown in the following table. Each payoff represents the present value of all future net profits.

A		B	
Probability (P_i)	Payoff (X_i)	Probability (P_i)	Payoff (X_i)
0.10	$-20	0.20	$10
0.50	20	0.40	20
0.40	50	0.40	30

The decision maker's utility function is $U = 100X - X^2$, where X is the dollar payoff.

1. Would you characterize this decision maker as risk seeking, risk neutral, or risk averse? Explain.
2. If the objective is to maximize expected net present value, which investment is the better choice? (For the moment, disregard risk.)
3. Evaluate the risk associated with the dollar returns for each investment.
4. If the objective is utility maximization, which investment should be chosen?

SOLUTION

1. Based on the utility function, it is seen that the decision maker is risk averse. This can be shown in the following way. Select any two dollar payoffs, say, $20 and $40, and arbitrarily assign them probabilities of occurrence, say, 0.4 and 0.6, respectively. The expected value of these payoffs is

$$\mu(\text{dollars}) = 0.4(20) + 0.6(40) = \$32$$

From the utility function, the utilities associated with $20 and $40 are 1,600 and 2,400, respectively. Thus the expected utility value is

$$\mu(\text{utility}) = 0.4(1,600) + 0.6(2,400) = 2,080$$

But if this person were offered $32 with certainty (i.e., a certain prospect having the same value as the expected dollar value of the investments), the utility would be 2,176. Because the utility is higher for the certain prospect, the person is risk averse.

2. The expected returns for each investment are

$$\mu_A = 0.10(-20) + 0.50(20) + 0.40(50) = 28$$
$$\mu_B = 0.20(10) + 0.40(20) + 0.40(30) = 22-$$

Thus A is the preferred choice because it has the highest expected value.

3. The evaluation statistics for risk and risk per dollar of expected return for both investments are

INVESTMENT A:

$$\sigma_A = \sqrt{0.10(-20 - 28)^2 + 0.50(20 - 28)^2 + 0.40(50 - 28)^2} = 21.4$$
$$\nu_A = \frac{\sigma_A}{\mu_A} = \frac{21.4}{28} = 0.76$$

INVESTMENT B:

$$\sigma_B = \sqrt{0.20(10 - 22)^2 + 0.40(20 - 22)^2 + 0.40(30 - 22)^2} = 7.5$$
$$\nu_B = \frac{\sigma_B}{\mu_B} = \frac{7.5}{22} = 0.34$$

The risk is greater for A ($\sigma_A = 21.4$ compared to $\sigma_B = 7.5$) and the risk per dollar of expected return is also greater for A ($\nu_A = 0.76$ compared to $\nu_B = 0.34$).

4. To make the decision assuming the goal is utility maximization, the payoffs must be transformed from dollars into utility using the utility function $U = 100X - X^2$. For example, the utility associated with a net payoff of -20 is

$$U = 100(-20) - 20^2 = -2{,}400$$

Repeating this for each outcome will yield two new probability distributions where the payoffs are in terms of utility.

Probability (P_i)	Payoff (U_i)	Probability (P_i)	Payoff (U_i)
0.10	−2,400	0.20	1,900
0.50	1,600	0.40	1,600
0.40	2,500	0.40	2,100

4. The expected utility returns are

$$\mu_A = 0.10(-2{,}400) + 0.50(1{,}600) + 0.40(2{,}500) = 1{,}560$$
$$\mu_B = 0.20(900) + 0.40(1{,}600) + 0.40(2{,}100) = 1{,}660$$

Hence, in terms of utility, investment B is the preferred alternative.

KEY CONCEPTS

- The market for insurance exists because many people are risk averse. The market for gambling exists because some people are risk seekers.

- Some people exhibit risk-seeking behavior and risk-averse behavior at the same time. One explanation for this is that they are risk seekers when relatively small amounts of money are involved but are risk averse when large amounts are at stake.

Adjusting Business Decisions for Risk

Although there are several ways to incorporate risk into the decision process, the most common method is to use a risk-adjusted discount rate in determining the present value of the future profits associated with an investment. Given the stream of future profits, π_t, the basic evaluation framework

$$PV = \sum_{t=1}^{n} \frac{\pi_t}{(1 + r)^t} \tag{14-4}$$

is modified by using an appropriate risk-adjusted interest or discount rate for r. Most investors are willing to accept greater risk only if there is the promise of greater returns when compared to an investment with less risk. For example, suppose that the typical return on an insured bank certificate of deposit is 10 percent per year. Clearly, no rational investor will invest in very risky ventures such as drilling for oil or mining for gold unless the expected return is considerably higher than 10 percent per year.

Suppose that the line R in Figure 14-6 shows all combinations of risk and return for which a hypothetical investor is indifferent. That is, this function shows the willingness of this investor to trade off risk against return. Clearly, the shape of this function will vary for different individuals, depending on their preference for risk. A very risk-averse person might have a trade-off function similar to the dashed line R'—any increase in risk must carry with it a significant increase in return. Conversely, another individual's trade-off function might be described by line R''. Here only a small increase in the rate of return is required to compensate for a rather large increase in risk.

Assume that the rate of return associated with a riskless investment is 10 percent. Recall that a riskless investment would have a standard deviation of zero. For the investor with trade-off function R, if the risk increases to, say, $\sigma = 1.0$, a 15 percent rate of return is required. The difference between this 15 percent return and the riskless rate of 10 percent is referred to as the *risk premium*. If $\sigma = 2.0$, the trade-off function R indicates that a 22 percent return is required for this person. Thus the risk premium is 12 percentage points. In evaluating investments, these differential discount rates would be used to evaluate the present value of future profits. That is, net cash flows for a high-risk investment would be discounted using a higher discount rate than would be used for a low-risk alternative.

It should be emphasized that there is no equation or table that relates risk and the discount rate. Clearly, there is a positive relationship between these two factors, but the relationship between them is strictly judgmental and must be made by individual decision makers.

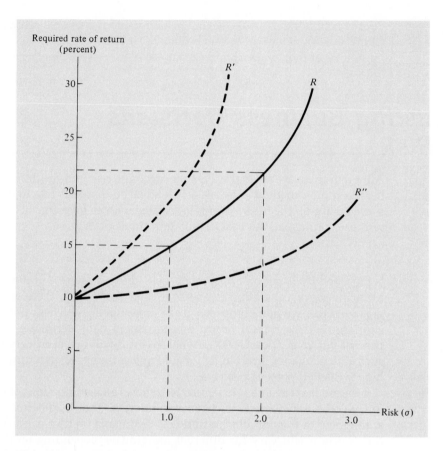

FIGURE 14-6 **Risk–Return Trade-Offs for Hypothetical Investors.**

EXAMPLE _____

Using Risk-Adjusted Discount Rates

Suppose that management at Showmax Theaters must decide whether to expand by building a few large theaters in large cities or building a number of minitheaters in small cities and towns. Each of the alternatives would require an initial invest-ment of $2 million. Although the large theaters have a greater expected return, this option has greater risk because there is more competition in the larger cities. In contrast, there is less potential for profit in the small markets, but in many of them there is little or no competition. The expected value of the net profits in each of the next ten years is $600,000 per year in the large markets and $500,000 per year in the small markets.

The value of σ is estimated to be 1.5 in the large markets and 0.5 in the small cities. Management has a risk–return trade-off function similar to that shown by curve R in Figure 14-6. This means that a rate of about 17 percent would be used to discount cash flows in the large-city alternative and a rate of about 12 percent would be used to discount cash flows in the small-city alternative.

SOLUTION

The net present value of an investment is determined by subtracting the initial cost of the investment from the present value of future profits. Note that the appropriate risk-adjusted discount rate is used in each case.

LARGE-CITY ALTERNATIVE:

$$NPV = \sum_{t=1}^{10} \frac{600{,}000}{(1 + 0.17)^t} - \$2{,}000{,}000$$
$$= \$2{,}795{,}162 - \$2{,}000{,}000 = \$795{,}162$$

SMALL-CITY ALTERNATIVE:

$$NPV = \sum_{t=1}^{10} \frac{500{,}000}{(1 + 0.12)^t} - \$2{,}000{,}000$$
$$= \$2{,}825{,}112 - \$2{,}000{,}000 = \$825{,}112$$

Although the nondiscounted cash flows each year are greater for the large-city alternative, when adjusted for risk, the present value of the cash flows is greater for the small-city alternative. Thus building minitheaters in smaller cities is the preferred investment.

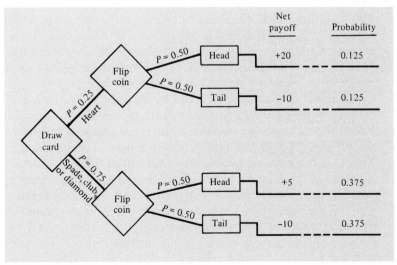

FIGURE 14-7 **Decision Tree.**

Decision Tree Analysis _____

The previous discussions of risk began with a set of outcomes for each investment and the probability of each outcome occurring. But some strategic decisions involve a sequence of decisions, states of nature, and possibly even subsequent decisions. Given this complexity, how are the alternative strategies to be evaluated? One approach is to use a decision tree that traces the sequence of events and/or decisions that lead to each outcome. Such a diagram shows two or more branches at each point where a decision or event (i.e., a state of nature) leads to the various outcomes. These branches are similar to those on a tree. Understanding the concept of a decision tree will help in understanding how the data in a probability distribution are determined.

To illustrate the concept, consider the following gambling game. An initial bet of $10 is made. A card is drawn from an ordinary deck of playing cards and then a coin is tossed. If the player draws a heart and then tosses a head, he receives $30, for a net payoff of $20. If a heart is not drawn, but a head is tossed, the player is paid $15, for a net payoff of $5. For all other outcomes, the player loses his initial $10 bet.

When drawing the card, the relevant probabilities are 0.25 that a heart is drawn (there are 13 hearts in a deck of 52 cards, so $\frac{13}{52} = 0.25$), and the probability that a spade, club, or diamond is drawn is 0.75. When tossing a coin, the probability of a head and the probability of a tail are both equal to 0.5.

The game can be analyzed using the decision tree shown in Figure 14-7. The probability of the outcome at each step in the process is shown on the branches of the tree. The probability of each final outcome is equal to the product of the probabilities along the branches leading to that outcome. For example, the probability of drawing a heart and then tossing a head for a net payoff of $20 is $0.25 \times 0.50 = 0.125$. By repeating this for each path along the decision tree, the probability of each outcome is determined. By associating the net payoff for each outcome with its respective probability, the probability distribution is determined. Then the usual evaluation statistics that describe expected return, risk, and risk per dollar of expected return can be computed.

The decision tree approach can be directly applied to managerial decision making. Suppose that a firm is considering entering a new market. This entry would require building either a large, medium, or small plant. This decision is shown in part I of Figure 14-8. A square is used at each branch to show decisions. Note that there are no probabilities associated with such decisions. A diamond is shown at those branches associated with the various states of nature that may occur. A probability must be assigned to each of these branches.

In this example, there are two stochastic elements associated with each decision (the term *stochastic* refers to an outcome that is determined by chance): (1) the reaction of a major competitor in the business and (2) the economic conditions that will prevail. Suppose it is learned that the competitor may respond to the new plant with a new national or regional advertising program or with no new advertising program. Assume that the probability of each occurring will depend

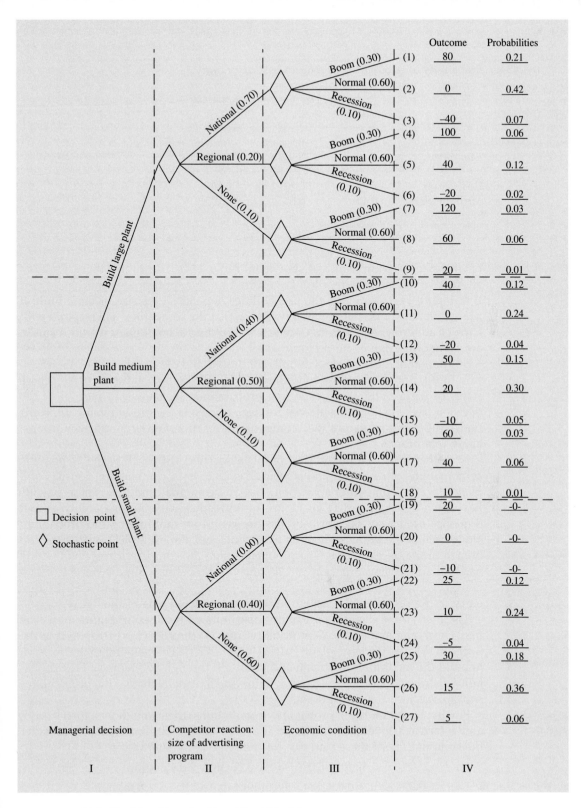

	Outcome	Probabilities
(1)	80	0.21
(2)	0	0.42
(3)	−40	0.07
(4)	100	0.06
(5)	40	0.12
(6)	−20	0.02
(7)	120	0.03
(8)	60	0.06
(9)	20	0.01
(10)	40	0.12
(11)	0	0.24
(12)	−20	0.04
(13)	50	0.15
(14)	20	0.30
(15)	−10	0.05
(16)	60	0.03
(17)	40	0.06
(18)	10	0.01
(19)	20	-0-
(20)	0	-0-
(21)	−10	-0-
(22)	25	0.12
(23)	10	0.24
(24)	−5	0.04
(25)	30	0.18
(26)	15	0.36
(27)	5	0.06

National (0.70), Regional (0.20), None (0.10)

National (0.40), Regional (0.50), None (0.10)

National (0.00), Regional (0.40), None (0.60)

Boom (0.30), Normal (0.60), Recession (0.10)

Build large plant

Build medium plant

Build small plant

☐ Decision point

◇ Stochastic point

Managerial decision

Competitor reaction: size of advertising program

Economic condition

I

II

III

IV

FIGURE 14-8 **Decision Tree for New Plant Decision.**

TABLE 14-5 **Probability of Alternative Responses by Competitor**

	Probability That Competitor Responds with:		
Plant Size	National Program	Regional Program	No New Program
Large plant	0.70	0.20	0.10
Medium plant	0.40	0.50	0.10
Small plant	0.00	0.40	0.60

on the size of plant built, as shown in Table 14-5. The probabilities for each alternative competitive reaction are entered on the appropriate branches of part II of Figure 14-8. Note that the probabilities depend on the size of plant built. If a large plant is built, the probability is high that the competitor will respond with a major advertising program. Conversely, building a small plant would result in a regional program or no program at all.

Suppose that the possible economic conditions and their probabilities are: recession (0.10), normal business conditions (0.60), and boom conditions (0.30). These states of nature and their respective probabilities are shown in part III of the decision tree. Finally, the outcome for each branch is the present value of profits under the states of nature (i.e., competitor's reaction and economic conditions) along that branch.

Note that there is a payoff (i.e., profit) associated with each of the 27 possible combinations of decisions and stochastic events. Each combination consists of a plant size, the competitor's reaction, and an economic condition. These payoffs have been listed in part IV of Figure 14-8 together with the probability of that sequence occurring. The probabilities are found by multiplying the probability along each of the branches leading to the outcome. For example, consider the top branch of the decision tree. The probability that the competitor responds with a national advertising program is 0.70, and the probability of an economic boom is 0.30. The product of these probabilities is 0.21, and this is shown as the first entry in the probability distribution on the right-hand side of the figure.

There are three distinct probability distributions outlined in Figure 14-8. The first, consisting of the payoff–probability pairs (1) through (9), corresponds to the decision to build the large plant. Pairs (10) through (18) correspond to the decision to build the medium-sized plant, and pairs (19) through (27) represent the probability distribution for the investment in the small plant. Note that the probabilities sum to one for each distribution.

Finally, based on these probability distributions, the evaluation statistics μ, σ, and ν for each investment alternative can be computed. For example, consider the computation of these statistics for the large-plant alternative:

$$\mu = 0.21(80) + 0.42(0) + 0.07(-40) + 0.06(100) + 0.12(40)$$

$$+ 0.02(-20) + 0.03(120) + 0.06(60) + 0.01(20) = \$31.8 \text{ million}$$

$$\sigma = \sqrt{0.21(80 - 31.80)^2 + 0.42(0 - 31.80)^2 + \cdots + 0.01(20 - 31.80)^2} = 43.60$$
$$\nu = \frac{\sigma}{\mu} = \frac{43.6}{31.8} = 1.4$$

These statistics for all three plant sizes are summarized in Table 14-6. As usual, the decision will not be an easy one for management. The expected return or expected net present value of all future profits increases with the scale of the plant, but so does risk, as measured by σ and ν. For example, the expected return on the large plant, $31.8 million, is higher than the expected return for the other two plant sizes, but the risk per dollar of return (1.4) is also the highest of the three alternatives. The manager's preference for risk will be a fundamental factor in making the decision.

Clearly, decision makers must keep the problem in proper perspective. One way is to include only those alternatives and outcomes that are relevant and significant in terms of both the probability of occurrence and the net payoff. Consider including the possibility of terrorist actions as a possible state of nature when evaluating a typical business investment decision. For military planners, this state of nature is both relevant and significant. However, for most business decisions such a possibility probably is not relevant, even though the payoff associated with this outcome could be a large negative number. That is, the firm may incur huge losses in the event of such an attack, but this outcome is sufficiently improbable that it is not relevant for most business decisions.

Even with careful attention to including only relevant decisions and stochastic factors, decision trees can easily become very large and complex. The total number of outcomes is equal to the product of the number of decisions or stochastic alternatives along each branch on the tree. For example, a decision to build a new plant might involve six different plant-size alternatives, five different ways a competitor might react, and three different economic environments. Hence the number of outcomes in this case would be 90 (i.e., $6 \times 5 \times 3$). One could easily imagine decision trees with thousands of possible outcomes. Whereas a computer would have no problem computing the probabilities and evaluation statistics for each of a large number of intricate decision trees, the manager's capacity to evaluate the options is limited.

TABLE 14-6 **Risk–Return Evaluation Statistics for Each Plant-Size Alternative**

	Alternative Plant Size		
	Large	Medium	Small
	(Dollar Figures in Millions)		
Expected return (μ)	$31.8	$21.3	$16.3
Risk (σ)	43.6	21.4	8.9
Risk per million dollars of expected return (ν)	1.4	1.0	0.55

KEY CONCEPTS

- A decision tree traces sequences of strategies and states of nature to arrive at a set of outcomes. The probability of any outcome is found by multiplying the probabilities on each branch leading to that outcome.
- There is a probability distribution for each choice included in a decision tree.

Summary

A decision maker faces risk when there are several outcomes associated with a decision and the probabilities of those outcomes are known. The greater the variation in those outcomes, the greater the risk. The set of outcomes and their associated probabilities comprise a probability distribution. If the probabilities of the outcomes are not known, the decision maker faces uncertainty.

The evaluation of a decision where risk is present is made by determining the expected value (μ), the standard deviation (σ), and the coefficient of variation (ν) of the probability distribution for the investment. The expected value estimates the expected return, the standard deviation measures risk, and the coefficient of variation measures risk per dollar of expected return. In general, decisions that promise higher expected returns also carry greater risk.

Behavior is said to be risk averse if the certainty equivalent of a gamble is greater than the expected dollar value of the gamble. In contrast, behavior is risk seeking if the certainty equivalent of a gamble is less than the expected dollar value of the gamble. A market for insurance exists because many people are risk averse. A market for gambling exists because there are risk-seeking individuals. Some people buy insurance and also engage in gambling games because they are risk seekers when small amounts of money are involved and risk averse when larger amounts are at stake.

A utility function indicates the amount of utility or satisfaction a person receives from wealth or income. It can be used to determine the individual's preference for risk. Risk aversion is indicated by a utility function that increases but at a decreasing rate. A risk neutral person has a utility function that is linear, and the utility function for a risk-seeking person increases at an increasing rate.

The most common method for compensating for risk when making decisions is to add a risk premium to the rate used to discount future profits. The risk premium increases as the risk associated with the decision increases. An alternative method for adjusting for risk is to evaluate the certainty equivalent of a risky decision.

A decision tree traces the sequence of strategies and states of nature to determine the set of outcomes associated with a decision. The probability of any outcome is found by multiplying the probabilities on each branch leading to that outcome. There is a probability distribution for each choice included in a decision tree.

Discussion Questions

14-1. Explain how the principle of risk aversion can be used to explain why the owner of a business would buy insurance on the life of a key employee.

14-2. Assume the risk-free interest rate (e.g., the rate on 91-day Treasury bills) is 5 percent. What interest rate would you use to discount the projected profits for each of the following investment? Explain. (Hint: What risk premium would you add to the risk-free rate in each case?)

a. A new motel in your city.

b. An exploratory oil well in an unproven oil field.

c. A video tape rental store in your home town.

14-3. One manager has said: "Because an individual's utility cannot be measured, there is no reason to consider it when making decisions." Do you agree or disagree? Explain.

14-4. Provide two examples of decisions made by administrators at your college or university where a decision tree could have been used.

14-5. In what areas can a firm use insurance to reduce risk?

14-6. Firm A sells one product to a single group of consumers, whereas firm B sells a variety of products to different groups of consumers. Which firm is taking more risk? Explain.

14-7. What are two examples of decision making under risk and two examples of decision making under uncertainty?

14-8. Consider a gamble that involved winning or losing an amount equal to your entire initial wealth. Would you take this gamble if the probability of each outcome was 0.5? What does this imply about your preference for risk? Explain.

Problems

14-1. Do each of the following distributions meet the requirements for a probability distribution? Why or why not?

(a)	P_i	X_i	(b)	P_i	X_i	(c)	P_i	X_i
	−0.10	10		0.30	−40		0.20	4
	−0.20	15		0.30	−50		0.40	8
	0.30	20		0.40	−200		0.30	0
	0.50	40					0.15	12
	0.50	50						

14-2. For each of the following probability distributions, calculate the expected value (μ), standard deviation (σ), and coefficient of variation (v).

(a)	P_i	X_i	(b)	P_i	Y_i
	0.8	20		0.1	10
	0.2	−5		0.2	20
				0.4	15
				0.3	30

14-3. For each of the following probability distributions where P_i is probability and X_i and Y_i are outcomes, determine the expected values (u_x and u_y), the standard deviations (σ_x and σ_y), and the coefficients of variation (v_x and v_y).

(a)	P_i	X_i	Y_i	(b)	P_i	X_i	Y_i
	0.20	−5	15		0.10	0	50
	0.40	0	20		0.20	10	40
	0.10	10	30		0.60	20	30
	0.30	20	50		0.10	30	20

14-4. Given the following probability distribution for returns on an investment in the common stock of two firms:

	Percentage Returns	
Probability	*Amalgamated Gold*	*First National Bank*
0.2	−20	−5
0.4	−10	4
0.3	20	6
0.1	40	8

Compute the expected value, standard deviation, and coefficient of variation for each investment.

14-5. Given the following probability distribution for the percentage returns on the common stock of General Motors and S&P 500 Index, determine the expected return, and standard deviation for each.

	Percentage Returns	
Probability	*General Motors*	*S&P Index*
0.2	−10	0
0.3	10	5
0.5	20	10

14-6. A gamble consists of a choice between two games. The first game requires rolling an ordinary die and receiving $10 times the number shown. The second game involves flipping a coin and receiving $70 dollars if it comes up heads and nothing if it comes up tails. Which game would be selected by a person with utility function $U = \ln W$? What choice would be made if the utility function is $U = W^2$?

14-7. Consider a person with initial wealth of $1,000 who has a utility function
$$U = \ln W$$
where W is wealth. Suppose this person is offered a gamble that involves winning $100 with probability 0.50 and losing $100 with probability 0.50.

    a. Compute the level of utility at the initial wealth.

    b. Given that the gamble is accepted, compute the expected wealth, the utility of expected wealth, and the expected utility of wealth.

    c. Will this person take the gamble? Explain.

    d. What is the certainty equivalent of the gamble.

14-8. A sales representative for the Rapid Vacuum Cleaner Company knows from past experience that she will sell a vacuum cleaner in two of every five homes in which she gives a demonstration. In a typical day she will give demonstrations in ten homes. If it costs $15 to give each demonstration (this includes all implicit and explicit costs) and if her commission is $60 for each cleaner sold, determine expected net profit per day.

14-9. The Lac DuFlambeau Corporation manufactures a broad line of fishing tackle and accessories. The firm has surplus cash and is considering the acquisition of a firm that manufactures flyrods. A broker identifies two firms, Flyrite and Perfect-Rod, that could be purchased for the same amount. The probability distributions for the present value of all future profits for each of these acquisition candidates are as follows:

Flyrite		Perfect-Rod	
Probability	Outcome	Probability	Outcome
0.40	200,000	0.20	100,000
0.20	200,000	0.50	200,000
0.40	500,000	0.30	250,000

    a. Make a complete investment analysis of each investment (i.e., compute the expected present value of all future profits, a measure of risk, and a measure of risk per dollar of expected returns).

    b. Which of the two firms should be acquired? Why?

14-10. For each of the following functions relating utility (U) and money (M), determine if the function implies risk-averse, risk-seeking, or risk-neutral behavior. Explain.

    a. $U = M + 0.25M^2$

    b. $U = 10M$

    c. $U = 500M - 2M^2$

14-11. United Steel, Inc., has experienced losses for several years. The production department has determined the only hope for reversing the negative trend in profits is to build a new plant outside the United States. Two alternative locations have been identified. Production in country A would be very efficient and low-cost, but the government is unstable. In the event of a revolution, United's assets might be appropriated. Country B has a much more stable government, but production costs are considerably higher than in A.

    The following data show the probability distribution for the present value of all future profits for each alternative.

Country A		Country B	
Probability	Profits (millions)	Probability	Profits (millions)
0.40	$ 0	0.40	$10
0.20	20	0.40	20
0.40	60	0.20	30

a. Make a complete analysis of both alternatives. Which alternative should be chosen? Why?

b. If the collective utility function of the board of directors is

$$U = 200X - X^2$$

where X is measured in millions of dollars of profit, which alternative should be selected? Explain.

14-12. Management at Unique Publishing has been paying an annual premium of $3,000 for fire insurance on their $100,000 plant. Net profit for Unique consistently is $100,000 per year after deducting the insurance premium. Any uninsured loss due to fire would be an expense in computing net income. A study has shown that the probability of fire during a year is only 0.004. (Assume that any fire would destroy the plant.) A consultant suggests that Unique cancel its fire insurance. Evaluate this recommendation for each of the following assumptions:

a. The sole objective of management is to maximize profit (i.e., no consideration is given to risk).

b. The sole management objective is maximizing utility and the relevant utility function is $U = 100\pi - 0.5\pi^2$, where π is net profit in thousands of dollars.

c. Given the utility function from part (b), compute and compare the expected utility of profit and the utility of expected profit. What does this tell you about the risk preferences of management at Unique Publishing?

14-13. State University is considering an evening MBA program. Dean Stephens determines that a minimum enrollment of 100 in a graduate program is necessary for a breakeven operation. As the only MBA program in the state, enrollment probably would be 125 students. Southwestern, a private university, is the only other school in the area that offers graduate programs. The dean thinks the probability is about 0.67 that Southwestern would respond to the State program with their own MBA program. If it did, enrollment probably would only be 70 students in the State program. However, if State offered both MBA and MPA (Master of Public Administration) programs, Dean Stephens thinks that enrollment would be 175 with no competition and 90 if Southwestern offers a program. Because of similarities in course requirements, the dean thinks that the MBA and MPA programs could be run as one graduate program. The dean believes that offering both degrees would reduce the probability that Southwestern will enter the MBA degree market to about 0.2.

a. Construct a decision tree that shows each possible outcome and the probability of its occurring.

b. Determine the expected number of students in State's MBA program if offered by itself and as a combined MBA–MPA program, where both degrees would be offered.

14-14. Acme Manufacturing is considering three alternatives, A, B, and C, for a new plant. Cost data for each of these plants are shown here. The cost of shipping one unit of output to the market will vary because each plant would be at a different location.

	A	B	C
Annual fixed cost	$100,000	$200,000	$300,000
Production cost per unit	20	18	15
Shipping cost per unit	5	6	6

The quantity sold will depend on economic conditions for the next year, as indicated here:

Economic Condition	Probability	Quantity Sold
Normal	0.8	100,000
Recession	0.2	80,000

The per-unit price of the product will depend entirely on the price set by Zenith Steel, the primary competitor in the market. It is thought that the probability of various prices being set will depend on the plant built by Acme, as shown here:

Acme Builds Plant	Probability That Zenith Responds with a Price of:		
	$20	$25	$30
A	0.10	0.40	0.50
B	0.30	0.30	0.40
C	0.60	0.20	0.20

Because of Zenith's dominance in the market, whatever price it sets will be followed by Acme.

a. Construct a decision tree showing the first-year net profit for Acme for each combination of plant size, economic condition, and pricing reaction.

b. Determine the expected first-year profit for each plant alternative. Ignoring risk, which plant should be built?

14-15. Sharp Products, a major paper recycling firm, must replace its processing equipment. The only alternatives are the Century Processor, a very efficient but somewhat unreliable machine, and the Sureshot Processor, a less efficient but almost repair-free piece of equipment. The two machines have equal initial costs and have a three-year life. Due to rapid technological change, the machines will have no salvage value at the end of that period. Sharp's engineering department has estimated the expected net cash flows associated with each machine over their three-year lives.

	Expected Net Cash Flows for Year		
Machine	1	2	3
Century	300	400	400
Sureshot	250	350	450

The management at Sharp uses a 14 percent discount rate for most equipment purchases. However, because of the unreliability of the Century Processor, a discount rate of 18 percent is appropriate for that machine. Which machine should be purchased? Explain. (Assume that all cash flows occur at the end of each year.)

Microcomputer Problems

The following problems can be solved by using the microcomputer program TOOLS, available in the study guide, or by using other computer software.

14-16. High-Risk Strategies, an international commodity trading company, is faced with four alternative strategies for trading wheat. The profit for each strategy will depend critically on the weather conditions (i.e., the state of nature) prevailing during the next 12 months. The set of profit outcomes for each strategy–state of nature combination is outlined here:

Weather Conditions (Probability)	Strategy			
	A	B	C	D
Hot–dry (0.10)	$-2,800,000	$1,700,000	$-2,410,000	$-3,625,000
Warm–wet (0.20)	-7,400,000	1,920,000	$-3,440,000	$-5,100,000
Warm–dry (0.30)	-4,520,000	1,800,000	2,140,000	1,460,000
Cool–wet (0.20)	-2,900,000	1,400,000	6,240,000	7,800,000
Cool–dry (0.20)	-2,100,000	1,100,000	5,110,000	6,125,000

Evaluate each alternative and determine which strategy should be implemented.

14-17. United Fabricated Products is faced with the decision to build a new plant near the site of a proposed new steel mill. Three plant sizes are under consideration—small, medium, and large. Unfortunately, if United is to build the plant, it must make the commitment now before it is certain that the steel mill actually will be built. If United delays the decision, its option on the only available site will expire and a major competitor, Walters Steel Products, will exercise its subordinated option on the land. The best estimate available suggests that the probability that the mill will be built is 0.75. The costs are: small plant, $12.1 million; medium plant, $18.0 million; and large plant, $25.7 million.

The profit outcomes for each possible outcome and the initial cost of each plant site are shown here:

	Present Value of Profits (Millions) for Each Plant Size		
Steel Mill	Small	Medium	Large
Built	$14.6	$29.4	$45.7
Not built	−3.4	−11.5	−26.5

Should United build a plant and, if so, which size? Explain.

14-18. Secure Money Managers limits its investments to five securities. The annual estimated rate of return on each of these for each state of the economy is shown here. The probabilities of the latter are: recession, 0.12; moderate economic growth, 0.65; and rapid economic growth, 0.23. Compute the expected return, risk, and risk per unit of return for each security.

	Security				
	(1)	(2)	(3)	(4)	(5)
Economic	International	United	Outland	Southern	HAL.
Condition	Meats	Trucking	Steel	Telephone	Inc.
Recession	11.4	−14.0	−9.5	11.1	5.0
Moderate growth	11.9	9.7	11.0	12.0	13.0
Rapid growth	12.2	21.6	16.2	12.4	14.2

14-19. Chi-Town Promotions must select a rock group for its next concert tour. The financial and marketing vice-presidents have estimated the following probability distributions for profits for each of four groups. Which should be selected?

(1) Electric Banana		(2) Zinc Dirigible		(3) The Grandpas and the Grandmas		(4) Hug	
Prob.	Profit	Prob.	Profit	Prob.	Profit	Prob.	Profit
0.73	$−2,450,000	0.42	$−5,400,000	0.22	$1,705,000	0.12	$−3,825,000
0.17	−1,400,000	0.21	1,650,000	0.23	2,124,000	0.23	$−1,024,000
0.10	−1,200,000	0.13	4,800,000	0.55	1,925,000	0.29	2,950,200
		0.24	6,450,000			0.36	8,100,200

Capital Budgeting

Preview

Most of the principles of managerial economics covered thus far have focused on short-run decisions. For example, determining the profit-maximizing price and output rate and deciding the optimal amount of labor to employ are important short-run decisions. Of equal importance are decisions about the nature of the firm in the long run. What new items should be added to or eliminated from the product line? Should old capital equipment be replaced? Should a new plant be built or should a competitor be acquired to broaden the product line or retail outlets?

Decisions such as these are absolutely crucial to the long-run profitability of the firm. Recall that the objective is to make those decisions that will maximize the value of the firm, which has been defined as the present value of all future profits or net cash flows. To meet this objective, assets must be continually deployed and redeployed to capture new profit opportunities. For example, General Motors' entry into the credit card market and the development of cable television services by several of the regional telephone companies (e.g., NYNEX and Bell Atlantic) represent significant new resource commitments by these firms.

In this chapter, the firm's long-run decisions are considered. First, the nature of capital budgeting decisions and the process of making long-run investments are considered. Next, alternative evaluation techniques for evaluating capital projects are developed and applied. Several special topics are considered, including capital budgeting in an inflationary environment and allocating limited capital funds under capital rationing. Methods for estimating the cost of capital funds are reviewed, including the Capital Asset Pricing Model (CAPM), which has proven to be one of the fundamental developments in the modern theory of finance. Finally, mergers and acquisitions are discussed. This topic is a special case of capital budgeting. For example, a firm may decide to enter the microcomputer business by building a new plant, staffing it with new production personnel, and developing a marketing force. Alternatively, the firm may seek to acquire (or merge with) an existing firm that already is in the computer market. Consideration of either alternative requires the application of capital budgeting principles.

Value Maximization and Capital Budgeting

Capital projects are those that are expected to generate returns for more than one year. Capital budgeting refers to the process of planning capital projects, raising funds, and efficiently allocating resources to those capital projects. Examples of capital projects include new factories, machines, automobiles and trucks, and computers. Outlays for research and development and advertising programs are also capital expenditures if the returns on those projects will flow for more than one year.

It is useful to categorize capital projects in the following way:

1. *COST REDUCTION:* investments in training, machinery, or other capital assets that reduce the cost of producing output.
2. *OUTPUT EXPANSION:* investments that accommodate increased output in response to actual or expected increases in demand.[1]
3. *EXPANSION BY DEVELOPING NEW PRODUCTS AND/OR MARKETS:* expenditures for the development and production of new products and/or the development of new markets by adding sales staff or by opening new outlets.
4. *GOVERNMENT REGULATION:* expenditures made to meet government safety, environmental, and other rules.

Capital projects typically are very costly. Indeed, many firms seek external financing to implement a capital spending program. Furthermore, most capital spending projects are not easily reversed. For example, once a new manufacturing plant is built, it may have no other use than the one intended. Thus it would be difficult to sell if a change in market conditions rendered it unnecessary. For these reasons, capital planning decisions may determine the course for the firm for many years to come. The problems associated with a poor pricing decision or incorrect estimate for one production run may be rectified quickly. Generally, this is not true for a major capital project. If capital spending decisions are poorly made, the firm's existence may be threatened.

Capital budgeting requires information on sales, production costs, advertising, and availability of funds, and therefore generally involves all areas of management. Furthermore, because of its critical long-run importance, the capital budgeting process usually is reviewed on a continuous basis by the top management of the firm.

The principle underlying capital budgeting decisions is that expenditures are made until the marginal return on the last dollar invested equals the marginal cost of capital.[2] Recall that the value of the firm is equal to the sum of all future net profits reduced to their present value using an appropriate discount rate, that is,

$$\text{Value} = \sum_{t=1}^{n} \frac{R_t - C_t}{(1 + r)^t}$$

where R_t is revenue in the tth period, C_t is cost, and r is the discount rate, which is the firm's opportunity cost of the funds used to make the investment. The basic capital budgeting question is: Will the capital expenditure, which itself will increase the firm's costs, increase revenue and/or reduce other costs sufficiently to increase the value of the firm? If the rate of return on the project is greater

---

[1] The same investments may result in both output expansion and cost reduction simultaneously. This certainly would be true if there are increasing returns to scale in production. In that case, an increase in output due to a capital expenditure necessarily would reduce the average cost of output.

[2] The cost of capital is the rate that must be paid on money raised externally by the firm (e.g., by borrowing or selling stock) or the opportunity cost (i.e., the foregone return) on funds the business has that it would have invested elsewhere or that the owners could have spent on consumption.

TABLE 15-1 **List of Hypothetical Capital Expenditures**

Project Description	Type of Capital Expenditure	Cost (Millions)	Rate of Return (%)
1. Replacement of obsolete equipment on an assembly line	Cost reduction	$4.5	18
2. Opening of three new stores on the East Coast	Market expansion	6.2	17
3. Formal training programs for all production employees	Cost reduction	1.5	14
4. Replacement of outdated heating and air-conditioning system	Cost reduction	3.9	12
5. New production facility	Output expansion	5.1	10

than the marginal cost of capital, the value of the firm will increase, and therefore the proposed capital project should be implemented.

Suppose that management has identified and evaluated each of the capital projects shown in Table 15-1. The projects are listed in decreasing order of rate of return. The schedule can be used to determine the quantity of capital demanded by the firm depending on the cost of capital. Thus these data represent the firm's demand for capital function, which is shown in Figure 15-1.

Using the marginal revenue/marginal cost principle, the firm will invest as long as the return on an investment is equal to or greater than the cost of capital. For example, if the cost of capital is 20 percent, none of the investment projects would be implemented because that cost exceeds the highest return (18 percent) available on a capital project. Thus if the firm borrowed $4.5 million at 20 percent interest to implement the first capital project, the annual interest of $900,000 would exceed the average annual return ($810,000) on the project, and profit would be

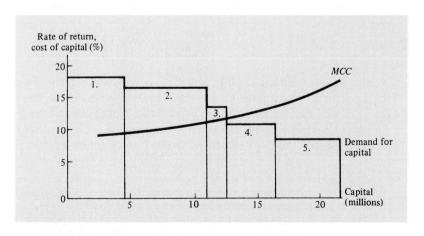

FIGURE 15-1 **The Demand for Capital and Cost of Capital Functions.**

reduced. Clearly, the value of the firm would be reduced if the firm made a capital investment that returned less than the cost of capital. However, if the cost of capital was 15 percent, both projects 1 and 2 would be implemented because their rates of return are 18 and 17 percent, respectively. In this case, the firm would spend $10.7 million on these two capital items. If the cost of capital was lower, the firm would make even more capital outlays.

The marginal cost of capital function (*MCC* in Figure 15-1) shows the cost to the firm of obtaining various amounts of capital. Determining the firm's cost of capital is discussed later in the chapter. The cost is shown as a gradually rising function because most firms are required to pay a higher cost to obtain increasing amounts of capital. For example, if the firm is borrowing those funds, the more that is borrowed, the greater is the risk that the firm will be unable to repay the lender. To be compensated for taking that additional risk, the lender must earn a higher return, which is accomplished by increasing the interest rate charged to the firm.

Figure 15-1 indicates that the firm would make investments 1, 2, and 3 because the rate of returns exceeds the cost of capital for these projects. Note that the rate of return on investment 3 is 14 percent, and the rate of return on investment 4 is 12 percent. However, because the firm's cost of capital is now more than 12 percent, investment 3 is made but 4 is not (i.e., in the figure, the *MCC* curve lies above the demand for capital schedule to the right of project 3).

KEY CONCEPTS

- Capital budgeting refers to the process of planning capital projects, raising funds, and efficiently allocating those funds to capital projects.
- Capital expenditures are made in order to reduce cost, increase output, expand into new products or markets, and/or meet government regulations.
- In general, capital expenditures are made until the rate of return on the last dollar invested equals the marginal cost of capital.
- The demand for capital function shows the amount of capital spending that will be made at each cost of capital.

The Capital Budgeting Process

In most firms, capital budgeting is a continuous process, with proposals being made regularly in all areas of the organization. Typically, each level of the organization has authority to make capital expenditures up to some dollar limit. Proposals in excess of that limit must be screened and approved by higher levels of management to ensure that the projects are consistent with the overall plan for the firm. For example, the production line foreman may have authority to make capital expenditure decisions up to a level of $25,000. Proposals above that amount must be approved by the plant manager, who may be able to authorize expenditures up to $250,000 but must have approval from the division vice-president for projects that cost more than that amount. Thus the larger the dollar cost of the proposal, the more screening steps it must go through.

The first step in this evaluation is to determine the cost of the project. Next, the net cash flows associated with that capital project are estimated. Finally, evaluation techniques are used to compare cash inflows to the cost of the project. In the following, it is assumed the cost of the project has already been determined so that the focus is on projecting and evaluating the cash flows.

Projecting the Cash Flows

Suppose that a firm is considering the addition of a new product line. It is estimated that the cost of new production machinery, reorganization of the production line, and additional working capital for inventory and accounts receivable will require an initial investment of $20 million. The breakdown of these costs is as follows:

Machinery	$15,000,000
Reorganization	2,000,000
Working capital	3,000,000
Total	$20,000,000

Sales revenues from this product are projected to be $12 million the first year, but because the new product is a substitute for one of the firm's existing products, the incremental sales revenue will be only $10 million. That is, the new product will add $12 million to sales, but sales of an existing product will fall by $2 million, yielding a net or incremental sales increase of $10 million. The marketing staff estimates that sales revenue will increase 10 percent each year. The research and development department has indicated that in five years, it can develop an entirely new product to replace the one under consideration. Therefore, management has decided to assume a five-year life for this product and that any evaluation of the proposed project be limited to a five-year period.

The production and engineering departments of the firm have developed the following incremental production cost estimates. Variable costs will be 40 percent of revenue and additional fixed costs will be $100,000 per year. The finance department reports that for depreciation purposes, the new machinery has a five-year life and that the straight-line depreciation method will be used. That is, the annual depreciation charge against income is one-fifth of the initial cost of the machinery, or $3 million per year:

$$\text{annual depreciation charge} = \frac{\text{cost}}{\text{years}} = \frac{\$15,000,000}{5} = \$3,000,000$$

The financial vice-president also indicates that the combined federal and state marginal income tax rate for the firm is expected to be 40 percent. Note that depreciation is a noncash expense that is included as an expense in computing income taxes but is then added back in to determine the net cash flow. The only reason it is considered is because of its effect on the firm's income tax liability. The salvage value of the equipment at the end of the five years is estimated to be $4 million. Also, at the end of the five-year life of this project, the $3 million that was needed for additional working capital is recovered. To simplify the

TABLE 15-2 **Projected Incremental Cash Flow for Proposed Capital Investment**

	Year				
	1	2	3	4	5
Sales	$10,000,000	$11,000,000	$12,100,000	$13,310,000	$14,641,000
Less: Variable costs	4,000,000	4,400,000	4,840,000	5,324,000	5,856,400
Fixed costs	100,000	100,000	100,000	100,000	100,000
Depreciation	3,000,000	3,000,000	3,000,000	3,000,000	3,000,000
Profit before tax	$ 2,900,000	$ 3,500,000	$ 4,160,000	$ 4,886,000	$ 5,684,600
Less: Income tax	1,160,000	1,400,000	1,664,000	1,954,400	2,273,840
Profit after tax	$ 1,740,000	$ 2,100,000	$ 2,496,000	$ 2,931,600	$ 3,410,760
Plus: Depreciation	3,000,000	3,000,000	3,000,000	3,000,000	3,000,000
Net cash flow	$ 4,740,000	$ 5,100,000	$ 5,496,000	$ 5,931,600	$ 6,410,760

Plus: Salvage value of machinery	$ 4,000,000
Recapture of working capital	3,000,000
Net cash flow (year 5)	$13,410,760

analysis, it is assumed that all revenues and expenses occur at the end of each year.

The detailed cash flow projection for each year is shown in Table 15-2. Note that there has been no consideration given to the costs of financing this project. The definition of cash flow when making capital budgeting decisions is the after-tax cash flow, assuming that the firm has no debt. The reason for this is that when using an appropriate evaluation technique, future cash flows are discounted at a rate equal to the firm's cost of capital. This automatically accounts for the financing costs. To include such costs as a subtraction from the net cash flows would effectively account for them twice and would be incorrect.

Evaluating the Capital Project

The remaining problem in this example is to rationally compare the projected net cash flows to the initial $20 million investment that is required so that the proposed project can be accepted or rejected. In order to maximize the value of the firm, the evaluation technique should

1. Consider all relevant cash flows.
2. Discount cash flows using the firm's opportunity cost of capital.
3. Select the one project from a set of mutually exclusive projects that maximizes the value of the firm.[3]
4. Allow each project to be evaluated independently of all others being considered.

[3] Mutually exclusive means that the selection of one project from a set of alternative projects precludes the others from being implemented. For example, a firm may be considering alternative design proposals for a new plant where only one will be selected.

Three evaluation techniques will be considered: payback period, internal rate of return, and net present value. As will be shown, the payback period method, although still used in some circles, fails to meet any of the four criteria just outlined and will be dismissed as a viable method. Under most circumstances, the internal rate of return method yields value-maximizing results but it fails to meet criterion (2) and sometimes (3) and (4). Thus, it is inferior to the net present value method because that approach meets all four criteria and will always guarantee that the project or projects selected for implementation will maximize the value of the firm.

PAYBACK PERIOD   Under this method, the number of years that it takes for the net cash flows (undiscounted) to equal the cost of project is defined as the payback period. The decision rule is to select the project that has the shortest payback period. Consider the projected net cash flows for two proposed capital projects, A and B:

Project	Initial Cost	1	2	3	4	5	Payback Period
A	1,000	500	500	1,000	1,000	1,000	2
B	1,000	250	250	500	5,000	10,000	3

Note that for project A, the sum of the cash flows equals the cost of the project in two years, whereas it takes three years in the case of project B. Thus, using the payback period rule, project A would be selected. However, even the most casual analysis would indicate that project B should be preferred because it has much larger cash flows in periods four and five. The net present value will be higher for B than for A for any normal discount rate. The payback period method fails because it does not consider all cash flows and does not discount those flows to their present value. Obviously, this method is a poor evaluation technique that warrants no further consideration.

INTERNAL RATE OF RETURN   The implicit rate of return on a capital expenditure can be measured using the internal rate of return (IRR) evaluation method. The internal rate of return is that discount rate that equates the present value of the cash flows with the initial investment cost. Define A_t as net cash flow in year t, C as the initial cost of the project, and n as the life of project. Now the IRR is determined by setting

$$\sum_{t=1}^{n} \left[\frac{A_t}{(1 + r^*)^t} \right] = C \tag{15-1}$$

and solving this equation for r^*, the internal rate of return. The decision rule is that if r^* is greater than the cost of capital, the investment should be made. That is, profits, and therefore the value of the firm, will be increased by making this investment because the firm is using capital that costs, say, 12 percent to earn a return greater than 12 percent.

Clearly, solving equation (15-1) for r^* by hand is not a trivial problem when n

is greater than 1. Fortunately, financial calculators and easily used computer programs are available that can solve *IRR* problems quickly. In their absence, trial-and-error methods can also be used. To illustrate the trial-and-error approach, arbitrarily select a discount rate and evaluate the present value of the cash flows. If the present value is higher than the cost, increase the discount rate and repeat the process. If the present value is lower than the cost, reduce the discount rate. By gradually adjusting the discount rate, this iterative process will ultimately lead to the *IRR*.[4]

Again using the data from the example in Table 15-2, the *IRR* method would require setting up the equation

$$\frac{4,740,000}{1 + r^*} + \frac{5,100,000}{(1 + r^*)^2} + \frac{5,496,000}{(1 + r^*)^3} + \frac{5,931,600}{(1 + r^*)^4} + \frac{13,410,760}{(1 + r^*)^5} + = \$20,000,000$$

and solving for r^*, which yields $r^* = 0.179$, or 17.9 percent. Because this rate exceeds the cost of capital (12 percent), the investment should be made.

NET PRESENT VALUE   The net present value (*NPV*) method of evaluation consists of comparing the present value of all net cash flows (appropriately discounted using the firm's cost of capital as the interest rate) to the initial investment cost. If the present value of the cash flows exceeds the cost, the proposal meets the evaluation criterion; that is, the value of the firm will be increased by making the investment. Equivalently, the rate of return on the capital expenditure exceeds the firm's cost of capital, and thus future profits will be higher if the investment is made. Using the *NPV* method, the rate of return on the invsetment is not determined explicitly. Therefore, it is referred to as an *implicit rate of return*. If the net present value is negative, the implicit return is less than the cost of capital.

Formally, the *NPV* rule is that if

$$NPV = \sum_{t=1}^{n} \left[\frac{A_t}{(1 + r)^t} \right] - C > 0 \qquad (15\text{-}2)$$

the capital expenditure should be made. For the example shown in Table 15-2, suppose that the firm's cost of capital is 12 percent. The net cash flows at the end of each year are given in the table. Note that at the end of the project's life (i.e., five years), the cash inflow from the salvage value of the machinery and the recapture of dollars tied up in inventory and accounts receivable is included. Based on a cost of $20,000,000, the *NPV* calculation would be

$$NPV = \left[\frac{4,740,00}{1.12} + \frac{5,100,000}{(1.12)^2} + \frac{5,496,000}{(1.12)^3} + \frac{5,931,600}{(1.12)^4} + \frac{13,410,760}{(1.12)^5} \right] - 20,000,000$$

$$= 23,589,040 - 20,000,000 = 3,589,004$$

[4] There are special cases where it is possible that two or more discount rates will equate the present value of the cash flows to the cost. That is, multiple values of the internal rate of return are obtained. This can occur in unusual situations where cash flows vary from positive to negative from one period to another. Such cases are so special as not to be of concern in this text. This interested reader is referred to T. Copeland and J. Weston. *Financial Theory and Corporate Policy*. 3rd Edition (Reading, Massachusetts: Addison-Wesley), 1988.

As the $NPV > 0$, the proposal passes the test. This means that the return on the new product line exceeds the firm's cost of capital, and the investment should be made because it will increase the value of the firm.

COMPARISON OF *NPV* AND *IRR* EVALUATION METHODS   Generally, when evaluating a single project, the *IRR* and *NPV* methods will yield consistent results. That is, if the net present value is positive, the internal rate of return will be greater than the firm's cost of capital, and vice versa. This is because for net present value to be positive, the implicit rate of return on the project must be greater than the discount rate. Therefore, for any single project, the two approaches usually give the same accept/reject signal.

However, in the case of two or more mutually exclusive projects (i.e., where only one of the investments will be made), the two evaluation techniques can result in contradictory signals about which investment will add more to the value of the firm. Consider the cash flow and evaluation criteria values for investments *A* and *B* in Table 15-3. Project *A* has a lower net present value but a higher internal rate of return. The reason for this inconsistency is that there is a difference in the implied reinvestment rate for the annual cash flows each year. That is, the cash returns that flow from the capital project each year are reinvested, but the rate earned on those reinvested dollars is not known. Therefore, an assumed rate must be used. In the *NPV* approach, it is implicitly assumed that the cash flows are reinvested at an interest rate equal to the firm's cost of capital. Under the *IRR* method, the implicit reinvestment rate is the computed rate of return. This is a somewhat optimistic assumption because the rate of return on the firm's investment opportunities in future years may not be as high as the investment being considered. Thus the *NPV* method offers the more conservative approach.

The NPV method meets all of the four criteria presented previously and will always select that project or projects that maximize the value of the firm, whereas under some circumstances, the IRR technique will not. For this reason, the NPV approach is preferred. Essentially, the value of the firm will be maximized by

TABLE 15-3 **Cost, Cash Flow, and Evaluation Criteria Data for
Two Hypothetical Capital Investments**

	Project A	*Project* B
Initial cost	$1,000	$1,000
Net cash flows (year)		
1	450	−300
2	450	0
3	450	600
4	450	600
5	450	2,000
Evaluation criteria		
NPV (12% discount rate)	622	675
IRR	34.9	24.2

aggressively developing capital project proposals, carefully estimating their initial cost and future cash flows, discounting those flows using the firm's opportunity cost of funds, and then implementing all proposals having a positive net present value.

CASE STUDY

Capital Budgeting in the Real World

Surveys have been made concerning the procedures used by managers to evaluate proposed capital projects. A summary of the results from one survey on the primary and secondary methods used is shown here:

	Percentage of Firms Using Method	
	1959 %	1985 %
Primary evaluation method		
Net present value	7	21
Internal rate of return	—	49
Payback period	42	19
Other	51	11
Secondary evaluation method		
Net present value	1	24
Internal rate of return	1	15
Payback period	15	35
Other	82	26

Although most firms now use the net present value and internal rate of return techniques, a significant number still rely on the payback and other methods that do not use discounted cash flow analysis. However, when compared to the results obtained some 26 years earlier, there has been a marked increase in the number of firms using the better evaluation approaches. In 1959, less than 10 percent of the firms surveyed were using discounted cash flow analysis (i.e., either NPV or IRR). By 1985, about 70 percent were using one or the other as their primary method and 39 percent were using one of them as their secondary method.

Competitive pressures will ensure that managers will adopt state-of-the-art techniques in all phases of their business operations. To do otherwise will result in lower profits and perhaps even losses. The firm that is not efficient in all areas, including capital budgeting, is not likely to be successful in a competitive business environment.

SOURCE: Suk H. Kim, Trevor Crick, and Seung H. Kim. "Do Executives Practice What Academics Preach?" *Management Accounting*. November 1986, pp. 42–52.

KEY CONCEPTS

- Using the net present value evaluation technique, if the present value of all future cash flows (discounted by the firm's cost of capital) exceeds the initial cost of the project, the investment should be made.
- The internal rate of return is that discount rate that equates the present value of all future net cash flows to the cost of an investment. If the internal rate of return on an investment exceeds the cost of capital, the investment will increase profits.

- The use of the NPV technique will always lead to investment decisions that maximize the value of the firm.
- Generally, the NPV and IRR methods yield consistent accept/reject signals. However, when comparing two mutually exclusive projects, the relative ranking of the projects can be different using the two methods because the IRR technique assumes that future cash flows can be reinvested at the internal rate of return for the project being evaluated.

Capital Rationing and the Profitability Ratio

To this point it has been assumed that the firm would make all capital expenditures that meet the criteria that $NPV > 0$ or that $IRR >$ cost of capital. However, for many firms, the total amount of money the firm has and that can be obtained by borrowing or selling stock is less than the total that would be spent if all projects were undertaken. In this case, choices must be made among those projects that meet the evaluation criteria. That is, available capital funds must be rationed among these competing projects.

There are several reasons why a business may be subject to capital rationing. First, the sheer number of capital proposals, if they all were implemented, may exceed management's ability to develop and manage them. Clearly, there is a limit to the scope and number of projects that can be effectively monitored at any given time. Seocnd, internal funds are limited and management may prefer not to take the risk associated with additional borrowing and/or the possible reduction in control associated with the sale of additional shares of common stock. Finally, an operating unit of a larger firm may arbitrarily be assigned a maximum capital expenditure budget for the year.

Strict adherence to the *NPV* evaluation approach (i.e., selecting the project with the greatest *NPV*) can lead to nonoptimal decisions if capital is rationed. Suppose that the firm's capital budget was limited to $20,000 and it was considering the three investments shown in Table 15-4. Further, assume that the firm's policy is to rank projects by their NPV and then implement projects beginning at the top of the list and continuing down until the available funds are exhausted. This approach would be suboptimal because only project *A* would be selected, thus

TABLE 15-4 *NPV* **Data on Three Capital Expenditure Projects**

	Project A	Project B	Project C
Investment	$20,000	$10,000	$10,000
Net cash flows (year)			
Period 1	9,000	4,700	4,700
Period 2	9,000	4,700	4,700
Period 3	9,000	4,700	4,700
NPV (12% discount rate)	1,616	1,289	1,289

adding $1,616 to the value of the firm. But if projects B and C were selected instead of A, the sum of the net present values would be $2,578. That is, the combination of investments B and C would add more to profit than would invest-ment A. The problem here is that the basic NPV approach does not compare the relative magnitudes of the net present value and the initial cost of the project.

Consider another set of capital projects where each has a positive NPV but where capital rationing restricts choice to some subset of the entire array of projects. Under these conditions, the problem reduces to finding all combinations of projects that meet the capital constraint, summing the NPVs for each combina-tion, and selecting that subset that has the highest sum of the individual NPVs. Initially, consider the set of individual projects A through F, in Table 15-5 and assume that total capital spending is limited to $1 million.

TABLE 15-5 **Profitability Ratio Analysis**

Project	PV of Cash Flows	Initial Cost	NPV	Profitability Ratio (R_p)
A	300,000	250,000	50,000	1.20
B	510,000	500,000	10,000	1.02
C	790,000	750,000	40,000	1.05
D	600,000	500,000	100,000	1.20
E	280,000	250,000	30,000	1.12
F	310,000	250,000	60,000	1.24
G	1,020,000	800,000	220,000	1.28

The subsets of projects that meet the $1 million capital budget, their cost, and total NPV for each set are listed here:

Combination	Cost	Σ NPV
A, B, E	$1,000,000	$ 90,000
A, B, F	1,000,000	120,000
A, C	1,000,000	90,000
A, D, F	1,000,000	210,000
B, D	1,000,000	110,000
B, E, F	1,000,000	100,000
C, E	1,000,000	70,000
C, F	1,000,000	100,000
D, E, F	1,000,000	190,000

Clearly, the combination A, D, F, which yields a combined NPV of $210,000, is the choice that maximizes the value of the firm.

What if another project (G) were added to the list that had an initial cost of $800,000 and a net present value of $220,000? Note that implementation of this project would preclude investing in any of the others. As its NPV of $220,000 is higher than for any other feasible combination of projects, G should be implemented and the remaining $200,000 in the capital budget left in the firm's bank account.

An equivalent but less cumbersome approach uses the concept of the profitability ratio (R_p) to rank projects. The profitability ratio is computed as one plus the present value of all future cash flows divided by the initial cost of the project; that is,

$$R_p = 1 + \frac{NPV}{COST} \qquad or \qquad R_p = \frac{COST + NPV}{COST} \qquad (15\text{-}3)$$

If the firm ranked the projects A through F in Table 15-5 by the profitability ratio, projects F, A, and D would be identified directly as those to be implemented. That is, F has the highest ratio (1.24); A and D are next, both having a ratio of 1.20. The total cost of these three projects is $1 million, which exhausts the capital budget. When project G is included, it has the highest profitability ratio (i.e., 1.28) and has an NPV greater than any other feasible combination of the other projects. Thus, it should be selected even though it does not exhaust the available budget of $1 million. The profitability ratio approach is much more efficient than the alternative of determining the cumulative net present value of each feasible combination of projects.

KEY CONCEPTS

- If the number of efficient capital projects exceeds the funds available, the firm faces capital rationing. In this case, the firm must select that combination of projects that maximizes the sum of the net present values.
- The profitability ratio, computed as one plus the net present value divided by initial cost, can be used to rank alternative investments when the firm is subject to capital rationing.

The Cost of Capital

The use of the net present value and internal rate of return methods requires that future cash flows be discounted by the firm's cost of the funds used to pay for the costs of the project. The cost of such funds is referred to as the cost of capital. In general, the cost of capital is the return required by investors in the debt and equity securities of the firm. Basically, there are three sources of funds to the firm for capital spending: retained earnings, debt, and equity. In the following, the cost of debt financing and the cost of equity financing through the sale of common stock are considered. The cost of using retained earnings for capital spending is approximately the same as the cost of common stock, so the cost of retained earnings is not discussed explicitly.[5]

---

[5] A naive manager might view the cost of retained earnings as being zero. This clearly is not the case, if for no other reason than that there is a significant opportunity cost to the owners of the business, who could use those funds for personal consumption or for investment in some other business.

Cost of Debt Capital

There is little controversy about the cost of capital raised by borrowing from banks or by selling bonds. That cost is the net or after-tax interest rate paid on that debt. Because interest, unlike dividends on stock, is deductible from income when computing income taxes, it is the after-tax cost that is important. For a given interest rate (i) and marginal tax rate (t), the after-tax cost of debt (r_d) is given by

$$r_d = i(1 - t) \tag{15-4}$$

For example, if the firm borrows at a 10 percent interest rate and faces a 40 percent marginal tax rate, its after-tax cost of debt capital is

$$r_d = 0.10(1 - 0.40) = 0.06$$

or 6 percent.[6]

Two important considerations should be mentioned. First, if the firm is not earning profits, the pretax and after-tax interest rates will be the same because the marginal tax rate is zero. Second, the concern is with the marginal cost of capital and not the average cost of capital for the firm. For example, that the average cost of debt in the firm's balance sheet is 9 percent is irrelevant. The only important consideration is the cost of raising new capital. This is because the investment decision requires comparing the rate of return on new projects (i.e., the marginal return) with the cost of acquiring additional capital (i.e., the marginal cost of capital).

Cost of Equity Capital

In general, determining the cost of equity capital from retained earnings or sale of common stock is more complicated and more controversial than determining the cost of debt. In the following, three approaches to estimating this cost are presented. Note that dividends are not deductible from income when computing income taxes, so the firm's tax rate does not play a direct role in determining the cost of equity capital.

METHOD I: THE RISK-FREE RATE PLUS RISK PREMIUM   Generally, investment in common stock is considered to be riskier than investment in bonds. The firm has a contractual obligation to make interest and principal payments to bondholders, and such payments must be made before dividends can be paid to stockholders. If profits rise and fall, it is likely that dividends also will fluctuate. However, except in the case of severe financial problems, bondholders will be paid. Thus it is thought that investors will demand a return on equity (r_e) composed of a risk-free return (r_f), usually considered to be the rate of return on long-term government bonds, plus a premium for accepting additional risk. This premium reflects the two sources of risk. First, there is the risk associated with investing in the securities of a private company as opposed to buying federal government

[6] Note that in the equations, the decimal equivalent of the interest rate is used. That is, a 10 percent rate of interest appears as 0.10 in an equation.

securities. Second, there is the additional risk associated with buying stock rather than bonds of a business. The premiums associated with the two types of risk are labeled e_1 and e_2. Thus the cost of equity capital is

$$r_e = r_f + e_1 + e_2 \tag{15-5}$$

One way to measure the first type of risk (e_1) is to use the difference between the rate of interest on the firm's bonds (r_d) and the rate of return on government bonds (r_f). This difference should increase as risk of default increases. For e_2 a rule of thumb is used to approximate the risk of buying the common stock of a firm rather than bonds. Necessarily, this is based on judgment rather than any formula or equation. A typical approach used by financial analysts is to assume that the return on a firm's common stock should be about 3 to 5 percentage points greater than on its debt. Using the midpoint of this range (i.e., 4 percent) as an estimate of e_2, the total risk premium (e) would be calculated as

$$e = e_1 + e_2$$

or

$$e = (r_d - r_f) + 0.04$$

For example, suppose that the risk-free rate is 8 percent and the firm's bonds are yielding 10 percent. Therefore, the total risk premium would be 6 percentage points, that is,

$$e = (0.10 - 0.08) + 0.04 = 0.06$$

and the firm's cost of equity capital would be

$$r_e = r_f + e = 0.08 + 0.06 = 0.14$$

or 14 percent.

METHOD II: DISCOUNTED CASH FLOW   Method I includes risk but fails to consider the possibility of growth in dividends and the value of common shares over time. An alternative approach is the discounted cash flow method. Just as the value of the firm is the present value of all future profits, the value of a share of common stock is the present value of all future dividends using the investor's required rate of return (r_e) as the discount rate. That is, one share of stock entitles the owner to receive a series of payments (i.e., dividends) roughly equivalent to an annuity. Thus the value of that share should equal the present value of the annuity. If the current dividend per share (D_0) is expected to remain constant, the value or price (P) of a share will be

$$P = \sum_{t=1}^{\infty} \frac{D_0}{(1 + r_e)^t}$$

or

$$P = D_0 \left[\sum_{t=1}^{\infty} \frac{1}{(1 + r_e)^t} \right] \tag{15-6}$$

It can be shown that the bracketed term reduces to

$$\frac{1}{r_e}$$

so that the value of a share of stock is simply the dividend rate divided by the required rate of return, that is,

$$P = \frac{D_0}{r_e}$$

However, if the dividend is expected to increase over time at an annual rate of g, it can be shown that the price per share will be given by

$$P = \frac{D_0}{r_e - g} \tag{15-7}$$

Solving equation (15-7) for r_e yields an equation for the cost of equity capital:

$$r_e = \frac{D_0}{P} + g \tag{15-8}$$

That is, the return required by the investor is equal to the current dividend yield on the common stock (D_0/P) plus an expected growth rate for dividend payments. The estimate of that growth rate might be the historic rate of growth for the firm or, perhaps, the consensus growth rate being used by financial analysts who study the firm.[7]

For example, suppose that a firm is paying a dividend of $8 per share on common stock that sells for $100 per share and that there is agreement among financial analysts that the growth rate of dividends of this firm will be 6 percent per year. Using this approach, the firm's cost of equity capital is estimated to be 14 percent. That is,

$$r_e = \frac{8}{100} + 0.06 = 0.14 \qquad \text{or} \qquad 14\%$$

Obviously, variations in the price of the stock will change the firm's cost of capital. For example, if investors bid up the price of this stock from $100 to $120 per share, the cost of capital will fall to 12.7 percent. That is,

$$r_e = \frac{8}{120} + 0.06 = 0.127 \qquad \text{or} \qquad 12.7\%$$

METHOD III: CAPITAL ASSET PRICING MODEL (CAPM)   The capital asset pricing model, widely used in the world of quantitative finance, emphasizes not only the risk differential between common stock and government bonds but also the risk differential among stocks.[8] The risk differential between stocks and government bonds is estimated by $(r_m - r_f)$, where r_m is the return on the average common stock and r_f is the rate on risk-free U.S. government securities.

---

[7] Most firms that have issued common stock that is actively traded in organized markets are followed by one or more analysts in banks, brokerage companies, mutual funds, and other financial institutions. Their forecasts are readily available and managers usually make it a point to keep track of what these analysts are predicting for their firm. For some large firms, there may be hundreds of analysts who follow each company.

[8] The theory underlying the development of the capital asset pricing model was an integral part of the revolution that transformed the world's financial markets in the 1970s and 1980s. William Sharpe, Harry Markowitz, and Marton Miller shared the 1990 Nobel Prize for their pioneering work in this area.

Relative risk among stocks is measured using the beta coefficient, β, as a risk index. The beta coefficient is the ratio of variability in return on a given stock to variability in return for all stocks. Return on a stock for a period of time, typically one year, is the dividend plus the change in the value of the stock during the period. Using k_i^s as the total return in the ith period on an investment in one share of common stock of company S and k_i^m as the total return on all common stocks (or a representative sample) in the ith period, the beta coefficient is determined by estimating the parameters of the following regression equation:

$$k_i^s = a + \beta k_i^m$$

The estimated value of β is the beta coefficient.

A stock with average risk will have a beta value of 1.0, meaning that the returns on that stock vary in proportion to returns on all stocks. A higher-risk stock might have a beta of 2.0, meaning that the variation in returns on that stock is twice that of the average stock. For example, if $\beta = 2$, when the returns on an average stock increase 10 percent, the returns on this risky stock increase by 20 percent. Conversely, a beta of 0.5 would be associated with a low-risk stock where returns varied only one-half as much as for the average stock.

Using the capital asset pricing model, the cost of equity capital is the risk-free rate (r_f) plus a weighted risk component, that is,

$$r_e = r_f + (r_m - r_f)\beta \tag{15-9}$$

In this model, the overall risk premium for common stock is measured by $(r_m - r_f)$ and the beta weight (β) then adjusts for the risk associated with the specific firm in question.

For example, suppose that the risk-free rate (r_f) is 8 percent and the average return on common stock is 11 percent. For a firm having a beta of 1.0 (i.e., the risk for the firm is the same as that for the market average), the cost of equity capital is

$$r_e = 0.08 + 1.0(0.11 - 0.08) = 0.11 \quad \text{or} \quad 11 \text{ percent}$$

Conversely, the cost of capital for a firm having a beta of 2.0 would be significantly higher. That is,

$$r_e = 0.08 + 2.0(0.11 - 0.08) = 0.14 \quad \text{or} \quad 14 \text{ percent}$$

Estimates of beta for many publicly traded companies are available from various financial service companies. For example, the Value Line Investment Survey reports estimated betas for several thousand firms.[9] Recent estimates for some major U.S. corporations are listed here.

American Telephone & Telegraph (0.85)	BankAmerica Corp. (1.25)
Consolidated Edison (0.65)	Delta Air Lines (1.10)
Ford Motor Corp. (1.10)	General Mills (1.00)
Nike (1.25)	Pepsico (1.05)
Sears, Roebuck (1.05)	Zenith Electronics (1.45)

[9] Value Line Publishing Company, New York.

Note that American Telephone and Consolidated Edison offer below-average risk, while Nike, BankAmerica, and Zenith carry significantly above-average risk.

The Composite Cost of Capital

Many firms attempt to maintain a constant or target capital structure. For example, management of a manufacturing business may prefer a capital structure that is 30 percent debt and 70 percent equity. In contrast, managers of an electric utility company may prefer a 60 percent debt and 40 percent equity structure. In either case, capital would be raised periodically both by incurring debt and by selling stock. The differences in capital structure reflect the preference for risk on the part of owners and managers and the nature of the business. A capital structure heavily weighted toward debt implies greater risk because of the greater interest and principal payments that are required. Public utilities tend to have a higher percentage of debt than most other firms because they have a monopoly position and usually the product they sell is a necessity. This means that the firm will have a reasonably stable and dependable flow of revenue and profit, and this offsets part of the high risk associated with a large proportion of debt in their capital structure.

A firm with a target capital structure may maintain two separate ledgers—a list of capital projects and a list of financing plans (borrowing, sale of stock, etc.). A particular financing option, say selling bonds having a cost of 10 percent, is not tied to one capital project. Rather, the firm uses an overall or composite cost of capital as the evaluation criterion for each capital project.

This composite cost of capital (r_c) is a weighted average of the after-tax cost of debt (r_d) and equity (r_e) capital. The weights are the proportions of debt (w_d) and equity (w_e) in the firm's capital structure. That is,

$$r_c = w_d r_d + w_e r_e \tag{15-13}$$

For example, suppose that a firm's target capitalization structure is 40 percent debt and 60 percent equity. Over the next twelve months it plans to raise $100 million by selling $40 million in bonds at a cost of 8 percent and issuing $60 million of stock at $60 per share at a cost of 12.5 percent. Thus the firm's weighted or composite cost of capital would be 10.7 percent. That is,

$$r_c = (0.40)(8) + (0.60)(12.5)$$
$$r_c = 10.7$$

The composite rate of 10.7 percent would be used to evaluate all the proposed capital expenditure requests to ensure that they are profitable.

KEY CONCEPTS

- The cost of capital is the return required by investors in the debt and equity securities of the firm.
- The cost of debt capital is the after-tax interest rate on the firm's bonds or borrowing.

- Three methods of determining the cost of equity capital are
  1. The risk-free rate plus a risk premium.
  2. Discounted cash flow.
  3. The capital asset pricing model.
- The composite cost of capital is a weighted average of the cost of debt and equity where the weights are the proportions of debt and equity in the firm's target capital structure.

CASE STUDY _____

Measuring the Cost of Equity Capital

Having several ways to determine the cost of equity capital can lead to different cost estimates, depending on the method used. The differences can be significant and may make the difference in a decision to make or not make a capital expenditure. Also, a public utility such as a gas or electric company generally has to offer evidence on the cost of capital in hearings about the rates the companies may charge. Obviously, in such cases, the company may want to document a high cost of capital to justify higher rates. In contrast, the staff of the regulatory body, who are supposed to represent the interests of the consumer, may use lower estimates of the cost to keep the rates down.

Although many cases could be cited, a good example is an application for a rate increase by South Central Bell Telephone Company before the Tennessee Public Service Commission. A financial expert hired by the telephone company used the discounted cash flow method to estimate the cost of equity capital at 14 percent. A member of the commission staff used the same technique to estimate the cost at about 11 percent. The explanation for the discrepancy was that the two experts differed in their opinions about the growth rate of dividends.

Clearly, the choice of a growth rate was important. The difference between an 11 percent and a 14 percent cost of equity capital translated into $20 million in annual profits for the firm. In its decision, the commission opted for a rate of just over 11 percent.

SOURCE: *Public Utilities Reports*, 4th Series, Vol. 22, pp. 257–280.

Mergers and Acquisition _____

The growth of the firm can occur internally or externally. When the firm builds a new plant, it is growing internally. For example, General Motors' construction of a new plant is an example of internal growth. Alternatively, the firm may grow by purchasing the assets of another firm (i.e., growth by acquisition) or by agreeing to join with that other firm under single ownership (i.e., growth by merger). Mergers and acquisitions are special cases of capital budgeting.

Types of Mergers

Mergers typically are divided into three categories: horizontal, vertical, and conglomerate. *Horizontal mergers* involve firms that directly compete for sales of

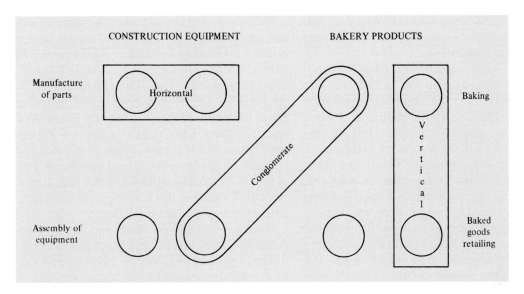

FIGURE 15-2 **Three Types of Mergers.**

similar products or services. A merger of General Motors and Ford would be a horizontal merger. *Vertical mergers* occur when firms that had been operating at different stages in the production and distribution of a product combine to form a single firm. Vertical mergers may consist of a firm acquiring a seller of its output, such as IBM purchasing a chain of computer stores that sell the firm's microcomputers. Often this is referred to as *downstream* integration. Another type of vertical merger is the acquisition by a firm of a supplier of resources or components needed to make its product. An example would be IBM purchasing a manufacturer of computer chips or disk drives. Mergers with suppliers often are referred to as *upstream* integration. Finally, *conglomerate mergers* involve the joining of firms producing unrelated products. An example would be a merger between Delta Airlines and the Levi Strauss Corporation.

Figure 15-2 depicts the three basic categories of mergers. It shows two industries, construction equipment and bakery products. A horizontal merger is represented by the joining of two manufacturers of parts. The combination of a bakery and baked goods retailer would be a vertical merger. The merging of an equipment assembly firm and a bakery would constitute a conglomerate merger.

CASE STUDY _____

The Poker Game for Gulf Oil

In March 1984, Standard Oil of California (Socal) and Gulf Corporation signed a preliminary agreement to merge. The terms were that Socal would pay $80 per share—a total of over $13 billion—for Gulf's stock. The result was a merger between the nation's ninth and tenth largest industrial corporations. Together, the two firms had 1983 assets of $45 billion and sales of nearly $60 billion.

The Socal–Gulf merger emerged as the product of a concerned effort by Gulf to avoid a hostile takeover by an investment group headed by T. Boone Pickens, Jr., the chairman of Mesa Petroleum. In late 1983, Pickens and his colleagues purchased 13 percent of Gulf's stock with the avowed purpose of restructuring the firm in order to increase profits. In response, Gulf's management convened a special shareholders' meeting to change corporate rules in order to make a takeover more difficult. About the same time, Gulf announced that it was considering the acquisition of Superior Oil Co. Although never completed, this merger would have increased Gulf's size and made a takeover more difficult because of the higher cost of the combined firm.

In February 1984, the Pickens group announced that it would pay Gulf's stockholders $65 per share for 13.5 million shares of stock. If completed, this purchase would have raised the group's stock ownership to over 20 percent and might have enabled it to replace some of Gulf's directors with individuals loyal to Pickens at the firm's annual stockholder meeting in May.

Gulf's public reaction to the offer by the Pickens group was to label it as "unfair and inadequate." Privately, the company's management began to contact other firms that might be interested in acquiring Gulf. By March, the list of prospective suitors had been pared to three: Socal, Atlantic–Richfield, and an investment firm, Kohlberg, Kravis, Roberts, and Co. Representatives of each of these firms were invited to come to Gulf's headquarters in Pittsburgh and make a careful examination of the firm's records. Following this investigation, each firm submitted a sealed offer for Gulf Oil.

Socal's bid of $80 per share was higher than Atlantic–Richfield's $72 but less than the $87.50 offered by Kohlberg, Kravis, Roberts, and Co. However, the Socal bid was accepted because the firm had access to the $13 billion necessary to complete the purchase, whereas the Kohlberg firm would have required several months to assemble the necessary funds.

Lest one feel sorry for the unsuccessful effort of T. Boone Pickens and his associates, it should be noted that Socal's offer enabled them to earn a capital gain of $760 million on the Gulf stock that they owned.

Merger Incentives

Some acquisitions take place because managers embark on the creation of a vast empire over which they can preside. The experience of James Ling, former president of Ling–Temco–Vaught, a conglomerate involved in the defense industry, is a case in point. In 1960, LTV ranked as the 335th largest firm in the United States on the basis of assets. After a flurry of acquisitions, the corporation had climbed to 22nd place by 1968. Mr. Ling's merger efforts were well rewarded in the stock market. In 1963, the price of LTV common stock was $9 per share. In 1967, the price reached a high of $169.50 per share. Unfortunately, the bubble finally burst as cutbacks in defense spending after the Vietnam War and the prospect of legal actions against the firm caused the share price to plummet to about $7 in 1970.

Although ego and empire building sometimes play a role in merger activity, usually mergers take place because managers believe that the value of the combined firm is greater than that of its constituent parts. Among the possible sources of this synergy are the following.

INCREASED MARKET POWER A merger between two competing firms can result in increased market power for the combined firm. In some cases, this increased market power stems from the elimination of an aggressive competitor. Consider an industry dominated by a few large firms. If one firm aggressively reduces prices, the other firms may be forced to respond with price reductions of their own. The result of this price competition generally will be reduced profit levels. However, one firm may acquire the aggressive rival by merger. By eliminating the source of active competition, the result may be higher prices, and hence increased profit, for all firms in the industry, albeit at the cost of reduced consumer surplus to buyers of the product.

In other situations, a horizontal merger may increase market power by eliminating excess capacity in an industry. Consider the tobacco industry at the turn of the century. In 1890, five cigarette manufacturers formed a cartel to stabilize prices. In 1898, the cartel expanded its activities into chewing tobacco by purchasing five other manufacturers. One year later, production facilities of thirty other chewing tobacco manufacturers were purchased and immediately closed. The result was a classic example of monopoly in action. By restricting output, the cartel was able to increase prices and profits.

TECHNICAL ECONOMIES OF SCALE If technological conditions in an industry result in increasing returns to scale, firms with large production facilities will be able to produce at lower average cost per unit than will smaller firms. Thus, small firms that merge may be able to reduce per-unit costs by expanding the scale of their operation. Such technical economies of scale may result from increased specialization of labor, greater use of automated production techniques, and/or sharing of overhead and management expenses.

PECUNIARY ECONOMIES OF SCALE Pecuniary economies of scale are cost savings that result from increased monopsony power of large firms. That is, large buyers may be able to obtain lower prices for inputs that they purchase. Consider small farming operations seeking to ship fruits and vegetables. If the firms merge to form a single corporation, the resulting firm may require a significant proportion of total trucking capacity in its region. Because the single corporation has greater market power, it is in a better position to negotiate favorable rates with truckers than would many small firms acting independently. The same principle applies in capital and advertising markets. As a major borrower, a firm such as AT&T may be able to obtain lower interest rates than those offered to smaller borrowers. Similarly, with aggregate expenditures in excess of $1 billion, Procter & Gamble is able to obtain volume discounts for advertising time and space. Firms acquired by AT&T or Procter & Gamble also would be able to buy at lower prices. These cost savings provide an incentive to merge.

REDUCED TRANSACTION COSTS Vertical mergers may reduce transaction costs for the acquiring firm. In the absence of vertical integration, purchasing inputs from suppliers or selling to distributors can involve substantial transaction costs. First, suitable trading partners must be located. Changing prices or needs may dictate periodic reassessment of the suitability of these partners. Next, the terms of transactions with these partners must be established. Because the interests of the trading partners may differ, skill and time may be required to reach agreement. When all parties are satisfied, there is still the problem of monitoring performance. Dissatisfaction by one party may result in a termination of the agreement or costly litigation.

The difficulty of negotiating and maintaining agreements with trading partners is compounded by the incomplete flow of information. Each firm will use caution to avoid disclosing facts that might allow competitors an advantage or permit the trading partner to better its relative position. Even the attempt to be completely open may be partially thwarted by differences in training and procedures of each firm.

Vertical integration reduces transaction costs by establishing permanent linkages among the different stages of production. Thus there is less need to search for suppliers and distributors, and the details of interaction between divisions can be dictated by the management of the firm. Similarly, a common set of procedures can be specified for use throughout the firm. Being vertically integrated also reduces the risks associated with depending on only one or two firms for the supply of important inputs.

RISK SPREADING   Conglomerate mergers may be a means of spreading risk. By diversifying its product line, managers can reduce fluctuations in profit rates. Consider a hypothetical merger between Holiday Inn and the Twentieth-Century Fox Corporation. The hotel and resort business is adversely affected by gasoline shortages and increasing travel costs. In contrast, motion picture producers tend to benefit from conditions that keep people close to home, where they are more likely to attend movies. Thus a merger between these two firms could produce a conglomerate with smaller fluctuations (i.e., a lower variance) in profits than for either of the firms operating independently. This reduced variability in profit should imply a lower beta value and, hence, a reduced cost of capital for the combined firm.

In this example, there may also be complementarity in the two product lines. Holiday Inn could show Twentieth-Century Fox movies in its motel rooms and Twentieth-Century might include references to Holiday Inns in its movies.

VALUATION DISCREPANCIES   There may be a substantial discrepancy between the acquisition price of a firm and its value to a potential merger partner. In some cases, an acquiring firm may be able to purchase production capacity at a much lower cost than it could build comparable capacity. In other circumstances, resources may be available at a bargain price. The merger between Gulf and Socal discussed in the case study on pages 517–8 is an excellent example. In early 1984, the exploration cost of crude oil was about $12 per barrel. But by acquiring Gulf, Socal increased its oil reserves by over 1.5 billion barrels at a cost of about $5 per barrel.

KEY CONCEPTS

- Horizontal mergers involve the combination of two or more firms that produce and sell similar products or services.
- A vertical merger occurs when a firm acquires a seller of its product or a supplier of materials used to manufacture the product.
- Conglomerate mergers combine two firms producing unrelated products or services.
- Horizontal mergers may result in increased market power by eliminating an aggressive competitor or by taking excess capacity from the market.
- Mergers may reduce costs as a result of
  1. Technical economies of scale.
  2. Pecuniary economies of scale.
  3. Reduced transaction costs.
  4. Valuation discrepancies.
- A merger may be a way of reducing fluctuations in profits, thus reducing risk.

Merger Procedures

Typically, three basic steps are involved in a merger. First, a suitable acquisition candidate must be identified. Second, the value of the target firm to the acquiring company must be determined. Finally, the managers and/or stockholders of the target firm must consider and approve the offer.

IDENTIFICATION OF A MERGER PARTNER   Several factors must be considered in selecting an acquisition target. One is the size of the prospective merger partner. Normally, a merger with a small firm is easier than with a larger firm because fewer dollars are involved. For example, the acquisition of Gulf cost Socal over $13 billion. To consummate the merger, Socal had to establish a multibillion-dollar line of credit with banks around the country. A number of other firms were interested in Gulf but were unable to arrange the necessary financing. Possible antitrust problems also favor the acquisition of small firms. If the participants in a horizontal merger control a substantial share of the market, the combination may be prohibited by the courts. Antitrust law and its application to mergers are considered in Chapter 19.

The expected reaction of the owners and managers of the target firm is another factor to be considered in selecting a merger partner. Although hostile takeovers have become more frequent in recent years, this type of acquisition is more difficult than if both parties favor the action. Again, the Socal–Gulf merger is a good example. Gulf's management strongly opposed a takeover by Mesa Petroleum. The firm issued public statements advising shareholders not to tender shares to Mesa. At one point, Gulf's managers went so far as to change the corporation's rules to make a takeover more difficult. In contrast, when Socal expressed interest in a merger, Gulf cooperated in every way. Thus time and dollar costs for an acquisition by Socal were much less than they would have been for Mesa Petroleum.

The extent that resources and facilities of a target firm complement those of the acquiring firm is a third factor in selecting a merger partner. A firm needing a stable cash flow to finance expansion or modernization of its facilities may seek out a merger partner with substantial cash reserves. A firm that perceives that it has an important gap in its product line will be attracted to a producer of a product that fills that gap. Similarly, firms requiring specific resources are likely to select the owners of those resources as targets for acquisition.

Finally, acquiring firms tend to select merger partners that appear to be the best bargain. It may be possible to purchase a firm at a price substantially below its potential value if its owner wants to retire or if the firm has encountered financial difficulties because of poor management or unfavorable economic conditions.

CASE STUDY

Merger Specialists

A merger between two large firms can be a complex undertaking involving billions of dollars. The following table shows ten of the most important mergers (by purchase price of the acquired firm) in the United States in recent years.

Because of the substantial amounts of money involved in mergers such as those listed in the table, firms frequently engage the services of merger specialists to help them identify prospective candidates for acquisition, structure the offer, and participate in the negotiations. Often, this assistance is extremely expensive. For example, the merger and acquisition group of First Boston Bank participated in Texaco's purchase of Getty Oil. The firm's fee for 79 hours of work was about $10 million. This translates to an hourly rate of $126,582.

Recent Large Acquisitions in the United States

Target Firm	Buyer	Acquisition Price (Billions)
Gulf Oil	Chevron	$13.3
Getty Oil	Texaco	10.1
Standard Oil	British Petroleum	7.6
Beatrice	Kohlberg, Kravis, and Roberts	6.3
RCA	General Electric	6.1
Superior Oil	Mobil	5.7
Shell Oil	Royal Dutch / Shell	5.7
General Foods	Philip Morris	5.6
Safeway Stores	Kohlberg, Kravis, and Roberts	5.3
Hughes Aircraft	General Motors	5.0

DETERMINATION OF THE VALUE OF THE TARGET FIRM   Once the merger partner has been identified, the value of the firm to the acquiring company must be determined. Conventional analysis suggests that the value of an enterprise is equal to the present value of future profits. That is, annual profits over some planning horizon are estimated and then discounted back to their present value. This amount would represent the maximum price that should be paid for the firm.

But mergers take place because of an anticipated synergism between the two firms. Thus the value of the target firm to the acquiring firm may be considerably greater than the present value of its profits as an independent entity. Hence an acquiring firm may be willing to pay a premium price. Fundamentally, the maximum price should still be based on an analysis of the present value of profits. However, in this circumstance, it is incremental profit to the acquiring firm that is the relevant consideration. That is, management should estimate its profit over the planning horizon with and without the merger. The discounted value of the difference is the maximum price that should be paid.

For example, assume that the present value of all future profits is estimated to be $400 million for Acme Inc. and $200 million for Peabody and Co. if the two firms continue to operate independently. Also assume that if Acme acquires Peabody, the combined business could take advantage of economies of scale and that the present value of Acme's profit (including the acquisition of Peabody) would be $800 million. Thus the present value of the incremental profit for Acme would increase by $400 million as a result of the merger. If Peabody had 5 million shares of stock outstanding prior to the merger, Acme could bid as much as $80 (i.e., $400 million ÷ 5 million shares) for each share of Peabody's stock.

Theoretically, the value of the firm as an independent entity should be approximated by the market value of its outstanding stock. For example, with the present value of profit equal to $200 million, the market value of Peabody's stock should be about $40 per share (i.e., $200 million ÷ 5 million shares). If this is true, the likelihood of a merger will depend on the amount of synergism associated with the merger. If the merged firm is no more valuable than its constituent parts, there is no incentive for the acquiring firm to offer a price greater than the current market price for the target. In that case, owners and managers of the prospective merger partner will not benefit and the combination probably will not take place. In contrast, if there are substantial synergistic benefits to the merger, a premium over the market value of the target firm can be offered. Because the benefit to managers and owners of the target firm can be significant, the merger offer may be viewed favorably. In the example, owners of Peabody's stock could receive as much as $80 per share for stock that was selling for $40.

PRESENTATION OF THE OFFER Once the maximum value of the target firm has been determined, the next step is to formulate a plan to facilitate the acquisition. If the management of the target firm is favorably disposed to the merger, the procedure should be relatively straightforward. Managers from both firms will meet to determine the details of the arrangement. Once an agreement has been reached, they will make a joint statement indicating the terms of the merger and urging acceptance by the acquired firm's stockholders.

The offer for the shares of stockholders may be in cash or it may be structured as an exchange of stock. A cash offer usually includes a premium over the current market price of the acquired firm's stock. Offers to exchange stock specify that shareholders of the target firm will receive a specified number of shares of the acquiring firm's stock for each share that they hold. The actual number of shares depends on the relative stock price of the two firms and the extent of synergistic benefits of the merger. Consider the hypothetical acquisition of Peabody by Acme. Suppose that Acme's stock is currently selling for $80 per share, while that of Peabody is at $40 per share. If these market prices accurately reflect the values of the firms as independent corporations, one share of Peabody stock would be worth as much as two Acme shares. But if combining the two firms increases their joint value, Acme will be willing to offer a more favorable exchange rate. For example, Acme may be willing to offer as much as one share of its stock for every Peabody share. The greater the synergistic benefits, the more attractive the rate of exchange can be made to Peabody's stockholders.

If the management of the target firm opposes the merger, the endeavor is more complicated. In this case, the acquiring firm must make its appeal directly to the target firm's stockholders through a tender offer. Such an offer typically indicates that a certain price will be paid for a specified number of shares of the acquiring firm's stock exchanged for that of the target firm. Frequently, the offer has a fixed termination date and is valid only if a minimum number of shares are submitted, or tendered, to the acquiring firm. For example, suppose that Peabody's management opposed the Acme takeover. Acme responds with a tender offer to purchase Peabody's stock at $60 per share. However, the offer is to be valid for only sixty days and is conditional on at least 51 percent of Peabody's stock being tendered to Acme. If Acme obtains the necessary 51 percent, the voting rights associated with this majority interest can be used to elect a new board of directors who will favor the merger. If sufficient shares are not tendered, the offer may be withdrawn and the shares returned to their original owners.

KEY CONCEPTS

- Prospective merger partners are evaluated in terms of size, anticipated reaction to a merger proposal, price relative to value, and extent of complementary resources.
- The maximum value of a target firm is the present value of the additional profits that would be earned by the acquiring firm after the merger.
- An acquiring firm may offer cash or an exchange of stock for the shares of a target firm.

CASE STUDY

The White Knight and Other Antimerger Strategies

Hostile takeovers can be extremely bitter and costly. As a means of thwarting such actions, several defenses can be used by managers of potential target firms. One option is to identify another firm, referred to as a white knight, that agrees to purchase the target firm to prevent its acquisition by a less favorable merger partner. A good example is Gulf, which used Socal and Atlantic Richfield as white knights to ward off unwelcome advances by Mesa Petroleum.

Another strategy is the sale of previously authorized but unissued shares to a sympathetic firm, financial institution, or group of investors. By having more shares outstanding, it is more difficult to obtain the number of shares required for a takeover. A related tactic is to initiate a merger with another firm. The advantage of this approach is that the resulting larger firm may be more difficult to acquire and perhaps less attractive with the new addition.

Then there is the Pac-Man strategy. It requires that the firm that is the target of a hostile takeover retaliate by using a tender offer of its own for the shares of the aggressor. That is, the target firm becomes the hunter instead of the hunted, as with the Pac-Man video game. Using the earlier example, if Acme had offered to pay $60 for Peabody shares, Peabody might respond with an offer to buy Acme shares for $90.

A firm subject to an unwanted takeover may swallow a poison pill to reduce its attraction to the other firm. One form of poison pill is to borrow money to buy its own stock. As the firm increases its debt and reduces its equity, it becomes a more risky business. That is, the likelihood of insolvency increases. As such, it becomes a less desirable merger candidate.

Finally, managers may protect themselves against the consequences of a hostile takeover by the inclusion of a golden parachute provision in their contracts. Such provisions are simply short-term employment contracts that become effective when there is a change of corporate control. They provide displaced managers with compensation in the event that they are replaced as a result of a merger. A list of the ten largest golden parachute payments to executives in a recent year included the following:

1.	John M. Richman, Vice-Chmn.	Philip Morris	$22,400,000
2.	Robert M. Price, CEO	Control Data	13,500,000
3.	R. Gordon McGovern, CEO	Campbell Soup	11,200,000
4.	Garth H. Drabinsky, CEO	Cineplex Odeon	7,400,000
5.	Joseph G. Temple, Exec. V-P	Dow Chemical	6,500,000
6.	Terrence D. Daniels, Vice-Chmn.	W.R. Grace	5,800,000
7.	Jan Leschly, Pres.	Squibb	5,400,000
8.	Myron I. Gottlieb, Vice-Chmn.	Cineplex Odeon	4,500,000
9.	Horst W. Schroeder, Pres.	Kellogg	3,800,000
10.	Kenneth J. Thygerson, CEO	Imperial Corp.	2,600,000

SOURCE: ''Pay Stubs of the Rich and Corporate.'' *Business Week,* May 7, 1990, pp. 56–64.

Summary

Capital projects are those investments that are expected to generate returns for more than one year. Capital expenditures are made to reduce costs, increase output, expand into new products or markets, and/or meet government regulations. Capital budgeting is the process of planning capital projects, raising funds, and efficiently allocating those funds to capital projects. In general, the firm continues to make capital expenditures until the rate of return on the last dollar invested equals the marginal cost of capital.

The capital budgeting process consists of two phases. First, the net cash flows are estimated, and second, evaluation techniques are used to compare those cash flows to the initial cost of the project. The payback method determines the number of years necessary for the cumulative net cash flows to equal the cost of the project. Because it fails to account for all cash flows and does not discount these cash flows at the firm's opportunity cost of capital, the payback method is an inferior evaluation technique. The net present value (NPV) and internal rate of return (IRR) concepts are the two most commonly used evaluation methods. Using the NPV method, a capital project is determined to be profitable (i.e., would increase the value of the firm) if the present value of all future cash flows exceeds the initial cost of the project. In contrast, the internal rate of return is the discount rate that equates all future cash flows and the project's cost. An investment should be made if the IRR exceeds the firm's cost of capital.

Generally, the NPV and IRR methods yield consistent accept or reject signals for proposed capital projects. However, the IRR method has several problems. For example, it sometimes results in multiple solutions for the internal or implicit rate of return. Also, it discounts future cash flows at the rate of return for the project being evaluated and not at the firm's opportunity cost of capital. Because of this, if the firm is subject to capital rationing (i.e., where the firm has more feasible capital projects than it can finance from both internal and external sources), the IRR method may not select that project that maximizes the value of the firm.

The profitability ratio is defined as one plus the ratio of net present value to initial project cost. It is used to rank the relative profitability of projects where the firm is subject to capital rationing.

The cost of capital is the return required by investors in the debt and equity securities of the firm. The cost of debt is the net (after-tax) interest rate paid on that debt. Alternative methods for estimating the cost of equity capital include (1) the risk-free rate plus a risk premium, (2) discounted cash flow, and (3) the capital asset pricing model. The last method uses the beta coefficient (a measure of the variability in return on a given stock relative to variability in return on the average stock) to measure relative risk among the common stock of different companies.

As firms often use both debt and equity financing sources, a weighted cost of capital measure is used. The composite cost of capital is a weighted average of the cost of debt and the cost of equity capital. The weights are the proportions of debt and equity in the firm's target capital structure.

Merger is defined as the joining of two or more firms under single ownership. Usually, mergers take place because management believes that the value of the combined firm is greater than the sum of its individual parts. Horizontal mergers involve firms that compete directly for sales of similar goods or services. Vertical mergers occur when firms that had been operating at different stages in the production and distribution process combine to form a single firm. A conglomerate merger combines essentially unrelated firms.

From the standpoint of the acquiring firm, a merger may be a means of increasing its market power by eliminating competitors. Other incentives to merge include cost reductions resulting from economies of scale, reduced transaction costs, and valuation discrepancies. A merger also may be a way of smoothing fluctuations in profits.

Several factors affect the choice of a target for acquisition. A merger with a very large firm may present financial problems and raise antitrust issues. If management of the target firm is expected to oppose the merger, the acquisition is likely to be more costly and difficult than if the proposal is accepted by those managers. The best merger partners are those that have complementary resources and can be purchased at low cost relative to their value to the acquiring firm.

The maximum price that one firm would be willing to pay for another is the present value of the additional profits that managers estimate would result from the merger. An acquiring firm may offer cash or it may propose an exchange of its stock for that of the target firm.

Discussion Questions

15-1. What is the basic principle underlying the approach used by a profit-maximizing manager to capital budgeting decisions?

15-2. Why is the marginal cost of capital schedule or function upward sloping for most firms?

15-3. Contrast the net present value and internal rate of return approaches in the evaluation of capital projects. In general, if the NPV is greater than zero, what does this imply about the internal rate of return?

15-4. Why is it that the net present value and internal rate of return methods can yield contradictory results when evaluating two mutually exclusive investments? Develop an example of two investments when this would happen.

15-5. What is the relationship between a firm's marginal income tax rate and the net cost of debt capital to the firm?

15-6. Some analysts claim that the cost of debt capital is lower than the cost of equity capital for most firms. If this is true, why don't firms rely exclusively on debt financing and not sell any common stock? Explain.

15-7. One firm in an industry may have 50 percent debt while another may have no debt. Why do some firms in the same industry have substantially different capital structures? Why do most firms in some industries (e.g., public utilities) have a large debt component in their capital structures while most firms in other industries have relatively little debt?

15-8. What is synergy as it applies to mergers? How does it affect the amount that one firm would be willing to pay for another?

15-9. Give at least one example (other than those used in the chapter) of each of the following types of mergers:
a. Horizontal.   b. Conglomerate.
c. Vertical.

15-10. How could a conglomerate merger be used to reduce risk?

15-11. Explain how a vertical merger between an electric utility and a coal company could reduce transaction costs for the combined firm.

15-12. What are three strategies a firm might use to avoid being acquired by another company?

15-13. Suppose that the capital market has correctly valued the price of a firm's stock. Why would an acquiring firm be willing to pay more than the market price? What would determine the premium over the market price that the firm would be willing to pay?

Problems

15-1. Staff members of the financial analysis department of Davis Electronics have determined the rate of return on each of the following capital projects.

Capital Projects	Required Investment (Millions)	Internal Rate of Return (%)
A	5.2	12.9
B	8.6	15.2
C	3.4	10.0
D	5.1	14.8
E	11.2	19.0
F	6.5	7.9

The firm's marginal cost of capital is given by the function

$$r = 8 + 0.10C$$

where r is rate of return (in percent) and C is millions of dollars of capital raised for investment.

a. Graph the firm's marginal cost of capital function and the firm's capital demand function.

b. Which capital projects should be implemented? What should be the firm's total capital investment?

c. If a general tightening in the financial markets shifts the firm's marginal cost of capital function to

$$r = 8 + 0.35C$$

determine which projects should be implemented and the total amount spent on capital items.

15-2. Tarnutzer Construction Company must replace its front-end loader. The initial cost and annual net cash flows for the two models under consideration are shown in the table. Given the heavy use of the machines, they will be completely worn out at the end of five years and have no salvage value. The firm's cost of capital is 12 percent.

	Model	
	Heavyduty	Sure Shovel
Initial cost	$10,000	$10,000
Net cash flows (year)		
1	5,000	−4,000
2	5,000	0
3	5,000	6,600
4	5,000	6,600
5	5,000	20,000

Use both the IRR and NPV methods to evaluate these capital proposals. Which should be purchased? Explain. (Except for the initial cost, assume that all cash flows are received or paid at the end of each year.)

15-3. Top management at Transworld, Inc., a large conglomerate, uses the net present value method for evaluating capital expenditure proposals. The firm's cost of capital is 16 percent. Currently, the following eight proposals are under review:

Proposal	Initial Cost (Millions)	Net Present Value (Millions)
1	$11.6	$ 3.6
2	9.4	−1.3
3	8.7	2.2
4	13.2	2.4
5	14.0	2.0
6	7.5	1.4
7	6.5	1.7
8	9.5	−2.4

a. If the corporation has a capital spending budget of $100 million for the coming year, which capital projects should be implemented? Explain.
b. If the capital spending budget is limited to $47.5 million, which projects should be undertaken? Explain.

15-4. The board of directors of Alder Enterprises wants to maintain a capital structure that is 30 percent debt and 70 percent equity (i.e., retained earnings and common stock). For the current year, the firm expects to earn $2 million after taxes (the firm's marginal tax rate is 40 percent) on sales of $15 million. Company policy is to pay out 50 percent of net after-tax income in dividends to the holders of the firm's one million shares of common stock. Management and outside analysts project a growth rate of 8 percent for sales, profits, and dividends. The market value of the firm's common stock is $20 per share.

The average dividend yield on all common stocks is 14 percent, and the interest rate on U.S. government securities is 12 percent. Both management and the firm's investment advisers, Saunders & Wennergren, agree that Alder could sell bonds at an interest rate of about 14 percent. The estimated beta coefficient for Alder is about 1.5.
a. Determine the cost of debt capital for Alder Enterprises.
b. Determine the cost of equity capital using each of the three methods described in the chapter.
c. Determine the composite cost of capital for the firm using the capital asset pricing model to compute the cost of equity capital.

15-5. Quickstor, Inc., builds and manages storage units that are rented to individuals and firms. Typically, the firm builds a number (usually 200 to 500) of these garage-like units at sites on the periphery of growing urban areas. Most of the time the storage units are demolished and the site cleared for housing and/or commercial development within five to ten years.

Management is deciding whether to build a 300-unit storage center between Oklahoma City and Norman, Oklahoma. Currently, similar units in the area are being rented for $85 per month. Each unit would contain 400 square feet and the construction cost per square foot, including site development costs, would be $8. The operating costs of the project (i.e., insurance, management, property taxes, electricity) are estimated at $0.125 per square foot per month. Both the rental rate and operating costs are expected to remain constant for the foreseeable future. Quickstor's cost of capital is 10 percent and its marginal income tax rate is 30 percent.

Because of the growth of the University of Oklahoma in Norman, it is likely that the storage units will be demolished after ten years to make room for student apartments. Demolition costs will be insignificant, and there would be no salvage value for any of the materials. The entire cost of the project will be depreciated in ten years, using the straight-line method. There is no alternative use for the land for the next ten years.

a. Given that Quickstor's objective is profit maximization, should this project be implemented? Use both the NPV and IRR evaluation criteria.

b. If your answer to part (a) is that the project should not be implemented, determine the maximum initial investment that could be made such that the project would be profitable.

15-6. P. T. Barnum, the head of the marketing department (who has had no training in capital budgeting), has proposed a new direct telephone advertising program that would require an initial investment of $100,000 in equipment and $50,000 per year in additional labor costs. It is estimated that the program would be effective for five years and would increase revenue in each of those years by $75,000 over the current level. After five years, the equipment would be obsolete with zero salvage value and the advertising program ineffective because of the entrance of new competition. Barnum argues that the four-year payback period makes the proposal a "can't miss" proposition. Use the NPV method to evaluate this proposal. Do you have any comments on Barnum's evaluation procedure? (Note: The firm's cost of capital is 20 percent, it uses straight-line depreciation, and the marginal tax rate is 50 percent.)

15-7. The engineering department of McDougal Steel has developed the following capital project evaluations:

Project	Present Value of All Future Net Cash Flows	Initial Cost
A	$190,000	$200,000
B	210,000	150,000
C	600,000	500,000
D	490,000	400,000
E	350,000	300,000

a. Assuming an unlimited capital budget, which projects should be implemented? Why?

b. Due to a change in top management philosophy that precludes additional external financing of any kind, the department is faced with a capital budget constraint of $500,000. Which projects should be implemented? Explain.

c. Five minutes before the department head is to take the results from part (b) to the corporate capital budgeting meeting, Smith comes in with a revolutionary new capital item that has a cost of $450,000 and an NPV of $120,000. Assuming Smith's analysis is accurate, what should the department head do? Why?

15-8. Given the following information on three major corporations, determine the cost of debt and the cost of equity capital for each firm using the three methods described in the chapter (i.e., the risk-free rate plus risk premium, the discounted cash flow, and the capital asset pricing model).

Firm	Tax Rate	Rate on Long-Term Bonds	Price of Common Stock	Beta	Annual Dividend	Dividend Growth Rate
Chrysler	36%	8.9%	21	1.30	0.60	10%
Johnson & Johnson	30	7.9	44	1.05	0.92	14
Detroit Edison	36	8.5	33	0.65	1.98	5

Assume that the risk-free interest rate is 5 percent and that the average return in the stock market is 12 percent.

15-9. The common stock of Throckmorton Machinery is currently selling for $40 per share, while the price of McKnight Equipment stock is $10 per share. Top managers at McKnight are planning an offer for the shares of Throckmorton. They believe that by applying their considerable managerial talents, the value of Throckmorton could be increased 25 percent by a merger with McKnight.

a. If a cash offer is to be made to owners of Throckmorton common stock, what is the maximum price that McKnight's managers should offer?

b. If the acquisition is to be made by an exchange of stock, what are the most favorable terms that McKnight should offer?

c. What will probably happen to the share price of Throckmorton's stock when the offer is announced? Explain.

Microcomputer Problems

The following problems can be solved by using the microcomputer program TOOLS, available with the study guide or by using other computer software.

15-10. National Communications offers discount long-distance telephone service to businesses in the southeastern United States. To meet the improved service offered by its competitors, National must upgrade its entire switching system.

Three alternative systems are available. The initial cost and estimated net year-end cash flows over the ten-year lives of the systems are shown here. Use both the net present value (NPV) and internal rate of return (IRR) criteria to determine which system should be selected. The firm's cost of capital is 13.4 percent.

System	Interstate	Scrambler	Regent
Initial Cost	$300,000	$135,000	$130,000
Net profits (year)			
1	45,620	−40,000	5,200
2	51,900	−22,000	8,100
3	55,800	−6,900	10,500
4	60,100	5,500	8,100
5	61,000	30,200	10,500
6	60,000	40,800	8,100
7	55,900	60,400	10,500
8	52,000	80,200	88,100
9	50,600	90,000	105,000
10	40,200	75,400	115,200

15-11. Margaret Vangilder manages the annual bazaar at the Pacific United Church. The most recent bazaar resulted in profits of $10,000, but shoppers had to be turned away because the church recreation room is too small. Given population and income growth in the area, profits could be expected to increase by 10 percent each year if the church could be expanded. A local contractor estimates that such an expansion would cost $35,000. The market interest rate is 10.125 percent, and the church will be torn down at the end of ten years to make room for a football stadium. Should the investment be made?

15-12. The Sloan Corporation is considering two projects with the following cash flows:

	End of Year:					
Project	0	1	2	3	4	5
X	$−100,000	$125,000	0	0	0	0
Y	−100,000		0	0	0	$228,000

a. Compute the net present value for each project using discount rates of 5, 7, 9, 11, 13, and 15 percent. Graph the net present value of each project as a function of the discount rate.

b. Determine the internal rate of return for each project. For what range of discount rates is the ranking based on the internal rate of return criterion consistent with a ranking based on net present value?

15-13. A temporary dam being planned by the federal government has an initial cost of $60 million and will have net cash benefits extending over a twelve-year period as shown.

Year	Net Cash Flow (Millions)	Year	Net Cash Flow (Millions)
1	0	7	15
2	0	8	15
3	5	9	20
4	5	10	20
5	10	11	25
6	10	12	25

a. Assume a discount rate of 10 percent. Compute the net present value and the internal rate of return for the project.

b. Repeat part (a) using discount rates of 5 and 15 percent. Does the choice of the discount rate significantly affect the evaluation of the project? Explain.

15-14. A new technique has been proposed for surfacing roads to prevent potholes. It can be used for a maximum of ten years, but its effectiveness decreases somewhat over time. The initial cost to resurface the road is $90 million and the future net cash benefits are shown below.

Year	Net Cash Flow (Millions)	Year	Net Cash Flow (Millions)
1	0	6	16
2	20	7	16
3	20	8	16
4	20	9	16
5	20	10	16

a. Assume a discount rate of 10 percent and that all benefits accrue at the end of the year. Compute the net present value and the internal rate of return for the proposal.

b. Repeat part (a) using discount rates of 5 and 15 percent.

CHAPTER *16*

Technological Change in a Global Economy

Preview ————————————————————————

During the 1970s, Alvin Toffler authored an influential book called *Future Shock*.[1] A central thesis of this work is that change occurs so rapidly in modern society that people find it difficult to adapt to their evolving environment. He argued that the average person is emotionally and intellectually left behind by the rapid pace of technical and cultural change. If Toffler's ideas had any relevance for the 1970s, they are even more applicable as society moves toward the year 2000. The last two decades brought radical changes in world political alignments, different societal values, and the availability of thousands of new and improved products because of advances in technology.

Faced with rapid change, many firms have found it difficult to keep pace. The demise of communism opened new markets in the Commonwealth of Independent States and Eastern Europe but also reduced the demand for some products (such as military hardware) and intensified global competition as firms sought to take advantage of emerging opportunities. Complicating the situation is the need for firms to stay abreast of new developments within their own industry. Electronics companies must be competitive in using the new digital technologies for their audio and video equipment. Automobile manufacturers survive only if they keep costs down by using advanced robotics for assembly. Computer suppliers can stay profitable only if their machines include state-of-the-art chips, display terminals, and storage devices.

This chapter focuses on technology in today's global economy. The first section examines the impact of technological change. The second evaluates the relationship between the rate of technological change and alternative market structures. Section three considers characteristics of innovation and factors that result in successful innovation. The final section describes techniques that can be used to forecast future technological and societal changes.

The Impact of Technological Change ————————

Technological change may involve new products, improvements or cost reductions for existing products, or better ways of managing the operations of a business. In some cases, the changes may seem simple and the results rather trivial, such as coating paper clips with colored plastic to prevent them from leaving marks on a page or tapering one side of the buttons on a shirt to make them easier to fasten.

In other cases, the technological advance may be brilliant and the impact on society highly significant. Consider the development and evolution of the electron microscope. The best optical microscopes can focus on objects as small as 1,000 angstroms in width.[2] During the 1930s, scientists learned to focus streams of electrons in the same way that optical devices focus light. The first electron

---

[1] Toffler, A. *Future Shock*. (New York: Random House, 1970).
[2] An angstrom is a unit of measurement equal to one ten-billionth of a meter.

microscopes achieved resolution of about 100 angstroms—ten times better than the optical microscopes. During the next sixty years, research efforts significantly improved the instruments. Today, commercially available electron microscopes can focus on objects as small as one angstrom—a thousand times better than the best optical devices. This capability has allowed biologists, chemists, and physicists to make important discoveries. For example, it has enabled medical researchers to examine and manipulate bacteria, viruses, and genetic structures as they search for cures for diseases.

Technological Change and the Production Function

Technological change can be thought of as altering the firm's production function. Consider a product with an isoquant for 100 units of output, as shown by QQ in Figure 16-1a. This isoquant shows all the possible combinations of labor and capital that, if used efficiently, could produce 100 units. Often, technological change allows the firm to use fewer inputs. This possibility is illustrated by the 100 unit isoquant $Q'Q'$ in Figure 16-1a. Note that improvements in technology allow the same 100 units of output to be produced using less labor and capital. Technological change has caused a shift in the production isoquants.

The isoquants in Figure 16-1a suggest that improved technology is neutral, that is, it allows equal reductions in both inputs. This could occur, but it is usually not the case. Some technological advances are primarily labor-saving, while others are mainly capital-saving. For example, the use of industrial robots in automobile

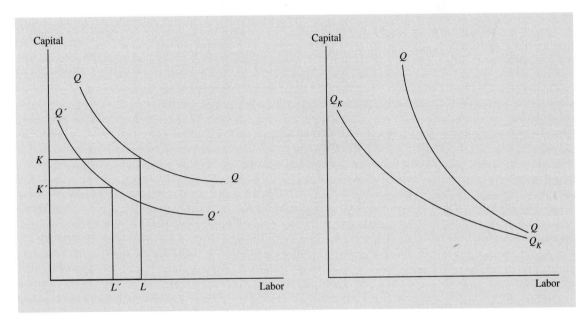

FIGURE 16-1a **Neutral Technological Change.**   FIGURE 16-1b **Non-Neutral Technological Change.**

manufacturing reduced the number of workers needed. In contrast, the development of the transistor conserved on capital by eliminating expensive and unreliable vacuum tubes and mechanical switches from television sets, radios, and other electronic equipment. Non-neutral technological change is illustrated by the isoquants in Figure 16-1b. The isoquant $Q_K Q_K$ depicts technological change which increased the marginal product of capital relative to the marginal product of labor.

Technological Change, Productivity, and Economic Growth

Economists use several measures to assess the performance of the economy. One of the most important is *productivity*, defined as the ratio of output to one or more inputs. Productivity is a key concept because it determines the standard of living that a country can achieve. In any given year, the total value of income received by individuals is based on the total value of goods and services produced. Thus, the only way for all consumers to have more real income is for the productivity of the inputs used to produce those goods and services to increase.

The most common productivity measure is *labor productivity*—output divided by the quantity of labor. If labor productivity can be increased, workers may be able to earn higher wages. Labor productivity has increased over time. However, there have been significant differences between countries. Percentage changes in labor productivity between 1970 and 1989 are provided in Table 16-1 for selected countries. Note that the rate of increase for the United States is less than every nation except Canada and Sweden. Slow growth in labor productivity has been a major concern in the United States in recent years.

Technological change is an important source of increased labor productivity. By shifting production isoquants to the left, labor-saving technological change allows the same number of workers to produce more output. However, technological change is not the only component of increased labor productivity. Productivity increases as workers accumulate more human capital and as the capital stock of the economy increases. Changes in relative input prices can also affect the mea-

TABLE 16-1 **Percentage Increases in Labor Productivity**

Country	Increase: 1970–1989
United States	2.9%
Canada	2.5%
Denmark	3.3%
France	4.1%
Italy	4.9%
Japan	6.0%
Netherlands	4.9%
Sweden	2.9%
United Kingdom	3.8%
Germany	3.2%

TABLE 16-2 **Sources of Growth in Real GNP**

Source of Growth	Percent Attributable to Source
Increase in inputs	
Labor	20%
Education	19%
Capital	14%
Technological change	31%
Other factors*	16%
Total	100%

* Economies of scale, improved worker safety and
  health, pollution abatement, and fewer labor dis-
  putes.

sured rate of labor productivity. For example, if capital becomes relatively more
expensive, firms will use more labor and less capital. Thus, the ratio of output to
labor input will decrease. Conversely, higher wage rates tend to reduce labor
usage and to increase the measured rate of labor productivity.

The output–labor ratio is commonly used to measure productivity because it
is easy to quantify. However, a better indicator is *total factor productivity*, which
compares changes in output with changes in both labor and capital inputs. Using
this approach, it is possible to identify the sources of economic growth over time.
A study by Denison focused on economic growth as measured by the change in
real income in the United States between 1929 and 1982.[3] The average annual
growth rate in real income over the period was 2.8 percent. The estimated components of growth are shown in Table 16-2.

Note that the single most important source of economic growth between 1929
and 1982 was technological change. Almost one-third of the increase is attributable
to improvements in technology. It is also important to observe that about 20
percent of growth was due to higher education levels of workers. Clearly, knowledge, whether associated with new or improved products or embodied in workers,
is crucial to economic progress.

KEY CONCEPTS

- Technological change allows the firm to produce the same rate of output using
  fewer inputs.
- Technological change may be input-neutral, labor saving, or capital saving.
- Labor productivity is the ratio of output to labor input.
- Total factor productivity compares changes in output to changes in both capital
  and labor.
- The single most important source of economic growth in the United States has
  been technological change.

[3] Denison, E. 1985. *Trends in American Economic Growth*. Washington: Brookings Institution.

CASE STUDY _____

Labor Productivity: Automobile Production in England and Germany

In the early 1980s, the Ford Motor Company opened automobile plants in England and Germany. The two production facilities produced the same vehicle and, in fact, were identical. They had the same projected capacity and used the same robot welders, automated body presses, assembly lines, and other capital goods.

But when the plants began operation, the actual results were much different. The English plant produced 716 cars per day with 11,315 workers—an average of about 16 workers per car. In contrast, the Germany facility produced 1,027 cars per day using only 7,789 workers—an average of about eight workers per car. Using identical equipment, labor productivity was more than twice as great in Germany as in England. What caused this dramatic difference?

Basically, it was the result of technical inefficiency in the English plant. When Ford officials began to compare the two facilities, they determined that there were differences in worker attitudes and behavior. Even a casual inspection of the plants revealed that the English employees weren't working as hard. Absenteeism was high and "goofing off" while on the job was frequently observed. In addition, featherbedding in the English plant had increased the number of workers. For example, a British doctor had certified that two men were required to lift the hood onto the car body, but typically one person did the lifting while the other stood by and watched.

Once they understood the problems, Ford management took steps to increase efficiency in the English plant. Employees were brought together in small groups and told that facility would be closed if productivity did not improve. British workers were flown to Germany to observe the operation of their sister plant. The firm also set up employee/management committees to assist in resolving conflicts.

By 1988, productivity at the English facility had markedly improved. Daily output increased to 1,130 cars with only 8,458 workers—matching the eight workers per car produced at the German plant earlier in the decade. However, productivity also increased in Germany. By 1988, that plant was using less than six workers per car per day. Thus, although significant improvement occurred in England, if the German facility is used as a standard, there was still technical inefficiency at the British plant.

Technological Change and Market Structure _____

The importance of technological change in facilitating economic growth is generally accepted. But an issue that has not been completely resolved is the relationship between alternative market structures and technological change. One question is what type of market structure best facilitates the generation of new knowledge? Another is the direction of causality. Does the market structure determine the rate of technological change or does the nature of technology dictate which market structure will prevail?

The Effect of Market Structure on Technological Change

Some economists believe that market power is a necessary condition for rapid technological change. They argue that most modern research and development activities require huge investments and can take years before they yield results. Small firms operating in competitive markets may not have funds to allocate to such efforts and may be unable to take advantage of scale economies associated with complex R&D projects. Also, firms in competitive markets may be unable to capture all the economic profits resulting from their efforts. If competitors can easily imitate new products and product improvements, firms will be less likely to allocate their resources to R&D.

One of the most vocal advocates of this view is John Kenneth Galbraith. Using language reminiscent of Adam Smith's "invisible hand," Galbraith wrote:

> A benign Providence . . . has made the modern industry of a few large firms an almost perfect instrument for inducing technical change. . . . There is no more pleasant fiction than that technical change is the product of the matchless ingenuity of the small man forced by competition to employ his wits to better his neighbor. . . . Technical development has long since become the preserve of the scientist and the engineer.[4]

Clearly, large firms have been responsible for many important developments. AT&T's Bell Labs devised the transistor and Dupont introduced nylon. But small firms have also had an impact. Steven Jobs started Apple in his garage and revolutionized the computer industry. Photocopying was invented by a patent attorney, Herbert Carlson, and commercialized by a small firm that later became the Xerox Corporation. A study by Jewkes, Sawers, and Stillerman investigated the origins of 70 major inventions since 1880. They found that 54 percent of those inventions could be attributed to people working alone and another 11 percent involved individuals working with research institutions. Only about one-third of the inventions came out of industrial research laboratories.[5]

The case can be made that small firms in competitive markets might be more progressive than larger firms with monopoly power. Small firms may be more likely to provide an environment in which new ideas can flourish, while larger firms may impose bureaucratic rules that stifle creativity. Also, a young, small firm may have to be innovative to survive. In contrast, large, established firms that are partially insulated from competition may have very little motivation to change their product lines or production methods.

In evaluating the effect of market structure on technological change, the key is to consider both the ability and the incentives to be progressive. Ability involves being able to fund expensive R&D projects, withstand failures, and wait for results. Incentives include the need to remain competitive and being able to capture the rewards of technological advance.

---

[4] Galbraith, J. K. *American Capitalism.* (Boston: Mifflin, 1952), p. 91.

[5] Jewkes, J., D. Sawers, and R. Stillerman. *The Sources of Invention.* (New York: Norton, 1969).

STATIC VERSUS DYNAMIC INEFFICIENCY Large firms with market power have an advantage in facilitating technological change. They are also better positioned to capture the rewards. However, freedom from the need to compete may cause firms to be inefficient. In Chapter 9, it was argued that allocative inefficiency results when firms with market power set prices above marginal cost. Market power can also cause technical inefficiency if firms incur additional costs because they do not need to compete. Some economists believe that *static efficiency* (obtaining the maximum welfare from resources at each point in time) is less important than *dynamic efficiency* (increasing total factor productivity over time).

Assume that a monopoly continuously wastes 10 percent of its inputs because of static inefficiency. However, because the firm is heavily involved in research, total factor productivity increases at a rate of 6 percent per year. Also assume that if the firm operated in a more competitive market, static inefficiency would be eliminated but productivity increases would average only 3 percent per year. For a given quantity of resources, if the firm's maximum output is 100 units for the first year, output in subsequent years for each scenario is shown in Table 16-3. In the fifth year and beyond, the higher rate of growth in factor productivity overcomes the static inefficiency associated with market power and output is greater in scenario II.

Obviously, the numbers in Table 16-3 are hypothetical. If the static inefficiency was less, scenario II output would exceed scenario I output sooner. However, if the productivity differences were smaller, the inefficiency depicted by scenario II would take longer to overcome.

The issue of the optimal condition for promoting technological change has not been completely resolved. However, the theoretical arguments and empirical evidence suggest that no one market structure or firm size is clearly superior. Rather, diversity appears to be a virtue because each size and structure has its own advantages and disadvantages.

R&D AND THE PRISONER'S DILEMMA In addition to traditional static and dynamic inefficiency, there are situations where research and development efforts

TABLE 16-3 **Effects of Static versus Dynamic Inefficiency**

Year	Scenario I Output — Static Efficiency and 3% Growth in Factor Productivity	Scenario II Output — Static Inefficiency and 6% Growth in Factor Productivity
1	100.00	90.00
2	103.00	95.40
3	106.09	101.12
4	109.27	107.19
5	112.55	113.62
6	115.93	120.44

TABLE 16-4 **Research and Development Payoffs**

		Firm B	
		R&D	No R&D
Firm A	R&D	80, 40	160, −40
	No R&D	−40, 120	120, 80

can be wasteful. Consider the case of firms in a duopoly. Each firm has the option of being involved in R&D to find ways to reduce production costs or just using its existing technology and saving the R&D expense. If one firm cuts costs and the other does not, the more efficient firm will have a competitive advantage. But if both firms find ways to reduce costs, assume that competition between them causes savings to be passed on to consumers and the firms receive little benefit. The payoffs to R&D efforts are shown in Table 16-4.

Table 16-4 is a classical example of the prisoner's dilemma discussed in Chapter 11. If both firms choose the R&D option, their expenditures will be partially self-cancelling. But if one firm is involved and the other is not, the non-R&D firm will lose money. Thus, each firm will engage in R&D. But both firms could earn more profit if they could agree not to spend for R&D. Unfortunately, this is not very likely. It is more difficult to monitor a competitor's R&D efforts than other activities such as pricing and advertising. Also, unlike prices and advertising, successful R&D efforts cannot be quickly and easily matched.

The prisoner's dilemma characterizes R&D efforts in many concentrated industries in the United States. Firms spend huge sums of money on research activities that duplicate those of competitors. Antitrust laws prevent them from engaging in joint research efforts and the fear of falling behind makes it impossible for them to cut back. In contrast, in Japan the federal government encourages joint R&D and large firms are much more likely to share information with each other about new products and processes.

The Effect of Technological Change on Market Structure

Market structure can affect the rate of technological change, but technology can also significantly affect the structure of the market. Telecommunications is a good example. The basic telephone patent was issued to Alexander Graham Bell in 1876. This patent right provided the Bell System a monopoly until it expired in 1893. For a few years, there was vigorous competition in some cities, but the available technology soon caused the industry to evolve into a virtual monopoly. In each city, the local network required that lines be deployed to every home and business in the community. This involved obtaining rights of way, putting wires under streets, and erecting thousands of telephone poles. Establishing a nation-wide long-distance network required that tens of thousands of miles of copper wire be run over great distances and through often difficult terrain. The necessary capital equipment was extremely expensive and there were significant economies of scale associated with the endeavor. As a result, smaller firms were unable to compete and AT&T was the dominant firm for almost one hundred years.

In the late 1960s, development of microwave technology provided opportunities for competitors. As an alternative to running cable, firms could establish communication links by setting up microwave towers every twenty or thirty miles. Microwave Communications, Inc. (MCI) offered the first serious challenge to AT&T by offering data transmission service between St. Louis and Chicago. After ten years in court and numerous challenges to the Federal Communications Commission, MCI finally established itself as a viable competitor. More recently, satellites and fiber optics have emerged as alternative technologies. Today, AT&T still dominates the long-distance market, but it faces significant competition from firms such as MCI, Sprint, and TelAmerica.

At the local level, technological change is having a similar effect on telecommunications market structure. Until the mid-1980s, most industry analysts believed that local telephone networks were natural monopolies and that regulation would always be necessary. But in the last few years there have been some dramatic changes. Large businesses have begun to establish their own microwave, satellite, and fiber optic links to meet their communication needs. Cellular systems provide an alternative to using the Bell networks. Potentially most important, many cable companies are installing new technology that allows two-way communications. In the near future, it is very likely that cable and telephone companies will be competing with one another. The cable firms will offer telephone service and the telephone companies may offer movies, games, and shopping services to their customers.

Some casual observers of the industry have suggested that the recent dramatic changes in telecommunications market structure are primarily the result of changes in regulatory policy as the courts and Federal Communications Commission have permitted competition in markets where monopolies had been protected. But a closer examination reveals that government was simply responding to the forces of technological change. When telecommunications technology no longer dictated the existence of natural monopoly, it was impossible for bureaucrats to perpetuate this structure. The new technologies made increased competition inevitable.

The same forces have caused structural change in the computer industry. Technological change has resulted in smaller and faster computer chips and storage devices. This has changed the market because many applications that previously required a large mainframe computer can now be performed on personal computers that fit on a desk. The result is that the industry has evolved from an oligopoly dominated by a few firms such as IBM into a much more competitive market with hundreds of firms selling personal computers. As with telecommunications, the new market structure reflects changes in technology.

KEY CONCEPTS

- Large firms with market power may be more innovative because they can afford the large investments, take advantage of scale economies, and capture the rewards from their efforts.
- Arguments that small firms will be more progressive include the need to innovate to survive and lack of bureaucratic constraints on creative activity.
- R&D efforts may be wasted in oligopolies if firms engage in efforts that duplicate the activities of other firms.
- Changes in technology, by reducing or increasing economies of scale, can alter market structures.

Industrial Innovation

To this point, the term *technological change* has been used rather loosely. Sometimes it can be useful to distinguish among invention, innovation, and diffusion. *Invention* can be thought of as the creation of new ideas. *Innovation* represents taking those ideas and transforming them into something that is useful for society. *Diffusion* is the process whereby the new product or process becomes available throughout the society.

In many cases, inventions never get to the innovation stage. In other cases, innovations fail to become widely adopted. Sometimes the problem is that an invention or innovation provides no real technical advantage or is not economically viable. But there are also instances when truly beneficial ideas languish for many years. In the early days of sailing, scurvy was the worst killer of sailors. In 1601, an English sea captain found that two or three teaspoons of lemon juice a day provided almost complete protection against the disease. His finding was quite well known at the time, but it was not until 1865, over two hundred and fifty years later, that the remedy was widely used and scurvy ceased to be a threat among British sailors.

Product versus Process Innovation

Innovation can be divided into two broad categories. *Product innovation* involves the bringing of new goods or services to the market, while *process innovation* is concerned with new techniques that reduce costs of producing and distributing existing products.

For a successful product innovation, the good or service will generate a stream of economic profit, such as that shown in Figure 16-2. In the early years, the firm may lose money as it attempts to launch the product and gain consumer acceptance. Later, there may be a period of rapid growth as the good or service becomes widely used and competitors provide substitutes. After the product has been available for a number of years, sales may stagnate or even decline.

In evaluating a product innovation, the firm can use the techniques of capital

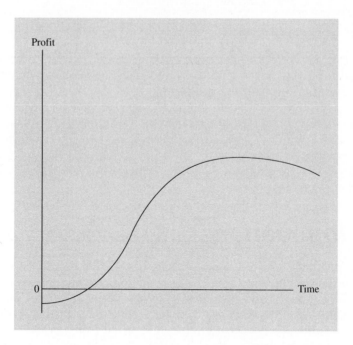

FIGURE 16-2 **Stream of Economic Profit for a Product Innovation.**

budgeting. An innovation usually involves a substantial initial cost and a stream of future profits. Basically, the question is whether the present value of profits is likely to exceed the upfront cost of bring the product to the market.

Evaluation of process innovation is similar. The initial cost of implementing the innovation must be balanced against the future cost savings that will result from the improved process. If the net present value is positive, then the new technique should be incorporated into the production process.

To illustrate the firm's decision, consider the example of a new process that could reduce the fuel cost of producing electricity. Suppose that an electric utility has generators that have been in service for many years. At present, there is no capital cost—the total cost of generation is the cost of fuel plus the firm's operation and maintenance expense. If the new generating technology is adopted, the firm could reduce its operating costs but would have pay the initial capital cost. For the process innovation to be profitable, the operating cost savings would have to be greater than the initial cost.

Assume that in deciding to use the new generators, managers consider costs for the next T years. Also assume that there is no inflation and that the equipment will produce Q kilowatt-hours of electricity each year. The operating cost per kilowatt-hour with the new equipment is estimated to be OC_N and the operating cost using the old generators is projected to be OC_E. Because the new generators are more efficient (i.e., use less fuel and will have lower maintenance costs), it is known that $OC_E > OC_N$. However, in calculating the operating cost saving, the time value of money must be considered—a dollar saved ten years from now is less valuable than a dollar saved today. This is taken into account by discounting the cost savings.

For the existing equipment, the present value of operating costs ($PVOC_E$) is given by

$$PVOC_E = Q \cdot \sum_{t=1}^{T} \left[\frac{OC_E}{(1 + r)^t} \right]$$

where r is the discount rate. The present value of operating costs for the new generating process ($PVOC_N$) is given by

$$PVOC_N = Q \cdot \sum_{t=1}^{T} \left[\frac{OC_N}{(1 + r)^t} \right]$$

Hence, the present value of the operating cost saving ($PVOC_S$) is

$$PVOC_S = Q(OC_E - OC_N) \sum_{t=1}^{T} \left[\frac{1}{(1 + r)^t} \right]$$

Let the initial cost of the new generating technology be IC and the present value of the salvage value of the old equipment be SV. The innovation decision should be based on a comparison of the purchase cost less salvage value versus the present value of the cost saving. Specifically, if $IC - SV < PVOC_S$, the firm should adopt the innovation. Otherwise, it should continue to use the existing technology.

CASE STUDY _____

Successful Innovation: The Gillette Sensor Razor

Gillette's Sensor razor is an example of successful product and process innovation. In the mid-1980s, engineers at Gillette perfected the design of a new hand razor with flexible twin blades that adjusted to the contours of the shaver's face. The new design provided a closer and smoother shave than any razor on the market.

When it was introduced in 1990, the Sensor was a near instant success. In the first two years, the company sold 50 million razors and more than two billion of the twin-blade cartridges. Today, the product is by far the top-selling razor in the United States, with over 40 percent of the market for nondisposable razors—nearly triple that of its nearest competitor.

The design of the new product was the easy part of the Sensor project. The challenging prob-

lem was finding technology that would allow the firm to profitably manufacture millions of razors and blade cartridges each year. With that volume, a reduction of even a tenth of a cent per unit could mean a large increase in profit.

One of the problems was that a Sensor blade cartridge has ten parts, while other twin blades have no more than six. More importantly, the blades must be mounted on a spring that permits them to move up and down but not laterally. Assembling the product at high rates of speed with margins of error between parts as small as one-thousandth of an inch was a difficult challenge. Gillette succeeded by using high-technology laser welding equipment that can precisely complete the necessary 15 welds on each cartridge in less than one-fifth of a second.

Quality control is also an important part of the manufacturing process. Each Sensor cartridge undergoes 100 mechanical or electronic inspections before it leaves the assembly line.

The firm's use of state-of-the-art technology and attention to detail has paid off in cost control. In the first two years since it started making Sensor, Gillette cut unit costs by 30 percent and hopes to reduce costs by another 10 percent over the next two years. Even the smallest detail can make a difference. A product inspection team noticed that a very small percentage of defects in a clip used to anchor the cartridge assembly was causing periodic slowdowns on the assembly line. The problem was detected only after analyzing the data from millions of assemblies. By making a slight design change, the firm was able to increase its rate of output by four percent with no increase in costs.

The Sensor's success illustrates the connection between product and process innovation. The flexible blade design was a brilliant design concept, but it became profitable to Gillette only after a series of process innovations reduced costs.

Requirements for Successful Innovation

Often, the firm that initially introduces a new product does not reap the rewards. For example, Bowmar Instruments was the first to develop pocket calculators, but the firm went out of business because it was unable to withstand competition from Texas Instruments, Hewlett Packard, and other large firms. RC Cola was the first company to sell cola drinks in a can and also the first to introduce a diet cola, but Coca-Cola and Pepsi-Cola responded so quickly that the smaller firm never gained any significant advantage from its innovation. In the early 1970s, Electrical Musical Industries, a small English firm, first developed CAT-scan technology, which provides a cross-sectional view of the internal organs of the human body. The technique is probably the most important advance in radiology since the discovery of the X-ray in 1895. But the firm had little marketing capability and no involvement in medical electronics in the U.S. The result was that firms such as General Electric soon introduced their own scanners and Electrical Musical Industries was forced out of the business in less than ten years, after losing more than $50 million.

The key to successful innovation is the ability to capture the rewards of new product or process developments. This can be difficult because technology, which is basically just information, has some of the characteristics of a public good. Once a new idea has been conceived, many people can use the information simultaneously. For the information to be valuable to its creator, there must be some way to prevent or at least delay others from gaining access to it.

Patents can provide some protection, but frequently they can be "invented around" and are usually not very effective for process innovations. In general, the keys to capturing the rewards of new process innovation are secrecy and being first to use the process. The advantage of being first is that the innovator can accumulate experience, which allows it to keep costs below those of other firms. For new product innovation, the keys to success often are the ability to market the product and, depending on the nature of the good, provide high-quality service to consumers.

Product innovation typically evolves through several stages. In the early period, the first firm to the market may have a temporary monopoly. As imitators appear, there may be several competing designs available. Over time, designs that are more costly to produce or less attractive to consumers will be dropped and the market will enter an era of product standardization. In the early days of the automobile industry, firms produced vehicles with both steam and internal combustion engines. History records that the internal combustion design was the winner. When video cassette recorders were first introduced, there were two competing technologies—Beta and VHS. The Beta technology actually had advantages but never gained a large market share and now has been completely abandoned. A crucial future battlefield is high-definition television (HDTV). Consortiums of American, European, and Japanese manufacturers are developing television technology that can provide a significantly sharper picture. But their approaches are mutually incompatible. As a result, two of the groups are destined to lose and one HDTV technology will emerge as the industry standard.

Once a (more or less) standard design for a product has been determined, the next phase involves developing better manufacturing processes that can reduce costs. At this point, economies of scale and scope can become important. Firms able to produce at high rates of output may be able to eliminate their small, less efficient competitors. Firms with experience in manufacturing similar products may be able to transfer their resources and expertise to producing the new good. Typically, a firm has a set of core competencies or areas where it has advantages over other firms. Innovation is more likely to be successful when the firm stays

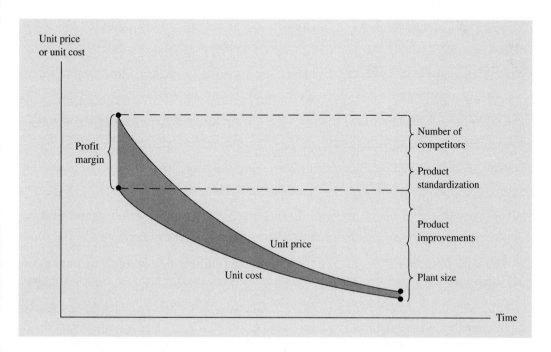

FIGURE 16-3 **Causes of Price Declines Over Time.**

with these core competencies. Although there are exceptions, companies that attempt to innovate in areas unrelated to their previous business experience often fail. The case of Electrical Musical Industries cited earlier in the chapter is a good example. The firm simply did not have the needed background to become involved in the health care field.

Figure 16-3 summarizes the primary sources of price declines over time for new products. The main causes of cost reductions are larger plant sizes and improvements in the production process. But profit margins also tend to decrease because product standardization eliminates the product differentiation advantage of early innovators and because of increased competition resulting from the entry of new firms into the market.

KEY CONCEPTS

- Innovation involves developing useful products. Diffusion is the process whereby new products become widely available.
- Product and process innovations should be evaluated by comparing the initial cost to the present value of the expected incremental profit.
- Often, the keys to successful product innovation can be marketing and the ability to provide service. Profitable process innovation involves secrecy and being able to exploit economies of scale and scope.
- Innovation is more likely to be successful if the firm stays within its core competencies.

CASE STUDY

The Qwerty Dilemma

Until the late 1800s, there was no standard arrangement of the keys on a typewriter. In 1873 Christopher Scholes developed the QWERTY layout, named after the six letters in the top left row. Ironically, the QWERTY keyboard was designed to increase rather than reduce typing time. During that era, all typewriters were mechanical and keys tended to jam if they were struck too rapidly. The placement of letters on the QWERTY keyboard made typists do more reaching and slowed their speed.

With today's electronic typewriters and word processors, the jamming problem not longer exists. The upper limit of speed is now constrained by human and not mechanical factors. In 1932, August Dvorak used time and motion studies to develop a new keyboard layout, which allowed faster typing. The Dvorak keyboard was set up so that the fingers rested on the letters, A, O, E, U, I, D, H, T, N, and S. Letters that were used less frequently were placed on other rows. The result was that about 70 percent of typing was done on the home row. In contrast, the QWERTY keyboard uses the keys on which the fingers rest for about 30 percent of strokes. The Dvorak board even takes into account the differential strength of fingers by placing keys so that the stronger fingers are used more often. It also is engineered so that successive key strokes use alternate hands. While one hand is hitting a key, a finger on the other hand can be reaching to strike the next key. It is generally agreed that the Dvorak keyboard can reduce typing time by as much as 10 percent and that it also reduces hand fatigue.

Because of its clear superiority, the Dvorak keyboard should have become the dominant design. But it didn't work out that way. In fact, it is difficult to find a Dvorak typewriter. The problem is that the QWERTY board has been the industry standard for many years. The existing base of equipment is almost entirely QWERTY and few typists know the Dvorak system. Because there is little demand for the improved keyboards, manufacturers do not produce them. But, because they are not available, typists have little opportunity to retrain. The result is a vicious circle that perpetuates the use of inferior technology.

Patents and Innovation

Advocates of a patent system usually make their case on the argument that market forces may fail to provide sufficient economic incentives to reward innovation. If imitators are able to move in rapidly and capture a substantial share of the market, the initial profits earned by innovators may not provide adequate compensation for the costs and risks that are borne. However, if there is a substantial delay between the time of innovation and successful entry by competitors, the economic profits earned in the interim may make invention and innovation a more attractive activity. The patent system, by establishing a period of time during which the firm faces reduced competition, increases the expected return for innovative effort.

By stimulating technological change, the patent system can increase the flow of new products and processes to the market. The case for patents rests on a benefit/cost analysis. The assumption is that new products and processes available because of the patent incentive more than compensate society for the higher prices that temporarily result from the monopoly status given patent holders.

In the United States, patents confer the exclusive right to the use of an idea for a period of 17 years. Under U.S. law, "any new and useful process, machine, manufacture, or composition of matter, or any new and useful improvement thereof" can be patented. However, there are three criteria that must be satisfied to obtain a patent. First, the invention must be new. Specifically, it must not have been known to the public before the inventor completed it or for more than one year prior to a patent application. Second, it must be useful. In practice, this test can be satisfied if there is at least some indication that the idea can be put to a practical use. Finally, it must be nonobvious. This provision has been controversial, but the present standard is that an invention cannot be patented if "the subject matter as a whole would have been obvious at the time the invention was made to a person with ordinary skill in the art."

A secondary reason for granting patents is to provide for widespread disclosure of new ideas and techniques. One of the requirements to obtain a patent in most countries is that the applicant must describe his or her invention in sufficient detail to permit others "skilled in the art" to use it if they had permission. A firm must take care submitting a patent application. The claims must provide enough information to satisfy the patent examiner but not enough to allow potential competitors to invent around the patent. The document must also be sufficiently broad to give the company latitude in marketing the product or process but narrow enough to avoid being rejected because it conflicts with the claims of existing patents.

Once a new patent is granted, its value may be tested in the courts. The U.S. Patent Office grants the patent but provides no other legal assistance beyond that point. If the owner of a patent believes that someone has infringed on a patent right, to get redress, the person or firm must sue the other party. An interesting recent example is the long legal battle that inventor Robert Kerns waged against the automobile industry. Kerns held the patent for a windshield wiper system used on almost all U.S. cars and trucks. He charged that the automobile industry was illegally using his invention without paying him royalties. After 14 years, in 1992, the courts ordered Ford to give him $10.2 million and Chrysler to pay $11.3 million in compensation. Not all infringement decisions favor the patent holder. In fact, about 20 percent of all court cases involving patents ultimately result in the patents being declared invalid.

One of the difficult aspects of U.S. patent law is the principle that a patent is issued to the person who conceives the idea rather than the person who first files for a patent. Although this may seem fair, it complicates the issuance of patents because the patent office (and often the courts) must decide who was the original inventor. The United States is alone in using this criterion. Every other country awards patents based on who is the first to file an application. In the next few years, it is likely that the United States will conform and adopt the first-to-file principle.

A second important international issue involving patents and also copyrights is countries that allow firms to steal and copy protected ideas. Computer software and hardware companies, pharmaceutical firms, book publishers, watchmakers, and shoe manufacturers in the United States and other countries lose billions of dollars each year because imitations of their products are sold to unsuspecting consumers. Among the worst offenders are firms in Korea, Taiwan, India, and Thailand. Either because of a lack of interest or resources for enforcement, governments of these nations seldom prosecute local firms for patent and copyright violations.

KEY CONCEPTS

- By creating a lag between innovation and imitation, patents increase the incentive for innovation.
- U.S. patents have a duration of 17 years.
- To be patented, an invention must be new, useful, and nonobvious.
- The award of a patent does not guarantee that the patent holder's rights will be upheld in court.
- U.S. patents are awarded based on who is first to conceive of an idea, while other nations use a first-to-file standard.

Technological and Environmental Forecasting

One of the requirements for effective long-term planning by managers is to assess the changes in technology and environmental conditions that could affect the firm. Technological forecasting involves anticipating development of new products and processes and the time it will take for them to be widely adopted. Environmental forecasts focus on factors such as population growth, resources, and social and political trends that may affect the firm's future.

All predictive activity is subject to error, but technological and environmental forecasting is particularly difficult because it often involves assessing ideas and relationships that do not exist at the time the analysis is being performed. For example, nuclear fusion is a technology for energy generation based on the joining of atomic particles. For the last thirty years, scientists have been predicting that commercial fusion would soon be available. But the fusion researchers are still in their laboratories and the breakthroughs have not yet materialized.

Although the techniques discussed in Chapter 5 have some value for long-term forecasting, most are better suited for predicting performance a year or two in the future. Long-term technological and environmental forecasts require special methods. By their very nature, they are less precise and rely heavily on the skill of the analyst. Two broad categories of techniques are discussed here. The qualitative methods focus on subjective judgments of individuals, while the quantitative approaches attempt to manipulate the limited data that are available.

Qualitative Forecasting Methods

When there are no empirical data, technological and environmental forecasts must be based on the best guesses of people who are knowledgeable in the field. In Chapter 5, the Delphi method was introduced as a technique for refining expert opinion. To use this approach, a group of experts is asked to assess a particular situation, presented with the judgments of others in the group, and then asked to reevaluate their individual positions based on what they have heard. This process may continue through several iterations until a consensus is reached or until it is apparent that there will be no consensus. The Delphi method has been successfully used to forecast the nature and timing of technological change. Gerstenfeld describes the following application.[6]

Round 1. A panel was requested to list inventions and technological changes that they thought were both needed and achievable in the next 50 years. From their responses, a list of 49 items was prepared.

Round 2. The group was presented with a list of time periods and asked to forecast the interval in which there was a 50 percent chance that each

[6] Gersenfeld, A. "Technological Forecasting." *Journal of Business*. (January 1971):10–18.

of the 49 developments would first be available. For example, one panel member might respond that there was a 50 percent chance of a cure for all forms of cancer 11 to 20 years in the future. Another might choose a 21- to 30-year interval.

Round 3. On items for which there was no consensus, the experts were asked to indicate the reasons for their estimates. After assessing the views of others, they were given an opportunity to change their responses.

Round 4. The process of rounds 2 and 3 was repeated. The ultimate result was a narrower range of estimates for most breakthroughs.

The Delphi method is not the only way to assist experts in making subjective assessments of the future. Sandoz, a Swiss manufacturer of pharmaceuticals, used subjective probabilities as a basis for R&D planning decisions. Twice each year a small group of managers and scientists was asked to estimate the probability of success for each of the firm's R&D projects. One of the problems the firm experienced was that the group had difficulty in making numerical estimates of the probabilities.

To assist the experts, an indirect method of quantifying probabilities was used. A wheel was divided into two colored sections, one blue and one orange. The wheel was adjustable so that the relative proportions of the two colors could be changed. In the center was a pointer that could be spun. Each expert was asked which event was more likely: (1) that the spinner would stop on the orange section or (2) that a specified R&D project would succeed. If the answer was (1), the wheel was adjusted to decrease the relative size of the orange. If the answer was (2), the orange portion of the wheel was made larger. The procedure was repeated until the person believed that the two events were equally likely. The portion of the wheel that was orange was the expert's subjective probability that the R&D project would be successful. The probability wheel provided no new information, but it did give the scientists and managers a frame of reference for making their decisions.

Forecasts of future technology can also be made using analogy methods. The concept is that experience with existing technology may provide insights in predicting what will happen with a new product or process. One possible application involves forecasting new technology in commercial aviation. Historically, the most advanced aircraft have been military because the perceived needs of defense have resulted in billions of dollars being spent for R&D. However, many of the resulting innovations have later been incorporated into commercial aircraft. Thus, by tracking the trends in military aviation, it may be possible to forecast future developments in the commercial aviation area.

The analogy method can be used if there are technologies that are expected to follow similar paths. The use of solar heating was analyzed by examining historical experience with heat pumps, and the diffusion of color television sets was predicted using sales trends for black and white sets. Similarly, the future rate of adoption of high-definition television sets could be evaluated based on experience with large-screen TV sets.

CASE STUDY

Megatrends 2000

In 1982, John Naisbitt wrote a popular and influential book, *Megatrends*, in which he predicted ten social trends that would affect the future. His analysis was based on a method called content analysis, which was developed during World War II. During the war, intelligence personnel wanted to obtain information on trends and opinions in enemy nations. In the United States, such information could be collected by developing and administering an opinion poll, but that option was not very feasible in Germany at the time. The best alternative was to perform an in-depth analysis of items appearing in German newspapers. As the war continued, information about the economy and public morale was pieced together and used to evaluate conditions and trends in Germany. The project was so successful that it was also used by the U.S. government to analyze Japan, Korea, and Vietnam during wars with those countries.

Naisbitt and his associates use this same technique to forecast the directions in which U.S. society is heading. For years, his staff has been extracting information from big-city and small-town newspapers. Relevant articles are clipped and assigned to one or more categories. By analyzing developments and changes found in their files, they attempt to identify important trends. Firms and other organizations subscribe to this service and receive forecasts pertaining to a specific area.

In 1990, Naisbitt published a second best-selling book called *Megatrends 2000.** His approach was the same, but this time the ten most important trends for the 1990s were identified. Following are his predictions.

1. A global economic boom during the 1990s.
2. A renaissance in the arts.
3. The emergence of free-market socialism.
4. A trend toward global lifestyles, but at the same time, intense nationalism.
5. The privatization of state-owned firms.
6. Increasing importance of the Pacific Rim countries.
7. A decade of women in leadership.
8. Increased importance of biotechnology.
9. A religious revival.
10. A greater emphasis on the individual and on freedom.

Naisbitt's forecasts have been criticized as being obvious and so generalized that they provide no real help in decision making. Still, looking at the list, there is some indication that the 1990s are unfolding as he predicted.

* Naisbitt, J., and P. Aburdene. 1990. *Megatrends 2000.* (New York: William Morrow, 1990).

Quantitative Forecasting Methods

Lack of empirical data can make technological and environmental forecasting difficult. However, there are techniques that allow an analyst to make quantitative forecasts based on limited data.

ESTIMATING THE LEARNING CURVE In some industries, a firm may be able to reduce its costs as it produces more and more units of a product. This is often referred to as the learning curve effect. This concept is different from economies of scale. Scale economies involve cost reductions associated with current output. The learning curve reflects efficiency gains resulting from the cumulative total of all output produced to date. Figure 16-4 shows an example of a learning curve for a manufactured product. Note that average costs decline as cumulative output increases. However, also note that the rate of reduction decreases as cumulative output increases.

If the learning curve is known or can be estimated, the information could be extrapolated to forecast future costs. Consider a firm that has been producing a product for a period of time and has collected the following data on average costs and cumulative output:

Average Cost	Cumulative Output
1.00	100
0.90	200
0.82	300
0.76	400
0.72	500

To determine pricing strategy, the firm wants to project average costs when it reaches a cumulative output of 600 units. In general, the learning curve can be expressed as

$$AC = BQ^\alpha \tag{16-1}$$

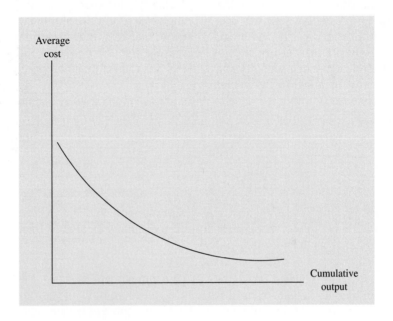

FIGURE 16-4 **The Learning Curve.**

where AC is average cost and Q is cumulative output. This functional form is selected because its graph corresponds to the learning curve of Figure 16-4.

Taking the logarithm of each side, equation (16-1) can be expressed as

$$\log(AC) = \log(B) + \alpha\log(Q) \tag{16-2}$$

Because equation (16-2) is linear, its parameters can be estimated using least squares. In original form, the estimated regression equation is

$$AC = 2.6164Q^{-2.055}$$

Substituting $Q = 600$, the predicted cost is $0.7027 per unit.

Not all products exhibit a significant learning curve effect. Experience may result in little or not cost reductions for low-technology goods and services. But there may be a significant saving over time for items that require new and complicated production processes.

DIFFUSION MODELS   The diffusion of new innovations often follows a fairly predictable pattern. When a new product or process is first introduced, potential users may be somewhat uncertain about its purpose, effectiveness, and/or safety. Consequently, the proportion of people or firms using the innovation is very limited at first. As the initial users gain experience, other begin to adopt the innovation. Thus, the second phase of diffusion is characterized by more rapid growth. Finally, as the market becomes saturated, the rate of growth declines. This pattern can be depicted by the S-shaped curve in Figure 16-5.

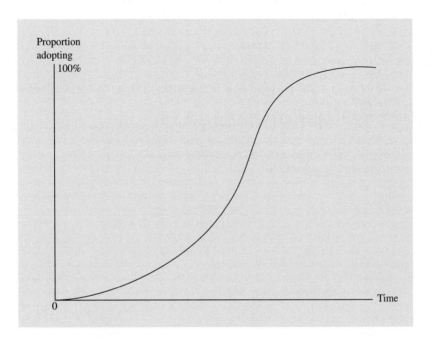

FIGURE 16-5 **The Diffusion Curve.**

During the early 1940s, Ryan and Gross studied the adoption of hybrid corn seed.[7] The new variety increased yields by 20 percent compared to the seeds most farmers were using at the time. The two researchers conducted personal interviews with 259 Iowa farmers and found that all but two had switched to the new seed between 1928 and 1941. From 1928 to 1933, the adoption rate was only 10 percent. But during the next three years, an additional 40 percent made the change. Thereafter, the rate of adoption began to level off because fewer farmers remained to adopt the new idea. Ryan and Gross were pioneers, but their methods have been used many times since then to evaluate the diffusion of new products and processes.

The S-shaped diffusion curve can be used to estimate the probability that any given firm or individual will be using an innovation at some point in time. The mathematical equation that depicts the curve is given by

$$P(t) = \frac{1}{1 + e^{-(B+at)}}$$

where $P(t)$ is the proportion of adopters at time t and B and a are the parameters that reflect the rate of adoption for a particular innovation. For example, if $B = -5$ and $a = 1$, then $P(t)$ for t ranging from 1 to 9 is

$$P(1) = 0.02$$
$$P(2) = 0.05$$
$$P(3) = 0.12$$
$$P(4) = 0.27$$
$$P(5) = 0.50$$
$$P(6) = 0.73$$
$$P(7) = 0.88$$
$$P(8) = 0.95$$
$$P(9) = 0.98$$

Thus after nine periods, the innovation will have been adapted by 98% of the group involved.

The statistical methods are beyond the scope of this book, but techniques are available that allow the coefficients of B and a to be estimated. Once the parameters of the equation have been determined, the proportion of adoption at a future time can be predicted.

KEY CONCEPTS

- The Delphi method is frequently used for making forecasts of technological and environmental change.
- Analogy methods predict trends for one innovation based on historical experience with a related innovation.

[7] Ryan, B., and N. Gross. "The Diffusion of Hybrid Corn Seed in Two Iowa Communities." *Rural Sociology* (1943), 8:15–24.

- The learning curve reflects cost reductions based on the cumulative output produced by a firm. The curve can be estimated using regression techniques.
- Diffusion of many product and process innovations follows an S-shaped curve. This curve can be used to forecast future rates of adoption.

Summary

Technological change can involve new products, improvements or cost reductions for existing products, or better ways of managing. Technological change can be represented as a leftward shift of the production function. Labor-saving change economizes on human inputs and capital-saving technology reduces the need for capital.

Labor productivity is the ratio of output to labor input. Increases in labor productivity may reflect technological change or increases in human capital and the stock of capital goods. A better measure is total factor productivity, which compares changes in output with changes in both labor and capital inputs. Over time, the single most important source of economic growth has been technological change.

Concentrated industries with large firms may facilitate technological change because of the large investments required, scale economies associated with research and development, and the ability of firms with market power to capture the rewards of innovation. The increased dynamic efficiency of firms with market power may offset any technical and allocative inefficiency that exists. However, small firms may provide an environment that is better suited for the development of new ideas. Also, firms facing competition may be forced to innovate to survive. Firms in oligopolistic markets may engage in wasteful duplication of R&D efforts.

Although market structure can affect the rate of technological change, the technology used in an industry can also affect market structure. Changes in technology have made the telecommunications and computer industries much more competitive.

Innovation involves taking new ideas and transforming them into useful products and processes. Diffusion is the process whereby innovations become available throughout society. An innovation should be adopted by a firm if the present value of profits exceeds the initial cost. For new processes, the keys to successful innovation are secrecy, maintaining some lead time over competitors, and taking advantage of economies of scale and scope. For new products, keys include being able to effectively market the product and providing good service. Innovation is more likely to succeed when the firm remains within its core competencies.

Patents provide a 17-year period during which innovators are provided legal protection from competition. To be patentable, the invention must be new, useful, and nonobvious. U.S. patents are awarded based on who is first to conceive of an idea. A patent may be invalidated by a court challenge.

The Delphi method has often been used to forecast the nature and timing of new technology and future social conditions. Another approach is to forecast one event based on historical experience with a similar or related event.

For some new products, average cost may go down with increases in cumulative output. This learning curve can be estimated by using regression techniques. Diffusion of new ideas may be represented by an S-shaped curve. The proportion of individuals or firms will have adopted the innovation at any time can be predicted by estimating the parameters of the curve.

Discussion Questions

16-1. Could the development of a completely new product be thought of as shifting the production function? Explain.

16-2. Does most technological change tend to be labor saving or capital saving? Explain.

16-3. What is human capital and how does it enhance labor productivity?

16-4. How could a large firm create a work environment that would allow new ideas to flourish?

16-5. How has technological change affected market structure in the automobile industry?

16-6. Innovators have the advantage of being first. Are there any advantages to being an imitator rather than the first firm to market a product or use a new process? Explain.

16-7. Recently, biologists have learned to manipulate genes. Should such discoveries be patentable? Why or why not?

16-8. Which of the trends listed in the *Megatrends 2000* case study seem accurate today? Are there some that appear to be inaccurate? Explain.

16-9. How does rapid technological change affect the value of input/output analysis as a tool for forecasting?

16-10. Think about the diffusion study for hybrid corn seed. Why did some farmers use it almost immediately, while others waited almost ten years?

Problems

16-1. A firm's production function is given by $Q = 20K^{0.5}L^{0.5}$. The price of capital is $10 and the price of labor is $5.

   a. Determine the expansion path. (Note: The expansion path is discussed on pages 199–202.)

   b. Assume that neutral technological change improves efficiency by 10 percent. Write the new production function and determine the new expansion path.

16-2. A firm's production function is given by $Q = 50K^{0.2}L^{0.9}$.

   a. What do you know about returns to scale?

   b. Assume that neutral technological change improves efficiency by 25 percent. How does this affect the answer to (a)?

16-3. Fawson Enterprises uses labor and materials to produce its product. In 1992, the firm used 10,000 hours of labor and 8,000 pounds of materials to produce 4,000 units of output. In 1993, 9,800 hours of labor and 7,900 pounds of materials were used to produce 4,200 units of output. In both years the price of labor was $20 per hour and materials cost $15 per pound.

a. What was the percentage increase in labor productivity between 1992 and 1993?

b. What was the percentage increase in total productivity between 1992 and 1993? Hint: Consider cost per unit.

16-4. A truck is driven 20,000 miles per year. Considering the fuel and maintenance expense, it is estimated that the vehicle costs $0.30 per mile to operate. A new truck would cost $15,000, but operating costs would be only $0.20 per mile. The trade-in value of the old truck is $4,000. The owner uses a planning horizon of eight years and a discount rate of 12 percent. Should the new truck be purchased? Assume that fuel and maintenance costs are paid at the end of the year.

16-5. A homeowner is considering spending $1,000 to purchase a new fuel-efficient furnace. In a typical year, the cost of heating with the existing furnace is $400. The new furnace will cut heating costs by 25 percent. The owner expects to live in the house for five more years and believes that the fuel-efficient furnace will increase the value of the home by $700 when it is sold. Assume that there is no difference in maintenance costs and that a discount rate of 10 percent is used to evaluate the decision. Also assume that all heating bills are paid at the end of the year. Should the new furnace be purchased?

16-6. The learning curve is estimated to be $AC = 5.00Q^{-1}$, where AC is average cost and Q is cumulative output. What is the estimated average cost for 800 units of output? For 900 units?

16-7. The diffusion curve for a new production process is given by $P(t) = 1/(1 + e^{-(B+at)})$, where $P(t)$ is the proportion of firms using the process at time t, $B = -3$, and $a = .5$. About how many years will it take until about 20 percent of firms are using the process? Until 50 percent are using it?

Problem Requiring Calculus

16-8. A firm's production function is given by $Q = 30K^{0.7}L^{0.5}$.
a. Calculate the marginal products of labor and capital.
b. Assume neutral technological change improves efficiency by 20 percent. Recalculate the marginal products.

Microcomputer Problems

The following problems can be solved by using the microcomputer program TOOLS, available with the study guide, or by using other computer software.

16-9. Bailey Manufacturing is contemplating adopting a new quality control system. The incremental revenues and costs over the firm's 12-year planning horizon are as shown here. If the firm uses a 10 percent discount rate for decision making, should the innovation be adopted? Repeat the exercise for discount rates of 5 and 15 percent. What discount rate would make Bailey essentially indifferent about using or not using the quality control system?

Year	Profit	Cost
0	0	500
1	5	15
2	10	15
3	15	15
4	25	15
5	40	15
6	60	15
7	90	15
8	100	15
9	110	15
10	115	15
11	120	15
12	120	15

16-10. A firm has collected the following data on average costs and cumulative output:

Average cost	Cumulative Output
$150	100,000
140	150,000
132	175,000
127	200,000
124	225,000
122	250,000
122	275,000

a. Estimate the firm's learning curve.
b. What is the difference between the actual and predicted average cost for 200,000 units of cumulative output?
c. What is the predicted average cost for 300,000 units of cumulative output?

CHAPTER 17

Locating the Firm in a Global Economy

563

Preview _____

The economic analysis developed thus far neglects an important factor—the effect of the spatial dimension and its implications for locating the firm. Locating a business in the right place is important because the cost of moving output and people across space is significant. For example, the best site for a retail store generally is one that is in close proximity to a large number of people who are the potential customers of the store. In contrast, a manufacturing firm may combine raw materials from several source and ship manufactured output to customers at other sites. In this case, an important location criterion is the cost of obtaining raw materials relative to the cost of shipping final output.

Another consideration is that all firms employ workers who must travel from their homes to the firm each working day. The firm must locate in close proximity to that labor supply or face the prospect of paying premium wages to compensate workers for traveling long distances and/or providing housing and other amenities for workers at the employment site. The latter are characteristic of installations located in remote locations such as offshore oil drilling platforms and some mining operations.

Clearly, some locations for the firm are better than others, and there are numerous examples of business failures that can be directly attributed to the selection of a poor location. In this chapter, five topics in location theory are discussed. First, the basic theoretical principles of industrial location are considered. Next is a discussion of the determination of the market area for a firm; that is, given the location of firms in a region, what share of the market will accrue to each? The third section covers the principle of threshold analysis, which explains why certain economic activities are found in some areas but not in others. In the next section, the relative importance of a variety of location factors is discussed. Finally, principles guiding the location of the firm in the global economy are developed.

Basic Location Principles _____

In this section, the fundamental principles of industrial location are outlined.[1] Consider, for example, the problems that would be associated with locating a manufacturing firm that used several different raw materials, each of which could be obtained from suppliers in many parts of the country, and that sold several different products to many customers in a number of locations. Seeking the location that minimized the total transportation costs for raw material and output could become a very complicated problem.

The simple models discussed here, however, provide the flavor of location theory and illustrate some important location principles. One principle is that

_____

[1] For an excellent summary of the basic principles of location theory, see W. Alonso, "Location Theory," in W. Alonso and J. Friedman, eds., *Regional Policy: Theory and Applications.* (Cambridge, Mass.: MIT Press, 1975).

there is a tendency for firms and individuals to locate together in particular areas. Even the most casual observer of geography is struck by the concentration of economic and human activity in cities. There are a variety of reasons for this concentration, but one of the most important is economic in nature. By locating in close proximity, the costs associated with moving people, goods, and information are reduced. Furthermore, these concentration forces tend to be mutually reinforcing and can cause a cumulative buildup of population and economic activity in an area. For example, suppose that a shopping center locates near a concentration of people. As a result of the employment and shopping opportunities provided by this center, more residents are attracted to the area, which creates demand for even more stores. This cumulative process is one explanation for the development of urban areas.

In the following discussion, several alternative models are developed to demonstrate the optimal location for a firm under specified market conditions. In all these models, there is a tendency for the firm to locate at a central point, such as an urban area where output is sold or at the site of a supply of raw materials. Although the models are very basic, they illustrate many of the key principles of location theory.

Locating in a Linear Market

If demand for a firm's output does not vary with location, the problem of locating a plant or service center reduces to one of cost minimization. Suppose that the letters A through I in Figure 17-1 represent households located on a highway. Such a distribution of customers is referred to as a *linear market*. Assume that each customer must be served once each month by delivering one truckload of output (e.g., coal or fuel oil for heating) to each home. Where should a firm locate its distribution center to minimize the total transportation costs of servicing these consumers?

The cost-minimizing solution is to locate at the median point, where there are as many customers on either side of the distribution center. Costs are minimized at this point because moving the firm in either direction adds more distance to people on one side than it substracts from people on the other. The median location is at the five-mile mark, where there are four customers on either side of the firm. The total mileage required to serve all customers is 70 miles, computed as the sum of a ten-mile round trip to A plus an eight-mile round trip to B, and so on. No other location will allow each customer to be served and result in fewer than 70 miles driven.[2]

---

[2] A logical, but incorrect, answer might be to build the facility at the average or mean location. To find the mean location, start at point zero on the highway and find the average distance traveled if all customers are served. That is, customer A is zero miles away from the endpoint, B is one mile away, and so on. The total number of miles is $0 + 1 + 2 + 4 + \cdots + 12 = 54$, and thus the average distance is six miles (i.e., 54 miles divided by nine customers). Using this criterion, the firm would locate at the six-mile mark and would make nine trips each period, totaling 72 miles. That is, one 12-mile round trip would be made to A, one ten-mile round trip to B, and so on. But this solution requires two additional miles of driving compared to the median solution.

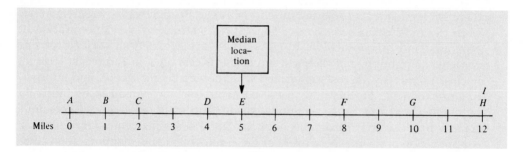

FIGURE 17-1 **Location of Consumers Along a Linear Market.**

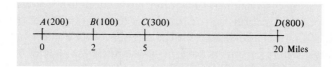

FIGURE 17-2 **Number of Consumers at Each of Four Cities Along a Highway.**

Consider another example of a linear market. Suppose that a firm is seeking a location to serve four cities, *A*, *B*, *C*, and *D*, along a highway. The number of customers in each city is shown in Figure 17-2. Using the principle of median location, the firm will minimize transportation costs by locating at *D*. Technically, the median location would be at some point on the west side of city *D*, where there are as many customers to the west as there are to the east.

Now, extend this analysis to another case where two firms are seeking locations along a linear market. Suppose that this market is one mile long with customers distributed uniformly along it. An example would be swimmers at a beach. Two vendors, *A* and *B*, sell ice cream to these swimmers using easily moved stands. Each consumer buys one ice cream bar each day, the price is the same at both stands, and consumers will patronize the closest vendor. Assume that the sellers initially set up their stands at the 0- and 0.25-mile marks along the beach, as shown in Figure 17-3.[3]

Because both sellers charge the same price and the swimmers go the closest stand, initially *B* will have 87.5 percent of the market because all swimmers to the right of the 0.125-mile mark will buy from *B*. But this is not an equilibrium location pattern. As the stands are easily moved, *A* can capture most of *B*'s market by moving his stand just to the right of *B*, say, to the 0.26-mile mark. This would give *A* about 74 percent of the market. It is likely *B* would respond by moving to the right of *A*. Then *B* would move just to the right of *A*, capturing perhaps 73 percent of the market. Such continuous relocation would continue until both

---

[3] This example was originally developed in a classic article by H. Hotelling, "Stability in Competition." *Economic Journal* (1929), 39:41–57.

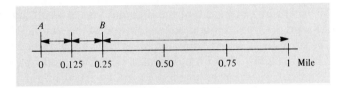

FIGURE 17-3 **Initial Location of Ice Cream Vendors.**

stands were located adjacent to one another at the 0.5-mile mark, as shown in Figure 17-4a. This is the equilibrium location pattern in this market because both sellers now have 50 percent of the market and neither seller can increase market share by moving.

Although this example is somewhat simplified, one can think of many cases where a number of competing firms all locate in one part of an area. For example, some urban areas have a theater district where a number of stage and movie theaters are located together. Shopping centers cluster a number of retail stores together. Once again, principles of location economics suggest a concentration of economic activity.

Although the location of both vendors at the 0.5-mile mark is the free-market equilibrium solution, it is not socially optimal because total transportation costs for all swimmers walking to the ice cream stand are not minimized. With the swimmers evenly distributed along the beach, the average distance to the nearest ice cream stand will be 0.25 mile if both stands locate at the 0.5-mile mark. This distance can be reduced by one-half, to 0.125 mile, by a regulation requiring that the vendors locate at the 0.25- and 0.75-mile marks, as shown in Figure 17-4b. In this case, the sellers would be located at the median locations of each half of the market. Note that both sellers still retain 50 percent of the market, but the average distance traveled by swimmers is reduced. Generally, free-market solutions to economic problems result in socially optimal outcomes. This is one case where that principle does not hold.

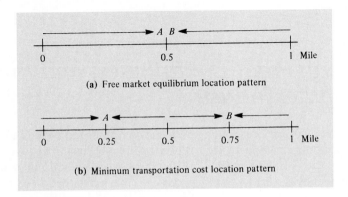

(a) Free market equilibrium location pattern

(b) Minimum transportation cost location pattern

FIGURE 17-4 **Alternative Locations for Ice Cream Vendors.**

Thus far it has been assumed that the demand for ice cream by each swimmer is one per day and does not depend on the location of the stands. This is somewhat unrealistic because the quantity demanded would probably be inversely related to distance from a stand. A swimmer located near the stand might have three or four bars, whereas a swimmer located 0.5 miles away might decide that it is simply too far to walk and thus not purchase any. That is, the price, including transportation costs, is too high for that individual.

Assume that the maximum distance a buyer would walk is 0.25 miles. In this case, the vendors would each sell twice as many bars by locating at the 0.25- and 0.75-mile marks (each having one-half the market) than by both locating at the center. In the latter case, each would have 50 percent of the entire market (i.e., one would have that part from the 0.00- to the 0.5-mile marks, while the other one would have that part of the market from the 0.5- to the 1.00-mile marks). Given these demand conditions, which probably are more realistic than those assumed in the previous example, the profit-maximizing and the socially optimal solutions are the same.

In general, there is a tendency for firms to locate in the middle of market areas. In larger urban areas, there typically is a central business district that serves the entire city with certain goods and services and a number of smaller business districts (e.g., shopping centers) that serve a submarket of the city. In any case, the principle of median location helps to explain the concentration of these businesses at particular points.

The principle of median location is one reason why the urban centers in the world have grown so much in the past fifty years. These cities are the median, or at least central, locations for many types of economic activity. For example, the downtown areas and suburban shopping centers of urban areas often have a number of the same type of store located very close together. All have sought the median location at the center of a market area. Obviously, one finds stores scattered at various points in urban and even rural areas. However, the growth of urban centers and the concentration of economic activity at points within those centers suggests a strong tendency to locate businesses at or near the median location within those markets.

CASE STUDY _____

Location Theory, Product Attributes, and the Personal Computer Industry

Firms producing similar goods or services tend to locate in close spatial proximity. Similarly, in many industries, there is little variation in the attributes of the products sold by the firms. That is, there is close proximity of attributes. The personal computer industry is a good example. When the industry began to develop in the early 1980s, there were several major manufacturers producing machines that were not compatible. For example, Osborne, Kaypro, Victor, Apple, and IBM all built personal computers, but each required some specially designed peripheral equipment, and software for one generally could not be used on the others. However, IBM quickly became the industry leader and attributes of the IBM-PC became the standard against which other computers were judged. As a result, other computer manufacturers began to develop and market their computers in terms of their "IBM compatibility." This compatibility stressed the extent that these computers would run software written for the IBM but also involved features such as the ability to use expansion boards and peripheral devices designed for the IBM. Once basic compatibility was established, other features, such as lower price or greater memory, could be promoted in order to differentiate the product from the IBM-PC.

The task of these competing manufacturers was a difficult one. They had to position their product close enough to the IBM-PC to convince potential purchasers that it could do virtually anything that the IBM computer could do. But the product had to be differentiated enough to establish a reason for buying it instead of the IBM product. Advertisements often stressed greater speed or lower price than comparable IBM products.

At the present time, there are more than 100 manufacturers of standard desktop personal computers that are all "IBM-compatible." In addition, a number of other manufacturers have given up trying to compete in this market. As suggested in Chapters 9 and 10, the economic profits being earned by Apple, IBM, and some of the other early entrants attracted numerous firms into the industry, including such giants as AT&T. Although the market has grown tremendously, fierce competition has resulted in much lower prices and most firms in the industry probably are not now earning economic profits.

The tendency for product attributes of different firms to be similar is not unique to the computer industry. Indeed, it is a characteristic of most mass-produced products. A television set must have most of the features of other makes. New automobile models seldom represent radical departures from competing models that are already on the market. Most new textbooks try to retain most of the features of texts that have been successful in the past. In each case, the explanation is the same as for the locational clustering of firms. If the product is too different, that is, too far from the "center" of the market, it is likely to attract fewer customers than if it has more traditional attributes.

KEY CONCEPTS

- Location of business is important because the cost of moving resources and output across space is significant.
- In general, principles of location theory suggest that firms and individuals benefit by locating close together and that these location forces tend to result in concentration of economic activity in urban areas.
- If demand does not vary with location, two firms serving a linear market will both tend to locate at the center of the market, resulting in higher transportation costs for their customers than if they located at separate points.
- If demand is inversely related to distance from the seller, the two firms will tend to locate in the center of each half of the market.

Firm Location: One Market and One Raw Materials Source

In the previous examples, the focus was on minimizing only the transportation costs associated with sending final output to consumers. No consideration was given to the cost of shipping ice cream bars to the vendors. This section considers a more realistic but still simple case of location decision for a firm that obtains raw materials at one site (M), processes them, and distributes to customers in a city (C). As shown in Figure 17-5, the raw materials and market sites, M and C, respectively, are T miles apart.

Assume that production cost, the price of output, and the quantity sold are the same regardless of where the firm locates the plant. The only variables are the total costs of transporting raw materials and output. Therefore, the problem reduces to determining that location that will result in minimum total transportation costs.

Let S_m be the cost per mile of shipping enough raw materials to make one unit of output (referred to subsequently as one unit of raw material) and S_o be the cost per mile of shipping one unit of output. The cost function for shipping raw materials is $S_m t$, which determines the cost of shipping one unit of raw material from M to any location t miles to the right of M. If the plant is located at the raw materials site, then $t = 0$ and the cost of shipping raw materials is zero. The output shipping cost function is given by $S_o(T - t)$, which defines the cost of shipping one unit of final product from any location $(T - t)$ miles to the left of C to that city. If the plant is located at C, the value of $(T - t)$ is zero and the shipping costs for output are zero.

At any intermediate point between M and C, there are shipping costs for both raw materials and output. The sum of these two costs is defined as total transportation costs. As price and other production costs are assumed to be constant at all locations, the problem reduces to choosing that site with the lowest total transportation costs.[4] In the example shown in Figure 17-5, the per-mile cost of shipping one unit of raw materials is assumed to be greater than the cost of shipping one unit of output. Thus total transport costs are minimized at the raw materials site M. In contrast, had transportation cost per mile for raw material been lower than for one unit of output, the lower total transportation costs would be achieved by locating at C.

This principle can be demonstrated mathematically. The total transport cost (TC) of locating the plant at any site t miles to the right of M is the sum of shipping costs for raw material and output, that is,

$$TC = S_m t + S_o(T - t)$$

or

$$TC = (S_m - S_o)t + S_o T$$

---

[4] Clearly, production costs and demand may vary among alternative locations, but this assumption simplifies the problem, allowing the analysis to focus on the transportation-related issues.

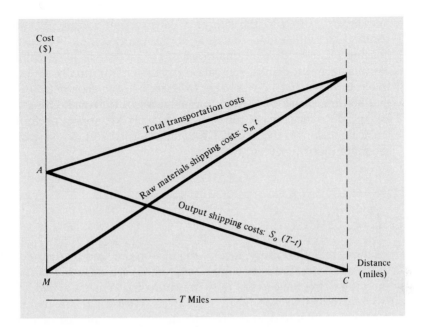

FIGURE 17-5 **Location Analysis.**

Recall that the plant will be located at some point t where $0 \leq t \leq T$. As the objective of the plant location decision is to minimize TC, it should be clear that if $S_m > S_o$, the value of t should be made as small as possible. This is accomplished by locating the plant at M, where $t = 0$. Alternatively, if $S_m < S_o$, total costs are minimized by making t as large as possible (i.e., $t = T$) and locating the plant at C.

If $S_m = S_o$, the total cost function would be horizontal and the firm would be indifferent about locating at any point between M and C. However, if there are costs associated with the loading and unloading of raw materials and/or output onto trucks, rail cars, or ships, then even if $S_m = S_o$, any intermediate location will have higher costs than at M or C because of the additional terminal costs incurred. For example, by locating at M, the loading of raw materials is avoided, and by locating at C, the loading of final output is avoided. If an intermediate location is selected, both of these costs will be incurred. Thus industrial location tends to take place either at a raw materials site or at the market. This phenomenon once again suggests the natural tendency for economic activities to be concentrated at certain places.

In general, products that tend to be "weight losing" in the production processes are associated with locations at the raw materials site. For example, the processing of gravel involves screening and washing large quantities of rock, dirt, and other debris to separate that part of the load that qualifies as gravel. The usable gravel may only be one-third of the material processed. Invariably, this process takes place at the raw materials site and then the finished product is taken to the marketplace, often to the site of a construction project. In contrast, "weight-gaining" activities tend to locate at the marketplace. For example, soft-drink bottling plants add small quantities of concentrate to large volumes of water to manufacture soft drinks. As water is available in virtually all locations at a relatively low cost but is expensive to transport, the economics of location dictate that bottling plants be located in market areas. Indeed, bottling plants are found in virtually every area of the country. The market area of each plant is relatively small because it is too expensive to ship bottled soft drinks very far, since they are more than 90 percent water.

CASE STUDY

Locating the Steel Industry

In the early part of the twentieth century, location decisions in the iron and steel industry were based primarily on minimizing the costs of the raw materials used in production, specifically coal and iron ore. At that time, it took approximately two tons of coal and one ton of iron ore to manufacture something less than one-half ton of steel. Clearly, this was a weight-losing process and the shipping costs of raw materials dominated the location decision. The steel industry also uses large quantities of water—about 65,000 gallons per ton of steel produced—for cooling and processing. Although much of this water is continually reused, there must be large supplies available. Thus locations on rivers or lakes were definitely preferred. Because western Pennsylvania had abundant supplies of coal and water available at low prices, virtually the entire U.S. steel industry located there and Pittsburgh became the nation's steel capital.

Improvements in technology steadily reduced the amount of coal required to process a ton of iron ore, and by the mid-1970s less than one ton of coal was used per ton of ore. While the industry remained tied to raw materials sources, it became relatively more important to locate near the sources of iron ore, much of which was mined in the Upper Great Lakes area.

Taking advantage of low-cost water transportation for both coal and iron ore and large water supplies, major steel-producing complexes developed at Cleveland, Youngstown, Detroit, Buffalo, and Chicago—all cities located on the Great Lakes. Smaller complexes developed later at St. Louis, Birmingham, and Fontana, California.

More recently, the use of scrap metal as a raw material has become important. The existence of large supplies of scrap metal in Detroit and Chicago helped the steel industry to grow in those areas. In fact, relatively small steel mills that depend almost entirely on scrap metal have been developed in places never thought to have potential as steel industry locations.

KEY CONCEPTS

- If other factors are held constant, a firm that uses raw materials from a site A and sells output in the market at B will locate at A if the cost of shipping raw materials is more than the cost of shipping final output. Otherwise, the firm will locate at the market, B.

- Even if the transportation costs are the same for raw materials and finished output, the lowest-cost location will be at either the raw materials site or the market because additional loading and unloading costs would be incurred at any intermediate location.
- Production activities that are weight losing tend to locate at the source of raw materials, whereas production activities that are weight gaining tend to locate at the market.

Market Area Determination ———————————

The market area for any one seller will depend on relative production and transportation costs. In the following, market areas for two competing firms will be determined under different assumptions relative to those costs.

Market Area: Equal Production and Transportation Costs

Suppose that two competing firms, A and B, have located production facilities in a region and that both have the same production and transportation costs. The price at the plant is set equal to production costs, and transport costs are paid by the consumer. Consumers will buy from that plant for which the delivered price (i.e., price at plant plus transport cost) is lower. Figure 17-6a shows delivered price functions for firms A and B located at points A' and B' along the distance or horizontal axis. Production cost is $0P$ at both plants. Any buyer located at point A' or B' pays $0P$, but more distant buyers must pay $0P$ plus the transportation cost from the plant. For example, if S is the per-mile transportation cost per unit of output, a buyer located t miles from A must pay $0P + St$. Thus the delivered price functions shown in Figure 17-6a have a slope equal to S.

Because consumers seek the lowest price, all those located to the left of point D will buy from A and those to the right of D will buy from B. Looking down on this two-dimensional market area, as shown in Figure 17-6b, it is seen that the line FG separates the two market areas. Along this market boundary, the delivered price is the same for both plants. To the right of this line, the price is lower for B, and to the left, it is lower for A. Point D in Figure 17-6a corresponds to point D^* in Figure 17-6b.

Market Area: Unequal Production Costs—Equal Transportation Costs

Suppose that firm B's production cost per unit increases while the costs at firm A remain the same. Figure 17-7 depicts the market areas for the two firms where A is able to produce at a lower cost than is B. As a result, the price at the plant is lower for A than for B. Per-mile transport costs are assumed to remain equal for both firms. Thus the slope of the delivered price functions is the same, but

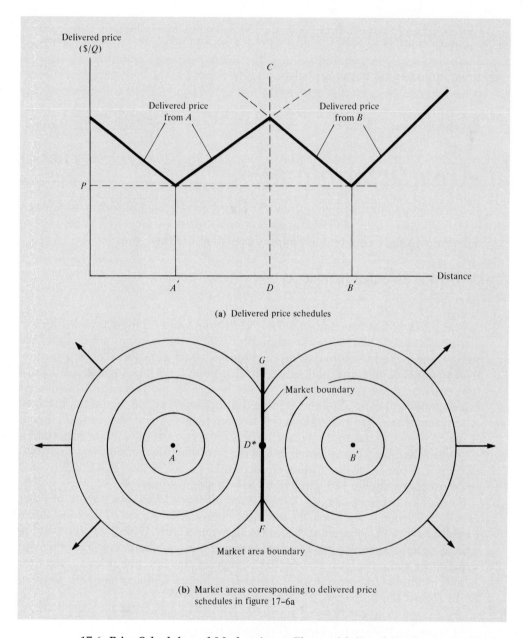

(a) Delivered price schedules

(b) Market areas corresponding to delivered price
schedules in figure 17–6a

FIGURE 17-6 **Price Schedule and Market Areas: Firms with Equal Production and Transportation
Costs.**

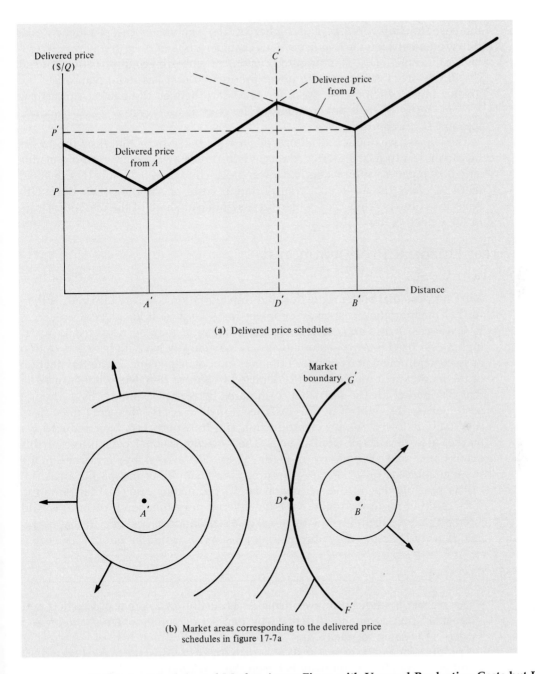

(a) Delivered price schedules

(b) Market areas corresponding to the delivered price
schedules in figure 17-7a

FIGURE 17-7 **Price Schedule and Market Areas: Firms with Unequal Production Costs but Equal Transportation Costs.**

the cost function for firm B is higher by the amount of the production cost differential between the two firms. This change results in A's market area increasing significantly. That is, now some customers who are geographically closer to B will buy from A because the lower production cost has more than offset the greater transportation cost. Also, the boundary betwen the markets, the curve $F'G'$ in Figure 17-7b, is now nonlinear. The point D' in Figure 17-7a corresponds to point D^* in Figure 17-7b.

The large share of the U.S. automobile market taken from American producers by Japanese producers located thousands of miles away is an example of this situation. Japanese automakers had lower production costs that more than enabled them to offset the additional transportation costs of shipping their output to American buyers. Thus they took over a significant share of the market for cars in the United States.

Market Area: Unequal Production and Transportation Costs

Next suppose that both production and transportation costs are lower for A than for B. Transportation costs may be lower for A because it has developed access to lower-cost barge and/or rail service, whereas B may be restricted to using higher-cost truck service. Alternatively, B may simply have higher costs due to obsolete equipment and/or poor transportation management. The determination of the market area for each firm is depicted in Figure 17-8. Note in Figure 17-8a that B's market area is restricted to the area between D'' and E'. Even though customers to the right of E' are closer to B' than to A', the delivered price from A actually is lower. A's lower production and transport costs have reduced B's market area to a small circular area. The two-dimensional perspective of this market area analysis is shown in Figure 17-8b. The market area for firm B is the small circular area B^*B^*. Firm A captures the remainder of the market areas.

It is possible that further reduction in A's production and/or transportation costs could occur to the point that the delivered price function for firm A would intersect that for firm B below the level of B's production cost $0P'$. In that event, firm A would capture the entire market area and B would be out of business.

KEY CONCEPTS

- The market boundary for two firms is a function of relative production and transportation costs and is defined by that set of points where the delivered price is the same for each firm.
- If production and transport costs are equal for both firms, the market boundary will be a straight line midway between the two producers.
- If production costs are higher for one firm but transportation costs are equal, the market boundary will be a curved line around the higher-cost plant.
- If both production and transportation costs are higher for one plant, its market area will be reduced to a circular area around its plant site.

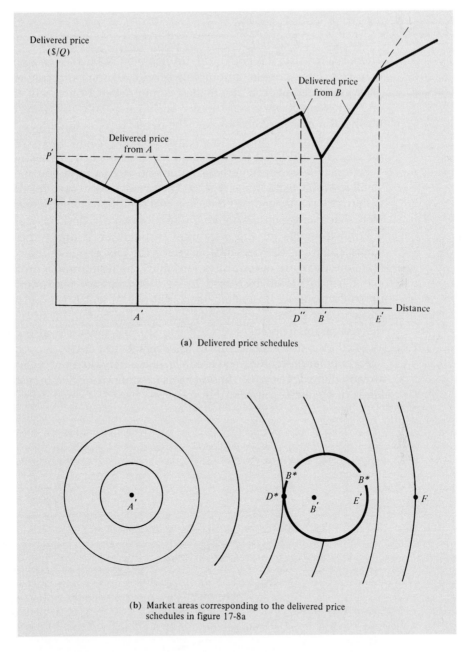

(a) Delivered price schedules

(b) Market areas corresponding to the delivered price
schedules in figure 17-8a

FIGURE 17-8 **Price Schedules and Market Areas: Firms with Unequal Production and
Transportation Costs.**

Threshold Analysis _____

There is a consistent hierarchical arrangement of businesses among cities of various sizes. For example, automobile service stations and convenience stores are generally found in even the smallest communities. Conversely, to find symphony orchestras and gourmet restaurants, one must usually go to large cities. The reason for this is a matter of economics. The demand for symphony orchestras in small cities simply is not great enough that revenue would cover costs. When that is the case, it is said that the threshold level for the activity has not been reached.

Figure 17-9 shows hypothetical demand curves for a gourmet restaurant in a small town (D_T) and in a city (D_C). The average cost curve for the restaurant also is shown. It is assumed that the same cost conditions would prevail in both places. Note that average cost is above the small-town demand curve at all points. Thus it is not possible for the restaurant to break even under these conditions. In contrast, part of the demand curve for the city is above the cost function and therefore there are output rates for which the restaurant is profitable.

If the small town increased in size, demand for restaurant services would probably increase. If demand increased to D_T^*, which is tangent to the average cost curve at point E, a threshold has been reached and it would be possible for the restaurant to break even. Of course, this threshold also could have been attained by a downward shift in the average cost curve.

As population centers increase in size, not only do more businesses of the kind already there develop (i.e., another service station or drive-in restaurant), but new kinds of businesses appear. For example, banks or small department stores are

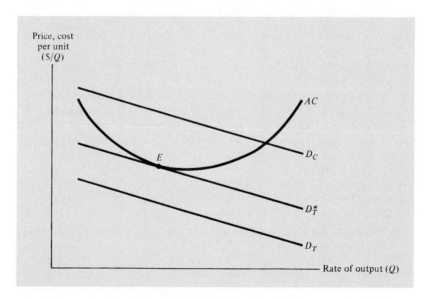

FIGURE 17-9 **Demand and Average Cost Functions for a Restaurant.**

often found in small cities but not in the smallest towns. As the latter grow, these activities appear when the threshold level is reached.

Selecting an Industrial Location

Obviously, the process used by managers to select a location for a store or plant is more involved than that suggested by the preceding theoretical discussion, but the process is consistent with that theory. Typically, the firm has a general idea about the set of possible locations for the facility. For example, a firm may find that a particular regional market such as the West Coast has grown so rapidly that a production facility can now be justified in that area. Often, a professional consultant with a particular expertise in facility location is brought in to make the evaluation. The firm provides that consultant with a rating of the importance of all location factors. For example, there may be specific requirements for rail service, large quantities of skilled labor or other input, or educational facilities that are found only in a few places.

In general, all significant factors that will influence the profitability of the proposed facility are evaluated at each location under consideration. Because both revenue and cost may differ at each location, the analysis must consider each location's attributes as they affect these two key variables. These locational factors are classified as primary and secondary.

Primary Location Factors

The locational attributes described here are fundamental in the decision to locate an industrial facility.[5] Although for particular firms some are more important than others, a significant shortfall in an area's ability to provide even one of these may greatly reduce the attractiveness of that site.

LABOR   The availability, cost, and productivity of labor are very important location determinants. Some think of a new business as attracting labor into an area rather than the business being attracted by existing labor supplies. This does happen, but in many cases, a new facility is not built in a location unless management is convinced there is an adequate supply of workers available who have the training and experience needed for the planned operation. The cost of that labor is also important, although low labor cost is not necessarily an advantage if the workers are poorly educated and trained because that may mean that productivity is low. Labor availability, cost, and quality must all be taken into consideration.

---

[5] For a detailed discussion of the industry location process and the importance of each locational attribute, see E. W. Miller. *Manufacturing: A Study of Industrial Location.* (University Park, Pa.: Pennsylvania State University Press, 1977).

ENERGY RESOURCES Some manufacturing processes use large quantities of energy per dollar of final output. For example, the processing of bauxite into aluminum requires large quantities of electricity. Thus it is not surprising that aluminum manufacturers have tended to locate in areas that offered low-cost electric power. The Pacific Northwest with its low-cost hydroelectric power plants and some areas in the South served with low-cost power from the Tennessee Valley Authority have been attractive locations for this industry. The availability of large supplies of low-cost coal for firing blast furnaces was a primary factor explaining the concentration of iron and steel manufacturing in western Pennsylvania.

TRANSPORTATION Transportation cost also is an important factor in industrial locations decisions. In the early history of the United States, locations near water and rail transportation were very important. This is evidenced by the rapid rate of growth of cities that offered good access to these transport modes. The relative growth of the service sector, which is not heavily dependent on transportation, and the emergence of truck transport have greatly expanded the range of good industrial locations. For example, the manufacturing activity that has developed in smaller communities and in suburban areas of large cities has depended largely on truck transport and the development of the interstate highway system.

PROXIMITY TO MARKETS FOR OUTPUT In general, it is advantageous for firms to be able to serve their customers quickly and at low cost. Clearly, one way to do this is to locate close to these customers. Also as indicated previously, firms need to locate near their employees, and people need businesses as places of employment. By locating together, the cost of transporting both people to work and products to consumers is reduced, as is the cost of communications. These forces combine to ensure that many firms will locate in population centers. Except for firms that are tied to raw material sites (e.g., where the production process results in large weight losses during manufacturing), there are strong economic forces pushing firms toward locations in urban centers.

GOVERNMENT REGULATION Federal, state, and local governments are assuming a more aggressive role in determining where industry can locate. Many local governments have used zoning laws to regulate the location of businesses within the city. More recently, air and water quality rules imposed by federal and state governments have been important in determining where polluting industries can locate. Although such controls have benefits, if taken too far, they discourage new business from locating in an area and may actually encourage some firms to move. The combination of their tax structure and government regulation of business has resulted in some areas of the country being regarded as pro-business and others as being antibusiness.

RAW MATERIALS AVAILABILITY Many businesses depend on materials of various types, such as unprocessed raw materials for use in manufacturing and finished goods for inventory in wholesale and retail establishments. The availability and cost, including transportation costs, of these materials are critical location factors.

Secondary Location Factors

There are other factors that influence location decisions but are of secondary importance. Two examples are the physical environment and government attitudes and policies.

PHYSICAL ENVIRONMENT   The climate, scenery, and environmental quality of an area may affect a location decision, especially if the other more fundamental characteristics are approximately the same as in the other locations being considered. Although there have been reports of an industrial location being selected simply because the company president enjoyed the scenery of the area, such cases are probably few in number. The competitive pressures of the marketplace would drive out firms whose important decisions were based on whim or personal preference rather than economics.

STATE AND LOCAL GOVERNMENT ATTITUDES AND POLICIES   Much has been written about the climate for business in the various states. Some states in the Northeast and Midwest are thought by some to be antibusiness, whereas others, especially in the South, are so pro-business that they offer subsidies to new firms to locate plants in their states. These subsidies may take the form of property tax reduction, free sites for factory construction, low-interest loans, and even the construction and lease of buildings at below-market rates. Despite claims about the importance of these subsidies, most evidence suggests that they play a secondary role in the location decision. Sometimes, however, businesses are able to obtain such subsidies by threatening to go elsewhere even though they have already decided to locate in the area. Their objective is simply to achieve a further reduction of their costs. In other cases, a firm may have decided to locate in a region and then will go shopping among the communities in the region for the best set of subsidies.

It should be recognized that low taxes in an area are not an advantage to a business if they are associated with a low level of public services. Poor schools, inadequate water and sewer systems, and/or limited police and fire protection may be the product of low taxes. These are not the characteristics of a good industrial location and the firm may have to incur additional costs to offset these inadequate public services. For example, elementary and secondary schools are important to the business because they influence the quality of the local labor force and are an important consideration for managers and other workers who might have to be recruited by the firm. Also, if the schools are not good, it may be very difficult to attract workers to the area. Thus, wage rates may have to be increased substantially to attract these workers, at least partially offsetting the advantage of low taxes.

CASE STUDY _____

Ranking Industrial Location Determinants

A number of surveys of managers responsible for industrial location decisions have attempted to determine the importance of various factors in choosing an industrial location. The relative importance of these factors as reported in a recent study is shown in the following table.

Geographic location cleary was the most important factor. This attribute captures the effects of being close to markets, to supplies of labor and raw materials, and to sources of specialized business services such as those provided by law and engineering firms. Worker productivity, availability of skilled labor, and a low union profile are also thought to be important. It is interesting that land (i.e., truck) transportation availability is generally regarded as much more important than is rail and water transport. In the past, rail and water would have been regarded as much more important. This change reflects the combination of better highway systems and changing technology in the transportation industry.

Relative Importance of Location Factors

Location Factor	Percentage of Executives Surveyed Who Rated the Factor as Being Vitally Important in the Industrial Location Decision
Geographic location	64
High worker productivity	59
Availability of land transportation	54
Low union profile	49
Stable state government	38
Skilled labor availability	32
Energy sources	30
Raw materials availability	28
Tax exemptions	27
Tax credits	26
Unskilled labor availability	22
Availability of air transportation	21
Water supply	17
Availability of rail transportation	16
Availability of worker training programs	10
Availability of water transportation	5

SOURCE: M. L. Goldstein, "Choosing the Right Site," *Industry Week*, April 16, 1985.

The Industrial Location Decision

Deciding where to locate an industrial facility generally is based on a comparison of the characteristics of that facility to the attributes of the various locations being considered. The first step usually involves an inventory of an array of locational factors at each area. This is followed by an evaluation of how the characteristics

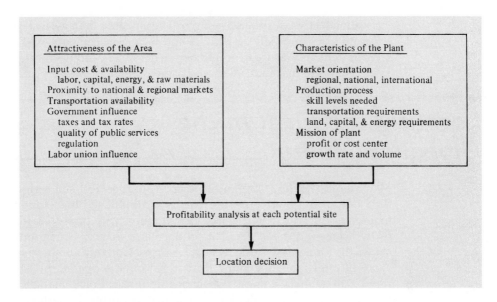

FIGURE 17-10 **The Plant Location Decision Process.**

of the proposed facility mesh with the area's locational attributes. The objective is to determine the present value of all future profits over the life of the plant at each location under consideration. This process is described in Figure 17-10.

Many government units in the United States have local development groups that promote the industrial development attributes of their area. This is done by advertising in business publications, direct contact and solicitation of industry, and making improvements in the area's locational attributes. Examples of the latter might include improvement of highways, establishment of vocational training centers, and development of land for new plant sites. These promotional activities, sometimes referred to as smokestack chasing, are perhaps the most visible part of the industrial location process.

Firms also spend a considerable amount of time and money evaluating various parts of the country for plant locations. Analysts may develop projected income statements for a proposed plant for each of a number of possible sites. Generally, the site that maximizes the present value of all future profits over the estimated life of the plant is selected.

KEY CONCEPTS

- The threshold level for an activity in an area occurs when the demand curve is tangent to the average cost function.
- Primary location factors include raw materials availability, cost and availability of labor and energy resources, transportation alternatives, and proximity to the markets of output.

- Location factors of secondary importance include the physical environment and the attitudes and policies of state and local governments.
- Firms generally evaluate a number of possible locations for a new facility and select the site that maximizes the present value of future profits.

Locating the Firm in the Global Economy

Many large U.S. and foreign firms now produce and sell a significant share of their output in other countries. This is accomplished by setting up subsidiaries in foreign countries, entering into joint ventures with producers in those countries, or by licensing foreign firms to produce and market their products. Table 17-1 shows the foreign sales of selected U.S. firms. Not only are these sales a significant share of total sales, for many firms their foreign operations have grown more rapidly than their domestic revenues as international market penetration has increased. The explanation for the expansion of firms throughout the global economy lies in three areas: developing and maintaining raw materials supplies, extending market power, and comparative advantage.

Raw Materials Supplies

Firms that are heavily dependent on particular raw materials need to ensure that they have continued access to dependable supplies. In some cases, materials are only available in foreign countries. An example is bauxite, which is the basic raw material used in producing aluminum. Virtually all of the deposits of this mineral are located outside the U.S.

TABLE 17-1 **Total Revenue and International Sales of Selected U.S. Corporations, 1992**

Firm	Total Revenue (Billions)	Foreign Sales (Billions)	Foreign Sales as of Percentage of Total Revenue	Type of Business
Caterpillar	$10.1	$ 6.0	59%	Earth-moving equipment
Ford	72.1	30.3	42	Automotive equipment
General Electric	43.1	15.1	35	Appliances; technology; communications
General Motors	$91.6	$14.7	16	Automotive equipment
IBM	$64.8	$32.4	50	Information-processing equipment
Rohm and Haas	$ 2.7	$ 1.2	45	Specialty chemicals
Texas Instruments	$ 6.5	$ 2.3	36	Electronic products

Many firms simply buy such raw materials directly from companies in the foreign countries. In other cases, the domestic firm will set up its own operation in the country. This reduces the risk of supply interruption because the domestic company has greater control of the foreign operation. Of course, other problems can arise that threaten such supplies, including war or government appropriation of the firm's property. These risks can be reduced by diversification, that is, by developing raw materials sources in several countries.

Extending Market Power

As discussed in Chapters 9 and 10, some firms have a degree of market power that gives them some control over the price of their products and may allow them to earn economic profits. This power may arise because the large size of the firm enables it to produce at lower cost than smaller rivals (i.e., economies of scale are present); the firm may have proprietary technology that results in low-cost production or even the monopoly production of a product; and/or the firm may have achieved a degree of product differentiation that allows it to sell above the price that would prevail in a competitive market. To some extent, the large multinational firms are able to use all three of these sources to increase their profits by expanding into foreign countries.

Consider the production of automobiles. Efficient production requires that large plants be used that incorporate assembly-line techniques to mass-produce cars. That is, there are significant economies of scale in this industry. Only very large firms are able to finance such facilities. Further, the production equipment and techniques are very sophisticated and require substantial technical expertise that is not generally found outside the staff of the firms in the industry. Finally, brand-name recognition also is very important; nameplates such as Chevrolet, Ford, Toyota, and Honda have come to have important meaning for most consumers and make it difficult for new entrants to gain consumer acceptance for their cars.

In recent years, Japanese auto producers such as Honda, Mazda, and Toyota have opened large manufacturing plants in the U.S. All of these firms are large enough to build large plants that allow efficient production, they have the technical capability to organize and run those plants efficiently, and their products are differentiated. Thus, their location in the United States is a natural extension of their market power into the U.S. economy.

Comparative Advantage

Finally, firms locate facilities in foreign countries to capture the *comparative advantage* offered by that country. Comparative advantage refers to a situation where the opportunity cost of producing two goods differs between two countries. One country is said to have a comparative advantage in the production of those goods for which the opportunity cost is lower than in the other country. Consider the following hypothetical production data for two countries, Japan and the U.S., which are assumed to be producing only cars and boats. If the U.S. used all of its resources to produce cars, assume that maximum production would be 100, and if it only produced boats, maximum production would be 200. In Japan, assume that maximum production could be 300 cars or 50 boats. That is, maximum production in each country is

	U.S.	Japan
Cars	100	300
	or	or
Boats	200	50

The opportunity cost of producing each product in each country in terms of foregone production of the other good is

	U.S.	Japan
Cars	2 boats	1/6 boat
Boats	1/2 car	6 cars

Note that Japan has a comparative advantage in producing cars (i.e., each car costs only 1/6 boat compared to two boats in the U.S.) and the United States has a comparative advantage in producing boats (i.e., each boat produced in the U.S. costs 1/2 car compared to 6 cars in Japan). When the opportunity cost of production differs between two countries, both can be better off by specializing in the production of the one product where they have a comparative advantage and then by trading with the other country.

For example, assume that both countries produce both goods and there is no trade between them. One possible production combination is shown here:

	U.S.	Japan	Total
Cars	50	180	230
Boats	100	20	120

Because there is no trade, the production in each country also represents the amount consumed in that country. Now assume that Japan produces only cars and the U.S. producers only boats; the maximum production is now

	U.S.	Japan	Total
Cars	0	300	300
Boats	200	0	200

Note that total production in the two countries has increased by 70 cars and 80 boats compared to the original levels.

Consumers in the U.S. and Japan want both cars and boats, so boats are traded for cars and vice versa. One possible final consumption pattern is

	U.S.	Japan	Total
Cars	60	240	300
Boats	120	80	200

This means that of the 300 cars produced in Japan, 60 were exported to the U.S. and 240 consumed in Japan. The U.S. produced 200 boats, of which 120 were exported to Japan.

Now consumers in both countries have more of both goods than they did before specialization and trade. Economic welfare has been enhanced with no increase in the amount of labor and capital employed; these factors of production have simply been reorganized so that each country captures its comparative advantage.

Usually, one need not know anything about the amount of resources devoted to the production of any good to determine which country has the comparative advantage in producing a particular good. If a country has a large share of world production and exports much of its output, it is probable that that country has a comparative advantage. Japan appears to have an advantage in electronics equipment, while the United States has a comparative advantage in the production of agricultural products.

The principle of comparative advantage will determine where multinational corporations locate their production facilities. Particular products will be produced in those countries where the opportunity cost of production is low.

CASE STUDY

Matsushita: The Ultimate Multinational Firm

Matsushita Electric Industrial Company, Ltd. is the largest producer of consumer electronics and industrial communications and information products in the world. Annual sales for this firm total about $60 billion. The firm was organized in 1935 by the late Konosuke Matsushita, whose corporate philosophy was based on the principle of ". . . contributing to the peace, happiness, and prosperity of mankind through the abundant supply of quality consumer goods at reasonable prices." If sales volume and annual payrolls are any indication, consumers and workers are happier and more prosperous because of his efforts.

The firm began the post-World War II period making washing machines and refrigerators. Later it developed new products, including color television sets, stereo equipment, air conditioners, microwave ovens, and a variety of other products for both consumers and industry. Its single biggest success was the video cassette recorder (VCR), which it pioneered along with the Sony Corporation. This product has changed the entire entertainment industry in the past 15 years and has generated enormous sales and profits for Matsushita. Consumers quickly recognize the firm's brand names, such as Panasonic, Technics, National, and Quasar.

Often products sold by other firms under other brand names came from a Matsushita factory.

The company is truly multinational in scope. Its 343 factories are scattered throughout the world, as are its 300,000 employees. The 220,000 stockholders in the firm bought their shares on markets in North America, Europe, Japan, and other parts of Asia. Until 1988, the company's accounting, finance, and marketing operations were controlled from headquarters in Japan, but recognition of the company's worldwide orientation led to a decentralization of these central functions to a variety of offices in the United States, Europe, and Japan.

In 1991, Matsushita made a major diversification move by acquiring MCA, Inc., a U.S. firm that is a major producer of movies, television shows, and recorded music. Not only are these products complementary with most of the company's electronics products, this acquisition allowed Matsushita to benefit from the comparative advantage of the entertainment industry in the United States.

Summary

Selecting the location for a business is important because the costs of moving output, workers, and customers across space are significant. To economize on these costs, people and firms tend to locate together. The urbanization process observed in the United States reflects the economic advantages of concentrating people and business.

A firm serving a linear market should locate at the median location, where there are an equal number of customers on both sides of the firm. Such a location will minimize the total transport costs associated with serving those customers. If two firms serve a linear market where buyers are evenly dispersed along the market and demand does not vary with the seller's location, both will tend to locate at the midpoint. If demand is inversely related to distance from the seller, the two vendors would tend to locate closer to the socially efficient points.

Firms that use raw materials from one source and sell finished output at another site choose a cost-minimizing location that depends on the cost of shipping raw materials relative to the cost of shipping output. Because of additional loading and unloading costs, firms tend not to locate at points intermediate between raw material sources and markets. Products that are weight losing in production tend to be produced at the raw materials site, whereas firms that produce weight-gaining products usually locate at the market.

The market areas served by competing firms depend on their relative production and transportation costs. Firms with lower production and/or transportation costs have larger market areas than their competitors. The cost differentials can become so great that the higher-cost firm loses its entire market area to the lower-cost firm.

Firms do not locate facilities in an area until the threshold level of demand has been achieved. This threshold is defined as the tangency of the average cost function and the demand curve. At that point, price covers average cost and a normal profit is possible. Some activities have low threshold levels and are found in even the smallest towns. Conversely, other activities tend to be found only in larger urban areas.

The industrial location decision involves a comparison of the characteristics of the proposed facility to the locational attributes of the areas being considered. Location factors can be classified as primary or secondary. Primary factors include geographic location, skilled labor availability, the cost and availability of energy resources, and availability of land transportation. Secondary factors influencing location include an area's physical environment and government attitudes and policy. Usually, differences in state and local taxes are of secondary importance in selecting an industrial location. Generally, firms select that location that will maximize the present value of future profits.

Firms locate plants and other facilities in foreign countries to provide dependable sources of raw materials, to extend market power, and/or to capture the comparative advantage of producing in those countries. A country has a comparative advantage if its opportunity cost of producing a product is lower than it is for other countries.

Discussion Questions

17-1. Why do businesses tend to locate together?

17-2. What location factors would be of primary importance and which would be of little significance to a firm in each of the following industries: retailing, oil refining, higher education, and lumber?

17-3. Is it wise for a local government to subsidize industries that locate in its city? What advantages and disadvantages are associated with such action?

17-4. In the 1970s and 1980s, technical and vocational education programs were expanded rapidly in states that were aggressively seeking new industry. What connection, if any, do you see between such education programs and the industrial location decision?

17-5. What is the market area for your university or college? That is, from what geographic area do most of the students come? Did the location of the school influence your enrollment decision? Explain.

17-6. What would you estimate to be the market area of each of the following firms?
   a. General Motors Corporation.
   b. A soft-drink bottling plant.
   c. Chase Manhattan Bank.
   d. First National Bank of Manhattan, Kansas.

17-7. Consider your community and two others that you are familiar with—one half as large and one twice as large (if there is one). What goods and/or services are available in your city that are not available in the smaller one? What is not available in your city that is found in the larger city? What is the explanation for this distribution of economic activities?

17-8. In the chapter, microcomputers and automobiles are used as examples of products for which firms tend to produce a median product. What other goods and services have similar median product characteristics? Explain.

Problems

17-1. Customers of a firm are located along a road as indicated by the letters A through J in the following figure.

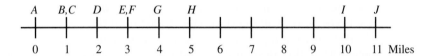

To service these customers, two truckloads of material must be delivered to each customer every week. The cost of making a delivery is $1.50 per mile.
a. Determine the cost-minimizing location for the firm.
b. Determine the total transportation cost each week assuming that (1) the firm locates at the median location; and (2) the firm locates at the mean location.

17-2. United Express makes weekly deliveries to each of a number of customers located in cities along an interstate highway. The location of these cities, A, B, etc., and the number of customers in each is shown in the following figure.

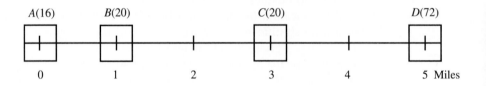

On one trip, four customers can be serviced. The transportation cost is $1 per mile.
a. Determine the median location for locating the company's delivery center.
b. Determine the total transportation costs at the median location.

17-3. Suppose that 500 swimmers are evenly distributed at intervals of two feet along a beach 1,000 feet long (i.e., one at the two-foot mark, one at the four-foot mark, etc.). Initially assume that each will buy one hot dog during the day from the nearest vendor.
a. If two hot dog vendors, A and B, locate at each of the following distances from the end of the beach, how many hot dogs will each sell during the day and what will be the total distance walked by the customers?

| Alternative | Location of: | |
	A	B
III	200 ft	400 ft
III	500 ft	500 ft
III	250 ft	250 ft

b. Repeat the exercise of part (a) under the assumption that demand is inversely related to distance. Specifically, assume the following demand schedule for hot dogs:

Distance of Swimmers from Nearest Vendor	Number of Hot Dogs Purchased
Within 100 ft	3
101 to 200 ft	2
201 to 300 ft	1
More than 300 ft	0

17-4. U.S. Cement, Inc., uses two tons of raw material (i.e., limestone, clay, coal, and gypsum) to manufacture one ton of cement. All of the raw materials are available at site A and all final output is sold in a market (B) located twenty miles away. The transportation cost per ton of raw materials is $0.40 per mile, while the per-ton cost of transporting cement is $0.60 per mile. Assume that rail is the only transportation alternative.
  a. Determine equations for the raw materials, output, and total transportation cost functions and plot these on a graph.
  b. Determine the location that minimizes total transportation costs (i.e., site A, B, or an intermediate location).

17-5. Consider two competing plants located at points A and B that are ten miles apart. Determine and sketch an equation for the market boundary separating these plants for each of the following cases:
  a. Product price is equal at both plants (i.e., $P_A = P_B = 20$) and per-mile transport costs per unit of output from each plant are the same (i.e., $s_A = s_B = 2$).
  b. $s_A = s_B = 2$ but $P_A = 25$ and $P_B = 20$.
  c. $s_A = 2$, $s_B = 3$, $P_A = 20$, and $P_B = 24$.

17-6. Mario's Fine Foods, a chain of ethnic restaurants, is considering locating a restaurant in Millville and Yorktown. The total cost and marginal cost functions of one of their restaurants are

$$TC = 1,000 + 2Q + 0.005Q^2$$

and

$$MC = 2 + 0.01Q$$

where TC is total cost, MC is marginal cost, and Q is the number of meals served per week. The following demand and marginal revenue functions for each city have been estimated using data from market surveys:

MILLVILLE: $P = 10 - 0.005Q$, $MR = 10 - 0.01Q$.
YORKTOWN: $P = 6 - 0.005Q$, $MR = 6 - 0.01Q$.

  a. Determine an equation for the average cost function. Sketch the average cost function and the two demand functions on the same graph. Use selected points from $Q = 0$ to $Q = 1,000$.

b. What output rate in terms of meals per month would minimize the average cost per meal?

c. Using the principles of threshold analysis, is a Mario's restaurant feasible in Millville? Yorktown? Explain.

d. For either or both cities where the restaurant is feasible, determine the profit-maximizing price–quantity combination, total revenue, total cost, and total profit.

17-7. The maximum production rate of wheat and nuts (both measured in bushels) for each of two countries is shown here:

	A	B
Wheat	1000	2000
	or	or
Nuts	4000	1000

a. What is the opportunity cost of production of each good in each country? Which country has a comparative advantage in wheat and which in nuts? Explain.

b. If the countries specialize in producing that product for which they have a comparative advantage, determine the amount produced in each and the total production for both countries combined.

c. With specialization and trade, demonstrate that consumers in both countries can be better off than under a "no specialization—no trade" arrangement.

d. What are the implications of your analysis in parts (a)–(c) for the location of industry between these two countries?

VII

Business Decisions and Government

CHAPTER 18

Taxes and Managerial Decisions

Preview

A large business may be required to pay dozens of different taxes and fees. At the federal level, there is the corporation income tax, the employer's contribution to the social security or payroll tax, and various excise taxes. The state government is likely to utilize a sales tax, excise taxes, its own corporation income tax, and a payroll tax used to pay unemployment compensation. At the local level, firms may face property taxes, license fees, and other assessments.

In addition to providing revenue to finance the activities of government, the various taxes have something else in common—each can affect managerial decision making. Taxes affect managerial decisions in several ways. Sometimes tax considerations determine the legal form selected for a business enterprise. For example, a desire to avoid payment of the federal corporation income tax may cause a firm to continue to operate as a partnership rather than to incorporate. Taxes can affect methods of doing business. Effluent taxes (i.e., taxes on pollution) provide incentives to change production methods, and property tax rates may affect location decisions. Taxes can also be an important determinant of the demand for a product sold by a business. For example, for many years an excise tax imposed on margarine made it difficult for that good to compete with butter. In contrast, a substantial income tax credit available to the purchasers of solar heating systems allowed such equipment to become more competitive with other methods of heating.

This chapter uses the tools of economic analysis developed in previous chapters to analyze the ways that taxes affect managerial decisions. First, the impact of an excise tax on equilibrium price and quantity is discussed. Next is a consideration of optimal strategies when a profits tax is imposed. The third section examines how taxes on inputs affect production decisions, and the fourth analyzes the effect of the property tax. The chapter concludes with an evaluation of preferential tax treatment, such as the income tax deduction for interest expenses, investment tax credits, and accelerated depreciation.

Excise Taxes

An *excise tax* is a sales tax levied on a particular good or service. For example, the federal government imposes excise taxes on gasoline, cigarettes, and liquor. Most states tax these three commodities, and many utilize excise taxes on other goods and services, such as soft drinks, hotel lodging, and theater tickets. In addition to providing revenues, excise taxes are sometimes used to decrease the quantity demanded for a product by increasing its effective price. Substantial excise taxes levied on cigarettes and liquor have always been justified as a means of reducing consumption of those products. Similarly, taxes on gasoline are used as a means of encouraging energy conservation. This approach is common in Europe, where excise taxes on motor fuel may cause retail prices to be double or triple the wholesale price of gasoline.

_____

Taxing Beer in Thailand and Gasoline in Washington, D.C.

Using excise taxes to alter consumer behavior can be a tricky undertaking. Sometimes the results are not as intended. Recently, the government of Thailand imposed a heavy excise tax on beer. The tax was designed to raise revenue and to reduce beer drinking. As a consequence of the tax, the price increased from $1.25 to $1.75 per pint and beer consumption dropped by 50 percent. But because the tax applied only to beer, other alcoholic beverages became relatively less expensive. For example, a pint of whiskey could be purchased for about the same amount of money as a pint of beer. The result was increased consumption of substitute beverages such as whiskey and other hard liquors. Thus by taxing beer, the government inadvertently encouraged people to switch to beverages with a higher alcohol content. Consequently, the consumption of alcohol may actually have increased as a result of the tax.

In 1980, the city of Washington, D.C., imposed a 6 percent excise tax on all gasoline sold within the District. Because the elasticity of demand for gasoline is low, it was expected that the tax would generate substantial revenues, which would help the city reduce a large budget deficit. But six months later, the tax was repealed. What happened?

Washington, D.C., is only ten miles square. Rather than pay the gasoline tax, motorists on the edges of the District simply bought their fuel at lower prices in the suburban areas of Maryland and Virginia, which surround the city. During the first month the tax was in place, the amount of gasoline sold in Washington, D.C., dropped by about one-third. Consequently, the anticipated tax revenues did not materialize and D.C. gas station owners lost sales and profits.

_____

Typically, it is the ultimate responsibility of the seller to pay an excise tax. Consider a federal excise tax of 20 cents per pack on cigarettes. A stores that sells cigarettes must remit 20 cents to the federal government for each pack sold. Now suppose that the tax is increased to 50 cents per pack. The store may raise the price of cigarettes by the amount of the tax increase, maintain the price at the pretax level, or increase the price by a part of the tax increase. The pricing policy used by the store does not matter to the government as long as the seller pays 50 cents in tax for each pack of cigarettes sold.

How should the store determine the price to be charged for cigarettes? A first reaction might be that the choice is obvious; the price should be increased by the full amount of the tax. But that would not necessarily be a wise decision. In fact, it might be a very poor choice under certain conditions. Basically, proper pricing policy requires consideration of the demand and supply functions for the product being taxed.

Suppose that before the excise tax increase, the retail demand and supply schedules for cigarettes are as shown in Table 18-1. Note that supply equals demand at $3.00 per pack. Thus the equilibrium quantity is 16 billion packs and the equilibrium price is $3.00.

TABLE 18-1 **Supply and Demand Schedules for Cigarettes (Billions of Packs Per Year)**

Price	Quantity Demanded	Quantity Supplied (Before Tax Increase)	Quantity Supplied (After Tax Increase)
$2.55	22	10	6
2.70	20	12	8
2.85	18	14	10
3.00	16	16	12
3.15	14	18	14
3.30	12	20	16
3.45	10	22	18

Now consider the 30-cent increase in the excise tax from 20 cents to 50 cents. Let the prices shown in Table 18-1 be the total amount received by the seller. At each price level, the seller must now pay an extra 30 cents in tax. Hence the net amount retained by the seller at any price level is 30 cents less than before. For example, if the consumer pays $3.00, from the perspective of the seller the price is the same as a price of $2.70 before the tax increase. But sellers' decisions are based on the amount of money actually received. Thus at a price to consumer of $3.00, only 12 billion packs per year will be supplied. Similarly, a price of $3.15 generates the same supply response as did a price of $2.85 before the tax increase. Thus the quantity supplied will be 14 billion. The other entries in the fourth column of Table 18-1 are determined in a similar manner.

The second and fourth columns of Table 18-1 can be used to determine the new equilibrium price. Note that supply and demand are equal at $3.15 per pack. This equilibrium price is 15 cents higher than the equilibrium before the 30-cent tax increase. The implication is that the tax increase is being shared by consumers and sellers. Consumers are paying 15 cents more for each pack of cigarettes and sellers are paying the other 15 cents. As expected, the new equilibrium quantity (14 billion packs per year) is less than the previous equilibrium amount (16 billion).

Figure 18-1 is a graphical representation of Table 18-1. The supply response to the tax increase is shown by shifting the supply curve up by the amount of the tax (30 cents). This shift (shown in the figure at $S'S'$) reflects the increased cost to the firm of selling cigarettes. The new supply curve indicates that less is supplied at any price than before the tax increase. The new equilibrium price of $3.15 occurs at the intersection of DD and $S'S'$.

In general, an excise tax is not borne equally by consumers and sellers. The actual impact of the tax depends on the relative slopes of the supply and demand curves of the product being taxed. Consider Figure 18-2a. In this case, the demand curve is vertical, indicating that demand is totally inelastic. Before the increase in the excise tax, the equilibrium price is $3.00. After the increase, the new equilibrium price is $3.30, while the quantity remains unchanged. Note that the price has risen by the full amount of the tax increase. There is no sharing of the tax

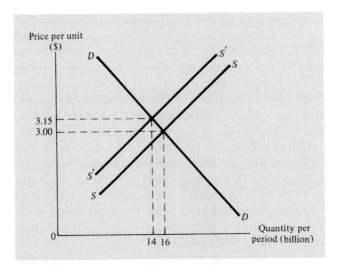

FIGURE 18-1 **An Excise Tax Shared by Consumers and Sellers.**

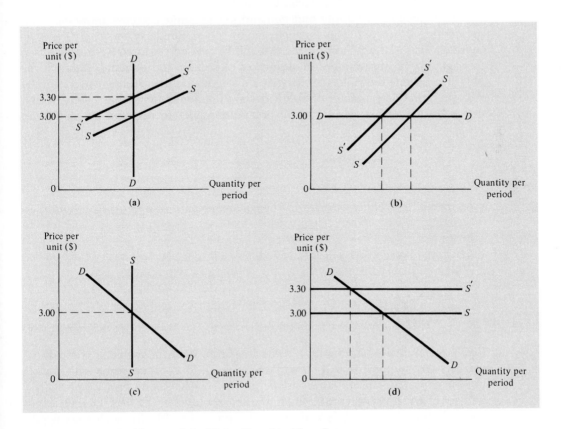

FIGURE 18-2 **Incidence of the Excise Tax: Limiting Cases.**

increase; consumers pay the entire 30 cents. The explanation is that quantity demanded is totally insensitive to price. The quantity demanded at a price of $3.00 per pack is the same as $3.30 per pack. Thus the entire tax increase can be passed on to the consumer with no loss of sales to the producer.

Figure 18-2b depicts an upward-sloping supply curve and a horizontal (perfectly elastic) demand curve. As a result of the tax increase, the quantity decreases, but the equilibrium price does not change. Thus the seller pays all of the tax. The reason is that because demand is totally elastic, any price increase will cause quantity demanded to be zero. Hence no portion of the tax increase can be passed on to the consumer. The entire tax must be absorbed by the seller.

Figures 18-2c and d show the incidence of an excise tax for vertical and horizontal supply curves. If supply is totally unresponsive to price (Figure 18-2c), there is no shifting of the supply curve in response to a tax increase. Equilibrium quantity remains unchanged and the entire tax is paid by the seller. In contrast, if the supply curve is horizontal (Figure 18-2d), consumers will bear the entire burden of the tax. This is because any decrease in the revenue per unit retained by the seller would cause quantity supplied to be zero. Thus the price increases by the full amount of the tax change.

In general, the effect of an excise tax on the price of a good or service depends on the elasticities of supply and demand. As demand becomes more elastic, a greater proportion of the tax must be paid by sellers. Similarly, as supply becomes more elastic, a larger share of the tax will be passed on to consumers. Thus if managers have information on elasticities of supply and demand, they will be able to anticipate the effects of changes in excise tax policies and plan accordingly. Although precise estimates of elasticities are not always available, even a rough guess can aid managers in making pricing decisions in response to changes in taxes.

KEY CONCEPTS

- As demand becomes less elastic, the consumer pays a larger proportion of an excise tax. With completely inelastic demand, the entire tax is paid by the consumer.
- As supply becomes less elastic, sellers pay a larger proportion of an excise tax. With completely inelastic supply, the entire tax is paid by the seller.

Taxes on Profit

In Chapter 9 it was shown that in the long run, firms in perfectly competitive markets earn no more than a normal rate of profit. In contrast, firms with market power may earn substantial economic profit. This economic profit represents a transfer of wealth from consumers to the shareholders of the firm. One means of redistributing this wealth is to impose a tax on profits. Ideally, such a tax would be paid only by firms that earn economic profits. As a practical matter, it is not possible to identify precisely the amount of economic profits being earned. Thus such taxes usually are structured as a percent of total accounting profit earned by a firm.

The purpose of this section is to analyze how a tax on profit affects pricing and output decisions of managers. It will be shown that the impact of such a tax depends on the objectives of managers. Specifically, it will be demonstrated that managers attempting to maximize total revenue respond to a profit tax differently than managers whose objective is profit maximization.

Profit Maximization and Profit Taxes

The profit-maximizing price and quantity for a monopoly are shown in Figure 18-3. Also shown is total profit earned at various output rates. Note that profit increases to output rate Q_m and declines for higher output rates.

Now assume that a proportional tax of t percent is levied on each dollar of profit. After-tax profit is also shown in Figure 18-3. Note that the effect of this

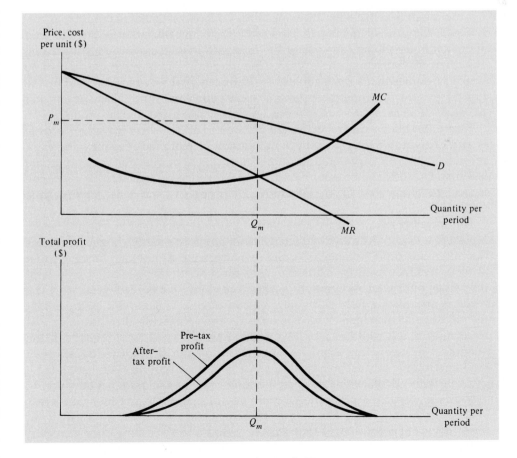

FIGURE 18-3 **Profit Maximization and the Profit Tax.**

tax is to reduce total profits by t percent at each output rate. However, it should also be observed that although profit is less than before the tax, the output rate that results in maximum profit has not changed. The firm maximizes after-tax profit by producing Q_m units as before. Because the profit-maximizing quantity is the same, the price set by the firm for the product will not change either. The profit-maximizing price is still P_m. In the short run, the implication is that the entire tax is absorbed by the firm in the form of reduced profits. None of the tax is passed on to consumers in the form of higher prices.

However, a tax on profit can affect prices and output in the long run. Such a tax reduces the net return on investment. This means that less investment will take place and hence the amount of capital in an industry will be reduced. A result is that productive capacity will increase less rapidly than if the tax had not been imposed. Thus, because quantity supplied will be less, in the long run prices are likely to be higher because of the tax on profit.

Revenue Maximization and Profit Taxes

The models of firm behavior developed thus far have assumed that profit maximization is the goal of managers. However, profit maximization is not the only approach to developing models of the firm. Alternative assumptions regarding objectives of managers can be used. One alternative is revenue maximization, which presumes that a manager acts to maximize total revenues received by the firm. Use of the revenue-maximization assumption can result in conclusions that are quite different from those obtained by assuming profit maximization.

Figure 18-4 shows that revenues are maximized at Q_1, where marginal revenue is zero. This result follows from the definition of marginal revenue—the extra revenue that results from producing one more unit of output. For any output rate less than Q_1, additional output increases total revenue because marginal revenue is positive. But beyond Q_1, marginal revenue is negative and hence total revenue declines.

The lower panel of Figure 18-4 shows profit at each rate of output. Let π_0 represent a target return set by management. Suppose that this target represents the minimum profit acceptable to the owners of the firm. Note, however, that profit is less than π_0 at Q_1. Thus managers must act to increase profit to at least the target return. In recognition of this constraint, a modified version of the revenue-maximizing hypothesis may be considered. This variant assumes that the objective of managers is to maximize revenue subject to the constraint that the firm earn at least its target rate of profit. Output rate Q_2 in Figure 18-4 is the quantity that meets this objective. Any output greater than Q_2 yields less than the target profit. Because marginal revenue is positive, output rates less than Q_2 generate reduced total revenue. Corresponding to the output rate Q_2 is the price P_2.

Now suppose that a proportional profit tax is imposed. Figure 18-4 shows that after-tax profit at Q_2 is now less than π_0. Thus, to maximize revenue while satisfying the target profit constraint, output must be reduced to Q_3 and the price increased to P_3.

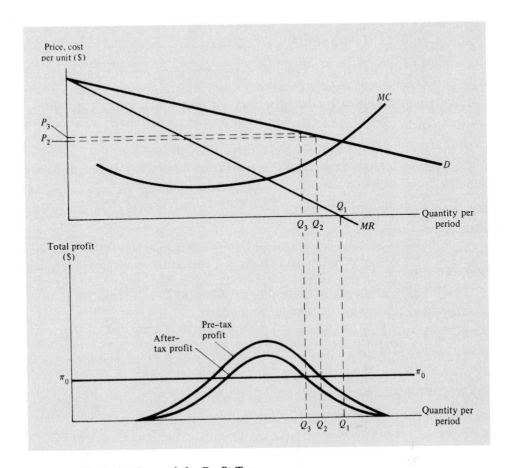

FIGURE 18-4 **Revenue Maximization and the Profit Tax.**

Note how the effect of the profit tax depends on the assumed objective of managers. For profit maximization, there is no short-run change in price or quantity as a result of the tax. In contrast, a revenue-maximizing manager subject to a target profit constraint will reduce output and increase price in the short run in response to a higher tax on profit.

KEY CONCEPTS

- If the firm's objective is profit maximization, the optimal price and quantity in the short run will remain unchanged if a profit tax is imposed. However, in the long run, a profit tax may cause firms to reduce their investment in productive capacity.
- For revenue-maximizing managers subject to a target profit constraint, a profit tax will result in reduced output and higher prices.

Taxes on Inputs

A firm may be taxed or required to make other payments to government based on the amounts of certain inputs utilized in its production process. One example would be a state excise tax on energy use. Another is money paid (based on the firm's total wage bill) to unemployment compensation or disability funds for those workers who lose their jobs or are injured while at work. An effluent tax based on emission levels of certain pollutants is a third example of a tax on inputs. It can be thought of as a tax on the use of water and air as depositories for waste materials.

Cost Minimization and Input Taxes

When a tax is levied on an input, information is provided to managers that relative prices of inputs have changed. Specifically, managers are signaled that the price of the taxed input is relatively higher than before the imposition of the tax. If managers are attempting to minimize costs, the tax may cause a change in the mix of inputs used for production.

Consider a firm that uses two inputs, capital and labor, to produce its product. Assume that the objective of managers is to minimize the cost of producing any given rate of output. Figure 18-5 depicts an isoquant for Q_0 units of output. As

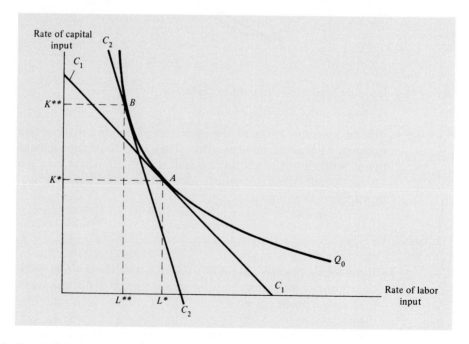

FIGURE 18-5 **Cost Minimization and Taxes on Inputs.**

discussed in Chapter 6, this isoquant shows all the efficient combinations of capital and labor that can be used to produce Q_0.

Let w be the cost of labor and r be the cost of capital. The isocost line C_1 shown in Figure 18-5 indicates the combinations of capital and labor that can be purchased for a given total expenditure, C_1. the slope of this isocost line is $-w/r$. For input prices w and r, the most efficient combination of capital and labor to produce Q_0 units is at point A, where the isocost line C_1 is tangent to the isoquant. Point A specifies use of L^* units of labor and K^* units of capital.

Now suppose that a tax of $\$t$ is imposed on each unit of labor used by the firm. What will be the least-cost combination to produce the specified rate of output, Q_0? The tax raises the price of labor to $(w + t)$ and changes the slope of the isocost line to $-(w + t)/r$. As before, the cost-minimizing rates of capital and labor are determined by the point where the lowest isocost line is tangent to the isoquant. The lowest isocost line is now C_2. Thus the optimal combination of inputs to produce Q_0 is at B, where C_2 is tangent to the isoquant. Point B indicates K^{**} units of capital and L^{**} units of labor. This combination includes more capital and less labor than before the tax. Thus the impact of a tax on labor is that managers substitute capital for labor in the production process.

This result is true in general. If technology allows substitution between inputs, a tax imposed on one input will cause greater use of the other inputs in the production process. One implication of this result is that input taxes can be used as a tool for public policy. For example, a tax levied on energy use would encourage energy conservation.

Effluent Taxes

If private costs of production are less than the total costs imposed on society, too many resources may be allocated to an activity. The production of paper is a good example. A paper mill generates residuals in the form of chemicals, particulates, and odors that are discharged into the environment. The high level of pollution resulting from paper production occurs because the firm does not consider all the costs of its activities. The problem is that the prices of some of the inputs used by the firm do not reflect their true social cost. Specifically, the air and water used for waste discharge may be considered free goods by the managers of the firm.

Excessive levels of pollution occur because of the lack of markets for air and water used in the production process. A business that uses energy or labor must pay for these inputs. But no one can exert an effective claim to ownership of the air, oceans, large lakes, and important rivers. Because there are no well-defined property rights, some individuals and firms can make free use of these resources. Further, there is no market mechanism to force them to take into account the social costs of their actions.

One approach to the problem of excess pollution is the use of effluent taxes. Under this approach, firms are allowed to choose the level of emissions but are taxed for the privilege. A tax on pollution can be considered as a tax on the use of water and air. By raising the price of water and air in this use, policymakers encourage managers to substitute other inputs in the production process. If a tax on emissions is set high enough, a firm will find it can reduce costs by installing pollution-control equipment that reduces the amount of emissions.

An advantage of effluent taxes is that they encourage the efficient allocation of resources. First, the divergence between private and social costs can be reduced or eliminated because the firm is forced to take into account the total social cost of its actions. Second, by allowing firms to select the optimal trade-off between polluting and paying taxes, variations in the cost of emission abatement can be taken into account. Firms with high control costs may find it profitable to make smaller reductions and pay larger amounts of effluent taxes. These funds can be used to compensate those who are affected by the firm's pollution. In contrast, firms that can easily reduce their polluting may find it less costly to make substantial reductions in discharges and thus avoid the tax.

Although they have promise, effluent taxes are not a complete solution. It can be very difficult to determine the optimal rate of the tax. Theoretically, the marginal tax rate should be equal to the marginal benefit of pollution abatement. Thus firms would devote resources to reducing emissions until the marginal cost exceeded the marginal benefit. In actual practice, marginal costs are very difficult to determine and any assessment of marginal benefits must be rather speculative. Effluent taxes have been used in Europe but have not found wide acceptance in the United States.

EXAMPLE

An Effluent Tax on Sulfur Dioxide Emissions

A community is experiencing serious air pollution resulting from emissions of sulfur dioxide (SO_2) from heavy industry in the area. The cost of reducing the emissions is not the same for all polluters. For some firms the cost is relatively low, while for others it is quite high. Assume that there are five sources of SO_2 pollution—A, B, C, D, and E—and that each emits 10 tons per day. Costs per ton of SO_2 removed from the air are assumed to be constant (i.e., for each polluter the first ton removed costs the same as the last ton) and are $100, $200, $300, $400, and $500, for sources A, B, C, D, and E, respectively. How could an effluent tax be used to reduce sulfur dioxide air pollution by 20 tons per day?

SOLUTION   The following figure illustrates the effect of a tax on SO_2 emissions. If an effluent tax were imposed, each pollution source would have the option of spending the money to eliminate pollution or paying the tax. Thus the decision faced by a profit-maximizing manager would be to select the least-cost option. For example, if the tax were set at $250 per ton, it would be cheaper for sources A and B to make the changes to eliminate their pollution. In contrast, for C, D, and E it would be less expensive to continue to pollute and to pay the tax. The net result would

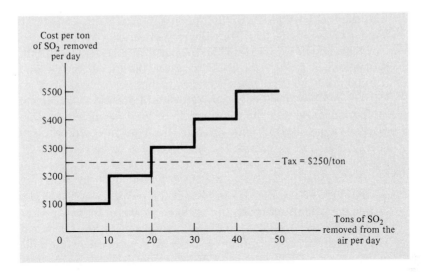

The Effect of a Tax on Sulfur Dioxide Pollution.

be a reduction of SO_2 emissions of 20 tons per day and $7,500 per day collected from effluent taxes (i.e., 30 tons of pollution per day from C, D, and E times $250 per ton). The tax revenue would be available to reduce pollution further or to compensate these affected by the pollution.

Property Taxes

Property taxes generate most of the revenues for local governments. Typically, the property tax is levied on land, structures, machines, and vehicles owned by a business. But there is considerable variability in property tax rates from one locality to the next. In one section of the United States the annual property tax assessment may represent about 1 percent of the market value of the property. In another location the property tax may be as high as 5 percent of market value. These variations in property tax rates can affect the value of the firm and also decisions of managers. Such effects are the focus of this section.

Fixed Property

Certain types of property are essentially fixed in location. Land and permanent structures, such as large buildings, are the best examples. Once constructed, it would be extremely costly and difficult to move a large manufacturing facility or an office building to a different location.

Assume that an economy has two taxing jurisdictions, A and B. Consider a parcel of land in A, which has an exact counterpart in B. With no property taxes, suppose that both pieces of land have a market value of $1,000,000 and generate annual rents of $100,000. Thus the rate of return of each parcel is 10 percent.

A $50,000 tax is levied on the property in jurisdiction A, but no property tax is assessed in jurisdiction B. As a result, the owner of the land in A must pay $50,000 in taxes every year. This means that net income for that property will be $50,000 and the after-tax rate of return will decline to 5 percent.

Now suppose that the two parcels of land are listed for sale at their pre-tax market values of $1,000,000. Clearly, the land in B would be preferred because of its higher rate of return. For the land in A to be competitive, its price would have to decline substantially. In fact, if the taxing policies of the two jurisdictions are not expected to change, the price would have to drop to $500,000. At this price the $50,000 in after-tax income of the property in A would provide the same 10 percent rate of return as the untaxed property in jurisdiction B.

When taxes are reflected in the value of property, the tax is said to be *capitalized*. The degree of capitalization of a tax is a function of the efficiency of capital markets in equalizing the rates of return on different assets. It is also dependent on the extent that the tax is perceived as permanent. For example, if the 5 percent tax is expected to be eliminated after one year, the effect on property values would be much less than if the tax is expected to be maintained at the 5 percent rate indefinitely.

Basically, the effect of taxes on land and other property that cannot be moved is to cause a one-time reduction in the value of the property. Hence the full impact of the tax will fall on the owner of the property at the time the tax is imposed. Because any subsequent owner will acquire the property at a reduced price, only the original owner will experience a loss of wealth.

CASE STUDY

Proposition 13 and Property Tax Capitalization

In 1978, voters in California approved a statewide tax limitation initiative known as Proposition 13. The measure was intended to provide homeowners with some relief from the high property tax rates that existed throughout the state. The key provisions of the initiative were (a) a one percent ceiling on the property tax rate that any local government could impose, (b) a rollback of assessed property values to their 1975 levels, and (c) the requirement that property taxes in an area could not be increased without approval by a two-thirds majority in a local election. The net effect of the initiative was to substantially reduce property taxes for many California homeowners. Fortunately, at the time, the state government had a large budget surplus, which was used to compensate local governments for the loss of property tax revenues. Consequently, there was no immediate reduction in the quality of services provided by cities, counties, and other local governmental units.

The concept of property tax capitalization suggests that the reduction in property taxes mandated by Proposition 13 should have increased the value of houses in California. In fact, if the property tax was fully capitalized, the price of a house should have increased by the present value of the tax cut. Is the evidence consistent with the theory?

A study by Rosen examined the effects of Proposition 13 in the San Francisco area.* He collected data on house prices and property tax payments before and after the passage of the initiative. Using regression analysis, Rosen estimated that the degree of capitalization was approximately 22 percent. That is, housing prices in San Francisco increased by about one-fifth of the property tax saving resulting from Proposition 13.

Economists have conducted dozens of studies of property tax capitalization. Although the exact percentages differ, almost all of these studies conclude that property taxes are partially, but not completely, capitalized. Typically, the finding is that the degree of capitalization is from 20 to 40 percent.**

* Rosen, K. "The Impact of Proposition 13 on House Prices in Northern California." *Journal of Political Economy* (1982), Vol. 90, pp. 191–200.

** For an excellent summary, see Yinger, J., et al. *Property Taxes and House Values.* (Boston: Academic Press, 1987).

Mobile Property

Some property can be moved from one location to another. For example, a large firm can easily transfer its vehicles among different offices. It may also be possible to relocate machines and other capital equipment. If there is a significant variation in property tax rates between taxing jurisdictions, the firm may have an incentive to move capital from the high-tax to the low-tax area.

The effect of this reallocation of capital is shown in Figure 18-6. Suppose that the firm has a fixed amount of capital, as measured by the length of the horizontal line from O_A to O_B. The relocation of capital from jurisdiction B to jurisdiction A

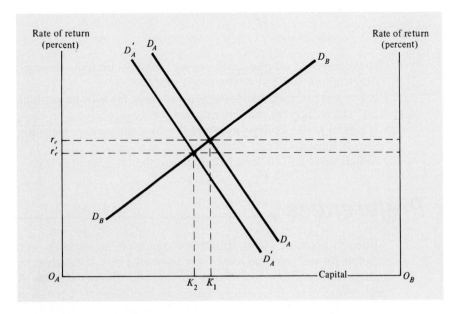

FIGURE 18-6 **Mobile Capital and the Property Tax.**

is shown as a movement to the right along the horizontal axis. Similarly, the relocation of capital from A to B is shown by a leftward movement. For example, at O_A all capital is in jurisdiction B and at O_B all the firm's capital is in jurisdiction A. The curve D_A depicts the pretax rate of return earned by capital in location A. The curve is downward sloping from left to right in recognition of diminishing productivity as additional capital is employed in A. The pretax rate of return for capital in jurisdiction B is shown by D_B. This curve is read from right to left and is also downward sloping. If capital can move freely between the two jurisdictions, adjustments will be made until the rates of return, r_e, are equalized. This equilibrium is shown by point K_1 in Figure 18-6. Thus the optimal amount of capital in A is $O_A K_1$, and the amount in B is $O_B K_1$.

Now consider a 5 percent property tax imposed on capital in jurisdiction A. This tax reduces the after-tax rate of return on capital. The new rate of return is shown by D_A'. The impact of the tax is to cause capital to be moved from A to B until the rates of return are again equal. This occurs at K_2. Thus the tax causes $K_2 - K_1$ units of capital to be shifted from A to B. Note that the rate of return, r_e', earned in both areas is lower than before the imposition of the tax. Thus the property tax on mobile capital has caused a decline in wealth for the owners of capital in jurisdiction B as well as those in A.

In general, a property tax can be considered as a tax on certain inputs. As such, its effects are similar to those described in the preceding section. If substitution between inputs is possible, then, by increasing the relative costs of land and capital, the property tax tends to decrease the use of these inputs. But if the amounts of land and capital are fixed, production techniques remain unchanged and the property tax simply reduces the market value of the assets.

KEY CONCEPTS _____

- A tax imposed on one input causes a cost-minimizing manager to use more of other inputs and less of the taxed input.
- If property is fixed in location, a property tax will be capitalized. That is, the tax will reduce the market value of the asset.
- If capital is not fixed in location, it will tend to move from high-tax to low-tax jurisdictions until the rate of return is equalized. The rate of return in both jurisdictions will be lower than before the tax was imposed.

Tax Preferences _____

Although taxes extract a substantial share of the earnings of most firms, it is possible for managers to reduce tax payments by taking advantage of various tax preferences that have been incorporated into the tax system. As used here, tax preferences refer to business activities, decisions, or conditions that are given preferential treatment under tax laws. Three examples embodied in certain income tax laws are considered in this section. First the provision that allows deduction of interest expenses is discussed. The second tax preference analyzed is an investment tax credit. Finally, the implications of using accelerated depreciation to compute tax liability are considered. In each case, the objective of the analysis is to show how these provisions affect managerial decisions.

Interest Deductions

Firms obtain money for investment using a combination of debt and equity finance. But these sources of funds are treated differently with respect to tax laws. Interest payments on debt are considered as expenses and can be deducted in computing tax liability. In contrast, the dividends paid to stockholders and funds kept by the firm as retained earnings are not deductible.

The preferential treatment of debt under the corporation income tax affects the optimal capital structure used to finance the firm. Consider a corporation that needs to obtain X dollars to pay for a new production facility. The investment is to be financed using a combination of debt and equity. Thus

$$D + E = X$$

where D is the amount of debt and E is the amount of equity.

If the cost of \$1 of debt is r_d and the cost of \$1 of equity finance is r_e, the total cost of financing the investment is given by $r_d D + r_e E$. But if the tax is imposed, the total cost becomes

$$(1 - t)r_d D + r_e E$$

where t is the rate of the corporation income tax. Note that the effective cost of debt is $(1 - t)r_d$ because deduction of the interest expense reduces the firm's tax liability by tr_d per dollar of debt.

Suppose that the objective of management is to minimize the total cost of financing the investment. One approach to the problem is to start with the assumption that only equity financing is to be used and then consider the effect on total cost of substituting dollars of debt for dollars of equity. Initially, it is assumed that r_d and r_e are not affected by the relative proportions of debt and equity.

Adding one more dollar of debt finance costs the firm $(1 - t)r_d$ while reducing equity finance by the same amount generates a saving of r_e. Hence the net effect on total cost of financing the \$1 is

$$(1 - t)r_d - r_e \tag{18-1}$$

If costs of debt and equity finance are equal ($r_d = r_e$), then because of the tax deductibility of interest, the use of additional debt continually decreases the total cost. Generally, however, the cost of debt is less than the cost of equity because debt holders assume less risk than do those who have equity holdings. This is because interest on debt must be paid before any money can be paid to a firm's stockholders. As compensation for the greater risk they bear, shareholders demand higher rates of return. If it is assumed that $r_d < r_e$, the advantage of debt finance is even greater.

Equation (18-1) has a somewhat surprising implication. In that additional dollars of debt always decrease the total cost of financing the X of investments, costs will be minimized by using only debt finance. Clearly, this result is not consistent with actual practice. In fact, most firms have capital structures with more equity than debt. Other than utilities, relatively few large corporations have a capital structure with as much as 50 percent debt.

It should also be noted that the costs of debt and equity capital are probably not independent of the firm's capital structure. As relatively more debt is used, the level of risk also increases. This can be demonstrated by a simple example. Consider a corporation that earned $1,000,000 after payment to all inputs except capital. Suppose that the firm has an interest expense of $500,000. Thus the amount of income left for dividends and retained earnings is $500,000. Note that earnings can decline substantially without impairing the firm's ability to meet its interest obligation. Of course, a decline in earnings would reduce the dollars left for dividends and retained earnings.

Now suppose that the firm's capital structure included proportionately more debt and that total interest expense was $950,000 instead of $500,000. If earnings are $1,000,000, the firm can still make its interest payments. But a relatively small decline in earnings can cause serious problems. If earnings drop by more than $50,000, the firm will be unable to meet its interest obligations. If this situation continues, the business may be forced into bankruptcy.

Investors require compensation for the increased risk associated with high debt/equity ratios. Thus, as more debt is used in the capital structure, the costs of both debt and equity finance increase. Let the higher costs of debt and equity (in comparison to the 100 percent equity case) by Δr_d and Δr_e, respectively. This increased cost is applied to the total dollars of debt (D) and the total dollars of equity (E). Thus the effect on total cost of using $1 more debt is given by

$$(1 - t)(r_d + \Delta r_d D) + (-r_e + \Delta r_e E)$$

which can be written as

$$[(1 - t)r_d - r_e] + [(1 - t)\, \Delta r_d D + \Delta r_e E] \qquad (18\text{-}2)$$

Equation (18-2) is easily interpreted. The first term in brackets is identical to equation (18-1) and represents the basic cost advantage of an additional dollar of debt finance. Note that for $r_d \le r_e$, this term is always negative, indicating that total cost is reduced by using more debt. The second term in brackets is always positive and reflects the increased costs of capital associated with higher debt/ equity ratios. As additional debt is utilized, $(1 - t)\, \Delta r_d D$ and $\Delta r_e E$ both become greater and thus the risk premium increases.

Equation (18-2) can be used to determine the optimal capital structure. Additional debt should be added until the basic cost advantage of debt is just offset by the risk premium required for a higher debt/equity ratio. Initially, the risk premium will be small and total costs will be reduced by using more debt. But beyond some point, adding debt increases the total cost. This result is shown graphically in Figure 18-7. With no taxes (i.e, $t = 0$), the curve indicates that financing costs are minimized when the capital structures includes D percent of debt.

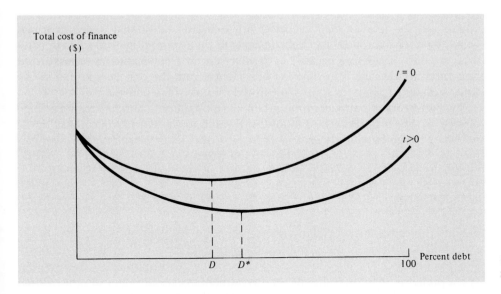

FIGURE 18-7 **The Cost-Minimizing Capital Structure.**

Equation (18-2) shows how the tax preference for interest expenses affects the optimal capital structure. If $t = 0$, debt will be used only as long as the pretax cost advantage of debt $(r_d - r_e)$ exceeds the risk premium. But for $t > 0$, by reducing the cost of debt relative to equity, the tax system provides an incentive for managers to use more debt. Hence, as shown by D^* in Figure 18-7, debt/equity ratios are likely to be higher when there is a tax preference. Note that the tax preference reduces the total cost of finance for all debt/equity ratios.

Tax-Exempt Fringe Benefits

Fringe benefits are compensation to workers in addition to their wages or salaries. Examples include paid vacations, medical and dental insurance, life insurance, and retirement programs. In the past 30 years, fringe benefits as a proportion of the total wage bill have increased, especially in union contracts. In 1960 employers of union workers paid 21 cents in fringe benefits for every dollar paid as wages. By 1992 that cost had nearly doubled, to 37 cents per wage dollar. The popularity of fringe benefits can be partially explained by tax preferences for such benefits.

In hiring workers, a manager must consider the total cost of the compensation package being offered. This package includes a salary plus various fringe benefits. In evaluating a job offer, workers may be willing to trade salary for additional benefits. However, the terms of trade can be affected by the tax treatment of fringe benefits.

Certain fringe benefits are exempt from the personal income tax. For example, medical insurance and retirement contributions can be provided by an employer and not considered as taxable income to the worker. Thus because of the tax advantage, the worker may be better off taking an additional dollar in fringe benefits rather than in salary. But the costs to the firm are the same. There is no tax advantage to the firm because both salary and fringe benefits can be deducted in computing the firm's income tax bill. Hence from the cost perspective of the firm, a dollar of salary is equivalent to a dollar of fringe benefits.

The preferential treatment of fringe benefits may alter the compensation package offered by the firm. Because the after-tax value to the worker of an additional dollar of fringe benefits is greater than an extra dollar of salary, the firm can provide the same total compensation to the worker at a reduced cost by offering relatively more fringe benefits than if the tax advantage were not available.

Investment Tax Credits

Business investment is crucial to a market economy. Without sufficient investment there will be little economic growth and existing facilities will soon become obsolete. Tax policy can be used to stimulate investment. One approach is the granting of tax preferences for investment. An investment tax credit is an example of such a preference. This credit allows businesses to reduce their corporation income tax liability by some fraction of the firm's investment spending during the year.[1]

In Chapter 15 it was argued that firms should undertake only those investments that have positive net present value. Consider an investment that requires an initial outlay of C dollars and has a useful life of T years. If the discount rate is r and the after-tax revenue resulting from the investment in a given year is $(1 - t)R_i$, the net present value of the investment is

$$NPV = \sum_{i=1}^{T} \left[\frac{(1 - t)R_i}{(1 + r)^i} \right] - C$$

If $NPV > 0$, the investment is profitable for the firm.

Now suppose that the provisions of the corporation income tax are changed to allow a 10 percent tax credit for investments made during the tax year. This credit would allow the firm to subtract $0.10C$ from its income tax payment, meaning that the actual cost to the firm of the investment would be only $0.90C$. Hence the net present value of the investment is now

$$NPV = \sum_{i=1}^{T} \left[\frac{(1 - t)R_i}{(1 + r)^i} \right] - 0.90C \qquad (18\text{-}3)$$

Because costs are reduced, the net present value increases. Thus one effect of the investment credit is to make profitable investment proposals more profitable. Another is to stimulate investment in projects for which net present value had been negative but that now are profitable because the net present value is positive. A third effect is to cause substitution of capital for other inputs in production. Because the effective after-tax cost of capital equipment is less than it would be without the credit, capital becomes relatively less expensive. Hence costs can be reduced by using more capital and less of other inputs.

[1] The general tax credit provision of the Federal Corporation Income Tax was repealed by the Tax Reform Act of 1986. However, investment tax credits still exist at the state level and for certain types of equipment at the federal level.

Solar and Conservation Credits: Incentive or Windfall?

Tax credits can be used to alter consumer purchasing decisions. During the late 1970s, there was a strong sentiment in Congress to conserve energy and promote the use of alternative energy sources. Legislation was enacted that allowed taxpayers a credit against their income taxes of 15 percent of the cost of home energy conservation expenditures to a maximum tax saving of $300. A credit was also allowed for the purchase of solar, wind, and other alternative energy systems. This credit was set at 40 percent of the cost of the system, with a maximum tax saving of $4,000.

The effect of the conservation and alternative energy system tax credits was to reduce the cost of such investments. By making them less expensive relative to use of conventional fuels such as oil and gas, the intent was to induce consumers to increase their conservation and alternative energy system expenditures.

However, one concern about the consumer tax credits is whether they significantly change consumer purchasing patterns. Those consumers who would have invested in conservation or alternative energy systems even without the tax credits receive a windfall benefit. In evaluating the credits, the windfall must be compared to the benefits to society of the additional investment that was induced by the tax credits.

Although the evidence is not definitive, the case for conservation tax credits appears weak. Survey information collected by the authors suggests that almost all conservation expenditures would have been made even without the tax credits. In contrast, credits for alternative energy investments seem to have played an important role in stimulating investment in this area. Only a small proportion of the survey respondents said they would have bought solar or wind energy systems if the credits had not been available.*

* H. C. Petersen, "Solar Versus Conservation Tax Credits," *Energy Journal* (1985), 6(3):129–135.

Accelerated Depreciation

In computing corporation income tax liability, depreciation expenses are deductible. Thus, when depreciation is taken into account, the net present value of an investment is given by the expression

$$NPV = \sum_{i=1}^{T} \left[\frac{(1-t)R_i + td_iC}{(1+r)^i} \right] - C$$

where d_i is the fraction of the total cost of the investment that can be depreciated in the ith year. Note that the depreciation allowance for any given year increases the net present value of the investment by $td_iC/(1+r)^i$. The reason is that the present value of the firm's tax liability is reduced by that amount. The expression for net present value an also be written as

$$NPV = (1-t) \sum_{i=1}^{T} \left[\frac{R_i}{(1+r)^i} \right] + tC \sum_{i=1}^{T} \left[\frac{d_i}{(1+r)^i} \right] - C \qquad (18\text{-}4)$$

For given C and t, note that the net present value increases as $\sum_{i=1}^{T} [d_i/(1 + r)^i]$ increases. But $\sum_{i=1}^{T} d_i = 1$. Thus the magnitude of $\sum_{i=1}^{T} [d_i/(1 + r)^i]$ depends on the size of the individual d_i. Because the depreciation benefit is discounted to the present, a method that allows larger write-offs in the early years of the depreciation period will result in greater net present value than if the depreciation rate is constant over the useful life of the investment. Thus if a firm is allowed to depreciate its assets more rapidly, otherwise unprofitable investment proposals may now show a positive net present value. The result is that additional investment may occur.

The straight-line method is the simplest technique for computing depreciation allowances. For a depreciation time of T years, this approach would specify $d_i = 1/T$ for all i. For example, if $T = 5$ and the cost of an investment is $100,000, the annual depreciation allowance is one-fifth of $100,000, or $20,000.

To stimulate additional investment, firms are sometimes allowed to use accelerated depreciation methods. The double-declining-balance technique is one example. Instead of deducting C/T in the first year, the firm is allowed to deduct $2/T$ of the total amount in the first year and $2/T$ of the remaining balance in subsequent years. For the example just given, 40 percent of the $100,000 could be depreciated in the first year ($40,000), 40 percent of the remaining $60,000 in the second year ($24,000), 40 percent of $36,000 in the third year ($14,400), and 40 percent of the remaining $21,600 in the fourth year ($8,640). The final $12,960 of the original $100,000 would be written off in the lst year of the depreciation period.

Although the total amount of depreciation is $100,000 under both schemes, the present value of the tax saving is greater with accelerated depreciation. If the tax rate is 50 percent and the discount rate is 10 percent, the present value of the tax saving for straight-line depreciation is

$$(0.50) \left[\frac{20,000}{(1.10)^1} + \frac{20,000}{(1.10)^2} + \frac{20,000}{(1.10)^3} + \frac{20,000}{(1.10)^4} + \frac{20,000}{(1.10)^5} \right] = \$37,900$$

while the amount using double declining balance is

$$(0.50) \left[\frac{40,000}{(1.10)^1} + \frac{24,000}{(1.10)^2} + \frac{14,400}{(1.10)^3} + \frac{8,640}{(1.10)^4} + \frac{12,960}{(1.10)^5} \right] = \$40,515$$

Note that the net present value of the investment increases by $2,615 under the double-declining-balance method. Thus the investment is more likely to have a positive net present value if accelerated depreciation is allowed for tax purposes.

KEY CONCEPTS

- Deductibility of interest payments on debt has the effect of increasing the amount of debt in a firm's optimal capital structure.
- Investment tax credits may stimulate investment by reducing the cost and hence increasing the net present value of an investment.

- By increasing the present value of tax savings, accelerated depreciation increases the net present value of an investment. Thus the rate of investment will increase.

Summary

By increasing the effective price, an excise tax can be used to decrease the demand for a good or service. However, the effect of an excise tax on the profit-maximizing price charged by a firm depends on conditions of supply and demand. The proportion of the tax that can be passed on to consumers is inversely related to the elasticity of demand. If demand is totally elastic, an excise tax must be absorbed by sellers. Conversely, the price increase that is caused by an excise tax is directly related to the elasticity of supply. If the supply curve is horizontal, consumers will pay the entire tax.

The effect of a tax on profit depends on the objectives of managers. If the goal of managers is to maximize profit, a tax on profit will not affect the optimal price and quantity in the short run. However, if the objective is revenue maximization subject to a profit constraint, a profit tax will cause a reduction in output and an increase in price in the short run.

Excise taxes may be imposed on inputs used by a firm. Such taxes signal managers that the relative prices of the inputs have changed. If technology allows substitution, a tax on one input will cause other inputs to be substituted for the input that is taxed.

Property taxes reduce the rate of return earned on the taxed property. If the property is fixed in location, the property tax will be capitalized and the market value of the property will decline. But if the property can be moved from one location to another, firms will shift property from jurisdictions with high tax rates to those with lower rates. This adjustment will continue until the after-tax rates of return are equal in all jurisdictions.

Interest payments on debt can be deducted in computing income taxes. This preferential treatment of debt reduces its after-tax cost relative to equity. Hence the tax system causes relatively more debt to be used in the corporation's capital structure. But higher debt/equity ratios mean greater risk for those who provide funds to the firm. Thus the costs of debt and equity capital increase. The implication is that there is a cost-minimizing debt/equity ratio for the firm.

The popularity of fringe benefits can be partially explained by tax preferences. Because certain benefits are exempt from the personal income tax, a dollar of such benefit is worth more to the worker than a dollar in salary.

Investment tax credits are used to stimulate investment in capital goods. They allow the firm to reduce its income tax by some fraction of the cost of an investment. By increasing their net present value, some investments that would have been unprofitable without the credits may now be undertaken by the firm.

By treating depreciation as a deductible expense, the tax system increases the net present value of an investment by an amount equal to the present value of the tax saving. But methods of accelerated depreciation, such as the double-declining-balance approach, increase the present value of the tax saving. As a result, they stimulate investment demand and encourage the substitution of capital for other inputs.

Discussion Questions

18-1. An excise tax is imposed on a product for which there are few good substitutes. Who will pay the tax, the firm or the consumer? Explain.

18-2. If there is no minimum profit constraint, how does the revenue-maximizing firm select the optimal rate of output?

18-3. A good is produced using capital and labor. Suppose that a tax is imposed on capital. What is the relationship between the convexity (i.e., curvature) of the isoquant and the effect of the tax? Explain.

18-4. What does it mean to say that a tax has been capitalized?

18-5. A tax on capital used in jurisdiction A could reduce the rate of return on capital employed in jurisdiction B even though there is no tax on capital in B. Explain.

18-6. New legislation eliminates all taxes on profit. How would this change affect the optimal proportions of debt and equity in the capital structure of firms?

18-7. Why does the marginal cost of both debt and equity increase if relatively more debt is used in the firm's capital structure?

18-8. A firm operates in a country that imposes a highly progressive tax on profit. Interest paid on debt can be deducted from taxable income and there is an investment tax credit. How is the effect of the interest deduction related to the profitability of the firm? How is the effect of the investment tax credit related to the profitability of the firm?

18-9. For tax purposes, firms are allowed to use accelerated depreciation. In evaluating investment decisions, how is the effect of accelerated depreciation related to the discount rate used by the firm in decision making?

Problems

18-1. The market supply and demand functions for videotapes are given by

$$Q_S = 100 + 20P$$
$$Q_D = 300 - 5P$$

where Q is quantity and P is the price of tapes.
a. What are the equilibrium price and rate of output?
b. If an excise tax of $2 per tape is imposed on the seller, what will be the new equilibrium price and rate of output? What proportion of the tax will be paid by purchasers of the tapes?

18-2. In a small, isolated college community, there are 2,000 apartments. In the short run, the only use of these apartments is for rental to students. The college has a large summer school program that results in a 100 percent occupancy rate throughout the year. The demand for apartments by students is given by

$$Q_D = 4,000 - 2P$$

where Q_D is the number of apartments demanded and P is the average monthly rental rate.

Graffiti painted on walls and sidewalks is a serious problem in the community. The mayor thinks that college students are responsible and that they should pay for the cleanup. Because students occupy all of the town's apartments, she proposes a monthly tax of $25 on each apartment rental.

a. On an annual basis, how much revenue will the tax provide?

b. Evaluate the tax as a means of forcing students to pay for cleanup of their graffiti.

18-3. Fred Merkle and Co. is the monopoly supplier of old movies in a region. Over a year's time, the demand for movies is given by

$$P = 100 - Q$$

where P is the price of movies and Q is the quantity demanded per year. The firm's total cost (TC) and marginal cost (MC) functions are

$$TC = 800 + 20Q + Q^2$$

and

$$MC = 20 + 2Q$$

a. What are the profit-maximizing price and rate of output?

b. What are the revenue-maximizing price and rate of output?

c. If the objective is to maximize revenue with a constraint that total revenue be greater than or equal to total cost, what are the revenue-maximizing price and rate of output?

d. Repeat part (c), assuming that a 10 percent tax is imposed on profit. Is your answer consistent with the discussion of the profit tax in the chapter? Explain.

18-4. A firm manufactures a product using both capital and labor. A federal tax credit is available for capital expenditures. Use isoquant analysis (see Figure 18-5) to show how the optimal combination of inputs used to produce Q_0 units of output would be affected by the tax credit.

18-5. A parcel of land has a market value of $100,000 and is located in a county with no property tax. Assume that a permanent $500 per year property tax is imposed on the land. If the tax is fully capitalized, approximately what will be the market value of the land after the imposition of the tax? Assume that investors use a discount rate of 10 percent.

18-6. Managers of Quick Foto of Fargo, North Dakota, are considering the purchase of a new device for processing film. The cost of the machine is $10,000; it has an expected useful life of ten years and a salvage value of $1,000. The firm's managers believe that the machine will increase Quick Foto's revenues by $2,000 per year. Operating expenditures are projected to be $500 per year. Assume that revenues and operating expenditures are incurred at the end of each year and that managers use a 14 percent discount rate in making investment decisions. The firm's marginal tax rate is 20 percent. What rate of investment tax credit would be necessary to cause managers to purchase the machine? Assume that the credit is received at the time of purchase.

18-7. A new cement truck would cost the Sure Stick Concrete Company $100,000. The law allows the firm to use either straight-line or double-declining-balance depreciation for tax purposes. The truck can be depreciated over five years and the discount rate used by managers is 12 percent. The firm's marginal tax rate is 30 percent. What effect does the choice of a depreciation method have on the net present value of the investment in the truck?

Problems Requiring Calculus

18-8. A property tax of T dollars per year is placed on a piece of urban property. If the tax is fully capitalized,
   a. Write a general equation showing the change in the market value of the property as the amount of the tax changes.
   b. Write a general equation showing the change in the market value of the property as the discount rate used to capitalize the tax changes.

18-9. Acme Manufacturing produces a product using labor and capital as inputs. The firm's production function is given by

$$Q = 25K^{0.1}L^{0.9}$$

The price of labor is $10 and the price of capital is $20.
   a. If the product is to be manufactured at minimum cost, for any rate of output, how much labor should be used for each unit of capital employed?
   b. Suppose a 10 percent tax is imposed on capital. How much labor should be used for each unit of capital?
   c. Starting from the initial prices, if a 10 percent tax is placed on each input, how much labor should be used for each unit of capital employed?

CHAPTER 19

Antitrust, Regulation, and Price Controls

Preview

Because competition benefits society by reducing prices and improving the efficiency of resource allocation, a top priority for government action should be the implementation of policies designed to enhance competition. In the United States, the primary public policy approach to increasing competition is through the use of antitrust laws. These statutes give enforcement agencies the power to alter existing or proposed market structures and to impose penalties for certain types of business conduct determined to be anticompetitive.

To avoid litigation, it is important that managers understand the scope and limits of antitrust law. Thus, the first section of this chapter considers antitrust activity in the United States. The objective is to make the reader aware of business activities that may violate antitrust statutes. The discussion begins with a review of basic U.S. antitrust laws and enforcement procedures. Next is a consideration of antitrust law as it applies to monopolization, mergers, collusion, and price discrimination. Finally, remedies and penalties used in antitrust enforcement are discussed.

Antitrust laws deal with industry structure and conduct. In contrast, the regulatory approach to public policy focuses on industry performance. It is based on the presumption that there may be circumstances where competition is not possible or is not desirable. Thus to prevent adverse consequences from the lack of competition, government may regulate firms so that they perform in a socially acceptable manner. Regulation may take the form of requiring approval for price changes, limiting entry or exit, or prescribing standards that a product or service must meet. The second major section of the chapter examines public utility regulation in the united States. The first topic considered is the need for public utility regulation. Following that is a brief overview of regulatory procedures.

Price controls are another tool that can be used by government to control business activity. Generally, they are used to combat inflationary pressures and expectations. The last section of this chapter evaluates the impact of price controls. Of particular importance is the differential effect of controls in competitive and concentrated industries.

Antitrust Policy

Most industries do not meet the criteria for perfect competition as discussed in Chapter 9. Moreover, the complexities of markets and the politics of decision making make it unlikely that any reasonable set of public policies could generate the conditions for perfect competition. Thus public policy must be content with a more limited objective. It has been suggested that a realistic goal for policymakers is workable competition. It may not be necessary for all the requirements of perfect competition to be met to achieve results that approximate those of competition. Markets may fail to meet one or more of the criteria and still be "workably" competitive.

The achievement of workable competition is the goal of antitrust activity. The antitrust approach acknowledges that imperfections exist in many markets but is directed toward narrowing the gap between actual conditions and the competitive ideal. The philosophy underlying antitrust enforcement is that by modifying the structure of markets and conduct of participants in markets, performance can be improved without direct government involvement in the daily decision making of managers. Prevention of a merger between two large corporations is an example of a structural modification. A fine assessed for fixing prices illustrates antitrust policy intended to alter business conduct.

U.S. Antitrust Laws

The Sherman Act and the Clayton Act (as amended) represent the primary legal basis for antitrust activity in the United States. The most important provisions of these two statutes are discussed here.

SHERMAN ACT   The Sherman Act was enacted in 1890 and has remained basically unchanged for over 100 years. It has two main sections:

> *Section 1.*   Every contract, combination in the form of a trust or otherwise, or conspiracy, in restraint of trade or commerce among the several states, or with foreign nations, is hereby declared to be illegal. Every person who shall make any such contract or engage in any such combination or conspiracy shall be deemed guilty. . . .

> *Section 2.*   Every person who shall monopolize, or attempt to monopolize, or combine or conspire with any other person or pesons, to monopolize any part of the trade or commerce among the several states, or with foreign nations, shall be deemed guilty. . . .

These two sections focus on different types of undesirable business behavior. Section 1 is intended to prohibit firms from conspiring to initiate and maintain practices not in the public interest. For example, an agreement among managers to fix prices would violate Section 1. The Sherman Act, Section 2, is designed to reduce market dominance. Firms that aggressively act to gain control of their markets may be in violation of Section 2. For example, in 1911 Standard Oil of New Jersey was found guilty of illegal monopolization of the market for refined oil. As a result, the firm was split into 30 separate companies. Most of the large oil companies in the United States today are the result of the Standard Oil dissolution.

CLAYTON ACT   The Clayton Act was enacted as a supplement to the Sherman Act. The intent of Congress was to provide legislation to prevent firms from obtaining monopoly power and also to specify specific business practices that are prohibited. The most important provisions of the act are contained in Sections 2 and 7.

> *Section 2.*   It shall be unlawful for any person engaged in commerce, to discriminate in price between different purchasers of commodities . . . where the effect of such discrimination may be to substantially lessen competition or tend to create a monopoly in any line of commerce. . . .

Section 7. No corporation engaged in commerce shall acquire, directly or indirectly, the whole or any part of the stock or other share capital of another corporation engaged also in commerce where the effect of such acquisition may be to substantially lessen competition between the corporation whose stock is so acquired and the corporation making the acquisition or to restrain such commerce in any section or community or tend to create a monopoly of any line of commerce.

These two sections each deal with a specific type of business practice. Section 2 is directed against certain types of price discrimination. Setting prices below cost to eliminate competition in a market is an example. Section 7 of the Clayton Act imposes restrictions on merger activity. A merger between General Motors and Ford could (and probably would) be prevented based on Section 7. Notice that the language of the Clayton Act is not absolute. That is, price discrimination and mergers are prohibited only if they tend to "substantially lessen competition or create a monopoly in any line of commerce."

Two important amendments have modified the original Clayton Act. In 1936, the Robinson–Patmen Act was passed to broaden the Section 2 provisions against price discrimination. The new act was aimed at large retailers who could undersell their smaller competitors because they could buy merchandise at lower prices from manufacturers and wholesalers.

In 1950 the Celler–Kefauver Amendment was enacted to supersede the provisions of Section 7 of the Clayton Act. The original Section 7 focused on competition "between the corporation . . . acquired and the corporation making the acquisition." This wording caused the courts to ignore the broader issue of a general lessening of competition. The result was that enforcement agencies found it difficult to prevent vertical and conglomerate mergers under the Clayton Act. Congress responded to this problem by passing the Celler–Kefauver Amendment, which amended Section 7 to read:

That no corporation engaged in commerce shall acquire, directly or indirectly, the whole or any part of the stock or other share capital and no corporation subject to the jurisdiction of the Federal Trade Commission shall acquire the whole or any part of the assets of another corporation engaged also in commerce, where in any line of commerce in any section of the country, the effect of such acquisition may be substantially to lessen competition, or to tend to create a monopoly.

Note that the amendment reduced the emphasis on reduced competition between the merging firms and stressed the idea that the demonstration of a lessening of competition "in any line of commerce in any section of the country" could be used to prevent a merger. The effect of the change was to make vertical and conglomerate mergers subject to antitrust action.

Antitrust Enforcement

Antitrust proceedings are initiated in four ways. First the Antitrust Division of the Department of Justice may file a suit. If the suit is continued to the point of formal litigation, it is first heard in a federal district court. If either party wishes to contest the decision of the district court, the matter is taken to a circuit court of appeals and, if the justices are willing to hear the case, to the Supreme Court. The Antitrust Division's responsibility is limited to initiating and prosecuting a case. The courts must determine guilt and penalties.

The second path of antitrust enforcement is through the Federal Trade Commission. When the commission staff decides to issue a formal complaint and the matter is contested by the defendant, an initial hearing is held before an administrative law judge who is a part of the FTC. If the judge decides for the defendant, the matter is dropped. However, if the decision is to uphold the complaint, the case can be appealed to the five FTC commissioners. If their decision is again against the defendant, the matter can be appealed to the federal courts.

A third enforcement procedure involves state antitrust legislation. Most states have their own antitrust statutes. Typically, complaints are prosecuted by the state attorney general's office and decided by state courts. Appeals from decisions by the state supreme court can be taken to the federal court system.

The fourth method for dealing with alleged antitrust violations is litigation by private parties. Individuals or firms may file suits in the federal district courts. For example, a firm that believes it has been overcharged because its suppliers have fixed prices could sue under Section 1 of the Sherman Act. Appeals are heard by a circuit court of appeals and, ultimately, the U.S. Supreme Court. Currently, about 2,000 private antitrust suits are filed in the United States each year. Private suits represent over 90 percent of all antitrust actions.

Rule of Reason Versus Per Se Offenses

The standard of proof required for conviction in antitrust prosecutions differs with the nature of the alleged violation. Sometimes, although an apparent antitrust violation may have occurred, it is not clear that there has been a net injury to society. Such cases are decided under a *rule-of-reason standard*. In rule-of-reason proceedings, successful prosecution requires not only the demonstration that the act has been committed, but also that society will be better off by prohibiting, modifying, or punishing the act. In contrast, certain activities are judged illegal without the requirement that the specific antisocial effects be shown. These acts are referred to as *per se offenses.*

The per se and rule-of-reason standards represent different points along a continuum. They differ in the volume and detail of evidence required for a successful prosecution. Rule-of-reason cases require extensive evidence proving that an act has been committed and demonstrating the damage that has been caused. Per se cases only require proof that the offense has been committed. In a sense, per se violations can be thought of as being judged as if the nature of the offense automatically dictates that the social costs of the act are clearly greater than any possible benefits. Thus the only real issue to be decided is the remedy or penalty in the case.

Not all antitrust violations fit into the tidy categories of being per se or rule-of-reason offenses. Still, there are some examples that can be cited as illustrations of each. Generally accepted as per se offenses are agreements to fix prices, divide markets between sellers, and to restrict or pool output. Activities evaluated under the rule-of-reason standard are mergers and monopolization of a market by a large firm or firms. As a rough guide, violations involving business conduct for which there is no strong justification are decided on a per se basis. In contrast, cases involving the structure of an industry usually are judged using the rule-of-reason approach.

KEY CONCEPTS

- Section 1 of the Sherman Act prohibits unfair business practices such as price fixing. Section 2 deals with monopolization.
- Section 2 of the Clayton Act (as amended by the Robinson–Patman Act) limits price discrimination.
- Section 7 of the Clayton Act (as amended by the Celler–Kefauver Act) is used to prohibit mergers that may result in a substantial lessening of competition.
- Antitrust actions can be initiated by the Department of Justice, the Federal Trade Commission, state officials, or private parties.
- Conviction of rule-of-reason offenses requires proof that the act has been committed and that social costs exceed benefits. Per se offenses require only a demonstration that the act has been committed.

Monopoly

Section 2 of the Sherman Act prohibits monopolizing, attempting to monopolize, and conspiring to monopolize. However, it is important to note that the economic and legal definitions of monopoly differ. In the study of economics, monopoly is defined as a single seller. The legal interpretation is much less restrictive. As used in antitrust proceedings, firms are viewed as having monopoly power if they have a high degree of control over the price of a good or service.

Since its enactment, the most controversial point with respect to Section 2 has been the standard of proof required for successful prosecution. The issue has been whether the Sherman Act made monopoly power in and of itself an offense or whether the showing of industry dominance had to be accompanied by evidence of illegal practices. During the past 100 years, the Supreme Court has accepted both points of view. The position taken by the Court at any given time has had an overwhelming effect on the use of Section 2. When proof of illegal acts to achieve monopoly power has been required, there have been few Section 2 convictions. For example, between 1920 and 1945, the Court seemed to require some evidence of illegal activity. During that period there were very few successful Section 2 cases. When the Court has held that the government only had to show the existence of monopoly power, Section 2 cases have been more frequent and more successful.

The current interpretation of Section 2 represents a compromise between the two extreme positions. The mere existence of monopoly power is not sufficient for successful prosecution under Section 2. However, the government no longer is required to show that a firm has engaged in acts that, considered by themselves, represent antitrust violations. Instead, prosecutors can focus on patterns of business behavior that have the net effect of allowing a firm to gain and maintain a monopoly position. Under this interpretation, practices that would be legal when considered in isolation or when used by smaller firms may be grounds for conviction if used by a firm judged to have dominance in an industry. That is, the standard used by the courts to judge large firms is more rigorous than that applied to smaller firms. For example, aggressive price cutting in markets with competition, coupled with price increases in other markets, probably would be ignored by antitrust officials if practiced by a small firm. But the same actions by a firm with a large market share could result in a suit for illegal monopolization.[1]

It should also be noted that the Supreme Court is unlikely to receive many new Section 2 cases in the future. Over the last ten years, the Justice Department and the Federal Trade Commission have essentially abandoned initiating cases requesting dissolution or divestiture of dominant firms. Their reluctance results from the substantial time and dollar commitment required to prosecute such cases, uncertainty as to their outcomes, and a perception that such cases are seldom necessary to protect consumers in today's global economy.

On those rare occasions when Section 2 cases are initiated, three conditions should be satisfied. First, substantial monopoly power must exist and must have been exercised. High market shares and findings of above-average profits are necessary but not sufficient conditions to satisfy this criterion. Second, possession of market power should be the result of more than just superior products sold by the firm or outstanding business ability displayed by its management. There should be evidence that the firm has used its market power to suppress competition. Even then, a careful evaluation of the firm's practices is required to determine that they have no efficiency-enhancing effects on the economy. Third, a case should not be initiated unless there is some identifiable remedy that will provide net benefits to society. This is crucial because once an enterprise has been restructured, any efficiency benefits may be lost forever. If the social costs associated with the status quo are small or are likely to be transitory, Section 2 remedies may not increase social welfare.

Most students of antitrust policy would agree that Section 2 of the Sherman Act has probably been a modest deterrent to high concentration in an industry. However, the main impact may come not from the results of litigation, but as firms modify their plans to avoid the costs and uncertainties of possible prosecution. It has sometimes been suggested that the ghost of Senator Sherman sits in every corporate boardroom.

CASE STUDY

The Great Antitrust Doubleheader

In January 1969, the Justice Department brought suit against IBM under Section 2 of the Sherman Act for illegal monopolization of the general-purpose computer market. The government

---

[1] For example, see *United States* v. *Grinnell Corp.*, 384 U.S. 563 (1966).

proposed that the firm be split into several competing companies. It took six years for the case to come to court. One reason for the delay was the discovery process whereby the government was required to make available over 25 million pages of documents to IBM and the firm provided over 60 million pages of documents to be used by the government in case preparation. The trial at the District Court level lasted six more years and generated 300,000 pages of testimony and exhibits.

In 1972, the Justice Department initiated litigation to force the American Telephone and Telegraph Company to sell off its manufacturing arm, Western Electric, and its local operating companies. The government charged that AT&T had used unfair practices to eliminate competition in the markets for telephone equipment and long-distance telephone service. The case has been referred to as the most important antitrust proceeding of all time because it sought the breakup of the largest privately owned enterprise that the world has ever known. At the time the suit was filed, AT&T employed several hundred thousand people and had revenues greater than the gross domestic product of all but 12 nations.

On January 8, 1982, the Justice Department announced resolution of both suits. The IBM suit was dropped because of changing conditions that had reduced the firm's market share and hence diminished the government's chances of obtaining a conviction. The AT&T suit was settled by a consent decree that required the firm to divest itself of all its local operating companies. These operating companies, such as Pacific Telephone and Telegraph, represented about two-thirds of AT&T's total assets. In return, the firm was allowed to keep Western Electric and its long-distance operations and to become an active competitor in selling computers, an activity that had been prohibited by an earlier consent decree.

The settlement of the two cases on the same day probably was not a coincidence. While dropping one suit, the government could claim victory in another, thus avoiding political criticism. Also, although the IBM suit was terminated, a powerful new competitor, AT&T, was freed to compete with IBM in the computer industry.

The objectives of these antitrust actions have been only partially realized. Competition in many telecommunications markets has increased, and consumers have a wider range of choice than before divestiture. However, AT&T has found it difficult to be an effective competitor in the computer industry.

Merger

It is more difficult to constrain existing market power than to halt monopolization in its formative stages. Because industry dominance has frequently been achieved by acquiring other firms, merger policy is an important tool for antitrust action.

EVALUATION OF MERGERS Mergers between large firms create the potential for abuse of the market power obtained by the combined firm. This abuse may take the form of higher prices, actions to deter entry or to eliminate competitors, or exercise of monopsony power to obtain price reductions from suppliers.

The primary argument in support of mergers is the possibility of efficiency gains. These efficiency effects may result from several different factors. The merged firm may be able to reduce its cost of production and distribution by realizing economies of scale. Inefficient techniques may be abandoned as firms gain access

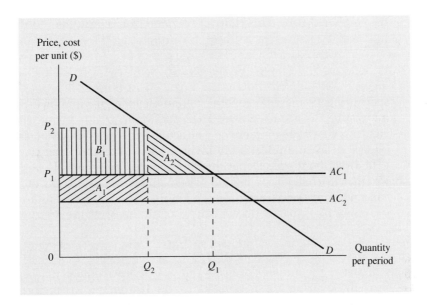

FIGURE 19-1 **Evaluation of Horizontal Mergers.**

to the patent rights and technical expertise of their new partners. Mergers may also concentrate assets under the direction of superior managers who have the ability to operate the firm more efficiently.

Although there may be other considerations, the basic decision to allow or prohibit a merger should rest on an evaluation of the costs of increased market power versus the social benefits of improved efficiency. Williamson has suggested a simple model for quantifying this trade-off.[2] Consider the demand and cost curves shown in Figure 19-1. Suppose that a merger shifts the newly combined firm's cost curve down from AC_1 to AC_2, while providing market power that is exercised by increasing prices from P_1 to P_2. The welfare trade-off is shown in the figure. The crosshatched area A_1 represents the resource saving associated with producing Q_2 units at the reduced average cost, AC_2. The crosshatched area A_2 is the deadweight loss stemming from increasing the price from P_1 to P_2. It represents the loss in consumer surplus as the higher price reduces the quantity demanded from Q_1 to Q_2. The merger can be evaluated by comparing the cost saving and the deadweight loss.[3] If the deadweight loss is greater than the efficiency gain, the merger should not be allowed. But if the resource saving more than offsets the deadweight loss, there may be a net benefit to society from the merger.

However, income distribution effects may also be important in evaluating a merger. Prior to the merger, the rectangle B_1 was part of the surplus value received by consumers. After the merger, this area represents economic profit earned by

[2] Williamson, O. "Economies as an Antitrust Defense: The Welfare Tradeoffs." *American Economic Review*, 58(March 1968): 18–36.

[3] Consumer surplus and deadweight loss are discussed on pages 319–321.

the combined firm. This transfer of value from consumers to the owners of the firm may be viewed as a reason for prohibiting the combination.

MERGER GUIDELINES A merger between large corporations is a costly undertaking. Considerable expense is involved in finding a proper merger partner, structuring the merger proposal, communicating information to shareholders, and integrating the acquired firm. This cost can be greatly increased if the merger is challenged by the government. The actual expense of litigation can be substantial, but the delay and uncertainty involved are even more costly.

In 1984, the Justice Department announced guidelines to be used in deciding whether to challenge a merger. These guidelines are based on overall industry concentration as measured by the Herfindahl Index. This index is computed by summing the squared market shares of all the firms in an industry. That is,

$$HI = \sum_{i=1}^{m} X_i^2$$

where m is the number of firms and X_i is the percentage market share of the ith firm. By squaring the market shares, the Herfindahl Index gives greater weight to large firms in an industry. For example, an industry with 10 firms each with a 10 percent market share would have a Herfindahl Index of 1,000. The index for an industry that has a dominant firm with a 50 percent market share and five smaller firms each with 10 percent shares would be 3,000.

The first step in applying the guidelines involves an examination of the Herfindahl Indexes for the industry. If the postmerger index is less than 1,000, the merger ordinarily will not be challenged. Mergers where the postmerger index is between 1,000 and 1,800 and where the increase in the Herfindahl Index as a result of the merger is less than 100 points are unlikely to be challenged. But if the postmerger index is between 1,000 and 1,800 and the increase is greater than 100 points, or if the postmerger index is greater than 1,800 and the increase is greater than 50 points, the Justice Department is likely to challenge a horizontal merger. These rules are summarized in Table 19-1.

Although industry concentration as measured by the Herfindahl Index is the starting point in using the guidelines, other factors are also considered by the

TABLE 19-1 **Likelihood of a Justice Department Challenge Based on 1984 Guidelines**

	Postmerger Herfindahl Index		
Increase in the Herfindahl Index	*Less than 1,000*	*1,000–1,800*	*Greater than 1,800*
0	Will not*	Unlikely	Unlikely
50	Will not*	Unlikely	Likely
100	Will not*	Likely	Will*

* Except in extraordinary cases.

Justice Department in deciding whether to challenge a horizontal merger. These are incorporated into the decision process in recognition that market shares are not the only data that affect the competitive effects of mergers. Other factors include ease of entry into the industry, the financial condition of the firm being acquired, the impact of foreign competition, and possibly efficiency gains from a merger.

EXAMPLE
_____

Horizontal Mergers: To Challenge or Not to Challenge?

An industry consists of eight firms with the following market shares:

Firm	Market Share (%)
1	30
2	10
3	10
4	10
5	10
6	10
7	10
8	10

Firm 1 announces that it intends to acquire firm 2. Will this merger be challenged by the Justice Department? Would a merger between firm 2 and firm 3 be challenged?

SOLUTION

Prior to any mergers, the Herfindahl Index for the industry is $30^2 + 7(10^2)$, or 1,600. After a merger between firm 1 and firm 2, the index would be $40^2 + 6(10^2)$, or 2,200. Because the Herfindahl Index is greater than 1,800 and the increase is more than 100, the Justice Department would challenge the merger.

If firm 2 and firm 3 were to combine, the postmerger Herfindahl Index would be $30^2 + 20^2 + 5(10^2)$, or 1,800. Because the index increased by more than 100 points, from 1,600 to 1,800, the merger is likely to be challenged. However, in making a final decision, Justice Department officials would consider other factors, such as efficiency gains that might result from the merger.

_____

PRESENT MERGER POLICY Horizontal mergers between large direct competitors are often challenged by the government. On most occasions, the courts have supported the government and prevented such mergers. The outcomes of proposed vertical and conglomerate mergers are less certain. During the 1960s and early 1970s, the government frequently was successful in challenging such mergers if they involved large firms. But during the late 1970s and 1980s, antitrust enforcement agencies have shown less interest in preventing vertical and conglomerate mergers. At present, unless it appears that such mergers would increase horizontal market power, they are unlikely to be challenged.

Recently, federal antitrust officials, instead of simply blocking certain large horizontal mergers, have allowed the mergers to proceed after eliminating any anticompetitive effects—an approach that has been referred to as "fix it first." For example, as a condition for not opposing a merger between two large oil companies, the federal government might require the acquiring firm to sell off those operations where the firms were direct competitors with substantial market shares. This divestiture could involve refineries, pipelines, and/or service stations.

KEY CONCEPTS

- Practices considered acceptable when practiced by small firms may represent antitrust violations if used by a large firm with considerable market power.
- One method of evaluating a merger is to compare efficiency gains with the social costs of increased market power. The income distribution effects may also be important.
- The Herfindahl Index is computed by summing the squares of the market shares of all firms in the industry. It takes into account the size distribution of firms.
- Mergers are likely to be challenged by the federal government in industries if the postmerger Herfindahl Index is greater than 1,800 and where the change in the index is greater than 100.
- Historically, the government has been very successful in preventing horizontal mergers between large direct competitors. Recently, antitrust officials have used a "fix it first" policy with respect to many such mergers.

Collusion

Another important goal of antitrust activity is to prevent collusion. Firms in oligopolistic markets have an incentive to collude. But the actual decision is based on a benefit–cost calculation by the firms involved. An important form of collusion is price fixing. The potential benefit of price fixing is obvious—increased profit. The costs fall into four interrelated categories. First, there is a cost associated with setting and changing industry price structures. Each firm in a cartel is in a different position, has different expectations, and has varying economic power in the industry. Hence it may be difficult to reach agreement. A second cost of collusion is that imposed by the inevitable cheating that will occur. Although profits can be increased by collusion, one firm can earn even greater profit by cutting its price slightly below the agreed level. Unless there is a mechanism for detecting and punishing cheaters, the cartel will soon fail as members cut prices to preserve their market shares.

A third cost of cartelization is that nonprice competition may replace price competition. For example, members of a cartel may engage in expensive advertising as a substitute for active price competition. Legal penalties imposed on convicted colluders are the fourth cost of price fixing. These may take the form of fines, prison sentences for executives, damage awards to private parties, or court orders to alter certain business practices.

The objective of antitrust policy is to reduce the net benefits of collusive activities. As the likelihood of conviction and the magnitude of penalties increase, the expected cost of violating antitrust laws increases. Also, if firms perceive that they are being actively scrutinized by antitrust authorities and that penalties from conviction will be severe, they will tend to adopt less easily detectable and less effective methods of collusion.

The courts have consistently taken a hard line against collusion. The precedent-setting case (*United States* v. *Trenton Potteries Co. et al.*) involved 23 manufacturers of bathroom fixtures who had conspired to fix prices. Through their trade association, the manufacturers published standardized price lists, met to consider prices, and pressured one another to sell only at list prices. When the association was brought to trial, it claimed that the agreement had not injured the public. The trial record supported this position, indicating that fixtures were often sold below the established prices. But the Supreme Court rejected the request for a rule-of-reason interpretation of price fixing. The justices argued that

> the reasonable price fixed today may through economic and business changes become the unreasonable price of tomorrow. ... Agreements which create such potential power may well be held to be in themselves unreasonable or unlawful restraints, without the necessity of minute inquiry whether a particular price is reasonable or unreasonable.[4]

The strong per se condemnation of price fixing has consistently been reaffirmed by the courts. Agreements to fix prices are a violation of the Sherman Act without regard to their effect. The prohibition applies not only to fixing minimum prices but also maximum prices and price differentials. Firms are simply not allowed to act in concert in determining prices.

Illegal price fixing costs billions of dollars each year in higher prices. Although explicit collusion has not been eliminated by antitrust efforts, the fact that it is judged by the courts as a per se violation of the law has had a significant impact in reducing the most effective forms of price fixing, group boycotts, and market allocation. Conspirators have been forced to abandon overt methods and to settle for less easily detectable and less efficient methods of collusion.

CASE STUDY

The Electric Machinery Conspiracy

In the early 1960s, 29 corporations were successfully prosecuted for fixing prices of electrical equipment such as transformers, generators, and switchgear. The indictments alleged two primary types of conspiracies. For sales involving open bids, the firms simply met to fix the prices that would be charged for different types of equipment. It was the sealed bid sales to the government that made the case intriguing. The intent of the conspiracy was to raise prices while allowing firms to maintain a predetermined market share. For example, GE was allocated 42

---

[4] *United States* v. *Trenton Potteries Co. et al.*, 273 U.S. 392 (1927).

percent of the market for switchgear, Westinghouse 38 percent, Allis-Chalmers 11 percent, and ITE Circuit Breakers 9 percent. Market shares were maintained by rotating bids so that each firm became the low bidder the requisite percentage of the time. This was accomplished by changing the order of bids about every two weeks or "with the phases of the moon."

To avoid detection, the conspirators engaged in elaborate precautions. Only first names were used and mail was always sent in plain envelopes to the homes of the executives. Calls were made from pay phones. Each firm was referred to by a code number. Expense-account vouchers were disguised by making them out for cities that were approximately as far from the firm's offices as the actual location of the conspiratorial gathering. The meetings themselves were often held in out-of-the-way places—a favorite was Dirty Helen's Bar in Milwaukee. Above all, company lawyers were never told anything.

As part of its investigation of the conspiracy, the Justice Department subpoenaed the records of the ITE Circuit Breaker Company. Nye Spencer, an employee of ITE, served as the scribe for the switchgear conspiracy. Spencer had kept detailed records of the conspiracy meetings to assist him in training his assistant. Confronted with the request for information, he turned over all his files to the government. Larger cracks in the dike appeared as lower-level executives cooperated with the investigation rather than implicate themselves further. Thus the government was able to assemble a strong case that the conspirators decided not to contest. Following sessions of plea bargaining, an agreement was reached whereby the firms were allowed to enter reduced pleas to some of the indictments in return for pleading guilty to others.

In the penalty phase of the case, the judge sent seven defendants to jail for thirty days and granted suspended sentences to twenty others. Never before had business executives been sent to jail as a result of Sherman Act violations. The firms were also required to pay nearly $2 million in fines. However, the greatest cost to the corporations involved was 1,900 private suits, resulting in damage awards of over $400 million.

Price Discrimination

Price discrimination can be used to discourage entry and weaken existing competitors. Predatory pricing is an important example. Consider the case of a large firm selling a single product in a number of distinct geographical markets. In some of the markets the firm has a monopoly, whereas in others it faces competition from smaller rivals operating in only a single area. The large firm can cut prices below cost in competitive markets and subsidize its losses from monopoly profits earned where the firm is the only seller. The smaller firms in the competitive markets may be forced from the market or into a merger if the dominant firm keeps its prices down. When the smaller firms have either gone out of business or been acquired, prices then are increased to the monopoly level.

Potential entrants into a market can also be deterred by the threat of predatory pricing. If the existing firm can create a credible threat that it will cut prices below cost if a new firm enters the markets, all but the largest potential competitors may be discouraged. Used in this manner, predatory pricing may be a useful tactic to prevent entry in an industry where natural barriers are not effective.

The courts have not been entirely consistent in defining what constitutes predatory pricing. However, recent court decisions have started from the premise that

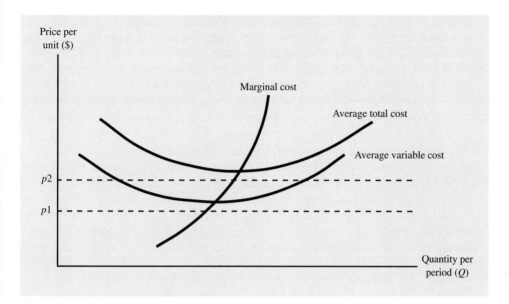

Price per
unit ($)

Marginal cost

Average total cost

Average variable cost

p2

p1

Quantity per
period (Q)

FIGURE 19-2 **Predatory Pricing.**

predation has occurred if price, p^1, is a set below average variable cost, as shown in Figure 19-2. From the perspective of economic theory, this position is defensible. In the short run, average variable cost represents the threshold between continuing to produce and shutting down an operation. If a price is below average variable cost, entrepreneurs can cut their losses by ceasing to produce. However, if price exceeds average variable cost, it is better to continue producing even if price is below average total cost, as shown by p^2 in Figure 19-2. The reason is that the excess can be used to pay a portion of the fixed costs. Thus a price that is above average variable cost but below the firm's average total cost can be justified. In contrast, a firm that sets its price below average variable cost and continues to produce can be logically viewed as having other motives, such as the elimination of current or potential competitors.

Price discrimination suits may involve considerable disagreement as to whether a firm has used predatory pricing. In some cases an important issue has been whether there is evidence of intent to exclude competitors. But if the court determines that predation has occurred, the defendant will usually be found guilty of an antitrust violation.[5]

Remedies and Penalties

Alleged antitrust violations are resolved in a number of different ways. The most common remedies and penalties are discussed here.

[5] Predatory pricing is not the only form of price discrimination that may violate U.S. antitrust laws. For a more extensive discussion of price discrimination and antitrust, see Petersen, H. C. *Business and Government.* (New York: Harper-Collins, 1993), pp. 189–196.

CONSENT DECREES   Most antitrust actions are resolved by consent decrees. These are agreements worked out between the government's attorneys and those of the defendant. Usually, they specify certain activities that the firm must or must not do. In return, the government agrees not to prosecute. In accepting a consent decree the firm, in essence, says: "We didn't do it, but we won't do it again." An important advantage of consent decrees is that they cannot be used as evidence of guilt in other proceedings, such as a private antitrust suit.

DISSOLUTION AND DIVESTITURE   In monopoly and merger actions, the court may use dissoluton or divestiture as a remedy. In 1911 the Supreme Court split Standard Oil of New Jersey into 30 smaller firms. This was an example of disolution, whereby the firm loses its identity. In contrast, a divestiture order requires the firm to sell certain of its assets, but the firm retains its identity. In approving a 1984 merger between Socal and Gulf Oil, the Department of Justice required Socal to sell off several thousand Gulf retail gas stations. This was an example of divestiture.

INJUNCTIONS   In ruling against a defendent, the court may issue an injunction that prohibits or compels certain actions on the part of the firm. For example, as a result of a price-fixing suit, a trade association may be prohibited from the collection and dissemination of information that was used to fix prices.

FINES   Firms convicted of Sherman Act violations may be fined up to $1,000,000 per violation. Officers of the firms may receive fines to a maximum of $100,000. However, in some price-fixing cases, each day is considered a separate offense. In this way, the potential fines can be much greater.

PRISON SENTENCES   A 1974 amendment to the Sherman Act made criminal convictions under Section 1 felony offenses and set the maximum prison sentence at three years. However, actual periods of incarceration for Sherman Act violations are usually less than one year. Convictions based on the Clayton Act are civil rather than criminal offenses and do not involve prison sentences.

TREBLE DAMAGES   Both the Sherman and the Clayton acts include provision for award of treble (triple) damages. If a private party can demonstrate that the antitrust laws have been broken and can prove the amount of damages sustained, the offending firm may be required to pay the plaintiff three times the amount of damages. Assume that Johnson Inc. and Mack Manufacturing are convicted of price fixing by the government. Firms that purchased the products of these firms at inflated prices could sue for damages. A successful government suit is prima facie evidence that the firms had violated the law. Thus the task of the plaintiffs would be to show the amount of damages. Suppose that it is determined that a specific firm purchased $1,000,000 in supplies from Johnson Inc. during the price-fixing period and that the total price would have been $900,000 in the absence of collusion. Thus the plaintiff has been overcharged by $100,000 and would be entitled to claim three times that amount, or $300,000. The prospect of treble damage awards may be the most important deterrent to antitrust violations.

KEY CONCEPTS _____

- The courts have consistently ruled that price fixing is a per se violation of the antitrust laws.
- Predatory pricing is a means of weakening competitors and deterring entry into an industry. Recent court decisions have defined predation as existing if price is set below average variable cost.
- Most antitrust suits are settled by consent decrees.
- Cases that go to court may result in dissolution or divestiture, injunctions, fines, imprisonment, and / or the award of treble damages.

CASE STUDY _____

Collusion in the Ivory Towers of Academia

In August 1989, the Department of Justice initiated an investigation involving 23 of the most prestigious private colleges in the United States. The allegation was that they were engaged in a conspiracy to raise tuition and to limit financial aid offered to students.

With respect to tuition, the charge was that the institutions shared information with one another regarding proposed increases. For example, an administrator at Harvard might have informed his counterpart at Yale that Harvard was contemplating raising tuition by 6 percent for the next year. Yale would use this information and similar data from the other Ivy League schools to determine its tuition rate. The result was that tuition rates were very similar. For 1989–1990, tuition, fees, and room and board at Yale were $19,310, while at Harvard they were just $85 more, at $19,395. Comparable totals at Dartmouth, Columbia, and the University of Pennsylvania were between those at Harvard and Yale.

The financial aid issue was somewhat more complicated. For many years, representatives of the nation's elite universities had met to coordinate the amount of assistance they would offer to outstanding students who had applied to more than one of the institutions. As a result of these discussions, students would be offered essentially identical amounts of aid from each school. The schools defended this practice as a way of allowing students to make their choices based on educational objectives rather than financial considerations. They also argued that it prevented bidding wars and allowed limited financial aid dollars to be spread among a greater number of deserving students. Although these are laudable goals, another effect of the practice was that it reduced the amount of aid offered to top students.

In 1991, the universities being investigated agreed to refrain from sharing tuition information, and the financial aid discussions were not held for the first time in 35 years. Although the schools avoided prosecution by the federal government, they are still vulnerable to private suits. At present, a class action is pending on behalf of individuals who received less aid money because of the collusive scheme.

Public Utility Regulation

In contrast to antitrust activity, the regulatory approach to public policy directly alters industry performance by setting prices and establishing conditions of entry and exit. Although regulation extends to many industries, it is most common in dealing with public utilities. It is difficult to define precisely what makes a business a public utility. However, there seem to be two general characteristics. First, the industry provides a product or service of particular importance. Either the day-to-day livelihood or the future growth of a region depends on the continued and reasonable provision of the product or service. Second, the nature of the production process is such that competition is seen as yielding undesirable results such as duplication of facilities. The public utility designation is usually applied to firms providing electric power; local water and sewage supply; telephone, telegraph, and cable communications; and urban passenger transportation.

The Need for Regulation

The traditional view of public utility regulation is that it serves the public interest by protecting consumers. The need for regulation exists when a supplier has a natural monopoly or to prevent price discrimination.

NATURAL MONOPOLY   Certain industries are sometimes referred to as *natural monopolies*. The term is used to describe production systems where technology results in continually declining average costs that provide a substantial cost advantage to larger firms. Because a firm can decrease its average cost by increasing its rate of output, the only stable market structure is that of a single firm serving the entire market. Smaller firms are either forced from the market or acquired by the dominant firm. Consumers in the market are then subject to the economic power of the resulting monopolist. Figure 19-3 depicts a natural monopoly. Note that the shape of the cost curves implies that a larger firm will be more efficient than a smaller one because it will have lower average costs at the optimal rate of output.

The existence of a natural monopoly poses something of a dilemma for public policy. One alternative is to let the firm operate as a monopoly. If the firm faced the demand curve DD, as shown in Figure 19-3, the monopoly price would be P_M and the quantity, Q_M. The firm would then earn economic profit, as indicated by the area of the rectangle P_MABC. Compared to marginal cost pricing (i.e., setting the price equal to marginal cost), the monopoly-pricing scheme would result in a deadweight loss and also a transfer of consumer surplus from consumers to producers.[6]

If the firm is not allowed to act as an unconstrained monopolist, there are several alternatives available to the policymaker. One is to invoke antitrust laws and divide the firm into smaller competing firms. But it is not clear that the public

---

[6] Deadweight loss and consumer surplus are discussed on pages 319–321.

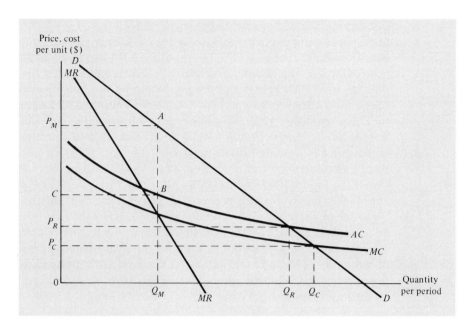

FIGURE 19-3 **Natural Monopoly.**

interest would be served by this action. The inefficiency of these small firms (because of their higher average costs at lower output rates) requires that they charge a high price just to earn a normal return on capital. There is no guarantee that the price required by such firms to earn a normal return would not be higher than the price that the more efficient monopolist would charge to maximize profits. Thus the antitrust approach may not be a desirable solution.

A second alternative is to allow the firm to maintain its monopoly position but require it to price at marginal cost. For the demand and cost curves in Figure 19-3, this would result in a price of P_C and a quantity of Q_C. At this level of production there is no deadweight loss because production is increased until the cost of producing the last unit is equated to the value of that unit. There is also no transfer of surplus from consumers to producers. In fact, the problem is quite the reverse. Because the monopolist is producing in a region of decreasing costs, its marginal cost is less than its average cost. Being required to price at marginal cost, the monopolist is unable to earn a normal return on capital. This is easily seen by observing that at the output rate Q_C, the average revenue as shown by the demand curve is less than the average cost.

If a policymaker requires a firm with decreasing costs to price at marginal cost over a long period of time, some provision must be made to compensate the investors in the firm for the losses that will be sustained. One way of doing this is to provide a subsidy. This approach is sometimes used with publicly owned bridges. The marginal cost of allowing another car over the bridge approaches zero. Thus cars are permitted to pass without charge or at nominal cost, and the cost of building and operating the bridge is paid from tax revenues. In the United States, providing explicit subsidies to business from public funds has never been very popular. There have been exceptions, such as subsidies for airlines, urban transportation, and telephone service to rural customers, but the general philosophy has been that public utility services should not be subsidized.

The most common method for pricing the products of a natural monopoly in the United States represents a compromise solution. The nature of the compromise is depicted by Figure 19-3. A simple description of public utility price regulation is that price is set equal to average cost. That is, the firm is allowed to charge a price that allows it to earn no more than a normal return on its capital.[7] This is shown in Figure 19-3 by the price, P_R, and the quantity, Q_R. The regulatory approach is a compromise because the price is less than the monopoly price but higher than marginal cost. There is some deadweight loss because price is not equated to marginal cost, but the deadweight loss is far less than if the firm were allowed to act as a monopolist. Because the firm earns a normal profit, there is no need for the subsidy that would be required with marginal cost pricing. Thus this mechanism achieves some of the gains from marginal cost pricing without requiring a subsidy.

UNDUE PRICE DISCRIMINATION   Price discrimination occurs when consumers are charged different prices for a product and the differences in price cannot be accounted for by cost differentials. As discussed in Chapter 12, the three requirements for successful price discrimination are that consumers have different demand elasticities, that markets be separable, and that the firm has some power over price.

The telephone industry provides an example of successful price discrimination policies by a public utility. Rates for basic telephone services are higher for business users than they are for residential users. There is no particular reason to assume that the cost of installing and maintaining a phone in an office is different from putting one in a kitchen. There are, however, possible differences in demand elasticity for business versus home phone customers. Consider the case of a stockbroker. The vast majority of orders for the purchase or sale of stock come to the broker by phone. There is no way the business could be conducted without a phone. In contrast, if there is a neighbor's phone that can be used in an emergency, it is quite possible to get along without a telephone in one's home. In economic terms, the stockbroker is said to have more inelastic demand for telephone service than does the residential customer.

The other conditions for price discrimination are also met in the telephone industry. Because there is a physical connection between the customer and the phone company, there is no way that low-cost home telephone service can be resold to a business customer. Also, if the stockbroker does not interconnect with the local phone company, there is no practical way to have access to customers calling in orders.

---

[7] Recall that average cost includes a normal return to capital. Thus if price is set equal to average cost, the firm will be earning a normal return.

The consequence of price discrimination provides an argument for regulation. Perhaps government should intervene to protect the commercial user from an unfair situation. The issue is not one of efficiency, but of fairness. The presumption is that the monopolist should not be allowed to use its power to unduly discriminate against some consumers. Although some discrimination may be acceptable, government intervention may be necessary when that discrimination becomes excessive. But there is no clear definition of the distinction between due and undue discrimination. In the end, undue price discrimination is whatever the regulatory commissions or the courts determine it to be.

KEY CONCEPTS

- Public utilities are firms that provide an essential service and that have limited competition.
- When there is a natural monopoly, the most efficient market structure may be a single firm serving the entire market.
- Public utility regulation as practiced in the United States is based on setting prices equal to average cost.
- Regulation may be needed to protect consumers from high prices and undue price discrimination by firms with market power.

Regulatory Procedures

Public utility regulation occurs at both state and federal levels. Federal regulation focuses primarily on wholesale and interstate transactions, while state regulatory activities concentrate on the intrastate retail market. Commissions responsible for public utility regulation typically consist of two basic divisions: the commission staff and the commissioners.

The commission staff is an adversary of the regulated firm in hearings before the commissioners. The staff must evaluate the evidence presented by the firm and make its own recommendations. Although consumer groups are becoming increasingly important in regulatory proceedings, it is still the commission staff that has the major responsibility for presenting the public's case to the commissioners. In contrast, the commissioners consider evidence and recommendations of the staff, the regulated firms, and other groups and then formulate the commission's policies.

Probably the most visible function of the state and federal regulatory commissions is setting prices for the products and services of the industries they regulate. The procedure used for price determination is a quasijudicial exercise called the *rate case*. There are two basic objectives in the rate case. The first is to find a general level of rates or prices that will allow the firm to earn no more than a fair or normal return on its capital. This occurs in the revenue requirement phase of the proceeding. The second objective is considered during the rate structure phase and involves setting rates that do not unduly discriminate against any class of consumers.

THE REVENUE REQUIREMENT PHASE OF THE RATE CASE   The rate case is concerned primarily with equity or fairness. If prices are raised and profits increase, stockholders of the firm benefit at the expense of consumers. If the firm is not allowed to raise prices or if the increase does not cover increased costs, the benefits to consumers from lower rates are obtained at the expense of lower returns to investors. If a general increase in profits to the firm is granted while keeping prices to some groups low, higher prices must be paid by other groups. The rate case is basically a zero-sum game in which one group can benefit only at the expense of others. Thus it becomes an adversary proceeding, with each of the parties involved trying to get a bigger share of the pie.

The procedure for determining the general level of prices in a rate case is easily described in theory, if not in practice. The firm is to be granted overall revenues sufficient to allow it to earn just a fair return on its capital. The procedure can be reduced to the following simple equation:

$$RR = E + s(RB - DEP) \tag{19-1}$$

where

$$
\begin{aligned}
RR &= \text{revenue requirement} \\
E &= \text{expenses} \\
s &= \text{fair return on capital} \\
RB &= \text{capital or the rate base} \\
DEP &= \text{depreciation}
\end{aligned}
$$

Equation (19-1) specifies that total revenue allowed by the regulatory commission should be sufficient to allow the firm to cover its expenses plus earn a fair return on the depreciated value of its capital base. Essentially, the public utility rate case is a cost-plus form of price setting. Revenues are set to cover the firm's costs of operating plus an add-on as a return to capital. In the rate case, each of the components of equation (19-1) is determined. The commission must decide on the firm's allowable expenses, a fair rate of return on capital, the depreciated capital or rate base to which the fair rate is to be applied, and finally, the revenue requirement necessary to cover the sum of expenses plus return to captial.

THE RATE STRUCTURE PHASE OF THE RATE CASE.   The emphasis of the public utility rate case has shifted over time. In the early days of regulation, the major area of controversy was the valuation of the rate base. Later, attention shifted to the fair rate of return. Until recent years, commissions paid relatively little attention to the structure of rates. The need for increases in total revenue often was met simply by adjusting all rates on a nearly proportionate basis. Commissions considered the structure of rates primarily in response to complaints received from specific groups of consumers. Basically, it was the firm that took the lead in determining what the structure of rates should be.

In recent years, much more attention has been paid to the structure of rates. As commissions have become more involved in determining the rate structure, they have required that firms provide additional information about the cost of serving individual categories of consumers. Often, the commission will request that the firm compute the rate of return being earned for each category of service or for each product that is provided. These data are then used by the commission in making rate adjustments. This is called *cost-of-service pricing*. For example, if a particular service or product is shown to be earning a very low rate of return under existing rates, the commission may approve a larger rate increase than for a service or product that is earning a higher rate of return. The commission's attempt to equalize rates of return is consistent with its mandate to prevent undue discrimination.

KEY CONCEPTS

- In a rate case, the regulatory commission must determine prices that generate revenues sufficient to cover expenses and allow the firm to earn a fair return on its rate base.
- In determining the structure of rates, most regulatory commissions use cost-of-service pricing, which focuses on equating the rate of return earned by providing service to each customer class.

Interest Groups and Regulation

Some scholars do not accept the idea that regulation effectively protects consumers. They believe that the effects of regulation can best be explained in terms of regulators responding to pressures from various groups who have an interest in the outcome of a decision. Stigler is a leading proponent of this view.[8] He considers the regulatory process as a means of redistributing wealth. This redistribution occurs as commissions make decisions that tend to favor one group over another. The power of regulatory commissions could be used to confer benefits on any segment of society, but Stigler argues that industry is more effective than consumers in affecting the outcomes of decisions. Thus regulation usually will favor industry at the expense of the consumer. But the main contribution by Stigler is not his conclusion that regulatory decisions are biased toward industry. It is his analysis that concludes that some groups are always likely to be better represented in regulatory proceedings than others. His work has evolved into a general theory of how interest groups affect the outcomes of political decisions.[9]

Modern interest group theory starts from the premise that regulation can have important effects on the distribution of wealth. As a result, those who will be affected by regulatory decisions have an incentive to try and influence those decisions. This can be accomplished by means such as lobbying, providing data, hiring expert witnesses, and conducting publicity campaigns. The responsibility of regulators is to sift through the information received and differentiate between arguments that reflect only special interests and those that support the public interest as the policymakers perceive it.

[8] G. J. Stigler, "The Theory of Economic Regulation." *Bell Journal of Economics and Management Science* (Spring 1971), pp. 3–21.

[9] See R. G. Noll and B. M. Owen, eds., *The Political Economy of Regulation: Interest Groups in the Regulatory Process* (Washington, D.C.: American Enterprise Institute, 1983).

Limited budgets and staff force regulators to make decisions at least partially on the basis of information that is supplied by various interest groups. Thus, those groups that do the best job of representing their interests are most likely to receive favorable treatment by the regulatory body. But such representation can be a time-consuming and expensive process. As a result, certain types of special-interest groups may have an advantage in regulatory proceedings. Factors affecting the degree to which a group will be well represented in a regulatory decision include degree of self-interest, size, homogeneity, and uncertainty.

DEGREE OF SELF-INTEREST   The more important a decision is to a group, the more effort the members of that group will expend to influence the decision. For example, an electric utility that is requesting a $100 million rate increase has a much greater stake in the decision of the regulatory commission than does the consumer whose monthly electricity bill will increase by $3.50 if the rate increase is approved. As a result, the utility will spend a great deal of time and effort trying to sway the commission, while an individual consumer may do little more than grumble when the higher bill comes.

SIZE OF THE GROUP   All other thing being equal, a smaller group is better able to promote its views than a group consisting of many people or firms. The reason is that organizational problems increase with size. Also, large groups tend to have more serious problems with free riders. A single consumer, asked to contribute to a fund to lobby for reduced electricity rates, may rationalize that his or her failure to contribute will have no noticeable effect on the effectiveness of the group. In contrast, in a consortium of three or four firms, one defector might spell the difference between success and defeat.

GROUP HOMOGENEITY   If all of the members of a group are in a similar position and have similar objectives, then the group does not have to spend time and money hammering out compromise positions for presentation before the regulatory body. All of the resources of the group can be marshaled to achieve the common goal.

UNCERTAINTY   If the results of a particular decision are predictable, then members of a group will be more willing to make contributions than if the results are uncertain. For example, if there is a lack of information as to whether deregulation of an industry will lead to higher or lower prices for consumers, then consumer groups may have little impact on the decision process.

Stigler's early formulation of interest-group theory predicted that regulation is biased toward producers. The modern theory is roughly consistent, but somewhat more general. Existing firms in an industry are likely to have a high stake in regulatory decisions, be relatively few in number, hold similar objectives, and have a good idea about the outcome of regulatory decisions. Thus, the views of those firms are likely to be well represented in the regulatory process. In contrast, consumers, small firms attempting to enter a regulated industry, and those advocating the use of new technologies are likely to be poorly represented. As a result, the theory predicts that there will be a tendency for regulatory decisions to favor the existing firms in a regulated industry. The theory also suggests that small, one-issue consumer groups such as environmentalists and senior citizens can have an important impact on the outcomes of decisions.

KEY CONCEPTS

- The regulatory process can be used as a means of redistributing wealth.
- Interest-group theory predicts that small, homogeneous groups that are significantly affected by a regulatory decision are likely to be favored by those decisions.

Price Controls

During periods of rapid inflation, price controls may be used to reduce the rate of price increases. In some cases, they are imposed on selected industries (such as rent controls or interest rate ceilings), while in other circumstances they have been used in virtually all industries.

Price Controls in Competitive Industries

Figure 19-4 depicts the supply and demand curves for a competitive industry. Each firm is considered to take as given the market price determined by the interaction of the supply and demand curves. The equilibrium price is P_e and the equilibrium quantity is Q_e. Suppose that public policy limits the price at which the product can be sold to P_c. The lower price reduces the amount that will be supplied to Q_s and induces additional consumers to enter the market so that the quantity demanded increases to Q_d. The amount that consumers want to purchase is now greater than the available supply, so there is a shortage of the price-controlled product.

In the free market, prices act as a rationing device to equilibrate supply and demand. Some consumers drop out of the market as prices increase. At the same time, quantity supplied will increase as production becomes more profitable. But when prices are set below the equilibrium level, another method of rationing must be found. Historically, alternative rationing schemes have taken many forms. The most common has been the black market. If products can be purchased at low prices by consumers who value them less than others who cannot obtain them, an opportunity to profit from exchange exists. The low-valuation consumers can sell the product to the high-valuation consumers, and both will be better off than if the black-market transaction had not occurred. The existence of black markets requires that there be people who are willing to break the law and risk incurring the penalties of running a black-market supply organization. It also requires that there be some consumers who are willing to purchse goods illegally. There has never been a documented case of effective price ceilings that was not accompanied by some sort of black market.

In many countries, the common manifestation of prices artificially kept below the market level is long queues of people waiting to purchase the limited supplies of goods. Such queues are common in poor nations and have periodically occurred

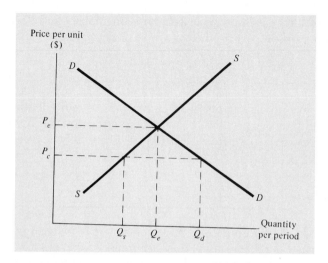

FIGURE 19-4 **Price Controls in Competitive Industries.**

at gas stations in the United States when price controls were in effect. Queues are a form of rationing in the sense that only those people willing and able to stand in line get the product. The inefficiency of this type of rationing is apparent when the value of time is considered. Suppose that the price of a product as determined by market forces would be $2 but the controlled price is set at $1. If the purchaser's time is valued at, say, $5 an hour, he has to stand in line only 12 minutes per unit purchased to lose the gain of being able to buy at a lower price.

Thus far, only the short-run implications of price controls of firms in competitive markets have been considered. The long-run impacts on investment may be far more important. One of the functions of prices is to signal needs for transferring resources from one sector of the economy to another. If prices are rising because of demand-induced pressures in one industry, capital tends to flow to that industry to increase supply. Rising prices also generate internal investment funds for expansion by firms within the industry. But if prices are kept at artificially low levels, the necessary signals are not provided to capital markets and sufficient internal funds are not generated. As a result, if controls are imposed for a long period of time, shortages become more acute because of the lack of expansion in the industry. When controls are lifted, pressures of excess demand may result in a significant price increase.

CASE STUDY _____

Rent Controls in Paris

Rent controls have been imposed by many city governments. In almost every case, the result has been a shortage of rental units and a deterio-

ration in the quality of rental housing. A dramatic example is Paris after World War II. Those lucky enough to have rent-controlled housing in Paris seldom had to pay more than 4 percent of their income for housing. Today, it is not uncommon for housing costs to take 30 percent of a family's gross income.

Unfortunately, quantity demanded far exceeded quantity supplied. For those who did not already have a low-rent unit, there were none available. The death of someone living in a rent-controlled unit was about the only possibility. Search for an apartment sometimes involved reading the obituaries or making agreements with undertakers for early notification of a death. Old people were often accosted by young wives wanting to make a "down payment" on future space. The rights to a rent-controlled apartment were sold for as much as $5,000 (in terms of 1993 dollars) per room. This high price is an indication of the misallocation of resources caused by the rent controls.

Another consequence of rent controls in Paris was the deterioration of the rental housing stock. With rents so low, it did not pay to build additional units, nor did it make sense to spend very much to maintain existing units. Between 1914 and 1948, the increase in rental rates was 6.8 times, while the cost of repairs increased by 120 times. As a result, repairs and other maintenance were neglected.

Price Controls and Firms with Market Power

On the basis of the theoretical discussions of the previous pages, the attempt to apply controls to competitive industries is not very promising. However, even casual observation of business in any developed nation reveals that many goods and services are not produced under conditions that satisfy or even approximate the perfectly competitive model. Rather, much of the economic activity in industrialized nations involve firms with some power to set the price of their product. This power is not complete because such firms have rivals, but it sometimes is enhanced by formal or informal price collusion among firms.

Where firms have power to affect prices, some of the traditional objections to price controls become less compelling. For economists who express concern about the loss of freedom resulting from price controls, a relevant question in this case is "Whose freedom?" For firms with market power, the invisible hand no longer functions as envisioned by Adam Smith. The loss of freedom caused by price controls is that of firms who have been exploiting the consumers of their product. For such firms, price controls might be viewed as limits on operations that markets do not effectively constrain.

Figure 19-5 depicts the application of price controls to a firm with market power. If left to maximize profits, the firm sets price at P_m and produces the quantity Q_m. By setting a price ceiling where the marginal cost curve crosses the demand schedule (point A), it is possible to constrain price without creating a shortage. The profit-maximizing firm chooses a quantity such that marginal revenues and marginal costs are equal. If the maximum price allowed is P_c, the firm has a new marginal revenue curve, P_cA, out to quantity Q_c. Because P_c is below the demand curve for all quantities less than Q_c, the firm can increase production from zero to Q_c by selling additional units at the same price. That is, the marginal revenue curve is given by the horizontal straight line P_cA. The firm should continue to increase its production as long as marginal costs are less than P_c. Thus the profit-maximizing quantity is Q_c. If price is set at P_c, there is no shortage or excess. The

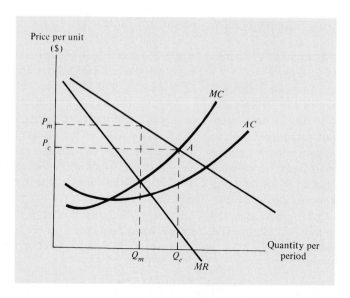

FIGURE 19-5 **Price Controls in Concentrated Industries.**

firm maximizes profits by producing Q_c, which is the same amount as consumers want to purchase at the controlled price.

It should be noted, however, that analyzing price controls is much easier than their actual implementation. Regulators seldom have good information on demand and costs. Thus it would be unlikely that policymakers could consistently identify the precise level at which the demand and marginal cost curves intersect. If price is set below this level, shortages will result. A price above that level means that prices are higher than necessary to equate demand and supply.

KEY CONCEPTS

- Price controls in competitive industries tend to result in shortages.
- In industries where firms have market power, if price is set equal to marginal cost, it may be possible to impose price controls without creating shortages.

Summary

The Sherman Act prohibits unfair business practices and the illegal monopolization of a market. Price discrimination and mergers are two important actions covered by the Clayton Act. The Robinson–Patmen Act broadened Clayton Act provisions against illegal price discrimination, while the Celler–Kefauver Amendment put vertical and conglomerate mergers under the jurisdiction of the Clayton Act.

Antitrust suits may be initiated by the U.S. Department of Justice, the Federal Trade Commission, state government officials, or private parties. For successful prosecution, per se offenses require only showing that the act has been committed. In contrast, rule-of-reason offenses also require a demonstration that the social costs of the act are greater than the social benefits.

The current interpretation of Section 2 of the Sherman Act is that practices that are acceptable when used by small firms may constitute antitrust violations if used by firms with substantial market power. Mergers contested under the Clayton Act should be evaluated to determine if the effect of increased market power exceeds any efficiency gains that may result from the merger. Income distribution effects may also be a consideration.

In deciding to challenge a merger, the Justice Department relies on guidelines based on the Herfindahl Index. A horizontal merger between large firms is likely to be prohibited, but vertical and conglomerate mergers will probably be allowed unless they increase horizontal market power.

Price fixing is usually considered a per se violation of the law. Predatory pricing can be used to weaken competitors and deter entry. Recent court opinions have defined predation as setting prices below average variable cost.

Most antitrust suits are settled by consent decrees before going to trial. Other remedies and penalties include dissolution or divestiture, injunctions, prison sentences, fines, and treble-damage awards.

Firms with continually declining average cost curves are referred to as natural monopolies because the only stable market structure is that of a single firm supplying the entire market. In the United States, the approach used to deal with natural monopolies is to give price-setting power to a regulatory body. Such bodies also protect consumers by prohibiting undue price discrimination.

In the revenue requirement phase of a rate case, a regulatory commission must determine the total revenue that will allow the firm to cover its expenses plus earn a fair return on its rate base. In the rate structure phase, a cost-of-service approach is often used whereby the commission adjusts rates to equalize the rate of return earned by each class of service. Modern interest group theory predicts that decisions of regulatory bodies will tend to favor small, homogeneous groups that will be significantly affected by the decision.

Price controls in competitive industries tend to cause shortages and result in queues and black markets. In contrast, in industries where firms have market power, by setting the controlled price equal to marginal cost, it may be possible to impose price controls without creating shortages.

Discussion Questions _____

19-1. How could private antitrust suits be used as part of a firm's strategy in dealing with its competitors?

19-2. Why are some antitrust violations judged using a per se standard?

19-3. How could the definition of the relevant product market affect a court's decision in an antitrust case?

19-4. Consider an industry with a large, dominant firm and a number of smaller firms. Suppose that a merger of two of the small firms would result in a Herfindahl Index greater than 1,800. Is there a basis for allowing the merger?

19-5. Trade associations are often involved in collusive agreements to fix prices. Why?

19-6. In the Trenton Potteries case, what did the Supreme Court mean by the statement "the reasonable price fixed today may through economic and business changes become the unreasonable price of tomorrow"?

19-7. How would the value of a good relative to its transportation cost affect the success of a large, multimarket firm using predatory pricing? Explain.

19-8. Can a monopoly be maintained in an industry that does not have continually declining average costs? Explain.

19-9. In a public utility rate case, how could a commission use the structure of rates to redistribute income? Give an example.

19-10. How might price regulation affect the rate of innovation in an industry?

19-11. How should a regulatory commission determine what constitutes undue price discrimination?

19-12. In competitive industries, when prices are kept below the equilibrium level by price controls, incorrect signals are provided to consumers and resource owners. Explain.

19-13. How do elasticities of supply and demand affect the magnitude of the shortages created by price controls imposed on competitive industries?

19-14. Would controls be more successful in keeping prices down during wartime than during a period of peace? Why or why not?

Problems _____

19-1. Bentley Manufacturing can produce desks at a constant average cost of $200 per unit, including a normal profit. Because of intense competition, the company sells desks for $200 and is able to sell 100,000 units per year. Bentley's managers have initiated a merger with New Top, another desk manufacturer. The merger will allow the combined firm to produce at an average cost of $190 per unit. The combined firm's additional market power increases the profit-maximizing price to $250, but only 80,000 units will be sold at that price. The proposed merger is being evaluated by the Department of Justice.

    a. If the demand curve is linear between a price of $150 and $250, will the deadweight loss exceed the efficiency gain resulting from the merger?

    b. What other factors should antitrust officials consider in deciding whether to challenge the merger?

19-2. An industry consists of eight firms. Sales for each firm in 1983 and 1993 are shown. Use the Herfindahl Index to determine whether the industry became more concentrated from 1983 to 1993.

	Sales (Millions)	
Firm	1983	1993
1	100	240
2	90	90
3	80	60
4	80	50
5	50	50
6	40	40
7	30	40
8	30	30
Total	500	600

19-3. Market shares for the firms in two industries are as follows:

Firm	Industry I	Industry II
1	5%	5%
2	5	5
3	20	5
4	5	60
5	5	2
6	20	3
7	20	5
8	20	15

Compute the Herfindahl Index for each industry.

19-4. An industry consists of eight firms of equal size. Two of the eight want to merge. Based on the merger guidelines used by the Department of Justice, will the merger be challenged? What if the merger involved four of the eight firms in the industry? Explain your answers.

19-5. A firm's demand function is given by $P = 100 - 4Q$. Marginal costs are constant and equal to $20. Competitive conditions in the industry require the firm to price at marginal cost. Scale economies resulting from merging with a competing firm would reduce the marginal cost to $19 and allow the firm to increase its price to $28. Use the Williamson model to evaluate the merger.

19-6. Malko Electronics is a manufacturer and distributor of Korean-made video recorders. The firm's most popular model sells for $250 in California. Shipping costs from Korea to the United States are $10 per unit. Fixed costs plus a normal rate of profit are $100 per recorder, and the average variable cost is $170. A competitor, Wagner Video, sells a comparable recorder in California for $280. Wagner has filed a price discrimination suit, charging that Malko is engaged in predatory pricing intended to drive Wagner from the market. The charge is based solely on the contention that Malko is selling below cost. What will be the important issues in the case? Is Malko likely to be found guilty of illegal price discrimination?

19-7. A regulated telephone company utility has a depreciated rate base of $500 million. The utility's capital structure consists of 40 percent equity and 60 percent debt. The after-tax cost of debt is 8 percent, the firm's common stock is currently selling for $8 per share, the dividend is $1, and the expected dividend growth rate is 2.5 percent per year. The firm's total expenses are $400 million.

a. If the regulatory body sets an allowed rate of return that is equal to the firm's cost of capital, what rate of return will the commission allow? Assume the commission uses the discounted cash flow method to compute the cost of equity capital.

b. Based on your answer to part (a), what is the revenue requirement of the firm?

19-8. Pilfur Oil has a monopoly on the sale of oil in Transylvania. Demand for the firm's product is given by

$$P = 100 - 20Q$$

where P is the price of a barrel of oil and Q is measured in thousands of barrels of oil per day. The marginal cost function for the firm is

$$MC = 10 + 5Q$$

a. What are the profit-maximizing price and rate of output for Pilfur?

b. The government of Transylvania decides that Pilfur's price is too high. The firm is required to set the lowest price that will not result in shortages. What will be the price and rate of output that meet these conditions?

TABLES

TABLE I Present Value of $1.00

$$PVIF_{i,n} = \frac{1}{(1 + i)^n}$$

Interest (Discount) Rate (i)

Periods (n)	1%	2%	3%	4%	5%	6%	7%	8%	9%	10%
1	.9901	.9804	.9709	.9615	.9524	.9434	.9346	.9259	.9174	.9091
2	.9803	.9612	.9426	.9246	.9070	.8900	.8734	.8573	.8417	.8264
3	.9706	.9423	.9151	.8890	.8638	.8396	.8163	.7938	.7722	.7513
4	.9610	.9238	.8885	.8548	.8227	.7921	.7629	.7350	.7084	.6830
5	.9515	.9057	.8626	.8219	.7835	.7473	.7130	.6806	.6499	.6209
6	.9420	.8880	.8375	.7903	.7462	.7050	.6663	.6302	.5963	.5645
7	.9327	.8706	.8131	.7599	.7107	.6651	.6227	.5835	.5470	.5132
8	.9235	.8535	.7894	.7307	.6768	.6274	.5820	.5403	.5019	.4665
9	.9143	.8368	.7664	.7026	.6446	.5919	.5439	.5002	.4604	.4241
10	.9053	.8203	.7441	.6756	.6139	.5584	.5083	.4632	.4224	.3855
11	.8963	.8043	.7224	.6496	.5847	.5268	.4751	.4289	.3875	.3505
12	.8874	.7885	.7014	.6246	.5568	.4970	.4440	.3971	.3555	.3186
13	.8787	.7730	.6810	.6606	.5303	.4688	.4150	.3677	.3262	.2897
14	.8700	.7579	.6611	.5775	.5051	.4423	.3878	.3405	.2992	.2633
15	.8613	.7430	.6419	.5553	.4810	.4173	.3624	.3152	.2745	.2394
16	.8528	.7284	.6232	.5339	.4581	.3936	.3387	.2919	.2519	.2176
17	.8444	.7142	.6050	.5134	.4363	.3714	.3166	.2703	.2311	.1978
18	.8360	.7002	.5874	.4936	.4155	.3503	.2959	.2502	.2120	.1799
19	.8277	.6864	.5703	.4746	.3957	.3305	.2765	.2317	.1945	.1635
20	.8195	.6730	.5537	.4564	.3769	.3118	.2584	.2145	.1784	.1486
21	.8114	.6598	.5375	.4388	.3589	.2942	.2415	.1987	.1637	.1351
22	.8034	.6468	.5219	.4220	.3418	.2775	.2257	.1839	.1502	.1228
23	.7954	.6342	.5067	.4057	.3256	.2618	.2109	.1703	.1378	.1117
24	.7876	.6217	.4919	.3901	.3101	.2470	.1971	.1577	.1264	.1015
25	.7798	.6095	.4776	.3751	.2953	.2330	.1842	.1460	.1160	.0923
26	.7720	.5976	.4637	.3607	.2812	.2198	.1722	.1352	.1064	.0839
27	.7644	.5859	.4502	.3468	.2678	.2074	.1609	.1252	.0976	.0763
28	.7568	.5744	.4371	.3335	.2551	.1956	.1504	.1159	.0895	.0693
29	.7493	.5631	.4243	.3207	.2429	.1846	.1406	.1073	.0822	.0630
30	.7419	.5521	.4120	.3083	.2314	.1741	.1314	.0994	.0754	.0573
35	.7059	.5000	.3554	.2534	.1813	.1301	.0937	.0676	.0490	.0356
40	.6717	.4529	.3066	.2083	.1420	.0972	.0668	.0460	.0318	.0221
45	.6391	.4102	.2644	.1712	.1113	.0727	.0476	.0313	.0207	.0137
50	.6080	.3715	.2281	.1407	.0872	.0543	.0339	.0213	.0134	.0085
55	.5785	.3365	.1968	.1157	.0683	.0406	.0242	.0145	.0087	.0053

TABLE I **(continued)**

Periods (n)	12%	14%	15%	16%	18%	20%	24%	28%	32%	36%
					Interest (Discount) Rate (i)					
1	.8929	.8772	.8696	.8621	.8475	.8333	.8065	.7813	.7576	.7353
2	.7972	.7695	.7561	.7432	.7182	.6944	.6504	.6104	.5739	.5407
3	.7118	.6750	.6575	.6407	.6086	.5787	.5245	.4768	.4348	.3975
4	.6355	.5921	.5718	.5523	.5158	.4823	.4230	.3725	.3294	.2923
5	.5674	.5194	.4972	.4761	.4371	.4019	.3411	.2910	.2495	.2149
6	.5066	.4556	.4323	.4104	.3704	.3349	.2751	.2274	.1890	.1580
7	.4523	.3996	.3759	.3538	.3139	.2791	.2218	.1776	.1432	.1162
8	.4039	.3506	.3269	.3050	.2660	.2326	.1789	.1388	.1085	.0854
9	.3606	.3075	.2843	.2630	.2255	.1938	.1443	.1084	.0822	.0628
10	.3220	.2697	.2472	.2267	.1911	.1615	.1164	.0847	.0623	.0462
11	.2875	.2366	.2149	.1954	.1619	.1346	.0938	.0662	.0472	.0340
12	.2567	.2076	.1869	.1685	.1372	.1122	.0757	.0517	.0357	.0250
13	.2292	.1821	.1625	.1452	.1163	.0935	.0610	.0404	.0271	.0184
14	.2046	.1597	.1413	.1252	.0985	.0779	.0492	.0316	.0205	.0135
15	.1827	.1401	.1229	.1079	.0835	.0649	.0397	.0247	.0155	.0099
16	.1631	.1229	.1069	.0930	.0708	.0541	.0320	.0193	.0118	.0073
17	.1456	.1078	.0929	.0802	.0600	.0451	.0258	.0150	.0089	.0054
18	.1300	.0946	.0808	.0691	.0508	.0376	.0208	.0118	.0068	.0039
19	.1161	.0829	.0703	.0596	.0431	.0313	.0168	.0092	.0051	.0029
20	.1037	.0728	.0611	.0514	.0365	.0261	.0135	.0072	.0039	.0021
21	.0926	.0638	.0531	.0443	.0309	.0217	.0109	.0056	.0029	.0016
22	.0826	.0560	.0462	.0382	.0262	.0181	.0088	.0044	.0022	.0012
23	.0738	.0491	.0402	.0329	.0222	.0151	.0071	.0034	.0017	.0008
24	.0659	.0431	.0349	.0284	.0188	.0126	.0057	.0027	.0013	.0006
25	.0588	.0378	.0304	.0245	.0160	.0105	.0046	.0021	.0010	.0005
26	.0525	.0331	.0264	.0211	.0135	.0087	.0037	.0016	.0007	.0003
27	.0469	.0291	.0230	.0182	.0115	.0073	.0030	.0013	.0006	.0002
28	.0419	.0255	.0200	.0157	.0097	.0061	.0024	.0010	.0004	.0002
29	.0374	.0224	.0174	.0135	.0082	.0051	.0020	.0008	.0003	.0001
30	.0334	.00196	.0151	.0116	.0070	.0042	.0016	.0006	.0002	.0001
35	.0189	.0102	.0075	.0055	.0030	.0017	.0005	.0002	.0001	*
40	.0107	.0053	.0037	.0026	.0013	.0007	.0002	.0001	*	*
45	.0061	.0027	.0019	.0013	.0006	.0003	.0001	*	*	*
50	.0035	.0014	.0009	.0006	.0003	.0001	*	*	*	*
55	.0020	.0007	.0005	.0003	.0001	*	*	*	*	*

* *PVIF* < .00005.

TABLE II **Present Value of an Annuity of $1.00 Per Period**

$$PVAF_{i,n} = \sum_{t=1}^{n} \frac{1}{(1+i)^t}$$

Periods (n)	Interest (Discount) Rate (i)								
	1%	2%	3%	4%	5%	6%	7%	8%	9%
1	0.9901	0.9804	0.9709	0.9615	0.9524	0.9434	0.9346	0.9259	0.9174
2	1.9704	1.9416	1.9135	1.8861	1.8594	1.8334	1.8080	1.7833	1.7591
3	2.9410	2.8839	2.8286	2.7751	2.7232	2.6730	2.6243	2.5771	2.5313
4	3.9020	3.8077	3.7171	3.6299	3.5460	3.4651	3.3872	3.3121	3.2397
5	4.8534	4.7135	4.5797	4.4518	4.3295	4.2124	4.1002	3.9927	3.8897
6	5.7955	5.6014	5.4172	5.2421	5.0757	4.9173	4.7665	4.6229	4.4859
7	6.7282	6.4720	6.2303	6.0021	5.7864	5.5824	5.3893	5.2064	5.0030
8	7.6517	7.3255	7.0197	6.7327	6.4632	6.2098	5.9713	5.7466	5.5348
9	8.5660	8.1622	7.7861	7.4353	7.1078	6.8017	6.5152	6.2469	5.9952
10	9.4713	8.9826	8.5302	8.1109	7.7217	7.3601	7.0236	6.7101	6.4177
11	10.3676	9.7868	9.2526	8.7605	8.3064	7.8869	7.4987	7.1390	6.8052
12	11.2551	10.5753	9.9540	9.3851	8.8633	8.3838	7.9427	7.5361	7.1607
13	12.1337	11.3484	10.6350	9.9856	9.3936	8.8527	8.3577	7.9038	7.4869
14	13.0037	12.1062	11.2961	10.5631	9.8986	9.2950	8.7455	8.2442	7.7862
15	13.8651	12.8493	11.9379	11.1184	10.3797	9.7122	9.1079	8.5595	8.0607
16	14.7179	13.5777	12.5611	11.6523	10.8378	10.1059	9.4466	8.8514	8.3126
17	15.5623	14.2919	13.1661	12.1657	11.2741	10.4773	9.7632	9.1216	8.5436
18	16.3983	14.9920	13.7535	12.6593	11.6896	10.8276	10.0591	9.3719	8.7556
19	17.2260	15.6785	14.3238	13.1339	12.0853	11.1581	10.3356	9.6036	8.9501
20	18.0456	16.3514	14.8775	13.5903	12.4622	11.4699	10.5940	9.8181	9.1285
21	18.8570	17.0112	15.4150	14.0292	12.8212	11.7641	10.8355	10.0168	9.2922
22	19.6604	17.6580	15.9369	14.4511	13.1630	12.0416	11.0612	10.2007	9.4424
23	20.4558	18.2922	16.4436	14.8568	13.4886	12.3034	11.2722	10.3711	9.5802
24	21.2434	18.9139	16.9355	15.2470	13.7986	12.5504	11.4693	10.5288	9.7066
25	20.0232	19.5235	17.4131	15.6221	14.0939	12.7834	11.6536	10.6748	9.8226
26	22.7952	20.1210	17.8768	15.9828	14.3752	13.0032	11.8258	10.8100	9.9290
27	23.5596	20.7069	18.3270	16.3296	14.6430	13.2105	11.9867	10.9352	10.0266
28	24.3164	21.2813	18.7641	16.6631	14.8981	13.4062	12.1371	11.0511	10.1161
29	25.0658	21.8444	19.1885	16.9837	15.1411	13.5907	12.2777	11.1584	10.1983
30	25.8077	22.3965	19.6004	17.2920	15.3725	13.7648	12.4090	11.2578	10.2737
35	29.4086	24.9986	21.4872	18.6646	16.3742	14.4982	12.9477	11.6546	10.5668
40	32.8347	27.3555	23.1148	19.7928	17.1591	15.0463	13.3317	11.9246	10.7574
45	36.0945	29.4902	24.5187	20.7200	17.7741	15.4558	13.6055	12.1084	10.8812
50	39.1961	31.4236	25.7298	21.4822	18.2559	15.7619	13.8007	12.2335	10.9617
55	42.1472	33.1748	26.7744	22.1086	18.6335	15.9905	13.9399	12.3186	11.0140

TABLE II *(continued)*

Periods (n)	Interest (Discount) Rate (i)									
	10%	*12%*	*14%*	*15%*	*16%*	*18%*	*20%*	*24%*	*28%*	*32%*
1	0.9091	0.8929	0.8772	0.8696	0.8621	0.8475	0.8333	0.8065	0.7813	0.7576
2	1.7355	1.6901	1.6467	1.6257	1.6052	1.5656	1.5278	1.4568	1.3916	1.3315
3	2.4869	2.4018	2.3216	2.2832	2.2459	2.1743	2.1065	1.9813	1.8684	1.7663
4	3.1699	3.0373	2.9137	2.8550	2.7982	2.6901	2.5887	2.4043	2.2410	2.0957
5	3.7908	3.6048	3.4331	3.3522	3.2743	3.1272	2.9906	2.7454	2.5320	2.3452
6	4.3553	4.1114	3.8887	3.7845	3.6847	3.4976	3.3255	3.0205	2.7594	2.5342
7	4.8684	4.5638	4.2883	4.1604	4.0386	3.8115	3.6046	3.2423	2.9370	2.6775
8	5.3349	4.9676	4.6389	4.4873	4.3436	4.0776	3.8372	3.4212	3.0758	2.7860
9	5.7590	5.3282	4.9464	4.7716	4.6065	4.3030	4.0310	3.5655	3.1842	2.8681
10	6.1446	5.6502	5.2161	5.0188	4.8332	4.4941	4.1925	3.6819	3.2689	2.9304
11	6.4951	5.9377	5.4527	5.2337	5.0286	4.6560	4.3271	3.7757	3.3351	2.9776
12	6.8137	6.1944	5.6603	5.4206	5.1971	4.7932	4.4392	3.8514	3.3868	3.0133
13	7.1034	6.4235	5.8424	5.5831	5.3423	4.9095	4.5327	3.9124	3.4272	3.0404
14	7.3667	6.6282	6.0021	5.7245	5.4675	5.0081	4.6106	3.9616	3.4587	3.0609
15	7.6061	6.8109	6.1422	5.8474	5.5755	5.0916	4.6755	4.0013	3.4834	3.0764
16	7.8237	6.9740	6.2651	5.9542	5.6685	5.1624	4.7296	4.0333	3.5026	3.0882
17	8.0216	7.1196	6.3729	6.0472	5.7487	5.2223	4.7746	4.0591	3.5177	3.0971
18	8.2014	7.2497	6.4674	6.1280	5.8178	5.2732	4.8122	4.0799	3.5294	3.1039
19	8.3649	7.3658	6.5504	6.1982	5.8775	5.3162	4.8435	4.0967	3.5386	3.1090
20	8.5136	7.4694	6.6231	6.2593	5.9288	5.3527	4.8696	4.1103	3.5458	3.1129
21	8.6487	7.5620	6.6870	6.3125	5.9731	5.3837	4.8913	4.1212	3.5514	3.1158
22	8.7715	7.6446	6.7429	6.3587	6.0113	5.4099	4.9094	4.1300	3.5558	3.1180
23	8.8832	7.7184	6.7921	6.3988	6.0442	5.4321	4.9245	4.1371	3.5592	3.1197
24	8.9847	7.7843	6.8351	6.4338	6.0726	5.4510	4.9371	4.1428	3.5619	3.1210
25	9.0770	7.8431	6.8729	6.4642	6.0971	5.4669	4.9476	4.1474	3.5640	3.1220
26	9.1609	7.8957	6.9061	6.4906	6.1182	5.4804	4.9563	4.1511	3.5656	3.1227
27	9.2372	7.9426	6.9352	6.5135	6.1364	5.4919	4.9636	4.1542	3.5669	3.1233
28	9.3066	7.9844	6.9607	6.5335	6.1520	5.5016	4.9697	4.1566	3.5679	3.1237
29	9.3696	8.0218	6.9830	6.5509	6.1656	5.5098	4.9747	4.1585	3.5687	3.1240
30	9.4269	8.0552	7.0027	6.5660	6.1772	5.5168	4.9789	4.1601	3.5693	3.1242
35	9.6442	8.1755	7.0700	6.6166	6.2153	5.5386	4.9915	4.1644	3.5708	3.1248
40	9.7791	8.2438	7.1050	6.6418	6.2335	5.5482	4.9966	4.1659	3.5712	3.1250
45	9.8628	8.2825	7.1232	6.6543	6.2421	5.5523	4.9986	4.1664	3.5714	3.1250
50	9.9148	8.3045	7.1327	6.6605	6.2463	5.5541	4.9995	4.1666	3.5714	3.1250
55	9.9471	8.3170	7.1376	6.6636	6.2482	5.5549	4.9998	4.1666	3.5714	3.1250

TABLE III **Values for Student's *t* Distribution**

| Degrees of Freedom | Confidence Interval | 90% | 95% | 99% |
	Significance Level	10%	5%	1%
1		6.314	12.706	63.657
2		2.920	4.303	9.925
3		2.353	3.182	5.841
4		2.132	2.776	4.604
5		2.015	2.571	4.032
6		1.943	2.447	3.707
7		1.895	2.365	3.499
8		1.860	2.306	3.355
9		1.833	2.262	3.250
10		1.812	2.228	3.169
11		1.796	2.201	3.106
12		1.782	2.179	3.055
13		1.771	2.160	3.012
14		1.761	2.145	2.977
15		1.753	2.131	2.947
16		1.746	2.120	2.921
17		1.740	2.110	2.898
18		1.734	2.101	2.878
19		1.729	2.093	2.861
20		1.725	2.086	2.845
21		1.721	2.080	2.831
22		1.717	2.074	2.819
23		1.714	2.069	2.807
24		1.711	2.064	2.797
25		1.708	2.060	2.787
26		1.706	2.056	2.779
27		1.703	2.052	2.771
28		1.701	2.048	2.763
29		1.699	2.045	2.756
60		1.671	2.000	2.660
120		1.658	1.980	2.617
inf.		1.645	1.960	2.576

SOURCE: R. A. Fisher, *Statistical Methods for Research Workers*, 14th ed. Reprinted with permission of Macmillan Publishing Company. Copyright © 1970 University of Adelaide.

Index